LUSITANIA

An Illustrated Biography

LUSITANIA

An Illustrated Biography

J. Kent Layton

AMBERLEY

Frontispiece: *The prow of the* Lusitania *is an imposing sight within her New York berth, around late 1908 or early 1909.*

Above: *c. 1908 port profile of the* Lusitania *anchored in the Mersey in Liverpool between round-trip voyages.*

In memory of Walter Layton, Richard Henry, and Barbara McDermott,
& to the Gilded Era, which came to its sudden end with World War One.

First published 2010; Second Edition 2015

Amberley Publishing
The Hill, Stroud
Gloucestershire, GL5 4EP

www.amberley-books.com

ISBN 978 1 4456 4262 8 (print)
ISBN 978 1 4456 4272 7 (e-book)

British Library Cataloguing in Publication Data.
A catalogue record for this book is available from the British Library.

Typeset in 10pt on 12pt Crimson Text
Typesetting and Origination by Amberley Publishing.
Printed in Great Britain.

Contents

To purchase other copies of this book,
or for the interactive experience, please visit:
www.atlanticliners.com

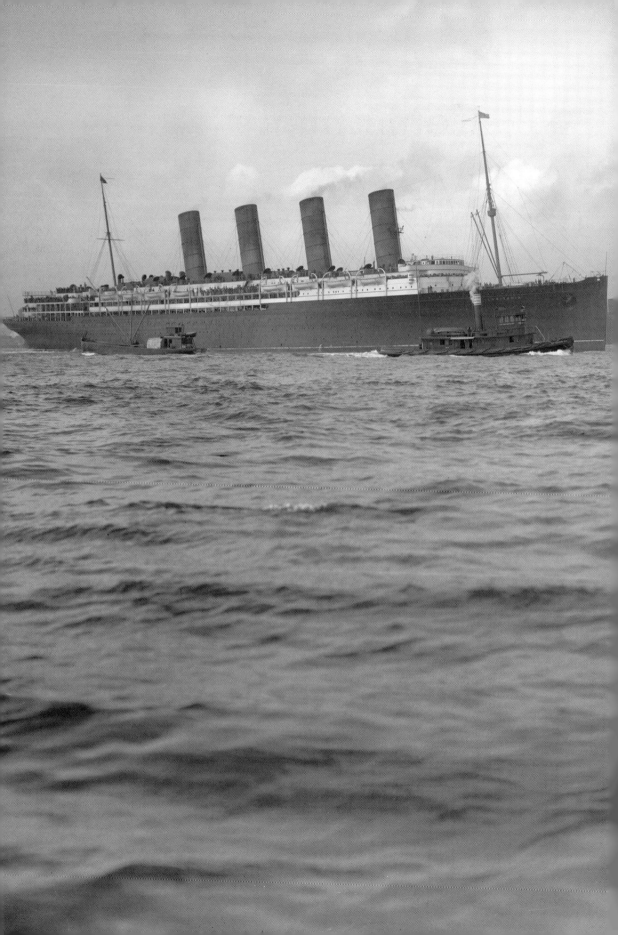

Centennial Note

There are moments in history that are true turning points, paradigm shifts that there is no coming back from. The sinking of the *Lusitania* on May 7, 1915 is one of these. Looking back over the course of 100 years, with two full world wars, a cold war, and all of the modern horrors of terrorism between us and that spring day, it is easy to lose perspective, to miss what a sad moment in human history the tragedy truly was.

The *Lusitania* was not the first merchant vessel sunk by a submarine during the Great War, nor was she the last to be sent to the bottom by those silent hunters of the deep. However, she was the first crack Atlantic liner, a ship whose name was known all around the world, to be sunk by a U-boat. Her lengthy passenger list of nearly two thousand souls, and the startling speed and violence with which she went down, guaranteed the horrendous death of twelve hundred lives. While many ships have followed in her tragic footsteps, and some have taken more lives in the process, the *Lusitania* was truly the start of a downward spiral. From that point forward, no one could hide behind the illusion that war was anything but a dirty business, or that innocent civilians could hide behind a badge of neutrality when they were caught in the wrong place at the wrong time.

Over the last century, the *Lusitania* has again been the victim of those who perpetuate the most absurd myths, inaccuracies, half-truths and conspiracy theories. From tales that the German submariners surfaced to shoot survivors, and rumors of clandestine explosive cargo, to political intrigue that supposedly sent the ship into harm's way in the hopes that she would be sunk, very few other ships have had their memories stained by such utter nonsense. Most school textbooks in the United States recite the "fact" that it was the sinking of the *Lusitania* that brought that country into the First World War when, in reality, over two years separated the points in history. The centennial anniversary of the disaster will no doubt prove fodder for a rehash of long-debunked or highly dubious "facts" – which, unfortunately, still grab headlines – in the hopes of selling a few books or documentaries.

This book has a different focus. While there is a great deal of information on the disaster, and many historical facts which really go a long way to showing why such conspiracy theories really make little or less than no sense, the majority of this book is devoted to a long-ignored chapter of the *Lusitania*'s history: her revolutionary construction and technology, and her resoundingly successful 7½ years in service with the Cunard Line. The introduction of the *Lusitania* and her sister *Mauretania* in late 1907, and the spectacular careers they enjoyed, literally saved that company and helped to ensure their survival for years to come. This book was originally self-published under a lengthier title in 2007, and then went to press with Amberley Books in late 2010. However, for this special commemorative edition, the text has been revised and expanded to add detail or correct errors. Some new and rare images have been selected to help supplement the original material and keep things fresh and visually interesting, while we've worked hard to retain the overall character and flavor of the original book.

As we count down the days to the one hundredth anniversary of one of the saddest chapters of human history, let us never forget those whose lives were brought to a tragic end or were forever altered by those events … events that the world was shocked by, and part of a war that the world never truly recovered from.

J. Kent Layton
December 2014

Opposite: *Escorted by a New York Central tug, the* Lusitania *steams up the North River toward Pier 54 after the conclusion of her second west-bound crossing.*

Above: *A beautiful photograph of the* Lusitania *at sea, traveling at high speed, around 1910 or 1911.*

Below: *A fine portrait of the* Lusitania *on her early trials, in July of 1907.*

Survivor's Note

By Barbara McDermott

"It was a beautiful ship; a true ocean liner. But it was a tragedy. I am very grateful that I was saved. It should never be forgotten. Why did they have to torpedo it? I hope people always remember the *Lusitania* and those poor people at the bottom of the ocean."

Barbara Anderson McDermott
Lusitania *Survivor*

Left: *Barbara Anderson was born in June of 1912, and was traveling with her mother, Emily (Mrs. Roland Anderson). Mrs. Anderson was aged 26 at the time of the sinking, and expecting another child. Barbara was rescued by Assistant Purser William H. Harkness, aged 25. She is shown with her rescuer in this photograph taken just after the sinking.*

Below left: *Mrs. McDermott in more recent times.*

Below right: *A beautiful portrait of Emily Anderson, Barbara's mother.*

Introduction

By Mike Poirier & Jim Kalafus

When Mr. Layton asked us to write a foreword for his book, it was with immediate enthusiasm, and without a second's hesitation, that we said "yes."

The history of the *Lusitania* in contemporary print began promisingly enough with A. A. and Mary Hoehling's *The Last Voyage of the Lusitania*, but subsequent works on the subject were a mixed bag and, unfortunately, by the century's end she was best remembered for fostering endless – and irresolvable – conspiracy debates. When we read Mr. Layton's manuscript, we were glad to see that he has succeeded in telling the long-neglected story of the liner's creation and service history in a manner that is both informative and readable. Her horrible fate aside, the *Lusitania*'s story is still interesting, for she was a ship of many distinctions and achievements. According to an article in the *Cunard Daily Bulletin* from summer 1913, the *"Path of Milestones in Shipbuilding"* that began with the Cunard Company's wooden *Britannia*, had culminated with the *Lusitania* and the *Mauretania* "ushering in a new era of ship-building."

Turbine driven, each proved to be a record breaker, although it was the *Lusitania* that first reclaimed the coveted Blue Riband from Germany. The *Lusitania* and the *Mauretania* were, by far, the must luxurious ships Cunard had constructed at the time of their introduction, and would remain so through the advent of the *Queen Mary* in 1936. One contemporary description stands out:

> These superb ocean greyhounds constitute the ultimate word in the way of passenger service. There are gymnasia where daily exercise in a great variety of beneficial forms can be enjoyed. There are verandah cafes, sun decks, smoking and drawing rooms, libraries and new 'lounges,' so called, where light refreshments are served at any time of the day or night. The best cooks to be found in the world are on board, and the menu is unsurpassed. A doctor is at your disposal, chiefly for social purposes, as it seldom happens that anyone is sick, because everyone is happy. Sleeping accommodations of the Cunard Steamships are most excellent. The passengers' quarters are located amidships. Perfect ventilation is the rule. Even the lowest staterooms are at least twenty feet above the level of the sea. Special Cabins de Luxe, marvelously appointed with the completest and most luxurious of everything that can contribute to the comfort and well being of the occupants can be engaged in advance. The quadruple screw and the magnificent size of these floating palaces cause them to cleave the ocean waves with a barely perceptible motion, so that *mal-de-mer* is a thing that will interest you in an academic way only. Here is health, joy, information, education, growth, outlook, that will inspire you for the rest of your life, give you topics of conversation, things to write on and talk about, and put you in touch with the best that the world has seen and said and done. Aboard ship you can depend upon it you will meet a charming and select company of ladies and gentlemen ... everything that can add to the pleasure, diversion and education of its guests has been provided, in ample measure, by the Cunard Steamship Company. These behemoths of the vasty deep ply between New York and Fishguard and Liverpool. This is the most expeditious route to and from the Old World.

> *Are You A Citizen of the World?*
> Elbert Hubbard, two page essay/ad.

> Mr. Hubbard, and his wife Alice, died aboard the *Lusitania* on May 7, 1915

Although larger ships appeared soon after, she remained a favorite and when one reads through the passenger manifests, one cannot help but notice the large number of repeat customers. The *Lusitania* may not have been the sole means of crossing the Atlantic, but as Mr. Layton illustrates, she proved to be a favored way of doing so.

Opposite: *The Lusitania arriving at her New York pier on her maiden voyage, September 13, 1907.*

This book engagingly chronicles the highs and lows of the *Lusitania*'s nearly eight-year service life. There is the triumph of the Blue Riband, and the embarrassment of the severe vibration that made extensive reconstruction necessary before her maiden voyage. There are accounts of skyscrapers 'black with people' eager to view the new giant upon her first arrival in New York City, and accounts of potential epidemics breaking out on board. Passengers such as Olga Petrova speak with enthusiasm about Captain Dow, while at the same time a long-term and trusted crew member is systematically robbing First Class travelers. Records are broken and too-shallow toilets spill water with the movement of the ship. And, at long last, a picture of the once-beloved ship that was the *Lusitania* emerges from the obscurity to which her violent death, and so many years of conspiracy theories, have relegated her.

We are confident that readers will find much new and interesting in Mr. Layton's work. Thanks to him, there is now a first-rate book by which to remember Cunard's brilliant but tragic flagship.

Opposite top: *Sir Edward and Lady Morris on the* Lusitania's *Boat Deck, just outside the First Class Entrance.*

Opposite bottom: *A wide-angle photo of the John Brown shipyards in early 1907, as the* Lusitania *was nearing completion.*

Above: *The* Lusitania *at Pier 54 in New York during an early stay.*

Below left: *A stern view of the* Lusitania *on her builder's trials in early July of 1907.*

Below right: *This view shows the rudder and propellers of the* Lusitania *prior to her launch.*

"Hail, 'Lusitania,' the first new leviathan twin to wed the ocean; fleet, strong and luxurious, a challenge to the world's mercantile marine. May she have a long career, maintaining prestige and profit to the nation and her Company."

1

A Matter of Honor

In the bustling metropolis that never slept, in the midst of momentous times, there were many newsworthy marvels of men to keep reporters busy. The age of the skyscraper had truly come to life there during the last few years. Names like "Flatiron" and "Singer" were watchwords of the day. Each one represented an enormous undertaking and a remarkable ongoing accomplishment by the human race. The dawn of the 'aeroplane' and the Marconi wireless radio, not to mention the rise of the horseless carriage, or 'auto-mobile', kept this city enthralled. The music of the day was rag-time. Its king-composer was Scott Joplin, an African American – or 'Negro', as the vernacular of the day had it – who would soon undertake a move to the city. The popularity of his music was especially enthralling because it proved just how far the nation had come in the preceding six decades, when a war had divided it primarily on the issues of race and slavery.

These three views of New York City, taken just after the dawn of the twentieth century, show it to be a hub of progress and excitement. Opposite: *In a view taken from a ferry in the North River in 1908, the Singer Building stands out as the tallest structure in the world, a title it would retain until the next year.* Above left: *A 1902 portrait showing the Flatiron Building under construction.* Above right: *The Flatiron Building towers over Broadway in this 1903 view.*

So on the day after the noteworthy event, it was not surprising that a story about it appeared in the pages of one of the world's most famous newspapers, which was named after the city it sprang from, *The New York Times*. The article was small, only three paragraphs in length, and it was buried deep on the eighth page that late-spring morning. However, it was enthralling for what it meant for technology and human progress:

WORLD'S LARGEST LINER
THE *LUSITANIA* SUCCESSFULLY LAUNCHED
AT CLYDEBANK
GLASGOW, Scotland, June 7. – The new Cunard Line steamer *Lusitania*, the world's largest liner, was successfully launched at Clydebank to-day, and was named by Dowager Lady Inverclyde. Hundreds of visitors from all parts of the country, besides thousands of the local population, witnessed the ceremony.[1]

Most of the details which followed in the remaining two paragraphs were a consideration of the basic points of the new ocean liner's statistics, and most of it was either incomplete or wholly inaccurate. It would be quite some time before the *Lusitania*'s presence was actually felt in New York, over a year to be exact; however, as time passed and the preparations leading up to her arrival continued, the New York press would really begin to whip up public excitement over the new liner.

Naturally, the actual event had been even more exciting to those in England, particularly to those who attended. The actual launch at the Scottish shipyards had taken place at 12:30 in the afternoon, and was followed promptly by a luncheon in the shipyard's lavishly decorated moulding loft. There were over five hundred VIP guests and dignitaries present; now they listened as representatives of the owners-to-be and the firm that was building the ship exchanged verbal bows with one another. Champagne-filled glasses were raised again and again in agreement with these wholehearted congratulations.

It was a monumental day for both the builders of the *Lusitania* and her owners-to-be. Indeed, everyone in attendance had every reason to feel proud over the accomplishment. The "heartiest congratulations," of "many notable shipbuilders and ship-owners from all parts of the Kingdom" were tendered. Sir Charles B. MacLaren, the Deputy Chairman of the builders, Messrs. John Brown & Company, Limited, proposed a toast to the "success of the *Lusitania* and Prosperity to the Cunard Company."

William Watson, the Chairman of the Cunard Company, rose to respond to Mr. MacLaren's toast. Watson was new to the Chairmanship of Cunard; the previous Chairman – and the driving force behind the idea for the *Lusitania* and her sister – namely Lord Inverclyde, had passed away on October 8, 1905. Watson paused with a note of soberness to thank Inverclyde's widow, Lady Mary Inverclyde, for having come down to the shipyard to ceremonially launch the ship. While it was "one of the saddest of things" that he had not lived to see this triumph, Watson told Lady Inverclyde that the Cunard Board was grateful to her for honoring her husband's memory in agreeing to participate in the festivities, albeit "at considerable cost to her feelings."[2]

William Watson.

The press throughout the United Kingdom was ecstatic with the latest maritime accomplishment of their country; in the preceding decade, the ocean liners of rival Germany – a new and upstart nation, which was now under the aggressive leadership of Kaiser Wilhelm II – had taken maritime pride from the 'Ruler of the Waves,' Britain. In what was now a matter of honor, the *Lusitania* had become the return salvo to Germany's prestigious Atlantic liners. In creating this new vessel, Britain had given birth to a new era in oceangoing technology.

The day that the *Lusitania* was launched also brought the world one step closer to an uncertain future, for this simple matter of honor would soon become a full-blown world war, with Great Britain and Germany grimly facing each other on the open battlefields of France. In the course of that conflict, the *Lusitania*'s name would become synonymous with tragedy. On that Scotch late-spring day of June 7, 1906, however, the word "*Lusitania*" meant only one thing: progress.

Lord Inverclyde.

For a full century, Great Britain had been – both in naval terms and in terms of merchant shipping – the dominant power in the world, and especially on the Atlantic. This was a matter of necessity, as England was a small island that depended on trade and naval power to maintain its power; it was also a national fetish. A British statesman reportedly once said in Parliament: "Ships, ships, ships. By them we exist as a nation, by them we advance, by them we exalt our national dignity. In area, England is small, but England owns the Atlantic – the Atlantic is a British pond." And this was no exaggeration.

Throughout the nineteenth century, tremendous advances in seagoing technology had arrived on the scene, and the transatlantic passage across "the pond" slowly turned from a weeks-long ordeal with the possibility of being drowned into a regular routine filled with unprecedented comfort and ever-increasing safety. Potential passengers were advised to take a sea voyage "as a rest and air cure ... Taking it all in all, sea trips [were] very strongly recommended as important hygienic factors," for the "invigorating effect of the ocean climate." One American book of the era put the popularity of taking a "foreign tour" to Europe this way:

But a few years ago a tour Around the World was beyond the reach, and almost beyond the ambition, of all save the very wealthy. Today, however, up-to-date machinery has almost annihilated time and distance, so that it is now one of the easiest, and certainly the most charming way of acquiring practical knowledge of other countries and other peoples under the most delightful conditions.

... The foreign tour has now become a yearly function of the large contingent of American pleasure-seekers, and the volume of travel is steadily increasing year by year. Within a very few years pleasure travel Around the World has more than quadrupled, and a girdling of the earth is now the grand tour which a little round of Continental Europe used to be. Today the latter is hardly more than a short excursion. Perhaps it would be safe to say that five hundred persons now go abroad to one who would venture the trip ten or twelve years ago.

Every Spring a huge exodus sets in, and then everybody seems to be going abroad. Friends and acquaintances plan ahead and make appointments from one year to another for reunions, etc., in London, Paris or other cities.[3]

Because of the technological advances in maritime construction, passengers were informed that they no longer had to worry about the dangers of an ocean passage:

After fighting the sea and its terrors for thousands of years, man has at last succeeded in conquering the sea, this wildest and most unruly of Nature's children. Against the modern iron or steel ship, which is equipped with every measure of protection that science and engineering can devise, the sea is almost powerless. Smaller vessels and sailing craft still feel its fury occasionally, it is true, but the enormous ships of the present day forge their way through the mighty ocean at high speeds.[4]

Although the French, Germans and Americans all had shipping interests on the Atlantic, and had even set up respectable transatlantic steamship companies, it was really the British companies that had set the benchmark in this trade. Halifax businessman Samuel Cunard had inaugurated the Cunard Line in 1840 in order to capture a Royal Mail subsidy. Thomas H. Ismay had founded the White Star Line on January 18, 1868, and the two British companies quickly became the most renowned in the world.

When the White Star liner *Teutonic* of 1889 entered service, she was the pride of Great Britain's mercantile fleet. On August 3 of that year, while participating in the Spithead Naval Review, she was inspected by the Prince of Wales and Kaiser Wilhelm II. Kaiser Wilhelm was the grandson of Queen Victoria, by way of her daughter Victoria, Empress Frederick of Germany. Born in 1859, he was but thirty when he boarded the *Teutonic*. Young and ambitious, Wilhelm was dearly devoted to his grandmother, but was also eager to see his own nation become a rival to Great Britain – perhaps even to usurp her position of dominance on the world scene. While touring the *Teutonic*, he was apparently heard to remark: "We must have some of these."

Germany had two main merchant lines, Hamburg-Amerika and Norddeutscher Lloyd (North German Lloyd). In 1897, North German Lloyd fulfilled the Kaiser's dreams when they introduced the new liner *Kaiser Wilhelm der Grosse*, named in honor of the Kaiser's own grandfather. The *Kaiser Wilhelm* was the longest and largest liner afloat at the time, and also proved to be the fastest, quickly taking the Blue Riband – the much-coveted yet non-corporeal prize for the fastest ship on the Atlantic – away from Great Britain's liners. Following in the wake of the *Kaiser Wilhelm* was a string of German liners that were the largest, fastest and most prestigious of the day.

In 1902, American financier John P. Morgan bought out the White Star Line, solidly placing one of the two great British lines under American ownership. Morgan also tried to buy out Cunard, but Cunard's Chairman, Inverclyde, was firmly opposed to the takeover. His company's position was unenviable, however; Morgan's new combine, the International Mercantile Marine, had the prestigious White Star Line in the fore. They were planning new and startlingly luxurious ocean liners for the Atlantic service. At the same time, the German lines held the Blue Riband, and were also trend-settingly luxurious. Then a rate war heated up, with competitors cutting the prices for travel across the Atlantic at a speed with which Cunard could barely keep up.

Cunard's front-running liners just before the turn of the century were the *Campania* and *Lucania*, both of 1893 and quite modest in comparison with the German and White Star ships. Cunard could not maintain their prestigious position on the Atlantic without putting new superliners into service, but neither did they have the resources to follow through on this notion. Their new *Ivernia* and *Saxonia* were the largest Cunarders ever built when they entered service in 1899 and 1900, respectively; still they could not compete with the other ships on the Atlantic at the time. More was needed – much more.

Inverclyde needed a backer, and the deepest pockets on hand at the time were controlled by Parliament under Prime Minister Salisbury; by July of 1902, the stewardship of the Government had changed, as Salisbury had been succeeded as Prime Minister by his nephew, Arthur Balfour. Appealing to feelings of bruised patriotic prestige, Inverclyde proposed to Parliament that the British Government provide Cunard with a loan in order to give them the fiscal fluidity needed to construct the largest and fastest vessels in the world. These vessels would, in turn, re-capture the mercantile pride from Germany.

No earthly government moves quickly, but before the summer of 1902 was out, Balfour's Government had at least conditionally agreed to the idea; even with the formal agreement pending, however, it was clear that they felt it necessary to back Cunard in order to salvage British prestige on the Atlantic. At last, in July of 1903, the final agreement was reached.

The formal agreement specified that the Government would supply a sum not to exceed £2.6 million in the form of a 20-year loan, at an interest rate of 2¾ per cent – less than half of the going rates at the time – in order to fund the construction of the two vessels. Additionally, a £150,000 sum was to be paid to Cunard every year to fund the ships' operation and upkeep. Under this agreement, the Cunard Line was to remain a British-only operation, with "no foreigner" being "qualified to hold office as a director of the company or to be employed as one of the principal officers of the company; and no shares of the company" were to be held by, "or in trust for, or be in any way under the control of any foreigner or foreign corporation, or any corporation under foreign control." A mail contract was also included in the arrangement. The company's leadership was altered to allow for three trustees to hold office. One would be elected by the Government, and a second would be elected by Cunard. These two trustees would then, in turn, elect a third member. Two nominees of the Government would also receive a single £20 share in the company, each man having somewhat unique shareholder rights and privileges.

On the other side of the equation, the Admiralty was to have complete approval over the ships' design. Each ship was to be capable of maintaining a minimum average speed of 24½ knots in moderate weather. If the

Arthur Balfour, British Prime Minister from 1902 to 1905.

speed of the new ships fell below that mark, but did not fall below 23½ knots, then a deduction from the annual £150,000 payment would be made. A speed of less than 23½ knots could mean further penalties, or even the complete rejection of the ships. The new liners were to be liable for charter by the Government in time of war, and were to be designed for conversion into high-speed auxiliary cruisers with formidable armament, should the need arise. Additionally, the charter of all Cunard ships by the Government was also assured under the provisions of the deal.

Once Cunard had signed on the proverbial dotted line, everything was ready for Cunard to proceed with the designs of and orders for the *Lusitania* and *Mauretania*. However, this was no simple process; much work had already been done on the project – even before the agreement was finalized – and still more lay ahead before the first ship's maiden voyage could commence.

2
The Birth of the *Lusitania*

Time was of the essence for Cunard in moving ahead with their new ships, because the more time passed, the greater their competitors' lead over them would be. Instead of waiting until the British Government had made a final agreement with them to fund the new ships, Cunard – working with ship-building firms that might eventually win the contracts to build the sister ships – began to start working on initial plans for the liners.

One English shipbuilding firm of the time was C. S. Swan & Hunter, Ltd., located at Wallsend-on-Tyne. Although they had not yet broken in to the list of top-notch shipbuilding firms of the day, they had already built for the Cunard Company the intermediate steamers *Ultonia* of 1899, of some 8,845 gross registered tons, and the *Ivernia* of 1900 and 13,799 grt. When she entered service, the *Ivernia* was paired up with the slightly larger *Saxonia*, of 14,197 grt, which had been built by John Brown & Company on the Clyde River. The order for a third ship of that class, the *Carpathia*, was placed with C. S. Swan & Hunter.

Based on their already-established relationship, it was natural that Cunard contacted C. S. Swan & Hunter very early on in the process of planning their response to White Star and the Germans. Cunard's General Superintendent, James Bain, and their resident naval architect, Leonard Peskett, had drawn up plans for liners 700 feet in length, designed for a service speed of 24 knots. The plans were submitted to Swan & Hunter in 1901, but no further action was taken at the time, for Inverclyde was still trying to secure financial backing from the British Government to follow through on the venture.

When the Government gave their conditional agreement to Cunard in 1902, the line's directors found that the specifications for the steamers they had originally proposed were no longer adequate, and went back to the drawing board. Eventually, they worked up a rough outline for a ship of 750 feet between perpendiculars[1] by 76 feet wide; additionally a speed of 25 knots, instead of 24, was now the goal that they set. For the sake of practicality, they decided to farm out the construction of each of the two new ships

to a different yard; this would allow for simultaneous construction. Cunard conferred with four competing shipyards: John Brown & Company of Clydebank in Scotland; the Fairfield Shipbuilding & Engineering Company of Govan, Scotland, also located on the Clyde; Vickers Sons & Maxim, Ltd. of Barrow-in-Furness; and finally – after the firm's Chairman, George Hunter, convinced Cunard to allow his firm a chance at the contract – C. S. Swan & Hunter. The four shipyards, in turn, performed elaborate model tests and mathematical computations to find the best overall size and shape for the vessels, and then submitted their results to Cunard for review.

At the time the Clyde River, which both John Brown and Fairfield yards fronted, was inadequate to handle vessels of the size being considered. In order to seriously pursue the contracts, the companies informed the Clyde Navigation Trust – a public statutory body responsible for maintaining and improving that river – that a contract for one of these liners could not be accepted "unless there was an absolute certainty that the channel leading from the yards concerned to the sea was deepened and widened to a certain extent". The Trustees "at once gave their assurance that there would be sufficient water by the launching date."[2] With that assurance, both companies were able to pursue a contract to build one of the new behemoths.

On December 18, 1902, the Cunard Board of Directors reviewed the four proposals. The most favorable ones were from C. S. Swan & Hunter and Vickers Sons & Maxim. Fairfield was forced to drop out of the running in January 1903, but John Brown still remained in the running at that point. Swan & Hunter had proposed a ship of 760 feet (b.p.) by 80 feet, while Vickers' proposal was for a ship with a slightly slimmer beam. Each ship would be powered by three sets of tandem quadruple-expansion five-cylinder reciprocating engines outputting over 60,000 h.p. Messrs. John Brown & Company, of Clydebank, proposed a vessel of 725 feet (b.p.) by 80 feet; model tests of this form brought back poor results, however. Meanwhile, the Swan & Hunter model tests showed that their design required 7 per cent less power to achieve the

This photo was taken during relatively early stages of construction, looking forward from the stern. The keel has been laid through the entire length of the ship, and the double bottom is likewise taking shape. Work on the bow section is advanced over work astern.

same speed as that of the Vickers design. However, some stability problems were encountered with their platform, and so it was decided that the new vessels' breadth should be increased to 87.5 feet. After further tank tests under the supervision of Sir Philip Watts, the Director of Naval Construction to the Admiralty, which were concluded in April 1904, the length b.p. of each ship was increased to 760 feet, while a working draught of 33.5 feet was settled on.

In July of 1903, the Cunard Company entered into the formal agreement with the British Government. Now, with adequate funds at their disposal, the time had arrived for Cunard to choose the companies that would build the new liners. Although Vickers Sons & Maxim had been an early contender, at a formal meeting with representatives of Vickers, Swan & Hunter, and John Brown, Cunard had indicated a clear preference for selecting John Brown and Swan & Hunter. As long as the two companies could 'collaborate with a view to producing duplicate ships', or sister vessels based on the same general design, those two companies were all but assured of receiving the contracts. With this affirmation, in order to prepare for the project ahead, Swan & Hunter agreed to merge with the nearby shipyard of Wigham Richardson, thus creating the firm with the preposterous-sounding name Swan, Hunter & Wigham Richardson. Vickers Sons & Max-

im, it was reported, simply could not build a ship with the increased breadth settled upon by Cunard after the tank testing. On April 30, 1904, Cunard's directors met with representatives from Swan, Hunter and John Brown, and informed them that they should 'regard the order as having been placed' with them. Both shipyards immediately began work on their respective projects.

Before the first keel plate of John Brown's ship could be laid, an appropriate slip to accommodate her unprecedented size needed to be built. The first issue that had to be tackled was that the Clyde River in front of the John Brown yard was only slightly over 600 feet in width – far too narrow to launch the nearly eight-hundred-foot hull of the *Lusitania* into. However, the frontage of the yard also came into close proximity with the confluence of the Clyde and Cart Rivers. Thus, the new slipway – replacing two previous slips – was built on an angle of forty degrees to the line of the river, to maximize this fortuitous position and allow a comfortable launch run of twelve-hundred feet. The keel blocks were built at a declivity of 7/16" per foot, spaced three feet apart from center to center. Bilge blocks were built to support the port and starboard extremes of the double bottom, and as the time drew near to launch the ship, the standing ways were constructed between the keel blocks and the bilge blocks.

This photograph was taken looking from the port stern toward the starboard bow of the Lusitania *at about the same time as the preceding photo. Workers are clearly visible installing the ship's hull plates while suspended from scaffolding.*

With these preparations complete, it was time for the real work to begin. The first keel plate for the new liner, John Brown Hull No. 367, to be laid down. This took place on Wednesday, August 17, 1904 – a ceremony that Cunard's Chairman, Lord Inverclyde, reportedly participated in.[3] From that time, work progressed quickly, and soon nearly the entire keel had been laid. Initial work was focused on the forward and midships regions of the vessel, as certain minor details of her final configuration – such as the positioning of bulkheads and some of the machinery seatings – had not yet been finalized.

As construction commenced, the ship – and her future running mate taking shape at the Swan, Hunter shipyards on the banks of the Tyne River – was without a name. It was not until February 15, 1906, at a meeting of Cunard's Board of Directors, that names were formally selected. Among the contending pairs of names were *Britannia* and *Hesperia*, *Britannia* and *Hibernia*, and *Albania* and *Morovia*. But in the end, the names *Lusitania* and *Mauritania* were selected. John Brown Hull No. 367 was to become the *Lusitania*, while the ship being built by Swan, Hunter, would be named *Mauritania*. The names were selected in honor of the names of former Roman Provinces located in Spain and Africa, respectively, and bore Cunard's traditional *-ia* suffix. The names were soon released to the public, but Cunard quickly realized that the spell-

ing of the Roman province whose name the Tyne ship bore was not *Mauritania*, with two i's. Instead, the correct spelling was *Mauretania*. They made the necessary alteration, thus confusing generations of maritime enthusiasts and researchers more familiar with the spelling of the modern nation Mauritania.

While the Cunard Company was deciding on names, the John Brown yards were alive with activity; pride in the project was running very high. This yard, these workers, were participating in the effort to build the world's largest and fastest ship – right there in Scotland. Naturally, the *Lusitania* was the pride of the British Empire; however, it was only natural that Scottish people felt a particularly strong attachment to her. The way that the Scottish people felt about the *Lusitania* is perhaps best summed up by a statement that one of her Scottish engineers made just as her Boat Deck was about to slip under the waves in 1915: "Och," he reportedly exclaimed, "but they can't sink a *Clyde*-built ship!"

At the English yards of Swan, Hunter, work on the *Mauretania* was ongoing. Although her keel was laid down only a day after the *Lusitania's*, she was progressing more slowly than her Scottish-built sister, and her form was lagging somewhat. Work on her was done underneath a large steel and glass enclosure, protecting workers from the often inclement English weather. At John Brown, on the other hand,

work continued in the open air. From a distance, it actually looked more as if the ship was simply sprouting from the muddy riverbank than from a carefully built slipway.

The deal to build the *Lusitania* meant that the yard would be bustling with work for a full three years, regardless of other projects that the company was carrying out simultaneously. However, there was also labor unrest at the time; no matter how proud the yard's employees were of their project, there were still several times when work on the ship was stopped due to strikes – one of these lasted a full seven weeks. During this particular strike, which occurred in late 1906 and was on the part of the boiler production crews and steel workers, the work was carried out by their apprentices; in due course, things returned to normal and work continued.

Despite the occasional spot of labor unrest, work on the *Lusitania* proceeded at a very good pace. Eventually, by the late spring of 1906, the ship's hull stood poised on the ways, towering above the shipyard and the River Clyde. All four propellers were mounted in their designated locations at the extremities of the tail shafts prior to the launch. To protect the delicate blades during the procedure, they were carefully bound in wooden casings that would be removed later on.

The preparations for the launch were extensive. At the bow, a strong cradle and fore-poppet had been constructed and firmly affixed to the shell plating; their purpose was to give the ship added stability during the critical moments when her stern was afloat and her narrow bow was balanced on the ways. These were fitted with tripping lines and bolts so that once the ship was afloat the entire structure could be easily removed. It

Opposite top: *This photograph shows the stern form of the* Lusitania *taking shape. The ship's stern post, the mount for the rudder, and the after propeller bossings are all clearly visible.*

Opposite middle: *This photo, looking astern, shows the plating on the Promenade Deck being installed.*

Opposite bottom: *This photo shows the liner's hull fully plated. Scaffolding still enshrouds the upper works along the sides as workers work to complete preparations for the launch. Astern, work on installing the ship's quartet of propellers is under way.*

Above: *The stern of the liner towers over the banks of the Clyde in this photo, taken as the launch date neared. Work is still under way around the propellers and rudder, and scaffolding still hangs over the sides of the ship.*

Below: *This photo was taken very close to the launch of the liner, and shows how far work has progressed since the photograph opposite.*

Opposite: *The mighty prow of the Lusitania towers over the shipyard, dwarfing everything in sight. The drag chains, which would help slow her hull after it had taken to the waters of the Clyde, have been attached to the eye plates along the ship's hull.*

Above: *Proud workers from the shipbuilding firm pose underneath the forward port propeller of the vessel, not long before the launch. The behemoth creation dwarfs its creators, giving some idea of the incredible effort already poured into the liner's construction.*

Below: *With most of the timber supports helping to balance the liner on the ways removed, this stern view shows the finished form of the hull in its entire splendor.*

was against this fore-cradle that the hydraulic cylinders would be used if the ship did not begin to move under her own weight when the time arrived. As the time for the event neared, the keel and bilge blocks were progressively removed until the ship was supported on the ways by the cradle.

The standing ways – positioned between the center keel blocks and the outer bilge blocks – were lubricated with a 3/8"-thick coating of Russian tallow and soft soap; the sliding ways, which were some 680 feet in length, were given a similar coating of lubricant. The sliding ways would bear an estimated pressure of about two tons per square foot during the launch. It was also necessary to provide a mechanism for initiating the ship's movement. Six electrically operated triggers – three to each side, about 180 feet apart – were positioned to release the ship on the sliding ways. Once these had been tripped, the ship would be motivated to begin its journey toward the water.

Getting the hull moving was one thing; stopping it was another. As the ship slid down the ways toward the water, its momentum would become a force to reckon with. Without some sort of stopping mechanism, the ship would simply careen across the full

Above: *The presence of a woman in the shipyard shows that this photograph was most likely taken on the day of the liner's launch, June 7, 1906.*

Below: *Spectators begin to gather in the yard to view the momentous event.*

width of the waterway and end up on the opposite bank of the river. Over a thousand tons of drag chain, including chains that were once used aboard Brunel's giant, the *Great Eastern*, were set up to act as this opposing force. The chains were set in groups and pairs along either side of the hull, resting on the ground in carefully arranged piles. Steel wire cables affixed the chains to the ship, and these were connected by chain plates bolted to the hull's outer shell plating. The drags were spaced at roughly ten-foot intervals, with the first being called into action as soon as the liner had traveled the full length of the ways; the heaviest drag pile was set to come into action last.

On the day of the launch, Thursday, June 7, 1906, the John Brown shipyards were buzzing with activity. The weather was sunny, all in all a beautiful late-spring Scottish day. While workmen carried out the final launch preparations, careful inspections were made all around the ship to ensure that everything was ready as it could be. Well-dressed, specially invited spectators began arriving, some six hundred all told. Some of these were allowed to venture down on the bank of the river, practically underneath the hull, to get a good look at the liner as it towered over them. Members of the press began arriving in droves, and thousands of spectators lined the banks of the Clyde

River along both sides, as well as on the decks of waterborne craft that, as the time approached for launch, stood off at a respectful distance from the 16,000-ton hull that would soon be entering the river.

Anticipation in the yard mounted as the predetermined hour approached, and everyone present took their places; all eyes were fixed either on the unbelievably large hull, or on Lady Inverclyde, who was standing on the launching platform near the bow. At the set time, 12:30 p.m., Lady Inverclyde pushed the specially rigged button that tripped the triggers, and smashed the bottle of wine against the prow, christening the unfinished ship to be the "*Lusitania*." Although a special indicator light was set up to show that the triggers had been successfully activated, it immediately became apparent that they had done their job. For the following twenty-two seconds, there was a tremendous creaking and groaning noise as the hull's weight shifted upon the ways. In the end, simple physics told the enormous hull which way it had to go; the ways were lubricated and the hull could not defy gravity, and so its only option was to follow the declining ways

into the water. During this twenty-two-second time of decision, the hull moved only one foot.

Then, during the subsequent sixty-four seconds of the launch, the hull began to move in earnest. The band present for the occasion struck up "Rule Britannia" on cue, and as she slid toward the water the Union Jack that hung from the prow stood out in earnest. It was, as one journalist later pointed out, an event of "national importance," not only because this was the greatest maritime achievement in history, but also because this ship would – it was hoped – put German maritime arrogance to shame.

It must have been a spectacular sensory experience; the bright sunshine and blue skies showed the scene in brilliant color. The white, black and dark red of the hull gleamed in all its newness as it ran toward and finally parted the waters of the Clyde River. The sound of the hull moving over the ways was thunderous, with the ship's hull groaning while the ways creaked under their respective stresses; next came the sound of the giant chains jangling as their connecting stays were brought taut, one after another, and the

Lady Mary Inverclyde has sent the bottle of champagne on course for the ship's prow. Within seconds, the liner would begin to slide down the ways.

Above: *This illustration shows the ship moving in earnest, her stern entering the water for the first time.*

Below: *This photograph shows the ship pulling away into the Clyde River. Her stern is in the water, and her prow still stands on the ways, balanced with the aid of the fore poppet. On the port side of the Forecastle, a workman waves his cap in salute to those watching. The British flag flutters proudly from the prow. The drag chains are already at work, slowly checking the great momentum that the hull had built.*

Opposite top: *A few seconds later, the* Lusitania *rides serenely on the river.*

piles began to drag along the riverbank. Then, in a moment, the launch had ended. The hull's movement stopped, the noise of the chains ceased, and only the cheers from spectators and the playing of the band remained. In the middle of the Clyde, the hull bobbed serenely in the water; without any fittings or machinery aboard, she rode unusually high, with the tops of her propellers yet exposed. Her prow sat 110 feet from the end of the ways.

During the primary 64 seconds of the launch, the ship had attained a mean velocity of 12.2 feet per sec-

ond, or just less than eight-and-a-half land miles per hour. In the end, the last pile of drag chains, which was also the heaviest, did not even find use before the hull was stopped in the river. In the moments shortly after the launch, six tugs hurried up and took positions around the giant form, attaching lines to the hull so that she could be warped into her fitting-out basin for the final stages of her construction. The pins holding the drag chains to the hull were released, and the hull of the *Lusitania* was safely brought to the fitting-out basin, successfully completing her first voyage.

Above: *Tugs begin to take the hull under their protective care, moving it slowly and cautiously toward the deepwater fitting-out dock.*

Right: *A montage from period Cunard publicity which shows several views of the launch. The photograph on the bottom shows the hull being towed stern-first to the fitting-out dock.*

Above: *On May 8, 1900, employees from the Engine Work & Patternmakers division of John Brown pose for this photograph. Doubtless many of these same individuals labored to bring the* Lusitania *to life just a few years later.*

Opposite top: *A portion of one of the liner's turbine casings arriving at the shipyard, where workers posed alongside of it to give some sense of scale.*

Opposite bottom: *In John Brown's Engine Works, the mighty turbines of the great liner are assembled.*

Although the festivities were grand that evening all around Clydebank, and newspaper reports throughout England thrilled readers with tales of the event, the truth was that the launching was only the beginning of the second half of the project of building the *Lusitania*. Work began afresh on the ship the next day, turning her into a finished and seaworthy ocean liner.

Fitting out the *Lusitania* was an enormous task. When she was launched, the ship was a mere shell. There were no engines, boilers, machinery, or equipment in place. Each deck was only a steel floor and a steel ceiling, with columns supporting the decks overhead – there was no internal subdivision other than the watertight bulkheads found below. Outside, the superstructure was only complete up to the floor of the Promenade Deck, while forward, a mere fraction of the Promenade Deck's enclosure and the flooring of the Boat Deck was in place. There was nothing above these points – no funnels, no masts … nothing. All of these items, as well as the ship's lavish appointments and furnishings, would be added during the fitting out.

The first step was to take the ship's machinery from shore, hoist it aboard the liner and put it into place. All of the boilers, uptakes, turbines, condensers, etc., had been produced in the Clydebank works ashore.

With the ship now ready to accept the machinery, each piece, in turn, was placed on small carts which ran on railroad-style tracks through the shops and out onto the wharf beside where the *Lusitania*'s hull was berthed. Once alongside the ship, a large crane would hoist the item off of its cart and into the air. This crane had been built by Sir William Arrol & Co., Ltd. It stood on the east side of the fitting-out basin, and had a lift capacity of 150 tons (Imperial).[3] Once the item was in the air, a delicate choreography followed: all along the decks of the liner, large openings gave access to the lowest regions of the ship. Eventually, these would all be sealed, used for funnel uptakes and ventilation spaces. With them still open, however, the crane operators could carefully lower the large machinery down into the bowels of the *Lusitania*'s hull, whereupon it was cautiously guided into its final mounts and secured to the ship. Eventually, all of the boilers, turbines, condensers, and machinery had found their way into the vessel. Following this, the large funnel uptakes and boiler flues were hoisted into place and attached, sealing the machinery in place.

When the ship was being designed, Cunard had given careful consideration to the idea of firing the ship's boilers with oil fuel, rather than coal. Sir

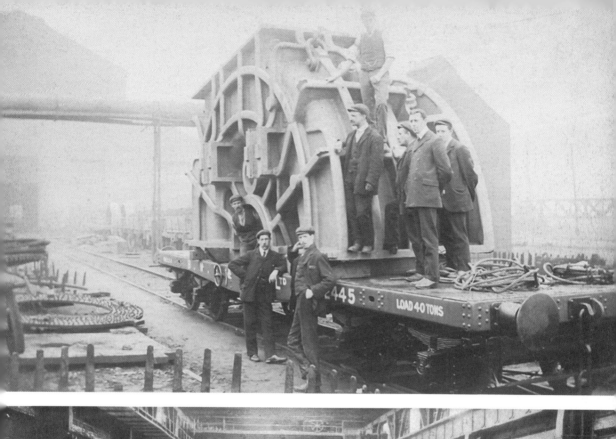

William White, a naval architect who consulted on the *Mauretania* project, later said that Cunard "recognized that by the use of oil there would be a considerable gain in weight and space required for fuel, large economies of labor in the stokehold and the numbers in its staff, easier regulation of steam, and more uniform production."[4] It would also be much easier to refuel the ship while she was in port, as moving coal aboard a liner was a notoriously grimy, labor-intensive, loud and messy task.

Despite these obvious advantages, Cunard could not obtain satisfactory arrangements for regular supply of oil fuel at an acceptable price; coal was still the standard of the time, and would remain such until after the First World War. Because of this, the decision was made to fuel the ships with coal instead of oil. Converting the *Lusitania* or the *Mauretania* to oil later on was still possible. It would be an involved and expensive undertaking, however. All of the coal bunkers would need to be made completely watertight and specially converted to carry liquid fuel rather than the solid type; heating and settling tanks would need to be installed, and provision made to pipe fuel to the boilers. If the boilers themselves were replaced entirely, then everything above them – including the funnels, the uptakes, and the boiler flues – would need to be removed to facilitate the change. Even if only the furnaces within the boilers were removed and replaced, that was quite an involved task. Such a conversion was performed on the *Mauretania* following the conclusion of the war, but the *Lusitania* was powered by coal throughout her career.

Once the *Lusitania*'s powerplant and machinery had all been installed, the ship's superstructure could be built, and the interior spaces could also be partitioned off and turned into finished cabins and public rooms. The final floor plan of the ship would primarily be laid out with yellow pine framing dividing the cavernous steel interiors of the unfinished decks. Once this framing had been finished, each subdivision would slowly be transformed into a completed reality.

The passenger accommodations of the *Lusitania* were unquestionably the most spacious and beautiful of their time. Although the ship was being funded on a Government subsidy, Cunard understood the need to create stunning and extremely comfortable spaces for their passengers, and they commissioned an architect named James Miller to design her interior décor.

James Miller was the son of George Miller, a farmer in the parish of Auchtergaven, Scotland. The Miller family moved to Cairnie, Forteviot shortly after James' birth.[5] Rising from humble origins, he was educated at Perth Academy; in time Miller became an associate of the Royal Scottish Academy, and also a Fellow of the Royal Institute of British Architects. Some of the other accomplishments that he would make during his career included work on the Canadian Pavilion for the Glasgow International Exhibition of 1901, an extension to the Glasgow Central Station Hotel (completed in 1907, in collaboration with Donald Mathieson), the Turnberry Hotel in Ayrshire, and the Prince of Wales Museum of Western India at Bombay (completed in 1915). By 1909, he had managed to achieve the distinction of being named one of Glasgow's "Who's Who" citizens. Today he is recognized as one of Scotland's greatest architects.

Miller created an overall theme that was very light in color. It made use of a lot of white, but it never grew boring to the eye, as the white was supported by gilt detailing, as well as gray and rose colored accents, combined with some use of natural French-polished woods of the finest quality. Overall, the décor was based on Louis XVI and Georgian themes. There

Left: *James Miller, a prominent Scottish architect, created a scheme of interior décor for the* Lusitania *which was considered "the highest conception of artistic furnishing and internal decoration."*

Opposite top: *In this photograph, workers leave the ship at the end of a long day's work. The liner's upper works are progressing well, with funnels and lifeboats already in place.*

Opposite bottom: *The First Class Writing Room & Library was rendered in the Brothers Adam style, and was designed to be a comfortable space for reading, letter-writing, or socialization with other passengers.*

The Writing Room.
s.s. LUSITANIA.

were instances where natural woods were used, left unpainted, but such woodwork was less in evidence in the Scottish ship than it would be aboard the *Mauretania*. This was because Cunard had farmed out the design of the *Mauretania's* décor to another architect, Harold Peto, who made much more use of natural-colored wood. In period black-and-white photographs, the use of natural-colored woods aboard the *Mauretania* appears dark and oppressive, but the reality was that Peto's work was in no way a disappointment. At the time of the *Mauretania's* maiden voyage it was said:

> Though the interior scheme of the *Mauretania* is like that of her sister ship, the *Lusitania*, there is an entire contrast in interior decoration. The color scheme of the *Lusitania's* decorations is white and gold, while in the *Mauretania* the natural color of the wood, combined with a darker and more somber tone of tapestries and upholstery, gives an effect of rich and substantial beauty.[6]

Regarding the *Lusitania's* interior décor, *Engineering* magazine noted: "The express Cunard liner *Lusitania*

... is not only a great step forward from the mechanical engineering standpoint, but marks the highest conception of artistic furnishing and internal decoration."[7] The *Lusitania's* décor was, indeed, extremely successful without overwhelming passengers with bombast, a trap that some German liners of the preceding decade had fallen into.

There were seven public rooms in First Class, five on the Boat Deck (A), a smaller one forward on the Promenade Deck (B), and one spanning the Shelter (C) and Upper (D) Decks. Since so much work went into creating them during this phase of the ship's construction, it would be appropriate to briefly consider them now.

Forward on the Boat Deck was the Writing Room & Library, which was positioned just in front of the Grand Entrance. With extreme dimensions measuring 52 feet wide by 44 feet long, a large amount of this space was taken up with the No. 2 Funnel Casing. Despite this, the room was an architectural masterpiece rendered in the eighteenth-century Brothers Adam style. The wood paneling was – like all other painted wood paneling in First and Second Classes – an ivory-white color applied in five coats. There were panels of gray silk brocade inset into the walls, and decorative Corinthian columns surrounded the steel supports holding up the decks above. The carpet was a rose color, while intricate decorative glass windows mounted inside of those overlooking the Boat Deck allowed light to pour into the space while providing a sense of "terra firma." There was a black and white marble fireplace along the forward wall,[8] while on the aft wall stood a twenty-three-foot-long mahogany bookcase. Standing some nine feet tall, only a foot and a half short of the ceiling, it contained a respectable lending library for the use of passengers during their crossing. Occasional tables and thickly padded horsehair-upholstered seats were provided, as well as writing desks. Sitting atop each of these writing tables was "a finely-chased and mercury gilt lamp," as *Engineering* magazine described it. Passengers could thus write to friends or loved ones on com-

Above left: *If one were to move from the Writing Room & Library into the First Class Entrance by going through the starboard set of double doors, this view would have presented itself. This was the prime people-moving feature of First Class life, with a staircase that descended from the Boat Deck (A) to the Main Deck (E). In the center of the stairwell was a pair of elevators, or lifts. The doors on the right led out to the Boat Deck through the vestibule.*

Left: *Looking forward and to port from the after starboard portion of the Entrance, the details of the elevator cages, skylight, and staircase are all clearly visible.*

plimentary Cunard stationary stocked and available on each voyage; as an alternative, they could also purchase *Lusitania* picture postcards for a nominal fee.

Moving just aft of the Writing Room was the First Class Grand Entrance. This was exactly what its name implied, and was designed to give First Class passengers access to any deck within their domain via the shortest possible route. There was a Grand Staircase along the forward end, encasing on three sides the center elevators' tracks. The floor was laid entirely in black and white India-rubber squares; although the tiles were laid diagonally to the ship's fore and aft axis, they were set to create a pattern that was aligned fore and aft. Surrounding the elevators and stairwell was an elaborate black wrought-iron rail offset with gilded decorations. A skylight sitting astride the stairway, some 21½ feet by 18 feet in size, allowed a glorious wash of light to fill the airy space, and settees in rose-colored upholstery complemented occasional tables and wicker chairs for those who wished to take a break from their ship-wandering. Palm trees lined the walls in convenient locations, and a rose-colored runner of carpeting descended the staircase. A fireplace was set in the aft wall, and over the mantle stood a tall arched

mirror. Corinthian columns some 9½ feet high covered the stanchions which supported the ceiling.

Astern of this highly functional yet beautiful space, through doors on either side of the Entrance's aft end, was the First Class Lounge & Music Room. Some 68 feet long by 52 feet wide, this beautiful room was covered with an enormous barrel-vaulted plaster and stained-glass dome rising to a peak of 18 feet in height from the floor. This plaster and glass masterpiece was divided into a dozen different panels, each one representing a separate month of the year. The overall scheme of the room was late Georgian. The walls were rendered in French-polished mahogany veneer, inlaid in specially selected and finely figured woods, while the carpeting and furniture were upholstered in light greens and yellows. At the fore and aft ends of the Lounge stood two enormous green marble fireplaces, each one 14 feet high, and both of them fully operational. A large grand piano was also installed. It was veneered and finished to match the overall scheme of the room, and sported an early double-leg design and cross-bracing between the legs and lyre just above the floor. This beautiful instrument truly made this public space a "Lounge & Music

If one continued aft from the Entrance, through the starboard set of double doors, there was the Lounge & Music Room. This was the center of First Class socializing during the voyage. Comfortable sofas and easy chairs clustered in small groups allowed for a pleasurable way to pass hours catching up with old friends or making new shipboard acquaintances. This view is looking aft along the starboard side.

Above: *The main portion of the First Class Smoking Room. The sole preserve of gentlemen, this space also had a fully functioning fireplace. It is clear that Cunard thought it necessary for the Smoking Room to be stunning. Architect Miller's initial scheme for the room was rejected by Cunard; they seem to have felt that it was not going to be impressive enough décor to set the stage as the most prominent men in the world socialized.*

Right: *The Verandah Café, astern of the Smoking Room, overlooked the Second Class spaces astern. This was a wholly nondescript and rather sanitary space that was never fully pleasing. It was the scene of some rather significant alterations and improvements in 1914.*

Room"; it was here that the ship's concerts were held on the last night of every crossing.

At the aft end of the Lounge, on either side of the ship, were two further sets of doors, allowing access to the First Class Smoking Room, astern. Although Cunard was trying to save money where they could in the construction of the ship, and they also felt that maintaining lightness of weight was a special point of consideration in both the construction and outfitting, the First Class Smoking Room was a special point of concern. Indeed, James Miller's original design for the space was rejected on the grounds that it was not outstanding enough; Miller went back to the drawing boards and in short order was able to design a room which more suited Cunard's tastes. When finished the Smoking Room was large, some 55 feet by 50 feet.

However, four banks of ventilating trunks, spaced from port to starboard across the forward half of the room, subdivided this space, creating a narrow portion fore and a large section aft. The sole preserve of gentlemen in this era, the Smoking Room was rendered in eighteenth-century style, with Italian walnut paneling and Queen Anne-style furniture. The general color introduced by the upholstery was referred to as "old Italian red." High-quality five-frame Brussels carpet runners covered over the parquetry flooring in the "traffic patterns" that were considered busiest. There was a bar and buffet, always well stocked, which was fitted with a sink, running water, and a small refrigerator to cool wines and mineral waters.[9]

From the Smoking Room, a doorway and hall led aft along the centerline of the ship, past the bar, and to the First Class Verandah Café. Some 49 feet 3 inches wide and 23 feet 6 inches long, this space proved problematic right from the start. It underwent numerous design revisions prior to construction; the first idea was to fit a Café with only a roof, and to leave all three sides open to the elements. This was clearly out of harmony with the harsh weather and temperatures often faced on the North Atlantic, and needed to be rethought, although the original large skylight in the roof was in the end retained. Cunard toyed with the idea of enclosing the three sides with folding screens, but found that it would actually be cheaper just to build solid bulkheads on the port and starboard sides and to place a trio of arched openings facing aft. The decision to go this route was made in February of 1907 at a point well along in the ship's fitting out. Although they ended up spending £1,100 on the room as it was originally fitted, it was rather a drab space, rather resembling a nondescript English train station more than anything else. It was filled with hardwood slatted benches, sturdy utilitarian furniture, and with the ship's outer deck planking undisguised on the floor. Improvements came soon, once the ship entered service. First it was noticed that even with three sides completely enclosed,

The Observation Room at the forward end of the Promenade Deck was to have been a very large space where passengers could relax while watching their ship combat the brutal elements of the rugged North Atlantic. In the end, the Observation Room was reduced to a narrow corridor – even narrower than this artist's depiction shows – by the last-minute addition of First Class cabins.

the room was still too open to the elements; thus removable screens were added to the archways to ensure that the space would be comfortable no matter what the weather. After the appearance of the *Olympic* (1911) and *Imperator* (1913), and with other, more luxurious ships fitted with Verandah Cafés entering service, as well, Cunard felt the pressure to improve the space dramatically. At first they considered converting it into a Gymnasium, but by early 1914 they settled for a less expensive option: at a cost just over half of the room's original price, they completely changed the décor. Wicker furniture was added, India-rubber tiling fitted to the floor, trellis work fixed to the walls, and a large number of hanging plants and greenery added.

One deck below, on the Promenade Deck, there was another, albeit much smaller public space, but one that is of note, nonetheless. This was the so-called Observation Room, which overlooked the Forecastle through a quartet of portholes. In the early days of the ship's design, this was envisioned as an actual room; when *The Shipbuilder* and *Engineering* magazines printed their general arrangement plans of the *Lusitania* and *Mauretania*, this was the layout that they showed in this area. In rather a last-minute decision, however, Cunard changed the design of the space. They decided to install two forward midships cabins, numbered B1 and B2; this greatly reduced the Observation Room, turning it into something more akin to a simple athwartship companionway than an actual room. Although modest in its finished reality, this idea was trend-setting. Later ships followed the notion, incorporating much grander and more luxurious Observation Rooms where passengers could watch their ship battle with the rugged North Atlantic head-on while ensconced in complete comfort.

The final primary public room fitted aboard the *Lusitania* was the focal point of all shipboard activity: the First Class Dining Saloon. This wonderful public space encompassed three decks, all told, with seating for passengers on the lower two, the Upper (D) and Shelter Decks (C), and a dome capping off the space on the third, the Promenade Deck (B). The main portion of the Saloon, on the Upper – also called the Saloon – Deck (D), was 85 feet in length by about 83 feet wide, and could seat 321 passengers; the higher, Shelter Deck portion was roughly 65 feet square, and could seat 143 passengers. The entire seating capacity of the Dining Saloon thus amounted to 470, or just slightly less than the ship's original First Class capacity of 552. The dome, elliptical in shape and rendered in plaster "of a very fine character," according to *Engineering*, was 29 feet in length and 23 feet 6 inches in width, with its peak rising some 27 feet 6 inches above the oak parquet floor of the Saloon's

Opposite: *A very early photograph of the First Class Dining Saloon. This extraordinary tall view shows the great feeling of spaciousness in the central portion of the room. The Saloon was located amidships between the Nos. 3 and 4 funnel uptakes. The space actually encompassed three decks; the dome was contained on the Promenade Deck, just below the Lounge & Music Room on the Boat Deck. The Shelter (C) and Upper Deck (D) levels were where passengers actually ate their meals.*

Another early view, this one taken from the balcony on the Shelter Deck. The dome above and the tables on the floor below clearly visible.

This photograph was taken from the aft and starboard side of the Shelter Deck level, looking forward and to port. Clearly visible in the center of the room is the central well which gave a vista to the goings-on below, on the Upper Deck level. In this view, tablecloths have been placed on the tables, and there is some evidence of decorative plants, as well, meaning that the ship was coming closer to completion.

In this view, taken on the Upper Deck (D), the room is completed. The tables are set and the room is fully prepared to receive hungry passengers. In this photograph, palms are plainly in evidence, adding to the elegant atmosphere.

lower level. Four paintings were located within the dome, rendered in the style of François Boucher and depicting the four seasons.

The Dining Saloon's overall scheme of decoration was Louis XVI, and like most of the other public spaces it was rendered in ivory white with muted gold offsets. In the one surviving color illustration of the Dining Saloon, the other point that stands out strongly is the rose-colored horsehair upholstery on the seats lining the tables and the matching Brussels carpet runners. The chairs surrounding the tables were firmly fixed to the floors, in keeping with the standards of the time, although they could swivel on their mounts for ease of entry and exit. Corinthian columns, which concealed the structural support pillars, rose from the floor, passed through the edges of the open oval well on the Shelter Deck, and finally met the base of the dome overhead. A mahogany sideboard, complete with brass fittings, was positioned on both levels of the Saloon, the one on the Saloon Deck being seventeen feet long, and the one on the Shelter Deck being only six inches shorter. A piano was provided on the Shelter Deck level, for the use of the ship's band at mealtimes.

Since it simply would not do for young children to be wreaking havoc in the First Class Dining Saloon, that space would become more or less the sole preserve of adults. Because of this, there was also a Louis XVI-style

Children's Nursery & Dining Saloon provided forward on the Shelter Deck, with an adjacent pantry; here the children's nurses could make sure that the young ones were well looked after while their parents enjoyed fine dining and dancing in the main Saloon.

The Second Class public rooms were less spacious and less ornate than those devoted to First Class, but they were quite comfortable for the time. The Lounge was situated on the Boat Deck, roughly square in shape and measuring 43 feet 6 inches in length and 39 feet in width. It was paneled in French-polished mahogany, and occasional tables and chairs were provided throughout the room for passengers' use. In the center of the room was an open well surrounding a staircase which descended to the Second Class Entrance on the Promenade Deck; this setup allowed the Second Class passengers easy access to all of their regions of the ship. When the ship's trials made it clear that severe vibration would be a problem in the Second Class areas, John Brown introduced some hasty structural reinforcements to try and cut down on the vibration. In the Lounge, this was most obvious in the new heavy brackets and arches that lined the room which, although paneled in mahogany to match the space, had all the appearance of the afterthought that they were. Much of the room's intended "open" feel was eliminated, but the alternatives were

The Second Class Lounge, prior to the installation of stiffening arches. Although necessary to combat the ship's vibration problems, the arches destroyed much of the open feeling in this photograph.

Above left: *The Second Class Ladies' Drawing Room.*

Above right: *The Second Class Smoking Room.*

Below: *The main level of the Second Class Dining Saloon, which was situated on the Upper Deck. The balcony above was for over-flow use, and was bordered by cabins. A piano was also located on the upper level.*

even more unpalatable, and the space was still quite comfortable even after the alterations.

Below on the Promenade Deck there were two other Second Class public rooms. Forward of the Entrance was the Ladies' Drawing Room, and astern was the Smoking Room. The Smoking Room was very similar to the Lounge in décor, with mahogany paneling and occasional tables. In a rather ingenious move, a dome was fitted up through the Boat Deck, and sprouted up just astern of the Lounge's deckhouse; this allowed bright sunlight into what would otherwise have been a rather enclosed space. The Smoking Room was 52 feet long and 38 feet wide at its widest point; its width tapered toward the stern to follow the contours of the ship's narrowing superstructure. The Ladies' Drawing Room, forward, was somewhat lighter in feel than the Smoking Room was, for as its name implied it was intended primarily for the use of ladies. It had a similar dome to that found in the Smoking Room. A cottage upright piano by Broadwood was provided for this space, and a high-quality Brussels carpet was fitted, once again in a rose color. The room was some 42 feet in width by 28 feet in length, and was provided with tables and writing desks, as well as chairs and

banquettes upholstered in the finest horsehair. During the alterations made to the Second Class regions of the ship to combat vibration, a large, fixed settee was installed in the center of the room. This settee took up a large portion of the floor space and replaced many of the chairs and tables.

Just below on the Upper Deck was the Second Class Dining Saloon, rendered in the Georgian style, and measuring some 61 feet in length by 74 feet in width. The Saloon could accommodate 259 passengers at a single sitting; since the Second Class accommodations were intended to take some 460, they would be served over the course of two sittings, instead of the single one found in First Class. A 24-foot 6-inch mahogany sideboard, rather similar to the ones in the First Class Dining Saloon, was fitted. A circular well above the main portion of the Saloon, lined with an elaborate white balustrade, led up to the Shelter Deck, and an enlarged Second Class Entrance. Here could be found another upright piano, as well as some space to create a makeshift secondary dining area, if the Second Class accommodations were particularly full for a crossing. White Corinthian columns lined the space on both decks, although some extra columns were installed during the pre-maiden voyage refit. It was quite obvious which ones had been pre-conceived and which ones had not, since the new columns, which concealed stiffening stanchions, actually cut right through the fixed lines of tables. Even with these afterthoughts added, the Saloon was quite a pleasant space to enjoy a meal, providing more room and even finer conditions than most First Class Dining Saloons of just a decade before.

It would be appropriate here to pause to consider a popularly held belief about the *Lusitania* and compare it with facts. Although much has been made over the years of the use of plaster in the ship, one can only imagine the amount of maintenance that would have been required on large quantities of plaster installed on a vessel that was sent through the mountainous seas of the North Atlantic, where her hull would flex and twist under the stresses imposed on her 787-foot length. In reality, most of the decoration in her First and Second Class public rooms was rendered in wooden paneling that was painted in an ivory white, to keep down on the maintenance. Only a select number of items, such as the dome over the First Class Dining Saloon, were rendered in plaster.

Third Class public rooms were far more Spartan than those of the other two classes. The Third Class Dining Saloon was located on the Upper Deck, like its counterparts in First and Second Class, but was forward near the bow. It was 79 feet 6 inches in length by 58 feet in width, with accommodation for only 332 passengers at a sitting, roughly one-third of Third Class's total capacity of 1,186. Thus, as in Second Class, meals were served in two sittings; if Third Class was booked heavily, the Third Class Smoking Room and the Third Class General Room – located just above on the Shelter Deck – could be converted for use as auxiliary Saloons. If these were put to use in this manner, primarily on westbound crossings with immigrants in high number, then the full capacity of Third Class could be served in just two sittings for each meal. An upright piano was fitted in the primary Saloon, but frills were lacking elsewhere. All of the furniture was solidly constructed and made for many years of use. The tabletops were of unvarnished canary pine, and the revolving chairs were 15 inches in diameter, set in rows with 22 inches between the centers of each seat. Hard slatted benches lined the outboard sides of the Smoking Room and General Room, although the ship's steel side was concealed beneath pine-framed walls. Overhead, the ship's deck girders were left bare, however, with only a number of coats of whitewash for decoration.

There was a semi-enclosed Third Class Promenade on either side of the Shelter Deck, just astern of the Smoking Room and General Room. This featured more slatted benches lining the outer bulkheads, and a bostwick gate at the aft end separated it from the open-air First Class Promenade just astern on either side. Much thought was given to the lavatories and baths for Third Class passengers; even so, their toilet luxuries were somewhat fewer in number than for passengers in the other classes. There were two baths for men and two for women installed in Third Class – one for every 275 or so Third Class passengers, as opposed to the standard of one bath for every 15 First Class Passengers and one for every 30 Second Class Passengers. Nevertheless, these baths, as well as the lavatories, were well equipped and offered a higher standard of cleanliness than most Third Class passengers were accustomed to in daily life. Overall Third Class accommodations were comfortable, clean, and of a high general standard; while light on the excess decorations, they did offer prospective Third Class passengers a more than decent trip between continents.

There were also cabins and staterooms to accommodate these passengers. In Third Class, when the ship entered service, there were some 302 rooms to accommodate 1,186: among this number were 4 eight-berth rooms, 21 six-berth rooms, 227 four-berth rooms, and 40 two-berth rooms. In Second Class, to accommodate the 460 passengers, there were 145 rooms: 85 four-berth and 60 two-berth. To care for the 552 First Class passengers, there were 260 rooms: 72 three-berth, 150 two-berth, and 36 one-berth.

Above: *The Third Class General Room, forward on the Shelter Deck. In this photo, it has been set as an overflow Dining Saloon. The difference between the upper two classes and steerage was quite a contrast.*

Below: *A typical First Class bath. Since the* Lusitania *was a British ocean liner, it is important to remember the differences in terminology between Britain and the United States. In England, a "bath" meant just that: a room with bathing facilities. On the other hand, a "lavatory" or "water closet" was a smaller room equipped only with toilets and sinks. In England, even today, one never asks to use someone's "bathroom" unless one actually wishes to bathe, whereas in the United States, if someone was to ask for a "water closet," "w.c.," or "the loo," most would not have the foggiest idea of how to respond.*

Third Class cabins were forward on D, E and F Decks; Second Class cabins were located astern, on C, D and E Decks; First Class cabins were housed along the extended midships region of the liner, on A, B, D and E Decks. Interestingly, not long after the ship entered service, more First Class cabins were ensconced on E Deck, forward of the Grand Entrance, at the expense of a number of Third Class cabins; this was because the First Class accommodations of the *Lusitania* proved even more popular than had been expected. The alterations were actually rather involved, necessitating far more than the removal of the old Third Class cabins and their replacement with new First Class ones, which was quite a complicated process alone. In addition to that, a watertight bulkhead (which was located at Frame 167 outboard, and jogged forward to Frame 169 inboard) had to be taken out, and a new one was installed in its place, further forward (at Frame 181).

Perhaps the most remarkable among the First Class passenger cabins were those installed on B Deck. Two Regal Suites, the premiere accommodations on the Atlantic in 1907, were fitted just forward of the First Class Promenades on either side of the ship. The port Regal Suite, cabins B48, B50, B52 and B54, comprised a dining room, drawing room, two bedrooms, and a private bath and water closet. The starboard suite was a similar, though reversed arrangement, with the cabins being numbered B47, B49, B51 and B53. If let as a complete suite, each could cost from $1,250 (US) out of season, to $1,750 in the intermediate season, all the way up to $2,250 in full season – prices which seem especially steep coming as quoted in 1912;[10] minimum First Class fare, by comparison, was a mere $115 US at the time of the maiden voyage. So expensive were these Regal Suites that only the super-wealthy or super-famous were able to let them out for passage, and frequently they went as individual cabins instead of the full suite.

For a little less money, the *en suite* rooms were another option. Each of these suites was comprised of a bedroom and sitting room, also with a private bath and water closet. When the ship first entered service, she sported six of these suites (B65 & 67; B68 & 70; B75 & 77; B76 & 78; B85 & 87 and B86 & 88); as the ship's career continued, the original six were given the designations of "Parlor Suites," and four new suites, given the original designations, were installed further aft (B89 & 91; B90 & 92; B105 & 109 and B104 & 110). Each of the Parlor Suites went for $700 US out of season and up to $1,500 US in season; to add a second person to each suite was an additional $100 US to the base price.[11]

In order to achieve this remarkable finished ocean liner, a lot of work went into her fitting out. Especially as the months progressed and the set time for

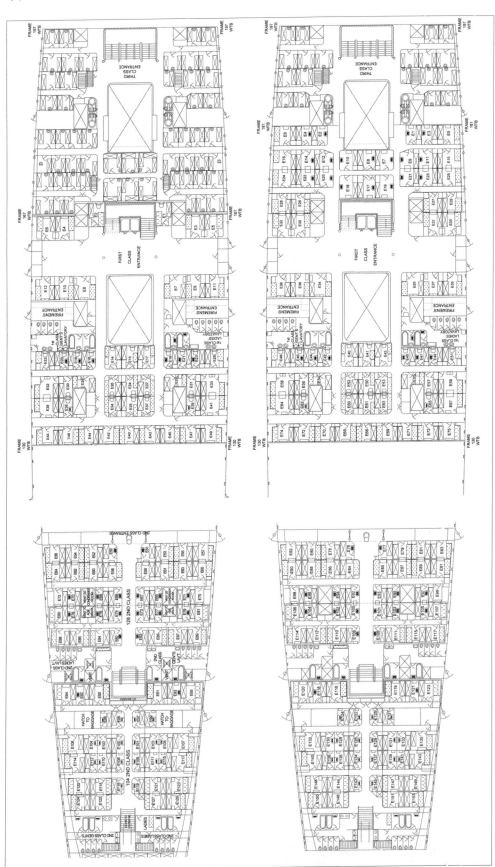

Two plans of E Deck's passenger accommodations. The upper plan is from when the ship entered service in 1907, while the lower plan is from later in her career. The alterations made in First Class include the removal of the watertight bulkhead from the area around the First Class staircase, the removal of Third Class cabins forward of that bulkhead, the installation of a new watertight bulkhead outboard of the No. 2. Funnel uptake casing, and the installation of new First Class cabins in the converted area. All of the cabins on the deck were renumbered, with the total number of First Class cabins jumping from 48 to 74. Superstitiously, no cabin on the Lusitania was numbered "13," a rather common practice on ships of the period.

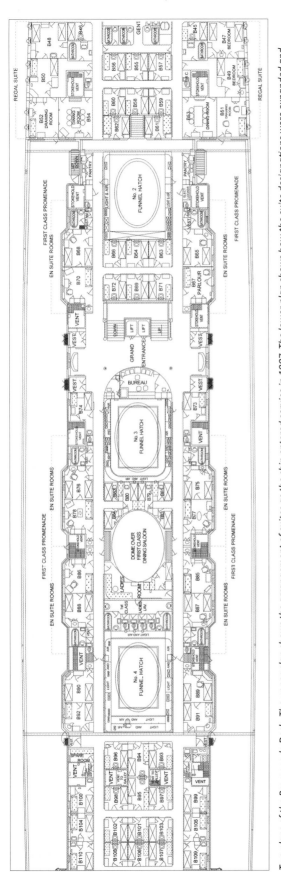

Two plans of the Promenade Deck. The upper plan shows the arrangement of suites as the ship entered service in 1907. The lower plan shows how the suite designations were expanded and altered during the ship's career.

This photograph was taken from the top of the fitting-out crane, looking at the bow half of the still-unfinished Lusitania. *The lifeboats are in place, swung out to allow maximum room for workers on the Boat Deck, and all four funnels have been installed. Work on the Sun Deck is under way, and workmen and materials can be seen all over both the Sun and Boat Decks.*

the maiden voyage began to near, things would have grown both enormously complex and frenzied. To add to the stress, regular inspections by representatives from the Cunard Line could, in a moment, halt all work on a certain area of the ship if it was not being done properly. There were bulkheads to build, carvings to make and mount, fittings and furnishings of all sorts to be carried aboard, wood floors to be laid, India-rubber tiles to affix, carpeting to unroll and carefully lay, elevator cages to install, light bulbs – and a lot of them – to mount. In every cabin, there was a need for coat hooks, a folding rack net for each berth, a brass door step, a white metal handhold over every upper berth, a brass mortice lock on each cabin door, and much more.

The ship's extensive plumbing system had to be installed, thoroughly tested, and absolutely leak-free. The ventilating systems needed to be installed, connected, tried and tweaked. Storm rails needed to be fitted in all of the ship's passages and companionways, and there were miles of them. Indeed, the list

of projects must have seemed endless – and at times, frustrating. Workers were no doubt vying for space in cramped quarters, as well.

Meanwhile, plans to accept the *Lusitania* and her sister ship in Liverpool and New York were also proceeding, and these preparations were running up against the same deadline, as well. Liverpool was designated both the registered home port and also the primary English terminus of the *Lusitania* and *Mauretania*; this was a logical decision since it was also Cunard's base of operations. The River Mersey ran in a rather southerly direction inland from Liverpool Bay. On the east bank was Liverpool proper, and on the west were the towns of Wallasey and Birkenhead. Along the eastern side of the Mersey were a series of piers, including the Prince's Landing Stage, or Prince's Dock. This was where the big Liverpool-calling Atlantic liners tied up to discharge passengers and luggage and to take on the fresh batch for the next outward-bound voyage.

The problem that now arose was that the depth of water alongside the Landing Stage would be insuf-

Top: *A period map of Liverpool showing the main shipping channel. The Prince's Landing Stage, as well as the Canada Dry Dock and most of the other principal docking facilities, were located on the east side of the Mersey. The Sloyne, not picked out on this map, was on the west side of the Mersey.*

Middle: *The Landing Stage at Riverside Station. Riverside Station was used specifically for boat trains, having opened in June of 1895. Via the London & North Western Railway (L.N.W.R.), passengers could make transit from 14th Street in New York to Euston Station, London, all under steam power. The trip from Riverside to Euston took eight hours.*

Bottom: *One of the two Cunard buoys made specifically for the* Lusitania *and* Mauretania *while they were at anchor in the Sloyne. In photographs of the* Lusitania *tied up to one, the buoy appears small, but this view shows just how large each one was.*

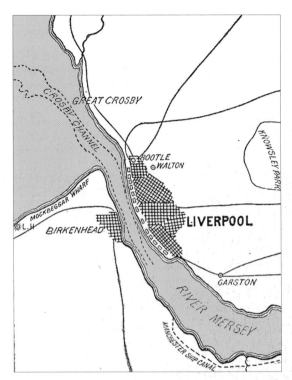

ficient for the new Cunarders. The Mersey Dock Board cooperated and managed to ensure that dredging operations were carried out prior to the *Lusitania*'s arrival in that port. This was no small task, encompassing over twenty square miles of the riverbed and removing roughly 200,000 tons of material, all told. Once it was finished, however, there was a depth of 36 feet below the lowest of low water – sufficient to allow the *Lusitania* and *Mauretania* to dock unless the weather conditions were remarkably poor. For times when the weather was too rough to tie up at the Landing Stage, or when the Landing Stage was in heavy use and there wasn't room to berth there, the *Lusitania* could dock in the Sloyne – an out-of-the-main-traffic backwater.

Liverpool was not an ideal port for ships of the *Lusitania*'s ilk, however. Far more often than could have been desired, poor weather did not allow the liner or her sister to tie up at the Landing Stage. Additionally, the bar at the entrance to Liverpool would not always allow the Cunarders a sufficient depth of water to enter the Mersey and gain access to their home port; if they arrived at a stage of the tide that was too low, they would have to wait until enough of the tide returned to allow them to enter port.

On top of this, the Sloyne had a strong current on the ebb tide of 4-5 knots. While this may not initially strike one as disastrous, because of this current and the enormous size and weight of the new sister speedsters, Cunard had been required to order two new buoys, which would be called North Cunard and South Cunard, for use in the Sloyne. The buoys were constructed by Messrs. John Bellamy, Limited, and supplied by Pintsch's Patent Lighting Company. When they were built, they were the largest buoys ever made, each with a 16-foot diameter, weighing in at 16¾ tons, and attached to 16 fathoms of 4½-inch stud-link cable chain. The new ships could tie up at these buoys and re-coal there, even offloading passengers and cargo by ferry if

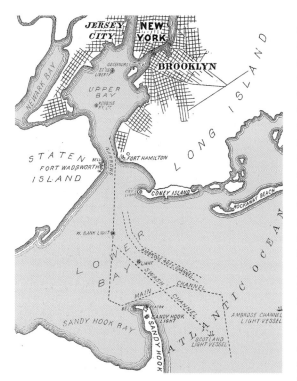

A period map of New York Harbor. The Main Ship Gedney Channel is the twisting course that passes just over Sandy Hook. The straighter, albeit unfinished, Ambrose Channel was a much simpler navigational option.

the ever-expanding size of seagoing vessels calling in the all-important American port. New York City resident John Wolfe Ambrose led the way in trying to improve the port's facilities; eventually it became an eighteen-year project that was not completely finished by the time he died. Existing channels were also deepened and improved. One of Ambrose's visions, however, was the creation of a first-rate deep-draught entrance to the harbor from Sandy Hook, the official "end-point" for westbound passages. The going was slow, but by May of 1899 – the same month that saw John Ambrose pass away – the contract to create the new channel was given by the U.S. Government to Andrew Onderdonk. In the 1901-1902 session of Congress, a bill was passed naming the as-yet-uncompleted channel in honor of Ambrose. The newly named Ambrose Channel project was slated to cost over $4,000,000, and involved the removal of some 42,000,000 cubic yards of muck from the bay. The original contract specifications called for some 4,000,000 cubic yards of material to be removed each year, but things had initially gone – as they usually do with this type of project – slower than expected.

The entire project was not officially completed until April 17, 1914, but Cunard hoped that enough of it would be finished so that the new *Lusitania* could use it on her maiden voyage in September of 1907. On August 2, 1907, the War Department told Cunard's New York men – a group headed by Manager Vernon H. Brown – that the *Lusitania* could use the Ambrose Channel on her way in, albeit at her own risk. It was expected that the new giant would draw 32 feet of water on arrival; although other large liners had left New York drawing that much water via the older channel, Cunard still wanted to bring the *Lusitania* in via the Ambrose Channel. For one thing, it was a much straighter cut, and for another, the new channel's current depth – between 35 and 40 feet – would, it was thought, allow for a larger margin for error. However, the course was not yet buoyed, and it was not even a sure thing that the necessary markers would be in place by mid-September.

Wanting to test the channel before the *Lusitania* arrived, the Cunard Line thought to send the *Caronia* out via the new channel when she left on Tuesday, August 27, 1907. Permission was obtained on Monday, August 26, and Manager Brown was aboard the liner for the event. Captain John Pritchard was in command of the ship, while the departure was overseen by Harbor Pilot Frank Cramer. Their presence was no accident. Pritchard would be taking the reins of the *Mauretania* that November; Cramer, one of New York's most experienced pilots, would be

it was necessary. Even so, there were occasions when the great *Lusitania* or her sister were swept along in the current despite having both main bow anchors in the riverbed; on such occasions, the liner would have to start her engines up, raise anchors, and head back to her original location before dropping anchor again. Coaling at the buoy was dangerous in poor weather, as well. Due to these disadvantages, White Star had moved their primary English terminus to Southampton in the late spring of 1907. Cunard stuck with Liverpool until after the First World War, but eventually followed suit. Thus, during the entirety of her career, the *Lusitania* ran out of Liverpool and returned there at the conclusion of each round-trip.

On the other side of the Atlantic, in New York, similar preparations were necessary, but not all of them had been in reaction to the *Lusitania*'s forthcoming arrival. Between Sandy Hook – the official entrance point into New York Harbor – and the Cunard piers in Lower Westside Manhattan, a new channel was being dredged to admit liners of the *Lusitania*'s size to the port. For some time the older Main Ship-Bayside-Gedney Channel had been the primary access to New York Harbor. However, by the early 1880s, it became obvious that this passage was not sufficient to care for

Captain John Pritchard, who took the Caronia *out by the new cut, would be the first Captain of the* Mauretania.

Even once the *Lusitania* had successfully entered the Upper Bay and found her way toward the Lower West Side Manhattan piers which were used by Cunard, facilities were not ideal. Work on extending Pier 54, where she was to tie up, was freshly completed in time for her arrival; yet it remained no more than a flat extension of land into the North River; there was no decent structure atop it to accommodate passengers as they landed, met friends and acquaintances, gathered luggage, and departed. Although Cunard put up a small temporary shed, there was no question that it simply would not hold all of the passengers once they had stepped ashore. Cunard officials could only hope that it didn't rain. The main pier structure would not be finished until very late in 1908, and in the meantime, the *Lusitania* would stretch the New York piers' capacity to the limit.

Meanwhile, back on the Clyde, things were progressing rapidly. In the spring of 1907, a new figure was introduced to the *Lusitania*. As spring turned to summer, he could be seen familiarizing himself with what was, in reality, "the first of a new class of giant passenger carriers." The man in question was Captain James B. Watt, and he was to be the *Lusitania*'s first Commander. Watt had just transferred from the *Carmania*, a vessel

bringing the *Lusitania* in on her maiden voyage in mid-September. As this "dry run" got under way, two leadsmen were kept busy taking soundings to warn of any hidden obstacles along the way. The atmosphere was clearly tense for those working to take the ship out, but the passengers thought that it was exciting to be aboard the liner for this historic voyage; they watched with a notable sense of superiority as the inbound *Kaiser Wilhelm II* wound her way about the twisting curves of the older channel.

In the end, the passage was successful, with Pilot Cramer claiming to have shaved a full half-hour off the trip to the open sea. However, there was still some question; the *Caronia* was only drawing 30 feet forward and 30 feet 3 inches aft at the time of her departure … would the *Lusitania*'s draught be too great at the time of her arrival to safely use the Ambrose Channel … too great to allow her to become the first of the Atlantic liners to come in to New York via the new cut? As the *Caronia* departed into the North Atlantic, and the dredging equipment resumed their task in her wake, the only certainty was that time would tell. Work on the Ambrose Channel would continue right up until the morning that the *Lusitania* arrived. The final decision to take her in by that route was only made on Monday, September 9, while the ship was in the middle of the Atlantic on her way to New York.

Captain James B. Watt, Lusitania's *first Captain, arrived at John Brown's during the spring of 1907 in order to familiarize himself with the ship before taking formal command.*

This photograph shows the Lusitania's *fitting out progressing well. All of the lifeboats are in place, the funnels installed, and the Boat Deck deckhouse underneath and forward of the aft funnel have all been erected. Construction on the First Class Smoking Room and Verandah Café still lags behind, however.*

which had entered service with Cunard in December of 1905, or just a year and a half previously. When the *Carmania* had entered service, she was the largest ship in Cunard's fleet, and boasted a service speed of 18 knots. To Watt, as he became familiar with the new *Lusitania*, the *Carmania* must have seemed a toy – she was only two-thirds the size of, and was seven knots slower than, the new vessel. The responsibility of commanding such a new and unique vessel must not have been lost on Watt, but the excitement must also have been palpable. On August 31, 1907, it was reported:

> It is appropriate that the man who will command [the *Lusitania*] is not only the commodore captain of the Cunard fleet, but we believe the commodore of the North Atlantic passenger trade … The responsibility of handling this great ship is of course an exceedingly grave one, inasmuch as her size and speed are beyond anything which a shipmaster has had the opportunity hitherto of becoming conversant with. Captain Watt, however, brings to bear upon his command a wealth of experience and skill that may be claimed to be unmatched. He is a type of commander which has made the British mercantile service honoured and admired throughout the world, and created almost sublime confidence amongst travelers.

Like many other successful shipmasters sailing out of Liverpool, Captain Watt is a Scotchman. He is a native of Montrose, and comes of an old seafaring stock. His early days were spent in sail, and he had a thorough experience in windjammers on the North Atlantic trade. He joined the Cunard Line as a junior officer in 1873, and has passed through every grade and through most of the principal ships of the company, including the *Umbria*, *Etruria*, *Lucania*, and *Campania*.[12]

The shipyard was a hive of activity, and the deadline for her maiden voyage – which was set for early September – loomed heavily as spring turned into summer. It was said:

> Four immense funnels, two tall masts, and a great dark hull alive inside and out with men is all that the public has yet been allowed to see of the great new Cunarder *Lusitania*, which, during June, was receiving the finishing touches in the tidal basin of Messrs. John Brown and Co.'s shipyard on the Clyde.
>
> By working day and night, and Sunday also, the builders of the newest, fastest and most luxurious ocean liner ever planned, hope to get the *Lusitania* ready to go down to the Tail of the Bank on June 27.
>
> Astonishing secrecy is being maintained in Glasgow and on the Clyde about the interior arrangements of this wonderful boat. The secrecy is ascribed in part to the fear lest rival companies should learn too much, and also to the fact that on

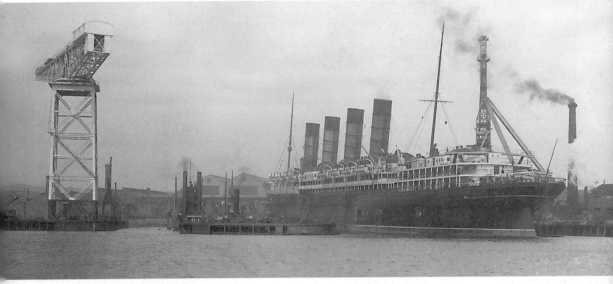

Top: *A view of the* Lusitania *during the later stages of her fitting out. In this photograph, her Smoking Room and Verandah Café have already been installed. On the left side of the fitting-out basin stands the 150-ton crane built by Sir William Arrol & Co. It was from the top of that crane that some of the overhead photographs of the liner fitting out were taken.*

Above: *A wonderful photograph of the* Lusitania *nearing completion.*

the stocks near her lies the new turbine cruiser the *Inflexible*, to be launched on June 26, and now guarded day and night by armed men.[13]

More than simply finishing the ship in time, there was another sobering obstacle that her shipbuilders had to face, as well: getting the massive liner to the sea. It was said that the task would be tremendous, and that the dangers posed by the trip were "a great weight of anxiety" to the firm.[14] The Clyde Trust and other river authorities had sent powerful dredging machines into the fourteen-mile passage for months, trying to

ensure a minimum depth of 23 feet at low water of ordinary spring tides. As the highest spring tide at Clydebank was never more than 11 feet, the total depth of high water available under even the best of conditions would never have exceeded 34 feet – very close to the *Lusitania*'s ordinary draft. The date set for her to venture from her birthplace for the first time was Thursday, June 27, 1907, and the selection of that date was not arbitrary. It was to coincide with the highest spring tide, to ensure maximum depth of water under the vessel's keel. Since such favorable circumstances would not repeat for some time, it was crucial that the

Above: *Another view taken from the top of the Arrol crane, looking down on the forward part of the ship. The vessel is all but complete, and much progress is visible since the similar photograph on page 46.*

Below: *Taken from the same location as the preceding photograph, this view shows the liner's stern decks from a unique angle.*

Lusitania make it out of Clydebank on that day, or she would be stranded there for some time afterward.

In order to minimize the ship's draft, only enough coal was put aboard to get her comfortably down to Gourock. When she departed, just before noon, she was drawing 29 feet 9 inches aft and only slightly less

than that forward. Although it was several feet less than she would ordinarily draw under load conditions, there were still great fears, particularly about the dangers in the tight curves of the river. Fortunately conditions on the chosen date were favorable. The ship made the trek at a cautious speed of about five knots, and with the assistance of a half-dozen tugs. Despite reportedly experiencing "great difficulties" – to the point that some papers later reported that she had actually gone aground – the *Lusitania* made the trip unscathed. She also gave the first hint of her capabilities during the two-hour passage. It was said that she "answered her helm with more than usual promptness."[15] With her first trip under her belt, she dropped anchor off Gourock, where she would spend the next few days. Although the official trials were

Above left: *An advertisement for Hall's anchors, manufactured by N. Hingley & Sons, Ltd. This firm supplied the* Lusitania's *anchors.*

Above right: *A length of the* Lusitania's *anchor chain with a worker standing beside it. The prow of the ship lies just visible in the distance on the right.*

Right: *One of the* Lusitania's *mighty anchors in the yard prior to installation.*

not scheduled until the end of August, John Brown wanted to conduct a series of 'secret' trials to find out exactly what kind of vessel they had built.

The first runs with the ship, carried out on Tuesday, July 2 and Wednesday, July 3, gave the first reason for optimism: she achieved twenty-five knots in speed for at least a time. It was also noticed that the ship's wake and the wave formation along her sides was "conspicuously small," indicating a well-formed hull, and "how remarkably low" the resistance against the hull was as she carved her way through the sea.[16] At the same time, however, the tests were also a disappointment of sorts: significant vibration was manifest in the Second Class areas of the superstructure, aft.

Returning to the Tail o' the Bank, John Brown carried out some stiffening of her structure to combat the vibration. When the ship once again took to open water at 5:00 p.m. on Monday, July 15, she was run at 25 knots in the direction of Liverpool; the vibration astern showed a marked improvement, but not enough

Top: *Smoke begins to drift out of the Lusitania's forward funnels. The ship is preparing to depart her birthplace for the first time; not all of the stokeholds have been fired, since the ship will be making the voyage at an ultra-cautious speed.*

Above left: *Having backed out of her berth, the Lusitania is carefully maneuvered down the Clyde toward open water. Visible just behind the ship's forward mast is the Arrol crane, at her fitting-out dock.*

Above right: *This photograph was taken shortly after the preceding one, and really gives some idea of just how cramped the passage was for the great liner. It is no wonder there were such great concerns about her reaching Tail o' the Bank safely.*

Above: *A view from the shore as the liner continues her passage down the River Clyde. Locals are clearly in evidence, crowding the pier on the right side of the photograph, bidding Clydebank's greatest achievement a fond farewell.*

Left: *Safe arrival. The Lusitania has anchored at Tail o' the Bank. Additional coal is already being loaded aboard the ship for her upcoming "secret" builder's trials.*

Below: *A starboard view of the ship at Tail o' the Bank, with smoke still emanating from her forward funnel, and lighters tied up alongside.*

Right: *A spectacular shot of the liner at her anchorage near Gourock.*

Top: *Another splendid view of the liner at Tail o' the Bank.*

Above left: *July 2, 1907. The* Lusitania *is taken in hand by several tugs, and moves steadily toward the open sea for the first time. Interestingly, the photographer mistakenly captioned the moment: "Mauretania's first trial".*

Above right: *A starboard bow view of the liner departing on her "secret" builder's trials.*

Below left: *A very rare image of the same event. The* Lusitania *is poised to prove herself to her builders and prospective owners.*

Below right: *Seen from shore, the* Lusitania *sports an impressive profile.*

Above: *With the tugs left behind, the liner enters open water for the first time.*

Below: *The liner moves into the loch and finds more and more room to build speed.*

Bottom left: *The turbulence behind the liner shows just how fast she is moving, and how much power she is thrusting into the water.*

Bottom right: *A spectacular July 2 view, showing all of the ship's mighty power and her grace. Smoke is now belching from all four funnels as she builds up a full head of steam for the first time. In this view, it is notable that although she is steaming at a good clip, there is very little disturbance along her flanks – she cuts cleanly and smoothly through the sea. This is an excellent omen for being able to achieve her designed speed of 25 knots … or more.*

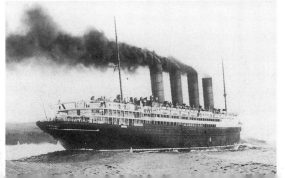

Above: *The* Lusitania *steams past Ailsa Craig headed south. Ailsa Craig is a small promontory jutting from the Irish Sea, south of the Isle of Arran, and less than fifty miles northeast of the entrance to the Belfast Lough. On August 2, under full steam, she would complete some additional speed trials in this vicinity, but in this photograph not all of her stokeholds seem to be fully operational, meaning that this photo was most likely taken during the liner's first journey down to Liverpool, England, on July 15, during the early evening hours.*

Right: *The Starting Platform of the* Lusitania. *It was here that her engineers awaited the command for "Full Ahead" for the first time.*

to prove satisfactory. John Brown reassured a nervous Cunard Line that they had more plans to combat vibration up their sleeves; among these would be the fitting of additional webs to the structure in the area of the forward propellers. Meanwhile, the *Lusitania* crossed the Bar and entered Liverpool at 5:00 a.m. on the morning of Tuesday, July 16. She anchored off the Landing Stage at Liverpool two hours later, entered the Huskisson deepwater dock later that day, and eventually was placed in the Canada Dry Dock. While she was drydocked, her underwater hull was thoroughly cleaned and repainted, since it was "heavily coated with the chemically-saturated mud of the River Clyde" and other growths which had accumulated on it during the previous year. This would allow for an accurate and unimpeded set of results during her formal acceptance tests.[17] It was also apparently here, during this stay in drydock, that her white-painted Shelter Deck hull strakes were painted black straight out to the prow, ostensibly to make her appearance better match the appearance of other Cunard vessels.

This photograph was apparently taken in the early morning of July 16, 1907, as the ship came into Liverpool for the first time, but before she was tied up in one of the Huskisson Dock's three branch docks.

Above: *Tied up in the Huskisson Dock, probably in the morning of July 17. This photograph most likely depicts the liner before she was moved to the Canada Dry Dock.*

Below left: *This very rare photograph was also taken in the Huskisson Dock as the ship waited to enter the Canada Dry Dock.*

Below right: *A rare and atmospheric bow view of the ship in the Huskisson Dock, still showing her proud white prow.*

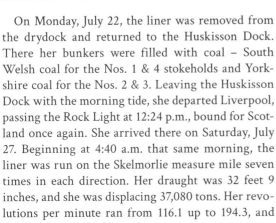

On Monday, July 22, the liner was removed from the drydock and returned to the Huskisson Dock. There her bunkers were filled with coal – South Welsh coal for the Nos. 1 & 4 stokeholds and Yorkshire coal for the Nos. 2 & 3. Leaving the Huskisson Dock with the morning tide, she departed Liverpool, passing the Rock Light at 12:24 p.m., bound for Scotland once again. She arrived there on Saturday, July 27. Beginning at 4:40 a.m. that same morning, the liner was run on the Skelmorlie measure mile seven times in each direction. Her draught was 32 feet 9 inches, and she was displacing 37,080 tons. Her revolutions per minute ran from 116.1 up to 194.3, and her speed ranged between 15.77 and 25.62 knots; at this latter speed, she was transmitting 76,000 horsepower into the water. These results were satisfactory, indeed. She returned to the Tail o' the Bank on that same Saturday afternoon and anchored.

Before the evening was out, the *Lusitania* was to depart on a "pleasure cruise" around Ireland. Aboard would be a specially selected group of about two hundred VIP guests, forty of whom were women. One of these guests was Mrs. Ethel Tweedie, a Queens College graduate and authoress. She had a special interest in philanthropy and served on several committees of the International Council of Women; in five years,

Above: *This photo shows the liner moving through the lock from the Huskisson Docks through to the Canada Docks. The lock clearance was only ninety feet, leaving a scant two and a half feet of room for the 87½-foot-wide liner to squeeze through. In this view, she is moving more or less north, parallel to the Mersey River. Once the ship had entered the Canada Docks, she would be turned to starboard and moved into the Canada Dry Dock.*

Below: *The ship has safely tied up in the Canada Dry Dock. A group of men gawk at the ship's unprecedented size. She dwarfs everything in sight.*

Top: *A large number of individuals crawl over the dock looking up at the massive liner. Was it possible that this behemoth would also slice cleanly through the North Atlantic as the fastest ship in the world? Many must have wondered.*

Left: *This prow-on view of the liner shows that the water has been pumped out of the drydock. Incredibly tall ladders allowed workers to gain access to the upper segments of the ship's underwater hull for the purposes of cleaning and applying anti-fouling paint. In this view, a worker stands atop one such ladder, along the liner's starboard side. Anti-fouling work is in progress.*

Above: *Another splendid view of the Lusitania in drydock. Work on the anti-fouling application continues, and the ship makes the people standing on the side of the dock appear very small, indeed.*

Left: *Workers go over every square inch of the ship's propellers, cleaning them and preparing them to drive the liner at her utmost during her upcoming formal trials.*

Above: *A view from the dock wall, looking at the starboard propellers and the bracing that helped stabilize the ship while she balanced on the narrow line of keel support blocks on the dock floor.*

Right: *A rare and superb view showing the liner in the Canada Dry Dock. The prow is still painted white in this view, but it would not remain so for much longer. Meanwhile, the after cranes – mounted on the Second Class Boat Deck – were also to be removed, deemed superfluous.*

Below: *A second view of the ship's knife-like prow while in the Canada Dry Dock shows that the application of the anti-fouling paint along her hull has come a long way during her stay.*

she would receive special recognition for rendering assistance to Sicilian earthquake victims. She later recalled of this trip:

We left Euston at 10 a.m. [on Saturday] ... for the Clyde, in a saloon train with every comfort, for it was a "Cunard special." A tug quickly conveyed us on board from Gourock ... Representative people of all kinds were on board ... there were members of the Government, Naval Attachés from different countries, distinguished lawyers, admirals, engineers of eminence (naturally interested in the new boat), with a sprinkle of politicians, literary people, and leading lights of various kinds. Nothing could have been more jovial or interesting than the company.

What a monster that great four-funnelled vessel looked as we came alongside. She was far too tall to allow us to reach her top decks by a companion ladder, and consequently a door on the side of the vessel, on a level with our tug, admitted a ship's gangway, across which we merrily tripped.

Once inside, we were somewhere just above the water-line, and were promptly hurled by a lift to our own particular deck, and found our way to our own particular cabin as indicated on each passenger's ticket. Brass bedsteads and silk eiderdowns were also innovations in the shipping world.

Above: *This photograph was probably taken as the* Lusitania *was removed from the Canada Dry Dock on Monday, July 22, 1907. Notice that not only has the prow been painted black, but the after set of cranes – previously mounted on the Second Class Boat Deck – has also been removed. Additionally a pair of stiffening stanchions has been installed astern during the ship's stay in dry-dock; by the time the ship had entered service, this would be increased to four stiffening arches in the vicinity. After departing the Canada Dry Dock on July 22, the ship was returned to the Huskisson Dock, where she was coaled prior to returning to Gourock.*

Below: *This view was probably taken on July 16 in Liverpool as the Cunard tender* Skirmisher *approaches. The Boiler Entrance gangway door on the starboard side of E Deck has been opened. This view, however, gives a splendid idea of how the great* Lusitania *would have looked to Mrs. Ethel Tweedie and other guests boarding the ship at Gourock for her round-Ireland cruise on the evening of Saturday, July 27, 1907. The only difference would be that by the time of the cruise around Ireland, the prow had been painted black.*

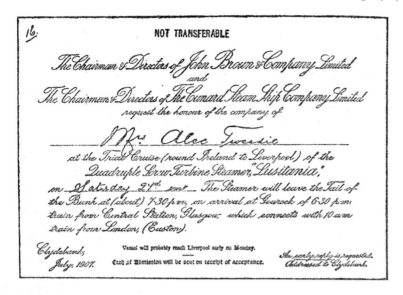

16.

NOT TRANSFERABLE

The Chairman & Directors of John Brown & Company Limited
and
The Chairman & Directors of The Cunard Steam Ship Company Limited
request the honour of the company of

Mrs Alec Tweedie

at the Trial Cruise (round Ireland to Liverpool) of the
Quadruple Screw Turbine Steamer, "Lusitania,"
on Saturday 27th inst. The Steamer will leave the Tail of
the Bank at (about) 7.30 p.m., on arrival at Gourock of 6.30 p.m.
train from Central Station, Glasgow; which connects with 10 a.m.
train from London, (Euston).

Clydebank,
July, 1907.

Vessel will probably reach Liverpool early on Monday.
—
Card of Admission will be sent on receipt of acceptance.

An early reply is requested.
Addressed to Clydebank.

to sea. [According to one official report on the ship's trials, the departure was at 6:55 p.m., and she passed Cloch Light at 9:10 p.m.] It was a glorious evening, the red sunset seemed to throw a halo of beauty over the first voyage of this great product of man's brain. It was as if a blessing smiled from that glorious sky …

This trial trip was an emblem of construction and attainment of a great feat. An action of satisfaction and congratulations. All was joy …

All Sunday we sped at twenty-two knots an hour, or three knots less than the colossal speed at which she was to cross the Atlantic. We saw the coast of Ireland clearly, although we were well out to sea … By dinner-time on Sunday we were actually passing Queenstown, and by eleven the next morning we had

Within a few minutes we heard the monster anchors weighed, and we were steaming as though it were an everyday occurrence, away down the Clyde in the evening light, past Arran and Kintyre, and out

---

Above: Mrs. Tweedie's formal invitation from the builders and prospective owners of the Lusitania *for the Irish cruise. Once she had made formal reply to this invitation, the companies sent her a special "Card of Admission" which would allow her to actually board the vessel.*

Below: This ultra-rare photograph, taken during the Irish cruise, shows a group of ladies lounging on the Promenade Deck. From left to right is Lady Pirrie, wife of Harland & Wolff's Lord Pirrie, Mrs. Ethel Tweedie, Lady Inchcape, and Lady Aberconway.

Cunard Daily Bulletin.

"Lusitania."

Vol 1., No. 1.   Her Trial Cruise, July 28th. to 30th, 1907   Gourock to Liverpool
Distinguished Company aboard

Left Tail of the bank. 8·50 p.m., Satur
day, Up to midnight, ... 58 miles
Sunday . . . . . . 488 miles
Monday . . . . 194 miles

Our First Impression.

Cunard enterprise keeps John Brown
marching on. Hail, "Lusitania, the first
new leviathan twin to wed the ocean; fleet,
strong and luxurious, a challenge to the
world's mercantile marine. May she h..ve
a long career, maintaining prestige and
profit to the nation and her Company :
(Editor).

A Really Modest M.P.

In reply to the constant enquiry,
"Who is the Member for Sark?"

The Member for Sark
Still keeps in the dark,
No candle illumines his features ;
But I have heard tell
Those who know him full well
Declare he's the best of God's creatures.
    TOBY, M.P

THE KENNEL,
BARKS.
July 27th, 1907

Marconigram.

Capt. Dow, " Campania." 90 miles West-
ward of the Fastnet sent the following
message to Capt. Watt, " Lusitania."
" Wishing all on aboard a pleasant trip."

Loose-itania.

The directing genii : Wat-(&)-son.
Lucy Tania ? A captivating ocean nymph
Kaid Maclean wires   " Am singing ' Rule
Lusitania "
Aid to appetite ? A blow on the Promenade
Deck.
Superb inertia. The Lounges.
" Comfort and courtesy," by Allison
" A luxurious shave " by Gadd
Compliments y to the cuisine   " I'm off
to dinner," · Lord Pirrie.
Hoblyn's choice : A full saloon
To get the bane off, consult Beynon

A Good Beginning.

Why is the " Lusitania's " first achieve-
ment one that may well make all our
distinguished statesmen envious ? Because
she has got round Ireland in one day

Unpardonable Omissions.

A vote of censure was passed on the
builders and the Cunard Company alike,
for one flagrant omission from the ship.
She has neither a grouse moor, nor a deer
forest aboard.

Atlantic Greetings.

On Sunday morning the " Lusitania "
was in communication with Anchor Line
" Caledonia," outward bound to New York,
170 miles west off Malin Head. Captain
Baxter sent his greetings and good wishes
to all on board. ·

The " Lusitania's " first Bulletin—all joy and happiness.

The very first edition of the Cunard Daily Bulletin *printed aboard the* Lusitania *includes a wealth of information about the goings-on aboard the trip. Captain Dow of the* Campania *had reportedly sent a congratulatory note to Captain Watt via wireless, as had the* Caledonia *of the Anchor Line. However, the guests were reported – jokingly of course – to have found an "unpardonable omission" from the ship's facilities.*

arrived in the Mersey – that is to say, we accomplished some seven hundred and forty miles in thirty-six hours. The *Lusitania* could do a good deal more than that, as she afterwards proved…

Somehow or other the *Lusitania* did not seem like a ship. Everything had been done to make her "unshippy."

After detailing her reminiscences of the ship's beautiful public rooms, the marvels of the new vessel's elevators and how greatly "appreciated" they were, she recalled of her traveling and dining companions:

We were the merriest party, and our little centre table was not the least merry. It was circled by Sir Charles (the builder) and Lady McLaren, The Chairman and Mrs. Watson, Mary Lady Inverclyde, who christened the boat, Mr. Gerald Balfour, Lord and Lady Pirrie, "Toby, M.P." and Mrs. Lucy, the Hon. Charles Parsons, of turbine fame, and myself.

Indeed, she recalled: "Nothing more sparkling can be imagined than the first glorious spell of rejoicing in the early days of the *Lusitania*, with a few hundred folk on board, and the air full of hope and pleasure of achievement."[18]

One of her fellow passengers, who was described only as "a prominent British shipbuilder," was equally enthusiastic. "Truly a magnificent vessel, not only in the perfection of her internal arrangements, furnishing and decoration, but the completeness of her structural detail is marvellous. I know nothing to equal her."[19] *Engineering* magazine simply concluded that the results of the tests on the shakedown cruise were "thoroughly satisfactory."

With the completion of the two-day 740-mile "pleasure cruise," the *Lusitania* found herself at the Mersey Bar off Liverpool at 9:37 a.m., Monday morning, July 29, 1907. There she sat, pristine in her freshly painted black hull and gleaming white superstructure, with her four majestic "Cunard red" and black funnels towering over the whole assemblage. The Cunard ferry *Skirmisher* brought more guests out to the ship, including technical staff from the Cunard Line and representatives of the Admiralty, and they were no doubt just as awed by her presence as the last party had been. She seemed to be moving even when she was at rest, even when her reflection sparkled in the undisturbed water sitting by her hull. Her appearance denoted that of a racer. She seemed to throb with life and energy.

Once the fresh guests had embarked, and Mrs. Ethel Tweedie and her party had disembarked – all via the *Skirmisher* – the liner then set off to prove herself in a more official capacity. She departed at 1:18 p.m. and steamed toward the Clyde at a speed of 15¾ knots to make consumption tests. The speed trials began at midnight that night, and ended at about 1 a.m. on Thursday, August 1; at the beginning, the ship's average draught was 32 feet 7 inches, and when she finished it was 30 feet 8 inches. This trial consisted of four runs over a measured course between the Corsewall Light on the Wigtown Coast and the Longship Light at Land's End. The weather was described as "favourable"; the days were bright and sunny, and the nights were just as brilliant. On both nights, however, there were stiff northwest winds running between Force 6 and Force 8. Since the ship was northbound on both nights, the wind had the effect of retarding her forward speed somewhat. On the other hand, everyone aboard must have been relieved because the wind prevented fog from rolling in and seriously affecting the tests.

The results of the four speed trials, with an accumulated distance of about 1,200 miles, were astounding. Southbound on the first run, she made an average speed of 26.4 knots, well above her design requirements. Northbound on the second, she averaged 24.3, a poorer showing but quite acceptable considering the interference from the northwest wind. The third run, with the *Lusitania*'s prow pointed south again, produced a run only two minutes longer than the first run south, at an average of 26.3 knots. Coming back up again on the fourth, she made 24.6 knots, a third of a knot better than her first run north. The average speed for all four runs was thus 25.4 knots, almost a full knot better than the average speed required by Cunard and the Admiralty. For all of this steaming, she had burned approximately 2,200 tons of coal. With all of these successes, John Brown must have breathed a tremendous sigh of relief.

However, the *Lusitania* had more impressive figures to turn in before the trials ended. Once the ship returned to the Clyde on Thursday, August 1, she made two additional runs between Corsewall Light and Chicken Rock at the southern tip of the Isle of Man. Over this 59-mile course, with a mean draught of 30 feet 2 inches, displacing 33,770 tons, the ship averaged 26.7 knots southbound and 26.2 knots northbound, for an accumulated average of 26.45 knots. This was an even more impressive performance than she had turned in on the four long-distance runs. More runs followed – a half-dozen to be exact – between Holy Isle, on the east coast of Arran, and Ailsa Craig Light. These tests showed further proof of the high speed of the ship and of her overall positive behavior in a working seaway. The weather on Friday, August 2 made it impossible to carry out the reversing and steering tests; instead, these would be carried out just prior to the maiden voyage.

Under normal conditions, when the ship met the speed criteria called for in her builder's agreement, she would have been accepted by her new owners. However, there was still the proverbial fly in the ointment: vibration. This was not to be taken lightly; Second Class regions of the ship were still nearly uninhabitable. This proved unacceptable to Cunard, and the ship's formal approval was postponed. Further alterations still needed to be made to the liner to reduce vibration. Naturally, the press and public alike were kept blissfully ignorant of this serious issue. Any rumors that did leak out were quickly minimized, particularly in maritime trade journals of the period, like *The Shipbuilder* and *Engineering*.

With the clock ticking and the maiden voyage only a month away, there was no time to build new propellers, which were under suspicion of being at the heart of the problem. However, something needed to be done in short order to strengthen and reinforce the stern frame of the ship so that the effect of the vibration could be reduced – otherwise the press reports surrounding the maiden voyage were sure to be marred with this particular nasty habit, and the ship's reputation would almost certainly suffer damage right out of the gate.

The ship was returned to the John Brown yards for some hasty, not to mention invasive, modifications. It was decided to add numerous stanchions and arches to the interiors of Second Class, bracing and stiffening the stern from within to combat the vibration. Extra support columns concealed beneath Corinthian-style pillars were enough in some areas, like the Second Class Dining Saloon. In other areas, the modifications were far more obvious, including large stiffening arches in the Second Class Lounge that destroyed the original "airy" feel of the space.

Vibration was not the only topic creating tension between Cunard and John Brown. Behind the scenes, financial problems were brewing as well. The original Government loan had totaled £2.6 million, to be divided evenly between the *Lusitania* and *Mauretania*; funds were withdrawn on a monthly basis by Cunard and sent to each shipyard after they had submitted monthly accounts. In the end, construction costs on both ships ran significantly more than Cunard anticipated, and exhausted the loan prematurely. The issue seems to have stemmed from the fact that these two ships were the most expensive ever built up to that time; there was no real precedent when the builders had submitted the price estimates which won them the contracts. Additionally, the contracts had been set at a cost-plus, rather than a fixed, price, and had not included sums for the liners' lavish interior appointments. Cunard had also approved some extra, and costly, upgrades to their designs during construction.

It was a recipe for disaster, and if both ships met the contract specifications during their trials, Cunard had no legal leg to stand on in denying payment or rejecting the liners. Cunard, already in a bad financial position, was forced to raise capital on debentures in order to maintain their monthly payments. During 1908, Cunard negotiated with John Brown for a rebate on the *Lusitania*'s total price, which had skyrocketed to £1.65 million. John Brown granted a £30,000 reduction, meaning that the final price they paid for her was £1,625,163 — some £325,163 over the portion of the loan allotted to her construction. However, as bad as things were with the *Lusitania*'s price, they paled in comparison to the cost overruns on the *Mauretania*, and the hostile situation which developed between Cunard and Swan, Hunter on the matter.[21]

All of these financial problems were kept carefully out of the public eye. Meanwhile, work on stiffening the *Lusitania*'s hull had continued. Once they were completed, the ship left the Clyde River bound for Liverpool on August 26, and over the course of that day and the next, the opportunity was taken to carry out her stopping and steering tests.

With the ship's engines turning at 166 revolutions, pushing her forward at 22.8 knots, the officers on the Bridge rang down "Full Speed Astern" on the Engine Room telegraphs; the engineers went to work quickly. The turbines were slowed and stopped in one minute and then reversed. In 3 minutes and 55 seconds the ship was brought to a complete stop, having moved forward about three-quarters of a mile, or roughly six boat lengths.

The turning tests were also carried out at a speed just below 23 knots. First was a "hard to port" order to the helm. The Quartermaster threw his weight into the wheel, and the tiller took some 18 seconds to go over some 34½°. The ship's stem shot to starboard, and she made a complete circle roughly 950 yards in diameter in 5 minutes and 48 seconds. When the tiller was put "hard to starboard," it took 20 seconds for it to travel 35½°, again resting against its stops; the liner's prow shot to port this time, and she made a nearly identical circle in 5 minutes and 53 seconds. Astern half-circles were also made. On the next day, August 27, the forward circles were made again, but this time at 180 revolutions per minute (roughly indicating 24 knots); she made the "port" order in 2 minutes and 46 seconds, and made the "starboard" order in 2 minutes and 35 seconds. These results were hailed as a vindication of the decision, made during design, to cut away the "deadwood" astern to add to her maneuverability.

During this two-day voyage, it was found that the new stiffening measures had helped the ship's vibration trouble, but had not entirely corrected it. Further corrective steps would have to be taken down the road, but now everything that could possibly be done prior to the maiden voyage had been seen to. Cunard formally accepted the ship, and she anchored in Liverpool's Sloyne; her official registration, numbered 124,082, was certified on August 30, 1907. With only a few days left before she would set out on her maiden voyage, public excitement over the new British greyhound was at what could only be described as a feverish level. There was only one question on the minds of everyone: would she have what it took to reclaim British maritime prestige and keep it there? The answer would follow in short order.

Before proceeding with a discussion of the ship's maiden voyage and career, however, it would be appropriate at this point to discuss the technical features of the *Lusitania*, to demonstrate just how unique she really was at the time when her career began, and how she changed throughout the course of her career.

This extremely rare photograph was likely taken shortly before the ship left the Clyde for Liverpool on August 26. The quartet of stiffening frames has been installed astern, and her prow is painted black. The ship's formal trials have been completed, but Cunard would not accept the ship until August 30. John Brown had toiled for about three weeks during August to carry out additional structural stiffening astern, and had managed to pull it off in time for the maiden voyage.

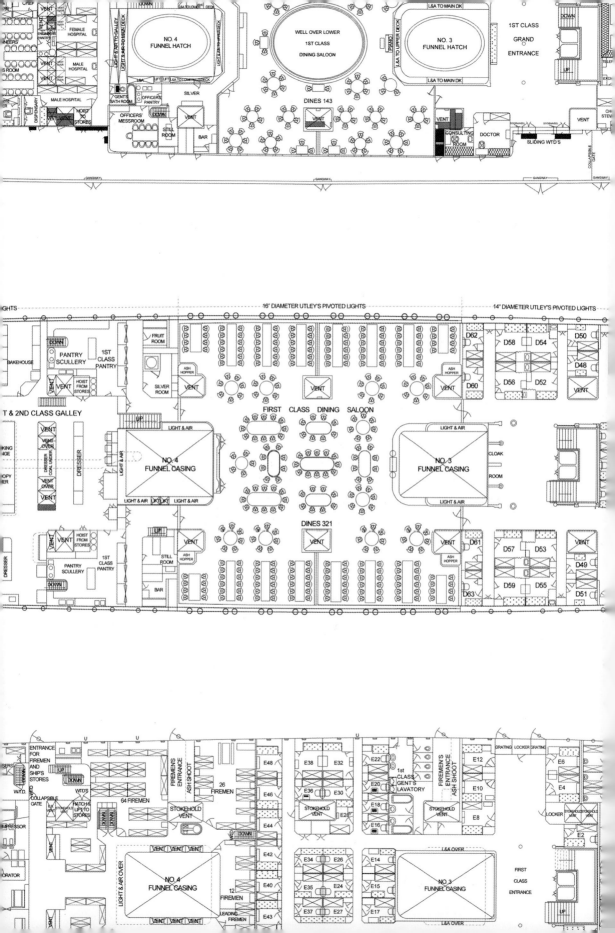

3
Lusitania: A Closer Look

Specifications & Overview: Royal Mail Steamer *Lusitania*

Built by: Messrs. John Brown & Co., Ltd.
Laid Down: August 17, 1904
Launched: June 7, 1906
Service Career: September 7, 1907 – May 7, 1915

Overall Length:	787.2 feet
Length Between Perpendiculars:	760 feet, 0 inches
Width:	87 feet, 6 inches
Draught:	33 feet, 6 inches
Moulded Depth:	60 feet, 4.5 inches
Gross Tonnage:	31,550.47 tons registered[1]
Net Tonnage:	8,514.59 tons registered[2]
Displacement:	44,060 tons registered[3]
	Ditto/inch immersion: 112.4 tons[4]
Powerplant:	Coal-burning Boilers
	(23 double-ended, 2 single-ended)
Engines:	6 Marine Steam Turbines
	(4 ahead, 2 astern)
Shaft Horsepower:	68,000 nominal
Screws:	4
Number of Decks:	10
	(Sun, Boat [A], Promenade [B],
	Shelter [C], Upper [D], Main [E], Lower [F],
	Orlop, Lower Orlop,[5] Tank Top)
Official Number:	124,082
John Brown & Co. Hull Number:	367
Carrying Capacity, Maiden Voyage:	
First Class:	552 (260 rooms)
Second Class:	460 (145 rooms)
Third Class:	1,186 (302 rooms)
Crew, Designed:	827
Total Carrying Capacity, Maiden Voyage:	3,025

THE CUNARD COMPANY QUA

R.M.S. L

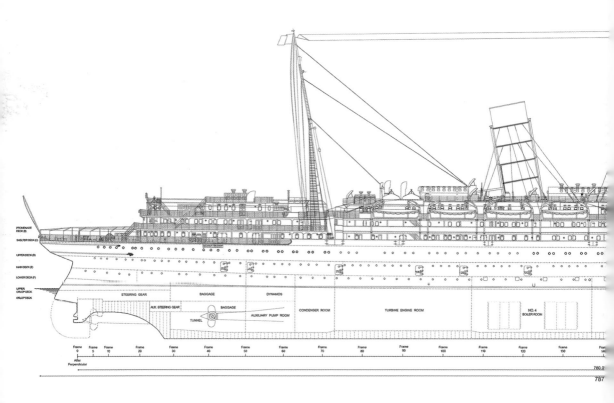

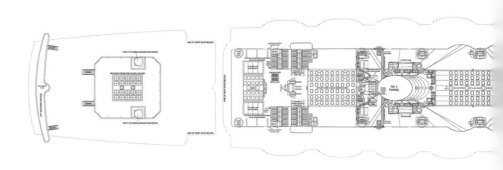

This and following pages: *General arrangement plans of the* Lusitania, *as built in 1907.*

UPLE-SCREW ATLANTIC LINER

USITANIA

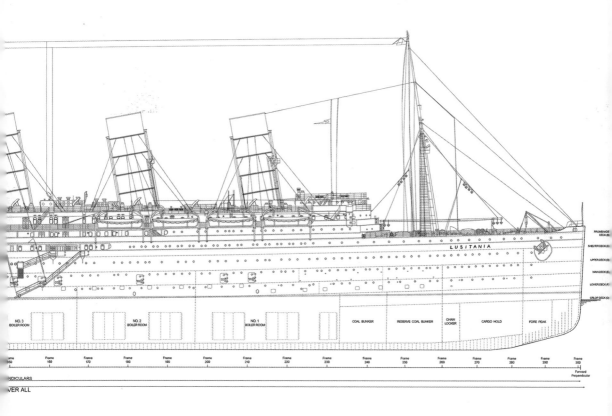

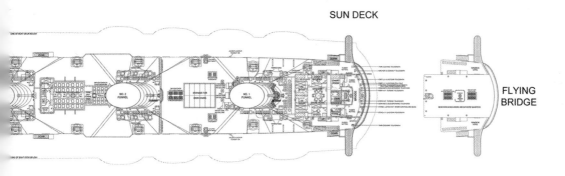

SUN DECK

FLYING
BRIDGE

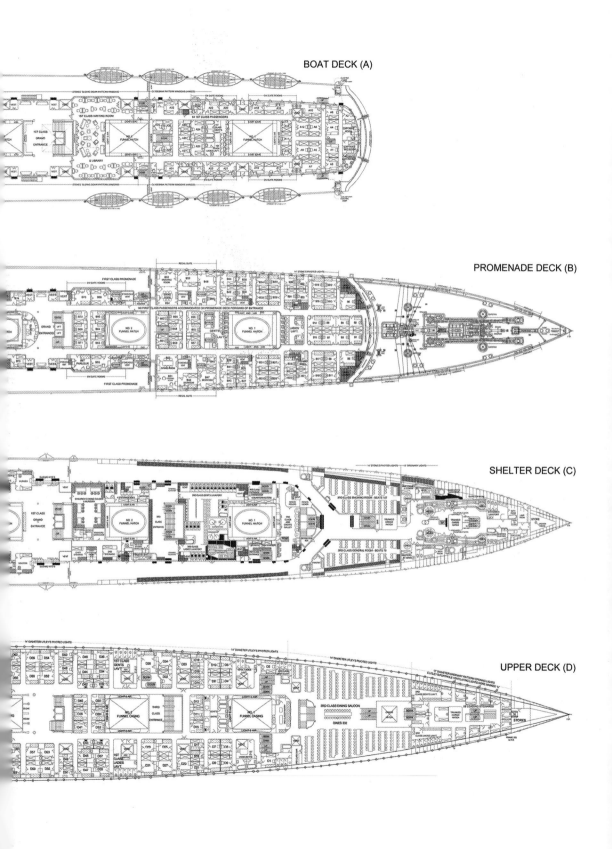

BOAT DECK (A)

PROMENADE DECK (B)

SHELTER DECK (C)

UPPER DECK (D)

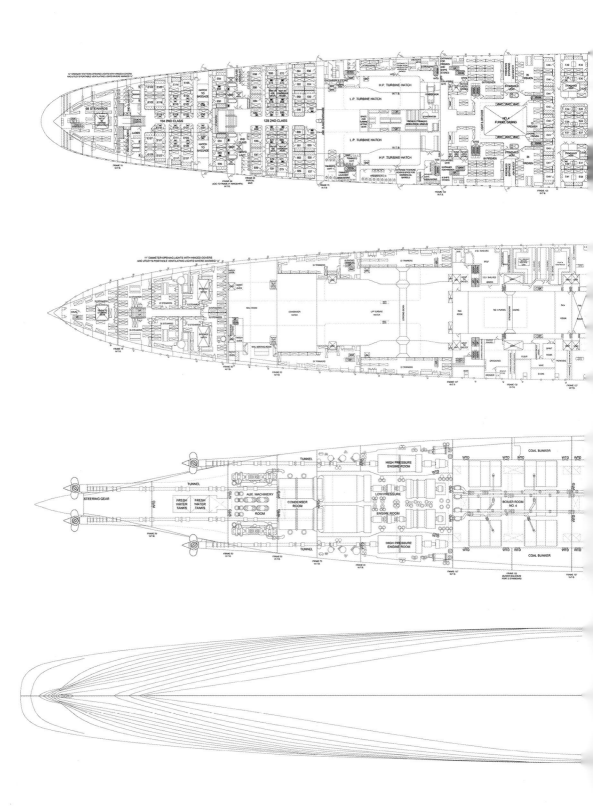

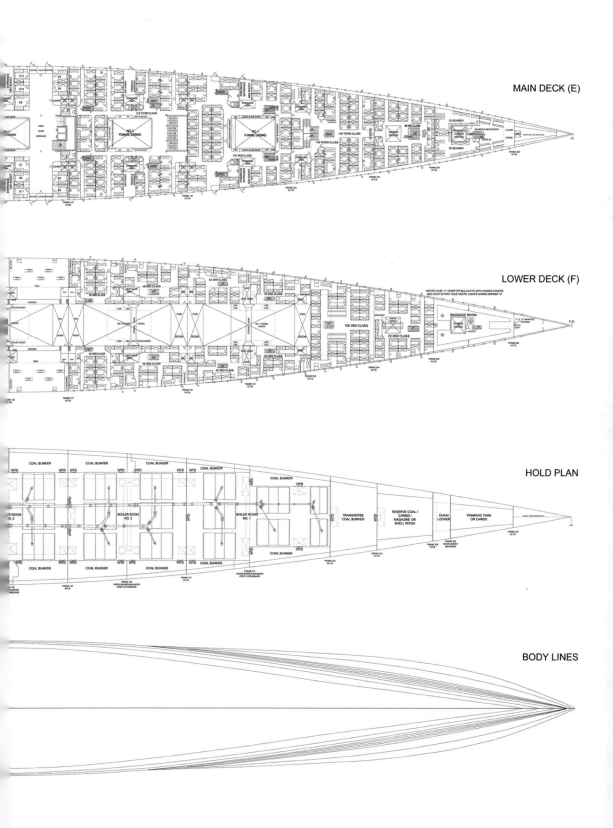

MAIN DECK (E)

LOWER DECK (F)

HOLD PLAN

BODY LINES

The Basic Structure of the *Lusitania*

The *Lusitania*, in finished form, was 787 feet in overall length, with a length between perpendiculars (b.p.) of 760 feet; her extreme breadth was 87 feet 6 inches. These dimensions were somewhat greater than those called for in Cunard's original 1902 draft: namely 750 feet b.p. by 76 feet in width. Even those smaller figures would have represented an immense increase in size from other ships of the time. For example, White Star's *Oceanic* of 1899 was some 685 feet in length b.p., while the German *Kaiser Wilhelm II*, which would enter service in 1903, was 678 feet in length b.p. Because of the *Lusitania*'s incredible dimensions, the Cunard Line was unquestionably in uncharted waters.

The process of taking these initial figures and transforming them into the finished form of the *Lusitania* was by no means arbitrary. Those involved in the task had to draw upon years of previous experience in ship design, and they also had to perform complex mathematical analyses of how different changes – even small ones – would change the vessel's overall characteristics. Once the mathematical studies were complete and some of the best potential dimensions were arrived at, it was time to put them to the test through model studies.

John Brown & Company, however, did not yet have a complete model-testing facility on their premises. Their model facility, then under construction, was unfinished and hence would be of no use in making an analysis; as there was no time to wait until it was completed to begin work, they approached the Admiralty with the conundrum. Persistence paid off, and eventually they were able to begin model tests for the project at Haslar, tests which the Mauretania's builders – Swan, Hunter & Wigham Richardson at Wallsend-on-Tyne – also had access to and participated in.

Perhaps never before in the history of shipbuilding had such great pains been taken to analyze the best possible form and final dimensions for a vessel. Different model shapes and sizes were tested to determine the best overall shape for the hull on the rough dimensions provided – best both for stability and for efficiency in attaining the high speeds required. Experiments were also made on the design of the ship's propellers, and the best possible placement of them in relation to the hull and to each other.

At the same time that the tests at Haslar were being carried out, John Brown had also managed to begin another and simultaneous set of model experiments; to accomplish this they had secured the cooperation of Messrs. William Denny & Brothers, of Dumbar-ton. This firm, not far from John Brown, happened to have a finished model experiment tank. Later, after John Brown's own model experiment tank had been completed on their own premises, they ran all of the tests again. Although these were done after most of the serious problems had been solved, they were able to provide further useful data, including the best possible directions to rotate the ship's propellers.

All of the model experiments compiled a veritable mountain of data. One early proposal made by John Brown was for a vessel of 725 feet b.p. by 80 feet, with a displacement of 32,900 tons and a block coefficient of 631. After the model tests, this rough design proved woefully inadequate and was rejected. Tests representing vessels of 760 feet b.p. and 80 feet in beam and of the same length but two feet narrower were also tested, but were also found wanting, particularly in stability. By increasing the models' represented beam to 88 feet on the same length between perpendiculars, satisfying stability was achieved. By next lengthening the ship's overall length to 787 feet (in the *Lusitania*'s case) or 790 feet (in the *Mauretania*'s), the necessary fineness of hull form could be maintained, as well. Extensive tests were also done to ascertain how much horsepower the different hull forms and sizes would need to drive them at the required 25 knots.

In the press of the period, and again in the years since her sinking, it has often been repeated that the *Lusitania* had an overall length of 785 feet.[6] At the other end of the spectrum, it was often stated, especially in period Cunard advertising which was repeated by some other publications, that the *Lusitania* and *Mauretania* both had an overall length of 790 feet. So what were the ships' true respective dimensions?

The *Mauretania*'s overall length was indeed 790 feet, and a cursory glance at the length between perpendiculars for the two vessels, identical at 760 feet, might initially lead one to believe that they also shared the same exact overall length.

Upon investigating the matter in a little more technical depth, however, the *Lusitania*'s true finished measurements have at last emerged:

From furthest point of ship aft to after perpendicular:	25 feet
Length between perpendiculars:	760 feet
From forward perpendicular to highest point of prow:	2.2 feet

The *Lusitania*'s complete overall length was, then, 787.2 feet, some three feet shorter than the *Mauretania*, even though their length between perpendiculars

was identical. This measurement's accuracy is borne out by the fact that both ships were registered as being 762.2 feet in length from the "forepart of stem to sternpost head." This measurement included the 760 feet between perpendiculars as well as the 2.2 feet of the ships' prows which extended forward from the waterline. The *Mauretania's* three extra feet in length were all contained within the stern of the ship abaft the after perpendicular.

Interestingly, the 787-foot dimension was by no means unknown at the time of her construction and entry into service. Two press reports read, with very great detail:

> The *Mauretania* is a sister ship to the *Lusitania*, though somewhat longer than the latter vessel, being 790ft over all, as against the *Lusitania's* 787ft, a fractional difference which, together with a trifling advantage in breadth, makes the *Mauretania* the largest vessel afloat.

This report was extremely detailed, even noting the slight six-inch advantage in the *Mauretania's* width over that of her sister. Another report stated at the time of the *Lusitania's* trials:

> The *Lusitania* is one of two ships built to the order of the Cunard Steamship Company to regain the blue ribband of the Atlantic … Their length over all is 787ft, breadth 87ft 6in, depth 60ft 4½in, and draught 32ft 6 in.[7]

Although the report was supposedly giving dimensions for both vessels, it is clear from the specific measurements of width and moulded depth cited that they were extrapolating from a set of the *Lusitania's* statistics and applying it to both vessels.[8] Another journal made a similar mistake at the time of the *Mauretania's* entry into service, taking the *Lusitania's* given overall length and applying it to the *Mauretania*, which they stated was "787½ feet long." Even though the figure was incorrect as applied to the *Mauretania*, it is clear that they were not simply pulling "787 feet" out of the ether. Finally, *The Daily Mirror* reported:

> The *Mauretania* is the largest, fastest, and most comfortable passenger vessel afloat. She is about three feet longer than her sister-ship, the *Lusitania*…[9]

When one compares the two ships' true dimensions, it is clear that the *Mauretania* held all the titles of dimension and measurement between the two. She was 2.8 feet longer, 6 inches wider, 387.22 tons greater in gross registered tonnage, and she also displaced 580 tons more than the *Lusitania* did. However, as the *Lusitania* was the first of the two to enter service, she alone held the title of "the world's largest ship" until the *Mauretania* entered service.

At such breathtaking dimensions, the *Lusitania* really was in a whole new dimension of engineering territory. Her hull would thus need to be unusually strong in order to cope with the enormous stresses that would be imposed upon it under North Atlantic circumstances. Additionally, as a merchant vessel which also had to be strong enough for Government service in time of war as an armed auxiliary cruiser, the strength of the *Lusitania's* hull needed to be more than just strong: it needed to be exceptional. This requirement was achieved in several ways.

For starters, the ship's frames were spaced closer together than was the norm for merchant vessels of the time, some 32 inches apart amidships, narrowing to 25 inches aft and 26 inches forward. This required that the holes in the intermediate longitudinals, designed to lighten the keel's overall weight, were placed with their larger dimension running vertically instead of horizontally.

The ship's cellular double bottom ran for almost the entire length of the ship, from the forward end of Cargo Hold No. 1 to the aft end of the Baggage Compartment behind the Auxiliary Machinery Room; the depth of this feature was five feet in the regions of the Boiler Rooms and Holds, and six feet underneath the Engine Room. It was subdivided by four longitudinal girders, two on either side of the keel, the second of which also capped off the top of the double bottom just past the turn of the bilge.

To aid in the ship's stability and comfort while at sea, a 36-inch-deep bilge keel was added to each side of the hull; it ran for just less than 230 feet. They were roughly centered along the fore and aft length of the hull, flanking Boiler Rooms Nos. 2–4.

The plating that formed the Tank Top, otherwise called the "inner bottom," was generally half an inch thick. Their thickness was slightly increased to $6/10$ of an inch underneath the supports which would bear the boilers' weight in due course. Underneath the seating for the turbines, additional stiffening girders were built in.

Stresses imposed on vessels like the *Lusitania* as they moved through the sea were astronomical, especially in bad weather. It is difficult to comprehend the figures and technical data, but a detailed look at one specific scenario that was calculated out during her design phase may help to understand these stresses. Perhaps the worst-case scenario for the *Lusitania* would be encountering a strong sea with wavelengths equal to the ship's length while in "arrival condition," with her coal bunkers depleted. Under this set of circumstances, not at all unheard of on the Atlantic, the ship would be the most prone to hogging, the term used to describe that moment when the ship's center was supported on the crest of a wave and her ends were unsupported in the troughs. When the *Lusitania* was 'hogging' in this scenario, it was calculated that the stresses on her uppermost structural deck, the Shelter Deck, would equal 10.6 tons per square inch amidships, while the compressive forces imposed on her keel would amount to some 7.8 tons per square inch.

To aid in combating this stress, the idea of incorporating a higher grade of steel in the ship's hull plates was considered. Tests were carried out to determine whether the adoption of high-tensile steel would actually be of use in strengthening the hull. The results showed that in general high-tensile steel would be more than one-third better – some 36% to be exact – than normal mild steel, which was commonly used in many liners of the period. It was decided to employ this type of steel over a great portion of the upper hull. This allowed the builders to reduce the scantlings slightly to save top weight; however, they reduced them by only 10%, leaving the hull of the ship considerably stronger than any previously seen in an ocean liner.

Typically, the *Lusitania's* hull plates were some 32 to 33 feet in length. Amidships, the high-tensile steel plates were some $^{22}/20$ inch thick. Toward the extreme bow and stern, where the frame spacing narrowed and the hull's form grew stronger, the plating was reduced to mild steel some $^{12}/20$ inch thick. Along vast stretches of the hull's upper midships section – at Upper Deck D and Main Deck E – her hull was again strengthened through "doubling," or the placing of one plate over another in high-stress areas of the hull. These high-tensile doubler plates were some $^{21}/20$ inch thick, making the total thickness of the shell plating in these areas $2^3/20$ inches, an astoundingly strong design.

Holding the plates together would be just over one thousand tons of rivets. Great care was taken in planning the connection of these plates to ensure maximum strength. The layout was precise, to say the least. The plans specified for the *Lusitania's* topside plating: "Edges treble riveted butts of outside plates double straps. Outer treble & inner quadruple riveted butts of inside plates strapped on inside & quadruple riveted uniform system of tack riveting between frames." From the Main Deck E to approximately ten feet below the waterline, the edges were to be "treble riveted, overlapped butts quadruple riveted." For the plating of the lower hull, plates were "worked clinker fashion for convenience in hydraulic riveting. Edges double riveted. Butts, double straps, outer double riveted & inner treble with openly spaced rivets in 3rd row."

Interestingly, while all this attention was paid to the nature of riveting the plate seams, a decision was made not to use high-tensile steel rivets. It was a common practice at the time to use soft iron rivets in merchant vessels' hulls; the Royal Navy, on the other hand, used much stronger high-tensile steel rivets. While deciding to adopt high-tensile steel for a good portion of the *Lusitania's* hull plating, it was thought that mild-steel rivets would suffice to hold them together. This decision seems questionable today. Indeed, even at the time, there was considerable controversy over the matter – logically speaking, an object is only as strong as its weakest component. One would think that the Admiralty, which had such a high level of interest in the *Lusitania's* design, might have pressed the matter, but in the end the decision to go with mild-steel rivets stood.

Partly making up for this, most of the rivets placed into the ship were driven in hydraulically, after the rivet-holes were specially reamed to ensure proper seating and reduce stress points. Only where the quarters were too cramped to allow the large, pincer-like hydraulic presses room to work were the rivets driven in the old-fashioned way.

The Shelter Deck was the topmost deck of the hull from the stern all the way forward to a point roughly

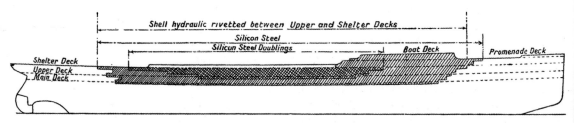

A profile showing the areas where hydraulic riveting, high-tensile steel, and high-tensile steel doublings strengthened the upper portions of the Lusitania's hull.

eighty feet forward of amidships, just behind the No. 2 funnel casing. From there forward to the tip of the prow, the hull was continued up to the Promenade (B) Deck. Everything above these points was only superstructure, which bore none of the ship's hull stresses. To save top weight, these decks and structures could, for the most part, be built of lighter materials than those used in the hull, aiding to the ship's overall stability. Interestingly, the original plan to have the Boat Deck (A) and Promenade Deck (B) overhang the rest of the hull by 20 inches on each side – an arrangement very similar to that finally adopted on the *Mauretania* – was dropped on the *Lusitania*. When she was finished, her Boat and Promenade Decks were flush with the remainder of her superstructure.

To prevent the superstructure from being torn apart by the movement of the ship's hull as it worked its way through the sea, two expansion joints were cut into the *Lusitania*, one just forward of the No. 2 funnel casing, and one just astern of the No. 4 funnel casing.[10] To cover these gaps in the deck, an ingenious design was conceived. On one side of the top of the opening, a brass plate wide enough to cover the gap even when it was stretched to its maximum was screwed directly into the decking. On the other end, this plate was left mobile and unattached. To prevent any squealing as the plate dragged over the decking, a small piece of greased leather was placed on the mobile side between the decking and the plate. Below the deck, a small plate trough was bolted into place on one end of the joint for exterior portions. Where the gap happened to cross through a passenger cabin, the plate trough was replaced with a leather trough.

Astern of the primary superstructure was a secondary superstructure some 130 feet in length. This separate structure, like the forward one, carried on the length of the Promenade and Boat Decks. Atop the Boat Deck area was a smaller deckhouse with its own short segment of Sun Deck. This subsidiary

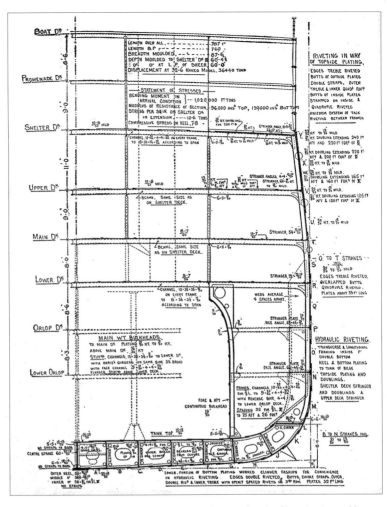

A midship section of the Lusitania *showing details of her riveting and layout.*

superstructure was completely given over to Second Class cabins and public rooms. Connecting the two structures was a short bridge, which spanned the five-foot gap at the Boat Deck level. A locked gate and sign notified Second Class passengers that they

This plan shows, in section view, a typical expansion joint.

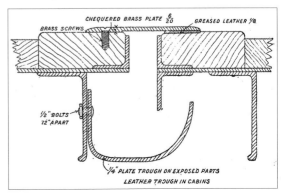

were not allowed to cross that point into First Class portions of the ship.

Atop the aft portion of the Second Class Boat Deck was the slightly curved Aft Docking Bridge, the ends of which overhung the sides of the ship by about four and a half feet. From this vantage point, officers and crewmen could have a full view over the stern of the vessel, over the sides of the ship, and forward along the Boat Deck all the way to the forward Bridge Wing; they could thus keep the Bridge crew informed on critical matters, especially during docking maneuvers in port. Underneath the center of the Aft Docking Bridge was a structure that helped support the upper fixture's weight. Housed within this structure was the Aft Wheelhouse, which housed the ship's third wheel and telemotor (two were fitted in the ship's Navigating Bridge, forward, and will be considered shortly); this allowed for a completely separate control over the ship's rudder and hence the ship's course in the event that the primary Bridge equipment became unusable for some reason. Placing the telemotor in the structure also precluded the necessity for any crewmen to stand exposed on the Aft Docking Bridge.

Because the Shelter Deck was the top deck of the hull for the majority of its length, it needed to be particularly strong to protect against hogging stresses, as described previously. It was also important that the upper decks of the hull should be strong for another reason. In the event of war, the Admiralty could exercise the option of converting the liner into an armed auxiliary cruiser. For such a service, she could be provided with twelve quick-firing 6-inch guns, four on the Forecastle (B) Deck, and the remaining eight on the Shelter (C) Deck.

To give some idea of just how extensive this armament would be, a comparison to other World War One-era Royal Navy vessels might put things into perspective. The H.M.S. *Nottingham* of 1914 was a light 'Town Class' cruiser of 5,440 tons. She sported only nine 6-inch guns – three less than the *Lusitania's* designed complement – with one thirteen-pound anti-aircraft gun thrown in for good measure. The H.M.S. *Hawkins* of 1919 was a cruiser of 9,800 tons which was some 605 feet in length. Her armament also consisted of only nine 6-inch guns, plus four 4-inch anti-aircraft and four three-pounder guns. This demonstrates the formidable level of armament planned for the *Lusitania*, if she was ever converted into active service for the British Government in time of war.

Six-inch guns like these were massive devices, weighing from five to seven tons each, for a total of 60-84 tons, depending on the exact specifications of the guns that could have been installed had she ever found active service. All of this weight had to be supported by the ship's structure. The decks also had to be capable of withstanding the powerful recoil of the guns when they were in use. This force was indeed something to reckon with: each gun had a muzzle energy of over 5,000 foot-tons, and it would be able to penetrate 4¾-inch armor at 5,000 yards (2.8 miles) range, and 6-inch armor at 3,000 yards (1.7 miles) range.

Specifics of the strengthening of the liner's Shelter Deck, where eight of the twelve guns would be installed, are telling. Amidships, stretching both fore and aft, the deck was not only plated with high-tensile steel, but was also doubled with a second layer of high-tensile steel, ranging from $13/20$ inch to $22/22$ inch in critical areas. In the eventuality, these guns would have been secured to the deck via circular mounts, or rings, which would allow them to rotate; such mounts were not originally built into the decks. At least some of these rings were installed aboard the ship in the spring of 1913; in the end, however, the guns themselves were never put aboard and the *Lusitania* was not armed at any point in her career. To save top weight, the decks of the superstructure – Promenade (B) aft of the No. 2 funnel casing, Boat (A) and Sun – which bore none of the stress that the hull did, were far thinner; their deck plating ranged between ¼ and ½ inch in width.

The ship's outer decks were sheathed in yellow pine planking, with only the margin planks in teakwood. The exception to this was on the Forecastle Deck, which was so exposed to the elements; here all the planking was teak. Many think that teak decking was the rule on Atlantic liners, but more often than not, it was pine. Teak was far more expensive to use, and for most areas of the ship's decks, pine did the job nicely. All of the *Lusitania's* decking – teak or pine – was of the highest quality, free from sapwood, knots and other imperfections. The Cunard Line specified to John Brown that the butts of the running deck planking was to be in all cases ten inches or more apart, unless there were two strakes between them, in which case the 10-inch rule could be reduced to five inches. Four strakes needed to separate planks that butted at the same length. Each strake of planking was four inches wide, and with a thickness of between two and three-quarters and three inches. The *Mauretania* and *Aquitania*, like the *Lusitania*, also bore pine deck planking.[11]

The *Lusitania* was designed as a "wet" ship, a term which succinctly described her behavior in rough weather. This was because the hull tapered to a fine point over a large portion of the ship's forward length.

Two views of the 6-inch guns installed aboard the Leviathan *during the Great War show just how massive the devices intended for the* Lusitania *were. Clearly, strong supports would be needed to hold them in place and to withstand their recoil during use. These photos also show just how impossible it would have been to conceal such weapons aboard the* Lusitania.

At the bow, as each deck climbed in succession out of the water, the hull did flare to a certain extent, but was quite fine by Atlantic liners' standards. This made the bow of the ship more or less slice through a large swell instead of attempting to climb over it in an exaggerated pitching motion. In rough weather, as the ship cut into the rolling sea, it tended to send water straight up off the sides of the bow, wetting the Forecastle thoroughly. In particularly foul weather, the whole bow and forward superstructure of the ship could bury itself in solid water.

Standard shipbuilding practice dictated building the liner's decks with a camber, or upward crown, with their highest point amidships and the lowest points along the port and starboard edges. This allowed any water that collected on the decks – due to weather or high seas – to wash out toward the edges of the ship, where it would drain away through the scuppers. On a "dry" ship, the camber, or crown, would naturally not need to be as great as on a "wet" ship. The later White Star liners *Olympic* and *Titanic* were designed as "dry" ships, and sported a 3-inch camber from outer edge to amidships for each of their decks. However, because large volumes of water frequently washed over the *Lusitania*'s open decks in dirty weather, her Boat, Promenade and Shelter decks were given an 18-inch camber, while a 6-inch camber was specified for all decks below that.

Along the centerline of the vessel, the height of each of the *Lusitania*'s decks was as follows:

Promenade Deck:	8 feet, 6 inches
Shelter Deck:	9 feet, 0 inches
Upper Deck:	11 feet, 0 inches[12]
Main Deck:	9 feet, 0 inches
Lower Deck:	8 feet, 0 inches
Orlop Deck:	8 feet, 6 inches
Lower Orlop Deck:	8 feet, 3 inches

The height of all public rooms on the Boat Deck varied depending on their location, as the height of the deckhouse structure was elevated from a point just forward of the No. 2 funnel to the aft end of the First Class Smoking Room.

Atop the Sun Deck stood the *Lusitania*'s crowning, and most identifiable feature, a quartet of proud smokestacks. Each of these was endowed with a coating of traditional Cunard livery. These funnels were designed to vent the exhaust gases from the boiler furnaces in the stokeholds. Each of the smokestacks bore five segments. The lower four were painted in Cunard's unusual orange-red color. Black bands separated each segment, and the topmost section was painted black. Each of the funnels stood roughly 65 feet tall in their own right;[13] being positioned atop the Sun Deck, they towered some 75 feet above the Boat Deck, a total of 120 feet from the designed waterline, and over 150 feet above the keel. The funnels had a fore-aft diameter of 24 feet, and were elliptical in shape, with their narrow dimension running port to starboard. Each structure was in point of fact a double funnel, with an inner casing separated from the outer casing by a minimum specified distance of six inches. The smokestacks were all raked aft at an angle of ten degrees.

Ship funnels may appear to be rock-solid structures, but they are, in reality, made out of very thin steel and are quite delicate. Because of their relative structural weakness, each of the *Lusitania*'s funnels was secured to the Sun and Boat Decks by a complex series of guy wires and chains. Thus secured, they could withstand anything that the harsh North Atlantic could throw at them.

The forward two funnels sported single-chime whistles in 1907, each one made of brass and standing some four feet high. The forward of the two whistles was eventually replaced by a double-chime setup to facilitate communication with tugboats, especially in New York Harbor which was often quite noisy. Even this was found deficient, and was again upgraded to a triple-chime whistle that looked remarkably like the setup sported by the *Olympic* and *Titanic*. In addition, two sirens flanked the whistle(s) on the forward funnel. All of this equipment could be controlled from the Bridge by the Captain and his Officers.

Early models for the ship, which was then slated to be powered by reciprocating engines in a triple-screw configuration, showed the *Lusitania* sporting only three funnels. However, when the ship's engine configuration was altered to turbines and the final boiler arrangement was laid out, it was deemed necessary to give the ship four funnels, instead of three. On the *Lusitania*, each funnel was tied to its own Boiler Room, and all four were real smokestacks. The *Lusitania*'s later competitors, White Star's *Olympic*, *Titanic* and *Britannic*, were each bestowed with four funnels, but only the forward three were connected to the Boiler Rooms, the fourth being primarily intended for visual impressiveness. In those days, the more funnels a ship sported the better; German greyhounds like the *Deutschland* sported four funnels, so it sat well with the management of the Cunard Line that the *Lusitania*, and her sister *Mauretania* and successor *Aquitania*, would all sport four, as well.

There is another interesting detail regarding the ship's funnels that is worth mentioning at this point. To all general appearances, the *Lusitania*'s four funnels were evenly spaced, a departure from the "double-pair" design of previous German ships of the era. A closer examination, however, showed that the *Lusitania*'s funnels were, indeed, paired. The space between the Nos. 2 and 3 funnels was just over two feet greater than the spacing between the Nos. 1 and 2 and the Nos. 3 and 4 funnels. Even these two gaps were non-identical, as the gap between the Nos. 1 and 2 funnels was a few inches greater than that between the Nos. 3 and 4.

Around the base of the four funnels, all along the Sun Deck, were some twenty-two hinge-topped ventilators, eleven on each side (two additional ventilators of this type sat astern on the roof of the Second Class portion of the superstructure). These primarily provided ventilation for the lower compartments of the ship, particularly the extremely hot Boiler and Engine Rooms. They also served as an escape route to the Sun Deck for anyone trapped below in the machinery spaces during an emergency.

These ventilators were truly unique in the annals of maritime construction. They presented a stream-

Above left: *A late 1908 photograph showing the whistles and sirens in their original configuration.*

Above right: *A photo from several years later showing the forward whistles changed to a triple-chime design.*

lined appearance quite different from the standard cowl-type ventilators; their low profile also made the four funnels of the ship appear taller to the casual observer. They were also the most easily identifiable difference between the *Lusitania* and *Mauretania*, for the younger, larger ship bore the standard cowl ventilators along her "top of the house." It is quite arguable that the *Mauretania*'s appearance suffered some from this arrangement, but the simple fact was that the standard cowl ventilators worked more efficiently. The canister-like lids of the *Lusitania*'s ventilators were quite often nipped cleanly off of their bases dur-

ing service in bad weather; they were progressively replaced with the more standard cowl ventilators as the ship's career continued.

Just forward of the No. 1 funnel, sitting astride the Sun Deck, was the ship's Bridge house, situated some ninety feet above the keel and some fifty-eight feet above the normal waterline. The overall rectangular structure of the Bridge sported a curved face toward the bow and was some fifty feet in length. In the stern section of this structure were the quarters for the ship's senior officers and the Officers' Smoke Room, which was serviced by its own pantry. The

Below: *The* Lusitania's *original vent configuration.*

Bottom: *A nearly identical view apparently taken during December 1912, showing which vents had been replaced with the cowl type.*

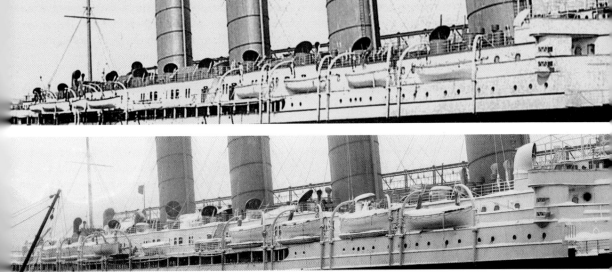

A beautiful view of the Lusitania's Bridge rising above the Forecastle, which was taken before her maiden voyage. Judging from the small amount of landscape visible behind the ship, as well as the angle of the sunlight, this view may have been taken at Gourock in late June or early July of 1907.

Captain's Suite was not located on this level, but was instead housed directly underneath the Bridge on the forward Boat Deck. It was comprised of a bedroom, day cabin and private water closet and bathroom. From here, access to the Bridge could be had via an interior staircase which led up into the Bridge house. Forward of the Officers' Smoke Room and Officers' Quarters there was a corridor which ran across the Bridge house, with a door to the exterior on either side. Just in front of this corridor, on the port side, was the Chart Room, while on the starboard side sat the bathroom and water closet for the officers. Lining the front of the Bridge structure, behind eleven square windows overlooking the bow and Forecastle, was the ship's main Bridge. This was the nerve center of the ship.

Most of the Bridge proper had rubber matting covering the deck to prevent slippage. Just behind the forward windows, arranged in a neat line, was all of the ship's main control equipment. All of these instruments were built to a higher standard than was the norm for the period in merchant vessels. This added expense was justified by the Admiralty, not because of the unprecedented size of the *Lusitania*, but instead because in time of war, she could be taken over for active duty as a naval auxiliary.

There were four telegraphs to control the turbine engines. The outboard telegraphs controlled the low-pressure and astern turbines, while the inboard telegraphs controlled the high-pressure ahead turbines. There were three controls for the ship's whistles, two pillar-style loud-speaking telephones (enabling the Officer of the Watch to speak to the Engine Room Starting Platform, Aft Docking Bridge, Crow's Nest and Forecastle Head), tell-tale indicators to show the operation of the turbine engines, a steering telegraph to show the position of the rudder, and a control for the watertight doors. Amidships there was a binna-

Above: *A beautiful and rare photograph taken on the Bridge of the* Lusitania. *The structure of the Wheelhouse stands on the right. On the left stand the ship's control instruments.*

Right: *A Duplex signal lamp indicator on the Bridge of the* Mauretania.

cle housing a compass. In the port-aft quarter of the Bridge was a Pearson's Fire Indicator, which was connected to a system of automatic and "break the glass and press"-type alarms. The Officer of the Watch could thus be immediately informed of a fire in any of the monitored areas of the ship. A similar indicator panel was located in the Engine Room, as well. In the starboard-aft quarter of the Bridge, there was the watertight door indicator, which kept the Officer of the Watch apprised of the position of each watertight door. The electrically powered indicating panel contained a faceplate with an engraved plan of the ship. Backlit ruby-colored discs were inserted into the plate to represent each of the monitored watertight doors. When the doors were opened, the discs were lit; when the doors were closed, the discs went dark.

Amidships, there was an enclosed Wheelhouse, with five forward-facing windows which looked out upon the Bridge. Within that Wheelhouse – accessed

Above: *An advertisement for Brown's Patent Telemotors, as fitted aboard the* Lusitania, *as well as the* Mauretania *and* Aquitania. *This company also supplied the telemotors for the Olympic-class ships.*

Left: *This photograph was taken on the Bridge of the* Mauretania, *and shows the controls for the watertight doors operated by the Stone-Lloyd system. The setup for this control on the Lusitania was quite similar.*

by a door to port and starboard, and with a third door aft leading into the Chart Room – stood the ship's wheel. There were two complete telemotors fitted in the Wheelhouse, which were operated from the central wheel. A clutch allowed each telemotor to be engaged separately; also located within the Wheelhouse was a locker for the ship's signal flags. A small patch of matting just behind the wheel added to the sheltered environment to make a relatively comfortable space for the duty Quartermaster to stand while he guided the ship on her course.

From the Bridge, a sliding door to port and to starboard led out toward the Bridge Wings. Rubber matting lined the decking outside the Bridge structure which led aft, to a staircase on the port and starboard sides that gave access to the Bridge roof; there, two skylights allowed light and, when the weather was good, fresh air into the Bridge House structure. There was a compass platform atop the Bridge, further removed from all metallic influence;[14] later in the ship's career, a second platform was installed a bit further aft, between the Nos. 1 and 2 funnels. Still later on, the compass structure atop the Bridge was raised even further to prevent magnetic interference. On the starboard side, just outside of the Bridge, was a docking telegraph, while a control for the ship's siren was mounted on the bulkhead of the Bridge, just forward of the door. On the opposite side there was a docking telegraph and an anchor and lookout telegraph. Another control for the ship's siren was located on the port bulkhead of the Bridge.

Stretching further outboard were the actual Bridge wings, which extended over the level of the Boat Deck and were supported by large columns at the outboard edge of that deck. They overhung the side of the ship by about four feet. From these vantage points, the Captain, officers, and in port the Harbor Pilot, could all see exactly what was going on around them; they could enjoy an unobstructed vista over the bow and Forecastle, as well as to each side of the ship; additionally, they could overlook the entire Sun and Boat Decks astern, to keep tabs on important goings-on such as lifeboat drills. Wooden gratings covered the decking of the actual Bridge wings; they were divided into four segments along each wing. Just behind the wings, staircases led down, allowing immediate access to the level of the Boat Deck.

Astern of the Bridge, also built atop the Sun Deck, was the ship's Marconi Shack. In this particular instance, the Marconi Shack closely resembled its name, being a basic rectangle in shape, and having all the appearance of an afterthought. It was situated between the No. 2 and No. 3 funnels directly abaft the skylight over the First Class Entrance. Its purpose was clearly shown to curious observers by the twin aerial wires that ran down to it from the dual aerials suspended between the masts. Within this small cubicle was the all-important Marconi apparatus, which connected the liner with the outside world and with other vessels while she was at sea. The ship's daily newspaper, which would be published aboard the ship during each crossing, would keep passengers informed of important events going on in the world even while they enjoyed their voyage.

There were actually two complete sets of wireless equipment; one was for transmitting and the other was for receiving. The receiving set was placed in a soundproof "quiet" room in one corner of the Marconi Shack. The ship's wireless sets were powerful enough to maintain communication with land for the entire voyage, except for a stretch of about three hours in mid-ocean. There was also an emergency apparatus available in the event that the ship's power was lost; during an emergency, wireless contact could thus be maintained with other ships in the area.

Two operators were employed by the Marconi Company to man the set, keeping a twenty-four-hour watch. This was the first time such a complete watch

Below left: *An early photograph of the* Lusitania's *wireless transmitting set.*

Below right: *A later photograph of the* Lusitania's *Marconi set.*

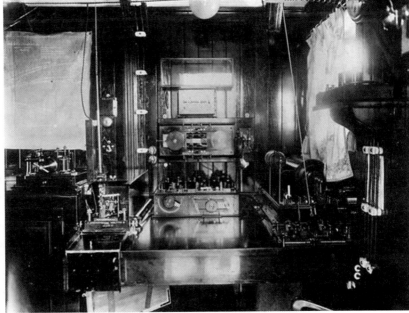

The Purser's Enquiry Office on B Deck. Located within the First Class Entrance, this is where passengers went to send telegrams.

order to gain physical access to the Bridge, a Marconi operator would need to go down to the Boat Deck level; in good weather, he could walk to the staircase just behind the Bridge Wing which then went back up to the Bridge area, while in poor weather, he could enter the First Class Entrance and make his way forward within the enclosed portions of the ship, finally re-ascending to the Bridge via the stairwell behind the Captain's Suite.

Supporting the twin aerials that served as the Marconi system's antennae was the ship's Foremast and Mainmast. Each of these masts rose roughly 170 feet above the waterline at their peak and, like the smokestacks, stood at an angle of roughly ten degrees from the ship's vertical fore and aft. The Foremast rose out of the Forecastle Deck, just behind the crew stairwell that led down to the Shelter Deck. The mast itself was hollow, with a ladder inside; this setup allowed lookouts to climb up to and down from the Crow's Nest, the base of which was over 85 feet above the waterline, enclosed and protected from the elements. Above the Crow's Nest was the ship's forward navigation lamp. Still higher, atop the very peak of the mast, there was an unusual weather-vane that was so small that it is nearly invisible in most photos. Attached to the Foremast were the crane booms that could hoist cargo from dockside up over the open cargo hatches and down into the holds. About five hundred feet aft of the Foremast was the Mainmast. This feature rose from the Shelter Deck between the First and Second Class segments of the superstructure, and its base was sunk solidly down into the Main Deck for structural strength. There was a navigational light attached to this mast, as well.

had been set up on an ocean liner, for a twenty-four-hour watch was not mandatory until after the sinking of the *Titanic* in 1912. Typically, the *Lusitania's* operators would have two six-hour watches a day.

Each Marconi-equipped ship or Marconi station was given its own unique three-letter call sign. Ships had call signs that began with the letter M, while fixed shore stations had call signs that began with the letter G. Land's End radio station, for example, was "GLD." The White Star liner *Titanic* received the now infamous call sign "MGY," while her sisters *Olympic* and *Britannic* were given the designations "MKC" and "MUW," respectively. The *Lusitania* was given the call sign "MFA," while the *Mauretania* was given the designation "MGA." Passengers wishing to send wireless messages could do so from the Enquiry Office. Charges varied greatly depending on the number of stations it had to be transmitted through; all wireless messages had to be pre-paid, and if the delivery failed, or needed to be re-routed through another station, the tolls were re-computed and collected from the sender.[15]

The Marconi Shack was connected with the rest of the ship via telephone on a 23-extension system that did not require a switchboard exchange. Communication could thus be made between the Shack and the Captain and officers, or with the First Class Bureau on B Deck, where passengers conducted necessary business with the ship's Purser and his staff and composed their wireless transmissions. Outside of the Marconi Shack was a staircase on either side of the Sun Deck which led down to the Boat Deck. Because of the bulwark all around the ship's Bridge House, in

Another unique design feature was incorporated into the design of the *Lusitania*, and into that of her sister. Because the *Lusitania* needed to be highly maneuverable if she was ever converted to serve as an armed merchant cruiser, it was decided to remove the keel of the ship for a distance of some sixty feet forward of the aft perpendicular, just fore of the rudder. This feature, referred to as 'removing the deadwood', thus created an arch in the hull, which would allow for her to make tighter maneuvers at high speed than she would otherwise have been able to perform.

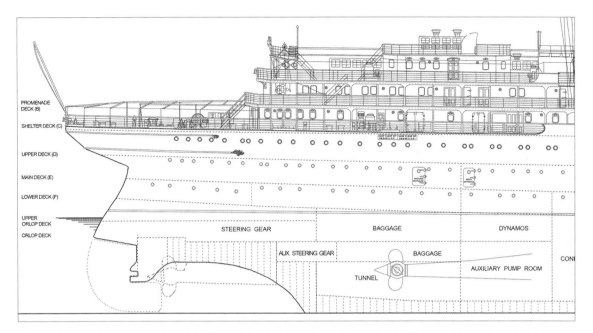

Above: *This plan shows the stern in profile. Clearly visible is the arch formed by cutting the "deadwood" away from the after hull. Although this certainly added maneuverability to the ship, stresses imposed upon the hull during drydocking were a point of concern with this break from traditional ocean liner design. In the end, the stern was more than strong enough to withstand the stresses imposed on it during such procedures.*

Below right: *A period photograph showing a steering engine and gear very similar to that found on board the* Lusitania.

There was a concern that because of this feature, the stern of the ship might not be able to support itself during a drydocking procedure, as the after 84 feet of the ship would be completely unsupported. Extensive calculations were performed to see how the stern would react under those circumstances, and how much pressure would be exerted upon the last keel block supporting the stern, the structural point which would act like a fulcrum for all of the stern's weight. Fortunately, it was discovered that the ship's stern would be sufficiently strong to support itself under these scenarios; it was even found that wooden keel blocks would be a preferable support material to steel ones, since the wooden ones were elastic and would help to distribute the weight of the ship more uniformly.

The Admiralty also specified that the entirety of the *Lusitania*'s rudder needed to be below the waterline, to protect it from any damage that it might otherwise sustain during enemy action. The design of the rudder adopted was the balanced type, supported by a single gudgeon and with a removable pintle. The actual rudder itself was comprised of three separate castings connected by horizontal flanges. These flanges had grooves, or recesses, called rabbets cut out of their edges to receive their opposite member; they were then heavily bolted. The rudder head was of forged steel, and its total area was some 420 square feet. The rudder's total weight was 126,336 lbs., or

roughly 63 tons.[16] Controlled by the elaborate steering gear, which is described later, it was able to move through 35 degrees on either side of the ship's main longitudinal axis (70 degrees in total movement), and up to 37 degrees (74 degrees in total movement) before physically jamming against its stops. The combination of the "deadwood" removal as well as the highly maneuverable rudder allowed the *Lusitania* to perform impressive turning circles on her trials and made it much easier to maneuver her during her service career.

The steering gear, in addition to the rudder itself, was a matter of concern to the Admiralty when the outline for the ship's design was initially drawn up;

all of the machinery for the steering gear and the rudder was placed below the waterline to prevent it from being damaged by enemy shellfire in time of war. The steering engines were mounted just forward of the tiller; they drove a cast-steel rack by means of worm-gear, a friction-clutch and spur-gear. The rack itself was made in three separate parts so that the teeth of the center section could be replaced independent of the other two when worn. There was a primary engine as well as a back-up engine, both engines being identical in design. Each set of engines had the capacity of exerting some 1,240 foot tons of pressure against the rudder-stock.

Also below the waterline, hidden from the eyes of spectators marveling at the liner's vast expanse from the outside, there was another important element of the *Lusitania* that saw great attention during her design. This was the watertight subdivision of the hull, something that was important during her peacetime career, but was even more of concern to the Admiralty in case she ever saw active service with the Royal Navy.

The *Lusitania* was subdivided into twelve primary compartments by eleven transverse (port to starboard running) bulkheads. Behind the Forepeak there were two Cargo Holds, which were followed by a transverse coal bunker, four Boiler Rooms (numbered 1–4 from bow to stern), the Engine Room, the Condenser Room, the Auxiliary Machinery Room, and the Steering Gear Compartment. These main bulkheads were built entirely out of high-tensile steel. In their lowest portions, they were fully ½ inch thick, and then thinned to $9/20$ inch up to the level of the Main Deck; above that level, they were $6/20$ inch thick. They were immensely strong, strengthened on one side by vertical channel stiffeners to the height of the Lower Deck, and by flanged stiffeners above that. They also had horizontal strengthening girders on the same side as the vertical stiffeners.

Even this high grade of watertight subdivision was not enough for the Admiralty. They knew that if the ship was ever converted into an armed auxiliary cruiser, it was conceivable that she could see enemy action, and even face a barrage of enemy fire. Normally the vessels which went into combat were purpose-built for such action, and sported heavy steel armor belts to prevent their flanks from being penetrated by enemy shells. However, this sort of armor plating was ponderous; the heavier and thicker the armor was, the slower the ship would be able to travel through the sea. As a passenger liner, slated to be the world's fastest to boot, the *Lusitania* could not be burdened with such armor. Yet without the armor, one

well-placed enemy shell could penetrate the ship's vital Boiler and Engine Rooms and wreak havoc on her machinery. In the Boiler Rooms, it would have been quite likely that the boilers or pressurized steam lines could have burst explosively; in the Engine Room, the six turbines could easily be damaged beyond repair. In either case, it would be quite likely that the ship's entire powerplant could be downed. This would force a drydock overhaul that could last months, or go so far as to jeopardize the ship's overall safety.

Some sort of protection had to be afforded the essential machinery spaces, and the Admiralty insisted that all such equipment be placed below the load waterline. Still not confident of adequate protection, the Admiralty further made sure that all of the Boiler and Engine Rooms were lined with longitudinal (bow to stern running) bulkheads in addition to the transverse ones. The longitudinal bulkheads were quite strong, being stiffened and braced to the side. When connected with the transverse bulkheads, the entire system contributed materially to the overall strength of the ship.

Adding these longitudinal bulkheads posed a problem, however: where would the six thousand tons of coal required to steam across the Atlantic be stored? It might seem strange that on what was going to be the largest ocean liner in the world, there was actually a premium of space. However, given the large quantity of coal required for each trip, the extreme size of the ship's powerplant and the fineness of the ship's hull it was nonetheless a sobering reality. There simply was no room to place transverse coal bunkers between each Boiler Room. To solve the problem, it was decided that the coal would be stored in the longitudinal wing compartments that lined the Boiler Rooms. This was not a problem for the Admiralty or, for that matter, for Cunard. The coal sitting in the bunkers would assist in shielding the machinery from enemy fire. At the same time, other Cunard liners had sported longitudinal coal bunkers, and it was found quite convenient since the coal was at all times very close to the boiler furnaces. Each coal bunker was further subdivided into two semi-autonomous compartments with a partial transverse bulkhead.

Through this arrangement, the *Lusitania* was endowed with 34 primary watertight compartments. In all however, when all of the subdivisions were accounted for, there were a total of 175 watertight compartments. Watertight decks at E and F Decks also topped off most of these compartments. The Forepeak was capped off by E Deck; Cargo Holds Nos. 1 and 2 was capped by F Deck. Astern, aft of the Turbine Engine Room, F Deck was again made watertight. There was also a watertight deck over the top of the outboard coal bunkers.

Considering the highlights of the ship's watertight subdivision brings us to a consideration of the *Lusitania*'s safety, stability, and comparisons to other ships of the era as well as to modern-day Safety of Life At Sea (SOLAS) regulations.

When the *Lusitania* entered service in 1907, she was hailed by *The New York Times* as being "as unsinkable as a ship can be ..." A pre-maiden voyage Cunard booklet likewise said: "In all, the *Lusitania* will have 175 watertight compartments, so that it may be claimed for her that she is as unsinkable as a ship can be." Indeed, the *Mauretania*'s watertight subdivision and basic structure was quite similar to that of the *Lusitania*, and she sailed the rugged North Atlantic from 1907 to 1934 – including time spent in war service – without ever being in critical danger or suffering serious structural defect. This testifies to the strength and overall high quality of the ships' designs. However, we also know that the *Mauretania* was never involved in a serious incident at sea, such as being struck by a torpedo or mine, colliding with an iceberg, like the *Titanic* did, or running into another large vessel. So how does the watertight subdivision of the *Lusitania* stand up under close scrutiny?

First of all, we should look at the effectiveness of the watertight subdivision between the wing coal bunkers and the interior Boiler Rooms. When the decision was made to adopt the longitudinal coal bunkers, it was not unprecedented by any means. The Royal Navy had been using this method of watertight subdivision for some time in their crack vessels. Many previous liners also had watertight bulkheads separating their coal bunkers from their boiler rooms. However, there were also risks. In order to pass the coal from the bunkers into the stokeholds, it was necessary to cut apertures into the base of these bulkheads, and through these openings it was possible for a flooded coal bunker to allow the sea into the inner compartment. Thus, these apertures were each fitted with a watertight door that could be sealed in the event of an emergency.

It was, however, a matter of historic fact that there could be problems in actually sealing these doors during a crisis. Let us review, briefly, the fate of the Cunard liner *Oregon*. The *Oregon* initially entered service with the Guion Line in October of 1883. She was 518 feet in overall length and was some 7,375 tons in size, and after her entry into service, she managed to take the Blue Riband with a westbound passage of 6 days, 10 hours and 10 minutes. When the Guion Line failed, the Cunard Line purchased the ship in May of 1884. Although she quickly lost the Blue Riband, she continued a successful and prestigious service with Cunard. On Saturday, March 6, 1886, she departed Liverpool with between 846 and 852 passengers and crew aboard.[17] In the early morning hours of March 14, eighteen miles off the coast of Long Island, a bedarkened schooner came out of the darkness like an apparition, right off the *Oregon*'s bow. The Cunarder's crew attempted to take evasive action, but the *Oregon* was struck. The schooner sank promptly and without survivors, having disappeared immediately after the collision; it has been

The Cunarder Oregon.

Above: *A period plan specifically showing the ship's watertight subdivision arrangements, and the locations of her watertight doors.*

Below left: *A photograph of one of the* Lusitania's *hydraulically operated watertight doors.*

Below right: *Another view of a similar door on a liner of the period.*

tentatively identified as the *Charles R. Morse*, which was also reported missing that night.

All attempts to stem the inflow of water through the three holes in the *Oregon*'s iron hull failed. An attempt was made by Captain Cottier to beach the ship on nearby Fire Island, but it was at this time that water entered the undamaged Boiler Room and put the powerplant out of commission. The ship was evacuated and sank about four hours after the collision.[18] Not a single life was lost in the incident. However, the reason water was able to enter the Boiler Room from the damaged outboard areas had to do with the failure of the watertight doors to properly seat themselves. Partly this was due to the distortion of the bulkheads in the collision, and partly it was due to the buildup of coal dust and debris that clogged the sills and tracks.

It was thus vitally important to ensure that the *Lusitania*'s watertight doors – particularly those which led from her wing coal bunkers into her Boiler Rooms – could be sealed effectively, reliably and quickly. The bulkheads of the ship were pierced and fitted with 69 watertight doors. The primary 35 doors (over 50%) were operated by the Stone-Lloyd system, which was constructed by Messrs. J. Stone and Company, Limited, of Deptford. It was operated on hydraulic power

(not steam, electricity or compressed air), the pressure of which was at all times maintained by two steam-driven duplex pumps located in the Engine Room. From there, a pressure main which circled the ship led to a powerful hydraulic cylinder attached to each door; the closing main of each door was controlled by an operating pedestal. This pedestal allowed pressure into the closing main, reversing the control valves and admitting pressure to the cylinders which operated each door. When the system was activated, either from the door lever or from the Bridge controls, a continuous warning bell sounded to warn crewmen in the area to get clear. Once the doors were closed, there was still a chance for members shut in the compartments to escape through the doors by using the control lever, raising the door for long enough for them to escape; it would thereafter close behind them as soon as they let go of the lever. The remaining 34 watertight doors were of the ordinary sliding pattern, worked by control rods and gearing from the Shelter Deck (C). A dial at the control point showed the position of the door at any given time. All of the Stone-Lloyd doors were also operable through this system in the form of a backup, as specified by the British Board of Trade at the time.

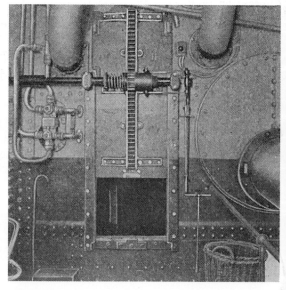

Notably, only the coal bunker doors in Boiler Room No. 3 were of the Stone-Lloyd system; that those associated with Boiler Rooms Nos. 1, 2 and 4 were of the older control rod type may not have seemed important at the time. However, the decision to fit only one-quarter of what were arguably the most critical watertight bulkheads in the ship with the hydraulic system could hardly be described as the wisest. Additionally, by way of hindsight – knowing that the *Lusitania*'s Boiler Room No. 1 and its starboard coal bunker was the one that bore the brunt of the torpedo's detonation – this decision seems particularly poor.

Assuming that all of the liner's watertight doors were closed in the event of an emergency, the *Lusitania* was designed to float with any two major watertight compartments flooded – even her largest ones. However, there were also flaws in the nature of her subdivision. Through the introduction of the longitudinal compartments, there was now the possibility of asymmetrical flooding. This type of flooding is extremely dangerous because as more water collects on one side of the ship as opposed to the other, the ship is pulled further onto the wounded side. This process could eventually end with the ship capsizing, a thoroughly unenviable scenario. Realizing this potential issue, the ship's designers made arrangements so that, through the use of pumps, the various watertight compartments in the ship's double bottom could be flooded. If the *Lusitania* took a heavy list to one side, then water could be pumped into the compartments on the other side in order to trim the list.

After the *Titanic* disaster, the practicability of various forms of watertight subdivisions and lifesaving appliances came into question. In particular, questions arose as to whether longitudinal bulkheads would have saved the *Titanic* from her fate after sustaining the damage from the iceberg. Naturally, Harland & Wolff's Edward Wilding – who had worked under the supervision of the Chief Designer of the *Olympic*-class ships, Thomas Andrews – was called on to testify at the British Inquiry. At the same time, Cunard's resident Naval Architect, Leonard Peskett – the team leader on the designs for the *Lusitania* and *Mauretania* – was also called on to testify as an expert on the subject. He was closely questioned regarding the safety of the *Lusitania* in various aspects. Coming some three years before the sinking of the *Lusitania*, but after the famous loss of the *Titanic*, the testimony is quite revealing.

Mr. Raymond Asquith: Will you give us your view about the comparative merits of the systems of longitudinal and transverse divisions?

21083. (The Commissioner.) You have a combination of both in those ships? – For ships of this class, I think that the transverse and longitudinal combined is best for all purposes, for very large ships.

21084. (Mr. Raymond Asquith.) That combination is best? – Yes, that combination is best.

21085. Were you in Court when Mr. Wilding was asked his views about some of the difficulties of longitudinal divisions? – Yes, I was.

21086. Did you hear him mention, I think, two difficulties, one of them being that there might be a tendency, if the ship was wounded at the side, for water to get in and cause a list, because there would be a difficulty in the water getting out again? – Yes, I heard that. That can be counteracted.

21087. In what way? – Supposing that any two compartments were flooded on either side, the opposite side could be filled in several ways; also you could flood the engine room and the compartment immediately abaft it; also the shaft tunnel aft.

21088. (The Commissioner.) But that is rather heroic, is it not? – There would be less trouble in doing that latter part than any of the other parts.

21089. (Mr. Raymond Asquith.) Have you made any experiments to see how far that is practicable? – No, no experiments have been made.[19]

Cunard's Naval Architect, Leonard Peskett. When once asked if he had designed the Lusitania *and* Mauretania, *he replied: "I had a great deal to do with it. The design was spread over a large number, but I was responsible."*

Even as late as 1912, then, "no experiments" had been made to demonstrate the practicability of this counterflooding system as installed in the *Lusitania*.

Even outside of the Mersey Inquiry's obvious interest in the matter, an enormous debate went on within the maritime community in general over which form of watertight subdivision was superior. Following the conclusion of the British Inquiry into the loss of the *Titanic, The Shipbuilder* magazine reported:

> The disadvantage of the longitudinal system is that, with several compartments flooded on one side only, the vessel will take an unpleasant list, and if she does not possess sufficient stability will completely capsize. It is our own opinion that the longitudinal arrangement is the better one, provided it is adopted in conjunction with a watertight lower deck and that the ship has a suitable metacentric height ... It seems to us ... that [counterflooding] arrangements would in most cases be ineffective, as owing to the list of the ship practically no water would run in on the undamaged side and the compartments on that side could only be filled by pumping up.
>
> Another danger with longitudinal bulkheads is that, as the side spaces are used as coal bunkers, the watertight doors through which the coal passes to the stokeholds will nearly always be open, and it might be difficult to shut them owing to the presence of coal in the openings. It is claimed that this difficulty has been largely overcome, and can be further minimized, by the provision of screens inside the bunkers placed above the doors, an arrangement always adopted in warships, but some doubt must always exist on this point. It would, therefore, be an advantage in this respect if oil were adopted instead of coal as fuel, in which case the doors could always be kept closed or dispensed with entirely.

Again the thinking on the matter at the time of writing is highly revealing. Even before the *Lusitania* was sunk, it was a known fact that her watertight subdivision and that of the *Mauretania* was potentially hazardous, because the sisters' metacentric height in an undamaged condition was only some two feet. *The Shipbuilder* magazine had commented on the metacentric height of the *Lusitania* and *Mauretania* in their special issues on them back in 1907:

> To gain steadiness at sea, it is usual to design passenger steamers with fairly small metacentric heights; but there are two objections to this course.

Firstly, such vessels when exposed to a beam wind often take an unpleasant list on account of their large exposed superstructure; and, secondly, if the ship gets damage the loose water in the compartment in communication with the sea may reduce the stability to a dangerous extent. Neither of these two defects need be feared in the *Mauretania* [or *Lusitania*], as the metacentric height is sufficient under all working conditions to prevent the ship heeling over under the action of a beam wind, while the great inertia due to her enormous weight and dimensions gives her a period of rolling equal to that of the steadiest liners afloat ...

> The stability when damaged has also been carefully investigated; and although the vessel may take an unpleasant list should two of the wing compartments be flooded when the bunkers are empty, she will always have a good positive metacentric height with a long range of stability.

This bit of material puts an obviously positive spin on the original calculations made by Leonard Peskett and his team. At the time that the designs for the ship were finalized, they had performed a series of stability analyses to ascertain how the ship would react under various scenarios of potential damage. These calculations demonstrated that if one coal bunker was flooded, the ship would be pulled over some seven degrees away from the vertical. With two flooded, that list would more than double, to fifteen degrees. Peskett's analysis further showed that with three coal bunkers flooded, the ship would become dangerously unstable. In fact, he advised that in the case of the ship assuming a list of more than twenty-two degrees and holding that position, she be abandoned without delay.

A modern stability analysis of the ship confirmed Peskett's original fears.[20] With one coal bunker flooded in her arrival (light) condition, the calculations showed the ship's metacentric height was 1.0 feet; with two flooded, that margin fell to .35 feet. With the third bunker flooded, that figure turned negative, moving to −0.21 feet. This meant that the ship would have become highly unstable in such a condition, unless quick action was taken through the intervention of "heroic" counterflooding measures. However, this process was fraught with complications: it depended on the presence of crew members to implement the orders, assuming that they had not already abandoned their posts; on the ability to communicate effective orders from the Bridge to those men; also on the operation of the ship's primary systems in order to provide motive power to the pump-

A period artist's depiction of the Justicia *as she would have appeared in service with the Holland-America Line as the* Statendam.

ing system. All of this, in retrospect, seems like something of a recipe for disaster.

Remarkably, the comparison between the two types of watertight subdivision – transverse only as opposed to transverse and longitudinal with coal bunkers in the outer compartments – left the realm of hypothetical and became a solid reality when the liner *Justicia* was torpedoed during World War One.

The *Justicia* was built by Harland & Wolff, of Belfast, Ireland. Laid down in early 1912 on the yard's No. 3 slip (the same one that the *Titanic* had been built on and launched from the previous year), she was originally ordered by the Holland-America Line as the *Statendam II*. Her hull number, 436, was only three digits removed from the last of the *Olympic*-class liners, the *Britannic*. Her relationship to the three *Olympic*-class vessels was undeniable.

The vessel was 776 feet in overall length, with a beam of 86 feet and a gross tonnage of 32,234. Being designed and built by Harland & Wolff to the same general lines as the *Olympic*, *Titanic* and *Britannic*, she was quite similar in size to the *Lusitania* (the Cunarder was 11 feet longer, 1.5 feet wider, and 684 tons smaller). She thus, for the purposes of our discussion, represents an 'alternative version' of the *Lusitania*. The intended Holland-America liner was

not built to Admiralty specifications, and thus had transverse longitudinal bunkers, without flanking wing bunkers along the outboard sides of the ship; her configuration was like that adopted by the *Olympic* and *Titanic*.

The *Statendam* was launched on July 9, 1914, but soon after the outbreak of war, the British Government requisitioned the unfinished liner for wartime service. The *Statendam* was renamed *Justicia* and handed over to the control of the Cunard Line – ironically enough, as recompense for the loss of the *Lusitania* – to serve as a troopship. However, the Cunard Line could not put a crew together quickly enough for the task, and she was, instead, handed over to the control of the White Star Line for the same governmental service. She was completed in April of 1917 and entered service in the dingy gray guise of a troopship. In early 1918, she was "dazzle"-painted to confuse submariners who might have been watching her through their periscopes, but the technique did not succeed. On July 19, 1918, while westbound as part of a convoy, and under the command of Captain Hugh David, the German submarine *UB-64* attacked her.

The single torpedo struck the ship on the port side at 2:30 p.m. The Engine Room, Dynamo Room and Cargo Hold No. 4 were all flooded. However, the ship

A dramatic view of the Justicia *sinking off the Irish coast. Not equipped with longitudinal bulkheads of the* Lusitania's *type, the* Justicia *withstood blows from three separate torpedoes over a period of 22 hours and 10 minutes.*

remained afloat. Two hours later, at 4:30, the same submarine attacked the ship again. Two torpedoes were launched this time. One missed, and the ship's gun crew deftly managed to detonate the other one before it could strike the ship. The *Justicia* was subsequently taken under tow, bound for the Lough Swilly. At 8:00 p.m., the *UB-64* attacked a third time. Once more, the gun crew made quick work of the torpedo before it could strike, and this time, depth charges from the *Justicia's* escorts damaged her attacker. The *UB-64* abandoned her five-and-a-half-hour molestation of the liner and withdrew. The tow project continued once the ship's nonessential personnel were evacuated.

At 4:30 a.m. the following morning – some fourteen hours after the initial attack – a second submarine, the *UB-124*, resumed the attack. Its torpedo was set to run too shallow, however, and missed the target completely. By 6:00 a.m., a dozen destroyers, as well as fourteen other vessels, surrounded the *Justicia*. The tow process continued, but was now hampered by poor weather. Finally, at 9:15 a.m., the determined *UB-124* attacked again; two torpedoes streaked toward the liner, and both struck the ship. The first one struck in Cargo Hold No. 3, while the second struck Cargo Hold No. 5. The ship now began to settle heavily by the stern and also to port, and the remaining crewmembers were forced to abandon ship. At 10:30 a.m., Captain David himself was evacuated; the tow

process continued, however, in the hopes that she could still reach shore. At 12:40 p.m., July 20, 1918, she finally succumbed to her wounds and sank.

Only sixteen crewmembers perished in the sinking. In all, seven torpedoes had been fired at the liner, three of which had struck the ship. From the time she took the first torpedo on July 19 to the time that she sank on July 20, some 22 *hours* and 10 minutes had elapsed. The *Lusitania*, as is so famously recorded for us through the pages of history, took one torpedo, immediately heeled over because her coal bunkers took on great quantities of water and counterflooding was impossible, sank in only 18 *minutes*, and took the lives of some 1,200 passengers and crew.

It is clear that the design of the *Lusitania*, under the supervision of the Admiralty, was focused on protecting the interior compartments from enemy shellfire. As submarine warfare was not really an essential issue before the outbreak of World War One, little or no investigation was done into the potential damage that a submarine-launched torpedo could cause to the ship. Under this rather un-anticipated scenario, it is clear that the *Lusitania's* design was highly vulnerable.

Interestingly, the *Aquitania* was designed along very similar lines to the *Lusitania* and *Mauretania*, albeit on the scale of the *Olympic* and *Titanic*. When she was built, the loss of the *Titanic* was fresh in mind, and her design reflected the new thinking on watertight subdivision. Leonard Peskett did an extensive analysis of her stability under certain damaged conditions on behalf of the Cunard Company and John Brown & Company, the builders of both the *Lusitania* and the new *Aquitania*. The most extreme scenario considered was the flooding of not one, two or three wing compartments, as had been considered with the *Lusitania* and *Mauretania*, but *all* of them. With some 5,300 tons of water filling these compartments, the ship would still only take on a list of 26° away from the vertical. This list would certainly be severe, but it was calculated that even under this "almost impossible" scenario, as *Engineering* magazine termed it, the ship's overall stability would not be in question as it would have been with only three flooded aboard the earlier ships.

Interestingly, the *Lusitania* and *Mauretania* would not meet modern SOLAS (Safety of Life At Sea) regulations on watertight subdivision. In one of the most remarkable twists of irony, the *Titanic's* watertight subdivision would pass such regulations. As *The Shipbuilder* stated in the above cited article on watertight subdivision, the inner skin should be far enough away ("10 to 15ft." or some 20% of the vessel's overall beam as specified by SOLAS in modern commercial ship design) from the exterior hull that damage to the outer shell does not similarly damage the inner shell. Specifically in the region of Boiler Room No. 1, this was a problem in the *Lusitania*.

As the bow of the ship narrowed in that region, it was found necessary to "step-in" the longitudinal bulkheads on either side of the ship at a point roughly forty feet forward of the compartment's aft transverse bulkhead. Because the outer hull was curved in at this point and the inner bulkheads were parallel to the ship's longitudinal axis, this meant that there were spaces in Boiler Room No. 1 where the bulkheads were dangerously close to the ship's outer hull. In the event of a torpedo detonating in this region of the ship, it was quite probable that the inner bulkhead would be severely compromised in the initial explosion, and that water would be allowed into the inner compartment either through damaged watertight doors or via direct damage to the structure of the inner bulkhead.

To summarize this discussion, it is clear that the *Lusitania's* system of watertight subdivision was not as good as it was commonly believed to be at the time of her construction, and that it left her vulnerable to a torpedo strike anywhere along the length of her boiler and engine compartments. This was especially true in the area of Boiler Room No. 1, which also happened to be the exact location that she was struck by a torpedo on that spring day in 1915. The design also left her quite vulnerable to asymmetrical flooding without proper planning to ensure a practical method of counterflooding.

As to the ship's stability and metacentric height, many allegations of poor design have been leveled against her designers, specifically Leonard Peskett, labeling the ship dangerously top-heavy. However, it is clear that her metacentric height was sufficiently good in an undamaged condition to ensure that rough seas or poor weather would not endanger the ship; the *Mauretania's* long service career in all sorts of situations at sea, and the *Lusitania's* own service between 1907 and 1915 proved that point. The *Lusitania* was also quite unthreatened by flooding of the ship's extreme forward or aft compartments, the ones not lined by longitudinal bunkers. Her design was even enough to withstand the asymmetrical flooding of two wing bunkers at any given time, as long as there were no other contributing factors to consider. However, with any additional damage or a third compartment flooded, the ship's stability immediately became critically suspect, particularly in the light of hindsight. All of the ship's remarkable strength, her high-tensile doubling steel plating, and her reinforced decks were not enough to save her from the one critical emergency situation that she actually faced during her career.

It is here that we will end our discussion of the ship's overall basic design and move into a discussion of the ship's revolutionary powerplant, something that quite deservedly stole the show when the *Lusitania* entered service in 1907.

The Heart of the *Lusitania*

There is no question that the powerplant of the *Lusitania*, the ship's heart and life, was revolutionary. As the nineteenth century progressed toward its conclusion, the evolution of the marine steam powerplant had undergone numerous refinements and improvements. Sails and paddlewheels had given way to double- and triple-expansion reciprocating engines and screw propellers. Ships with one propeller had eventually given over to those with two, giving a tremendous increase in reliability.

Right through the 1890s, all the first-rate express ocean liners had been double-screw vessels propelled by reciprocating engines. However, it was becoming clear as the new century came on the scene that the development of the reciprocating engine was reaching its zenith. There was only so much horsepower that an engine of this design could produce. They also had other disadvantages, including vibration at high speeds and that they took up enormous quantities of a ship's overall interior volume.

During the design phase of the *Lusitania*, questions thus arose: how much horsepower would be needed to propel the *Lusitania* up to the record-breaking speeds called for by the Parliamentary loan? Would reciprocating engines be able to supply the necessary power? When it was believed that the liner's width would be some 78 or 80 feet, it was found that some 60,000 horsepower would be required. To supply this amount of power, it was thought that three quadruple-expansion five-cylinder reciprocating engines could be used, each tied to its own propeller, creating a triple-screw design.

When it was discovered that the ships needed to be some 88 feet in width in order to create a more stable vessel, this changed the equation entirely. All new model tests and computations were carried out. Swan, Hunter – the *Mauretania*'s builders – did a rather unique set of model tests. Instead of using purely towed models, they also designed and constructed a $1/16$-scale battery-operated pine launch, which could actually hold operators and numerous recording instruments. They built this unusual craft and tested it at the Northumberland Dock on the north side of the Tyne River, looking to find the necessary indicated horsepower to drive the ship and also the best possible propeller design and layout. Even the effect of wind resistance against the superstructure was carefully noted; atop the motorized launch, special stand-ins for the basic shape of the vessel's deckhouses, funnels and superstructure were constructed and mounted. Tests were then carried out to see the effect that the wind would have upon the ship, depending on velocity and direction, and how much power would need to be allowed 'in reserve' for those times that the ship was running into the wind. The results were then scaled up to the ship's full size, and the numbers were telling: when traveling at 25 knots against a wind of 25 knots, the ship would require a full 12% more power than without the headwind. When traveling at 25 knots with a following wind of the same speed, she would need 4% less power than she normally would need. These results, as they applied to the *Mauretania*, would also very closely approximate the wind-resistance that the *Lusitania* would need to deal with during her career.

When all of these variables were taken into account, it was determined that the *Lusitania*, as well as the *Mauretania*, would now need some 68,000 nominal horsepower in order to drive them at the desired speeds. This was a problem since the original triple-screw design was already pushing the limits of reciprocating engine technology.[21] So how could the necessary 68,000 horsepower be achieved?

It turned out that there was another possible alternative, although it had never been tested on this sort of scale before. This new possibility was the marine steam turbine, pioneered by Sir Charles Algernon Parsons. Parsons' tests with the 100-foot test craft *Turbinia* at the 1897 Naval Review had achieved legendary status. Since then, other small- to medium-sized vessels had begun to experiment with this technology, and with good results.

Although the idea looked as if it could work on paper, the question was: would it actually work on this scale? The odds were enormous. If the *Lusitania* or her sister did not meet the speed requirements outlined by Parliament, there could be severe monetary penalties involved; the ships could even be rejected. Then, too, there was the question of reliability. There was simply not much data to go on yet, and certainly the proposed powerplants for the *Lusitania* and her sister were unprecedented in size.

In 1903, a committee was set up to investigate the propulsion matter thoroughly, and to make a recommendation to the Cunard Line and hence to the builders. This committee was comprised of specialists in the field of ship design and propulsion, and included James Bain, Marine Superintendent of the Cunard Company; Engineer Rear-Admiral H. J. Oram, C.B., Deputy-Engineer-in-Chief to the British Navy; J. T. Milton, Chief Engineer-Surveyor of Lloyds of London; H. J. Brock of Messrs. Denny, of Dumbarton, which company had experience building ships fitted with turbine engines under license from Charles Parsons. A representative of John Brown, T. Bell, of Swan, Hunter, Sir W. H. White, K.C.B., and Mr. Andrew Laing of the Wallsend Engineering Company, were also included. Lastly, and perhaps most importantly, Sir Charles Parsons himself was brought in to consult the subject.

After lengthy deliberations, in June of 1904 the committee reached their decision: Parsons-style steam turbines would be adopted in both new speed-queens. Inverclyde took his committee and some close friends to dinner at the Carlton to celebrate the momentous decision. Even so, there was much work ahead before the new behemoth sister ships were steaming on the North Atlantic at high speed. How large would the turbines be? How many propellers would she employ? How would her powerplant be laid out?

Data about the use of turbines in oceangoing steamships began to become available when the Allan liner *Victorian* made her maiden voyage in April

The *Carmania* proved generally faster than her more traditional sister. It was also reported that the turbine even proved more efficient than the reciprocating engine. While this may have been true at high speed, at lower speeds the tried-and-true reciprocating engine still had the cost advantage.

The timing of certain events leading up to the installation of the turbine engines in the *Lusitania* and *Mauretania* suggests a slightly different picture of history than is commonly supposed. It has often been said that the construction of the *Caronia* and *Carmania*, and the superiority of the *Carmania*'s powerplant, were the final factors in deciding to adopt turbines in the *Lusitania* and *Mauretania*. Certainly the *Caronia* and *Carmania* were experiments, and the data obtained from comparing the near-twins was very helpful to Cunard in determining at what point reciprocating engines were still more desirable in successive intermediate vessels. However, they were certainly not the deciding factor in favor of turbines, as has at times been repeated. The simple fact is that by the time the *Carmania* had entered service, Inverclyde's commission had long since made its decision in favor of turbines for the *Lusitania* and *Mauretania*. Additionally, by the time of the *Carmania*'s maiden voyage, the *Lusitania* had already been under construction for well over a year, and she would be launched into the Clyde only seven months later. By the time raw data was coming in from the *Carmania*, the *Lusitania* and *Mauretania* were already slated for use with turbines.

The decision to utilize turbine engines, made in 1904, was not based on the *Carmania*, but instead on necessity. While the originally intended trio of five-cylinder reciprocating engines might have been able to produce 60,000 horsepower, the only way to get a minimum of 68,000 horsepower was to add more engines to that design. A quartet of five-cylinder reciprocating engines, along with the boilers to fire them, would have consumed an incredible amount of interior space – far too much to be considered viable. The only alternative was to adopt turbine engines. Not only would they take up less room within the liners' hulls – allowing more room for paying passengers – but they would also be less prone to causing vibration, as even the best-built and most carefully balanced reciprocating engines were. Even more fundamental was that they would be capable of producing the horsepower required to drive the ships at speed.

In the meanwhile, work on the *Lusitania* and *Mauretania* progressed steadily after their keels were laid. All work had been focused on their bow and midships sections. It was reported by *The Shipbuilder*

Charles Parsons

of 1905. She was the first transatlantic vessel to use turbines, and was quickly followed by her sister ship, the *Virginian*. Cunard had also, some time previously, decided to construct their own test-beds to obtain hard facts on the efficiency of turbines. Doubtless the company wanted to see how the hypothetical translated into a reality that was nearly on the scale of the critically important *Lusitania* and *Mauretania*. These two new Cunarders were ordered from John Brown & Co., and were eventually known as the *Caronia* and *Carmania*. Both ships were nearly identical, sporting two funnels, and had very similar overall lines. The *Caronia* was 678 feet long and 72 feet wide, with a gross registered tonnage of 19,594. The *Carmania* was some three feet shorter in overall length, but bore the same width with a tonnage of 19,524. The primary difference between the two ships was in their powerplants. The first ship, the *Caronia*, sported typical double-screw reciprocating engine technology. The *Carmania*, on the other hand, sported turbine engines on a triple-screw configuration.

First down the ways was the conventional *Caronia*. She was launched on July 13, 1904, and made her maiden voyage on February 25, 1905. The *Carmania* was launched on February 21, 1905 and made her maiden voyage on December 2 of that year. Once the two ships had entered service, it was quite clear which powerplant was more capable of providing high speed, and this was the turbine.

that even after the final decision in favor of turbines, and even after the orders had been placed for both ships, "many details in regard to the propelling machinery were ... still in abeyance, and this explains why the photographs taken in the preliminary stages of the construction show a considerable advance in the progress of the work at the forward end ... At the after end the work was somewhat delayed, in order that the position of bulkheads, engine seatings, etc., could be fixed to suit the best arrangements for the machinery which had not then been finally settled." Although specifically discussing the *Mauretania*, the statement applies equally to both ships. Very minor details still needed to be worked out on them as construction began, but the major decisions were already solidly in place.

In the end, the powerplant installation on the *Lusitania* was quite different from that installed in the *Carmania*. It was decided that four of these turbines would be installed in the larger vessel for forward thrust; the power would be transmitted to the sea through four propellers, each propeller geared to its own forward-thrust turbine. The quadruple-screw arrangement in the *Lusitania*, adopted also by the *Mauretania*, was unprecedented. Previously, almost all crack Atlantic liners had been limited to two screws (still a major advantage over single-screw vessels of the mid- to late nineteenth century), and even the great *Carmania* had only three. Once more, the rather radical decision to use four had been prompted by necessity. To divide the 68,000 horsepower in four ways meant that each propeller shaft would need to transmit only about 16,000–17,000 horsepower. If fewer shafts had been employed, the torque stresses imposed on the shafts would have been well over the tolerable limits of even the finest-quality steels of the time. If a shaft had snapped or otherwise failed at sea, the results could have been disastrous: more than one ship has gone to the bottom after a snapped propeller shaft allowed the sea to flood the Engine Room.

After careful study, it was determined that two high-pressure turbines would drive the outboard set of propellers, while two low-pressure turbines would drive the inboard set. One drawback of adopting turbine engines is that turbines are irreversible for astern thrust. To offset this deficiency, two high-pressure turbines were installed just forward of the low-pressure turbines to work the inner propellers, thus making for a total of six turbines powering the vessel. By adopting four units for forward thrust, along with four screws, the machinery could thus be divided into two complete sets, one on each side of the ship. With the Engine Room subdivided into numerous compartments, this further ensured that even if damage was taken to one side of the powerplant, the other side would most likely be able to function.

The placement of the propellers was important in achieving success with the ship's desired speed. It was decided that the outer propellers would sit some seventy feet forward of the inner propellers.[22] The shafting for the inner propellers was entirely contained within the ship, and their framing was bossed out and supported by web frames. The forward propellers were also carried by heavy webs. Each propeller was given three bolted-on manganese-bronze blades, which were shaped quite roundly.[23] As originally fitted, the outer propellers had a diameter of 15 feet 0 inches and a pitch of 16 feet 6 inches, while the inner propellers had a diameter of 16 feet 6 inches and a pitch of 15 feet 9 inches.[24] The blades of all four propellers were contained within the beam-line of the ship, but all worked within free water. After extensive tests at the Clydebank yard's new experimental model tank, it was also decided to rotate the outer propellers in an inward direction, while at the same time having the inner propellers rotate outward, or in the opposite direction, to achieve optimum efficiency.

In order to determine the final dimensions of the turbines, it was necessary to decide just how fast the propellers would spin in order to achieve peak efficiency in transmitting the required horsepower into the sea. At the time, channel steamers and small craft had adopted a high speed of rotation. Mostly, this was because of space constraints and the need to adopt small turbines. There were those who felt that a high rotation speed meant losing a percentage of overall efficiency. However, after no small amount of study, it was decided to adopt a propeller rotation speed of about 185 per minute on the *Lusitania*. Working backward from this decision, the final dimensions of the ship's turbines could be calculated.

As built, the rotor-drums of the high-pressure turbines were 96 inches in diameter. The larger low-pressure turbines had rotor drums of 140⅜ inches. These were all hollow-forged, and the rotor-drums for the low-pressure ahead turbines were the largest of their type which had been constructed at the time. All of the rotor-drums were manufactured at John Brown's Atlas Works in Sheffield through hydraulic forging. The Atlas Works also made all of the *Lusitania*'s rotor spindles and propeller shafting.

The blades for the turbines ran from 2¼ inches up to 22 inches in length. For the longer blades, three rows of shrouding, consisting of circumferential strips laced with copper wire which was then soldered, was employed to give them both radial and lateral rigidity. To prevent distortion from the expansion of the drum and of the brass strip, expansion joints were included in these bindings. The strip was divided into shorter lengths, which were connected by brass tubes, within which they could slide. Great care was taken during the construction of the turbines to ensure balanced operation once they were installed aboard the ship.[25]

For times when maintenance needed to be carried out on the turbines, special lifting gear was designed, capable of hoisting 115 tons. The outer casings for the turbines could be lifted up by a height of 4-6 feet (depending on which turbine was under repair), and the rotors themselves could also be lifted if necessary, once the bearings had been removed. This could even be accomplished, if it was deemed necessary, at sea, and did happen on one occasion during her actual time in service.

After this consideration, one might wonder: just how closely did the turbines' performance match their anticipated performance? On the *Lusitania*'s trials, a torsionmeter calculated the amount of power being developed; this particular information recorded beginning on July 27, 1907, when the ship had a draught of 32 feet 9 inches and a displacement of 37,080 tons. This information was also compared to the ship's speed at the time of reading, the revolutions per minute and the rate of the propeller's slip through the seawater at the time. The results are astounding.

Time	RPM	Speed In Knots	Shaft Horsepower	Slip of Propellers
1st double run	194.3	25.62	76,000	17.2%
2nd double run	186.0	25.0	65,500	15.5%
3rd double run	174.2	23.7	51,300	14.5%
4th double run	161.5	22.02	40,500	14.3%
5th double run	147.6	20.4	29,500	13.1%
6th double run	131.1	18.0	20,500	13.7%
7th double run	116.1	15.77	13,400	14.6%

This information is even more remarkable when one considers the relative newness of the technology and the unprecedented proportions of the turbine powerplant placed aboard the *Lusitania*. The ship's builders were really in uncharted waters, and not only did they correctly design a powerplant that developed the needed horsepower and more, but through the efficient design of the ship's hull – notwithstanding the already-noted problems that this design created for comfort while at sea – she was able to exceed her mandated service speed. In fact, it was calculated after the ship's trials that in order to maintain a speed of 25.4 knots, the ship would need to develop some 68,850 horsepower; this is incredibly close to the original calculations following model tests that to maintain 25 knots the ship would need some 68,000 horsepower.

In order to motivate all of this turbine machinery, vast quantities of steam at high pressure were required. To provide this steam, a large powerplant was provided in the form of 23 double-ended and 2 single-ended coal-fired boilers. These 25 boilers were arranged in four separate watertight compartments, with Boiler Room No. 1 being the forward-most and No. 4 being the aft-most, closest to the Engine Room. Six boilers were arranged in each of the aft three Boiler Rooms

In this photograph on a ship of the period, perhaps even on the Lusitania *or* Mauretania, *a stoker tosses a shovelful of coal into the furnace.*

A photograph of one of the Lusitania's *stokeholds. At the far end are two of the watertight doors to the coal bunkers.*

(2-4), in two rows of three abreast. Because of the taper of the ship's hull in the region of Boiler Room No. 1, it was found necessary to adapt a different arrangement. In the stern portion of the compartment sat a single row of three double-ended boilers. Forward of these, where the longitudinal bulkheads stepped in, a second row of two double-ended boilers was installed. To provide the last fraction of steam required to develop the needed horsepower, two single-ended boilers were placed adjacent to the forward transverse bulkhead of the compartment.

The double-ended boilers were 17½ feet in diameter and 22 feet long. In each of these boilers there were 344 stay-tubes and 720 plain tubes for a total of 1,064. The total heating surface of each was 6,593 square feet and the grate area of each 168.65 square feet. The single-ended boilers were identical, except that they were slightly shorter at 12 feet. All told, the ship's 192 furnaces had a collective grate area of 4,048 square feet, while the total heating surface was 158,350 square feet. The boilers' shells were made of high-tensile steel, which had a maximum tensile strength of 36 tons per square inch.

Once the water within the boilers had been superheated into high-pressure steam, it was carried aft via a network of steam pipes which ran above the tops of the boilers, but which was still roughly ten feet below the load waterline of the ship.[26] Each Boiler Room had its own steam pipe. The feed for No. 1 Boiler Room was situated several feet to the port of the ship's centerline. No. 2's feed was situated several feet to starboard of the same point. The Nos. 3 and 4 feeds were situated just outboard of the first two, respectively to port and starboard. On the forward side of the forward Engine Room bulkhead, a stop valve was fitted

to each line. These valves could be worked both from the Engine Room and from the Boat Deck. Each boiler room was tied in to its own funnel to ventilate the coal smoke and fumes from the combustion chamber, and the funnels' height above the grate level was some 130 feet. With the powerplant operating under full steam, it was rated to deliver steam at a pressure of 195 pounds per square inch to the turbines.

Once the steam had passed through the turbines, it was sent to the condensers, to be condensed back into feed water before returning to the boilers to be reheated into high-pressure steam. The condensers were arranged in pairs, and had a total of 82,800 square feet of cooling surface between them. There were also two auxiliary condensers placed in the forward end of the Engine Room. These auxiliary units had a cooling surface of 4,000 square feet, and were given their own separate circulating pumps and air pumps.

It was estimated that the ship would burn about 1,000 tons of coal each day of her crossing, and enough bunker space was devised – through the outboard bunkers flanking each Boiler Room, and through the cross-bunker just forward of Boiler Room No. 1 – to give the ship a carrying capacity of some 6,000 tons of coal. Further arrangements were made to carry extra coal in the No. 2 hold and above Boiler Room No. 2 if the need arose for additional capacity. In actual service, the *Lusitania* at times burned coal somewhat less eagerly than anticipated, even dropping at times into the mid-800 tons per day range; at other times she used the full amount that she was designed to burn. The ship's Engine Room Log for her third west-bound crossing, in November of 1907, is telling. On the voyage from Liverpool to Queenstown, Ireland, she consumed 408 tons of coal; between Queenstown and New York, she burned 4,976 tons. Her galleys and auxiliary machinery burned 18 tons of coal during the voyage, for a total consumption between Liverpool and New York of 5,402 tons of coal. During each of the four full days of her crossing, she burned exactly 1,090 tons of coal, and her average speed for the entire crossing from Queenstown to New York was 24.25 knots, beating her previous average of 24.002 knots during her second westbound crossing when she had re-taken the Blue Riband from Germany.

After World War One, the *Mauretania*, like all of the other crack Atlantic liners, was converted to burn oil fuel. It economized the operation of her stokeholds, and improved her performance markedly. It would have been interesting to see how the *Lusitania* would have adapted to a similar conversion, had she survived the war. She doubtless would have enjoyed an increase in performance at least equal to that enjoyed by the *Mauretania*, although whether or not she could have rivaled the *Mauretania* is something that could be debated for decades to come.

There has been a longstanding feeling that the *Mauretania* was the vessel which proved to be the faster of the two sister ships. A brief investigation of this point is in order during our consideration of the ship's powerplant.

Let us start the investigation by comparing the trials of the *Lusitania* and *Mauretania*. Between midnight on July 29 and 1 a.m. on August 1, 1907, the *Lusitania* managed to make an average speed of 25.4 knots over a period of roughly 48 hours, in conditions described as "favourable, with cloudless days and starlight nights." In early November of the same year, the *Mauretania* managed to average 26.04 knots during a similar type of test, but in conditions described as a "moderate gale of force 7" during early portions of the event. This might seem conclusive, but another test shows figures that favor the *Lusitania*. On a shorter run of 59 miles made twice in each direction during her trials, the *Lusitania* averaged 26.45 knots. On the measured mile, run twice in each direction, the *Mauretania* averaged a speed of 26.17 knots, just slightly slower than her older sister.

It must also be pointed out that trials are not always indicative of actual service records. At the time of a vessel's trials, the crew is not always familiar with the machinery that they are operating, the layout of the ship, or even with each other. It is also important to point out that they were not always supplied with a grade of coal that was equal in quality to the coal that they would use while in service.

So, naturally, we must ask the question: what did the two ships prove during their actual service careers? The *Lusitania* entered service first, and took the Blue Riband on her second westbound crossing with an average speed of 24.002 knots, according to the Cunard Line's official statement.[27] In July of 1908, she bettered her own record again, this time at an average speed of 25.65 knots and a time of 4 days, 16 hours and 40 minutes. This average continued to improve as the ship became further broken in and her propellers were replaced with more efficient versions.

Captain S. G. S. McNeil, who served as Chief Officer of the *Lusitania* from late 1907 until the spring of 1911 during some 53 voyages, and who went on to serve the *Mauretania* as Staff Captain and Captain for nearly five years, felt that the *Lusitania* was not a bit slower than the *Mauretania*. He believed that this "wrong impression was probably brought about by the fact that the *Lusitania*, on her first eight voyages, did not have the type of propeller blade that the *Mauretania* had. When the new ones were shipped the former's averages improved considerably, and I

remember three of them were 25.89 knots [in average] with only a decimal difference."

The *Mauretania*'s two fastest eastbound pre-war crossings were made at 25.88 and 25.89 knots, respectively. The first of these two crossings, made on June 16, 1909, was completed in 4 days, 17 hours and 21 minutes; the second, made on August 4, 1909, was made in one minute less time. Her fastest pre-war westbound crossings, which were made fighting the prevailing current, were even faster. Departing Liverpool on her 26th voyage on September 25, 1909, she made the crossing in 4 days, 10 hours and 51 minutes at an average speed of 26.06 knots. It was on this crossing that she took the westbound Blue Riband from the *Lusitania*. On September 10, 1910, another westbound crossing proved even faster at 4 days, 10 hours and 41 minutes at an average speed of 26.06 knots. In May of 1911, she made an average of 27.04 knots (or just a shade over 31 land miles per hour) for a single day's run.

While Captain McNeil clearly felt that the *Lusitania* was not slower than the *Mauretania*, the simple truth of the matter is that after September of 1909, the *Lusitania* was never able to take the Blue Riband back from her slightly younger sister – an honor which the *Mauretania* held until June of 1929. There was certainly plenty

Sandy G. S. McNeil, pictured at the time he was Captain of the Ausonia.

of opportunity for her to take that coveted distinction back from the *Mauretania* after September of 1909; indeed, she could have done so at any point up until the Cunard Line reduced her top speed to 21 knots in November of 1914, and until that time, making the best speed possible was almost always desirable.

Only the ignorant would claim that the *Mauretania* was *significantly* faster than the *Lusitania* at the time that the two ships served together, or that the *Lusitania* was a slouch by comparison. However, upon a close inspection of the original records, it seems very clear that the *Mauretania* was the faster of the two ships, specifically during their pre-war service together.[28] Even so, the *Lusitania* was able to turn in remarkably consistent and swift speeds and was only marginally slower than the *Mauretania*.

From this consideration, it can clearly be seen that the powerplant of the *Lusitania* was not only a marked departure from the standard technology of the day, but that she was also a striking success, becoming a trendsetter for all the Atlantic liners that followed in her wake for the next forty years.

The Secondary Systems of the *Lusitania*

In addition to the primary systems that powered the *Lusitania*, there were numerous other systems that, while secondary, were absolutely essential to the operation of the ship, and to the safety and comfort of her passengers.

The Electrical Systems

Ever since the Cunarder *Servia* of 1881, all of the crack ocean liners had, to some extent or other, utilized electrical lighting. This was more than just a convenience: it also improved the safety of the liners. Previously open-flame light systems had been used aboard ship, with all of the resulting hazards, and fire at sea was rightly considered to be one of the worst nightmares for seafarers. As time had passed, electricity had become completely indispensable aboard crack Atlantic liners. More and more uses were found for electrically operated devices and equipment, and thus there was an ever-greater demand for electricity aboard ships by the time that the *Lusitania* was designed and constructed.

The electrical installation of the *Lusitania* was unprecedented in power and scale, and comparisons were made at the time to land-based generating stations for a city of 100,000 residents. While Swan, Hunter decided to have the electrical installation of the *Mauretania* fitted by an outside contractor, the John Brown & Company's Electrical Department undertook the complete project on the *Lusitania*.

A quartet of Parsons-style turbo-generators, rated at 375 kilowatts each, was placed in the Auxiliary Machinery Room, abaft the Turbine Engine Room on the Orlop Deck. The compartment was divided along the centerline of the ship by a longitudinal watertight bulkhead, with two of the turbo-generators being placed in each side. In this way, even if flooding in one compartment knocked out the first pair of turbo-generators, half of the electric-producing machinery would remain intact.

Each turbo-generator was capable of supplying some 4,000 amperes at 110 volts while turning at 1,200 rpm. The entire electrical-generating plant was operated off of steam produced by the boilers, a standard design of the day; unfortunately, it did mean that in the event of serious damage being done to the ship's powerplant or to the high-pressure steam lines which conveyed the steam to the equipment, the electrical-generating plant could fail, as well. In all fairness, it would be a catastrophic event, indeed, which would disrupt the steam-generating plant in such a manner.

From the turbo-generators, the power went to the primary switchboard, which was of the same design as those used in Royal Navy warships of the time. One board was fitted in each of the Dynamo Rooms, but the two boards could be coupled for tandem operation, or they could work independently of one another – a very important consideration in case one of the Dynamo Rooms was flooded or otherwise put out of commission. Governing the connection between the two boards was a double-pole 5,000-amp switch. Each board had a 4,000-amp main breaker, and a dozen 1,000-amp subsidiary breakers. In addition to these two primary boards, there were twelve auxiliary switchboards placed in other locations throughout the ship. Each of these subsidiaries was fitted with single-pole 150-amp switches as well as double-pole fuses of the Dixon blotter type. The electrical current was then carried to ancillary junction and distribution boards, and finally delivered to the instruments calling for current.

The main electrical cables were two inches in external diameter, and were insulated with vulcanized rubber, with a double covering of asbestos and jute braiding thrown in to aid in fireproofing. They were held in place by iron racks mounted on each side of the Engine Room and Boiler Rooms, and were some four miles long in total. In all, there were well over 150 miles of electrical cables installed throughout the entirety of the ship.

All of this was set up to power an unprecedented number of devices, at least on board an ocean liner. There were some 6,300 lamps of various ratings and designs, both for passenger cabins and public rooms. Additionally the ship's navigation lights and the red and green sidelights were all electrically operated. In the event that one of these lights experienced a burnout, a spare filament was automatically turned on, and an indicator on the Bridge immediately informed the ship's officers that the primary bulb had burned out and needed to be replaced.

One relatively novel feature was an arrangement of telephones aboard the ship for the use of both the crew and passengers. The Graham's loud-speaking telephones on the Bridge have already been described along with the other Bridge equipment. There was also an exchange-less system of 23 telephones to connect the Bridge, Marconi Shack, Purser's Bureau, as well as the quarters of the senior officers and stewards. Additionally, there were some 89 telephones fitted in the Regal and *en suite* First Class Staterooms, allowing the passengers to communicate with other rooms, and also to communicate with the Purser's Bureau, the Ship's Surgeon, Chief Steward, etc. To direct this flow of telephone traffic, there was a central exchange board. Additionally, while the ship was tied up in Liverpool or New York, this system could be interconnected with a landline. This astonishing provision allowed a passenger sitting in his or her cabin to communicate with friends and relatives ashore as long as the *Lusitania* was in port. It was said of the telephones in the First Class cabins:

> The telephone used on the steamship *Lusitania* is quite interesting. The induction coil, condenser, and bell of the instrument are enclosed in a small white enamel box, and the switch hook which projects from one side is provided with a special retaining device designed to prevent the receiver from being knocked off by the motion of the ship. The receiver is allowed to rock on the hook, otherwise the lever would lift and make a false connection when the ship was pitching and rolling.[29]

Another fitting specifically for the convenience of passengers was a system of cabin bells, 950 all told, to call a steward for assistance. There were some forty indicator boards, each series of cabins having their own indicator in the companionway. Additionally, there was a master indicator at the night steward's station, which would come in handy during the night when all of the normal stewards were off-duty.

There were also electric radiators fitted in the First Class staterooms, approximately forty of the 2½ amp-

type, and another fifty of the 7-amp type. Additionally, there were also over forty different electrically operated machines in the ship's Galleys, such as ice-cream freezers, potato peelers and dough-mixers.

There were four primary deck cranes, manufactured by Messrs. Stothert & Pitt, which were also powered by electricity. Each one of this quartet was capable of hoisting slightly over 1.5 tons (3,360 pounds). Two of the cranes had an 18-foot radius, and the other two had a radius of 26 feet. They were able to lift at a speed of 100 feet per minute, and were able to slew, or turn, at a rate 400 feet per minute. The lifting motors were rated for 15 brake horsepower each, while the separate slewing motors were rated for 2½ brake horsepower each. Both cranes were mounted atop the Boat Deck; the larger set was placed on the port and starboard sides of the First Class Boat Deck, just astern of the after lifeboats, with their jibs usually pointed aft over the space between the two primary portions of the superstructure. The smaller set was mounted atop the forward portion of the Second Class Boat Deck, usually stowed with their jibs pointed forward toward the larger set.

These cranes were used to hoist aboard the baggage and mails that the ship would usually carry, which were stored in the holds fore and aft. The two sets of primary cranes were mounted astern because that was where most of the baggage and mails would be stored during the ship's service. However, two electric winches were also provided on the Main Deck forward to service the fore holds; each of these winches was also rated for just over 1.5 tons. In addition, there were also two winches placed on the Forecastle, by each forward cargo hatch.

All four of the primary cranes were in place when the ship left Scotland in early July of 1907, and when she arrived in Liverpool. By the time she departed Liverpool on her maiden voyage, however, the after set had been removed, deemed unnecessary. In time it was found, however, that the second set was necessary after all, and they were later re-installed in their original positions.

There were also four electric lifeboat winches placed atop the Sun Deck, one on each side just abaft of the No. 1 funnel, and another pair just abaft the No. 4 funnel. These winches would be used in raising and lowering the boats, and were each rated for lifting just over 5½ tons (11,200 pounds) at some 40 feet per minute.

Also included aboard the ship were eleven lifts, or elevators. Electric lifts had been in use within land-based structures since the 1880s. In 1905, the first electrically operated passenger elevator was installed aboard the Hamburg-Amerika liner *Amerika*, built by Harland & Wolff of Belfast, Ireland. Thus, when the decision was made to equip the *Lusitania* with a pair of lifts in her First Class Entrance, it may not have been a surprise, but the decision was still something of a novelty on the Atlantic. The two passenger lifts were placed side by side in the central well of the Grand Staircase. The other nine lifts were primarily used for baggage and cargo, or to bring foodstuffs from storage up to the pantries and galleys. The table below gives more specifications on each of eleven elevators found throughout the ship.

Load Capacity	Speed, ft./minute	Travel	Motors, Rated B.H.P.
Two passenger lifts, 1120 lbs. each	150	From Main Deck to Boat Deck, 36 ft. 3 in.	8
Two baggage lifts, 4,480 lbs. each	100	From Orlop Deck to Shelter Deck	15
Two service lifts 1,120 lbs. each	100	From Lower Deck to Shelter Deck	5
Three food lifts, 224 lbs. each	60	10 ft. to 11 ft.	1½
Two ash hoists, 224 lbs. each	200	Approximately 60 ft.	3

The two passenger elevators interconnected the Main, Upper, Shelter, Promenade and Boat Decks. Each car was some 5 feet 6 inches deep by 4 feet wide. Most photographs taken that show the elevator spaces only show the protective grills which separated the stairs from the elevator and their machinery; the cars themselves were made of solid mahogany. Each lift had two steel lift cables, each of which passed through the space between the dome over the staircase and the outer skylight, ran forward horizontally to a point past the skylight over the First Class Reading & Writing Room, and connected with the winding gear. Below the winding gear were the counterbalance weights. If for any reason the lift's hoist wires failed, there was a special brake in order to hold it in place without allowing it to merely drop to the bottom of its shaft.

A lift call was supplied at each deck for each elevator car, with an electrical bell and indicator placed in the corresponding lift. A lift attendant, who worked a cylindrical switch with three positions – "up," "down," and "stop" – saw the call on the indicator and then operated the car in response, moving it to the desired location. The handle on the switch was self-centering, so that the attendant had to hold it in the "up" or "down" positions in order to proceed. If the handle was accidentally released, it would immediately revert to the center "stop" position, and the car would immediately stop its travel. If the handle were to be held down as the lift neared either extreme of its track, an automatic cut-off switch would also stop the lift. The gates that allowed access to the elevator could not be opened if the elevator was not in place on the other side. Another safety feature was to prevent the lift-gates from being left open while in operation through automated locks and electrical contacts. In May of 1915, it was these two safety features which apparently trapped the occupants of the elevators when the ship lost power.

Another system devised to maintain passenger and crew comfort had to do with the ship's ventilation. On the North Atlantic, liners had to contend with extremes in temperature and climate. In the summer, temperatures could easily rise into the eighties or higher outside, and in the winter, it was not uncommon for temperatures to plunge well below freezing. Today we take climate control aboard ships for granted, but as the nineteenth century progressed, such systems were still in their infancy; early ships were content to provide hatches and skylights that merely allowed access to light and external air. By the time that the *Lusitania* was constructed, however, climate control had become more important and also more technically proficient.

Heating the interior spaces of the Cunarder was far simpler than cooling them. The *Lusitania* was constructed at a time when air-conditioning systems were in their infancy; as early as 1889, refrigeration units were used in large cities to preserve things like foodstuffs. It was in 1902 that Willis Carrier built the first air conditioner in an attempt to reduce the humidity that built up inside a printing company; he patented his invention in 1906 as the "Apparatus for Treating Air." The actual term, "Air Conditioning" was coined that same year. It took some time, however, for air conditioning to really catch on. It was 1917 before two movie theaters – the New Empire in Montgomery, Alabama, and the Central Park in Chicago, Illinois – actually used air conditioning. However, whether heating or cooling, it was important

Left: *An advertisement for Waygood, the company that supplied the lifts for the* Lusitania *and* Mauretania.

Above: *A photograph of the* Lusitania*'s B Deck First Class Entrance, showing the position of the lifts in relation to the main staircase.*

at all times to provide adequate fresh air to even the deepest and most enclosed spaces of the ship.

On a large ship like the *Lusitania*, this system by necessity had to be extremely extensive. The "thermotank" type system was adopted aboard the liner. This system not only supplied fresh air to the interior spaces, but also heated and humidified it in dry or cold conditions. In all, the ship was designed with some 49 thermo-tanks – 24 servicing First Class areas of the ship, 9 in Second Class, 11 to Third Class, and 5 for officer and crew accommodations.[30] Most of these thermo-tanks were mounted around the funnels or atop the Sun Deck in other locations; others were positioned in open-air Promenade areas. The forward thermo-tanks were placed between decks, with their fresh air supply being drawn down from the after end of the Bridge deckhouse, since forward portions of the ship could frequently be buried under solid water in heavy seas.

The thermo-tanks were capable of changing the air by way of exhaust or supply every 7-10 minutes in the compartments that they were tasked to freshen. Exhausting air was done primarily along the Sun Deck, at the very top of the ship, while drawing fresh air into the ship was done along the Promenade Deck, to prevent foul discharging odors from water closets and galleys from being brought back into the interior spaces. Heating was performed by passing fresh air through hot steam-tubes heated by the boilers; under the old system, it had required some three hours to heat a room to a desired temperature, while with the thermotank heating system it required only a fraction of that

time, at fifteen minutes. A temperature of at least 65° Fahrenheit could thus be maintained at all times even under the coldest circumstances. The warm air was admitted to the interior spaces through vents placed high in the interior rooms, so that it could heat evenly as it cooled. Cooling interior spaces, on the other hand, was rather limited. Fresh air was drawn in to the system, and brought into the interior spaces along the floor, then being drawn out through the higher vents.

There were also a dozen high-power exhaust fans connected to the galleys, lavatories and water closets, which were able to completely exchange the air in any given space every four minutes. In all, there were over ninety heating or ventilating motors, to aid in the ventilation of both the passenger spaces and also the super-heated Boiler and Engine Rooms. Some of these fans were tied into the ventilating trunks that led to the canister-style ventilators along the Sun Deck, which have already been described.

This system may sound complete as described. However, when the *Lusitania* entered service in September of 1907, it immediately became clear that some portions of the ship were still uncomfortably warm during warm weather. Throughout the ship's career, upgrades were made to her system of ventilation in an attempt to combat this problem. It must also be stressed, however, that this type of problem was not uncommon in ships of the period. The *Olympic*, for example, was plagued with stuffy interior spaces in warm weather, and throughout her career, upgrades were made to her ventilation systems, as well.

Another vital consideration was to include methods of combating fire should a conflagration ever break out aboard the *Lusitania*. Atlantic liners of the period, filled as they were with combustible woods and veneers, would never pass modern fire codes. Due to varying circumstances – including the relatively primitive types of electrical wiring employed in ships of the day – it was not uncommon for even relatively new ships to suffer minor fires. It was thus important to make provisions to gain control over any such situation.

There were two complete systems of fire mains fitted, with hose connections on each deck. Each connection was fitted within a small box, the interior of which was painted red. Also contained within each of these boxes was a long leather hose, wound around a dispensing reel, and fitted with a spray nozzle. These setups were also used by the crew to wash down the decks. There were portable chemical fire extinguishers placed at strategic locations throughout the ship. Fire alarms were also placed in various locations on board. Each alarm was triggered by a button housed behind glass, the interior of the space behind the glass being painted red for ease of identification. To detect any fires that could be lurking in less frequented spaces of the ship – like the holds – there were also automatic fire alarms.

One thing that might not have been an obvious necessity aboard ship, considering her natural element, was water. Large quantities of water were needed for her boiler feed water as well as for the drinking, cooking and washing services for the crew and passengers. To meet this demand, two sets of distillers were provided aboard the *Lusitania*. Each of these two was capable of supplying 18,000 gallons of fresh water during any 24-hour period for cooking and drinking, and an additional 15,000 gallons a day could be provided for baths, toilets and washing purposes. Evaporators, not the distillers, provided some 240 tons of water a day for the boilers when operating in the compound manner, or up to 250 tons a day when operating at high pressure.

Lifeboat & Lifesaving Appliances

When the *Lusitania* was about to enter service, it was believed that she was "unsinkable," a term used by *The Shipbuilder*; several years later, they would use that term again in reference to the *Olympic* and *Titanic*. On the second occasion, they used the qualifier, "practically." In this instance, however, there was no qualifier and the Cunarder was merely dubbed "unsinkable." It was typically thought that the ship was so strong, and so remarkably subdivided by watertight bulkheads, that there was no chance that she could ever sink.

Regardless of this view, British Board of Trade regulations specified that she be endowed with lifeboat accommodations. These were the same regulations from 1897 that were still in effect when the *Titanic* sank in 1912, and although the *Lusitania* was not as large as the White Star liner, and did not have as high a passenger and crew capacity, she still surpassed those laws by a large measure. The top-end estimate considered under these regulations was for a ship of 10,000 tons; the new Cunarder was just over three times that size.[31]

Since the British Board of Trade had not changed the regulations in advance of the *Lusitania*'s arrival – and would not, in point of fact, change them until after the *Titanic* disaster in 1912 – the Cunard Line opted only to fit the "unsinkable" liner with enough lifeboats to meet

Below left: A photograph showing Boats Nos. 2, 4, 6 and 8 on the port Boat Deck.

Below right: A period plan showing a lifeboat configuration similar to the Lusitania's. The Lusitania was given standard round-bar radial-type davits very different from the Welin davits carried by the Olympic and Titanic. One obvious difference between this period plan and the installation aboard the Lusitania is that the davits on the Lusitania were set at the ends of the lifeboats.

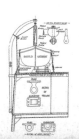

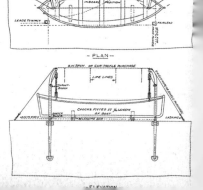

the regulations, not with enough to care for all passengers and crew in the event of an emergency. Consequently, some sixteen lifeboats were provided for the *Lusitania* when she entered service. These were mounted in four sets of four, along the fore and aft corners of the ship's Boat Deck. When the ship originally entered service, the boats were numbered rather oddly. Although the odd-numbered boats were on the starboard side, and the even-numbered ones were on the port side as usual, the high-numbered boats were toward the forward end of the ship. This unusual arrangement was eventually changed to the more standard numbering system with the high numbers at the aft end of the deck. The boats were each 30 feet long by slightly over 9 feet in maximum breadth, with a depth of about 3 feet 9 inches, although the exact width and depth dimensions of each lifeboat varied slightly. When empty, each boat weighed about five tons.

To move these large and heavy lifeboats over the side of the ship for lowering, some 32 round-bar radial-type lifeboat davits were installed along the outer superstructure of the ship, one on each side fore and aft of each lifeboat. These radial davits, the typical style used in most steamers of the day, each had their base set into a heel socket, which was riveted into the shell plating at the foot of B Deck. At the level of the Boat Deck, a collar that was similarly attached to the shell plating provided lateral support for the davit, and allowed it to rotate freely within its circular constraints.

The lifeboats were stowed along the deck and rested on chocks fitted to the decking. Most frequently they were found in this position, but during good weather it was not uncommon for the crew to swing them out at least partway over the water to make more room for passengers walking the deck. In order to prevent damage as they swung in and bumped the corner of the deck, a boom could be fitted between the two davits. Each boat was also fitted with a snubbing chain to prevent it from swinging too far out and away from the ship.

After the *Titanic* disaster, it was immediately clear that all ships would have to begin carrying an increased number of lifeboats. Multiple changes were made to the *Lusitania*'s lifeboat arrangement between 1912 and 1915. Collapsibles had to be fitted underneath the standard lifeboats; additional standard lifeboats were secured to the Boat Deck between the fore and aft sets, but for some time they had no davits to lower them to the water. These extra davits were fitted later; this new arrangement consisted of two sets on either side amidships, between the fore and aft quadrants, and one on each side astern, along the Second Class Boat Deck.

When the *Lusitania* departed New York on her final crossing on May 1, 1915, she had lifeboat accommodations for 2,605, in total – some 646 more than the official number of passengers and crew who were aboard for that final crossing – in 48 lifeboats. This lifeboat accommodation was broken down in the following way:

- 22 WOODEN LIFEBOATS — 11 on each side, ten of which were along the First Class Boat Deck, and one of which was mounted on the Second Class Boat Deck. Capacity: 1,323.
- 26 COLLAPSIBLE LIFEBOATS — 18 in all, stored beneath eighteen of the regular lifeboats, with the remaining 8 stored abaft the main lifeboats. *Capacity: 1,282.*

She was also endowed with some 35 life-rings, conveniently distributed throughout the ship. There were in addition a total of 2,325 life jackets placed aboard, 125 of which were specifically designed for children. Many of these were placed directly in passenger cabins, although there were also lockers on deck where additional numbers of them were stowed.

Below left: A 1914 photograph showing a stack of extra collapsibles. At first, the boats added after the Titanic *disaster were not under davits; eventually, more davit sets were added to make handling them in an emergency easier for the crew.*

Below right: The aft starboard Second Class lifeboat station. This photograph was taken on May 1, 1915.

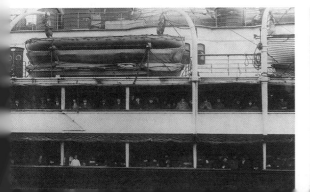

Above: *This photograph was taken shortly after the* Lusitania *returned to Liverpool from Gourock at the end of August 1907. Coaling barges are tied up alongside the port side, and they have begun the laborious task of filling the holds with fuel.*

Below: *Almost certainly taken at a similar time as the preceding photo, this view is unique because of its angle. While coal tenders still line the ship's side, the crew has rigged canvas screens along the entire length of the liner's B Deck First Class Promenade, closing it off from any inclement weather.*

4
A Distinguished Career

In early September of 1907 Liverpool, England, was the center of a storm of excitement. The maiden voyage of the *Lusitania*, arguably the most important event in the maritime community in a decade, was set to begin on Saturday, September 7. Her presence at her new home port was nothing if not obvious; the enormous liner sat anchored in the Sloyne, gleaming in all of her glorious newness. She was not tied up directly at the Prince's Landing Stage because the older Cunarder *Lucania* was tied up there at the time, and the smaller *Lucania* would depart Liverpool just before the *Lusitania*. As the *Lucania* was the fastest British merchant ship in service up to that time, there were wild rumors that the two ships would engage in a true side-by-side race across the Atlantic to New York. Cunard tried in vain to dispel the rumors, but were, no doubt, pleased with the excitement they created. Not only did the interest in this "race" arouse interest in the maiden voyage, but it also gave the *Lusitania* a slightly lower, albeit subsidiary, goal to her primary one: recapturing the Blue Riband from Germany.

The press eagerly participated in stirring the public, giving Cunard and the *Lusitania* more free publicity than the company could possibly have hoped for. One account lavished praise upon her in this way:

> A vast ship that is so splendid a palace of luxury that one can scarcely realise that one is not in a magnificently appointed West End hotel – that is a first impression of the Cunard Company's leviathan, the *Lusitania*, the largest, most powerful, most speedy, and most wonderfully equipped vessel of her kind in the world.
>
> Every detail of this mighty ship has been artfully designed to beguile passengers into the belief that they are on terra firma, and not crossing the wide Atlantic at all. How can one describe this wonder that has been created by the greatest geniuses of shipbuilding and decoration?
>
> ... The illusion of fashionable hotel life is carried out even to the tiniest details. One gazes out of one's cabin, not through the round port-hole of nautical tradition, but through a daintily curtained window. You turn in vain to seek the familiar bunk. Its place is taken by a comfortable, curtained brass bedstead. Arm-chairs invite you by their elegance and comfort and a shower bath is at hand, should you feel hot and fatigued, and the telephone is on your table ready for you to communicate instantly with any other part of the ship; or if you want to chat with fellow-passengers you may enter the lounge, the most superb piece of work on this remarkable vessel ...[1]

Cunard officials must have recognized, with something bordering on glee, that this high level of public excitement over the new speed-queen boded well for both the maiden voyage and a successful career to follow. In order to capitalize on this high level of public interest, Cunard set up a special event. On Tuesday, September 3, the *Lusitania* was opened to the public. Ferries were engaged to run people from shore to her anchorage in the Sloyne, each paying a half-crown for the privilege of seeing the world's newest, largest, and fastest ship. In about five hours, some ten thousand people visited the liner, and the proceeds were donated to charity.

Three days before the maiden voyage, representatives of the Cunard Company asked Ernest Wighton, manager of the Olympia Variety Theatre in Liverpool, if he could put together a variety show for some 800 guests aboard the liner before she entered service. Wighton accepted, took his entire company aboard, constructed an 18 foot by 9 foot stage in the First Class Dining Saloon, found a place for a full orchestra, and in essence set up a "miniature replica of our own stage performance." Among the performers in the show were a "musical comedian", a "musical sketch with songs and dances", and "The three Prestons, acrobats and humorists". The program was such a success that Cunard briefly entertained the notion of doing regular vaudeville theater shows aboard the *Lusitania* and *Mauretania* – a concept that American playwright Charles Frohman was keenly interested in.[2] Although the concept was never put in to practice, the fact that

Above: *This photo shows that the tenders have accomplished their refueling, as the ship's bow rides much lower in the water than it had before.*

Right: *Gulls flutter about the liner as she rests at anchor in the Sloyne. The ship was a hive of activity before the maiden voyage, and excitement was at an all time high.*

Above: *Although labeled as the "Mauritania," [sic] off Rock Ferry, the view is clearly one of the* Lusitania *in that location. The canvas screens along the promenade remain in place. The ship towers impressively above all other harbor traffic, and even makes the skyline of Liverpool look diminutive.*

Below: *This port-side view of the ship is impressive not only for its rarity, but also because of its razor sharp quality. At the bow rides one of Cunard's new pair of buoys for use in the Sloyne. The canvas screen remains in place along the side of B Deck.*

the normally-reserved and rather businesslike Cunard Company had engaged such a performance showed their excitement at having the largest, most luxurious, and hopefully the fastest ship in the world back under their house flag.

Pride in the new ship was running high throughout England, but especially in her home port. There was a great confidence that the *Lusitania* would re-claim the Blue Riband on this maiden trip. In some respects, this seemed well-founded, based on the results of her official trials; others, however – in particular the Germans – were adopting a 'we'll see' attitude toward the event. Bookings were extremely high aboard the *Lusitania*, and there would be quite a number of notables aboard; reporters were eager to discover what famous names might be included among her First Class passenger list, but the Cunard Line denied them the particulars. Cunard said that this was to "shield" those passengers from any "inconvenience." However, it is likely that Cunard also felt this shroud of secrecy would help to increase the sense of excitement among the press and public – and it did.

The *Lucania* had entered service with Cunard as their fastest ship in September of 1893, and it was the ship that the Germans had taken the Blue Riband from in 1897; although fourteen years of age and less than half the *Lusitania*'s tonnage, because of this excitement over the maiden voyage of the *Lusitania*, and the rumored "race" between the two, the *Lucania* had some 740 First and Second Class passengers booked. This was a very good showing, indeed; official word from Cunard, however, stayed the course: there would be no race.

Meanwhile, there was trouble behind the scenes. The *Lusitania* was not only the largest and, it was expected, the fastest vessel in the world. She was also the most expensive. As such she, and her sister *Mauretania* to follow, were the largest single risks for insurers to back. It was said:

> Although the London underwriting market is admittedly large, the brokers of the Cunard Line have found some difficulty in completing the insurances of the *Mauretania* and *Lusitania*. Under the builders' policies the *Lusitania* was insured for £1,500,000, to cover the risk of trials, etc., although the original policies on each steamer were £1,250,000. On the Cunard fleet policies the boats are valued at £800,000 each, and additional amounts are placed on what is called "Total loss, but including excess general average and salvage charges." The amount placed on in this way was £400,00 on each steamer. This is now being increased to £500,000, and one

result of such enormous lines being placed is that the rate gets stiffer, and, whereas liners of normal values could easily be covered at 21s per cent. for 12 months against total loss only, the rates of these steamers are now over 25s per cent.[2]

It was also reported that for the *Lusitania*, underwriters were having "considerable difficulty," and that "brokers found it to be impossible to complete their slip, rates double the ordinary being asked … So huge indeed have recent insurances been that but for the cooperation of anybody of any importance in the market they could not have been effected."[3]

Meanwhile, other plans for the maiden voyage continued. Preparations to feed the first batch of passengers during the crossing were well under way, and the list of items required seemed endless. There were orders for enough foodstuffs to feed an entire city. This list included, but was not limited to, "16,000 gallons of milk, 78,000 pounds of flour, 6,000 pounds of fish, 125,000 pounds of meat, 2,000 pounds of tea, 50,000 eggs, 9,000 pounds of butter, 10,000 pounds of bacon and ham, 10,000 fowls, 45,000 oysters, 1,000 pounds of turtle, 2,000 pounds of plums." To serve these meals, there were some "18,000 pieces of silver, 11,800 knives, 50,000 pieces of crockery," and much, much more.[4] It was elaborated:

> The service of plate … consists of 18,000 pieces. The patterns have all been specially designed and manufactured with a view to stability and to resist the hard wear inevitable on board such an immense ship. The spoons and forks are of the old English pattern. The coffee and tea pots, sugar basins, and cream ewers are in different sizes, from the usual breakfast and tea services to tete-a-tete sets for ladies' afternoon teas. The entrée dishes, vegetable dishes, cruet frames, butter coolers, sugar baskets, sauce boats, soup tureens, soufflé dishes, etc., all have had great care bestowed upon them. The beautiful dessert dishes are works of art in themselves, being of exquisite design and lined with gold. Each article is engraved with the well-known badge of the company.[5]

In the days leading up to the departure, the ship's officers came aboard, and her crew was also signed on. Captain Watt was no doubt enthusiastic about starting the maiden trip of his great new liner. Below, in the heat and noise of the Turbine Engine Room, was located the Starting Platform. This control center for the ship's engines was an assemblage of wheels, gauges, dials, and other controls. Vaguely resembling an H. G.

In this photo, the ship is straining at the buoy; the chain is taut, and it has wrapped its way across the prow, chafing the paint. Even at the time of departure, the chafe mark on that segment of the prow was still visible.

Wells time machine come to life, the Starting Platform was the direct purview of the Chief Engineer. Scots have long been recognized as wonderful engineers, and so for this Scottish-built marvel of technology, it was only proper that the *Lusitania*'s Chief Engineer was a Scot. This post was given to Alexander Duncan, formerly of the *Campania*, a ship that was then fourteen years old. That vessel had been the first Cunard liner to sport a twin-screw configuration, and bore a service speed of 22 knots. Now Duncan was upgrading to a much larger, faster liner, with four screws instead of two, and a completely different type of engine technology. The Renfrew native, however, proved more than competent at working the *Lusitania*'s newfangled powerplant as her career began.[6]

Arthur H. Rostron had been assigned as the ship's First Officer for the maiden voyage. This must have been truly exciting for him. However, the day before the trip was to begin, there came a last-minute change-up, and Rostron received a promotion. He was quickly transferred to his first command, the *Brescia*, on the Mediterranean route. Rostron must have been quite overjoyed at receiving his first posting as Captain, but at the same time no doubt felt somewhat dismayed over having to leave the world's largest liner behind for one of only 3,200 tons. Rostron's career would take off quickly, however; in less than five years, he would achieve fame as the Captain of the Cunarder *Carpathia*, and not long after that, he would serve as Captain of the *Lusitania* and later of the *Mauretania*.[7]

The crew complement needed to man a ship as large as the *Lusitania* was enormous. There were 69 in the Navigation Department, including the Captain, his eight officers, eight Quartermasters, three Boatswains, three Carpenters and Joiners, two Lamp-Trimmers and Yeomen, two Masters-at-Arms, two Marconi Operators, and forty Seamen. In the Engineering Department, there were some 369 spaces to fill: 33 Engineer Officers, 3 Refrigerating Engineers, 192 Firemen, 120 Trimmers, and 21 Greasers. These 438 men were necessary to run the ship between her ports in Liverpool and New York. Then there came the third category, those who looked after the needs of the passengers, and also the needs of the other crewmembers; these numbered some 389: the ship's Doctor, the Chief Purser and two Assistant Pursers, the Chief Steward and two Assistant Stewards, the Chef, two Barbers, twenty-eight Cooks and Bakers, two matrons, ten stewardesses, seven Postal Clerks, two Typists, fifty Leading Stewards, Barkeepers, and the like, and some 280 Stewards. All told, the ship's complete crew complement was some 827.[8]

With the entire crew complement signed on, and the ship coaled and victualed, the working plan for the day of the event was simple, or so it looked on paper: the *Lucania* was set to depart the Prince's Landing Stage at 4:30 p.m., after which the *Lusitania* would tie up there, embark her passengers, and depart at 7:00 p.m. Time would tell whether or not all would go as planned.

Whether or not the *Lusitania* departed on time, one thing was for sure: she would receive a fantastic send-off. Special police arrangements were made to control the large crowds expected that Saturday evening. Sure enough, all through the day, great throngs of sightseers and spectators came down to the waterfront to witness to the departure. "The huge floating landing stage and

In the early evening hours of September 7, 1907, the mighty Lusitania *is moved from her anchorage at the Sloyne, in the Mersey, to the Prince's Landing Stage. The Second Class gangway door on E Deck is already open. Tugs are pulling the nose of the vessel sharply toward the eastern shore.*

Above: *The Lusitania angles in toward the Prince's Landing Stage, which is already packed with people. The port anchor has been lowered to the waterline, and the tug at the bow is now checking the bow's progress toward shore, while another tug is pushing the ship's stern closer to the dock.*

Below: *This view was taken from the stage, looking over the crowd which had gathered and toward the towering side of the Lu-sitania. Although it was not taken on the evening of September 7, 1907 – as is evidenced by the after lifeboat being swung out, and not in place on the deck as the other September 7 photographs show – it does give some impression of the scene that night. At the bow, lines have been swung out over the side, preparatory to tying up.*

Opposite top: Another very rare photograph taken on September 7. The ship has just tied up; the First Class gangways on C Deck have been opened, but the gangway has not been extended to the side of the ship yet.

Opposite bottom: This view gives a good idea of what it looked like to gaze down upon the Prince's Landing Stage before the Lusitania left on her maiden voyage. The photo was purportedly taken from the Lusitania, and the crowds are quite large in number, but the photograph was taken later than 1907, since the Royal Liver building – completed in 1911 – stands apparently whole in the background. Beyond the Royal Liver building stands the Port of Liverpool building. The weather and fading daylight are also a similar match to that evening.

the river wall parades for miles down the stream on both banks were crowded with cheering spectators, who for hours waited to view the departure of the vessel," it was said.[9] This crowd eventually reached an estimated 200,000 in number.

Meanwhile, although the Cunard offices in Liverpool had been a busy scene in the days leading up to the departure, things really came to a head that Saturday. It was said that the "counter of the saloon [First Class] passenger department was almost unapproachable, whilst in the steerage department the crowd filled the room."[10]

In the event, the *Lucania* left a half-hour late, at 5:00 p.m., at which point the larger liner left her anchorage in the Sloyne and, under the assistance of tugs, moved north into the Mersey proper. It was low water, and the ship was drawing 33 feet 8 inches forward and 34 feet 8 inches aft, but there were no concerns of her grounding, since the depth of the harbor was 36 feet.[11] To save time once she was tied up, as she moved toward the Landing Stage, her Second Class Entrance gangway door on the starboard side of E Deck was thrown open, its white-painted interior surface standing out in stark contrast against her black hull. The vessel tied up at the Prince's Stage about an hour after the *Lucania*'s exodus. Soon, a gangplank had been stretched from the upper level of the stage's platform to the ship's First Class gangway doors on the Shelter Deck.

In short order, passengers began boarding the new liner in earnest. First Class passengers came aboard via their Entrance, roughly amidships on E Deck (Second Class came in astern, and Third Class forward). Once aboard, passengers, obviously awed by the *Lusitania*'s size and beauty, set off to find their way about her labyrinthine interiors. The goals were obvious: to find their assigned cabin, the Purser's Office – 'B Deck, just off the main staircase,' an obliging steward might tell them – or one of the outer decks to look down on the scene below. And what a scene it was: below, on the stage and on the waterfront, there was the great throng of spectators, and beyond were the buildings of the great city of Liverpool. As dusk began to settle over the city, one by one the lights of the *Lusitania* began to flicker to life; this wash of illumination bathed the spectators in the gathering darkness below her in a sea of light. Looking up at her enormous dark silhouette, seeing her lit up from stem to stern, the new *Lusitania* presented a "truly magnificent spectacle," to the crowds on shore.

The process of embarking passengers to the *Lusitania* that evening was more or less normal; however, it was complicated by the crew's unfamiliarity with the ship and her unprecedented size. There were also

Above left: Three stewards on a liner of the era.

Above middle: A genial stewardess was always ready to help passengers settle in for their journey.

Above right: An unusually wide-angle photograph of the B Deck First Class Entrance. It is not difficult to see why passengers were overwhelmed with the ship's spacious accommodations.

Above left: *Robert Balfour.*

Above right: *Mrs. Potter Palmer.*

a number of visitors who boarded the ship to see her splendor for themselves, adding to the volume of human traffic. There was some congestion noted at the gangways, but considering the large step forward she represented in the size of Atlantic liners and the number of passengers that could be carried, things did not go too badly.

Climbing the First Class gangway that evening were many prominent people of the day. There was Richard Croker, Jr., the son of the great ex-Tammany Hall chief and former New York boss, who had retired to an estate in Ireland, and who was traveling with his wife and daughter; Robert Balfour, a prominent Scotsman, Liberal M.P., prominent London businessman, and former resident of San Francisco from 1869 to 1893; the Countess of Dunmore and her daughters Lady Victoria Murray and Lady Muriel Gore Browne – prominent Christian Scientists in England; architect Louis Hay and his wife; Mrs. Bertha Palmer – the apparent "inventor" of the greatly beloved brownie – and her son, Potter Palmer, Jr., prominent Chicago citizens; Mr. and Mrs. Cyrus H. McCormick, also of Chicago; there was also E. H. Cunard, one of the Cunard Line's Directors, along with other Cunard VIP's; W. J. Luke, a naval architect from John Brown & Co., aboard with other John Brown employees to ensure the success of their firm's crowning achievement; American Senator George Sutherland (R-UT, 1905-1917); New Jersey State Senator E. R. Ackerman (R, 1906-1911, U.S. Representative from NJ, 1919-1931); Mr. & Mrs. Robert Goelet; a prominent Reverend from Pennsylvania, Joseph L. McCabe; George Peabody; the Consul General for Roumania at London, Count Ward; 82-year-old John H. Starin, former Rapid Transit Commissioner of New York

and prominent New York City businessman and democrat; George J. Capewell, Vice-President and Superintendent of the Capewell Horse Nail Company – and many, many others. There was even a group of 16 prominent British financial journalists, on their way to Ontario, eager to see the sights of New York City on their way there. Although no one had exercised the $4,000 option of booking either the port or starboard Regal Suites – the ship's premiere accommodation – as a complete set of rooms, they were let as separate apartments.

A special correspondent from the *Tribune* also climbed the gangplank, mingling with the passengers and touring the ship. He recalled: "It was like the hall of the Carlton hotel – a lift shot up and down; there were dainty decorations on the high walls; pictures flourished on the staircase; ladies sat at ease in lounge chairs; there was a post office and letter bureau. The further one went the greater grew the surprises. State rooms with brass beds, wardrobes, a telephone, and washing arrangements in a special compartment leading out of each room, music rooms, smoking rooms, tea rooms, writing rooms, a dining saloon so large and lofty that tables were set on the surrounding balcony, so that the passengers dined in two tiers – it was all so splendid and on so generous a scale that one readily gave the *Lusitania* pride of place as queen of the Western Ocean."[12]

Sailing scenes like that which transpired on that momentous September evening were vividly described in one period reference guide:

> The departure of an ocean liner presents a picturesque scene. The hurry and bustle; the excitement and confusion! The growling of stevedores, the chaffing of longshoremen, the swearing of cabmen and drivers, the ejaculations of belated passengers, the timid shrieking of hurried ladies, the grumbling of harried baggage-masters, the smothered inspections of truckmen, and the vociferous orders of officers, are discerned beneath the puffing of tugs, the swish of ferryboats, the whistles of excursion steamboats and pleasure craft, and the vibrant bass of escaping steam. A concert never to be forgotten ...
>
> ... Accompanying friends ..., who may go aboard for leave-taking, will have ample warning when to go ashore, and they should never be urged or allowed to linger after being warned to withdraw.
>
> "ALL VISITORS ASHORE!" – Hark, there goes the bugle! Now the stewards are shouting "all visitors ashore!" accompanied and emphasized by shrill shrieks from the ship's sirens ...

... JUST BEFORE SAILING.—The decks are one mass of passengers, enlivened by the gay costumes of ladies. Overhead on the bridge, the commander and his junior officers; at the bow and stern are the senior officers; the purser and the doctor attending to their manifold duties, all in rich uniforms, and the vessel is now ready to "cast off," amid the fluttering of innumerable handkerchiefs and the shouting of farewells ...[13]

With the *Lucania* departing a half-hour late, it was a given that the *Lusitania*, too, would be delayed from her scheduled 7 o'clock departure. In the end, she left just over four hours after the smaller liner, at 9:10 p.m. When the moment arrived for the liner to begin her maiden voyage, a new era in the history of Atlantic liners began in earnest. Captain James Watt ordered the ship's whistles sounded, telling those below that she was about to depart. Then the lines were cast off from the stage, and crewmen on the bow and stern reeled them back up into place; they would be used later to tie the ship up in New York at the conclusion of the crossing. With the Cunard tender *Skirmisher* at her bow, the *Lusitania* "dropped away stern first from the stage up river, and was then sheered slowly out against the incoming tide."[14]

As the gap between her hull and the Landing Stage began to expand, patriotic fervor reached the breaking point, and the crowd of 200,000 spectators burst spontaneously into the refrains of that favorite British patriotic song, "Rule, Britannia," "the refrain being caught up speedily by the passengers aboard the liner. At the same time all the shipping in the stream, large and small craft, saluted with shrill and hoarse soundings of their steam whistles, and the *Lusitania* proudly responded with a thrilling outburst from her own powerful siren signal," temporarily drowning out the continuing strains of "Rule, Britannia."[15] The correspondent for *The New York Times* reported:

> The scene as she sailed was a memorable one. Fully 100,000 [*sic*] spectators lined the landing stage and the river banks in the immediate vicinity and yelled themselves hoarse as the liner gathered headway down the river, and every steamer and riverside factory for miles along the Mersey joined in the chorus of good-bys. The din was deafening.

No one present would ever forget the sendoff that Liverpool gave the *Lusitania* that night. As the liner began to disappear "as a foreshortening glow into the night," it was termed "a brilliant departure.[16] Even

Top: *Chief Engineer Alexander Duncan. Even now, it seems thoroughly appropriate that a Scot was given oversight of the* Lusitania's *engines.*

Above: *A view taken on a Starting Platform in the Engine Room of a liner of the period. Although not taken aboard the* Lusitania, *it gives a good idea of the scene at the Starting Platform when, in response to the jangling of the Bridge telegraphs, the engines were started for the first time in service.*

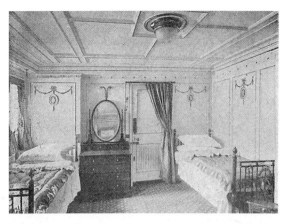 

Above left: *Looking forward in the bedroom of the port side Regal Suite, B48.*

Above right: *Looking aft in stateroom B92 on the port side. The door visible in the aft wall led out into the corridor. This was one of the rooms, when sold with B90 just forward, that would later be given the* en suite *designation, although the two rooms always had an interconnecting door.*

Liverpool, accustomed to the sight of the greatest ships by day and night, had never seen anything to equal it." As the "hurricanes of cheers" slowly faded, there was only one question on everyone's minds: would she, after all, recapture the Blue Riband for Great Britain?

Once the ship had cleared Liverpool waters and dropped off her pilot, she picked up speed, setting a course for Queenstown, Ireland. Overall, the ship was not pushed during this leg of the crossing, since it was not until she departed Queenstown that her crossing's timing actually began, and since she also encountered patches of fog down the Irish Channel, between Holyhead, Wales and Tuskar Rock Light, Ireland, near Wexford Bay. That night, the spacious

accommodations aboard the *Lusitania* were clearly too much for some of the passengers; quickly finding themselves lost in one of her apparently endlessly corridors, they had to be "rescued" by stewards and stewardesses and directed to their cabins or to the public rooms. The ship clearly felt rock-solid, and predictions ran high that there would be absolutely no seasickness during the crossing, no matter what the weather.

Some passengers were clearly disappointed that the ship was not making an all-out dash to Ireland. The officers and engineering staff knew better, of course – some crew hinted to passengers that they were holding everything in reserve for the next day, with their sights locked cleanly on the *Deutschland*'s speed

 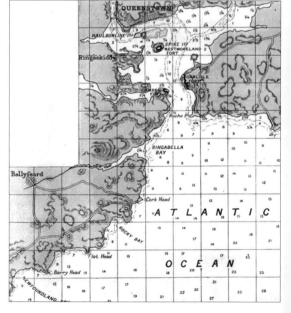

Above: *A typical Queenstown tender.*

Right: *A period chart of Queenstown Harbour.*

Above: *Walking the chilly decks often required being bundled up for protection against the elements.*

Right: *While passengers dressed for dinner, the Chef and his men slaved in the galleys to prepare their fare. This photograph shows the* Lusitania's *Chef's Office.*

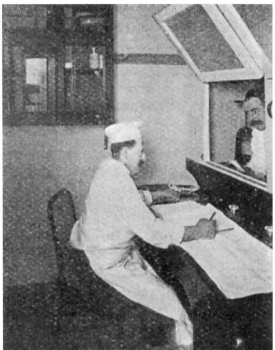

record. "Wait till we get to sea," one said. One of the Cunard Line officials aboard told another: "We are out to do things."

At 9:28 a.m. (Irish Time) on Sunday, September 8, the *Lusitania* arrived at her Irish port of call for the first time, and anchored "a cable's length" from the *Lucania*, just off Roche's Point.[17] It was said that the *Lusitania* "made a magnificent picture" as she lay at anchor beside the older liner. The two headlands at the mouth of the harbor were covered in people, some of whom had been waiting for three or more hours, to catch a glimpse of the mighty *Lusitania*. It was said that aboard the tender, as it "cleared the land and came into view of the four-funnelled monster lying outside a murmur of admiration went up from those on board." Some two hundred would-be passengers had descended upon the city with high hopes that they could take passage on the liner to New York. Unfortunately, there was no room aboard the already-booked ship; they could only watch as she transferred to the tender mail from Liverpool, took on 768 bags of mail bound for the U.S., and then left. The *Lucania* made it out of harbor fifteen minutes prior to the *Lusitania*; the new liner passed Daunt's Rock at 12:11 p.m. When the *Lusitania* left Queenstown in her wake, she had 486 First Class, 483 Second Class, and 1,121 Third Class passengers aboard, some 2,090 in total. When combined with some 800 crew members, there were nearly 3,000 souls aboard the liner for the crossing.

Anticipation was high for the ship to proceed at "Full Ahead"; however, hardly had the *Lusitania* cleared the harbor when sporadic fog descended upon her. Captain James Watt was clearly visible pacing the Bridge and Bridge wings all afternoon, and passengers lined the ship's rails, hoping to spy the older *Lucania* as they caught up to and passed her. All were resoundingly disappointed that the real start of the crossing was at a forced saunter instead of the thoroughbred pace they had expected. By 6:00 p.m., however, the fog had cleared, and Captain Watt gratefully passed word to the Engine Room for the engines to be unleashed in earnest.

That evening, as the ship revved up to high speed for the first time in service, the first full-dress dinner at sea was served; this was the first since, according to Atlantic tradition, the first and last nights after leaving port were not formal "dress" occasions. This custom allowed passengers time to settle in from boarding and to prepare for landing, respectively. Before dinner started, finely dressed passengers were still seen lining the rails on the chilly decks, hoping to see the *Lucania*. In the end, the older ship did not appear before they had to go down to the Dining Saloon.

The twin elevators in the Grand Entrance were found to be well used, especially at dinnertime. The Lift Attendants, in their gold-trimmed uniforms, were kept busy ferrying the well-dressed ladies and gentlemen up and down before and after dinner. One after another, the passengers all flocked to the

Saloon, either on the main, lower level, or the upper level with its balcony overlooking the scene below. A period reference paints the scene:

> The grand saloon, tastefully decked ..., forms a sight delightful to every sense of the most cultured. Not only are the viands tempting, but the paintings, the flowers, the music, the furniture, the napery, all must please the fastidious and hyper-critical. Passengers ... are served beyond the dreams of the epicure of a generation ago.[18]

Indeed, the picture was a splendid display of the Edwardian Era, white tie and tails for the gentlemen and beautiful ladies dressed in their finest gowns and jewelry. By this time, shipboard acquaintances had begun to grow, and old friendships were being refreshed once more. The mood in the Saloon was certainly genial that evening, as First Class passengers made their grand entrance in their resplendent finery and partook of the culinary delights presented for them. Sitting in the beautiful Saloon, listening to the music of the ship's orchestra, "it was difficult to believe one's self at sea," one passenger recalled. At least, with the ship's steadiness, there were very few cases of *mal de mer*. Although on this and subsequent nights it was noticed that there were too few Saloon Stewards to adequately care for all the passengers' needs, and service suffered a bit because of this, overall enthusiasm over the meal was high.[19]

Above: *The galley aboard a Cunarder of the era.*

Below: *The lower level of the First Class Dining Saloon, with all the tables set and prepared for starving passengers to dine.*

When ladies and gentlemen were finished eating their meals, they were – rather a novelty – allowed

A seat at the Captain's table was a coveted privilege, and remains so down to this day.

to smoke in the Saloon together while they listened to the orchestra playing from the balcony. Not long after 8:00 p.m., the orchestra left the Saloon, but the evening was far from over. After eating a hasty dinner, they moved up to the First Class Lounge & Music Room where, at nine o'clock, they began to serenade the passengers once more. Meanwhile, the other passengers enjoyed an after-dinner coffee or other drink in the Verandah Café, peacefully whiling away the hours while their ship sped smoothly along across the Atlantic. Gentlemen later moved on to the Smoking Room, without the accompaniment of their lady companions, to enjoy a drink, play some cards, have a good cigar and, naturally, to place wagers on the ship's pool.

The ship's pool was a longstanding Atlantic tradition, but the betting was particularly keen to guess correctly the ship's run, since all were hoping for a record crossing. Because of this anticipation, the higher numbers were the most popular. Some took a more middle-of-the-road number. Two men in the crowd, Messrs. Archibald S. White and Henry L. Doherty, took low numbers; the others present probably looked upon them as pessimists or as some form of traitor for this move, but only time would tell who was right and would pocket the money.

The much-touted "race" with the *Lucania* was over almost before it began: the older liner, which had a fifteen-minute lead on the *Lusitania* at Queenstown, was overtaken and passed in the middle of that Sunday night/Monday morning. By midday on Monday, the new liner had a lead of sixty-one miles. The *Lu-*

sitania's position at noon on Monday, September 9 was 51 °7' N latitude, 23 °3' W longitude. She had traveled 561 miles since 12:10 the previous day; not a match for the *Deutschland*'s best day's run of 601 miles, but certainly not a bad showing considering she had moved cautiously through fog for nearly six hours outside of Queenstown. Those who had bet on high numbers the previous night were disappointed; Messrs. Doherty and White made some £210 on their bet. Hopes were still high among all, however, for a record passage.

By this time, the ship's size had simply overwhelmed some of her First Class passengers. Instead of trying to physically find their friends when they needed to get in touch with them – to ask them to dinner, to a social gathering that evening before dinner, or merely for a stroll on deck – many decided to use the novelty of their cabin telephone; the switchboard was kept busy. Apparently, the British custom of greeting, namely, "Are you there?" prevailed over the American "Hello?" for opening these conversations.

Even busier, perhaps, was the ship's pair of Marconi Operators. On the average, a thousand words a day passed through the wireless aerials suspended over the ship's quartet of tall, proud funnels. Wireless was still something of a novelty at the time, and passengers were eager to convey to friends or loved ones on shore or aboard other ships information about their trip on the largest liner in the world. The reporters who were aboard were just as eager to transmit their tales and detailed information on the ship's progress to their respective editors; they were dismayed to find that Purser Lancaster was carefully monitoring all messages going out from the ship to make sure no one transmitted anything negative about the ship or her speed.

On Monday, one of the reporters found this out the hard way. Lancaster scoured through the man's report back to his paper, and quickly found something that he didn't like. He glanced at it severely, and asked: "What's this?" When the reporter explained, he still was not satisfied, crossed out the vexatious word, and wrote it down again. The stunned reporter asked if the Purser really was the press censor. Lancaster "drew himself dramatically up to his full height" of five feet one inch, and replied: "I am."

In the Smoking Room that night, after dinner, enthusiastic passengers were still optimistic for a high run; bets on 600 knots or better were taken quickly. The weather had been fine on Monday, and so it was hoped that the ship's speed had been ratcheted up a bit. On the other hand, Messrs. White and Doherty took the low field again, paying a mere £7.

Meanwhile, 64-year-old First Class passenger George Joseph Capewell found himself thoroughly enjoying his passage. Capewell had been born in Birmingham, England, but was educated in Connecticut. He was now the Vice-President and Superintendent of the Capewell Horse Nail Company; seven years before, an article had reported that his "tenacity of purpose [had] brought him to the top," and that it was Hartford, Connecticut's boast that he was one of the men who had put the city on the world map. Due to his extensive business interests on both continents, Capewell was a seasoned Atlantic traveler, having taken the White Star liner *Oceanic* across to Europe in June, and having been able to make crossings at one time or another on most of the newest Atlantic liners. It was thus quite significant that he was enjoying this passage more thoroughly than he recalled ever enjoying another such voyage. Capewell noticed that the waves and movement of the sea seemed to have no effect on the ship whatsoever; indeed, he was impressed to hear of the reports that no one had succumbed to *mal de mer*. Also notable was the fact that, with about three thousand people on board the liner, there was still plenty of room in the public spaces. Every detail seemed to be perfect; the ship's airy decoration was, to his tastes, a welcome departure from the pompous and dark interior spaces of many of the German liners of recent years. He found the ship very "light and cheerful." Indeed, she seemed more like a "great hotel" than a ship traveling the rugged North Atlantic at high speed. When Capewell retired at night he thought it difficult to discern, lying in his berth with no visual point of reference, whether the ship was traveling at twenty-five knots or standing still.

On Tuesday, one of the news correspondents on board gave Purser Lancaster – the admitted unofficial "press censor" – a shock when he announced that he was going to send his next wireless report in code. Lancaster pored over the message with extra thoroughness, and quickly spotted something he didn't like: the phrase, "We tank."

"Suffering Samuel Johnson," he exclaimed, "what's this cryptic sentence mean?"

To this uncharacteristic behavior on the part of a ship's Purser, the troublesome correspondent replied that it was merely his way of saying that the ship was going at twenty-five knots, her full speed. The explanation seems to have soothed the Purser somewhat on the matter.

This reporter's estimate of the ship's speed was misinformed, however. At noon, the day's run was calculated and then posted for passengers to see: 575

nautical miles – an improvement of only fourteen nautical miles over the previous day's run. Disappointment must have showed all over the ship, especially to those who had placed high-field wagers in the ship's pool the previous evening. Messrs. White and Doherty, however, must have been pleased when they pocketed £219 for their second bet. However, there was still hope for the optimists. Even at this 'easy' pace, the gap between the *Lusitania* and her forerunner, the *Lucania*, had widened to a full 120 miles – many still felt it possible that the ship would speed up and yet make the crossing a Blue Riband-winning one.

By this time, the routine aboard the ship was beginning to settle down a bit, and with the ship not making her maximum speed, some of those aboard began to look for ways to divert themselves. The reporters aboard noted that the *Cunard Daily Bulletin*, which was compiled by the Purser and printed each day right on board the ship, didn't have that certain 'punch' that their own newspapers ashore had. A contingent of them approached Purser Lancaster and offered to take the responsibility off his hands, turning it into a 'true' newspaper. It would be filled, they proposed, with the more interesting goings-on aboard, including the numerous shipboard romances that were already cropping up. Lancaster, somewhat surprised at the suggestion, flatly refused, and the ambitious reporters were left to find other ways to while away their time.

One made use of his time by interviewing Chief Engineer Duncan briefly. Duncan told the newspaperman that the turbines were working "splendidly," and that "there had not been the slightest hitch." When asked if the ship had done her best yet, Duncan replied: "Oh, no, we never expect to get the best results out of a ship on her maiden trip. When the engineers and stokehold staff get better acquainted with the engines and boilers we shall achieve far better results than we have done this trip." This was, of course, a standard response on the part of personnel of any line on any new ship that was expected to fetch the Blue Riband before the record was actually secured. While not a complete denial of attempting to recapture the record, it was a true statement that the *Lusitania*'s speed, like the speed of any ship on her maiden voyage, would only increase as time passed.

When asked whether it was probable that the *Lusitania* would take the Blue Riband back from the Germans, however, Duncan responded with resounding confidence: "Perfectly sure. There's not the slightest doubt of it." Even if the record was not recaptured on this crossing, every engineer and officer

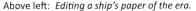

Above left: *Editing a ship's paper of the era.*

Above right: *A typical setup for printing a ship's paper like the* Cunard Daily Bulletin.

Right: *A* Cunard Daily Bulletin *from Tuesday, May 31, 1910, Crossing No. 81 West.*

aboard the *Lusitania* knew what she was truly capable of; taking back the Blue Riband for Britain was only a matter of time.

One reporter was able to spend quite some time of the crossing in the Marconi Shack on the Sun Deck, which he described as the "little brown cabin away on the upper deck" that few of his fellow passengers had taken note of. The cabin was quite small and was full to the point of brimming over with equipment. "No vessel," he told his readers, "has possessed such wonderful equipment for the transmitting of wireless messages ... [The cabin] is not big, and part of it is partitioned off for the sleeping berths of the two strenuous young electrical engineers. There is only just room to move about between brass handles, dynamos, glass tubes, mysterious wires which seem to lead nowhere, and cabinets with metal fittings containing secret and ghostly potentialities." Despite this lack of room, the two operators moved with an "easy swiftness" about the shack. They were kept so busy that the reporter recalled: "During the five days I was with them, each had but four hours' sleep out of the

24. Yet, in spite of their white, tired faces, they were not merely cheerful, they were happy. 'Wireless' to them had become a religion. So long as 'wireless' went well, they laughed at sleep." They listened intently as the various wireless messages came in over the headset. Sometimes the transmissions even interrupted each other. Many congratulatory messages came in, including one from the *La Lorraine.*

Suddenly, something else began to come through the set. It was at four o'clock in the afternoon of Tuesday. The operator's cleanshaven face went "tense with listening," and he "flung up a warning hand" to the others. "Quiet there, quiet," he said. "Here's the long-distance spark."

The other operator, who was standing "back among the brass handles and grim electrical coils," also gestured to the reporter for silence. Then he explained in a whisper: "We are within two thousand miles. That is America's first word." It was the first time that the *Lusitania* had established wireless contact with the New World.

Soon enough, the operator began transmitting again, resuming "his swift tap-tapping at the little ebony handle on his desk, filling the little chamber with an electrical crackle, like that of a coffee mill, lighting it up with blue sparks, which flashed from a glass cylinder in front of him, and told of the force which was flinging the message into the air."

Indeed, in an era when wireless telegraphy was the cutting edge of technology, the reporter thought that the Marconi Shack, isolated from the rest of the ship in its own little technological cocoon, was remarkable. To his mind, there was no other place "so magically equipped; no place that could provide such dramatic surprises."[20]

That same evening, there came an unpleasant change in weather. The sea turned rough, and a strong north-northeast wind descended upon the ship. Although some rough weather had been encountered during the ship's trials, this was the first time she had met up with anything but smooth seas in actual service, with actual paying customers aboard. According to passenger reports, the ship behaved beautifully; although the wind whistled around the outer decks, the *Lusitania* was completely unaffected. Indeed, State Senator Ackerman, traveling in First Class, later said: "On Tuesday night there was a bit of rough weather, but we only knew it because of a bulletin posted to that effect."

At noon on Wednesday, September 11, the ship's run was again calculated and posted, this time showing some 570 knots logged – some 1,700 run since leaving Queenstown, and officially showing that the ship had crossed the halfway mark of the crossing during the previous night. This run was slightly less than that shown the previous day, but considering the winds and seas encountered the previous night, this was not a bad showing by any means.

Not long after the day's run was posted, the ship's whistle sounded. Curious passengers rushed outside to see the reason for this commotion. After some searching of the horizon, they spotted a small steamer some distance ahead, but almost right in the giant Cunarder's path. Backing up the deafening whistle, a Scotch crewman with a powerful voice was heard to shout a warning out over the bow: "Ship ahoy. Get out of the road, or we'll sink you." It did not take long for the *Lusitania* to overtake and safely pass the smaller, significantly slower vessel, and leave her in her wake.

During the remainder of the day on Wednesday – while passengers enjoyed walking the decks, taking tea in their deck chair and watching the sea slip by, catching up on their reading, or listening to music from the ship's orchestra – it became clear that the liner's engines had been unleashed with a newfound vigor. Previously, some had reported feeling little or no vibration in First Class portions of the ship; Second Class passengers may have disagreed with that sentiment. With the ship's increase in speed, however, the vibration was now "perceptible in all parts of the ship"; aft spaces and the passengers occupying them would now have been suffering the full brunt of the flaws in the ship's propeller design.

That evening, the concert was held in the First Class Lounge & Music Room. This was a standard feature of every crossing on Atlantic liners of the day, and was usually held on the last night of the journey. Since the ship was scheduled to arrive Friday morning, this event would normally have taken place on Thursday night. However, with the ship's clearly increased speed, it may have been felt that, with weather permitting, the arrival might have been so early on Friday morning that a late-evening concert on Thursday might have left the passengers exhausted.

At the concert, two prominent passengers took center stage to praise the new liner's performance. It was U.S. Senator Sutherland who, during his speech, coined the now-famous phrase about the *Lusitania* being "more beautiful than Solomon's Temple," not to mention being "large enough to hold all his wives and mothers-in-law." This comment raised a hearty laugh since he hailed from predominantly Mormon, and hence polygamous, Utah – although he was neither. Robert Balfour, M.P., also spoke about the liner, and highlighted her as yet another link of friendship between America and England.

Above: *This photo, looking aft along the port side of the Lounge & Music Room, shows the Broadwood grand piano quite clearly. This was where the shipboard concerts were held on the last night of every crossing, and both the ship's orchestra and First Class passengers would have made use of the piano throughout the trip.*

Below right: *A scene showing passengers at a ship's concert.*

Once the concert concluded, many of the First Class passengers drifted off to their cabins for the night; some others remained awake, especially in the First Class Smoking Room, eager to make their wagers. Interestingly, whereas it had been the high numbers that proved most popular in the early days of the crossing, on this night, it was the low numbers that were going quickly. In point of fact, two men bid on the low number for £31, and there was some dispute as to which man had placed the wager first. The gentlemen present put it to a vote and picked one of the two, while the other man used the money he had saved to buy a round of refreshments for the rest of the group. Yet others were busy filling out their customs declaration forms, which were typically distributed by the stewards early on in the crossing; there were always those who procrastinated in filling out the forms until the last minute.

Fog moved in at 11:30 that night, forcing Captain Watt to slow his ship once more. Some of the more superstitious aboard began to wonder what it was exactly that had so "jinxed" the maiden voyage. In reality, there was nothing uncanny about it – the North Atlantic is not exactly a friendly environment for record-breaking. A good record run has to be comprised of two things: a powerful enough ship to make

the speed required and favorable weather conditions. The latter had merely been absent from important portions of this crossing. Another two hours were spent in fog on the morning of Thursday, September 12. Because of these fog banks, when the run was posted after noon on Thursday, the figure had not broken the 600 mark. At 593 nautical miles at an average of 23.86 knots, however, it was the best run of the voyage so far. Cheers went up from enthused passengers at the marked increase in mileage. Mr. Ohio Barber took £184 for a middle-of-the-road bet placed the previous evening.

With this respectable run under her belt, it still looked possible that the *Lusitania* could make a record. The benchmark crossing made by the *Deutschland* in September of 1903 was from Cherbourg, France, to New York over a course of 3,054 nautical miles. The *Lusitania*'s course was 272 miles shorter because she was coming in from Queenstown instead of from the continent direct. Thus, in order to be able to compare the two runs successfully, a certain time handicap for the *Lusitania* would have to be figured in, roughly eleven hours' worth. More accurately telling without complicated calculations would be the average speed for the complete crossing.

The German liner's record crossing had been made over the course of six runs: 417, 571, 578, 570, 583 and 335. Her average speed for the crossing was some 23.15 knots. With runs so far of 561, 575, 570 and 593, the *Lusitania*'s speed to noon on Thursday had been 23.11 knots – a difference in speed of only .04 knots. Her Wednesday-Thursday run was only eight miles short of the best single day's run ever, made by the *Deutschland* in 1901, of 601 miles. All she needed was one more good day's steaming, and the record seemed within her grasp – and this despite all of the foggy weather she had encountered through the voyage so far.

Anticipation of arriving in New York was beginning to grow all over the ship; it was reported that the Marconi Operators' daily regiment of a thousand words per day suddenly doubled on Thursday. Meanwhile, in New York, eagerness about the ship's arrival was growing, as well. Reports of the ship's position began streaming in from land-based wireless stations in touch with the liner. Estimates of the ship's final time made their way into papers; *The New York Times* predicted 5 days, 1 hour and 15 minutes. Enormous preparations were under way to greet the ship. Extra policemen were called out in Manhattan to perform crowd control in the area of the ship's pier. Large quantities of boats and pleasure craft, large and small alike, prepared to sail out to meet the ship in the harbor and escort her in. Friday's early edition papers reminded the general public of her due time so that they could be sure not to miss the event.

As it turned out, the *Lusitania* covered the last 483 nautical miles without incident. She arrived at Sandy Hook, the official end-point for the crossing, at 8:05 a.m. on Friday, September 13, 1907. Her crossing had taken 5 days and 54 minutes (only 21 minutes off of the estimate made by *The New York Times*). Her average speed for the trip had been 23.01 knots ... the *Deutschland*'s record was safe by only a half-hour's time. Having left Liverpool with some 6,500 tons of coal and arriving with just less than 1,500 tons remaining, she had burned roughly five thousand tons of coal at an average rate of 41 tons every hour.

In short order, Harbor Pilot Frank Cramer and Cunard's New York General Manager, Vernon Brown, met the liner. Cramer came aboard via the pilot cutter *New Jersey*. As he was coming aboard, someone aboard the nearby pilot cutter *New York* hoisted a sheet with the word "Scab" on it. Apparently, someone was disgruntled and jealous that Cramer had been given the honor of taking the *Lusitania* in via the new Ambrose Channel. Ignoring this snub, Cramer climbed aboard and eventually found his way to the Bridge, where he took up a position amidships; Cunard had specifically chosen him for this task, and he had run up and down the new Ambrose Channel several times in prepara-

Below: *A period view of Sandy Hook.*

Right: *The buoy marking the entrance to the Ambrose Channel.*

Above: *The pilot boat* New York. *It was from this vessel that Pilot Cramer was insulted while boarding the* Lusitania *to bring her in for the first time.*

Below: *A New York harbor pilot boarding a ship of the period. This view shows the long and perilous climb up the rope ladder that he had to undertake before arriving on the deck.*

tion for this momentous event. The situation was tense, and Cramer and the ship's officers were certainly extra vigilant to make sure that everything went according to plan. Captain Watt stood directly behind Cramer, keeping an eye on the goings-on around him. Junior Third Officer Dolphin and Fourth Officer Battle were at the port and starboard Engine Room telegraphs, respectively, prepared to relay orders to Chief Duncan at a moment's notice.

The ship entered the channel at a cautious eight knots. One after another, the temporary buoys came up and fell astern. As Pilot Cramer grew more confident with maneuvering the *Lusitania*'s bulk through the course, he gradually increased her speed; the ship was drawing only 30.6 feet of water at the bow and 32.3 feet at the stern, and the Ambrose was currently dredged to 32½ feet at low tide. Still, there was the factor of the unknown – never had a ship with a draught this deep navigated the Ambrose Channel in either direction, and there was very little margin for error. Eventually, she emerged from the new cut at twelve knots, and everyone on the Bridge sighed gratefully. The next stop was Quarantine.

The revenue cutter had already departed the Battery at 6:30, headed for Quarantine to intercept the inbound *Lusitania*. It was filled with customs men and reporters. Other boats soon showed up: the *Ellis Island*, an immigration boat; the *Dalzelline*, a customs cutter; the *Gov. Flower*, the Health Officer's tug, with Health Officer of New York Dr. Doty standing outside the pilothouse in his brilliant gold-laced uniform; there was the *Manisees*, the Army Engineer's tug, as well. There were also the unofficial members of the welcoming flotilla. The *Sirius*, a local steamboat operated by the Iron Steamboat Company, came up in short order carrying fifteen hundred sightseers. As the *Sirius* – some twenty-six years old at the time of the event – passed the *Lusitania*, all of the sightseers hurried to her starboard rails to watch the giant Cunard liner go by; the small vessel leaned ominously under the imbalanced weight.

A liner's maiden reception in New York is always a proud affair; this one stood out as special, however. As *Lusitania* appeared from the light morning mists at 9:25 a.m., spectators on the craft moving to greet her caught their breath. She was *enormous*; some later recalled that she looked "like a skyscraper adrift." When she turned slightly to make anchorage at Quarantine, she presented her full length for the first time, and it was obvious that she was even bigger than everyone had at first believed. And she was *beautiful*; her thoroughbred lines immediately put to shame the profiles of all previous liners. Sparkling in her new paint, she

Left: *The Statue of Liberty.*

Above: *A view taken from one of the high-rises of Lower Manhattan. Looking south across the bay toward the Statue of Liberty, a flotilla of craft – described by* The New York Tribune *as a "curious mosquito fleet" – are happily escorting the* Lusitania *to her Manhattan pier.*

looked particularly impressive. She came to rest at anchor at quarter of ten that morning.

Bedlam immediately erupted as every boat in sight – and there were plenty of them – cut loose with their whistles, holding long, sustained blasts of salute to the new Cunarder. As her passengers lined the decks, waving back at the hospitable greeting committee, the *Lusitania*'s own whistle sounded over and over again to return the salute. The Quarantine tug approached, carrying the health inspectors to look over the passengers for signs of disease and trachoma in particular. The inspection of the passengers took only a half-hour.

A mail boat tied up astern so that workers could begin transferring some 1,500 sacks of European mail that the liner had brought with her. Then the revenue cutter moved up and unleashed a tide of newspaper reporters and others upon the liner; each one hurried aboard with one goal in mind: get the story of the maiden crossing of the world's largest ship.

Once her call at Quarantine was finished, the ship began moving up the Upper Bay, toward her lower west side Manhattan pier. As the Statue of Liberty came up ahead, the reporters were busy moving from passenger to passenger, getting interviews and comments on their

Opposite: *The* Lusitania *raising anchor at Quarantine. She is dressed from stem to stern in celebration of completing her first transatlantic crossing.*

Below: *A stern view of the liner during her maiden arrival.*

Above: *The* Lusitania *steams past the Battery on Lower Manhattan, escorted by a flotilla of welcoming craft.*

Below: *Passing Lower Manhattan with the excursion boat* Sirius *running alongside.*

thoughts about the ship. Passengers were on the whole very free with their praise of the liner, her stability and – curiously enough – her lack of vibration. All were clearly disappointed that they had not been aboard for a Blue Riband-taking crossing.

One veteran North Atlantic passenger was Robert P. Porter, who was just concluding his eighty-sixth crossing. He said: "She has not done her best. She can, I believe, make 625 knots in twenty-four hours and break another record. A slight vibration was noticeable at her speed trial, but it was found that this was not caused by her machinery, but by the fact that the structure aft had not been sufficiently stiffened. This was done, and now there is practically no vibration. There was not a hitch with the turbines ... The great disappointment to many on board was the fact that

Above: *The* Lusitania *steams up the North River in this photograph taken from the top of the Singer Building. At the time, the Singer, standing at the corner of Liberty Street and Broadway, was the tallest skyscraper in the world. The largest of the welcoming vessels, just along her starboard side, is the excursion boat* Sirius.

Left: *The Singer Building was still incomplete, and would only be finished the following year.*

Below: *From a lower perspective at the waterfront, the liner looks much grander; her decks are lined with people.*

Above: *Another fantastic view of the procession of vessels, with the* Lusitania *at its core, as it moved up the North River.*

Below: *Due to the state of the tide, the liner had to move north, past Pier 54 – where she was to dock – and then turn around in order to be swung in correctly. This view shows her making the final turn toward the Cunard pier.*

Above: *A bevy of tugs push and pull the immense liner as she nears her berth.*

Below: *The bow starts to enter the dock, but her angle is not right quite yet, and more work lies ahead for the tugs.*

Above: *In this photograph, the prow has almost touched Pier 54, while the tugs are trying to pull her stern back out to line her up. Spectators on the pier, including officers of either the navy or the merchant marine, stare up at the great ship.*

Right: *As the ship lines up with Pier 54, more spectators watch her progress.*

Below: *As the ship comes into Pier 54, spectators line every square inch of the docks. Many cabs, personal carriages, and even the occasional motor car await the arrival of wealthy passengers as they disembarked the ship and made their way into the city.*

the *Lusitania* did not break all records. I am certain that she is 'going to do things.' The fog out of Queenstown and the two hours yesterday morning caused us a delay and, of course, that could not be helped." Robert Balfour told a reporter: "The Captain, the chief engineer, and the naval constructor are Scotch, like myself, and so I expect great things from this steamer." Senator Sutherland of Utah went further, saying that the liner was "as free from vibration and as steady as it is possible for a ship to be."

Ernest Cunard said: "I think that the *Lusitania* is a wonderful vessel, and has more than come up to our expectations. The turbines have acted splendidly in every way. Naturally there was some slight vibration when the ship was being driven at top speed, but it was nothing like the vibration of reciprocating engines. The engines have worked without a hitch during the entire trip." He added: "No ship ever makes her record passage on her maiden voyage. The *Lusitania* averaged 25½ knots on her trial trip for forty-eight hours, and there is no reason why she should not do better later on. We are very much pleased from every point of view with the latest addition to the Cunard fleet." Indeed, he pointed out that his reason for taking passage on this crossing was "to watch the working of the ship in order to see if we could improve the *Maretania* [sic], now nearing completion. I find that I shall have no suggestion to make."

Apparently, there was only thing that seemed to be worthy of complaint at the time; New York was in the midst of a late-summer heat wave. Although the mean temperature for New York in September during that era was a mere 66° Fahrenheit,[21] as the sun rose toward its zenith that day, the temperature moved well past eighty. The ship's ventilation system, though extensive, was simply unable to compete. In an era when day suits and full-length dresses were *de rigueur*, things grew uncomfortable quickly.

While the reporters were busy interviewing as many passengers as they could find, the ship continued to move toward Manhattan, still escorted by countless waterborne craft; the cacophony of steam whistles and shouting and cheering from those present did not cease throughout the entire journey. As the ship neared Lower Manhattan, the thousands of people who had congregated at the Battery caught their breath. Indeed, the ship was more impressive now, for she was fully dressed out: she flew the U.S. flag from her Foremast, the Cunard house flag from her Mainmast, the blue ensign of the British Royal Naval Reserve from the taffrail, and she was showing a full display of signal flags fore and aft to mark the occasion. The Singer Building, still under construction, was going to be the world's tallest; as the *Lusitania* moved toward Manhattan, an American flag was hoisted atop it in salute to her. The Cunard flag on the roof of Cunard's offices was doffed three times, and the *Lusitania*'s crew acknowledged this by lowering her own Cunard flag. From every window in

Above left: *This beautiful view was probably taken from the top of the pier shed, looking toward Lower Manhattan. It gives a wonderful impression of how things would have looked to passengers making their way down the gangplank to shore. The* Lusitania *towers over everything and everyone in sight.*

Left: *Another marvelous view looking up at the side of the liner. Passengers, crew and officers – standing on the starboard Bridge wing – wave down at the crowds below.*

This view looks northwest toward the mighty liner, and shows the woefully inadequate pier structure.

This unique view of the Lusitania *tied up at New York's Pier 54 was taken during one of her first two stays in that port. Some of the cobblestones visible in this photograph are still in place in the vicinity of Pier 54.*

Manhattan with a view of the scene, all activity slowed or ceased so that the moment could be absorbed, etched firmly in the memories of those present.

For those on board the liner, this reception was quite a surprise. To 64-year-old George Capewell, the tops of most of the big buildings in Lower Manhattan seemed to be "black with people." As those aboard the liner enjoyed the event, the ship continued to move past the Battery and up the North River. On the Bridge, Pilot

Cramer had her brought up past Pier 54 to a point where she could be turned around; due to the flow of the tide, this would ease her in warping into dock. For nearly an hour eight tugs pushed and pulled at her enormous weight, but eventually she was secured to the dock that would be her "home away from home" for the next seven and a half years. Spectators on the pier and at least five thousand more on the streets outside the pier waved and cheered; the scene was, initially at least, utter pandemonium. Some of the more deter mined individuals that pushed forward were "roughly handled" by the police as they were tossed back into the barely contained crowd. Only once the throng had begun to thin and the mounted police intervened was a measure of order restored.

With the situation quieting down, those who were still present could take the time to fully appreciate the size of the great liner. Her bow towered over the virtually empty pier and over most of everything else in the immediate area. New York was, even then, larger than life, and the enormous *Lusitania* instantly seemed to fit in well.

Passengers began to disembark slowly. The Countess of Dunmore and her daughters, Lady Murray and Lady Browne, disembarked the ship in somber mourning attire, for the Earl of Dunmore had passed away three weeks previously; their garb of woe did not harmonize, however, with the overall theme of celebration. Mrs. Potter Palmer – the driving force behind the invention of the brownie – and her son Potter Palmer, Jr. were tackled by reporters eager to confirm or deny rumors that she would marry King Peter of Serbia soon. In point of fact, there were many rumors surrounding Mrs. Palmer and various European heads of state at the time. Mrs. Potter denied the rumors rather wearily, and in the end, the gossip came to naught. The party of sixteen British financial journalists raced off the ship almost as soon as the gangplank had been lowered into place. They were met by automobiles and lunched at the famous Lotos Club before touring *The New York Times* building. Their stay in New York was an adventure-filled one, if short: their train for Canada departed that very evening.

While some were disembarking the ship, a very few special visitors and members of the press were allowed aboard, bucking the general tide as they climbed the gangplanks. Inevitably, they found their way to the Bridge, and Fourth Officer Battle patiently explained to them the details of how all of the Bridge instruments worked. Meanwhile, on the pier below, there were two sightseers of obvious rural origin; they were looking up at the ship in awe, with their jaws slack. One looked at the other and said: "No one will believe us when we go back and tell them about this ship. And by heck, I would not have believed it either."

After all the hype that had preceded the crossing, no one could believe that the ship had failed to take back the Blue Riband. Even now, at a century's remove, it seems out of place with the promise delivered during her trials. To explain this, it has often been repeated that it was the fog that prevented the *Lusitania* from making a record crossing. To an extent this may be

true, because she had been forced to slow up by the fog outside of Queenstown, as well as by the fog on Wednesday night and Thursday morning. While the ship was steaming at reduced speed, the half-hour's steaming that made the difference was lost. However, looking at the entire trip, it is clear that the *Lusitania* had not been driven flat out during the crossing, even when the weather was clear. As of noon on Thursday, the ship was only .04 knots in average speed behind the Blue Riband crossing held by the *Deutschland* – an average of 23.11 knots for the Cunarder up to that point, as opposed to 23.15 knots for the German ship. However, after noon on Thursday, the ship slowed her average speed considerably, so that by 8:05 the next morning, she had averaged 23.01 knots for the entire crossing. Why, one asks, was there such a significant reduction in speed on the last run?

Even before the *Lusitania* departed Liverpool, Cunard's New York agents had been trying to obtain permission for her to use the new Ambrose Channel to enter New York Harbor; the Main Ship Channel was simply too winding to accommodate the *Lusitania's* unprecedented length safely. The Ambrose Channel was far straighter and more direct, but was as yet incomplete; permission to use the channel had only been given by special exemption during the course of the maiden crossing. Even this special permission was limited in that she could only use the new cut after dawn and before dusk. With this fact in mind, if Captain Watt had maintained his higher speed of Wednesday-Thursday, the ship would have arrived much earlier at the Ambrose Lightship, during the night of Thursday-Friday; this would have necessitated waiting at the Lightship through the night until dawn the next day.

According to Vernon Brown, Watt had been informed prior to departing Liverpool that, "on account of tidal conditions, it was undesirable to arrive at Sandy Hook Bar until after daylight on Friday." Indeed, on Wednesday, September 11, Brown had sent Watt a Marconi wireless stating that he would meet the ship "outside the Bar about 8 o'clock on Friday morning, and for the Captain to be prepared to come in through the new Ambrose Channel at 9 o'clock." It seems that after a good day's run between Wednesday and Thursday, Captain Watt's intention was to take his intended time of arrival off Sandy Hook and work backward from that point to dictate the speed he needed for the rest of the crossing; the ship had not been pushed for a record at any point in her crossing.[22]

Although some in Germany celebrated the "failure" of the *Lusitania* to recapture the Blue Riband, and some in America and Great Britain were quick to pounce on the relatively sluggish speed of the liner when everyone was expecting her to smash all the records, naysayers were missing one very important point. If the Germans' record was safe by only half an hour when the *Lusitania* had not made anything like a true attempt at the Blue Riband, there was no real doubt that the trophy would soon be returned to Great Britain by their newest greyhound.

No one knew this better than the Germans, and they were sweating bullets. They tried to throw some cold water over the maiden voyage by telling the press that they would probably no longer even try to build record-breaking ships. They said that there was more profit in larger moderate-speed ships, and because record-breakers were invariably uncomfortable for their passengers. At the same time, the Assistant General Manager of Hamburg-Amerika's New York offices, J. P. Meyer, also questioned the official timing of the *Lusitania*'s maiden voyage. Calculating a run of 2,780 miles over 120.9 hours, he came up with an average speed of 22.994 knots, instead of the officially released 23.01 knots; then he went out and made a press statement on the difference. In the end, it became clear that he had miscalculated the length of the run by two miles, making the critical difference in average speed.

On Sunday, September 15, Vernon Brown issued a statement that read, in part: "The hasty adverse criticisms of our German friends might cause a suspicion that the wish was farther to the thought." Referring back to older Cunarders, Brown said that it took time – in some cases up to five years – to get a ship to perform at her absolute best. He did, however, predict that "the patience of our German friends" would not be so sorely tested with the new Cunarder. He also touched on another serious concern that had been expressed prior to the maiden voyage: coal consumption. Many felt that it was possible that the ship could smash through all speed records, but that the cost in fuel would be so enormous that it would negate the speed advantage. Brown was pleased to announce that the ship had arrived in New York with her bunkers only three-quarters depleted, proof positive, he said, that the *Lusitania* had not been driven for speed during the crossing. "No railroad train could have been more exact in following out its itinerary than was this ship in following out her instructions," he said.

Although Cunard was beaming over the *Lusitania* in the public, there were a few teething problems that had come to their attention during the maiden crossing. There were issues in the lavatories, for example; the stall doors had springs to hold them in place, instead of hooks, but the springs were not up to the ship's motion in a sea. The lavatory bowls were also too shallow, allowing the water within to slop out over the rim in response to the liner's roll. There was also some imperfection with the supply of fresh and salt water to the baths. These and other details would be seen to in short order, however, and considering the overall scale of the project that the *Lusitania* had been, they were all relatively minor matters.

The turnaround in New York was a busy period for the *Lusitania*'s crew … no one had ever performed this chore on a liner that big. To aid them in completing the task in good time, the ship was closed to the general public during her stay in that port. The re-coaling process was enormous all in its own right; while that was being handled, the ship's stewards and stewardesses were busy cleaning and prepping the accommodations in order to accept a fresh batch of passengers on the eastbound return to Europe, which was set to begin on Saturday, September 21. This eight-day period for preparations was truncated because the primary passenger areas of the ship had to be ready for public inspection by specially invited guests of the Cunard Company.

On Saturday, September 14, crowds of sightseers still swarmed over the streets in front of Pier 54, straining to get the best view of the ship and hoping in vain to be allowed onto the pier. By Sunday, the local fruit, lemonade and souvenir vendors caught on to the opportunity, and set up along Tenth Avenue close by the pier. Unlike the crush and confusion of Friday, the crowds were all very well behaved; even so, they swarmed over Pier 55 and the nearby *Charles Street* to get good broadside views of the ship. A few who had managed to procure boarding passes were allowed to go onto the pier and were observed with envious eyes as they climbed the gangplank. Even this visitation was short-lived; after 4:30 p.m., no one but ship's crew was allowed to go aboard.

On Tuesday, there was a luncheon aboard the liner for some four hundred guests of the line. These visitors were given the grand tour of the liner, including a specially prepared lifeboat drill. Chief Engineer Duncan even allowed his precious Engine Rooms to be inspected by the guests. On Wednesday, there was the main inspection by some 1,500 specially invited guests. The excited members of the public who had received this distinction boarded via the Second Class Gangway, and were given a tour of the First Class Dining Saloon, the Regal Suites, and the public rooms on the Boat Deck. A further few VIP's were taken aboard on Thursday. Among these was one Samuel Clemens, the author and satirist better known as Mark Twain. Twain – a former riverboat pilot and the man who had coined the term "the Gilded Era" to describe the exciting time that was then at its peak – was quite taken with the liner. With typical good humor and spontaneity, when his tour was finished, Twain said that he would tell Noah all about the *Lusitania* when he saw him. For those who had not been among the privileged few to get a boarding pass and guided tour of the ship during her first stay in New York, Cunard officials promised that at the end of her second westbound crossing, they would give the public more opportunities to see her splendor in person.

The whirlwind stay in New York came to its conclusion with startling speed. On Saturday, September 21, the ship began her second crossing of the Atlantic. She was scheduled to sail from her pier at 3:00 p.m. Captain Watt hosted a lunch for several prominent individuals, including Ernest Cunard, J. P. Morgan – owner of the competing International Mercantile Marine Group and White Star Line – Vernon Brown, and 71-year-old U.S. Senator Eugene Hale (R-Maine), the Chairman of the Committee on Naval Affairs. Hale had previously turned down a position as Secretary of the Navy, but during his career had done much for appropriations to help build up the United States Navy.

Bookings for the crossing were heavy: some 350 in First Class, 300 in Second and 980 in Third. Indeed, the *Lusitania* was taking home many of the same First and Second Class Passengers that she had brought over with her, included among them various reporters, Ernest Cunard and other Cunard Line representatives, John Brown employees, and notable men involved with the steamship industry. She was also carrying Mrs. Gertrude Eversfield and her ten-year-old son Charles. The woman and boy were returning to England after having arrived in New York only a few weeks previously, deported due to trachoma. Two other children, who did not have the eye disease, were remaining in the United States with their father, who was soon to become a United States citizen; they bade farewell to their mother and brother in the Ship's Hospital before being taken ashore.

Some two thousand spectators showed up around Pier 54 to see the liner off. To avoid confusion, Cunard refused to allow anyone onto the ship who did not hold a ticket for the crossing; hence, many farewells between passengers and their friends and relatives took place right on the pier.

Harbor Pilot Edward Young, one of the most experienced pilots in the service, had been selected to take the *Lusitania* out of New York waters through the Ambrose Channel. There was some concern in certain circles that the liner would ground on the bottom of the new cut while passing out, because her draft – with a full load of 7,000 tons of coal aboard – was now expected to be some 34 feet 5 inches. Young had been busy during the preceding week studying the navigation for the course so that he would be fully prepared when the time came. Others aboard for the trip down to open water included Vernon Brown and his assistant, J. H. Walker, Captain

A wonderful starboard profile of the Lusitania *departing New York Harbor. Judging from work on the Singer Building in the background, and on certain features of the ship visible in the photo, this would most likely date to her first or second departure from New York.*

Herbert J. Haddock of the White Star liner *Oceanic*, and two other Cunard skippers, Captain Irving of the *Pannonia*, and one Captain William Thomas Turner of the *Caronia* – a man who would himself later command the great *Lusitania*.

Just before departure, there was an incident that nearly ended in serious trouble. The liner was still held fast to her pier when one of the forward lines snapped with a loud crack. With the tide coming in, the current began to push the ship's hull forward, deeper into her berth. At that point the stern lines were rather slack, and as the ship began to creep forward, two of the gangplanks connecting ship to shore began to move forward, as well. There came a scramble to keep the platforms under their shore ends. Meanwhile, the Pier Superintendent noticed that there were people clustered around the tops of the gangplanks; if these bridges to the shore gave, with people standing at the gangway, there was no telling what could ensue. Showing remarkably quick thinking, he barked at the people in the gangways, warning them to get back; although there was no time to explain the situation, everyone obeyed the command promptly. The ship only ended up moving about ten feet before the stern lines grew taut and the ship came to a stop, and the gangways ended up holding fast to the ship and the shore; it was clear, however, that further precautions would have to be made in the future to prevent the ship from taking it in her head to shift position in her berth again.

By the time the ship was ready to depart, 3:00 had come and gone, and she was forty minutes late when she did back out into the North River. Cheers went up as the ship left New York for the first time, and American and British flags suddenly appeared both on shore and on the ship's decks. There were far fewer waterborne craft to salute her on the way out than had greeted her the previous week. The *Lusitania's* siren sounded only once when a ferryboat threatened to cut into her path. Once her nose was pointed downstream, she was poised, under Pilot Young's supervision, to get under way in earnest, in a scene closely paralleling this narrative:

> ... Slowly, but steadily, the craft moves, as though awakened from sleep and endowed with life. Like a leviathan she quivers ... Then, with majestic motion, the stately ship glides down on the broad bosom of the river, and soon the vista of the noble bay is unfolded to the wistful vision of all on deck. As our vessel passes between Governor's Island and the titanic figure of Liberty, gazing backward one gains a last view of those colossi of the metropolis, the lofty office buildings. Distance softens the outlines, and their skyline merges in a curve of grace with the grand contour of the Brooklyn Bridge. Out past the shores of Brooklyn and Staten Island; through the Narrows, past quarantine islands and Sandy Hook, away on the port side, the coast of Long Island; then a glimpse of Fire Island lighthouse, and we are on the bosom of the deep, with no more land to be seen till we reach the welcoming shores of the Old World.[23]

Here, where the New York channel waters gave way to the Atlantic, Pilot Young and the other temporary passengers disembarked the liner. Young had encountered no great difficulty in bringing the *Lusitania* out through the unfinished Ambrose cut, despite her additional draft, since the tide was in a very high state. At 6:41 p.m., she passed Sandy Hook Lightship and took to the open sea. Ahead lay the North Atlantic Ocean and, some twenty-eight hundred miles beyond, Queenstown, Ireland. Somewhere in that course, it was hoped, she would beat the eastbound record of the *Kaiser Wilhelm II*. That voyage was made in June of 1904 between Sandy Hook and Eddystone – some 3,112 nautical miles – over 5 days, 11 hours and 58 minutes at an average speed of 23.58 knots. Optimists taking interest in the *Lusitania's* crossing were hoping that she could make it in 4 days and 12 hours; more realistic estimates were put at slightly over five days. Since she had averaged just over 23 knots westbound, it was easily conceivable that she would be able to maintain an average return speed high enough to recapture the Blue Riband.

Instead, Captain Watt started the crossing at a speed that, for the *Lusitania*, was a downright saunter; by the time Fire Island was fifty miles in her wake, Watt had only ratcheted her speed up to 22 knots, and by noon the next day, she was making only slightly better than 22½ knots. Fog was encountered on Sunday morning, but speed was maintained because it was not particularly thick. At noon, a run of 369 miles from the Ambrose Lightship was posted. At about that time, however, the fog grew significantly denser, and the ship was slowed, her speed falling below twenty knots as she passed between Cape Sable and Sable Island. For the remainder of Sunday and through all of Monday, fog enshrouded the liner and by Monday at noon, she had only covered 524 knots. Her speed remained at 19 knots throughout late Monday. By noon on Tuesday, September 24, she had covered another 525 knots.

The weather had heretofore been relatively poor, but next it took a turn for the worse; on Tuesday night, the seas mounted until it was described as "very heavy." The liner rolled from port to starboard, reaching angles of twenty degrees away from vertical. Despite this heavy roll, she charged forward through the waves just as she had been designed to do, with

Above: *Safely at home port. An early port-side view of the liner in the Mersey.*

Right: *An early view showing the port Boat Deck of the great liner, as seen from the port Bridge wing.*

"the rhythmic ease of a cruising yacht," it was observed by one passenger. Indeed, when the ship's run was calculated at noon on Wednesday, it was found that despite the poor conditions, she had made her best run of the crossing to that point: some 530 miles.

By noon of Thursday, she had only covered another 523 miles. At last, the poor weather cleared, and although temperatures were quite chilly, the sky was clear, the sea was smooth, and there was only a light breeze from the east. At this point in the crossing, it began to become obvious that the transatlantic passage was nearing its end. On Thursday evening, Bull Rock off the southern coast of Ireland came into view. At 1:20 a.m. Friday morning, she passed Brow Head, another prominent Irish landmark. This signpost made it clear that Queenstown was only seventy miles ahead.

On Thursday evening, Captain Watt authorized a statement to be sent via wireless to the anxious press syndicates ashore. In part, it said: "Our maiden homeward passage has been satisfactory in every respect. The machinery has behaved magnificently throughout, and has performed its full duty without a single flaw … We attempted no record on our maiden voyages except the record of landing our passengers safe and happy." The ship covered the last 336 miles, arriving at Daunt's Rock at 3:56 a.m.; she thereupon entered the Irish harbor for the second time, setting up a routine that would last for much of her career. She had made the eastbound passage in 5 days, 4 hours and 19 minutes at an average of only 22.58 knots.

Once the ship departed Queenstown Harbour on Friday morning, Captain Watt decided to give his ship a full-throttle blast of high speed. Leaving at about 7 a.m., the ship surged forward, covering the 228 miles at an average speed of 25 knots and arriving in Liverpool at around 4 p.m. She landed her passengers in short order, and it was noted that those proceeding to the capital by the London & North Western Rail company arrived there just a bit after 9 p.m., not at all an unreasonable hour.

Because neither one of the *Lusitania*'s maiden crossings had taken the Blue Riband, many possible contributing factors to the ship's "failure" were advanced in the press at the time: these ranged from the fog and poor weather to stoker complacency and poor-quality coal. Even so, it is clear that the Cunard Company and Captain Watt never intended to drive the ship at full speed in either direction; there is simply no other way to interpret the data. However, it was also clear that in order to demonstrate that the *Lusitania* was indeed the fastest ship in the world, the upcoming crossings would have to be significantly faster – they would have to recapture the Blue Riband for England, if the weather cooperated.

Behind the scenes, the Germans were desperate to find out everything they could about the *Lusitania*'s powerplant. They had already begun to plan a response to the *Lusitania* and her forthcoming sister *Mauretania*, but in order to leapfrog ahead of the new Cunarders, they needed to divine everything that they possibly could about them. Many Cunard representatives had taken passage on the German record-breakers when they had first made their debut on the North Atlantic, trying to learn their secrets. The Germans thus decided to send a delegation of a dozen or more engineers on the liner's upcoming westward passage, all traveling as passengers, and all of them keen to find out information about the *Lusitania*'s breathtaking powerplant.

After being given a thorough turnaround in Liverpool between Friday, September 27 and Saturday, October 5, the great *Lusitania* was ready to embark on her next crossing of the Atlantic. Departing Liverpool, she made a swift 24-knot run out to Queenstown. After stopping briefly there, she took to the Atlantic with 1,994 passengers and crew aboard, only 96 fewer than had been aboard for the highly anticipated maiden voyage. She passed Daunt's Rock at 10:25 a.m. Captain Watt opened the speed-queen up on the ocean for the first time; the muzzle had at last been removed, and the liner was now lunging forward with the *Deutschland*'s record fixed firmly in her sights. Vibration astern was noted to be quite strong, a sure sign that the ship was moving at a high rate of speed. By noon she had logged 41 miles at a speed of 25.9 knots.

The Atlantic tossed rain, a westerly wind and heavy seas her way before Sunday evening was over, as if attempting to spoil the *Lusitania*'s plans, but it did not last for long; once she had cleared that stretch of poor conditions, things remained mostly clear for the rest of the crossing, with the exception of a slight fog on the morning of Wednesday, October 9. By noon on Monday, October 7, the ship had logged an additional 590 miles – only three miles short of the best run that she had made on her maiden westbound crossing three weeks previously, and a mere eleven miles short of the best day's run to date, made by the *Deutschland*.

Down below, the stokehold crew toiled in conditions that could only be called hellish. Temperatures in the four boiler rooms were astoundingly high; as the stokehold indicators sounded their relentless high-speed gong, the stokers opened the furnace doors and shoveled what seemed like endless quantities of coal into the furnaces before slamming the doors shut again. Wheelbarrow after wheelbarrow, shovelful after shovelful … aft, in the Engine Room, Chief Engineer Duncan watched the pressure gauges rise and kept a careful eye on the turbines as they spun at the upper ends of their designed rpm's. Would the ship break the best day's record run? The crew knew that if conditions held through the night and the next morning, the *Lusitania* was easily capable of doing so.

At noon on Tuesday, the ship's officers fixed the ship's position and calculated the day's run; immediately thereafter, they posted it in the companionways and Smoking Rooms across the ship for passengers blue with anticipation to see. The post told the tale: the *Lusitania* had traveled 608 miles since noon the previous day at an average speed of 24.32 knots. She had taken down the *Deutschland*'s record by seven miles. Passengers were described as "enthusiastic" upon receiving the news; the Blue Riband was a big step closer. Celebrations aboard even made it down into the usually all-business stokeholds. A bottle of ale was given "on the house" to each of the 323 members of the Boiler Room crew. This thoughtful generosity helped to celebrate an event which would not have been possible without the stokers' hard work and skill.

Just as on the previous westbound crossing, betting in the ship's pool was enthusiastic. At 9 o'clock each night in the Smoking Room, the auction was held and the wagers were placed. This time, however, high bidding seemed justified. On Tuesday evening, Colonel James Elverson bought the high number for $125. Over the night and through the next morning, the ship surged forward through the ocean. The ale given the stokers did wonders for the ship's speed, and when the run was posted on Tuesday, the ship had made 617 knots. Her position was 44 °north latitude by 54 °west longitude; her average speed for the previous day was some 24.76 knots. Perhaps moved by the alcohol they had received the previous evening, and the hope of more to come, the stokers had managed to wring another nine miles' worth out of the ship's machinery. Colonel Elverson took over six

SCHEDULE B.

FORM OF PASSENGER LIST.

6

SHIP'S NAME.	MASTER'S NAME.	Tons per Register.	Aggregate number of superficial feet in the several compartments set apart for Passengers, other than 1st Class Passengers.	Total number of Statute Adults, exclusive of Master, Crew, and Cabin Passengers, which the Ship can legally carry.	WHERE BOUND.
Lusitania	Jas B Watt	8514	19609	1220	New York

I hereby Certify that the Provisions actually laden on board this Ship are sufficient, according to the requirements of the Passengers' Act, for 1200 Statute Adults, for a voyage of 24 days.

Queenstown, Date 6th Oct 1907 (Signature) W Watt Master.

NAMES AND DESCRIPTIONS OF PASSENGERS.

N.B.—1st Class Passengers must also be included in this Schedule, after the other Passengers. Sec. 6 of 26 and 27 Vict., Cap. 51.

An official passenger manifest, filed in Queenstown on the ship's second westbound crossing. Signed personally by Captain Watt, the form also gives the "Tons per Register" as 8,514, the "Aggregate number of superficial feet in the several compartments set apart for Passengers, other than 1st Class Passengers" as 19,609, and the "Total number of Statute Adults, exclusive of Master, Crew, and Cabin Passengers, which the Ship can legally carry" as 1,220.

hundred dollars for his wager on the high number the previous night.

This second consecutive record-breaking run amply demonstrated that the *Lusitania* and her crew seemed highly determined to take back the Blue Riband; it further pointed, if conditions held, to a significant lowering of that record by the time Sandy Hook was reached. Naturally, based on the data from the ship's informal and formal trials, Captain Watt and his officers as well as Chief Duncan and his men knew just how fast the *Lusitania* was. Now, however, it was clear to everyone that the ship was every bit as fast as her trials had indicated she would be. Looking at these figures at a century's remove also demonstrates just how much Captain Watt and his officers had kept the *Lusitania* reigned-in during her maiden crossings.

The news of this second day of record-making was greeted in England with what could, with some reserve, be called great enthusiasm. The London offices of the Cunard Line posted an official notice advertising the remarkable 617-knot run. British newspapers speculated that the success of the *Lusitania* in returning the Blue Riband to the British Empire was almost a certainty. In New York, on Thursday, Vernon H. Brown said that the *Lusitania* still wasn't being pushed; she was, as he put it, "just jogging along." He denied that the liner was attempting to make a record, which was of course utter rubbish, but he did promise: "When the Cunard officials feel the time is ripe, then you will see what the *Lusitania* can really do in the way of speed."

If the stokers had been hoping for a second round of ale "on the house," they were to be disappointed Wednesday night when none appeared. That night, rumors abounded that a drop in speed the next day was to be expected due to this regrettable lack of celebratory refreshment, and the low number went to Colonel Elverson for $175. Showing that shipboard rumors often do have a base in fact, the ship's run at

This view of the Lusitania, *taken as she steamed up the North River toward Pier 54, was taken on her second arrival. She was now officially the fastest ship in the world.*

noon the next day was exactly 600 miles; her position was 41 °north latitude by 66 °west longitude, and her average speed for the entire crossing from Daunt's Rock had, to that point, been some 24.12 knots.

Colonel Elverson took $836 for his wager the previous evening. One of the ship's officers did his best to explain that the lower run had absolutely nothing to do with the supply of ale being cut off; instead, he pointed to the fact that with the coal supplies being much lower, it would take more work to get the fuel to the boilers, and that this might account for the change. Even with this slightly reduced run, it was still clear that nothing but an accident could prevent the ship from taking back the Blue Riband. Even the weather was co-operating, being clear and calm, with no further trace of fog.

At 5:25 p.m., New York time, the *Lusitania* charged past the Nantucket Lightship at nearly twenty-five knots. The passengers lined the rails and watched with great interest as they passed the moored vessel – a sure symbol of New York's proximity – at a range of only a mile and a quarter.

At dinner that evening, George Croydon Marks, M.P., a 49-year-old First Class passenger and representative of North Cornwall, was greatly moved by the *Lusitania*'s accomplishment. Since he was an engineer as well as a politician, Marks must have known full well just how certain it was that the liner was about to take the Blue Riband. In the great double-decked Dining Saloon, Marks gave a congratulatory speech. At one point, he turned to the dozen or so German engineers who were aboard, and pointed to them. His voice was shaking with emotion as he said: "England once more rules the sea; and we have to thank not only Mr. Parsons, who perfected the turbine, but the Cunard line and the British Government which financed this magnificent undertaking despite the sneers of German engineers, such as are now aboard this vessel taking notes and gathering information on the advanced science in shipbuilding."

A little later that evening, the ship's concert was held. Donations totaling $115 were made for the firemen and stokers, a special bonus of appreciation from the passengers to the crewmen who made their already record-

Above: *A beautiful wide-angle photograph of the Lusitania pulling into Pier 54 at the conclusion of her second westbound crossing. She was now officially the fastest ship in the world. The area parallel to the waterfront on the right side of the berth, looking north, would eventually become the Henry Hudson Parkway. Popularly called the "West Side Highway," the Henry Hudson is a main artery for traffic through New York City. The new pier structures, when completed, would hide the waterfront from those outside. The photograph might have been taken from the Strauch Bros. Piano Action factory visible in the photograph at the top of page 139.*

ABSTRACT OF LOG OF THE
Cunard Royal Mail Steamship "LUSITANIA,"
(CAPTAIN J. B. WATT)

FROM LIVERPOOL TO NEW YORK.

Date, 1907.			Distance.	Latitude.	Longitude.	Winds.
Saturday	Oct.	5	—			Left Liverpool Stage at 7-48 p.m.
Sunday	,,	6	228	To Q'stown		Arrived Queenstown at 7-45 a.m.
	,,	,,	41	From Daunt's	Rock L'ship.	Left Daunt's Rock 10-25 a.m.
Monday	,,	7	590	51·01 N	24·54 W	N W'ly
Tuesday	,,	8	608	48·38 ,,	40·10 ,,	S W'ly W'ly
Wednesday	,,	9	617	44·40 ,,	54·00 ,,	W'ly
Thursday	,,	10	600	41·20 ,,	66·02 ,,	W'ly N E'ly
	,,	,,	131	To Nantucket	Lightship.	
Friday	,,	11	193	To Sandy	Hook L'ship	1-17 a.m. Sandy Hook L'ship abeam
From Daunt's Rock L'ship to Sandy Hook L'ship			2780			AVERAGE SPEED 24·00

PASSAGE :
Daunt's Rock Lightship to Sandy Hook Lightship :—4 Days, 19 Hours, 52 Minutes.
ALL PASSENGER STEAMERS OF THE CUNARD LINE ARE FITTED WITH MARCONI'S SYSTEM OF WIRELESS TELEGRAPHY.

master of the ocean highway, and this English victory is one in which the whole world joins." He added: "We Americans also are in on the victory."

Colonel James Elverson, Jr., of Philadelphia – who in just four years' time would become the editor of *The Philadelphia Inquirer* – expressed his sentiments that the *Lusitania* was a magnificent achievement. Indeed, he felt that she was the noblest and best-appointed steamship afloat. George C. Marks, M.P., was also generous with his praise: "The idea of 'hands across the sea' has never been better exemplified than tonight. This trip is an international achievement, untinged with envy." Thanks were due to the stokers, to Thomas Edison, "the wizard of America," "some of the most persevering of the scientists of England," and Mr. Marconi, for contributing wireless communication. He also paused to "congratulate the Cunard Company on its perseverance and indomitable pluck. It is easy to copy, but very difficult to initiate; all the world may now copy this splendid ship."

Meanwhile, even as the concert and speeches wrapped up, the great liner continued forward on the last leg of her dash to New York. The vessel came into sight of Fire Island at 11:22 p.m., and passed the landmark at 12:07 a.m. on the morning of Friday, October 11. Then the final 324 miles of the voyage were completed; the ship arrived at Sandy Hook Lightship at 1:17 a.m. The *Lusitania* had made the 2,780-mile journey in 4 days, 19 hours and 52 minutes. The previous record crossing by the *Deutschland* had been at 23.15 knots; the *Lusitania* had averaged 24.002 knots, over three-quarters of a knot better. The westbound Blue Riband had returned to Great Britain for the first time in nearly a decade. It was also, simultaneously, the first time that a transatlantic passage had been made in less than 5 full days; she was hailed the "first of the four-day liners."

Because the Ambrose Channel was still not open to use without the benefit of daylight, the liner anchored about four miles off Sandy Hook until she could make her entrance to the Port of New York. With the arrival of dawn, and with the Harbor Pilot aboard, the liner moved up the channel, emerging from the cut after 7:00 and arriving at Quarantine by 7:40. After this pause, she resumed her journey north, reaching Pier 54 at 10:30 a.m. and tying up.

Passengers were liberal with their praise for the world's fastest ocean liner. Particularly telling, perhaps, was the fact that Mrs. Isaac (Julia Barnett) Rice, who had founded the "Society for the Suppression of Unnecessary Noise" the previous year, was pleased with her trip aboard the liner. Others stepping down the gangplank that morning included Senator Hale, returning from England after having gone out on the *Lusitania*'s

breaking passage possible. Indeed, it was suggested by one present following the concert's conclusion that an actual stoker be called up to accept the fund; not long after, an Irish stoker named Garry appeared, mumbled a few words of thanks, and proceeded to begin lighting his pipe. Purser Lancaster quickly ordered the man below for his impudence. It was later revealed that "Garry the Stoker" was none other than First Class passenger Bransby Williams, an actor and famous impersonator of Dickens characters. The performance, the garb, the accent – it had all been so well done that everyone, including officers who had not been told about the skit, were fooled into thinking that he was a real stoker.

There were also speeches given in honor of the powerful liner. Colonel H. I. Kowalski of San Francisco was the Chairman of the concert. He said that although the passengers applauded the *Deutschland* "as the pacemaker," they cheered the *Lusitania* for "beating her in this heroic struggle to wrest from the German giant the blue ribbon for speed. The lion is again

Above: *A stunning bow-on photograph of the liner at Pier 54 during an early stay in New York. It is easy to see how the great ship captured the attention, the fascination, and the admiration of the world in her first few months of service.*

Below: *This stunning and ultra-rare photograph was taken in Liverpool between the* Lusitania*'s second and third round-trip voyages. It shows the two Cunard fliers together for the first time. The* Lusitania *was, by this point, the fastest ocean liner in the world; the* Mauretania *was about to undergo drydocking prior to her official trials. Judging from the known dates for the movement of both the* Lusitania *and the* Mauretania*, the picture could only have been taken between October 25 and November 2, 1907. Soon would begin an unprecedented, if good-natured, competition between the sisters for record speeds.*

previous eastbound crossing; Viscount de Alte, Portuguese Minister to Washington; and the Honourable Claude Brabazon, a member of the British Aero Club who would soon be engaging in a 24-hour balloon flight between St. Louis, Missouri and Sabina, Ohio.

Inevitably, the reporters searched out and found Captain Watt himself. One asked: "What do you think of the *Lusitania?*"

He responded, "She's a daisy."

Another question followed rapidly: "Can she do better than this?"

With typical wit and good-humor, he replied, "Isn't this good enough?" Indeed, Watt, Chief Duncan, and others knew that the *Lusitania* was capable of even more.

As promised during the *Lusitania*'s maiden stay in New York, Cunard opened the ship up to visitors much more during this turnaround. On Wednesday, October 16, a crowd of up to 15,000 persons – there were so many that an accurate head-count proved impossible – were allowed aboard. There was so much chaos around the pier that it was reported that a woman actually fainted from over-stimulation.

After staying in New York for parts of eight days, the *Lusitania* began her return trip to England on Saturday, October 19, 1907. Three thousand gathered at her pier in Lower Manhattan to see her on her way, cheering wildly as Captain Watt time and again bowed graciously from his Bridge. She departed at 3:30 p.m. carrying 429 First Class, 340 Second Class, and 850 Third Class passengers, and passed Sandy Hook Lightship at 5:44 p.m. Ahead of her was the return voyage to Queenstown – and the eastbound record of the *Kaiser*

Wilhelm II of 23.58 knots. It was now clear to everyone that the *Lusitania* was capable of taking this record down. Although Captain Watt again stated that he was not going to push for a record, he did not think it unlikely that if the weather held she could take the eastbound Blue Riband, as well. Proof positive of such an attempt rested in the ship's coal bunkers; they were filled with a surplus of fuel so that she could perform at her maximum for a sustained period of time.

Although the weather was initially clear and fine, it grew poor quickly and stayed that way for two days, with strong southeasterly gales and high head seas. Even after those two days, when things eased up a bit, the seas remained heavy and the winds remained strong. Additionally, the ship also encountered heavy fog off Fastnet, Ireland. To noon on Sunday, *Lusitania* had made 405 knots, and this was followed by runs of 570, 540, and 532 by noon on Wednesday. By noon on Thursday, she had added another 570 miles, leaving only 190 further miles before she arrived at Daunt's Rock. Her navigation was spot on, exactly matching the 2,807-mile distance of her original eastbound crossing.

She arrived at the official end-point of the course at 9:37 p.m. on Thursday evening, October 24, 1907. Her time over the course was 4 days, 22 hours and 53 minutes at an average speed of 23.61 knots - .03 knots' higher average than the record which had been held by the *Kaiser Wilhelm II*. The *Lusitania* had beaten her own last eastbound crossing's time by 5 hours and 26 minutes, and her average speed for the entire crossing was just over a full knot better than she had made before. Arriving at Queenstown in the late evening of Thursday was far preferable to arriving there in the middle of the night, as she had on the last crossing. Even more astounding was the fact that all of these successes had been made despite poor weather – weather much more agitated than it had been on the previous eastbound trip.

Despite having already proved to be the world's largest, most comfortable, and fastest ship, Captain Watt and Mr. Duncan next showed that the liner had a lot more left in her. If a sense of routine was beginning to set in for Captain Watt and his officers and men, the upcoming crossing would go on to show that on the North Atlantic, nothing is ever routine.

The *Lusitania* began her third westbound crossing on Saturday evening, November 3, 1907, with a highly respectable booking, some 2,037 passengers in all. Included in this number were some from theatrical circles, most notably Mrs. Patrick (Beatrice) Campbell, her son Allan Urquhart, and Miss Julia Marlowe. 42-year-old Mrs. Campbell had made her stage debut in 1888, making her first appearance on Broadway only five years before. Her fame was unmatched, however, and in 1914,

Above: *Mrs. Patrick Campbell.*

Below: *John Dunlop of John Brown & Company.*

Right: *The arched boom rest on the Forecastle was destroyed by a monstrous sea on her third westbound crossing.*

Below: *This photograph shows the* Lusitania *entering New York during the first few months of service. A chute for the mails can be seen dangling from the Shelter Deck gangway doors. Passengers line the Boat Deck, and are especially in evidence underneath the Bridge.*

she would even go on to play the role of Eliza Doolittle in George Bernard Shaw's play *Pygmalion*. She was a shoe-in for the role since, although she was far older than the character, Shaw had written the part of Eliza specifically for her. Julia Marlowe was 41 years of age during the crossing, an English-born American actress noted for her Shakespearean portrayals, and also for her divorce in 1900 from her first husband, Robert Taber. Also aboard for the trip was Baron von Hengelmüller, the Austrian Ambassador to the United States, and his wife, as well as James B. Reynolds, Assistant Secretary of the U.S. Treasury. Another passenger for the crossing was John Dunlop, the Chairman of John Brown & Company, which had built the ship.

Purser Lancaster also had a very unique cargo under his direct supervision. Just prior to departure from the Prince's Stage, a special train had arrived from London. Carried on this train was some £2,472,230 of gold – worth some $12,361,150 in United States dollars at the time, or more than $250,000,000 in today's U.S. dollars. This was the largest single shipment of gold bullion aboard a liner in history up to that time, and the press had dubbed the *Lusitania* a "treasure ship." Most of this gold had only just arrived from South Africa the previous week for refining. Spread out over fifteen consignments, this particular shipment was going to the United States Treasury and U. S. bankers in order to make up for a sudden demand for currency there. This demand was so pressing that the Americans made the purchase from the British despite a currency disadvantage of almost five to one – £1 for $4.90 as of the stock market's close on Friday, November 2, to be exact.

One after another, some 334 wooden boxes sealed with iron security strips were manhandled off of the train and up the gangplank to the ship's Strong Room on the Lower Deck. Purser Lancaster watched as each box came aboard and carefully ticked each, in turn, off on his list. Once the consignment was safely stowed away and under lock, Lancaster gave a receipt to the head of the bullion bankers' delegation, who had primary responsibility for the consignment's safety. With the passing of that single receipt, it was now the Cunard Line that bore the liability for the safety of the gold. That accountability ultimately fell on Captain Watt, but it landed even more squarely on Purser Lancaster's shoulders. Once the ship had taken to the sea, there was not an awful lot to worry about in the way of thievery; where, one asks, would a thief aboard ship go, whilst carrying heavy gold bars, in the middle of the Atlantic? The ship did have to reach her destination safely, however, and it all had to be unloaded on the other side safe and sound. Until Lancaster could pass another receipt to those responsible for the cargo in New York, it was his charge.

The Cunard "treasure ship" made it to Queenstown by Sunday morning, departing from there at 11:30 a.m. By noon, she had logged 21 nautical miles at 24.24 knots; to noon on Monday, she had steamed 606 miles at an average speed of 24.28 knots; by Tuesday, 616 miles at 24.6 knots; by Wednesday, an additional 618 at 24.8 knots; at noon on Thursday, 610 more at 24.52 knots. Things seemed to be going very well.

Unfortunately, the weather had other ideas. Through Thursday and Friday, the liner came straight into a cyclone, steaming not through the perimeter of the tempest, but through its center. The *Lusitania* had seen rough weather before, but this was her first trial by fire in some of the foulest weather that the North Atlantic could toss her way. "It was as though all the demons of the deep pursued us," Captain Watt later recalled. The worst of it came at 4 p.m. on Thursday, November 7. Steaming through seas that were as high as her Bridge – or roughly sixty feet – the ship buried her nose in one of the waves, whereupon the wave crested and collapsed on her forward decks. John Dunlop, of John Brown, was no doubt keenly interested in the behavior and sturdiness of his firm's handiwork. He said that the ship shook from bow to stern as this sea crashed into her Bridge; it imploded three of the heavy-duty windows overlooking the Forecastle and twisted off the arched steel cargo boom rest on the bow; it next tossed spindrift higher than the forward funnel. On the Bridge, the First Officer was cut by flying glass, but his injuries were, fortunately, not severe. Although the overall situation was very trying, it was later reported that the *Lusitania* had reached every expectation of behavior. Later reports that the members of the crew toiling in the Boiler and Engine Rooms would never have supposed there had been a storm may have been slightly exaggerated; quite telling, however, is the fact that the ship maintained an average speed of over twenty-two knots despite this punishment.

The gyrations aboard were severe enough to cause the cancellation of the ship's concert on Thursday night, a regular highlight of each passage; this cancellation was especially disappointing since some of the theatrical people aboard were slated to perform in it. Despite the rough weather, Mrs. Patrick Campbell offered a reward of £100 to the members of the Engineering Department if they could stoke the fires enough to get the ship to Sandy Hook before midnight. Through Thursday night and Friday, the ship forged determinedly forward, carrying two thousand passengers, over eight hundred crewmembers, and some $12.3 million in gold bullion.

It was not until after the ship passed the Nantucket Lightship on Friday that the weather began to ease up a bit. She steamed the last 310 miles at 22.09 knots, arriving at Sandy Hook at 1:40 a.m. on Friday morning, November 8. She had thus averaged 24.25 knots over a 2,781-mile course in 4 days, 18 hours and 40 minutes. That she had cut 42 minutes and added roughly a quarter of a knot to her overall average speed over her previous record was pleasing enough. That she had done this despite a southerly gale during her last full day was even more astounding. Although the stokers were no doubt disappointed that they had not received Mrs. Campbell's reward by reaching Sandy Hook before midnight, it was no small point of satisfaction to be able to show that despite the battering, the liner had come through safely and in good time.

In New York, Thursday evening had been a marked contrast to the scenes on board the *Lusitania*. Notably, Anton Bruckner's (1824-1896) unfinished 9th Symphony in D Minor had debuted at Carnegie Hall, performed by the Boston Symphony Orchestra. It was a fitting way to open their concert season, and was well received. But on Friday morning, the excitement shifted, and once again focused on the mighty *Lusitania* as she pulled into her West Side pier.

Burly longshoremen moved toward the liner, climbed up the freight gangplank and headed toward the Strong Room. There, Purser Lancaster had a brief conference with the American representatives of the consigners before unlocking the doors to allow for offloading. Two men took each box, straining under the boxes' great weight as they went down the gangplank. The Purser, now standing on the pier, dutifully checked off each box as they went; two others backed him up, to ensure an accurate count. A special fence-

Above: *Navigating close to shore during her first year of service.*

Below: *A very early photograph of the* Lusitania *being maneuvered in one of Liverpool's Canada docks. Probably taken on July 22, 1907 (compare with the picture at the top of page 63), as the liner was leaving the Canada Dry Dock for the first time, this photo shows a number of interesting features. The stiffening members introduced along the edges of the Promenade and Shelter Decks in Second Class are clearly visible. At this point, there were only two such stiffeners. Two further sets would be introduced shortly thereafter. As in the other photo, the Cunard tender* Skirmisher *can be seen alongside. A number of ladies also stand on the deck, underneath the stern Docking Bridge. Notice that the propeller bumpers are in place during the movement of the ship.*

enclosed portion of the pier, close to the river, was set aside as a temporary landing stage for the gold. Spectators on the pier lined the rail, watching as the largest single shipment of gold ever carried aboard an ocean liner was unloaded.

Once the entire shipment had been discharged, and the count had been tallied and double-checked, Purser Lancaster signed the second receipt, passing responsibility for the gold back to the consigners. The gold was next moved from the pier to waiting trucks, where it would subsequently go to the Sub-Treasury and the Assay Office for distribution. The "treasure ship" reverted to the mere mortal status of "world's largest and fastest." Visibly sweating although he had not been doing any of the manual labor, Purser Lancaster was manifestly relieved as he wiped his brow. He said, "My, I am glad that's off my hands. Now I can go to luncheon."

The ship remained in New York until Saturday, November 16. Interestingly, on the day she left that

An early photograph of the Lusitania's *sister and competitor, the* Mauretania. *The two vessels were in a league of their own for several years on the North Atlantic, but the* Lusitania *was hard pressed to keep up with her sister's records.*

port for the third time, the *Lusitania* lost the title of "world's largest ship" in service; that very evening, her slightly larger sister *Mauretania* departed Liverpool on her maiden voyage. Immediately, the new ship seemed destined to take records away from the *Lusitania*. Not only was she larger and longer than her older sister, but she was also carrying what was now the largest consignment of gold ever carried on an ocean liner, some $12.9 million dollars' worth. Because of the miserable weather she encountered westbound, however – a trip that has now become infamous in the annals of maritime history – she did not take the Blue Riband from the *Lusitania* on that crossing.

At the same time that the *Mauretania* was picking her way westward through monstrous weather and enormously rough seas, the *Lusitania* was fighting her way east through the same weather. Despite the storms, she made very respectable time, comparable with her second eastbound trip. When she reached Queenstown at 8:25 p.m. on Thursday, November 21, the weather was still poor, and Queenstown Harbour was nothing if not tempestuous. Two tenders were sent to intercept the *Lusitania*, but the weather was so rough that after two hours of maneuvering, they had to give up altogether on the idea of coming alongside her. Instead, one of the *Lusitania*'s own lifeboats was lowered, took on the Liverpool pilot and the Queenstown dispatches, and then returned to the ship. Unable to land her Irish-bound passengers and mail, the *Lusitania* departed for Liverpool.

The *Lusitania* had set the standard, taking the Blue Riband in each direction after only a month of service. Yet, there was reason for the *Lusitania*'s crew to believe that they might be hard-pressed to keep up with the new liner. During the *Mauretania*'s sea trials, she managed to achieve speeds higher than those realized by her older sister during her trials. The *Mauretania*'s crew was also quite keen to beat the *Lusitania*. During the "*Mary*'s" trials, there were some "exciting moments" in the stokehold. One observer recorded:

The [*Mauretania*'s] men came from the north-east coast, and there was a powerful manifestation of rivalry between the Tynesiders and their comrades on the Clyde, who had been out with the *Lusitania* some weeks previously over the self-same course. I was in the stokehold while the *Mauretania* was running round the north end of Scotland on her way to enter the measured distance and test. The ship was running easy at the time, and a gang of eager giants of the black squad had gathered before one of the boilers which at the time was not working, and were holding forth strenuously upon the speed merits of the two ships. A stoker who hailed from South Wales, and accordingly had no interest in either riversides [*sic*], started the argument by extolling the performance of the *Lusitania* over the 1,400 miles round trip. He worked his north country comrades to such a pitch that at last one of the brawniest wielders of the stokehold shovel bawled out, "Look you 'ere, mate, we'll lick the '*Lucy*', even if we bust the '*Mary*' to do it!" To which there was such a vociferous and enthusiastic "Aye! Aye!" that I knew the *Mauretania* was destined to be put through her paces with a vengeance … and there was a shake of the head which told me that it would not be their fault if the liner did not do something striking. No brawn and muscle were spared on that 48-hours run in tossing the huge shovelfuls of coal from bunker to boiler furnace; the engineer never had the least doubt about the pressure of the steam within the boilers; the black squad below were seeing to that, because the pride and glory of Tyneside were at stake.[24]

Despite her failure to take the prize on her westbound maiden crossing, in returning to Europe the *Mauretania* took the eastbound Blue Riband from her older sister, making the passage in 4 days, 22 hours and 29 minutes at an average speed of 23.69 knots. The *Lusitania*'s best time over the same 2,807-mile course, by comparison, had been 4 days, 22 hours and 53 minutes at an average speed of 23.61 knots, a difference of 24 minutes and .08 knots.

With that single act, the *Mauretania* started a friendly rivalry between the two liners. Now that the two sisters were both in service, there grew a keen competition to see which of the two could take the record. Ultimately, it did not matter to the British – and to a lesser extent, the Americans as well – which of the ships held the Blue Riband; more important was that the Germans were strictly out of the race. However, to many, especially those who had a particular favorite between the two sisters, it was very important which ship held the prize. This was particularly true of each ship's respective crew and officers. It was also a competition between an English-built ship and a Scotch-built one, and this tended to raise some level of fervor between the two countries' citizens.

It has often been asked which of the two sisters was faster. The short answer is that it was the *Mauretania*. The long answer is involved; perhaps a brief review of some of the records made by each ship, in turn, would help to explain this.

Once the *Mauretania* had taken the eastbound Blue Riband, it seemed like the North Atlantic tried everything to prevent her from next taking the westbound honor; throughout the winter and early spring there were terrible storms, fog, high winds. Then, on April 11, 1908, *Mauretania* left Queenstown and, taking the long course to avoid icebergs, steamed 2,889 nautical miles to Sandy Hook in 4 days, 23 hours and 59 minutes. Her average speed was 24.08 knots, and she had

clipped a single minute, just sixty seconds, from the *Lusitania*'s best westbound record of 5 days flat. Now the *Mauretania* held both records.

The *Lusitania*'s crew didn't take well to this development; two westbound crossings later, the *Lusitania*'s nineteenth, she put up a valiant fight. First, on Wednesday, May 20, she set a daily record of 632 knots at a speed of 25.42. By the time she reached New York that Friday, she had steamed the same 2,889 nautical miles at an average speed of 24.83 knots, exactly three-quarters of a knot faster than her upstart sister. She had done the course in one hour and thirty-seven minutes less.

If the *Lusitania*'s crew thought they could relax, they were in for a shock. Just a week later, the *Mauretania* arrived in New York following her fifteenth crossing; she had made a great run and managed to recapture the prize from her older sister. She had shaved seven minutes off of the *Lusitania*'s time, steamed just one mile more over the same course, and had averaged .03 knots better. More astoundingly, the *Mauretania* did this on only three propellers, having damaged one of her port propellers earlier that month.

Clearly something would have to be done about that, the *Lusitania*'s crew must have grumbled. As bad as it was to lose the prize, it was just plain humiliating to lose it to a sister ship which was suffering from such a monumental handicap. To remedy the situation, she re-took the westbound prize on Crossing No. 23 west. When she reached Sandy Hook on July 10, she had taken 4 days, 19 hours and 36 minutes (an improvement over the *Mauretania* of 39 minutes) at an average speed of 25.01 knots. It was the first time that either ship had logged an entire voyage at an average over 25 knots; at the same time, this new record crossing had included a best day's record run of 643 nautical miles, some eight miles higher than the best that the *Mauretania* had logged to date. Just to make sure that the *Mauretania* stayed in second place, two westbound crossings later, the *Lusitania* beat her own record and brought the average speed up to 25.05 knots for the entire long course, logging a best day's record run of 650 nautical miles and making the whole crossing in 4 days and 15 hours flat.

The situation remained rather static all through the fall of 1908 and through the beginning of 1909; the *Mauretania* was in no condition to take back the *Lusitania*'s records on only three props. At the same time, the *Lusitania* simply could not take the *Mauretania*'s standing eastbound record. In September of 1908, the *Mauretania* damaged a second prop; it was promptly replaced, but the originally damaged one was not. Finally, at the end of October, 1908, the *Mauretania* was laid up and given entirely new outboard props; these new propellers were improved over her original screws in that they were made from a single-cast. Expectation was high that the rivalry would now resume, and when the *Mauretania* started her next crossing on January 24, 1909, it did.

The *Mauretania* did not take the westbound Blue Riband right out of the gate. On her return crossing, ending February 3, however, she lowered her own best time eastbound, bringing her average speed up to 25.20 knots; she maintained that average over 4 days, 20 hours and 27 minutes, steaming over the 2,934-mile long course. On her next westbound crossing, she then managed to take the Blue Riband back from the *Lusitania*. That new record crossing was 4 days, 17 hours and 6 minutes in duration – nearly two hours shorter than the *Lusitania's* best time over the long course. The average speed she made was 25.55 knots, exactly half a knot better than her older sister's best westbound speed. During that same crossing, she set a record for single day's steaming at 671 knots, 21 nautical miles better than the *Lusitania's* best day westbound. By August of 1909, the *Mauretania* had again increased that record to 25.84 knots.

Next came the return salvo from the Scotch vessel. On Saturday, August 28, 1909, the *Lusitania* left Liverpool on her fifty-ninth westbound crossing. Once she had cleared Daunt's Rock at Queenstown, she set her teeth into the task of taking back the westbound Blue Riband from her sister. She was armed with a quartet of new propellers that had been fitted during July; two four-bladed single-cast brass screw props

were on her outboard shafts, while two three-bladed manganese props were fitted inboard. Chief Engineer Duncan watched his equipment as the turbines drove the props into the water more and more quickly. For the first day, "the weather was rough, with a head sea …," her Captain, William Turner, recalled later, "… but after that we had a fine smooth passage." Turner took the ship across via the short course, inaugurating that run for the 1909 season; with this reduction in steaming distance, there was a possibility that the ship could land her passengers on Thursday night, rather than on Friday morning; if the liner could manage it, this would be a benchmark accomplishment.

One after another, the daily runs were posted: to noon Sunday, 61 miles; to noon Monday, 650; Tuesday, 652; and Wednesday, 651. On Wednesday, the weather deteriorated again, blowing first from the southeast before veering around all points to northwest. Captain Turner knew that this was beginning to slow the ship down – the question was, how much? Would she still be able to make a record crossing? That night it was obvious that she was steaming hard. The passengers were enthralled; at the concert that night, they unanimously adopted a resolution congratulating the Captain, Chief Engineer and crew on the record they felt sure was to be set, and noting their privilege to "cross in the steamship which breaks the transatlantic record between Europe and the United States."

The Lusitania *in the Mersey early on in her career.*

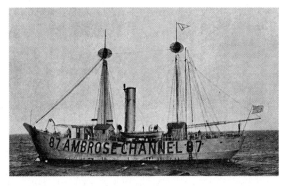

The Ambrose Channel Lightship.

Their optimism proved well-founded. At noon on Thursday a run of 647 was posted – only five miles short of the best run she had heretofore made during that crossing – in spite of the weather. The *Lusitania* triumphantly steamed the final 123 miles to the Ambrose Lightship, arriving there at 4:42 p.m., and having plenty of time to navigate up to her west side pier and land her passengers by eight o'clock that night. She had recaptured the prize, making the 2,783-mile passage in 4 days, 11 hours and 42 minutes at an average speed of 25.85 knots – just .01 knots higher than the *Mauretania's* newest record. The new propellers had given the liner the advantage she had needed, by a hair's breadth. As the victorious Cunarder steamed up New York's Upper Bay, past the Statue of Liberty – while the sun slowly set over the New Jersey skyline, illuminating the ship in a brilliant crimson evening's light – Captain Turner felt confident. Once he had docked, he told reporters that he thought that this record passage would "keep [Captain] John Pritchard busy with the *Mauretania* for a time."

Congratulations were offered from C. P. Sumner, the new General Agent for the Cunard Line in the United States, as well as from former General Agent Vernon Brown. Captain Turner replied to their sentiments with a sly smile, saying that he hoped to do even better in the future. Chief Engineer Duncan, beaming over the ship's triumph, refused "with the usual canniness of a Scot" to give out actual coal consumption figures during the trip. It was said "on good authority," however, that she had averaged 1,050 tons a day, including coal for the auxiliaries, or about 4,725 tons for the crossing.

Even with these new propellers and this new record, however, there was one detail of the passage that might have been unsettling to some: the best day's steaming by the *Lusitania* on this crossing had only been 652 miles – 21 less than the best day's westward steaming by the *Mauretania*. This significant

difference made it clear that even with the *Lusitania's* new props, she might still be unable to keep up with her younger sister.

In the end, the *Lusitania* only held the west-bound Blue Riband for a week. On the Saturday after the older sister had arrived in New York, the *Mauretania* left Liverpool and set her nose toward Queenstown; she departed there on Sunday, September 5, passing Daunt's Rock at 10:15 a.m., some fifteen minutes later than the *Lusitania* had on her previous crossing. The daily runs came in at 56, 653, 658, 643, 641 and 132. The ship arrived at the end-point for the crossing at 4:50 p.m., covering the same 2,783 miles as her sister, but shaving seven minutes off her sister's new record, at an average speed of 25.87. This was .02 knots better than the *Lusitania's* average. Although the weather overall had been more favorable to her than during her older sister's crossing, there was fog during the last day that held her up some two hours. She was also reportedly dealing with a poorer quality of coal, which was apparently full of stones. It was said that when Chief Engineer Currie reported this to Captain Pritchard, he replied with dismissive determination: "Never mind, Chief; we will beat the *Lusitania* even if we have only stones to get steam with," and he was right. Some months later, in March of 1910, and coming over the long course, the *Mauretania* upped the average westbound speed again, this time to 25.91 knots.

From September of 1909, the *Lusitania* was never able to take the Blue Riband from the *Mauretania* in either direction. This was not because she did not attempt to do so. On Crossing No. 75 West, March 19-25, 1910, she tried to take the coveted trophy, and this time she sported an even further improved set of propellers that were virtually identical to the *Mauretania's*. Earlier that same month, Chief Officer Sandy G. S. McNeil of the *Lusitania* talked to New York reporters about these props; he told them that he felt that with these new screws installed, the *Lusitania* would prove faster than her sister. Up to noon on Thursday, March 24, Chief Officer McNeil may have felt his point was being proved; the *Lusitania* was making excellent time. However, on the last day, she hit heavy fog and hopes for a record were dashed. Also telling was the fact that her best runs of the crossing before the fog were only 656 on Wednesday and 655 on Thursday. These still did not approach the *Mauretania's* best daily records.

Before the summer season was out, the *Mauretania* further reduced her westbound time over the short course, further complicating things for anyone hoping the *Lusitania* could take back the record. On her Crossing No. 79 West, beginning September 10, 1910,

Above: *The* Lusitania *entering Liverpool on an early crossing, passing the New Brighton Tower. Completed in 1900, the tower was over five hundred feet tall, and featured a ballroom underneath. Sadly, the tower was not maintained during the Great War, and was demolished between 1919 and 1921.*

Below: *This photograph shows the* Lusitania *at the Prince's Landing Stage, probably during 1909 or 1910. Construction on the Royal Liver building is progressing in the background, and would be finished by 1911.*

she took only 4 days, 10 hours and 41 minutes at an average speed of 26.06 knots. In this, she shaved off ten minutes from her previous record while showing the same average speed overall.

The late March, 1910 crossing of the *Lusitania*, during which she encountered poor weather, might sound like an unfair handicap. So what could the *Lusitania* do in perfect weather? On Crossing No. 91 West, September 17-22, 1910, she tried again and this question was answered. There were no difficulties or poor weather reported during the trip. However, when she arrived at Sandy Hook, she had only averaged 4 days, 13 hours and 26 minutes at an average speed of 25.40 knots; this was a full hour and forty-four minutes slower

than her own best time. Her highest run was only 647 miles. More proof came in after the turn of the New Year. On Crossing No. 99 West, in January of 1911, she again tried and failed to make a record. Despite the fact that she was favored by fair winds and smooth seas, the liner made the crossing in 4 days, 13 hours and 35 minutes, one of her fastest long-route passages ever, but still not fast enough to take the record from the *Mauretania*. Some fog had been encountered near the American coast, but the weather was reportedly not thick enough to retard her progress.

A stern view of the liner at the Landing Stage, probably around 1909 or early 1910.

Above: *A very busy scene at the Landing Stage, showing the frenzy that was arrival in or departure from Liverpool. The crane astern and the booms at the forward mast are in the process of being used, while a gangway connects both the First and Second Class sections of the ship to the shore.*

Below: *A photograph probably taken in early 1908 shows the alterations on the Forecastle deck. The forward anchor crane has been painted black rather than white, as it was during the maiden voyage. The original arched boom rest has been replaced, and only two booms are in evidence attached to the foremast.*

Lusitania or *Mauretania*:
Which Was More Popular?

Right from the start, there was competition in the making ... not between two enemies, but between two sisters striving toward a common goal. For starters, the two vessels had been built in different yards. The *Lusitania* was Scottish-built, while the *Mauretania* was English-built, forming a pride that fell along national boundaries within the United Kingdom. The *Lusitania* held the title of largest and fastest ship in the world from September through November of 1907. The *Mauretania*, however, was longer, wider, and heavier than her sister, and thus took the title of "world's largest" upon her entry into service. There was more to it than just the title of "world's largest," however. The crews of each wished to take the coveted titles of world's fastest and most popular, and in so doing they also served both the good of their owners and continued to establish British mercantile supremacy.

The *Mauretania* consistently triumphed over her sister's speed throughout their time in service together on the North Atlantic. It seemed that the *Mauretania* had bested her older Scottish-built sister in every sense ... save one: popularity. It has often been said that during their time together on the North Atlantic between late 1907 and the spring of 1915, the *Lusitania* was more popular with the traveling public – despite the fact that she was the marginally smaller, slower and older of the two sisters. Maritime writers, apparently at a loss to explain the reason for her apparent edge in popularity, gave credit to her "light" and "airy" interior décor in First Class. For many, many decades, that was the final word on the subject: the *Lusitania* was more popular with the traveling public and that was that.

But was she really?

There are a number of factors which might be weighed into a consideration of a ship's popularity. There is emotional attachment, both during a ship's life and in memoriam after they have passed from the rugged surface of the sea. This is certainly true of the *Titanic*, which sank on her maiden voyage and never completed a crossing of the Atlantic. Her much longer-lived sister *Olympic*, on the other hand, carried hundreds of thousands of passengers over a career that spanned parts of three decades. By comparison, the *Olympic* is vaguely remembered – if at all – as a ship that was nearly identical to the legendary lost liner.

A far more tangible way of ascertaining a ship's popularity, however, is to look at the numbers of passengers that they carried on their decks. Again, there are different ways of viewing the matter. For example, would one count the total number of passengers carried during their careers, or during their concurrent years of service only? Certainly the latter would seem to be the only fair way of doing things. However, what if the ships made a different number of crossings during the same year? What if one was laid up for some time, as the *Lusitania* was during the first half of 1913, while her sister continued plying the waves? Such circumstances would certainly distort the conclusion one way or another. However, if the vessels made a similar number of overall crossings during the period under examination, then the conclusions might not be so far off.

So let us examine the matter from the period when each liner entered service through to the end of the year 1914. By this standard of measurement, which of the ships proved more popular? From the time that she entered service in September of 1907 until the end of 1914, the *Lusitania* carried 240,959 passengers. The *Mauretania*, from the time she entered service in November of 1907 until the end of 1914, carried 247,971 passengers. By this method of calculation, the *Mauretania* came out some 7,012 passengers ahead of the *Lusitania*.

Some might still protest, however, saying that although the *Mauretania* came into the picture two months after her sister, that vessel was out of service for some time during 1913. Certainly if the *Lusitania* had been in service all through that time, she would have proved more popular, they would say. This leads us to our second method of calculation: to find an average of the number of passen-

Above: *This stunning view shows the two "Ocean Monarchs", as the photo was captioned, tied up alongside each other. The photograph was taken on October 14, 1909 in the Canada Dock during one of the rare times that the two sisters were together in port.*

Below: *A rare view taken as the* Lusitania *was being brought out Liverpool's Canada dock at the end of her October 1909 joint stay with her sister.*

gers carried per crossing for each ship. What do these numbers reveal?

From the start of her career in September of 1907 through the end of 1914, the *Lusitania* carried an average passenger list of 1,242. The *Mauretania*, from her maiden voyage in November of 1907 through the end of 1914, carried an average passenger list of 1,298. The average for the *Mauretania*, then, was higher than that of the *Lusitania* by some 56 persons.

After considering the matter very carefully, the truth becomes clear. The oft-told tale that the *Lusitania* was more popular because of her style of décor is nothing more than another old legend that has been repeated time and again until it has been accepted as reality. By both calculations, the *Mauretania* was a more popular ship than the *Lusitania* during their concurrent careers on the North Atlantic, although by a small margin.[25]

For four more years after that attempt – nearly half of her steaming career of 202 crossings or 101 round-trip voyages – she never took back the prize. After the Cunard Line reduced her speed by closing down her No. 4 Boiler Room in November of 1914, she did not get another opportunity to make an attempt at the Blue Riband. In 1932, Sandy McNeil – who served aboard the *Lusitania* from her fourth voyage in 1907 until the spring of 1911, and who later commanded the *Mauretania* between 1928 and 1931 – remembered in his memoirs that the *Mauretania* "was not a bit faster than the *Lusitania*." After reviewing the cold hard facts, however, it is clear that Mr. McNeil was mistaken. He mentioned that after eight voyages, the *Lusitania*'s propellers were improved, and that after that time, her speed improved significantly; he specifically recalled three voyages came in at "25.89 knots with only a decimal difference." However, by 1910, the *Mauretania*'s averages had crept above that mark, continuing to rise throughout her career, and she continued to hold the record until 1929.

Interestingly, the *Lusitania* did show that she still had a couple of remarkable tricks up her sleeve. In the late summer of 1911, a strike in Liverpool held up her scheduled departure from that port by eight days – a catastrophic delay for such a punctual service. She finally left on August 28, and began a marathon of back-to-back crossings in an attempt to put her schedule on track again. She returned to Liverpool on Saturday, September 9, holding a new record for a round-trip voyage across the Atlantic. She had managed the feat in just 11 days, 23 hours and 45 minutes – 12 hours and 32 minutes better than the *Mauretania*'s fastest round-trip record. This record was not due to any record-speed sailing – though, by necessity, her steaming was swift and the weather she encountered was favorable – but rather to an astounding 32 hour and 10 minute turnaround in New York. Still behind schedule, she departed Liverpool again on Monday, September 11, again after a very short stay in port, and arrived back in New York on Saturday, September 16. She had managed to cross the Atlantic three times in three weeks, and once she had made New York, her engines were finally given a rest and cooling-off period. That December, she again made another record-breaking round-trip – some 12 days and 17 hours over the long course – although this was again due more to a short turnaround than record sailing in either direction.

Perhaps even more astonishing was a feat that she managed in December of 1912. From the morning to the afternoon of Friday, December 19, she averaged 27 knots an hour; during that period, she charged for a full hour at close to 28 knots, making 207 revolutions in the process. Unfortunately, the high speed was not maintained throughout the entire crossing, or even through a full day's steaming; thus, this remarkable speed did not give her any tangible record. Even so, Captain Dow, her Commander at the time, described it as "her best work ... since she has been a ship," and added that he still thought it possible for the ship to make an Atlantic record.

In 1914, she did snatch one record back from the *Mauretania*. Eastbound, on Crossing No. 172, she established a new speed record for a single day's steaming in that direction. On March 12-13, she covered 618 knots at an average speed of 26.7 knots per hour, beating the *Mauretania*'s best eastbound day's steaming by four miles. Although Captain Dow had been confident of a new Atlantic record when he had left New York, the ship did not re-take the Blue Riband on that crossing. Her crew, however, was not about to give up. It was noted in *The New York Times* that they had "sworn with strange oaths in West Street, New York, and Scotland Road, Liverpool, to win the blue ribbon of the Atlantic for their countrymen and popular commander." When the war intervened only five months later, however, the records were still held by the *Mauretania*, and the *Lusitania*'s top-speed sailing days had pretty much reached their end. Having discussed the speed rivalry between the *Lusitania* and *Mauretania* in such close detail, there is now no question that the *Mauretania* had the advantage between 1907 and 1915; it is also clear that the *Lusitania* was hard on her heels all the way. Which ship could have proved faster after the War, when both were converted to oil, is a subject that is wide open to hypothetical debate.

Speed, however, was just one aspect of the *Lusitania*'s great career. On the North Atlantic, there is one primary enemy of speed, and that is the whims of mother nature herself. Most often, this capricious nature was manifested in fog, and quite frequently in simple "heavy weather," with a rolling sea. However, there were times when capriciousness turned to outright violence. This most often took place during those infamous winter months on the North Atlantic. Some of the weather that the *Lusitania* encountered during her career was downright breathtaking.

On Saturday, November 30, 1907, the *Lusitania* was preparing to depart Liverpool for Queenstown and New York; unfortunately, the Mersey was closed in with thick fog, and it was impossible for the ship to tie up at the Prince's Landing Stage to take on her passengers during the entirety of the day. By that night, waiting passengers were sent to local hotels;

Sunday morning, at 8:00 a.m., the liner was finally able to tie up at the stage and take on her passengers. She had just enough time to cast off and move out into the Mersey before the fog closed again, this time so thoroughly that she couldn't cross the bar and was forced to drop anchor. At 4:00 p.m., the fog lifted slightly, and over the next hour and a half, under the most careful pilotage, she managed to pick her way into open water. Even once this was accomplished, however, there was no way for her to make time in the thick weather, and it was Monday morning before she was able to drop anchor in Queenstown. She was, at that point, already a full day behind schedule.

If Captain Watt was expecting an improvement out on the North Atlantic, he was sorely disappointed. The ship had not traveled far from Queenstown when she encountered a westerly gale. From that point forward, the trip was an absolute nightmare, with one gale after another tossing the ship around like a child's toy. The Dining Saloon, normally the center of all shipboard activity, was virtually deserted. On Monday morning, a "mountainous sea" broke inboard and did a bit of damage to the ship. The bulwark of the forward Promenade Deck was dented, and the face of the Boat Deck deckhouse in the area of the Captain's Suite was heavily damaged. A support for one of the cargo booms was also twisted, and three of the booms went astray, taking a mast stay with them. Captain Watt was forced to stop the ship for several hours while repairs were made by brave crewmen weathering the elements on the exposed Forecastle. Off Cape Race, she found herself in the center of a cyclone sporting forty-foot seas. Wave after wave smashed over her bow, completely inundating the forward portion of the ship and sending spray higher than her funnels. The sight awed her officers; they felt that the waves were moving in "as though to bury" their ship. Captain Watt was impressed with what he saw, as well. When the ship docked safely in New York on Sunday, December 8, he said: "The weather was the worst I have experienced in years. We had every kind of a gale." He felt, however, that the *Lusitania* had behaved "admirably and proved her worth." Other ships fighting their way through the furious seas that week – like the American liner *Philadelphia*, the Hamburg-Amerikan Line ship *Amerika*, and the White Star liner *Cretic* – all suffered more severe damage and also had harrowing tales to tell.

In February of 1909, there was another astonishing storm that battered the *Lusitania*. Once again, the trouble began even before she had left Liverpool, where she had been in drydock for hull maintenance prior to the trip. When the time came, on Wednes-

day, February 3, to bring her out of drydock, gales moved in. The Mersey became much too rough for safe navigation, and it was decided that she should remain in drydock overnight. On Thursday, when the weather deteriorated instead of letting up, Cunard decided to prepare the *Lucania* in the speed queen's place. On Friday, there came a last-minute reprieve, and the *Lusitania* was cautiously eased out of the drydock and up to the Landing Stage. Once there, she began taking on coal and cargo, but even before this process was completed, fog closed the Mersey in completely. Her frustrated crew and passengers could do nothing but wait; in the event, the weather did not allow her to depart on Crossing No. 41 until nine o'clock Sunday morning. She fought her way to Queenstown in incredibly rough weather, and once she had arrived outside the entrance of the Irish port on Sunday evening, there was no sign of improvement. Captain Turner wisely decided not to enter the harbor until daylight, and dropped the starboard anchor in just over ten fathoms, or sixty feet, of water to wait. Astoundingly, at 10 p.m. that night, the 3¾-inch-diameter iron anchor chain parted because of the stresses imposed upon it. The port anchor was dropped in the hopes that it would hold better than its counterpart had; it did, and at daylight, the ship eased into harbor. There, she took on extra coal before leaving on Monday evening.

The poor weather continued right through Monday night and all during the day on Tuesday, and Turner nosed forward at a mere 14 knots. That night, the gale eased a bit, and the ship's speed was increased until noon on Wednesday, when the weather descended again with renewed vigor and a foul head sea. At five o'clock that afternoon, a tremendous wave – tall enough to stand over the upper Bridge – crashed over her bow. It struck with such force that the port-side steel crew ladder from the Promenade Deck to the Boat Deck was nipped cleanly from its bolted mounts; a piece of the teak rail on the forward Boat Deck was carved out, the rail on the port Bridge Wing was split, and the canvas windscreen and framework was torn away. The teak shutters for the Bridge windows were smashed, and the Bridge's structure was dented, as well. One First Class passenger, Andrew D. Provand, a former member of the Glasgow Parliament (Liberal), was nearly killed; standing on the forward Boat Deck against all better judgment, he saw the wave descending on him and turned to run. He reached the companionway and went to go inside, but slipped as he went, cutting his forehead as he entered the sheltered interior of the liner. Despite this punishment, the *Lusitania* was again reported to have

A very rare photograph taken from the Second Class decks of the Lusitania, *overlooking her fantail in bad weather. Although the* Lusitania *was one of the largest and fastest liners of the day, the raw power of the North Atlantic tested her mettle frequently throughout her career.*

"behaved splendidly." Only three passengers required the attention of the Ship's Surgeon for seasickness.

For centuries, sailors have reported run-ins with tremendous seas. One period reference work discussed waves of "'about 40 feet'" as a "common estimate of the height of the larger waves in a severe gale on the North Atlantic." However, it added:

> It is difficult to say what may be the greatest height of the solitary or nearly solitary waves that are from time to time reported by mariners. The casual combination of the numerous independent undulations running on the sea presumably sometimes produced two or three succeeding ridges or two or three neighboring domes of water of considerably greater dimensions than those of the ordinary maximum waves of a storm. Although these large cumulative waves may be frequently produced, yet they will be comparatively seldom observed, because so small a fraction of the ocean's surface is at one time under observation. There are seemingly reliable accounts of cases in which these "topping seas" have reached the height of 60 feet.[26]

In intervening decades, scientists began to scoff at these reports of "freak," "cumulative," "topping," or "rogue" waves; according to their mathematical computations, such waves could occur only once in ten millennia. In just the last few years, however, after incontrovertible evidence has come to light, they have begun to re-examine their conceptions on the matter. Indeed, the sixty-foot estimate referred to in this period publication is not by any means the maximum height of a rogue wave, and they can occur in poor weather or fair. Sailors who survived encounters with these waves reported that they would appear out of nowhere, as if by magic.

The wave which smashed into the *Lusitania* in February of 1909 was most likely one of these rogue waves. The North Atlantic had even more in store for the *Lusitania*, however. Looking back on the events of Monday evening, January 10, 1910, in latitude 51° north and longitude 23° west, during Crossing No. 71 West of the *Lusitania*, the pattern of a rogue wave seems to fit perfectly.

Only thirty-three hours out of Queenstown Harbour, the Cunarder was picking her way through the foul weather at fourteen knots. At 6 p.m., Captain Turner left the Bridge to go down to dinner, leaving Chief Officer McNeil in command. This was Turner's last round-trip voyage aboard the *Lusitania* before transferring to the *Mauretania*. When he left, the wind was out of the west – dead ahead – and the ship's bow was plowing through one mighty wave after another; Quartermaster Riddey was at the wheel within the enclosed Wheelhouse, Relief Quartermaster Harding was standing at his side, and Bridge Boy Tommy Hughes was present on the Bridge, as well. Third Officer Storey decided to brave the elements to climb up on the roof of the Bridge and read the compass there. No doubt all were relieved when the gangway door slid closed behind him, restoring a measure of calm to the Bridge.

Everything seemed foul but typical, but in a heartbeat, everything changed. First, the liner shipped a particularly solid swell, and her bow dropped down into the trough behind it. McNeil, already holding on for dear life, must have been horrified to see what was on the other side of the watery valley: an enormous "accumulative" wave. It was so mammoth that it shut out the sky and horizon from his vantage point, normally eighty feet above the water; outside, Storey had made it up onto the roof of the Bridge when he, too, spotted the wave coming. There was just enough time for the officers to see the wave's approach, but only a couple of seconds to react. McNeil rushed for the door to the Wheelhouse, ostensibly to give an order to Quartermaster Riddey; outside, Storey realized he could not get back inside before the ship was inundated, and threw himself flat against the deck, locking himself around a support for the compass platform; young Tommy Hughes had the same instinct, even though he was inside the Bridge. In that moment, the officers and men could do nothing but hang on for the ride and pray that the ship survived what was coming.

Before the *Lusitania* could rise up onto the monstrous sea, it broke above her and collapsed squarely onto her Forecastle and forward superstructure. The whole bow of the liner was pounded underneath the ocean, and solid water engulfed the Bridge before running down the length of the ship moving aft. In a matter of only a couple of seconds' time, the orderly control center of the liner turned into some sort of carnival funhouse run amok. The impact smashed the entire steel face of the Bridge in until it was flush with the row of telegraphs and instruments; it pulverized the windows overlooking the bow, and smashed their teak reinforcing screens into kindling. Suddenly, the wave was inside the Bridge, as well – the water was three feet deep and moving fast. McNeil was picked up by the water's force and tossed into the Wheelhouse through the door. In that shocking moment, Quartermaster Riddey chose to hold on to the ship's wheel, probably feeling that it was the least likely object in the area to be moved by the onrushing wave; he was no doubt quite surprised when the wheel was wrenched right off of the telemotor, and both were thrown into the Chart Room wall. Relief Quartermaster Harding was tossed like a rag doll, bruising his leg against a bulkhead. The water shorted out the electric lights, adding to the chaos.

Chief Officer McNeil struggled to his feet, pulling himself through the Wheelhouse door and back out onto the main Bridge. The scene must have been astounding, with three feet of water swishing about, and the raging wind outside howling in through

This bow-on view of the Lusitania *at her Sloyne anchorage was probably taken around 1911. She is being recoaled and prepared for another westbound crossing. The rogue wave which pounded the ship in 1910 was large enough to severely damage the Bridge, which is quite sobering to consider when looking at how far above the water that structure was.*

the shattered and disfigured windows. He spotted a white-gloved hand in the water that was swirling across the room. It belonged to Bridge Boy Hughes, who was just then being swept out in the current. At the last moment, his hand found a support stanchion and he clutched it, preventing himself from experiencing untimely demise. The force of the torrent within the Bridge was strong enough to embed a large fragment of teak wood two inches into the wooden case of the fire detection gear. From the Bridge and Wheelhouse, the water surged aft into the Officers' Smoke Room and the Officers' Quarters, inundating them, as well.

Outside, as the ship's bow rose back up out of the sea, Third Officer Storey must have been quite surprised to find he was still alive; as the remnants of the wave washed astern, it did an astounding amount of damage. The same short which had plunged the interior of the Bridge into darkness also knocked out the electrical masthead and sidelights. The starboard companionway from the Boat Deck up to the Bridge was torn right off; its counterpart on the port side was nearly torn away, and eventually had to be lashed in place. Boats Nos. 1 and 3 were smashed into the deck and damaged beyond repair, their enormous davits twisted like salt-water taffy. What little was left of Boat No. 1 swung in and almost completely blocked the Boat Deck.

With no wheel on the Bridge to control the ship's direction, a new problem presented itself, as the ship's bow began to drift to port until she was pointing south, presenting her broadside to the sea. The ship's engines were stopped until a measure of control could be regained. In the bedarkened Bridge, the water may have been draining away, but the mess left behind was astonishing; the sight of the dismounted ship's wheel and the crumpled, dazed form of Quartermaster Riddey in the corner of the Wheelhouse would, under other circumstance, have been humorous.

There was no time to laugh, however – the situation had to be brought under control quickly. Orders were given to get the aft steering station to control the rudder; meanwhile, Chief Officer McNeil and his men began to work on the lights and on re-attaching the wheel. After ten minutes, the wheel was back in place, and another five minutes passed before the lights were turned back on. It was only once these tasks had been completed that McNeil had a chance to get a good look at himself; he noticed that his uniform coat and shirt were not only sopping wet, but they were also bloodstained. He looked for the source of the blood, and found that his forehead had a long

A rare view of the liner tied up at the Landing Stage, displaying the additional compass tower on the roof of the Bridge.

THE "LUSITANIA" AT THE LANDING STAGE, LIVERPOOL.

gash across it, while his chin was also cut; in the rush and confusion of those fifteen minutes, he had never felt the injuries. Forty minutes after the *Lusitania* had survived her encounter with the rogue wave, the ship was again under way and in control, moving at a cautious ten knots.

A thorough inspection was done, and the Bridge was cleaned up. Captain Turner was no doubt astonished at his return to what had been, only a few minutes before, the organized nerve center of his vessel; what glances and words were exchanged between him and his Chief Officer can only be surmised. As cleanup continued, it was discovered that a good many items from the Chart Room had been washed out to sea, including the ship's log. The good news was that the ship was not taking on any water from burst seams due to the stresses imposed upon her hull; however, there was some disturbing evidence within her frame of the wave's strength. Bulkheads in crew spaces forward were bent, there were broken doors, and the copper pipes connecting the hoisting gear were bent out of shape.

By noon on Tuesday, the battle-scarred liner had logged only 319 nautical miles, and the weather continued foul. Ahead of her, on Saturday morning, the Nantucket Lightship broke loose from its moorings and it looked as if she and her nineteen crewmen could be swallowed up by the sea; the lightship's crew kept in constant contact with the Newport wireless station; the revenue cutter *Acushnet*, located near Wood's Hole, Massachusetts, was even put on notice to be ready to respond should she send a call for assistance. Despite the foul temper of the Atlantic, the *Lusitania* arrived at Sandy Hook on Friday morning; the weather was still too rough to enter New York Harbor, however, and she was forced to anchor until Saturday morning. Once she tied up at Pier 54, her passengers stepped gratefully ashore, most of them very glad that their ordeal was over and that they had found *terra firma* once more. One of the First Class passengers, The Honourable George Keppel, told incredulous reporters: "I enjoyed the trip, although we had big seas."[27]

The liner's return trip to Liverpool between Wednesday, January 20 and Tuesday, January 26, was also miserable. It started off all right, but on Sunday the ship steamed straight into a northerly gale. At the peak of the storm, a First Class passenger was tossed to the floor of the Dining Saloon, injuring his back, and a woman in Third Class 'temporarily lost her reason,' in the delicate vernacular of the time. The ship's call at Fishguard was cancelled, and she arrived in Liverpool a day late, but in safety. It had certainly been a memorable last round-trip for Captain Turner as the *Lusitania*'s Commander.

On Crossing 101 West, during February of 1911, Captain Charles brought the ship though another series of astoundingly rough gales which came from every point on the compass. The wind speeds, reportedly up to ninety miles per hour, matched those of a strong Category 1 hurricane; it blew so hard that the paint along the ship's sides was ripped right off of the steel plating. Once again, some of the waves were strong enough to nearly engulf the Bridge, but once again, the great ship survived relatively unscathed and landed her passengers safely.

Another frightful crossing by the *Lusitania* was made in late October of 1913. Picking her way westward toward New York, under the temporary command of Captain Arthur Rostron, the ship ran into what her log described simply as a "whole gale; high seas." With winds of eighty miles an hour and tremendous waves, the ship bravely forged forth. One particularly rough sea on the afternoon of Tuesday, October 28, when a huge sea swamped the ship's stern, sending solid water down into the Steward's Quarters astern and thoroughly dousing everyone and everything inside. Meanwhile, two Able Seamen – Patrick Daly and George Brown – found themselves assigned the unsavory task of trying to get the falls of the starboard emergency boat sorted out so that it could be swung back in. Just then, the ship lurched to starboard and shipped a huge sea. Daly saw it coming and leapt onto the deck and broke his thigh; Brown held on to the lifeboat for dear life as the wave took it and turned it completely upside-down, receiving some bruises in the process. Despite this mess, the average speed for the voyage turned out to be 23.74 knots.

Through all of this, it is clear that the Cunard speed queens were immensely strong and seaworthy liners; in February of 1913, the *Mauretania* was picking her way through a shocking storm, under the command of William Turner. Without notice, she suddenly found herself sitting with her bow and stern poised on two separate mountainous seas, with her midships portion sagging unsupported and her screws racing in the air before being reigned in by their governors. When the wave under the bow moved off, she dove into the ocean and the Bridge was inundated underwater, very much as the *Lusitania*'s had been three years before. This particular scenario was one that shipbuilders of the time had designed their vessels to withstand, but there was no known precedent for the event. Mr. Hunter, from Swan, Hunter, was aboard for the trip, and he later said that he was very pleased

This extremely rare, perhaps one-of-a-kind photograph, came from an amateur stereoview card. The photograph was taken on April 23, 1908, as the Lusitania *was coaling in Liverpool. It would appear that the black paint along her starboard hull has recently been retouched.*

with her performance. Not a rivet in her hull was slack, it was later discovered.

The two sisters may have been strong and safe in rough weather, but they were not always comfortable. With their ultra-fine bow lines and minimal ascending bow flare, they tended to cut more directly through large waves than other liners, which rose up over waves to a larger degree. This meant that great quantities of water were often shipped over the forward decks in bad weather, and often right up to or over the Bridge before running aft down the Boat and Promenade Decks. This produced rather a harsher ride for the ship's occupants than they might have wished for, but this fineness of hull at the bow was required to allow the ships to maintain a high rate of speed; it was simply a feature of their design, and never posed any real threat to their safety.

Sometimes poor weather could lead to other risks. Daunt's Rock, four miles off the coast of County Cork, Ireland, was not only the official starting and ending point of the transatlantic crossing, but it was also a known hazard to navigation, despite the presence of a lightship close by. The Cunarder *Ivernia*, picking its way toward Queenstown from Boston in a heavy fog bank on May 24, 1911, found herself afoul of Daunt's Rock. The ship's starboard bow was damaged badly, and the ship limped into Queenstown Harbor to offload her passengers. By the time that

had been completed, however, the ship had taken on so much water that she had to be beached. Temporary repairs were carried out, and the ship was later returned to service, but the whole affair prompted discussion about safety signals around obstacles like Daunt's Rock.

In the midst of this discussion of the subject in the press, Captain Turner recalled to a reporter from the New York *Outlook* a trip that he had recently taken on the *Lusitania*, which had also been rather hair-raising. All through the east-bound trip, the weather had been so foul that he had been unable to make a single celestial observation. Running on dead reckoning across the Atlantic, the time eventually came when he knew, almost as if by some sort of sixth sense honed by years of experience, that he was not far from running right into the Irish coast. Captain Turner was widely acknowledged to be "one of the most skillful navigators afloat," and yet he had to use every available tool at his disposal to bring the great liner through safely. "Soundings, fore and aft, were of no avail, so judging the ship to be near Kinsale he headed the huge liner round, went dead slow, and pointed for the shore," no doubt praying that his first sight of land wouldn't be when he grounded on it. Soon enough, he heard two gun signals sound in quick succession to starboard. "He threw the helm over to port, and told the officer on the bridge to time off six minutes, when again

A 1908 profile view of the Lusitania *departing New York. Some of the paint on her black hull seems to have been freshly touched up. Many passengers are in evidence on the Shelter Deck, but fewer are visible on the Boat and Promenade Decks.*

the two guns were heard, and that meant the Head of Kinsale was close at hand, and, twelve miles further on, Daunt's Rock." The *Lusitania* had been saved through the caution of her Captain on that occasion, but navigating in poor weather was always more dangerous than most of her passengers generally gave thought to. The article concluded, "The problem of safety at sea … is only half solved by that which is inventive and automatic. It still requires a man who makes no error of judgment, who is cool, calm, collected, and who knows the seas as if they were the streets of a mapped-out city." Captain Turner obviously had the experience and skills required to cope with any imaginable danger that the sea could throw her way.[28]

Storms, fog, and close calls in escaping the sea's wrath may have generated oft-told tales, but perhaps the most important part of life aboard the *Lusitania* was, for her officers and crew, a sense of order and routine. After the high-stress and excitement of the maiden voyage, things began to settle down quickly for her crew. What had once seemed enormous and overwhelming soon became familiar and mundane. Many of the ship's crewmembers stayed on board for numerous voyages. Of course, the officers were assigned by the Cunard Company, and they often stayed for quite lengthy tenures. Crewmembers in various departments, like stokers, stewards and the like, signed on for a single round-trip voyage at a time; nevertheless, the *Lusitania* was a good job, and she became much beloved by those who manned her.

Trip after trip found many of the same crewmembers working together. This created, in a very real sense, a home and family atmosphere aboard the huge ship. In turn, this "family" created an overall personality for the *Lusitania*. No doubt, to some extent, the crew's good rapport and positive sentiments toward their vessel had something to do with the fact that the *Lusitania* was remembered in later years as a "happy" ship. Other vessels over the years suffered from the reverse, and it showed. This sentiment, be it positive or negative, is just as real and tangible to passengers as if it was a physical object, and it is just as true today as it was a century ago.

This "family" started at the top, with the ship's Captain. Naturally, the senior officers also played a part in this family, but the Captain was the true driving force, the "father" figure aboard. The men who were appointed as Masters of the Atlantic liners during this era of history were an interesting breed of individual; in the time of the *Lusitania*, most of them were still from the ranks of sailing ships, a select group that grew ever smaller with each passing year. Most had colorful personalities of one type or another. Some loved to spend time with passengers, telling tales and associating with society's elite, while others viewed this social intercourse with indifference or contempt. Some were quite warm and personable, while others were gruff and short-tempered, especially toward officers and crewmen. Some were strict disciplinarians, driving their ship and crew to operate at peak efficiency, while others kept a somewhat easier eye on

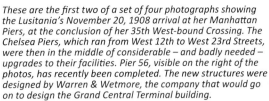

These are the first two of a set of four photographs showing the Lusitania's November 20, 1908 arrival at her Manhattan Piers, at the conclusion of her 35th West-bound Crossing. The Chelsea Piers, which ran from West 12th to West 23rd Streets, were then in the middle of considerable – and badly needed – upgrades to their facilities. Pier 56, visible on the right of the photos, has recently been completed. The new structures were designed by Warren & Wetmore, the company that would go on to design the Grand Central Terminal building.

the overall situation aboard; the crew viewed some of them with cool distaste, while other Captains inspired unswerving dedication and loyalty from their crew. Passengers also grew attached to certain Masters, even following them, in some cases, from ship to ship. Once disconnected from the umbilical of company management ashore, each skipper was free to run his ship with a certain personal flourish, and whether they were loved or hated by passengers and crew, all of them were skilled seamen; they were all also alike in that they seemed filled with a certain wanderlust in life, and found a home in their vessels, until the sea had become their natural element.

The *Lusitania* had several different commanding officers during the seven and a half years that she was in service. Her first Master was Commodore James B. Watt. When he took command of the *Lusitania*, Watt was 65 years old – two full years past Cunard's normal retirement age. However, special exemption had been granted to the Scotch Commodore so that he would be able to take the great new Scotch liner out and break her in. Watt's early days at sea were under sail; he had joined Cunard in 1873 and had risen through the ranks with distinction. Most of the previous crack Cunard ships, like the *Lucania*, the *Campania*, and the *Carmania*, had all come under his captaincy in preceding years. As the first skipper of the *Lusitania*, Watt set the tone for the ship's entire career; it was under his command that the liner and her crew truly began to settle into her routine of service. For nearly a year, Watt held the reins of the great ship.

By the late summer of 1908, however, it became clear that Watt's retirement was coming soon; with his departure from active service, Captain John Pritchard, of the *Mauretania*, would be left with seniority and would become the Commodore of the line. The decision was made to have Watt's position on the *Lusitania* filled by Captain William Thomas Turner, then Master of the *Caronia*. Watt's last round-trip voyage, the liner's seventeenth, began in late October of 1908. On the westbound crossing, the ship encountered strong seas; at one point, the liner buried herself so deeply in the sea that the wave swept down the decks and found its way into the First Class

Opposite top: *The liner continues to warp in to Pier 56, which is just north of Pier 54.*

Below: *With the Luitania safely berthed at Pier 56, she is still visible from the street, as the building which interconnected all of the piers is not complete between Pier 56 and Pier 54. On the extreme left, it is clear that construction on Pier 54 has not yet begun.*

Grand Entrance via an open door. Seawater cascaded down the elevator shaft, down the Grand Staircase, and thoroughly drenched some of the passengers as it went. But to Watt, that crossing was no doubt memorable for another reason: his daughter Helen was traveling to the United States for her wedding. Once the ship landed in New York, she would be married to her fourth cousin, a man named Gordon Watt, from Chicago.

In the early morning of October 30, 1908, Captain Watt stood on the Bridge of his ship as she steamed slowly up the Upper Bay under the eye of the harbor pilot. Watt's mind was no doubt churning; his face was noted as stern. As the skyline of New York came into view through the mists, filled with tall buildings of every sort, the moment must have been truly bittersweet to him. This was the last time that he would greet Manhattan, a city that had become a home away from home of sorts. The stay in New York and the return crossing to England went smoothly; once the *Lusitania* returned to Liverpool, Captain Watt turned command over to Captain Turner. In all, Watt had commanded the ship for one year and two months.

Captain Turner was a remarkable officer, and under his leadership, the *Lusitania* would attain some of her most remarkable accomplishments. Born in October of 1856, Turner was 51 years old when he took command of the great ship. He had gone to sea at the age of thirteen, working under sail for some time; although he was quite proud of having served aboard sailing vessels, he did not particularly relish his experiences during that period, recalling harsh words from superiors, weevil-infested biscuits, and severe punishments. His goal had always been to command a ship, and eventually he had taken a major step forward toward attaining this dream: in 1878, he joined the Cunard Line as Third Officer of the *Cherbourg*. With his career going in the right direction, he was married in August of 1883. Unfortunately, within a few years, he discovered that Cunard would not appoint an officer to command one of their ships unless he had commanded a vessel of another line first. So Turner returned to sail for a short spell in 1889, and was appointed as Master of the *Star of the East*. After one round-trip voyage to Australia aboard her, he went back to Cunard and continued moving up the ranks, serving with distinction during the Boer conflict as Chief Officer of the *Umbria* and earning a medal for his work. In 1883, he had saved a young boy from drowning in Liverpool, plunging into icy water to make the rescue; this service had earned him a second medal, this one from the Royal Humane Society of Liverpool.

His first Cunard command was the *Aleppo*, and in short order, he moved through the *Carpathia*, the *Ivernia* and the *Caronia*. Achieving command of the *Lusitania*, one of the two largest and fastest vessels in the world, must have seemed like a remarkable accomplishment to him, but he had proven his worth to Cunard. Turner was a skilled seaman, never having experienced a major emergency while in command. It was noted, however, that he had a somewhat gruff manner; in particular, he had little patience for First Class passengers, and apparently attempted to slip out of his social obligations whenever it was possible to do so. He was described as a man of medium height, with a bright, if weather-beaten face and he sported a distinctive row of crow's feet around his eyes when he smiled. His niece, 14-year-old (as of summer, 1909) Mercedes Desmore, lived in New York, and it was a favorite past time for him to spend time with her

Captain William Turner leaning on a ship's telegraph. Turner had been chosen by Cunard to replace Captain Watt when his tenure of command ended. Turner remained in command for over a year before moving on to take charge of the Mauretania.

while he was in port between crossings. Perhaps he lavished this attention on her because his family situation was not going particularly well. His wife had moved out of their home in 1903, and had taken their two sons with her. With things going poorly on the home front, at least Turner could take comfort in his career, being in charge of the mighty *Lusitania* – and better things were ahead for him.

In December of 1909, the Cunard Line decided that no man over the age of sixty would henceforth command the *Lusitania* and *Mauretania*. This policy alteration meant that Captain Pritchard of the *Mauretania*, who was over sixty, would be retiring almost immediately. His departure meant that Captain Robert C. Warr became Cunard's new Commodore. However, because Warr was 61 years old, he was placed in command of the *Umbria*, instead of one of the two crack sisters. Captain Turner was thus selected as the next skipper of the *Mauretania* – primarily because of his fine performance as Master of her older sister – and it was decided to bring 45-year-old Captain James Charles onto the *Lusitania* in his place. The change came swiftly. At the conclusion of the *Lusitania*'s Voyage No. 36, on January 26, 1910, Turner just barely had time to join the *Mauretania* on her next westbound passage.

It was another month before the *Lusitania* departed on her next crossing, but when she left Liverpool on February 26, 1910, Captain James T. W. Charles was resolutely in charge. Not only was he the youngest man that would ever take command of the *Lusitania*, but he would also hold that position longer than any other Captain during the ship's career. Charles was rather tall, standing almost a full head higher than most of the other officers who served aboard the liners. He stands out as a particularly likeable Captain. An example of his pleasant manner came during his first westbound crossing in command, when a 19-year-old stowaway was discovered aboard. He had boarded in Liverpool with the Third Class passengers, and had not been discovered until two days after the ship left Queenstown. When he told Captain Charles his story, it was obvious that Charles immediately took to the young man, commending him for his "supreme nerve," and even giving him a gift of some cigarettes when he met him on deck later. When the liner landed in New York, the young man was let go without prosecution.

In 1911, while in charge of the *Lusitania*, Captain Charles received the distinction of being appointed Sir James Charles; while he was taking the *Lusitania* out of New York as the new White Star giant *Olympic* was arriving on her maiden voyage, Charles failed

to give the incoming ship a customary salute; some felt that this was an intended snub, but others more charitably speculated that he was busy both with taking his ship out of dock and with absorbing the news of his new title. Captain Charles grew quite attached to the ships that he commanded; in 1928, Commodore Charles was on his final voyage in command of the *Aquitania*, and he passed away before the trip was over. Many believed that he, quite literally, died of a broken heart. While he was in charge of the *Lusitania*, Captain Charles did something rather unique, in that he made an endorsement for the Auto Strop Safety Razor; it was quickly run as a full-page ad in magazines, carrying his photograph in Cunard uniform. Captain Charles guided the ship on forty round-trip voyages, no less than eighty crossings, ending in October of 1912. These proved some of the most turbulent months of the *Lusitania*'s career before the Great War. There was a certain loss of prestige with the introduction of the *Olympic* into service, and there were months after the loss of the *Titanic* when big ships like the *Lusitania* were viewed with skepticism even after they were provided with enough lifeboats to save everyone aboard. Through it all, however, Captain

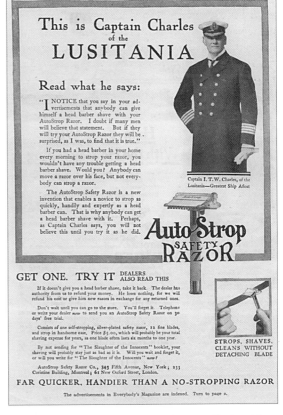

A razor advertisement featuring Captain James Charles while he was in command of the Lusitania.

Above: *Captain Arthur H. Rostron, temporary skipper of the Lusitania.*

Right: *Captain Daniel Dow, a Scotsman by birth, but raised in Ireland, loved to regale his passengers with humorous tales, and used his pipe as a prop when retelling them in his "racy Hibernian style."*

Charles watched over the ship and her passengers and crew, and the liner continued her successful service on the North Atlantic. When the *Lusitania* went in for work on her turbine engines in October of 1912, she was out of service for nearly two months, and change was in the air. Captain Charles was transferred and replaced by Captain Daniel Dow. The liner returned to service under Dow's care, departing Liverpool on December 13, 1912. She was, on this crossing, performing the annual Cunard Christmas mail-run in the *Mauretania*'s stead. Captain Dow's command of the *Lusitania* lasted only for the one round-trip voyage, for when the ship returned to Liverpool on December 31, she was laid up again, once more due to trouble with her turbine engines.[29] When she re-entered service on August 23, 1913, she was again under the command of Captain James Charles. This time, Charles was only to stay in command for two months, or three round-trip voyages. At the conclusion of this stint, Captain Turner was appointed to become master of the new *Aquitania*, Captain Charles was moved to the *Mauretania* in his place, and a gap opened up on the *Lusitania* once again.

On October 25, 1913, the *Lusitania* departed on her next round-trip voyage, No. 81; this time Captain Arthur H. Rostron, famed skipper of the *Carpathia* who had rescued the *Titanic*'s survivors a year and a half before – was in charge on her Bridge. Rostron's command of the liner was only eighteen days in length,

and included the foul-weather trip referred to previously. This was the shortest term that any Master would put in aboard the liner. After Rostron's single round-trip voyage, Captain Dow again took the *Lusitania*, starting with Crossing No. 163 West, which began on November 22.

Daniel Dow – a Scotchman by blood, but born and raised in County Cork, Ireland – was well known all over the Atlantic as "Paddy" Dow. He had acquired the nickname from the Liverpool Irish stokers that were acquainted with him. His other nickname was "Fairweather" Dow, because of his apparent tendency toward seasickness in all but the fairest of weather. Dow was well known as a skilled and cautious skipper, one who could always be relied on to make correct decisions in an emergency situation. He had served with Cunard since he was 28 years old; at that time, he had already been at sea for a dozen years. In the winter of 1914, while in command of the *Lusitania*, Captain Dow successfully coordinated a rescue of crewmembers from the *Mayflower*. For their efforts in this crisis, he and his officers received an official presentation at the Town Hall in Liverpool. He was described as rugged in appearance, and was known to run a tight ship. He was also noted to be quite sensitive and solicitous, a "genial gentleman" that simply did not get flustered no matter what the provocation. He was also strong-willed and was backed up by an "inexhaustible fund of shrewdness."

Unlike Will Turner, Dow relished socializing with his passengers. He was recalled as brimming with "lively anecdote," which he could tell in a "racy Hibernian style." Two of his frequent passengers were Olga Petrova – an accomplished Broadway and film actress and storywriter – and her husband, Dr. John Stewart. In her memoirs, published nearly thirty years after the event, she recalled Captain Dow as a "brilliant and tireless storyteller and a mine of information on the lives of the great men of the sea." She recalled that his "special hero was Lord Nelson and he would, if unchecked, be quite willing to sit up till dawn reciting his exploits," using his beloved pipe as a prop.[30]

Around Christmas of 1912, Captain Dow recalled rather nostalgically: "I passed my first Christmas at sea off Cape Horn in a snowstorm as apprentice on a 500-ton bark, and this will be my twenty-first at sea. The *Lusitania* could carry my old clipper packet on her after deck, but for all that the old days were happy days. The plum duff tasted far better to me without any music or frills, except a few chanteys from the star performers in the foc'sle and half deck, than it does these days, when liners have been transformed into floating hotels." Captain Dow remained in command until the conclusion of her 198th crossing. His term as Commander lasted some fifteen and

a half months, taking her right through the opening months of the Great War.

The shipboard "family" of the *Lusitania* was not only comprised of her Commanders, however, but also of her senior officers. Cunard's officer hierarchy was not exactly the same as the better-known one of the White Star Line. White Star placed immediately under the Captain a Chief Officer, and he was succeeded by six officers numbered First through Sixth in descending rank – eight men, in total. Cunard's chain of command bore the same number of officers, eight all told, but was arranged differently: immediately under the Captain was the Chief Officer, and he was succeeded by Senior and Junior First, Senior and Junior Second, and Senior and Junior Third Officers; the senior and junior concept might be somewhat confusing to the uninitiated. Each of these Executive Officers had to be equipped with Master's Certificates, and some of those who held these positions over the years had more than one to their credit.

Each of these men had specific duties to attend to at various times during the ship's routine. All but the Senior Second Officer were assigned specific watches to maintain during the course of the day. The first watch of each day began after sundown, at 8:00 p.m.,[31] and ran their course in this way:

A c. 1910-1911 photograph of the Lusitania *at the Landing Stage in Liverpool, showing a great deal of traffic in the Mersey.*

Watch	Time Period	Officers
First	8:00 p.m.–12:00 midnight	Junior First / Junior Third
Middle	Midnight–4:00 a.m.	Senior First / Senior Third
Morning	4:00 a.m.–8:00 a.m.	Chief Officer / Junior Second
Forenoon	8:00 a.m.–12:00 noon	Junior First / Junior Third
Afternoon	Noon–4:00 p.m.	Senior First / Senior Third
Dog Watches	4:00 p.m.–6:00 p.m.	Chief Officer / Junior Second
	6:00 p.m.–8:00 p.m.	

The Senior Second Officer was responsible for looking after the ship's mail cargo; however, if one of the officers were unable to maintain his watch, the Senior Second would do so in his place. Of the two officers who were on watch at any given time, the senior of the two men was specifically designated the Officer of the Watch. As such, everything that happened on board during his duty shift was his responsibility. If something unusual or extraordinary occurred, it was also his responsibility to inform the Captain on the matter. The Captain himself did not hold a set watch, but was on the Bridge quite often throughout the day, keeping a close eye on the goings-on. Additionally, in cases of fog or in emergency situations, the Captain

was expected to be on the Bridge until the danger had passed – a duty that, in sailing on the often foggy, often hazardous North Atlantic, could prove to be a mind-numbing marathon.

While the ship was in port, there were watches to keep as well; three senior officers kept a standard 9:00 a.m.–5:00 p.m. duty shift, although this could go either shorter or longer depending on the situation at hand. The junior of each of the two men who held at-sea watches together maintained that watch on their own while in port, as well. This allowed them to handle any situation that developed day or night and take appropriate action, and it also gave them valuable experience. While passengers were either embarking or disembarking from the ship, there was another set of duties to tend to. The Junior Third Officer was charged with the forward gangways and luggage; the Senior Third with the after gangways and baggage. The Junior Second was concerned with gangways and specie; the Senior Second also looked after specific gangways while keeping an eye on the mails, which also happened to be his primary at-sea responsibility. The Junior First Officer was stationed on the Bridge, while the Senior First Officer took charge of all the seamen. The Chief Officer held in his hands the reins for the entire embarking or disembarking operation.

Lastly, while entering or departing port, there was yet another round of operations to be handled. The officers were paired off with the same partner that they kept watch with. The Chief and Junior Second Officers were stationed on the Forecastle head. The Senior First and Third Officers took up position on the Stern Bridge and the after mooring station. The Junior First and Third Officers were positioned on the Bridge. The Senior Second escorted the pilot to and from the Bridge, and also had to keep an eye on the ship's shell doors, any tenders that were servicing the ship, and also had charge of the gangways and mails while docking.

These duties all constituted the course of routine shipboard operations; this was by far the way most time passed aboard, whether in port or at sea. However, there were also rare occasions when emergencies arose, and at such times each officer also had a

This photograph appears to have been taken in New York during a departure of the Lusitania *for Europe. It was probably taken in 1910 or after, as the stripe of black paint has been extended through to the end of the Promenade Deck, and the canvas rail covers are in evidence. The ends of the Cunard piers, even once the new buildings were constructed, were open at their extremity, and this could be where the photograph was taken.*

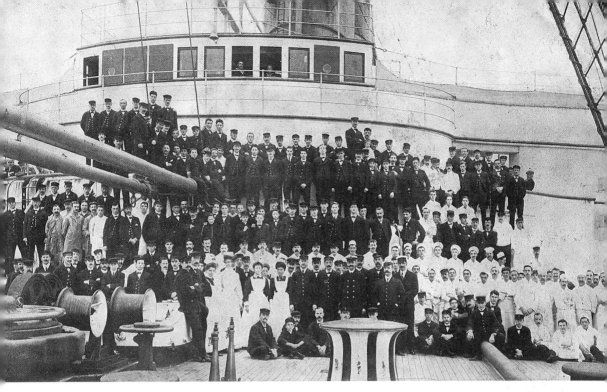

Above: *A photograph of the liner's crew standing beneath the Bridge and on the Forecastle. Judging from the features of the ship visible, it would appear that the photograph was taken around 1908. Also of interest is that four of the eleven windows of the Bridge have protective covers over them, either because they had been broken or to prevent them from being broken in bad weather. Three other windows in the Bridge appear to be open, and crewmen stare out through two of them.*

Following spread: *Another photograph of members of the crew, this time posing on the Second Class Boat and Sun Decks, while the photographer takes the picture from the Stern Docking Bridge. As in the photo on pg. 183, most of the crew members are stewards, stewardesses, members of the culinary department, and some bellboys. The ship's bugler stands holding his bugle over the Sun Deck rail; near him an older gentleman has spryly decided to stand outside the rail. In the background on the port side, a lad is visible washing down the deck. The port side staircase leading from the Sun Deck down to the Boat Deck was removed, apparently never to be replaced, although the starboard one remained in place permanently. As the roofs of Piers 56 and 54 are visible, the photograph was clearly taken while the ship was berthed in New York; since they are shown as completed structures, this photo was taken in 1910 or later, as Pier 54 was not finished before that year.*

specific duty to tend to. This could run the gamut from controlling fire extinguishing systems to rigging collision mats. These emergency situations were drilled quite frequently, and each officer knew that he was responsible not only for carrying out his assigned duties should the need arise, but also for doing so in a timely manner. In such situations, life and death – either for individuals or in some dire cases for everyone on the ship – quite literally came into their hands. This was a fact that these men knew only too well; each, no doubt, hoped every day that such a situation would not arise and that if it did, they were able to discharge their responsibilities well.

In addition to their regular watches, emergency preparedness, and navigation duties – which included not only taking regular fixes, but also keeping the ship's charts up to date – the officers of the *Lusitania* were heavyweight paper-pushers. No less than a half-dozen various ship's logs had to be regularly maintained; manifests had to be signed off on; reports had to be filled out and filed correctly. The list must have

seemed endless. The Captain was also busy; he kept a customary set of morning rounds, inspecting the ship from stem to stern with his senior officers before receiving reports from the various department heads. By the end of each day, the officers were exhausted; a junior officer from the White Star Line once put it this way: "You must remember that we do not have any too much sleep and therefore when we sleep we die."[32]

All of this work left little time for socializing with society's elite. Although there was a specific table set aside for the Captain and his officers in the First Class Dining Saloon, for obvious reasons it was never fully populated. When officers encountered passengers, they were to be courteous, informative, and agreeable. However, their responsibilities were simply too numerous to allow them to whittle away time in social niceties beyond those which were absolutely necessary. However, most of the ship's officers – from the Junior Third to the Captain – enjoyed a certain "he's in the club" sort of treatment from many of the First

Class passengers who traveled on their ship. This was despite the fact that a majority of them had worked their way up from extremely humble origins. Anything that they said was taken by even the wealthiest or most influential of passengers with extra consideration and thought; it must have seemed quite ironic to the officers that they were granted such a high status by their rich and famous passengers. It must also have appealed to their vanity at times, and there were no doubt occasions that they thoroughly enjoyed the at-sea hierarchy.

Although these young men frequently had girlfriends, fiancées, or wives on land, all of them were young men, no doubt frequently cursing their inability to linger and chat with some of the more ravishing ladies who were in their official, if detached, care. Conversation would frequently have turned to discussing these lovely ladies and commiseration over

not being able to make more leisurely contact with them. There would also have been some gossip and head-wagging over the often absurd incidents that took place on each voyage … *'The gamblers took how much from so-and-so?' 'You mean that there was an argument over who had made the first bid on that number in the ship's pool?'* … and the like. The officers talked about these goings-on in the Officers' Wardroom, around their meal table, and even on the Bridge during quiet moments. More specifically, quiet moments when the Captain wasn't around, because the Bridge was expected to be as quiet as a crypt unless conversation pertained to the ship's navigation. During their voyages together, these officers and men frequently formed solid friendships that lasted even when they were reassigned to other vessels.

On May 29, 1912, the Cunard Company's Board of Directors met and decided to add another member to

PICNIC & GAMES, R.M.S. "LUSITANIA" AUGUST 14TH, 1910, AT COLLEGE POINT, LONG ISLAND, N.Y.

PHOTO. BY. WURST.

Members of the Lusitania's *crew photographed while on excursion at College Point, Long Island in New York. The photo's date, namely August 14, 1910, places the excursion between Crossings Nos. 87 and 88. Interestingly, a number of the same crew members are visible in all three of these group shots.*

this family of officers. They created a new position, namely that of the "Staff Captain." About a week after the decision was made, the Directors of the Cunard Company noted that the Staff Captain was responsible for insuring the safety of passengers, primarily by keeping track of lifeboat drills and the general operation of the ship; the new position was doubtless created in direct response to the *Titanic* disaster of only six weeks before. "It will make a good deal of difference to the captain and will help the Chief Officer," Charles Sumner explained in New York.

The men appointed to this position were full-fledged Masters of other vessels, not ordinary Executive Officers, and would only serve aboard the *Lusitania*, *Mauretania* and the *Aquitania*, when she entered service. Smaller Cunarders, like the *Caronia*, would not be endowed with a Staff Captain, but rather would have an extra Executive Officer added to their lists.

Captain Samuel "Sandy" G. S. McNeil (R.D., R.N.R.), formerly the Chief Officer of the *Lusitania*, but now serving as Master of the *Albania*, received a letter from Cunard dated May 30, informing him that he would become the Staff Captain of the *Mauretania* on her next crossing, due to begin on June 1; this short notice certainly made for a hasty transfer. Captain Jerry F. Simpson of the *Veria* received an almost identical letter on June 6, informing him of his appointment as Staff Captain of the *Lusitania* beginning on her next crossing, which would start on June 8. The letters clearly pointed out that the Captain was still to be "in supreme command" of the ship, and that they were to consult him in any matters required, so that there could never be a conflict of interests. In consolation for their transfers, which might have seemed like a demotion of sorts, both men were given a raise in pay of £25 per year, for a full £300 annual wage. Attached to each letter the men received was a two-page list of some twenty-three separate duties that came with this position. These included the general discipline of the crew, the general cleanliness of the ship, to take charge of lifeboat drills, to handle passenger complaints, to see to the ventilation of the ship, to make the 10 a.m. rounds with the Captain, to make unscheduled visits to department heads throughout the day, and to preside over a table other than the Captain's in the First Class Dining Saloon. The Staff Captain's normal day would run from 7 a.m. to 9 p.m., after which time he would make his daily rounds through the ship; he would not

A photograph most likely taken around 1910 while the ship was at the Prince's Stage; just barely discernible is the missing set of stairs leading from the Second Class Boat Deck up to the Sun Deck on the port side. The Cunard tender Skirmisher *lies alongside the ship.*

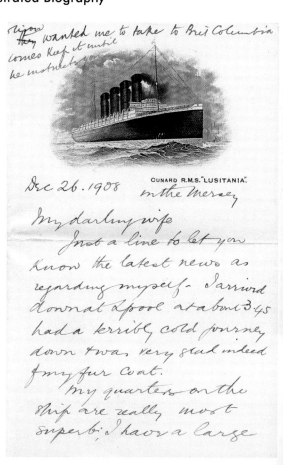

they wanted me to take to Brit Columbia
comes keep it until
he instructs you

CUNARD R.M.S. "LUSITANIA".

Dec 26. 1908   in the Mersey

My darling wife
   Just a line to let you
know the latest news as
regarding myself. I arrived
down at Lpool at about 3.45
had a terribly cold journey
down + was very glad indeed
f my fur coat.
   My quarters on the
ship are really most
superb; I have a large

Above: A c. 1911 photograph of the Lusitania at anchor in the Mersey. A much larger and more comprehensive structure stands atop the roof of the Bridge than was previously in evidence. This structure was most likely a canvas awning support, which would help to keep the Bridge and Officers' Quarters cool during hot weather. Such structures were usually portable, but this one is seen often on the Lusitania around this time period.

Opposite top left: A 1909 advertisement for travel to Europe aboard the Cunard fleet.

Opposite top right: This letter was written in December of 1908 from on board the Lusitania. It was penned by First Class passenger Austin Partner, and was addressed to his wife. Three-and-a-half years later, Partner would perish in the sinking of the Titanic.

Below: This fine port side profile of the Lusitania in Liverpool was probably taken around 1909.

Above: *Taken from the starboard Bridge wing, this photograph shows passengers enjoying the Sun and Boat Decks on a brilliant day.*

Below: *A scene on the Boat Deck. Looking at the photograph, something seems clearly amiss with the passenger walking forward along the deck, until one realizes that the ship is at sea and is heeled to port by as much as ten degrees.*

Above: *A group of First Class passengers pose on a chilly Boat Deck. The photograph was taken when the Lusitania's arrived in New York on Friday, February 3, 1911, at the end of Crossing No. 101 West. Second from left is Lady Catherine Decies. The man in the front is Lord Decies, her son, and on the extreme right is his sister, the Hon. Mrs. Barclay. The woman on the far left appears to be their other sister, Mrs. Wilkinson. Behind them stands the Hon. Seton R. Beresford. The group was arriving for Lord Decies' wedding to Miss Vivien Gould.*

Below: *A view looking forward along the port side of the Sun Deck from just behind the fourth funnel.*

Opposite top: *First Class passengers promenade along the Boat Deck. This view was taken on the port side and looks aft. In the foreground, a passenger enjoys the Atlantic vista from a wicker chair.*

Opposite bottom left: *A female First Class passenger pauses for a snap on the Sun Deck despite the cold weather.*

Opposite bottom right: *This rare photograph shows a crewman posing with two Second Class passengers on the starboard side of the Boat Deck.*

Below: *Antarctic explorer Sir Ernest Shackleton and his wife Emily, shown arriving in New York on the* Lusitania. *The photograph was taken on March 25, 1910, at the conclusion of Crossing No. 75 West. He had almost made it to the South Pole the previous January, and upon his return had been knighted by King Edward for his efforts.*

Bottom: *Sir Ernest Shackleton, photographed on the same day as the previous photograph. He is standing on the port Boat Deck, just outside of the Verandah Café.*

A DANCE

HELD ON BOARD

CUNARD R.M.S. "LUSITANIA,"

(Captain James B. Watt)

Tuesday, July 7th, 1908.

Dancing 9 to 11 p.m.

Music by "Lusitania" Orchestra.

C. Cameron, Musical Director.

M. C. - - Dr. J. J. Watson.

Mid-Atlantic.

Above: *A striking view of the Lusitania at the Landing Stage around the summer of 1911. The gangways are in place to move passengers from ship to shore.*

Below: *This photograph, from the same era, shows the ship preparing for departure.*

Right: *Held on July 7, 1908, on Crossing No. 23 West, this dance featured music by the Lusitania's orchestra, and ran until eleven o'clock that night. The Musical Director was one C. Cameron, while the M.C., or Master of Ceremonies, was Dr. J. J. Watson.*

Below right: *A First Class luncheon menu from the last day of Crossing No. 63 West, October 16-21, 1909.*

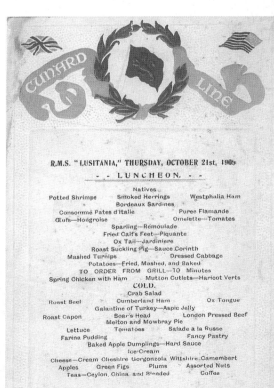

CUNARD LINE

R.M.S. "LUSITANIA," THURSDAY, OCTOBER 21st, 1909.

- - LUNCHEON. - -

Natives
Potted Shrimps   Smoked Herrings   Westphalia Ham
Bordeaux Sardines
Consommé Pates d'Italie   Puree Flamande
Œufs—Hongroise   Omelette—Tomates
Sparling—Remoulade
Fried Calf's Feet—Piquante
Ox Tail—Jardiniere
Roast Suckling Pig—Sauce Corinth
Mashed Turnips   Dressed Cabbage
Potatoes—Fried, Mashed, and Baked
TO ORDER FROM GRILL—10 Minutes
Spring Chicken with Ham   Mutton Cutlets—Haricot Verts
COLD.
Crab Salad
Roast Beef   Cumberland Ham   Ox Tongue
Galantine of Turkey—Aspic Jelly
Roast Capon   Boar's Head   London Pressed Beef
Melton and Mowbray Pie
Lettuce   Tomatoes   Salade a la Russe
Farina Pudding   Fancy Pastry
Baked Apple Dumplings—Hard Sauce
Ice-Cream
Cheese—Cream Cheshire Gorgonzola Wiltshire Camembert
Apples   Green Figs   Plums   Assorted Nuts
Teas—Ceylon, China, and Blended   Coffee

A close view showing the side of the liner towering over the Prince's Landing Stage. Many of the ship's portholes are open, and the gangways are stretched very nearly to their maximum height to reach the side of the Shelter Deck.

Lounging on the Boat Deck at sea.

be required to stand a four-hour watch, unless one of the other officers could not fulfill his shift.

From all of this, it was clear that Cunard was trying to take some of the social obligations and navigational details off of the hands of each of the Masters of their three largest ships. This would allow them to focus more on the safe navigation of each liner; the Staff Captain's duties regarding lifeboat drills show just how seriously Cunard was taking this sort of thing in the wake of *Titanic*. What was more, this decision was a wonderful public relations move; just knowing that Cunard was concerned enough to appoint an extra officer primarily to look after lifeboat drills reassured nervous passengers about their safety at sea. Both Staff Captain McNeil and Staff Captain Simpson wore the same uniforms as Captain Turner and Captain Charles, and they were given accommodations on A Deck forward, near the Captain's Suite, which had previously been for First Class passengers. When the *Mauretania* arrived in New York on June 7, 1912, Staff Captain McNeil showed that he was taking his responsibilities seriously by conducting a full lifeboat drill, lowering all of the craft to the water.[33]

Although it was the ship's senior officers who were most sought after by the passengers, it was far more likely that they would have the opportunity to spend time with the Ship's Surgeon, the Assistant Surgeon, the ship's Purser or one of his assistants. Although these men were not directly responsible for the navigation of the *Lusitania*, they were members of her senior staff who were specifically selected to spend

time with the passengers during each crossing; they were also closer to the inner sanctum of the officer corps than many others in the crew. "Avoid asking the officers questions about the navigation of the ship; remember that they have had to answer these questions many thousands of times, and eventually this becomes wearisome even to the most good-natured officers," passengers were advised.[34] Despite such reminders, how many times the Purser or other officers were asked about the minutiae of navigation or technical matters – or for the "inside scoop" on the next day's run – is a point that begs an incalculable answer.

When the company was fair, spending time with the passengers could be a joy to the Purser and his staff; when the company was dimwitted or outright annoying, it could be a curse. Only the best of "good-natured officers," who also had a flair for the diplomatic, were chosen to officially care for the First Class passengers on the *Lusitania*. Her first Chief Purser was Claude Lancaster. Lancaster had joined Cunard in 1879 as Third Officer of the *Brest*; poor eyesight, however, had taken him from the navigation department into the realm of Purser. He stayed with the *Lusitania* as Chief Purser from the time of her maiden voyage until the conclusion of her seventy-sixth round-trip voyage, in December 1912. The last officer to hold this post aboard the *Lusitania* was James A. McCubbin.

Down below decks, far away from the comforts of passenger accommodations, there was another group of elite men. Whereas the senior officers and Chief Purser and his staff had duties in socializing with the ship's passengers, it was the ship's engineering department that socialized with her machinery, making sure that the liner operated at peak efficiency at all times. The *Lusitania*'s first Chief Engineer was, appropriately enough, a Scotsman, Alex Duncan, who would later become the Chief Engineer on other prestigious Cunard liners like the *Berengaria*. Scotsmen seemed disproportionately, though appropriately, high in number in the *Lusitania*'s Scottish-built Engine Room; they knew and loved their ship and her beautiful engines. She, in turn, seemed to give them the respect and performance that they expected of her no matter what the weather. The last Chief Engineer to serve aboard the *Lusitania* was Archie Bryce, a good friend of Captain Will Turner.

And so it was, with this fine group of officers and a predominately happy crew, that the *Lusitania* plied the seas for those seven and a half years, covering the same route over and back each time. Deviations were few and far between, excepting those occasions when, due to poor weather, a stop at Queenstown – or later, at Fishguard – had to be cancelled. In the course of this routine, the ship typically left Liverpool on a Saturday, and made New York anywhere from Thursday night to Saturday morning, depending on the weather; the following Wednesday, usually at 10 a.m., she would depart New York on the return trip, arriving at Queenstown on Monday, usually before noon; she would then arrive in Liverpool by late Monday or early on Tuesday. That Saturday, some three weeks after she had begun the cycle, she would start the process all over again. Within this overall three-week routine, however, her schedule did change from time to time as the Cunard Line tried new approaches to pleasing their passengers.

As early as July of 1909, there was talk of adding Fishguard, Wales as an eastbound stop on the *Lusitania's* itinerary. Fishguard seemed an ideal port for a stop on the eastbound Atlantic route. Landing in the Welsh port would allow overland travel to London via the Great Western Rail lines on an estimated five-hour journey. If passengers wished to stay in Fishguard overnight, they could do so at the G.W.R. Co.'s Fishguard Bay Hotel. Surveyors were sent out to Fishguard to check over the harbor and ensure that it could handle the draught of the two largest ships in the world. They found sufficient water, and also that the Bay was well sheltered. It was protected on the east, south and west by headlands and hills several hundred feet high; to the north it was protected by a "substantial" 2,000-foot-long breakwater.

With the green light given to bringing the two ships into Fishguard, and *Mauretania* called there on August 30, 1909. She dropped anchor at 1:17 p.m. that afternoon. A mere eight minutes later, the mail

These photographs, taken in the summer of 1912 while the Lusitania was at New York, show some rare shipboard socialization between two officers and a pair of ladies. No back story on the photos has survived, giving the imagination free reign. Were the ladies passengers? If so, how did the officers manage this feat, since fraternization with female passengers was resoundingly discouraged? Were the women members of the crew dressed for a visit ashore during a rare period of "off-duty" time? Or were they friends or relatives of the officers, given leave to visit the ship while she was in port?

Above: *With the canvas awnings astern also in place and ready to help shield passengers from the sun, a crowd is beginning to form on the quay below, bidding the liner a fond farewell. Work on the Royal Liver Building, in the background, is progressing well, helping to confirm a summer of 1911 date of this photo.*

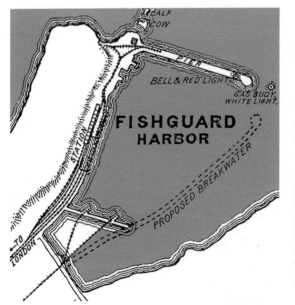

Left: *A period map of Fishguard Harbour.*

Below: *This period map shows the advantage of the overland route to London via Fishguard, Wales.*

tender was alongside. At 1:42 p.m., the mail tender departed with its cargo. Meanwhile, at 1:33, the passenger tender had drawn alongside the liner, and it departed at 1:57 p.m. At 2:00 p.m. on the nose, the *Mauretania* was able to raise anchor and resume her trip to Liverpool.[35] On Monday, October 4, on the last leg of Crossing No. 62, the *Lusitania* made her first stop in that port. It was found that the call at Fishguard allowed passengers to arrive in London about five hours earlier than if they had stayed with the ship all the way to Liverpool. Dropping the mails at Fishguard instead of at Queenstown also precluded

Above: *This view, taken August 30, 1909, shows the* Mauretania's *first call at Fishguard, Wales. The scene would have been very similar when the* Lusitania *called there for the first time just over a month later. The following six photos are from the same event.*

Below: *The baggage tender* Great Western *leaving to rendezvous with the* Mauretania.

delays in getting the mail to London due to rough weather. This was because it merely had to be transported overland via rail from Fishguard, whereas from Queenstown it had to travel cross-Channel.

Despite the addition of the Welsh port to the *Lusitania*'s eastbound itinerary, Queenstown remained a port of call three more times in the same direction; thereafter, the *Lusitania* ceased calling at the Irish port eastbound. The following summer, it was announced that Cunard had decided to cut out Queenstown as an eastbound stop for all of their express liners, not just the *Lusitania* and *Mauretania*. The Irish simply wouldn't have that, and brought pressure to bear upon Cunard in the hopes that they would restore the stop. Cunard met them partway, restoring the eastbound stop for all of their express liners except for the sister speedsters. The Irish Parliament was still not happy. They wanted the *Lusitania* and *Mauretania*, and continued to work on getting them back eastbound;

Above: *The tender* Sir Francis Drake, *seen here approaching the ship's side, would take the passengers ashore. The event is filmed for posterity by the cameraman standing atop the tender's Bridge.*

Left: *The mails were offloaded to the tender.*

Above: *An adventurous older gentleman grabs his belongings in one arm and firmly grasps the gangplank rail with the other hand as he disembarks to the tender.*

Below: *A stunning photograph of a G.W.R. tender tied up along the Mauretania's side during disembarkation. The Mauretania appears to be leaning somewhat to port, perhaps because all of the passengers are lining the rails on that side to watch the transfer.*

Above: *With the transfer complete, the ship was headed back out to sea a mere forty-three minutes after she had dropped anchor. Meanwhile, passengers bound for London stepped ashore and took a G.W.R. train to their destination.*

Right: *An artist's view of the Lower Manhattan skyline, with the Singer tower featured prominently, gives an idea of what it would have looked like to depart from the city aboard the* Lusitania *during one of her famed midnight sailings.*

meanwhile, Cunard continued to have the two liners call at Queenstown in the westbound direction.

Even with the addition of Fishguard as a port of call eastbound, with that port's convenient rail routes to London, there were still times that the *Lusitania*'s London-bound passengers did not arrive in the English capital until quite late at night. Additionally, there was also the matter of the Irish screaming for the two sisters to resume their eastbound stops at Queenstown. Cunard seemed to wrestle with this conundrum for some time before making a remarkable decision: instead of having the *Lusitania* sailed at nine or ten in the morning from New York, why not sail her out eight or nine hours earlier, at 1:00 a.m.? Surely this alteration would allow enough time for the sisters to stop at Queenstown once more, and would still get the passengers to London before it was too late. At the eleventh hour, however, the decision to restore the eastbound stop at Queenstown was dropped; although the late-night sailing time was retained, pas-

sengers bound for Ireland would land at Fishguard and take the ferry back to Rosslare.

In December of 1911 it was announced that both sisters would start this schedule at the end of February,

Top: *A scene on the Second Class Boat Deck at sea from before 1912. While some of the passengers are enjoying a game of shuffleboard, others are content to lean against the rail. Some crewmen stand nearby in discussion. It looks as if the weather was quite chilly, as everyone is warmly dressed.*

Above: *The actor Sir Charles Wyndham, and his longtime leading lady, the actress Mary Moore. The photo was taken upon their arrival on the* Lusitania *in New York on Crossing No. 69 West, December 24, 1909. In 1916, Wyndham would marry Moore.*

1912, with the *Lusitania* making the first of these so-called "midnight sailings" from New York. Although it was hoped by the Cunard Company that the sisters would "always sail at or near" that hour, the actual departure would be "left to the discretion of Capt. Charles of the *Lusitania* and Capt. Turner of the *Mauretania*, and if in their opinion the conditions should ever appear to be adverse they will have the power to delay the time of departure until the conditions are more fa-

vorable."[36] However, the Ambrose Channel was by this point fully illuminated at night, and all sorts of night-time traffic was coming and going through the cut in darkness. It thus seemed likely that the *Lusitania* and *Mauretania* could almost invariably make this sailing time. Cunard was confident that these "midnight sailings" would prove popular, and they did. A buffet was served from 9:00 p.m. to 12:00 midnight, just prior to departure. Many passengers, especially those booked

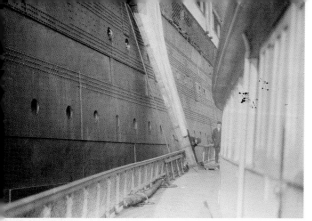

in First Class, spent their last few hours ashore at social events and parties. Despite the popularity of these nocturnal departures from New York, in practice it was found that passengers bound for London would still not always arrive before night fell in that city.

During the summer of 1913, Cunard made the decision to cut all stops at Queenstown for the *Lusitania* and her sister; Irish politicians renewed their protests with characteristic vigor, and delayed the actual implementation of this adjustment, although in the end their fuss was for naught. The last stop that the *Lusitania* would ever make at the Irish port came at the beginning of Crossing No. 167, westbound, on January 4, 1914. Although she was scheduled to stop there on the outbound leg of her next round-trip voyage, on February 1, she could not due to rough weather. On February 12, Cunard announced publicly that all stops at Queenstown for the two sisters were now a thing of the past.

Even with midnight sailings from New York, no call at Queenstown, and the stop at Fishguard with its express train service, Cunard still felt it necessary to further ensure that eastbound passengers would arrive in London at a reasonable hour. Thus, in March of 1914, they pushed the 1:00 a.m. Wednesday departure time back to 6:00 p.m. on Tuesday evening. The six o'clock sailing was only maintained through August of that year, and subsequently reverted to 1:00 a.m. before shifting back and forth between the two a couple of times. Finally, as a last change in her New York departure schedule, Cunard took to sailing her out on Saturday mornings at 10:00 a.m. She remained on this schedule for the remainder of her career. Despite all of these alterations to her schedule in departing New York eastbound, her westbound departure from Liverpool on every third Saturday never changed.

Within this rather malleable routine, there was the factor of the unexpected. One good example of this came during the summer of 1911. When the *Lusitania* arrived in Liverpool on August 15, the city was in chaos; widespread labor unrest had led to strikes, ri-

Drydocking was a matter of routine maintenance for the Lusitania. *While there, her hull was scraped and painted, thoroughly checked for storm damage, and various upgrades were also made. This view seems to have been taken around 1908, as the ship was leaving the Canada Dry Dock.*

oting and mob scenes that had plunged the city into a reign of terror which lasted for days. The *Lusitania* could not be docked upon arrival because the tugboat men were among those striking. The ship was not able to dock, victual, and take on coal immediately, and her crew was unable to get her ready for her next scheduled departure. She was not ready to depart Liverpool again until the evening of Sunday, August 27 – a catastrophic twelve-day delay that prompted the ship to run flat out in order to attempt to catch up some of the lost time. To do this, she made three full crossings by September 17. Turnarounds in New York and Liverpool between these trips were compressed to shockingly brief affairs, and the ship's turbine engines were not given a break at all during this period. When the ship tied up in New York at the end of that third crossing, she held a new record for making three back-to-back crossings in three weeks' time. It was reported that while she was in New York, her turbines would be given a proper chance to cool off; they would also be given a thorough inspection for damage due to the unusual length of sustained use they had endured.

On Wednesday, December 6 of that same year, there came another schedule disruption: a gale in Liv-

erpool caused the *Mauretania* to break loose from her moorings and ground in the Mersey. She was refloated late the next morning, but Cunard decided that she should have a thorough hull inspection before her next sailing. Because of this, the *Lusitania* was sent out to make the pre-Christmas mail crossing in her place. She departed Liverpool on Saturday, December 8 and arrived at her New York pier at 7 a.m. on Friday, December 15; after a high-speed turn-around in that port, she made the eastbound crossing, arriving back at Fishguard, Wales a very respectable 12 days and 17 hours after leaving Liverpool.

There were also technical problems that disrupted the *Lusitania*'s regular service schedule. One of these transpired at about 8:30 on a Monday morning in late March of 1909. Just a day out from Queenstown, the ship began to shudder violently for about four minutes. Concerned passengers left their breakfasts or came up from their staterooms in disarray, hoping to find the cause of the disruption. Down in the Engine Room, the reason was immediately apparent: one of the propellers had thrown a blade, and the imbalanced remaining portion of the screw was vibrating, creating the disconcerting effect. To prevent damage

This stunning photograph of the Lusitania tied up to Pier 56 was most likely taken in late December of 1912, between Crossings Nos. 153 West and 154 East – her first post-turbine-refit round-trip voyage. Post-Titanic lifeboats are in evidence on the Boat Deck, but no permanent provisions for their use have yet been made. Snow has accumulated on the ship's upper decks. A quartet of new cowl-shaped ventilators, the starboard two of which are visible here, have been installed during her layover.

Above: *Taken at the same time as the preceding photograph, the snow is very much in evidence, as is the starboard cowl vent just behind the Bridge. It was at the end of the upcoming return to Liverpool that the ship's turbines were severely damaged and she was taken out of service for eight full months of repairs. This was also the first crossing that she made without Chief Purser Lancaster, as he had just retired. By this point the ship had earned a record of nearly a half-million miles.*

Right: *This unusual photograph shows the port side Boat and Promenade Decks of the liner. Canvas has been stretched over the Promenade Deck to help keep inclement weather out. The late-1912 addition of the* Mauretania-*esque cowl ventilators has already taken place, but the vents just behind the Bridge do not appear to have been replaced yet. Judging from the rather shabby appearance of the paint along the decks and on the davits, the photograph may have been taken during her autumn of 1912 lay-up for turbine repairs, as the ship would never have been allowed to look so worn while in service.*

to the machinery, all of the engines were immediately stopped. Then, to discover which prop was the offending one, the engines were re-started; it was soon found to be the inboard starboard prop that had suffered damage. The day after she arrived in New York, divers were sent down to inspect the exact nature of the trouble. It was worse than it was originally believed. One of the three blades had broken off close to the head, and another had sheared at mid-blade.

A new pair of propellers would need to be installed, but it could wait until the ship returned to England. She made her next crossing eastbound on only three propellers; the new set that replaced the older pair was a marked improvement, being more akin to the *Mauretania*'s high-performance screws, and gave the *Lusitania* improved performance.

More tiresome than this rather commonplace mishap, however, was a protracted series of difficulties with *Lusitania*'s turbines. The troubles all began in June of 1912, on Crossing No. 141 West. There was probably a lot of talk about one passenger in particular, Mrs. Joseph Loring. She was a widow of one of the victims of the *Titanic* disaster, which had taken place just two months before. When the liner was ready to depart Queenstown on Sunday, June 9, all seemed well; the order was rung down to the Engine Room for "Half Ahead" on the low-pressure turbines which drove the inboard props. The engineering staff put steam pressure on the pair, but the port turbine wouldn't budge, not even with twenty thousand horsepower applied to it. There was no easy way to find the cause of the dilemma; answers would not be forthcoming without lifting the cover off the turbine. It was decided to hold off on repairs until the ship returned to Liverpool. However, the prop was frozen in place and was creating drag on the ship as she moved through the water. By Sunday afternoon, the Chief Engineer decided to de-couple the shaft at the neckpiece; this would allow the prop to spin freely in the water like a windmill, reducing the drag. After the engineers removed all but two of the connecting bolts, the vessel was stopped dead in the water. Once the last two bolts had been removed, the ship resumed course, and it was reported that the prop spun freely at about 100 rpm all the way to New York. When the *Lusitania* arrived in New York, 5 days, 20 hours and 50 minutes after leaving Queenstown, at an average speed of only 21.48 knots, it proved to be far from a record-breaking passage. She returned to Liverpool at a similarly slow pace, and her next crossing was canceled while her turbine cover was lifted to discover the source of the problem.

Following this incident, the *Lusitania* made a round-trip voyage in July all right, but on the following westbound passage, spanning from late July into early August, there came another episode. While en route from Liverpool to Queenstown in heavy weather, at about nine o'clock on the night of Saturday, July 27, it was discovered that the bearings of the port high-pressure turbine had overheated until the brass cap had begun to melt. The bearing – which weighed a ton and a half – would have to be removed and replaced with the spare, which was stowed all the way forward by the Firemen's Quarters. Extra men from every department aboard the ship were sent into the titanic effort as, by a system of pulleys, the replacement bearing was taken out of storage and slowly moved over to the port side. Then it was moved aft to the spot where it could be hoisted into position to replace the faulty bearing. The task took a full twelve hours, and by noon on Monday, the ship had made

only 469 miles. Although the new bearing worked all right, by the time she reached New York, her average speed for the crossing was a mere 21.19 knots.

With a second turbine experiencing catastrophic failure, it was clear that something was very amok with the *Lusitania's* engines. Beginning on October 15, 1912, she was removed from service for nearly two full months. John Brown was tapped to open up all of the turbines with the exception of the starboard high-pressure one, and to effect repairs and inspections of the equipment. Cunard invested £7,330 in this work, and the ship re-entered service when she departed Liverpool on December 13 on her seventy-seventh round-trip voyage.

It was during this west-bound crossing, on December 19, that she averaged a speed of 27 knots – including a burst of almost 28 knots for an hour, while turning out 207 revolutions on the engines – for a full day of steaming. While she did not manage to recapture the Blue Riband, she received high praise for the impressive feat, and the turbine work may have seemed eminently successful. She returned to Liverpool, completing the round-trip voyage, on December 31, and everything seemed all right to the public. Then there came a surprise: almost as soon as the liner had tied up in Liverpool, Cunard announced that her next crossing would be canceled. When inquiries were made as to the cause, Cunard responded simply that there had been a "slight derangement in the machinery."[37] That was all the public was told at the time.

Behind the scenes, the situation was quite serious. Fresh from two months of significant turbine maintenance and repairs, another serious turbine problem had occurred. It had happened as the *Lusitania* was approaching Fishguard Harbour on the afternoon of Monday, December 30. A steamer coming out of Fishguard got too close for comfort, and to avoid a collision, the helm was put hard to port. This attempted turn to starboard failed when the telemotor jammed up, and the *Lusitania* remained stubbornly on course. By then the situation was quickly becoming critical, and the order was given for "Full Astern" – without stopping the turbines before changing over to astern thrust. The engineers complied, and a collision was avoided. Once the situation had calmed, it was found that the reason the steering gear had failed was because a bit of marline had dropped into the telemotor and jammed the system up. If everything else seemed all right, that illusion was quickly shattered. When the time came for the ship to resume her trip toward Liverpool, it was found that the port low-pressure turbine, the blades of which

Above: *A stunning view of the* Lusitania *in the new Gladstone Graving Dock in Liverpool. The dock was opened in July of 1913 by King George V; in August of 1912, it had been announced that the* Lusitania *would be the vessel to inaugurate the dock. However, because of her extended lay-up for turbine repairs, it was the* Mauretania *that was instead given that privilege. Before the ship returned to service in late August of 1913, however, the* Lusitania *did apparently pay a visit to the new dock, and that may be when this photograph was taken. It was apparently during the 1913 lay-up that the mounts for her 6-inch guns were installed on the Forecastle, although the guns themselves were never put into place. The tarps on the Forecastle could be covering the new mounts while work on installing them progressed. Also of great interest is the fact that workers seem to be working on installing the new davits amidships on the First Class Boat Deck, to carry the extra post-*Titanic* lifeboats which had previously just been mounted to the deck. Another new pair can just be discerned along the edge of the Second Class Boat Deck aft, as well. A final alteration that was made around this time is that the after set of cranes – removed just prior to the maiden voyage in 1907 – was replaced, and they were thereafter visible on the ship through the spring of 1915.*

Left: *Viscount Haldane standing on the Boat Deck of the* Lusitania *upon her arrival in New York at the end of August 1913. This was her first appearance in that port since the previous December, following an eight-month lay-up in Liverpool to repair her damaged turbines. He is standing on the port side, by the forward window looking into the First Class Reading & Writing Room.*

Opposite: *A Second Class breakfast menu for the morning of arrival in New York at the conclusion of Crossing 159 West.*

had just been replaced, would not move. The ship limped back to Liverpool on only three props. Once she arrived at the mouth of the Mersey, tugs were called in to assist the ship in maneuvering in the narrow confines of Liverpool waters. A preliminary examination of the machinery revealed that the blades of the port low-pressure unit were twisted out of pitch. Additionally, the blades on both of the forward-thrust turbines on the starboard side had also been damaged.

Obviously a more thorough investigation was in order; repairs were going to take some time, but just how extensive they would have to be was not yet clear. The ship's forthcoming voyages were canceled, and she was replaced by shifting other vessels in the fleet about. The crippled *Lusitania* was soon placed in the Canada Dock so that a thorough inspection could be made of just how bad the situation was. It was hoped that the blades on the port low-pressure turbine could once again be replaced, and that the damaged blades on the other turbines could simply be straightened out without having to replace them. It was an enormous task, simply to find out what needed to be done; it took two full weeks just to lift up all the turbines' casings and ascertain the damage. When they did, they found a real mess. It was going to be impossible to simply patch up the turbines. Instead, they were going to have to completely re-blade and service all four of the ahead turbines. The contract for work was given to Cammell, Laird & Co., and Parsons & Co., and for some time she could be seen in the Canada Dock in Liverpool. She did not return to service on the Atlantic until late August of 1913, a full eight months from the time of the incident at Fishguard.

This latest round of turbine work cost Cunard some £7,639. £2,432 of that figure was spent in opening up the port and starboard astern turbines, inspecting them, and putting them back together with no repairs made. Other work was carried out on the ship during this extensive lay-up, and brought the total expenditure on this eight-month overhaul to over £50,000. This was an astounding sum, especially when one considers the vast amount of revenue lost in the liner's absence on the North Atlantic – which some estimates put at a half-million pounds. Cunard was also not particularly pleased that John Brown's 1912 repairs, which had cost over £7,000 in their own right, had not held up for more than a single round-trip voyage. Negotiations between the two firms commenced on the charge for the second set of repairs, and were concluded amiably by mid-October of 1913.[38]

These large-scale disruptions to the *Lusitania's* schedule were rare, however; more common were the less troublesome but always noteworthy occurrences that fell outside the purview of "ordinary." For example, the liner's departure from New York in January of 1908 became a scene of utter chaos. The first problem was that ticket agents, ever eager to sell cabins and make a commission on their sales, had overbooked the Cunarder's accommodations. Because of this, a great crowd of would-be Third Class passengers had to be turned away at the gangplank. Shortly thereafter, word was passed down that there were still some Second Class cabins available for an upgrade of only $13. The crowd rushed to the ticket office on the pier *en masse*, clamoring to take the cabins. While the beleaguered employees sorted through the mess, the *Lusitania's* whistle sounded; a horse pulling a cab on the pier started at the unearthly noise, and decided to charge right toward the horde by the ticket office. Traffic policemen reacted quickly and warned the crowd, which scattered quickly. One Italian gentleman, however, could not get out of the way in time, and was knocked down; fortunately, he suffered nothing more than a good bruising from his encounter with the frightened

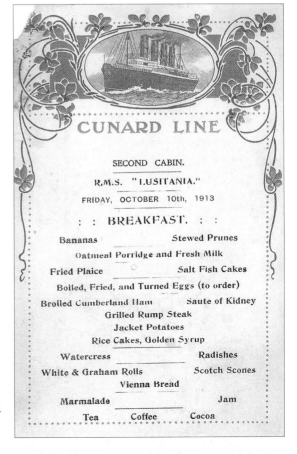

CUNARD LINE

SECOND CABIN.

R.M.S. "LUSITANIA."

FRIDAY, OCTOBER 10th, 1913

: : BREAKFAST. : :

Bananas   Stewed Prunes

Oatmeal Porridge and Fresh Milk

Fried Plaice   Salt Fish Cakes

Boiled, Fried, and Turned Eggs (to order)

Broiled Cumberland Ham   Saute of Kidney

Grilled Rump Steak

Jacket Potatoes

Rice Cakes, Golden Syrup

Watercress   Radishes

White & Graham Rolls   Scotch Scones

Vienna Bread

Marmalade   Jam

Tea   Coffee   Cocoa

Opposite page: A series of three photographs taken aboard the Lusitania *during Crossing No. 53 West, June 19-25, 1909.*

Top: *The Verandah Café, looking forward from the Second Class Boat Deck.*

Bottom left: *The First Class Boat Deck, looking forward. Again, because of the angle the passengers are walking at, it is apparent that the ship is giving a spirited ride.*

Bottom right: *A view looking forward along the Boat Deck. The view was taken from the Aft Docking Bridge.*

beast. A traffic officer eventually stopped the horse, and its driver was arrested for not having a proper cab license.

Sometimes the commotion came in a completely different way. That same July, a well-dressed and obviously well-to-do First Class passenger was unceremoniously escorted off the *Lusitania* before she departed New York. It seems that the man had caused a sensation soon after boarding; once comfortably ensconced in his stateroom, he made an aberrant attempt to call up the Tsar of Russia, the King of England, and the Pope in Rome, to inform all of them that he was on his way to pay them a visit. There were some lines of social behavior that one just didn't cross; Chief Surgeon Dr. Pointon was consulted, and recommended that the man's health was not robust enough to stand the ocean voyage – very likely an exaggeration, but a convenient loophole nonetheless. As the man was being escorted from the ship, he was described as highly excited; after he was refunded his ticket price, however, he left quietly.

There were the eccentric, and then there were the outright lawless. Customs inspectors in New York were renowned for their ability to sniff out passengers who felt adventurous enough to lie on their customs declarations forms, or who attempted to smuggle items into the country on their person. Despite the inspectors' vigilance, there were still people who tried to bend the rules, and with varying degrees of success. In June of 1910, four ladies traveling together in First Class failed miserably at this charade. First, they stated that they had nothing whatever to declare. This immediately roused suspicions, and an examination of their nine steamer trunks and hand baggage was set to begin. At the last moment, they changed their story to a declaration of $160. This was just too much to believe, and they were sent back aboard the ship for a thorough examination of their person. The women inspectors who were called in to carry out the examination emerged with a veritable treasure trove, worth about $3,500; they found nine items of jewelry in a bag strung on a girdle about the waist of one woman, and other items were found on the other three women in short order. All four of these female travelers were wealthy – one of them was even married to former Chicago Mayor DeWitt Cregier (Term 1889-1891). They were all taken down to the Federal Building for further questioning. Despite the damning evidence found on their person, all four women strongly denied that they had been attempting to defraud the government.

Other passengers were suspected of having perpetrated far more serious crimes. One particularly profound incident swept the *Lusitania* up into the middle of an international manhunt. It all began on Saturday, December 26, 1908 in Cunard's Liverpool offices on Water Street. With the *Lusitania* due to sail for New York that day, there were a large number of prospective passengers who required attention by the office personnel. At about 12:30 p.m., one particular gentleman, wearing a vicuna overcoat and top hat for protection against the cold, and who was of slim build, came into the office. Soon this man found himself being assisted by John Forsythe, the Manager of the Second Class department. He requested accommodations for him and his wife aboard the *Lusitania*. Forsythe pulled out a diagram of the liner's passenger accommodations, and offered the man cabin E76, which was an inside Second Class cabin, the rate for which would have been £12.

The gentleman did not seem particularly happy with the offer, explaining: "No, I do not like that, it is inside; it was offered by your agents in Glasgow." When he made the remark about the Glasgow agency, he seemed to immediately regret having mentioned it, and immediately added, "by your other agents."

Forsythe thought it a little odd that the man seemed to regret having mentioned Glasgow so much, but went back to the drawing board. Soon he had found an alternative, and offered cabin C1, which was just forward of the well overlooking the Second Class Dining Saloon, and which also had a view overlooking the after portion of the First Class decks. The price for this cabin was £28. Again, the gentleman was not particularly happy, this time with the price.

The Cunard agent stuck to his guns, however, and soon enough the man acquiesced and accepted cabin C1 for the £28. He paid with six £5 Scottish notes, and was given £2 in change. Forsythe asked his name.

"Otto Sando. S-a-n-d-o. It is not Sandow, the strong man," he said with a jocular smile.

Forsythe gave him an application form for tickets, No. 37/5, which the man filled out carefully. He gave his wife's name as Anna, his age as 38 years, and gave his profession as a dentist. He put down that he was from Germany, but was also a U.S. Citizen, and gave a Chicago, Illinois address.

The Cunard agent noted that Mr. Sando seemed a trifle nervous; at one time when the office door opened, Sando looked expectantly in that direction. It wasn't the first nervous passenger that Forsythe had seen, however, and he dismissed it from his mind. After exchanging another small amount of the man's money, Forsythe watched as the gentleman left the Cunard office to return to his hotel.

The Sandos boarded the *Lusitania* and the ship had cast off before the day was out. The weather during the westward passage, the outward leg of the ship's twentieth round-trip voyage, was decidedly foul, however – "very rough," as Second Class Bedroom Steward Thomas Atherton recalled. Second Class Stewardess Beryl Bedford recalled that she was very busy with the passengers in her care, as many of them – including "a great many ladies," as Bedford recalled – were seasick. Anna Sando stayed confined in her cabin for most of the trip, although her husband made it down to the Dining Saloon for his meals. He told Bedroom Steward Thomas Atherton that he had crossed the Atlantic a half-dozen times and "had not previously been sick."

Apparently, the Sandos were not pleased with the service that they received during the trip. Rather early in the voyage, Stewardess Beryl Bedford heard from the Chief Steward that they had complained of a "want of attention" to Mrs. Sando during her illness. The stewardess must have chafed at the complaint, no doubt being run ragged by the many ill passengers she had to divide her time amongst. She did not, however, confront the Sandos about their complaint when she returned to assist them, and they did not complain about the matter to her directly, either.

When the voyage had ended on the morning of January 2, 1909, it must have seemed like just another run-of-the-mill winter crossing, and Stewardess Bedford was no doubt pleased that the Sandos would soon be disembarking. However, as the *Lusitania* was picking her way up New York waters toward her pier, a revenue cutter approached and several lawmen and detectives boarded the liner. Something was amiss. It turned out that they were on a manhunt, looking for a "slim man, with a dark complexion, about 5 feet 7 inches in height, 35 years old, and with a crooked nose." When they came across Otto and Anna Sando, they found that he met the description of their wanted man. He was suspected in connection with the murder, on December 21, of Miss Marion Gilchrist, an elderly lady who had lived in Glasgow.

The man quickly admitted to the authorities that "Sando" was a pseudonym, and that his real name was Oscar Slater. As the ship traveled up the Bay and tied up at her pier, he and his wife were questioned. Slater admitted that they were traveling from Glasgow; when asked if he knew the deceased woman, he said no, he had never heard of her. His wife agreed that she had not known of the woman, either. Slater was next formally arrested, and when his person was searched, a pawn ticket from a Glasgow broker was found. It was for an advance of £60 on a three-rowed crescent diamond brooch, pawned on the day of the murder; a brooch was also known to have been stolen from Miss Gilchrist by the murderer. Slater told the authorities that the brooch he had pawned was a different one than Gilchrist's, and that he had it in his possession before the murder had even taken place.

Quickly realizing the gravity of his situation, and seemingly "becoming confused, [Slater] added that he knew the woman was murdered because he read about it in the papers before he left Liverpool." The authorities felt that the pawn ticket was "significant" evidence, and took Slater to the Tombs to set a hearing. His wife was taken to Ellis Island for further examination. Before she disembarked the *Lusitania*, she gave this statement to the press, speaking with what was described as a "slight French accent":

I was married to Mr. Slater in Glasgow on July 12, 1901. My maiden name was Miss Andrea Anton. I was a daughter of Malone James Anton, and lived in Paris. I came to America with my husband soon after the marriage. Two years ago we left here on the *Kaiser Wilhelm II*. We spent most of the time in France until three months ago, when we went to Glasgow, where my husband then established himself as a dentist. I myself have been to this country several times in my life.

Back in Slater's cabin, C1, Bedroom Steward Thomas Atherton began cleaning up in preparation for the next batch of passengers who would occupy it. Therein, he found a copy of the previous Sunday's *News of the World* newspaper, which was frequently brought aboard the vessel at Queenstown. Atherton picked up the newspaper, curious to see if he could find some mention of the Gilchrist murder in its pages, no doubt surprised at how he had suddenly and unwittingly been drawn into the case. He found that the article about the murder had been torn out of the paper; thinking little of it, however, he threw the newspaper away and continued to clean the cabin.

Subsequent to the foul-weather voyage on the *Lusitania*, Oscar Slater's story continued to unfold, gathering attention from the press and public alike. Although there was not enough evidence to warrant extradition back to Scotland for a trial, Slater agreed to the extradition, apparently believing that he could easily clear his name of the charges. Stewardess Bedford and Bedroom Steward Thomas Atherton were called to give witness in the subsequent trial, a trial which many believed was biased. Slater was found guilty of murder in May of 1909 and he was condemned to death. Because of public outcry, however, his sentence was commuted to life in prison.

A year later, a Scottish lawyer and amateur criminologist, William Roughead, published the book *Trial of Oscar Slater*, which showed clearly the flaws in the prosecution's case, including the irrelevancy of the "significant" pawn ticket from Glasgow. In 1912, Sir Arthur Conan Doyle himself – famed creator of the fictional detective Sherlock Holmes – became involved in clearing the man's name. He published *The Case of Oscar Slater*, in which he pled for a full pardon. *The Truth About Oscar Slater* was published, by William Park, and by July of 1928, the conviction was overturned. Slater was released and received £6,000 in compensation for the years of mistaken imprisonment.

Indeed, Slater's trial and imprisonment was a gross miscarriage of justice. Although he was no saint, as the saying goes, he certainly was not guilty of murdering Miss Gilchrist. Slater was a German-born Jew who had lived for some time in the United States. When he moved to Glasgow, and set up as a dentist, it soon became clear to people in the community that he was not a man of high reputation, and that he certainly was no dentist. He had already been married in 1901 or 1902 to a woman named May Curtis, but later separated from his wife, apparently because of her drinking problem. Apparently, she subsequently tried to keep in touch with him, and was later said to have been "always bothering him and came after him" for money. Slater lived his life as a club manager, and was also apparently involved in trading precious stones, associating with criminals in the process.

Around 1905 Slater had met a woman named Andrée Junio Antoine at the Empire Theatre in London. At the time, she was around eighteen years of age, but was already a prostitute, with the professional name of Madame Junio. Soon a romance bloomed between

them, and they found a new life in America, traveling there under assumed names, where he ran a club in New York City. It was said that they formed a "left-handed alliance," but whether this was a formal marriage or a common-law marriage is not known. Eventually, they returned to Europe, settling in Glasgow only a few months before the murder. Although he was not entirely of good reputation, Slater had never found himself on the wrong side of the authorities before being charged with the slaying. Numerous witnesses vouched for his innocence, including Miss Antoine, who provided an alibi for his whereabouts at the time of the murder. The couple's departure from Glasgow had nothing to do with fleeing the scene of a murder, but was instead planned for some weeks, and had more to do with finding someone who agreed to take their flat than it did with guilt. They were traveling under assumed names, just as they had before, in order to avoid detection by Slater's wife, who was apparently still looking for him. It was later concluded by impartial – and informal – investigators that Miss Gilchrist was murdered by her own nephew.

Slater's case was a sad miscarriage of justice. However, the connection between this notorious story and the *Lusitania* was remarkable and was perhaps the most incredible tie to a criminal investigation in the whole of her career. The connection between the Slater case and the legendary liner, however, was little-remembered in subsequent years.[39]

Lawbreaking wasn't confined only to the *Lusitania's* passengers. For several months in 1910, there was a suspicious rash of robberies aboard the ship. On crossing after crossing there were complaints from passengers of being robbed; on one voyage alone some $4,000 came up missing. There was no chance that the robberies could be by a single passenger, because it was spread out over such a protracted period of time. Finally, in November of that year, the perpetrator was caught: it was a Boatswain's Mate named Joseph Weavill, who had been with the ship since her maiden voyage. Weavill had moved through the ranks from Seaman to Quartermaster, and then by his own request to Boatswain's Mate. This particular job put him in the position to commit the robberies. He was arrested in Liverpool, and sentenced to six months in jail.

Captain Turner was also apprehended once, during the late summer of 1909, although for a far less nefarious reason. Turner's beloved niece, Miss Mercedes Desmore, was living in New York at the time, and one of Turner's favorite pastimes was to be a good uncle and spoil her at every opportunity. She boarded the liner to meet her uncle one Friday night, and when

Left: *A pre-1912 photograph taken along the First Class Boat Deck.*

Opposite: *The* Lusitania *tied up in New York. This photograph clearly shows Pier 56 to the left; it was taken from the Aft Docking Bridge.*

West Side Pier. Over a thousand people gathered at the dock to meet their friends and relatives as they disembarked. Only about fifteen minutes after the ship left, word came to return to Quarantine immediately. A Romanian passenger in Third Class had a disease which the Deputy Health Officer could not diagnose in short order. Over an hour passed before a simple communiqué reached the city:

> Am anchoring off Stapleton for the night. Have not been passed by the doctor. CHARLES.

There were 915 Cabin Class – Cunard's terminology for combined First and Second Class passengers – and 1,125 Third Class passengers aboard. As word passed around the ship, they expressed no small amount of concern over the situation at hand. There was a cholera scare on in Europe at the time, and no one wanted to be stuck aboard a ship with an ailing passenger if there was any possibility of becoming sick. Overnight, bacteriological tests were carried out on the Romanian passenger, and by morning, they came back negative for anything infectious. The ship was duly cleared at 9:20 in the morning, and docked just before 11:00 a.m. The scare was quite real; fortunately, the threat had not materialized into anything dangerous for the ship's passengers and crew.

Corporate espionage was also a constant reality, particularly 1907 and 1908. When the *Lusitania* and *Mauretania* entered service, they were far and away the most technologically advanced liners of the time, and the German steamship lines were desperate to find out more about their workings. Armed with such information, they could create the appropriate response in their next generation of liners – and they could discover whether such liners were even financially feasible without government subsidies. In early September of 1908, there was a group of steamship men on the floor of the New York Maritime Exchange, and their conversation turned to whether the new Cunarders were really turning a profit. The general feeling seemed to be that if the British Government had not been providing an annual subsidy, they would have been losing ventures.

At this, a representative of a German steamship company piped up. "I will show you this is not so," he

they disembarked at 6:30 p.m., she was carrying a gift from Turner: a half-pound package of chocolate. As they passed the customs gate, she happened to be holding it in her hand and eating a piece of it. One of the customs inspectors stopped them dead in their tracks and insisted that they could not leave until a duty had been paid on the offending chocolates, and took them right from the girl's hand. Turner was incensed. During his entire career with Cunard he had never been stopped at the customs gate; to be taken to task like a criminal in front of his niece – especially over such a trivial thing – was unbearable. He quickly stormed off and re-boarded the *Lusitania*, but left a profound impression on the zealous customs official. Later on the customs man decided to return the chocolates to Captain Turner with an apology.

Somewhat less humorously, in early September of 1910, there was quite a scare on board. The ship arrived in New York late on a Thursday night with a full complement of passengers; indeed, it was noted that demand for this crossing was high enough that she could have booked twice as many as she could carry. After making her customary call at Quarantine and being given release, she set her nose toward her

ABSTRACT OF LOG.

R. M. S. "LUSITANIA."
Commander J. T.W. CHARLES,
R.D., R.N.R.

NEW YORK TO LIVERPOOL via FISHGUARD.

Date, 1911.	Distance.	Latitude.	Longitude.	Winds.
Wednesday, May 31	15	Ambrose Ch.	L'ship abeam	at 10-55 a.m.
Thursday, June 1	550	40·29 N	61·30 W	S.E'ly to S.W'ly
Friday, ,, 2	557	40·55 ,,	49·16 ,,	S.W'ly
Saturday, ,, 3	581	45·11 ,,	37·42 ,,	S.W'ly
Sunday, ,, 4	576	48·58 ,,	24·45 ,,	S.W'ly
Monday, ,, 5	563	51·15 ,,	10·30 ,,	S.W'ly to W'ly
,, ,, ,,	90	to Daunt's	Rock L'ship	3-37 p.m. Daunt's Rock L'ht abeam
From Ambrose Ch. L'ship to Daunt's Rock L'ship	2932			
	133	Daunt's Rock	to Fishguard	AVERAGE SPEED 24·49.
	148	Fishguard to	Liverpool	

PASSAGE:

Ambrose Channel Lightship to Daunt's Rock Lightship :--4 Days, 23 Hours, 42 Minutes.

ALL PASSENGER STEAMERS OF THE CUNARD LINE ARE FITTED WITH MARCONI'S SYSTEM OF WIRELESS TELEGRAPHY

THE "LUSITANIA" AND "MAURETANIA" HOLD ALL EASTWARD AND WESTWARD RECORDS FOR HIGHEST DAILY RUNS FASTEST PASSAGES, SHORTEST PASSAGES, AND HIGHEST SPEED.

A log abstract card from Crossing No. 112 East, made at an average speed of 24.49 knots, shows an interesting and unique bit of advertising that only Cunard could employ. At the very bottom, it shows that the Lusitania and Mauretania *then held "all eastward and westward records for highest daily runs, fastest passages, shortest passages, and highest speed." Such bragging rights were a boon to the British line, as the Germans – thanks to their corporate espionage – knew only too well.*

said. To back his claim, he produced a detailed set of figures that showed just how closely his company had been studying the new British ships during the preceding year. He was able to prove that not only were the new sister ships making good money, but that the entire fleet of the Cunard Line had picked up traffic because of the boasting rights that the company held over having the world's largest and fastest in their proverbial stable.

The Germans had certainly done their homework. During 1908, a certain Second Class passenger was seen traveling on the *Lusitania* quite frequently. He was no ordinary passenger, but he was instead a German marine engineer employed by one of the great German steamship companies. For some time this engineer had been known to possess a developed ear for listening to the operation of ships' engines. It was said that he could tell by the engines' strokes just how much coal was being consumed, and that every sound had a definite meaning for him. After months of traveling on the great liner, with his ear glued to the bulkheads, he reported to his superiors in their New York office that the ship was more efficient than commonly supposed.

The Germans did not rely on ears alone. It was said to be rather common during late 1907 and through 1908 for stokers, oilers and firemen to be thrown off the *Lusitania* and *Mauretania* after evidence had surfaced that they were German spies trying to find out more details on the liners' technology.

Trying to steal a ship's secrets would hardly have caused a threat to the overall safety of the liner. However, in November of 1911 there did come a potential threat to the overall safety of the *Lusitania*. Shortly after departing Queenstown westbound for New York, the electrical light wires in a Second Class cabin short-circuited and started a fire. The crew of the liner put the conflagration out in short order, before the blaze got out of hand. Initially the press reported that passengers were driven to the decks by "thick, pungent smoke," with the lights in the Second Class regions of the ship going out almost immediately. In reality, the affair was far less dramatic; First Class passengers were not even aware of the problem until the ship had docked in New York.[40]

Less dangerous to the safety of the ship, but nevertheless an irritation, were the professional gamblers that menaced uninitiated or gullible First Class pas-

The Lusitania *tied up at Pier 56 during the Hudson-Fulton Celebration in late 1909. She is dressed out for the event. Grandstands have also been built outside the pier structure so that spectators could watch the river traffic coming and going.*

sengers looking to pass the time while they traveled. One period guidebook advised: "Gentlemen should be very cautious about playing cards, or other games, with strangers, as professional gamblers are constantly crossing the Atlantic, looking out for the unwary. There is nothing unusual in the captain posting a notice in the smoking room warning passengers against gamblers."[41] Indeed, such notices were prominently displayed on the *Lusitania*, and at times special warnings were posted, as well. For example, in January of 1911, when one well-known card sharp was spotted boarding the ship with a companion, the two men were confronted by the ship's officers; they reassured the officers that they were not aboard for work, but had instead undertaken the crossing for other reasons. Captain Charles was informed immediately, and he ordered that the men's descriptions be printed and posted in the main companionways so that the passengers would be aware of their presence and – it was hoped – refrain from playing games of chance with them.

Even these precautions did not always protect passengers from being duped – warnings could be posted, but if passengers decided to play, there was little that the Line could do to protect them. That is exactly what happened late that May: a pair of professional gamblers took an estimated $14,000 – over a quarter of a million in 2005 U.S. dollars – during Westbound Crossing No. 111. At some points, there was over $1,000 sitting in the pot at any given time; although it did not become widely known through First Class regions of the ship what was going on, some did take an interest in the gaming and sat in to watch events unfold. One man played for an hour, losing a thousand dollars for his efforts before he quit in disgust at his "ill-luck." Luck had nothing to do with it. Another passenger who was observing had lived in the Western United States for most of his life; this was an area as notorious now as it was then for its gambling and cheating. After the crossing he recalled that he had "never in his experience ... seen such quick action and such a passing of signals as had marked" this series of games. Those that were being taken were dealt very good hands, "hands which, had the game been on the level, would have been worth every bit of the risk taken upon them." These "good hands" caused the players to wager in full confidence; at each turn of the cards, however, an even better hand prepared by the professional gamblers would top them. The losers paid up in full, and the card sharps disembarked with their enormous take.[42]

As troublesome as these incidents proved to be, there were also remarkable events of a pleasant or interesting nature. Between September 25 and October 11, 1909, the State of New York commemorated the 300th anniversary of the discovery of the Hudson River in 1609, and the anniversary of Robert Fulton's first voyage on that river under steam

in 1807. The festivities were aptly christened as the Hudson-Fulton Celebration. British and United States navy vessels were entering or anchored in the North River to participate in the event. On the day before the occasion began, the *Lusitania* arrived in New York. Steaming toward her pier at about four o'clock in the afternoon, she came up on the H.M.S. *Inflexible*, which had not reached her anchorage yet. The pilot kept the *Lusitania* quite close to the British flagship, and the warship's band serenaded the *Lusitania*'s passengers with British and American patriotic airs as they steamed side by side for two hours. The warship's decks were manned in salute, and the *Lusitania*'s passengers cheered wildly; finally, the *Lusitania* pulled ahead and proceeded to her pier.

Five days later, on Wednesday, September 29, 1909, the *Lusitania* was preparing to depart New York eastbound amidst the same celebration. That same morning, famed aviation pioneer Wilbur Wright made three short but groundbreaking flights around New York City, taking off from Governor's Island. These flights became a real highlight of the overall event. During the second of these adventures, which took place just after ten o'clock and lasted just five minutes, the audacious Wright passed directly over the *Lusitania*, which

Top: *The Wright Flyer, piloted by Wilbur Wright, takes off from Governor's Island as the* Lusitania *departs New York.*

Above: *The Wright Flyer moving just above the ground of Governor's Island, with all the harbor traffic busily moving about in the background.*

1. An artist's conception of the Lusitania during late 1914 or early 1915 steaming in the open ocean. With concerns over the Lusitania's safety waning, her drab gray disguise had been dropped, and she was repainted in civilian colors. Her funnels are once again seen in their unusual "Cunard red" livery, and a new bronze-gold band circles her superstructure between the Promenade and Shelter Decks.

Top: 2. *A July, 1907 photograph of the Lusitania, steaming off Gourock on her preliminary builder's trials. The photo was re-touched and colorized, and then was released in postcard format. The correct overall length of the Lusitania, namely 787 feet, is noted in the corner of the card.*

Second row: 3. *Another early July photograph of the Lusitania, hand colorized for distribution to the public. Although many individuals who worked on tinting photographs during that period were content to splash the Lusitania's funnels as a deep red, this artist has taken pains to accurately reproduce the correct shade of the Lusitania's smokestacks.*

Above left: 4. *An early piece of Rosenvinge artwork of the Lusitania in port. The ship's height is exaggerated and her prow is painted white; some details of her finished structure are also inaccurate. However, the scene really is a spectacular view.*

Above right: 5. *This view of the ship is well known to Lusitania enthusiasts, and shows her at high speed off Scotland in July of 1907. What is more unusual, however, is that the original black and white photograph was colorized and gives a more vivid idea of how impressive the ship's appearance was that summer. Notice that the artist has even tinted the reflection of her funnels in the water.*

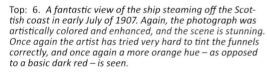

Top: 6. *A fantastic view of the ship steaming off the Scottish coast in early July of 1907. Again, the photograph was artistically colored and enhanced, and the scene is stunning. Once again the artist has tried very hard to tint the funnels correctly, and once again a more orange hue – as opposed to a basic dark red – is seen.*

Above left: 7. *The* Lusitania *entering the Canada Dry Dock in July of 1907. Most of the buildings visible around the dock have since been demolished. The railing on the dock wall, as well as the line of bitts on the dock, are still present.*

Above right: 8. *A modern photograph of the Canada Dry Dock in Liverpool, England. This is where the* Lusitania *was drydocked for the first time in July of 1907, and was the drydock that she used for most of her career. This view is looking out (in a generally westerly direction). Behind the mound of fill is the River Mersey.*

Bottom right: 9. *Another modern photo of the Canada Dry Dock, showing the raised portion at the head of the dock, and the staircase leading up to that platform. Notice that in the July of 1907 photograph (above) the same staircase and railing are visible.*

Above: 10. *A pre-maiden voyage view of the* Lusitania *in the Sloyne. Although the coloring of the funnels is far too dark, the view is stunning in giving some idea of the ship's presence.*

Below: 11. *The* Lusitania *towers over New York's Pier 54 immediately after her maiden arrival.*

Opposite: 12. *This splendid image was taken from the Crow's Nest, looking aft over the upper decks of the* Lusitania. *It clearly shows the extra compass tower that was installed atop the Bridge, and the frame for the sun shades which had been erected above it. Two men, who appear to be officers, stand on the starboard side of the Sun Deck, just abaft a ventilator.*

Above left: 13. *This Christmas greeting card featuring the* Lusitania *brings to mind scenes of Captain Dow sitting with his officers, enjoying their 1913 Christmas dinner of turkey and plum pudding, while Captain Dow regaled them with his famous stories, using his pipe as a prop to help inject life into the tale.*

Above right: 14. *The cover of the January 1, 1910 menu, the inner pages of which can be seen on page 226.*

Bottom right: 15. *A June 3, 1911 Second Class menu shows a two-funneled Cunarder off the French Riviera.*

Left: 16. *A startling starboard profile of the* Lusitania *at sea in late 1910. With smoke pouring from all four funnels, the ship is making good speed in calm weather.*

Bottom left: 17. *An artist's view of the* Lusitania *entering New York harbor at the conclusion of one of her late-1913 westbound crossings. Behind the ship are the high-rises of Lower Manhattan, including the Singer and Woolworth Buildings. New York was a "home away from home" for the* Lusitania, *and she became a fixture of that city's Lower West Side during her career.*

SECOND CABIN

R.M.S. "LUSITANIA."

SATURDAY, JUNE 3rd 1911

MENU.

Tomato Soup

Boiled Codfish, Parsley Sauce

Veal Cutlets with Ham, Sauce Piquante
Duckling en Compote, Green Peas

Roast Forequarter of Lamb, Mint Sauce

Spring Cabbage   Lima Beans
Boiled Rice   Boiled and Mashed Potatoes

Swiss Apple Tart   Assorted Pastry
Blancmange and Custard

Ice Cream

Cheese   Dessert

Tea   Coffee

18. *An artistically colorized photograph of the Lusitania's Lounge & Music Room. This photo shows the after fireplace, the Broadwood grand piano and, through the open doors, the First Class Smoking Room astern.*

19. *A spectacular hand-color view of the First Class Lounge. The treatment of colors is probably more authentic than the previous view, but the two illustrations together give a splendid idea of how the room really looked.*

20. *A Rosenvinge illustration of the First Class Smoking Room in use. Based on the high degree of accuracy in this illustration, it may have been based on an actual photograph which was then artistically colorized and enhanced.*

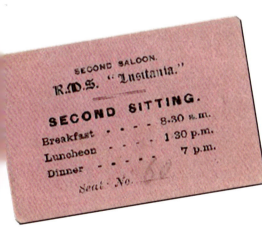

Top: 21. *This fine starboard-bow view shows the Lusitania on the open sea during the war. She has dropped her initial masquerade and returned to her civilian colors, but a gold band separates her hull and superstructure. Her funnels still retain their Cunard-red color, but that would change before she began her 202nd crossing on May 1, 1915. In service for over seven years, the ship still cuts an impressive profile.*

Above: 22. *A Second Class seating ticket for the second seating meals during the final crossing of the Lusitania.*

Right: 23. *The most beautiful illustration of the ship's interior ever produced shows the First Class Dining Saloon in all its glory. The red and gold colors present in the room really stand out from their appearance in ordinary black and white photographs. The picture is completed with the passengers, all dressed in their Edwardian best, taking their seats for dinner and socializing with fellow passengers. Interestingly, during construction, Cunard toned down the brightness of the gold adornment until it was an old French color.*

Above: 24. *The Lusitania closes the Irish coast on the afternoon of Friday, May 7, 1915. Visible in the distance is the Old Head of Kinsale. The ship loafs along at an easy pace, and the general feeling among many passengers is that the dangers of the crossing are coming to an end. Nothing could have been further from the truth. A seven-and-a-half-year career was coming to a close, and some two thousand people were about to be swept up in its violent final chapter. Twelve hundred men, women and children would not survive*

Opposite: 25. *The stern of the Lusitania rises from the sea as her bow plunges beneath the waves. Her propellers have breached the surface; in the chaos on deck, the officers attempt to fill and safely lower the lifeboats on the starboard side. The Irish coast lies tantalizingly close but, ultimately, too far away to offer refuge in shallow waters.*

26. *An outstanding, dramatic portrayal of the Lusitania's demise. Based on the original illustrations by* Lusitania *survivor Oliver Bernard found on page 324, this view shows the last moments of the sinking. Boat No. 11, carrying Oliver Bernard and many others, sits all too close to the dying liner; within moments, they would be pushing off from the No. 4 funnel as it slid past them. Boat No. 15, under the charge of First Officer Jones, is just a little farther away. Hundreds of people from all walks of life cling desperately to anything that they can; most would perish in the chill waters.*

Above: 27. *The wreck of the* Lusitania *on the seafloor, within hours of the sinking. It is very difficult to ascertain just what the wreck looked like that afternoon, because it is such a horrendous mess today. However, the positioning of the steam pipes leading to the funnels suggests that, contrary to some artistic depictions, the funnels were not dismounted until the ship was on or near her final resting place, indeed, that some of them were only dismounted from their position later. Some of the lifeboats were still attached to the ship when it sank, as seen here. The split in the center of the ship's hull is still visible today. Today the wreck is pancaked down to roughly half of its original width, and all of the upper superstructure is detached. Although some of this no doubt resulted from the forces in play as the ship sank, a lot of the damage seems to have been done when the wreck was used as depth-charging target practice during later years; in fact, some of these unexploded depth charges remain around the wreck today. Much of the damage visible was probably due to the depth charging, although the depth charging was almost certainly for less nefarious reasons than is commonly supposed. All of this means that it is likely that the wreck looked much the way portrayed in this view on the afternoon of May 7, 1915.*

Below: 28. *The* Lusitania's *prow is one of the few places easily recognized on the wreck today. She is a broken, tangled mess that bears no resemblance to her former glory, when she endured everything that the North Atlantic could throw at her, safely conveying her passengers from one side to the other for seven-and-a-half years over the course of 201 crossings.*

Above: 29. *A 2007 photograph of Cunard's longtime monarch* Queen Elizabeth 2 *in Liverpool, England. Her keel was laid on the banks of the Clyde River in July of 1965 as John Brown Hull No. 736 — the same company which had built the* Lusitania, *as well as other Cunard wonders such as the* Aquitania, Queen Mary, *and* Queen Elizabeth. *Pictured here some thirty-eight years after her maiden voyage, the QE2 is tied up almost exactly where the* Lusitania *tied up during her seven-and-a-half-year career (see the photograph on page 160). Clearly visible behind the ship's bow is the Royal Liver Building, with the Cunard Building and Port of Liverpool Buildings just to the right.*

Below: 30. *Seen in early 2007, the Royal Liver Building is awash in light, with the Cunard Building just to its right, and the end of the Port of Liverpool Building just visible at the photograph's extreme right. Although some of the other structures forming the city skyline are far more modern-looking, there are still elements of the city that would have been familiar to the* Lusitania *and her travelers during her career.*

Below left: 31. *The salvaged propeller of the* Lusitania *resting at the Merseyside Maritime Museum.*

Below right: 32. *This key belonged to the* Lusitania's *Wheelhouse. It was safely preserved through the sinking by Quartermaster Hugh Johnston, who was on duty at the ship's helm at the time of the disaster. Johnston stayed at his post until just moments before the Bridge was swamped.*

Bottom: 33. *Albert J. Byington's wine account from the last voyage, which he brought with him as he left the dying liner.*

Above: *A moonlit stroll on deck frequently led to shipboard romances.*

Below: *A wonderful view, from about 1911, of the ship re-coaling at Pier 56. Despite the presence of the coaling tenders, the aft lifeboats have been swung out preparatory to a lifeboat drill.*

ally made an impression on him. He later recalled that even from high in the air, he could feel their pounding vibration resonate through his body. The surreal moment passed quickly, but it was certainly noteworthy in historic context … just fifty short years later, aircraft would sound the death knell for transatlantic passenger trade.

The *Lusitania* also seemed to be gifted with the romantic touch. Because of her prestige and her proximity to New York and London society, it was quite common to find newlywed couples crossing in one direction or the other on a leg of their honeymoon. It was considered quite the thing to have an early morning wedding in one of New York's more notable churches, and then to take breakfast at Delmonico's before embarking on the *Lusitania* for her eastbound crossing. Every wedding day has its stresses, however; in October of 1908, Mr. Forbes Hennessy and Miss Margaret Sheehan had quite a shock when they found that the departure of the *Lusitania* had been moved up from 11:00 a.m. to 9:00 a.m. The ceremony had been planned at 8:00 that morning at St. Patrick's Cathedral, with the breakfast at Delmonico's set to follow. The three-month-long European honeymoon simply wouldn't wait, and it was decided to move the ceremony up to 6:45. The officiating monsignor was no doubt trying to stifle a yawn or two as he presided, and once the couple had been officially joined, they hastened to the ship directly, choosing to have breakfast in the First Class Dining Saloon of the *Lusitania*. Here the cuisine and the surroundings were no doubt

had just departed her pier and was moving down the North River toward open water. Wright had received many salutes from waterborne craft that morning, but it was the *Lusitania*'s triple-toned whistles that re-

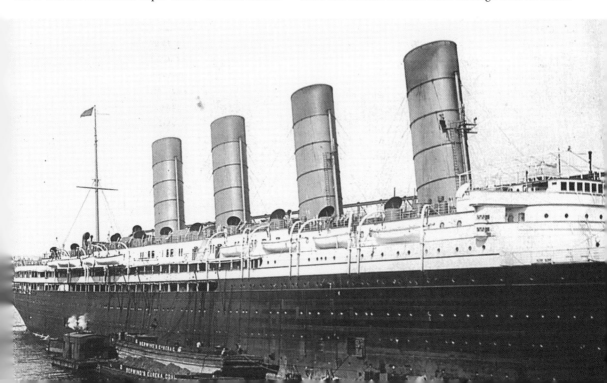

Mr. Jos. B. Black
Mr. Charles F. Bliss
Mr. M. Blum
Mr. M. J. Brandenstein
Mrs. Brandenstein and maid
Mrs. Ruth Brandenstein
Master Joseph Brandenstein
Mr. Abraham Bijur
Mrs. Bijur
Mr. Arthur Brichant
Mr. William Clinton Brown
Mr. D. E. Brown
Miss Hazel Brown
Mr. Henry A. Budd

Miss J. Callaghan
Mr. Thomas Carrick
Mrs. Carrick
Her Excellency Mme. de Carriere
Mr. B. Cerame
Mr. Chapman
Miss Mabel Charles
Mr. S. C. Childs
Mrs. Childs
Miss Marion Childs
Mr. Peter B. Chisem
Mrs. Chisem
Miss I. Chisem
Mr. Hugh Chisholm
Mr. William Lee Church

Mrs. Clark and maid
Miss Mary de Forest Clark
Mr. A. S. Coelho
Mr. J. Cohen
Mr. Howard Cohen
Mrs. Max Cohen
Miss L. Cohen
Mr. J. de Cordova
Miss M. de Cordova
Mr. E. W. Cramer
Mrs. Cramer and maid
Mr. Wm. F. Crawford
Mr. R. B. Cueto
Mr. C. Cueto
Mr. Thomas M. Curtis

Mr. V. F. Deacon
Mr. W. D. Denegre
Mrs. Denegre and maid
Miss Frances B. Denton
Mr. J. J. Desmond
Mrs. Desmond
Miss Marjorie Desmond
Master Lawrence Desmond
Mr. Rudolph Deutsch
Mr. W. L. Douglas
Mrs. Maldwin Drummond and maid
Mrs. John Duveen and maid
Miss Mildred Duveen and nurse
Master Ormond Duveen and nurse

Mr. T. R. Ellison
Mrs. James Elverson and maid
Mrs. L. Erdin
Miss J. Erdin
Mr. Ernest Eugster

Mr. Julian P. Fairchild
Capt. Chas. Fauvel
Mr. Charles Fochheimer
Mr. J. G. Findlay
Mrs. Findlay
Mr. Manuel Fernandez
Mr. W. Findley
Mr. J. Grant Forbes
Mrs. Forbes
Miss Marie Louise Field
Mr. de Fiorre
Mr. A. N. C. Freadgold
Mr. J. J. Friedman
Mrs. Friedman
Mr. Walter Fryer

Sir Frank Newnes, Bart
Mr. W. Newhouse
Miss E. K. Norris

Mr. Thomas O'Connor
Mrs. O'Connor
Mrs. McKinley Osborne and maid
Miss Elizabeth Osborne
Miss Francis Osborne

Mr. Adolph Hahn
Mr. Julius H. Hahlo
Mr. Oliver Ambrose Hales
Miss Clarissa Hales
Mr. James Marwick Hales
Mr. H. M. Harwood
Mr. Ho Ficoluka & Hasler
Mr. Walter Hately
Mrs. E. C. Hawkins
Miss Agnes C. Hawkins
Mr. Thomas Hayes
Mr. Leland Hayes
Mr. J. Leslie Hees
Mr. Ralph M. Helmer
Dr. W. A. Hennrich
Mr. D. W. Herrman
Mr. Arthur J. Herschman
Mr. J. Hislop
Mrs. Hislop
Mr. C. G. Hill
Mr. Fred. C. Hood
Mrs. H. C. Hoover and maid
Master Herbert Hoover
Master Allan Hoover
Mr. O. O. Howard
Mrs. Howard
Mr. Allan Hughes
Mr. Wm. Hutchinson

Mr. Charles Ickle
Mr. H. G. Imamura

Mr. C. M. Jackson
Mr. D. F. Jackson
Mr. Malcolm D. Jeffrey
Miss M. Jones
Miss Sadie G. Jones
Mrs. Pembroke Jones and maid
Miss Margaret Johnson
Mrs. Adolphe M. S. Johnston

Mr. L. Kaiser
Miss Marguerite Kaufman and maid
Mr. S. H. Kahn
Mrs. Kahn
Mrs. J. Kaufman
Mr. John A. Kelly
Mr. F. Kinnell
Mr. Geo. W. Kettle
Mrs. Kettle
Mr. Wm. A. Keys
Mrs. Keys
Mr. George F. Knuble
Mr. Bernhard R. Klug
Mr. Richard D. Knight
Mr. W. F. Knox
Mrs. Knox
Mr. Jacob Kohn
Mrs. Adolph Kramer
Miss Hilde Kramer
Master Eric Kramer
Mr. A. A. Kuhn

Mr. John Larkin
Mr. Herbert H. Lehman
Mrs. Lehman and maid
Miss Lilly Lena
Mr. Ben Lichtenstein
Mrs. Lichtenstein
Miss Liebenstein

Miss Maass
Mr. F. J. Mackey and valet
Mrs. Max Mandel
Mr. S. J. Marshall
Mr. Wm. L. Marshall
Mr. James Marwick
Mr. F. G. Matthews
Mr. J. Mead
Mr. Wm. B. Melish
Mrs. Melish
Mr. Jules Mendel
Mr. Mendel
Mr. John Meyer
Mr. Richard S. McCreary
Mr. Geo. E. Mac Donald
Mrs. Mac Donald
Mr. W. M. McIlvay
Mr. J. Lawrence McKeever
Mrs. Morton Mitchell
Mr. James Mitchell
Mr. H. J. Montefiore
Mr. H. A. Morgan
Mr. Palmer B. Morrison
Mrs. Morrison
Mr. G. G. Mosley
Mr. C. C. Murphy
Mrs. Murphy
Mr. Daniel Meese
Mr. Gurnee Munn
Mrs. C. A. Munn and maid
Miss Gladys M. Munn

Miss Ruby Raymond
Miss Leona Redd
Mr. Charles F. Richmond
Miss Elizabeth B. Rea and valet
Mr. H. J. Reckatt and maid
Mrs. Reckett and maid
Mr. George C. Riggs
Mrs. Riggs and maid
Mr. Edward Roberts
Mrs. Roberts
Mrs. Howard Roberts and maid
Mr. J. A. Robertson
Mrs. Robertson
Mr. Wm. Robins
Mrs. Robins
Mrs. J. Franklin Robinson
Mr. Annie D. Robinson
Mrs. David Roney
Mr. W. B. Rosskam
Mrs. Rosskam
Mr. Edward Rothschild
Mrs. Rothschild
Mr. Henry W. Rudd and manservant

Mr. Frank Samuel
Mr. Oswald Sanderson
Mr. A. Schwartz
Mr. S. Schluechterer
Mrs. M. Scott
Mr. Jose Seoane
Mr. Charles A. Sherman
Miss Hedwige Siefert
Mr. Samuel Slimowitz
Mr. J. G. Smith
Mr. Franklin G. Smith
Mrs. Smith
Mr. Frank L. Smith
Mr. F. R. Smith
Mr. B. F. Smith
Mr. John Spalekhaven
Mr. W. S. Spaulding
Mrs. Spaulding and maid
Mr. J. K. Spittal
Mr. John C. Spooner
Mr. Philip Spooner
Mr. F. B. Springer
Mr. B. Springer and maid
Miss Anita Springer
Mr. T. W. Stewart
Mr. H. A. Stillwell
Mr. B. B. Strassburger
Mr. A. A. Strassburger
Mr. W. A. Streeter
Mr. J. F. Sullivan
Mr. J. L. Sullivan

Mr. C. Carlisle Taylor
Mr. Geo. F. Tenaille
Mr. Sterling H. Thomas
Mr. Philip R. Thompson and valet
Count Leon D. Tolstoy
Mrs. John D. Tomlinson
Mr. Morris Toppelman
Mr. C. E. Trampler
Mr. A. R. Turner
Mrs. Turner

Miss Alma Upham

Mrs. H. A. Vernet

Miss Joan Waldron
Mr. W. H. Waldron
Mrs. Waldron
Mr. Henry Waiters
Sir Jos. Ward
Lady Ward
Mr. G. Ward
Miss Ward
Mr. Louis S. Waring
Mrs. Waring
Mr. W. T. Warren
Mr. Alexis Wasseleff
Mr. S. Whibley
Mr. F. W. Whitridge
Mrs. Whitridge and maid
Miss Joan Whitridge
Mr. J. Beaver White
Mr. A. P. Williams
Mr. Geo. D. Widener valet and chauffeur
Mrs. Widener and maid
Miss Eleanor E. Widener and maid
Mr. George D. Widener, Jr.
Mr. H. S. Winton
Mr. Francis Willey
Mr. H. R. Winthrop and valet
Mrs. Winthrop and maid
Mr. D. Wolf
Mr. R. B. Woodbury
Mr. H. K. Woodman
Mr. S. Woodman
Mrs. Wm. H. Young

Opposite top left: *A unique view of the ship docked in New York, looking down along the length of the ship.*

Opposite bottom: *This photograph shows the* Lusitania *in the Mersey around 1911. The anchor crane at the bow is in use, as are the cargo derricks connected to the foremast. Also of interest is that the hull is in the process of being repainted, with equipment over the side to assist the process.*

Opposite top right, this page above: *A First Class passenger list from Crossing No. 108 East. Among the passengers on the voyage were composers Irving Berlin and Jerome Kern.*

just as noteworthy as at their originally intended breakfast destination.

Crossings aboard the *Lusitania* even sparked frequent "shipboard romances," just as it did aboard other ships of the era. Such fraternization was almost always confined to members of a single traveling class, however, and not between those from op-

posite ends of society. Separating the classes was a series of bulkheads and gates of all sizes and shapes that were, by their very design, not meant to be circumvented. "First class passengers are not allowed to enter second or third class compartments, and vice versa, as complications might arise under the quarantine regulations. Visits to the steerage can only be made by special permission," prospective travelers were advised.[43] However, within the confines of a single class, there were many shipboard romances aboard the *Lusitania* in those years – whether it had to do with the invigorating sea air, the romantic atmosphere aboard the ship, or even just a moonlit stroll on the Promenade Deck, where there was never a "conjunction more fatal for an innocent flirtation," and where cupid marked "the spot and the scene for his own."[44] Although most of these romances faded with the crossing's end, others thrived for years to follow.

Sea voyages were always social affairs, even when romance was not involved; the "shipboard friendship" is legendary with good reason. One period piece of literature on ocean travel put it this way: "The forming of pleasant acquaintances passes away many agreeable hours ... With discernment and tact often a lifelong friendship is formed on an ocean voyage." By observing social amenities and courtesies, it was virtually guaranteed that the voyage would be "one of the most agreeable experiences of life."[45]

The world around the *Lusitania*, however, was changing during her career. Although the *Lusitania* was the largest "in service" passenger liner for less than two months in 1907, Cunard touted the two sisters as being "the world's largest steamships," in addition to being the fastest, in their advertising. After June of 1911, however, they could only claim the title of the "world's fastest steamships," for in that month, the White Star Line countered Cunard's challenge by putting into service the newest and largest steamship in the world: the *Olympic*.

The *Olympic* was far larger than either Cunard sister. She was 882 feet 9 inches in length – some ninety-five feet longer than the *Lusitania*, and over ninety feet longer than the *Mauretania*. She was also somewhat wider, at 92 feet 6 inches in maximum breadth. She sported a fuller figure than the Cunard sisters, with a much greater proportion of her hull bearing the full beam than did the hulls of the *Lusitania* and *Mauretania*. This was possible because she was designed primarily for comfort at sea, not speed. At 45,324 tons, she was nearly half again as big as the speed queens in enclosed volume. In size and grandeur, she truly trumped the competition. While the

Above: *A 1911-era photograph of the* Lusitania *at the Prince's Stage.*

Opposite page: *The White Star giant* Olympic *arrived in New York for the first time on June 21, 1911. As she entered port and was warped into Pier 59, White Star's pier, the* Lusitania *was departing on Crossing No. 114 East. She can be seen backing out of Pier 54 on the left side of each image. Interestingly, Captain Charles of the* Lusitania *did not salute the newer, larger liner during his departure. Some felt that this was a snub against the* Olympic; *others more charitably chose to believe that Captain Charles was simply too busy taking his ship out to offer this customary courtesy.*

Lusitania and *Mauretania* eagerly dove through and sometimes under heavy seas, the *Olympic* gracefully pitched over them. Her fuller beam supplied a higher rolling stability that was very forgiving to her passengers. Being kept out of the race for the Blue Riband, at a service speed just over 21 knots, the *Olympic* also lacked the noticeable vibration of the Cunarders. Her powerplant was unique in the annals of maritime shipbuilding: two four-cylinder triple-expansion reciprocating engines driving outboard screws, with waste steam vented into a single low-pressure turbine driving a center prop. The ship put some 46,000 nominal horsepower into the water, compared to the Cunarders' 60,000-plus each. *Olympic* was a true "floating palace," with plenty of space for the niceties and comforts that the Cunarders simply could not afford within their slim hulls.[46]

The *Lusitania* and *Mauretania* were hopelessly outsized; however, they had the advantage of good reputation. This advantage was further highlighted when the *Olympic's* sister ship, *Titanic*, made her maiden voyage beginning on April 10, 1912. The crossing ended ignominiously four and a half days later, after a collision with an iceberg. Fifteen hundred lives were lost in the disaster, primarily due to a lack of lifeboats; a lack of lifeboat drills and familiarity with their operation also seemed to dampen the attempts by her officers to get the boats loaded and lowered. In the end, the Cunarder *Carpathia* rescued the *Titanic's* survivors. The *Titanic* disaster was the worst in maritime history up to that point, and it sent shockwaves through the industry. The *Olympic* caught the brunt of the backlash, being so nearly identical to *Titanic*; she was removed from service and thoroughly overhauled, with additional lifeboats and watertight bulkheads being installed.

One of the *Titanic's* passengers, Benjamin Guggenheim, would have been alive if he had sailed as planned on the *Lusitania*; however, when the Cunarder's April sailing had been canceled so that she could be drydocked for maintenance, Guggenheim transferred to the *Titanic*. This was, in retrospect, a very poor decision. Minutes before the ship sank, Guggenheim is reported to have said of himself and his manservant,

On April 10, 1912, the second Olympic-class liner – Titanic – left Southampton on her maiden voyage. Her introduction in service meant more competition for the Lusitania; *five days later, however, the* Titanic *lay at the bottom of the North Atlantic. The sinking had dramatic repercussions on the entire shipping industry, and the* Lusitania *and other ships did not escape unaffected.*

"We've dressed up in our best and are prepared to go down as gentlemen."[47] Another passenger who was to sail in First Class on the *Titanic*'s disastrous maiden crossing had instead opted to go early on the *Lusitania* before she was laid up. This was none other than Guglielmo Marconi, founder of the Marconi Company, whose technology had enabled a rescue of the *Titanic*'s passengers. Because of his extremely fortuitous decision, he was in New York in the days immediately following the disaster, meeting *Titanic*'s surviving wireless operator and participating in the American Inquiry into her sinking.[48]

While the *Olympic* was suffering from the stigma of her sister, the entire shipping industry was suffering, as well. The *Lusitania* and her sister had, fortuitously, been in service for over four years, building a reputation for safety and reliability. Even so, neither sister had enough lifeboats on board for their full passenger and crew complement. Cunard quickly placed more collapsibles and lifeboats aboard the *Lusitania*, so that she would have lifeboat capacity for all. She sailed from Liverpool for the first time after the *Titanic* disaster on April 28, 1912. The additional lifeboat installation was nothing if not hasty; up to the last moment before departure, crewmen could be seen fitting the new lifeboats aboard the Boat Deck. The *Olympic*'s first sailing from Southampton after

A photograph of the starboard Boat Deck of the Lusitania, *with a man posing proudly beside Boat No. 7. In the wake of the* Titanic *disaster, lifeboats took on a previously unknown importance to passengers, crew, and ship owners. Wicker chairs are visible at left, a comfortable seating arrangement for passengers wanting to lounge on deck. On the Promenade Deck below were the more typical deck chairs.*

A stern view of the Lusitania, *probably in Liverpool. Her lower gangway doors are opened, and the ship seems to be making preparations for another crossing.*

the disaster had been canceled because a large portion of her Firemen had mutinied. Although the *Lusitania* did not carry any of *Olympic*'s intended passengers from that canceled trip, she did carry the mails that had been allotted to the *Olympic*. On the Cunarder's return trip from New York, she also carried some of those who had survived the *Titanic* disaster, including Sir Cosmo and Lady Duff Gordon. Cunard sent the *Lusitania* via the longer southward passage to further ensure that she avoided any encounters with icebergs. Additionally, Cunard quickly instituted the aforementioned role of the Staff Captain to oversee shipboard activities, especially lifeboat drills. During later refits, extra amidships davits – two on either side of the First Class Boat Deck, and one on either side of the Second Class Boat Deck – were installed as well, adding to the security her passengers could feel.

When the *Olympic* was removed from service late in 1912 for her complete refit and overhaul, the *Lusitania* and *Mauretania* were left as the unrivaled crack liners on the Atlantic trade once again. This did not last for a long time, however; in June of the following year, there came a new competitor, Hamburg-Amerika's *Imperator*. This monster ship was the first to exceed nine hundred feet in length, and sported a gross tonnage of 52,117, some twenty thousand tons more than the *Lusitania*. She could carry almost 5,800 passengers and crew within her cavernous interiors. Her First Class appointments were considered by many the finest and most luxurious ever installed on an ocean liner. It wasn't all bad news for Cunard, however. The *Imperator* proved to be a 'first rate hotel but a third rate ship,' in the words of Hamburg-Amerika's Director, Albert Ballin. She was horribly top-heavy – earning the dubious nickname *"Limperator"* – and rather prone to fire. In her first year of service, she never satisfied Hamburg-Amerika's hopes. During a major overhaul between 1913 and 1914, drastic measures were taken to reduce top-weight and increase stability. About ten feet were cut off the tops of each of her three funnels; less grandiose, lighter-weight materials were also substituted for many of her First Class appointments, and tons of cement were unceremoniously dumped into her double bottom.

In 1914, Hamburg-Amerika put a second sister into service: the *Vaterland*. She was even larger than the *Imperator*, and proved to be a much better-built ship, having been constructed in a completely different yard from the first vessel, and based on greater experience

This and following spread: *A series of nine photographs taken on Crossing No. 138 East, May 8-14, 1912. They show life on board the* Lusitania *within a month of the* Titanic *disaster. This was the return leg of her first round-trip voyage following the sinking.*

Opposite top: *Captain James Charles is clearly visible on the starboard wing, with two officers on his left and one to his right. The weather is clear and fair, not very different from that encountered by the* Titanic *on her first crossing.*

Opposite bottom left: *The photographer has turned to face aft, and is overlooking the starboard Boat Deck. Immediately apparent are the extra lifeboats resting on the deck. As the* Lusitania *was undergoing maintenance at the time of the White Star liner's loss, her crew had been able to install the extra lifeboats even before she had returned to the Atlantic. Some members of her crew had nearly decided to strike, as crewmen on the* Olympic *had done just after the* Titanic's *sinking. In the end, however, they were reassured enough on the reliability of the new extra lifeboats that they decided to make the trip. Because of the* Olympic *crew's strike and canceled voyage, some of the* Olympic's *mail had been transferred to the* Lusitania *on Crossing No. 137 West.*

Opposite bottom right: *On the port side of the Sun Deck, standing between the first and second funnels, looking aft. Just visible on the left is the second compass platform.*

Below left: *On the Sun Deck, looking forward from the vicinity of the fourth funnel.*

Below right: *From the Sun Deck, aft, looking forward along the port Boat Deck. This photo shows more details on the extra lifeboats; they included regular lifeboats, visible amidships, as well as collapsibles, which can be seen stowed underneath the original lifeboats.*

Top: *Third Class passengers promenading on the Forecastle. In rough weather, this space was uninhabitable.*

Above: *Standing on the Promenade Deck overlooking the fantail and stern.*

Opposite top: *The starboard Promenade Deck, looking forward.*

Opposite bottom: *Standing beside one of the lifeboats on the Boat Deck.*

Above: *An early photograph of the HAPAG giant* Imperator, *which entered service in early 1913.*

Below: *A menu from the* Lusitania, *January 1, 1910 – Crossing No. 70 East – celebrating the start of a new year for the liner. In pencil on the left can be seen a listing of individuals, probably those who were at the owner's Dining Saloon table.*

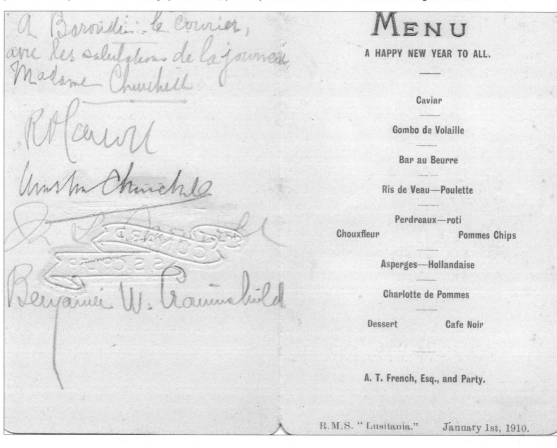

MENU

A HAPPY NEW YEAR TO ALL.

———

Caviar

Gombo de Volaille

Bar au Beurre

Ris de Veau—Poulette

Perdreaux—roti

Chouxfleur   Pommes Chips

Asperges—Hollandaise

Charlotte de Pommes

Dessert   Cafe Noir

A. T. French, Esq., and Party.

R.M.S. " Lusitania."   January 1st, 1910.

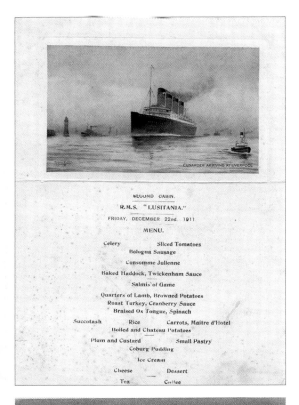

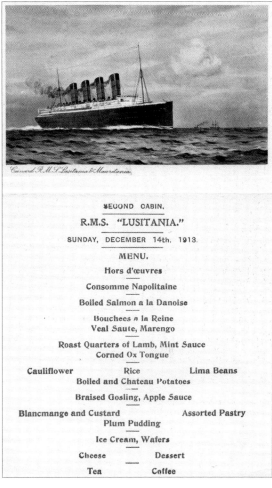

SECOND CABIN.

R.M.S. "LUSITANIA."

FRIDAY, DECEMBER 22nd, 1911

MENU.

Celery   Sliced Tomatoes
Bologna Sausage
Consomme Julienne
Baked Haddock, Twickenham Sauce
Salmis of Game
Quarters of Lamb, Browned Potatoes
Roast Turkey, Cranberry Sauce
Braised Ox Tongue, Spinach
Succotash   Rice   Carrots, Maitre d'Hotel
Boiled and Chateau Potatoes
Plum and Custard   Small Pastry
Coburg Pudding
Ice Cream
Cheese   Dessert
Tea   Coffee

SECOND CABIN.

R.M.S. "LUSITANIA."

SUNDAY, DECEMBER 14th, 1913.

MENU.

Hors d'œuvres

Consomme Napolitaine

Boiled Salmon a la Danoise

Bouchees a la Reine
Veal Saute, Marengo

Roast Quarters of Lamb, Mint Sauce
Corned Ox Tongue

Cauliflower   Rice   Lima Beans
Boiled and Chateau Potatoes

Braised Gosling, Apple Sauce

Blancmange and Custard   Assorted Pastry
Plum Pudding

Ice Cream, Wafers

Cheese   Dessert

Tea   Coffee

CUNARD
MUSIC
PROGRAMME

Top left: *A Second Class menu from Crossing No. 130 East, dated December 22, 1911.*

Above: *This Second Class menu was from Crossing No. 165 West. Certainly few passengers could have complained of a limited selection of culinary experiences while aboard the* Lusitania.

Left: *The cover of a "Cunard Music Programme" from the* Lusitania.

Next page: *A summer of 1912 photograph of the* Lusitania *docking at Liverpool. The officer on the pier is in his summer whites, while on the ship's side, nearly every porthole is open for ventilation.*

Left: *Countess de Bertier and her young son Arnaud arriving in New York on the* Lusitania *in January of 1914, at the end of Crossing No. 167 West. They are standing on the starboard Boat Deck; just behind them are the doors which lead into the First Class Grand Entrance.*

Below, inset: *A concert program from Crossing No. 171 West, in March of 1914.*

Below, main: *A bow view of the* Lusitania *arriving in New York at the conclusion of Crossing No. 171 West, on March 6, 1914.*

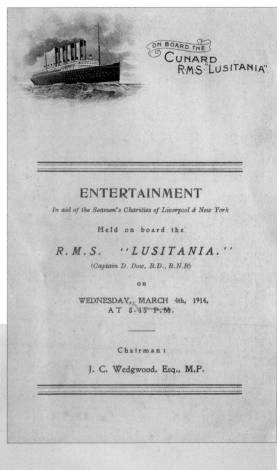

ON BOARD THE
CUNARD
R·M·S. "LUSITANIA".

ENTERTAINMENT

In aid of the Seamen's Charities of Liverpool & New York

Held on board the

R.M.S. "LUSITANIA."

(*Captain D. Dow, R.D., R.N.R.*)

on

WEDNESDAY, MARCH 4th, 1914,
AT 8-45 P.M.

Chairman:

J. C. Wedgwood, Esq., M.P.

with ships of her ilk. *Vaterland* was astoundingly spacious and luxurious, but the two Cunard sisters still had the advantage of speed.

On May 30 of that same year, a new Cunard liner, which was to be paired up with the *Lusitania* and *Mauretania*, began her maiden voyage. She was the *Aquitania*. At 901' 6" in overall length and 97' wide, she sported a gross tonnage of 45,647. Although not quite as large as the German sisters, she was longer than the White Star sisters *Olympic* and *Britannic* (which vessel was still unfinished), and was certainly competitive with the White Star and HAPAG giants.

She was not designed to be as fast as the *Lusitania* or *Mauretania*, but rather to make a somewhat more relaxed 23-24 knots. Having sacrificed those crucial 2-3 knots, she was intended to give her passengers a thoroughly comfortable ride. Her hull was designed to ride over swells instead of dashing through them; inside, her First Class public rooms were lavishly and tastefully decorated to compete with the other first-rate liners plying the Atlantic. Placed under the command of Captain William Turner, and with her engines under the watchful eye of Chief Engineer Archibald Bryce, the *Aquitania* was an instantaneous

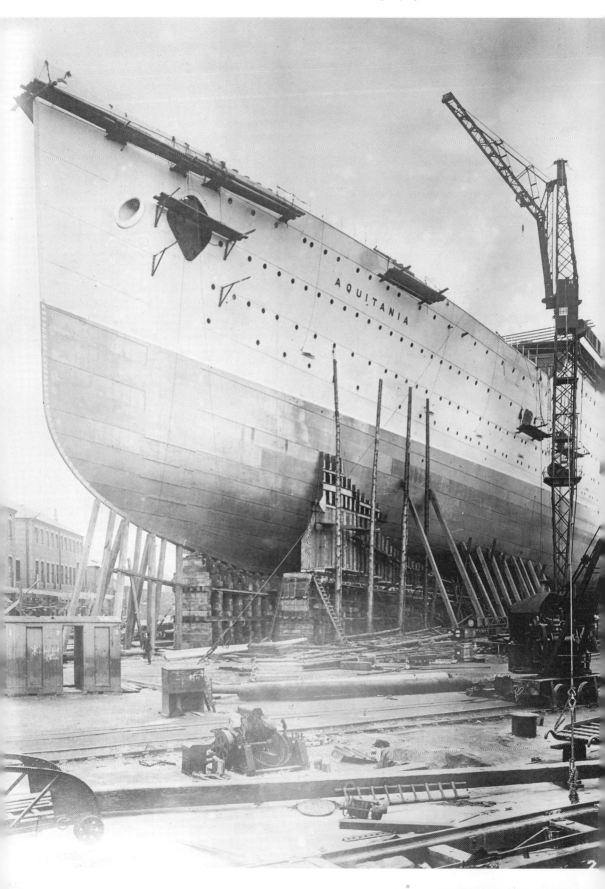

success. In her larger size and greater comfort, Cunard now had a well-balanced trio of ocean liners operating a weekly service between Liverpool and New York – the two fastest ships, and one of the most luxurious.

All of the excitement regarding the new *Aquitania* was still in the air when – quite suddenly and with very little warning – the whole of European civilization collapsed. Thus began a cataclysm that quickly engulfed the entire world and ended the era that had given rise to the *Lusitania*.

Opposite: *The bow of the third ship of the Cunard express trio,* Aquitania. *Here she is visible on the stocks at John Brown & Co., where the* Lusitania *had been built seven years before. Built on a similar, if scaled-up platform as that of the* Lusitania *and* Mauretania, *she was designed to be more spacious, more luxurious, but not quite as fast as her older running mates.*

Top right: *A 1913 advertisement for Cunard's forthcoming* Aquitania, *along with her two running mates,* Lusitania *and* Mauretania. *With White Star's loss of the* Titanic, *and only two of the HAPAG giants in service by the summer of 1914, Cunard certainly had a lead over the competition.*

Above: *This photo shows the new* Aquitania *on her trials. Although half again as big as the* Lusitania *and* Mauretania, *and different from the older liners' appearance in many ways, their familial connections are immediately obvious.*

5
The Last Days
Crossings 184-202 - August, 1914 - May, 1915

In the years leading up to 1914, there was obvious political tension on the European continent. However, there was a common belief that a large-scale war between the major European powers was not a genuine threat. This belief was fostered by at least two factors. First, all of the royal houses of Europe were tied together by blood relations. Second, international commerce between these nations was strongly entrenched, and seemed to support the economies of the entire world; a large-scale conflict, it was believed, would not be in the financial interests of those involved. This feeling of security, however, was only an illusion.

The road leading to war was long and complicated. On June 15, 1888, Wilhelm II was crowned Kaiser of Germany. Wilhelm's ascendancy to the throne was a bit unexpected; his father had died after only one hundred days in power. Young Wilhelm's mother, Victoria, Empress Frederick, was the daughter of Britain's Queen Victoria. Wilhelm was devoted to his grandmother, which seemed superficially to bode well for relations between the two nations. Unfortunately, Wilhelm was arguably ill-prepared for the realities of being Kaiser. His mother had tried to instill in him British political ideals, but he instead took after German autocratic ways. Being less than thirty years of age when he came to power, Wilhelm was young, and he was both energetic and ambitious. In particular, he was determined to displace Great Britain as the prominent world power. The British Royal Navy was the undisputed ruler of the waves, so Wilhelm decided to build a modern navy, the High Seas Fleet, which would challenge British naval supremacy. The Kaiser also closely backed Germany's two

Opposite: *A detail of the photo on page 214, showing the* Lusitania *in the Gladstone Dry Dock in Liverpool.*

Above left: *The Archduke Franz Ferdinand in a nautical setting. He is seen here with his wife – Her Highness Sophie, Duchess of Hohenberg – and the Countess Baillet de Latour.*

Above right: *In a remarkably ironic photograph, Kaiser Wilhelm II and Winston Churchill are seen attending German military maneuvers together.*

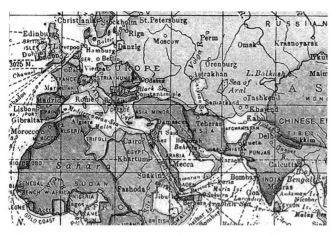

A 1913 map of the powder keg that was Europe.

primary merchant shipping lines, Hamburg-Amerika and North German Lloyd, in their desire to build sea-going passenger liners that were bigger, better and faster than those in the British White Star and Cunard fleets. With Wilhelm's support, the Germans had held dominance on the Atlantic shipping lanes for a decade, until the *Lusitania* and *Mauretania* had come upon the scene. Although relations between Germany and Great Britain remained polite, it was clear that the two countries were on a political collision course.

Meanwhile, all of Europe had been dividing itself into two armed camps. Throughout the last portion of the nineteenth century, treaties had been passed and alliances formed to create a "safety net." If one European country was attacked by one or two others, the alliances guaranteed that they would have a safety net to back them up. There was on the one hand the Triple Alliance – comprised of Germany, Austria-Hungary, the Ottoman Empire, and Italy – formed in 1882; on the other hand there was the Triple Entente, formed in 1907 between Great Britain, France and Russia. Additionally, Britain, France and Prussia had given their guarantee in 1839 that they would protect the neutrality of Belgium, should that country ever be threatened. The formation of these treaties, in point of fact, had the unfortunate effect of turning all of Europe into a "house of cards." It allowed for the possibility that a small conflict could erupt into a full-fledged European war in very short order, should the right circumstances arise.

Then there was the wild card: a group of radicals, now better known as terrorists, called the "Black Hand." This group had close connections with the nation of Serbia, which neighbored Austria-Hungary. In 1903, the leader of this group, Colonel Dragutin

Dimitrijević, had even played a pivotal role in bringing a new King to the Serbian throne. Austria-Hungary was clearly concerned with Serbia and the "Black Hand," and with good reason. The entire region was quite unstable. Two momentous conflicts, the First and Second Balkan Wars, had been fought between October of 1912 and July of 1913, and notably included in the combatants' list of both conflicts was Serbia. Fortunately, this conflict had not escalated into an all-out European war, but it was a portent of things to come.

In June of 1914, the Austrian army maneuvers were set to be held in Bosnia. Archduke Franz Ferdinand – the heir to the Austrian throne, and whose uncle was Emperor Franz Joseph – traveled there to oversee the operation. Following the exercise, Franz Ferdinand and his wife decided to pay a visit to Sarajevo, Bosnia's capital. The Black Hand armed three assassins and sent them to kill the Archduke. On the morning of June 28, while driving through Sarajevo toward the Governor's residence in an open-top automobile, the group struck. They attempted to make the kill by throwing a bomb at the vehicle; fortunately the bomb bounced off the car and the couple was spared. They arrived at the residence unscathed. In a blatantly foolish decision, they decided to leave in the same open-top vehicle. This time, their driver took a wrong turn and had to stop the car. In an astonishing twist of fate, he stopped right beside another of the assassins, who immediately stepped forward and shot the Archduke and his wife, killing both. The assassin fled, trying and failing to take his own life; he was quickly apprehended.

In the moment that these two members of Austrian nobility drew their last breath, the powder keg of Europe had been lit. Austria was moved to take action against Serbia when it became clear that the assassins had been tied in with the Black Hand and that Serbia had aided them. They went to Kaiser Wilhelm in Germany, and asked if he would back them in war against the Balkan nation. Wilhelm said that he would, if Austria decided on war. He judged, incorrectly in retrospect, that both Russia and France would not involve themselves in a conflict between Germany and Austria-Hungary on the one hand and Serbia on the other. The Austrians, now with German might solidly behind them, sent a note of ten demands to Serbia. Serbia planned to concede to all but one, but then it was discovered that Tsar Nicholas II of Russia was feeling inclined to back them if

Above: *A very rare photograph taken upon the Lusitania's last pre-war arrival in New York, on Friday, July 31, 1914, at the conclusion of Crossing No. 183 West. The picture was taken on the Boat Deck in the vicinity of the First Class Lounge, and shows actress Pansy Dowdall in the middle, with Cyrus McCormick on the left, and Marcella Andrews on the right. McCormick had been aboard the* Lusitania *during her maiden voyage nearly seven years before.*

Right: *The* Vaterland, *caught in New Jersey at the outbreak of war, along with other German merchantmen.*

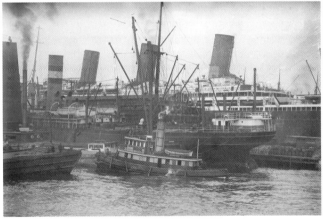

there came conflict; this moved the Serbians to reject the Austrian note outright. The Austrians had had enough, and declared war on Serbia on Tuesday, July 28 – exactly one month after the assassinations. The Russians began to mobilize to defend Serbia. Kaiser Wilhelm and German Chancellor Bethmann-Hollweg pleaded with Russia to cease their buildup. The Tsar complied on July 29, but was pressured by his advisors into re-mobilizing the next day. The Germans responded by issuing an ultimatum to Russia and France, and on August 1, they declared war on Russia. The French mobilized against Germany and asked Britain for their official position; the Brit-

ish stalled, waiting to see what would happen next. Germany responded to the mobilization of France by declaring war on that nation. The German war plans for a conflict against France called for them to march through neutral Belgium in order to reach the front and begin fighting, which they did on August 3. Great Britain declared war on Germany in response on the very next day, August 4.

Although now we can see the tragic repercussions of this conflict, the European populace in general greeted the news of war enthusiastically, even excitedly. As soldiers from each nation began shipping out to their respective fronts, the general feeling was that they would quickly 'clean the clocks' of their enemies, that their own nation would grow in dominance, and that peace would quickly follow. This hope quickly faded as reality began to set in.

Meanwhile, this fast-paced succession of events had caught the Atlantic shipping industry completely unawares. Once all of Europe had plunged into the fracas on August 4, ships of the transatlantic passenger ferry were in the middle of their normal routines, completely unprepared for the new political circumstances that now surrounded them. The *Olympic* and *Mauretania* were westbound for New York; the new *Vaterland* was at her Hoboken pier along with about ten other German merchantmen, and with another forty scattered throughout other U.S. ports; the *Lusitania* was in New York preparing to return to Liverpool. Mass confusion and wild rumors were rampant in New York. Sailing schedules were postponed or canceled until more details began to come to light. The obvious question was: would it be safe for the *Lusitania* to return to England?

While the British Expeditionary Force was preparing to cross the English Channel to assist the French, the British Government was also making plans to ensure that they maintained strict control over the seas. The Germans were quick to threaten that control. On the day after the British declared war, the Germans were caught illegally mining waters outside Britain's territorial waters. More mines were quickly laid off North Sea ports, as well as in the waters off the coast of Ireland. The continuation of these illegal operations posed a significant threat to the British; the Royal Navy lost the new battleship *Audacious* on October 27, 1914 to just such a minefield.

The Germans felt that they needed to resort to this tactic because although they had a very modern naval fleet, it was not as large as the Royal Navy. The British were expecting – indeed, were hoping for – a quick, full-on confrontation between the two fleets, because they knew that they would most likely prevail in a Trafalgar-like fashion. The Germans also knew the facts, and so they kept their High Seas Fleet at home and safely tucked away from the guns of the Royal Navy.

With the High Seas Fleet posing little immediate danger, the next thing that the British had to contend with was the matter of German merchant vessels that were scattered all through neutral and European ports. Would their crews manage to convert them into armed commerce raiders, as the Admiralty had planned to do with the *Lusitania* and *Mauretania* in time of war? The British wanted to make quite sure that they did not. They sent three *Monmouth*-class armored cruisers – the H.M.S. *Berwick*, H.M.S. *Lancaster*, and H.M.S. *Essex*, of nearly 10,000 tons each, and each sporting a speed of about 23 knots – to sit outside the entrances to neutral ports, including New York, just outside the three-mile limit of American territory. Liners like the Cunarder *Carmania* were quickly requisitioned by the Admiralty for conversion into armed merchant cruisers to back up this blockade.

This plan was not entirely effective. The day before the British declared war, August 3, the North German Lloyd steamer *Kronprinz Wilhelm* decided to squeak out of New York and give the British the slip before they were trapped in port. Her crew blocked up every porthole and extinguished every light in order to make her nearly invisible at night. The thirteen-year-old, 14,908-ton ship made it out of New York Harbor and steamed south into the West Indies. There, she rendezvoused with the German light cruiser *Karlsruhe*, which had already been based in the Caribbean when conflict erupted. From the cruiser she received her armament, and began a career of commerce raiding in the West Indies. The Hamburg-South Amerika liner *Cap Trafalgar*, only about a year old, was another German ship that was armed, activated and stationed in tropical waters; she was given a moderately light armament of two 4.1-inch guns and some machine guns.

Back in New York, there was anxiety over the *Lusitania*. There was obvious danger beyond the Ambrose Channel light; even if the ship made it back to Liverpool, would the Admiralty order her requisition, turning her into an armed merchant cruiser? The liner was due to sail on that fateful Tuesday, August 4, at 12:00 noon. Expectations were high that one of the inbound British cruisers would meet the *Lusitania* and provide her with protection on the Atlantic. However, at the planned sailing time, Captain Dow had received no word on whether he should proceed, and if so, whether to expect to be convoyed. He sent Chief Officer Johnson back ashore to inquire at the British Consulate whether he was cleared to depart. There were only two hundred passengers aboard bound for Europe, one hundred in First Class, and fifty in each of the lower classes; some of those who had come to see the liner depart began to speculate that the crossing would be canceled.

Nearly an hour passed before Johnson returned and hurried back aboard the ship. He had obtained clearance. Just minutes later, Captain Dow's voice was heard: "All lights out." The order was repeated up and down the decks until the ship was almost completely dark, with only her masthead lights and port and starboard running lights showing. Then she cast off and backed out into the North River. Once the tugs had gotten her nose pointed downstream, she began her journey into the now-dangerous waters of the North Atlantic. Passengers were informed that although they could go out onto the decks, they must show no lights after dark. In the passageways within the ship, oil lamps had been hung to replace her brilliant electrical illumination. Down below, a large stock of gray paint, which had been acquired from New York vendors, sat waiting for use.[1]

As the *Lusitania* departed New York, she passed the *Olympic* in The Narrows; the European world *Olympic* had left only a few days before had disintegrated in her wake. She had a rather large group of passengers aboard whose nationalities and sentiments fell on both sides of the new war, and she had poured on the speed during the last day in order to evade any German vessels hunting for her; in fact, on that last day, she had achieved – with strenuous effort – the remarkable speed of 25.1 knots.[2] Even as the *Lusitania* steamed east and the *Olympic* arrived in safety, there was further chaos in Hoboken. There, Pier Superintendent Bode heard a rumor that there was a plot to blow up the *Vaterland*. Fifty policemen were immediately sent out to take up station aboard the ship and around her; swift motor launches with powerful searchlights swarmed about in the river around the liner, and a perimeter was set up around the North German Lloyd piers. The ship's own crew began to search the river with the liner's searchlights.

As the *Lusitania* steamed east, there was some excitement. Minutes after departing the dock, there had been an audible "Whang!" that emanated from the ship's innards. Hardly had the pilot been dropped when it was discovered that the sound had come from one of the turbines running amok; with only three ahead turbines operating, the ship's top speed would be reduced, making it more difficult for her to evade any pursuing German cruisers. Rumors next began to spread among the nervous passengers that the turbine had been damaged by a German saboteur, who had hoped to slow the ship's top speed and make her "easy prey for a faster vessel that might be lying in wait."

On Wednesday, August 5, there came a thrill, which was later recounted by one of the *Lusitania*'s passengers:

> There was luckily a mist, for suddenly we sighted a warship on our port quarter, and as we watched her intently, not knowing what her nationality

was, we saw her swing round, and deliberately try to cut us off. At the same instant we changed our course and ran for it. She seemed to gain a little on us, but you could see the heavy seas breaking over her bows, and presently there was a puff of white smoke or steam, but we heard nothing. Just then, the mist came on thicker, and we gradually lost her. We heard afterwards that the captain had wired to the *Essex* to come to us quick, and that the puff of smoke, which many of us had thought was her steam-whistle, was probably a gun fired. We also heard that she signalled to us to lay to, which order we declined to comply with.[3]

Although certainly colored by rumor and anxiety, the account is fascinating nonetheless as it shows just how tense the situation was during the crossing. One of the ship's officers, who had been on watch during the encounter, was said to have told passengers: "I can only say that she was a destroyer, burning oil, and that she chased us." He told them that she had not flown a flag giving her nationality, but that she had signaled: "You are captured. Heave to."[4]

The Cunard liner *Pannonia* passed the *Lusitania* that same day, inbound to New York from Gibraltar. She reported that the "ship was dark, except for her running lights, and was being driven along at a high rate of speed." Soon thereafter, a British warship had informed the *Pannonia* that it was safe for her to proceed into harbor at New York, as "there were several British ships within wireless call." The *Pannonia*'s wireless operator, however, said that he could hear German cruisers communicating with each other.[5]

Meanwhile, back aboard the *Lusitania*, the wireless news reports coming into the ship's Marconi room were "perfectly crazy." There were rumors of a tremendous naval battle in the North Sea in which "nineteen German ships and six British vessels" were sunk. Captain Dow reportedly fretted for a friend, O'Callahan, who was assigned to the *Iron Duke*, but the following morning news came in that there had been no naval battle, after all. Not knowing what was really going on in Europe, and not knowing whether to trust inbound news reports or to view them as wild rumors, passengers were "left to play with their fears and surmises."

Interestingly, the *Lusitania*'s wireless does not seem to have been completely silent. When the oil tanker *Tonawanda* docked in New York on August 6, Captain Hart told reporters that "he heard the *Lusitania* in wireless communication with the British cruiser *Essex*, saying that a foreign cruiser was following her and asking the *Essex* to stand by."[6]

There was yet another surprise in store for passengers. As the ship began to come alive on Thursday morning, passengers emerging on deck were surprised to find that the funnels of the ship were being painted in gray with the stores of paint acquired back in New York. Crewmen were perched "in what seemed, to landsmen, most precarious positions" around the structures. The next day, the rest of the upperworks were also given this coat of gray; the crew was trying desperately to help disguise the Cunarder from enemy ships. Although coating the ship in this wash of gray might have been useful in preventing visual detection from a long distance, it would have done little to disguise her actual identity once spotted on the North Atlantic, since her profile was so well known.

Captain Dow informed the passengers that rumors were then circulating in New York to the effect that the *Lusitania* had been "blown up and sunk with all hands." The passengers fretted over what their relatives and friends would think had happened to them, and there were requests to use the wireless to inform those ashore that they were quite safe, and had not blown up at all. "We are under war orders," came the response. "Not a word may be sent by wireless."

War correspondent Herbert Corey, aboard for the trip, painted the scene aboard the vessel:

At night, the steamer crept along without a light showing. Even her green and red lights were off duty. Her windows were curtained. Her interior halls were dark. One groped to one's stateroom at night through gloomy passageways, colliding with shuddering stewards who spoke in whispers. It was a weird, an unusual experience. People who owned sensibilities began to feel them jerking. It brought home to them the fact that war is actually upon the seas – that after half a century of peace the privateer may again be regarded as a possibility, and that innocent people are exposed to the danger of capture as prisoners of war.[7]

No one knew what awaited them in Europe, or whether they would actually reach Europe at all. The customary stop at Fishguard, Wales was canceled, and the ship proceeded directly to Liverpool; indeed, Fishguard was left out of the ship's itinerary throughout the war months. The *Lusitania* arrived at her home port safely, successfully concluding her 184th crossing of the Atlantic. It was a slow passage, but at least she had made it in safety. She dropped anchor in

the Mersey at 10 p.m. That evening, passengers were delayed in disembarking, although two tenders were tied to her side for hours. When passengers asked why they were inconvenienced so, the reason given was quite simple: "War!" The next morning, as passengers still cooled their heels, they began to notice that the Mersey, usually filled with mercantile traffic, "seemed deserted." It was said:

> One began to sense the fact that a great war – a world war – is actually in progress. There is no surface patriotism. There are no cheers – no bubbling outbreaks of enthusiasm. Everyone is quiet and serious and thoughtful.
>
> "Only in the little wars do people laugh and talk," said Frederick Palmer, the war correspondent. "In big wars they are silent."[8]

It was not long, however, before the initial fears for the *Lusitania*'s safety on the North Atlantic quickly

Opposite: *Seen from the starboard Boat Deck, paint crews work eagerly on the No. 2 funnel, trying to camouflage the* Lusitania's *upper works and make her harder to spot.*

Below: *This photograph, taken from the Forecastle, shows the ongoing paint efforts. The forward superstructure is now gray, and passengers have come out, fascinated by their liner's transformation.*

began to fade. The reason for this was that there seemed to be no apparent threat to her safety anymore. The German Navy was bottled up in the North Sea and kept at bay by a long-range blockade by the Royal Navy. The threat of commerce raiding on the North Atlantic by converted German liners did not materialize, either. The *Kronprinz Wilhelm, Cap Trafalgar* and *Karlsruhe* all stayed in the tropics. The *Karlsruhe* blew up and sank on November 4. The *Kronprinz Wilhelm* was forced to put into Newport News, Virginia in late April of 1915, starved of supplies and resources. The *Cap Trafalgar* had an unfortunate ren-

dezvous with the converted Cunarder *Carmania* off the coast of Brazil on September 14, 1914. After a fierce battle, the *Carmania* sank the German liner, although the British ship was heavily damaged and put out of commission for over two months. Just ten days after the outbreak of war, the Admiralty declared: "The passage across the Atlantic is safe."[9]

Both the *Lusitania* and the *Mauretania*, along with a number of other liners, were activated by the British Admiralty on August 3, and several more were called up on August 6. By the time the *Lusitania* reached Liverpool on August 11, however, the Admiralty had decided that she and her sister were no longer required, and released them back to the Cunard Line. The reasons for this are not entirely clear; frequently the battle between the *Carmania* and *Cap Trafalgar* are cited, but that event had not yet occurred when the ships were released. The *Aquitania* was called up for service as an armed merchant

Left: *The* Carmania.

Below: *An artist's representation of the duel between the* Carmania *and the* Cap Trafalgar.

cruiser almost as soon as hostilities had erupted. On August 25, she was involved in a collision with the Leyland liner *Canadian*, and required months' worth of repairs in Liverpool; yet this event came later also, and could not have been a contributing factor.

More likely, the real reason that the Admiralty released the *Lusitania* and *Mauretania* in early August was that there was nothing for them to do as armed auxiliaries. The German Navy and threat of German commerce raiding had been effectively contained. At the same time, the speedsters were expensive to operate, gobbling vast sums of coal; what was more, the 1902 loan which funded their agreement stipulated that if either vessel was chartered by the Government, they would pay fees of 25s. per gross registered ton per month, or 30s. per gross registered ton per month if Cunard provided the officers and crew. With seemingly little for the liners to do at that point, and great expense to charter and operate them, it was a logical decision to allow them to remain in merchant service.

Thus, the *Lusitania* was to remain on the commercial route for the foreseeable future. This was good for Cunard, as the Company had plenty of employment for the liner; at the time, there was a strong demand for westbound passage across the Atlantic. Many Americans and others who suddenly found themselves vacationing in the middle of a war-torn Europe wanted desperately to get back to the safety of neutral ground. *Lusitania*'s Crossings Nos. 185 and 187 West, made in mid-September and early October, reflected that demand; both crossings, despite wartime hazards, showed strong bookings. The *Mauretania* made three round-trip voyages after the war's outbreak,[10] and the *Lusitania* and *Olympic* also remained in service. Once the demand for westbound travel had reached its natural conclusion, passenger numbers dwindled dramatically on the Atlantic. White Star decided, with revenue declining – and especially after the *Olympic* had a narrow miss with the minefield that sank the battleship *Audacious* – to remove the *Olympic* from commercial service. Accordingly, she was laid up in Belfast beginning in early

November of 1914. The *Mauretania* was laid up in late October. The final White Star titan, *Britannic*, was still incomplete at Belfast, and the final HAPAG giant, *Bismarck*, was in a similar condition at the Blohm & Voss yards in Hamburg. The *Vaterland* was stuck for the foreseeable future in Hoboken, and the *Imperator* was bottled up on the Elbe River.

With all of her running mates and primary competitors out of service, incomplete, or otherwise indisposed, the *Lusitania* was once again the largest and fastest ocean liner plying the North Atlantic. Although passenger revenues were significantly reduced, Cunard felt that with the German Navy bottled up, the risks on the Liverpool-New York run were not great enough to force them to withdraw the speed-queen from commercial service.

Unfortunately, there was another threat to merchant shipping developing. This time, the menace took naval warfare from two dimensions into three, because it came from underneath the surface of the water. The bigwigs in virtually every navy of Europe had initially viewed submarines with skepticism and no small amount of dubious uncertainty; not only were they "damned un-English," according to Rear Admiral Sir Arthur Wilson, but they were also quite prone to malfunction and technical problems that could render them dangerous to their own crew, not just to ships of an enemy nation. However, with the High Seas Fleet bottled up in German waters, the Germans were forced to begin to devise tactics to employ their submarine fleet against the British. Unlike a large surface fleet, these submarines could sneak in and out of German ports right under the collective noses of the Royal Navy; they were virtually undetectable.

The U-boats failed their first test against the British. On August 9, the *U-15* – a submarine barely two years old, on the eighth day of her first patrol – was spotted by the British light cruiser *Birmingham* off Fair Isle. The submarine was apparently attempting to move in to position to attack the cruiser. The *Birmingham* brought her guns to bear on the submarine, inflicting severe damage on her before turning into

The U-15.

her and ramming the fragile craft at an estimated twenty-five knots. The U-boat promptly sank, killing her entire crew of twenty-three men.

The following month, submarines proved a bit more successful, exacting revenge for the loss of the *U-15*. On September 5 the *U-21*, under the command of Kapitänleutnant Otto Hersing, found the British scout cruiser H.M.S. *Pathfinder* off the coast of Scotland in the North Sea. That sunny afternoon, Hersing fired a single torpedo at the cruiser at a range of 1,600 yards. The torpedo struck the ship's flank, and a boiler exploded. This blast tore into the ship's magazine, with predictable results. Following the two back-to-back explosions, the *Pathfinder* sank in only four minutes; of her 267 crewmen, only eleven survived. Hersing later noted in his log: "I believe I have shed the first blood using submarines within this war … My men are in great spirits because of our victory. I have spoken to many of them and they feel as if they are immortal." He also noted: "Though High Command believes this will be a swift and honourable war, I think otherwise. The recent enemies we have encountered show that it will be a bloody and deadly war." In making this historic entry in his log, he showed great perception.

Before the month was over, another U-boat inflicted an even more astounding attack. On the morning of September 22, the *U-9*, under the command of Kapitänleutnant Otto Weddigen, ran across three *Cressy*-class armored cruisers, the H.M.S. *Aboukir*, H.M.S. *Hogue* and H.M.S. *Cressy*. These three ships, ranging in age from twelve to thirteen years, of about 12,000 tons each, were part of what had become known as the "live bait" squadron; they were aged, unable to stand up to modern German surface warships, and their system of watertight subdivision was considered vulnerable. However, the Admiralty needed ships to maintain patrols, and so it was that the *U-9* came across them in the North Sea that morning. As if their age and watertight subdivision were not bad enough, they were ignoring orders to zigzag at 12-13 knots; instead, they were steaming in a straight line at only ten knots, complacent because no U-boats had been spotted in the area up to that point in the conflict. First to go was the *Aboukir*, at 6:25 a.m., struck by a single torpedo. Her captain assumed that she had been mined, and signaled the other warships for assistance. The *Hogue* was struck by two torpedoes as the *Aboukir* was going under, at about 7:00 a.m.; she sank in only ten minutes. Probably not believing his luck, Weddigen wasted no time in moving in on the third ship, the *Cressy*. In short order, she, too was struck by two torpedoes, out of three fired, and sank

in a mere fifteen minutes. Out of 2,296 men on the three ships, 1,459 were killed in the unprecedented attacks. These two separate incidents showed that the Germans were willing to use the U-boat against British warships. Some attacks on merchant vessels were also carried out, but almost invariably within the confines of the well-known "cruiser rules."

While all of this was going on, the *Lusitania* continued plying the route between New York and Liverpool. Her 185th crossing of the Atlantic – which began on Saturday, September 12, 1914 – proved newsworthy. It seemed that the liner's longstanding reputation for romance was still proving to be well founded. One of the passengers on the trip was 20-year-old Marshall Field III, grandson of Chicago's wealthy and famous merchant, and future heir of a $60 million dollar fortune. Another of the passengers was 24-year-old Miss Evelyn Marshall, a member of a well-established "old New York family." Miss Marshall was "noted for her beauty," and had even enjoyed the privilege of being presented at the Court

Below: *Marshall Field III.*

Opposite: *Miss Evelyn Marshall, pictured here after her marriage to Mr. Field.*

of St. James's in London in early 1914. Miss Marshall and her mother, Josephine, had been in Paris when hostilities broke out. Instead of running for home, as so many American citizens had, Miss Marshall remained and had become engaged in working in an American Hospital there.

Eventually, however, the time had come for her to return to the United States, and she and Mr. Marshall found themselves aboard the *Lusitania* during the late-summer voyage. It was later reported to have been a "brief but pretty romance" aboard the liner. The pair took long walks on the Promenade Deck which lasted long into the wee hours of the morning. According to fellow passengers, Mr. Marshall seemed "deeply smitten." Then, before the ship had landed in New York on Thursday, September 17, the young man had proposed, and Miss Marshall had accepted. The couple was married the following February.[11]

With what was ordinarily the busiest traveling season of the year winding down, and with demand for trans-Atlantic travel hitting other ships, it is no surprise that the *Lusitania's* numbers, too, were declining.[12] Although there seemed enough demand for travel to keep the ship in service, by mid-November 1914, the liner was losing nearly £2,000 per trip, partly due to falling passenger traffic and partly because of higher coal prices since the outbreak of hos-

tilities. The Cunard Company decided to economize the *Lusitania's* operating costs, by closing down Boiler Room No. 4, with its six boilers; this would save an estimated sixteen hundred tons of coal on each voyage. It also reduced the number of stokers required. This meant that the ship's top speed would not be twenty-one knots instead of twenty-five, but this was still a respectable speed.

The Admiralty agreed with Cunard's decision, and allowed the reduction in speed. Not only was German commerce raiding by converted merchant vessels out of the picture, but up until the spring of 1915, no U-boat had successfully attacked a moving vessel traveling faster than 14 knots – some seven knots slower than the *Lusitania* could still travel. Their agreement is a key point to consider, since the British Government still owned more than half of the *Lusitania* under the terms of the twenty-year loan which funded her construction. They had direct oversight of the ship's operation in order to give her the best protection possible, and changing her route, destination or speed was quite within the realm of their discretion. They, like the Cunard Company, apparently felt that the ship was quite safe at twenty-one knots instead of twenty-five, believing that this reduced speed was still fast enough. Although the decision was sanctioned, it was not announced by Cunard or the Admiralty to prospective passengers. Many who followed her progress during the next few months realized that she simply wasn't moving at her old speeds, but the exact cause for her sluggishness did not become widely known until later on.

Throughout the fall and winter months – both before and after the reduction in speed – Captain Dow's attitude toward the *Lusitania's* safety seemed to be similar to that taken by Cunard and the Admiralty: business as usual. On September 17, 1914, the *Lusitania* arrived in New York with 1,502 passengers, including 605 in First Class; she had made the crossing at an average speed of 23.17 knots despite a gale off the Irish coast. Among those who had traveled in First Class was Sir James M. Barrie, the famous Scotch playwright. It was Barrie's second trip to the United States, and he was coming to be re-united with some old theater friends. When theater actress Maude Adams had seen Barrie in England the previous summer, he had told her to convey a message to his old friend, an impresario named Charles Frohman: "Tell Frohman I will see him in his office in September." Ten years earlier, Frohman had produced a little play that Barrie wrote called *Peter Pan*; it had become Frohman's favorite production and a great classic of the stage and later of the screen. Other than this

Sir James Barrie, in a photograph taken between 1908 and 1915.

quick statement made to the actress, however, Barrie had given no further notice to Frohman of his visit, and ended up surprising him completely. The short notice did not stop the friends from dropping in at the Knickerbocker Theatre to see a play that evening. Despite this illusion of normalcy, things had certainly changed on the world scene. Barrie commented to inquisitive reporters on his arrival that he thought that the war would be a drawn-out affair, and that a German defeat would not come quickly. "Aside from this military spirit, the Germans are a magnificent nation," he said.[13]

In November of 1914, after the *Lusitania* encountered serious weather, Captain Dow joked to reporters that he was unfortunately unlike Kaiser Wilhelm, and could not "say to the winds, 'Peace, be still,' and be obeyed."[14] During that particular crossing, there were notables sailing among her total of 918 passengers, including George Booth, cousin of Cunard Chairman Alfred Booth. Most conspicuous among these notables, however, was Vincent Astor – son of John Jacob Astor of *Titanic* notoriety – his wife, and his sister Alice. Over the coming months,

more notables began showing up on the liner's decks, feeling that travel to England was more or less a relatively safe decision again.

Meanwhile the British tightened their grip on the seas in an attempt to force Germany into submission. They had already resorted to an illegal long-range blockade of Germany; this was, they explained to neutrals, a necessity, since the Royal Navy would be a sitting duck to German air and coastal defenses if it were stationed at the three-mile limit allowed for under international law. At this point, however, they broadened the scope of their blockade. On November 3, 1914, they announced that the entire North Sea was now "a military area," and that portions of it would be laced with mines. Neutral ships were warned that they could only enter the North Sea at their own risk. Instead of inspecting neutral shipping on the high seas for contraband headed toward Germany, the British began moving them into port, where a more leisurely inspection could take place. If contraband was discovered, it would be impounded; even if what the vessel was carrying was not contraband, the British typically paid for it and kept it for themselves, lest useful items fall into German hands. Neutrals protested, but nothing really changed as a result.

Next the British began taking liberties with the definition of wartime contraband. Previously, international law had provided three categories of goods – absolute contraband, conditional contraband, and non-contraband. Absolute contraband would include munitions and war materials. Conditional contraband could include items that could be used for either peace or war. Non-contraband was for items that were believed to have no effect on a conflict. As the months passed, the British began to declare more and more items absolute contraband, subject to seizure without indemnity. When the Germans, backed into a corner by the British blockade, declared grain supplies to be under Government control, the British said that this would mean foodstuffs would reach the German Armies before the German population, and would aid in the war efforts. Thus by March of 1915, even foodstuffs had been declared absolute contraband.

In response to this, the Germans continued to punch up their U-boat warfare. The question soon came to the fore: how could the British protect their shipping against U-boats? Anti-submarine warfare was in its infancy. If a warship found a submarine on or near the surface, they could attack with gunfire; they could also turn and ram the craft. Beyond that, there was not much that could be done – items like depth charges would not be invented until much later in the conflict. There were some measures that could be taken, however. On January 31, 1915, and again on February 10, the Admiralty issued top-secret instructions to merchant skippers, to help them understand how to defend their ships from the U-boat menace. These orders were in part defensive in that British ships would now attempt to resemble neutral ships to the extent possible, even flying neutral flags. In other areas, they were not as defensive. For example, merchant skippers were advised to turn toward and attempt to ram any U-boats that they saw.

The Germans almost immediately discovered these orders through their operatives in England, and they responded. If the British could starve the Germans with an illegal blockade while masking their own ships under neutral flags, the Germans now reasoned that they could starve the British with a similarly illegal U-boat blockade. They declared the area around the British Isles to be "an area of war," on February 4, 1915; a two-week grace period was granted, allowing neutral ships in the zone time to leave before the new blockade became active. They warned that *all enemy vessels* – whether warships or merchant ships – were liable to destruction with or without warning, and regardless of whether or not such attacks imperiled lives. The Germans also warned neutral shipping away, for even though the U-boats had "instructions to avoid violence to neutral ships in so far as they are recognizable," due to the British false flag order and the "contingencies of naval warfare," attacks on neutral shipping could "not always be avoided."

There was another contributing factor to this declaration of a War Zone. As the war began to drag on through the fall of 1914, American businessmen had been quick to seize the opportunity to make a tidy profit for themselves. In order to continue attacking one another on the field of battle, each side needed armament and war materials. Great Britain, in particular, was in desperate need of these munitions and war supplies, having consistently under-estimated the amount of ammunition British troops would need on the battlefield. British union workers seemed unwilling to increase production by hiring unskilled, non-union workers despite the national emergency. Thus, Britain took to ordering heavy quantities of munitions through the American Bethlehem Steel Corporation.[15] All of these munitions were shipped via the Atlantic route to England. In order to pay for the sales, American bankers were given tacit permission by the U.S. Government to extend financial assistance to the British. Instead of giving loans to a warring nation, which would have been illegal, these were instead called lines of credit – a ridiculous line of distinction that really meant nothing. Most of these "lines of credit" were arranged through J. P. Morgan & Co., headed by J. P. "Jack" Morgan, Jr. In the first year of this arrangement, over a billion dollars' worth of war materials was purchased by the British in this manner. The Germans were incensed, and protested. The U.S. Government declared that it was not actually arranged for by the Government, but rather through corporations and private individuals; as such, it was quite legal under the Hague Convention of 1907. The shipments continued. The Germans felt that they could at least put a damper on them by way of a U-boat blockade.[16]

Neutrals were angered by Germany's War Zone proclamation, and protested vigorously. In the forefront of this protest was the twenty-eighth President of the United States, Woodrow Wilson. On February 10, his Government sent a stern diplomatic note to Germany over this declaration of a war zone. Its content threatened that if "an American vessel or the lives of American citizens" were lost as a result of this war zone, the American nation would hold Germany to a "strict accountability." The exact actions that the United States would take were never outlined, and the note did not explain what the nation would do if American citizens were lost on a belligerent vessel as a result of U-boat warfare.

Wilson's Government was clearly acting more heavy-handedly with Germany than it was with Great Britain. When the British blockade of Germany went into effect, the United States had protested, but neither quickly nor with great vigor. It seemed that Wilson was pre-disposed to take offense with the German declaration because it threatened to take lives by action; the British blockade, on the other hand, merely created delays and stopped up revenue without taking life. The general population of the United States, on the other hand, was not so clearly pro-Allied; many of the population were German or Irish in background. The Germans sided with the Fatherland, and the Irish, hating the British as they did, also felt disposed to side with the Germans. Even so, the American public did not want to be actively involved in what was seen as a European conflict. The U.S. Secretary of State, William Jennings Bryan, saw that the Government was taking an un-neutral stand, and tried to steer them back on course; when he failed, he eventually resigned his post. In place of Bryan, his clearly pro-Ally assistant Robert Lansing was appointed as Secretary of State. The un-neutral spiral continued unabated.

Great Britain was also walking a fine line. American sentiment, particularly those of that country's

Left: *President Woodrow Wilson.*

Below left: *Secretary of State William Jennings Bryan.*

Above: *Bryan's successor, Robert Lansing.*

British Board of Trade, Walter Runciman, on February 12, 1915, just over a week after the Germans had announced their submarine-enforced War Zone. He stated: "It is most important to attract neutral shipping to our shores, in the hope especially of embroiling the U.S. with Germany."[17] In this note, many have seen Churchill making some sort of reference to an evil plot of having neutral shipping sunk and neutral citizens killed, thus bringing the United States into the war.

Other than the fact that it would have been very difficult for Churchill to pull the Germans' triggers in such a fashion, this theory really doesn't hold up under close scrutiny. It was quite clear to everyone involved – including high ranking members of the United States Government, Churchill and members of the British Government, and it was even clear to the Germans – that if the United States entered the war at that time, it would have been disastrous to the British, not the Germans. The new Secretary of State, Robert Lansing – who was decidedly pro-Ally – prepared a memorandum clearly outlining why this was so. The British Ambassador to the United States, Sir Cecil Spring-Rice, was also clear on this point, telegraphing London on May 9, 1915 that it was their "main interest to preserve U.S. as a base of supplies." He felt convinced that if the Americans entered the conflict, they would divert their munitions – then keeping the British afloat in the war – toward their own army. In the time that it took for the American Expeditionary Forces to be equipped, trained, and sent over to

German and Irish immigrants, had to be kept against the Germans so that they did not also begin pressuring the American government to take a more neutral position in the war. So the balance needed to stay exactly where it was for the time being. A young Winston Churchill, First Lord of the Admiralty, noted this when he wrote a letter to the President of the

Europe, the delicate balance on the fronts would be significantly upset, with potentially disastrous consequences to the British.[18] These facts are like a wet blanket that make any allegations of plots to sink the *Lusitania* seem rightfully preposterous.

Meanwhile, the *Lusitania* continued plying the North Atlantic. She was set to begin Crossing 195 West, the out-bound leg of her ninety-eighth round-trip voyage, on Saturday, January 16, 1915. Among the passengers who would be taking passage aboard the liner was Helen Losanitch, a 28-year-old woman who had left her parents and sister behind in Nish, Serbia. She was on her way to Canada, via the United States, traveling with a delegation of the Serbian Red Cross on a mission to help secure aid for her fellow Serbs. As she began to make her way toward the docks, she could see the *Lusitania* "gleaming white in the distance, her yellow smokestacks proudly towering over those of all the other ships around her." Once she got on board and the 9:00 p.m. sailing time approached, the scene was a busy one if nothing else. "All was confusion," Miss Losanitch recalled, "stewards and stewardesses guiding passengers with their suitcases to their staterooms, lifts going up and down, bustle, noise and hurrying everywhere." She found that her cabin was "small but most comfortable," and that it was "tastefully furnished."

That night, as the vessel headed out of Liverpool and into the chop of open water, the sea's force began to tell. The *Lusitania* rolled so much that Miss Losanitch became seasick, and put a poor first night in aboard. At dawn the next day, the sea grew calmer and soon blue sky appeared. Lounging in a deck chair, the young lady slowly began to regain her strength.

Far from the guns and trench warfare and atrocities being committed in Europe, and with the seas still being considered safe for the *Lusitania* and other liners flying the Union Jack, shipboard life on the great ship seemed like a haven of pre-war peace. It was a small pocket of tranquility, where the war seemed like a distant nightmare. Miss Losanitch wrote:

> Were it not for the ship's motion, one might think one were in some *de luxe* hotel on land. Tea is served at 5 P.M. in the large salon, fresh roses and carnations are on the small tables, and the passengers sit in comfortable easy chairs, some smoking, others reading the mail which awaited them aboard the ship, still others sipping tea and chatting, and all accompanied by the crackling of a huge log fire that blazed in an enormous fireplace at one end of the room. What a contrast to the life I had so recently

A view of the Lusitania *at Pier 54. This view was taken quite late in her career.*

left! It doesn't seem possible that elsewhere in the world people are homeless and starving.

On the morning of Monday, January 18, Miss Losanitch was on her way into the Dining Saloon for breakfast when one of the ship's bellboys approached and handed her a paper, saying, "Morning paper, Miss." At first she thought that it was a copy of the London morning paper, and when she expressed surprise, the bellboy grinned and explained: "Ship's paper, Miss. We print one every day."

On the evening of Friday, January 22, the customary seamen's aid benefit concert was held. After the concert, it was announced that Madame Slavko Grouitch, the American wife of a distinguished Serbian diplomat, and who was also with the delegation of the Serbian Red Cross, would speak to passengers about the Serbian plight. On Saturday, as promised, the meeting was held at 4 p.m., and "was a great success ... [The] lecture hall was absolutely packed with passengers, and their interest was so great that all stayed on until the dinner hour." After dinner, Miss Losanitch went up on deck for some fresh air, and spotted the Ambrose Lightship, silent sentinel of the entrance to New York Harbor, "barely visible in the fog and blackness of night." The other passengers "went wild" when they spotted it, whistling, clapping, and even throwing empty bottles over the ship's side into the water, "expressing joy at this symbol of their safe arrival, an arrival home for many of them." As she had never seen America before, spotting that light was her "first greeting from the New World."[19]

The ship pulled safely up to her New York pier and disembarked her load of over 600 passengers. Then began the process of turning her around for her next departure, which would be a week hence. No one could have known at the time that the upcoming

Above: *Miss Nona McAdoo and her traveling party aboard the* Lusitania, *January 30, 1915.*

Opposite: *The cover of the passenger list for the January 30 eastbound crossing.*

Below: *This photograph shows the* Lusitania *leaving her New York pier during the winter months of 1914-1915. The flag of the United States flies from her foremast. She has dropped her initial gray scheme of disguise, but a gold band now has been painted around the superstructure just above the black hull. A clear difference can be discerned between the black tops of each of her four funnels and the lower segments, indicating that her funnel color had been restored to their traditional Cunard livery. Interestingly, her two 'midship lifeboat stations are empty. On the right, the three smokestacks of the enormous German liner* Vaterland *tower in the distance.*

trip back to Europe would prove to be an astounding difference from the relative calm and peace of the preceding westbound passage. Nor could they have known that it would also be one of the most historically important in the *Lusitania*'s entire career.

Crossing No. 196 East began auspiciously on Saturday, January 30, 1915, five days before the Germans declared the new submarine-patrolled War Zone. She carried 753 passengers on the trip. Among these were some 370 in First Class, a number which was noted to be only two smaller than that which she had carried on a similar January crossing in 1914, before the war. Many came down to see family and friends off at the New York pier; it was "a matter-of-fact crowd, though rather gay, and the European war seemed a long way off," it was reported. There were many traveling for business, and others traveling merely for pleasure.

Among the most important passengers who were aboard for this trip were Colonel E. M. House, a friend and advisor to the President of the United States, and his wife. The couple was ostensibly "chaperoning" Miss Katherine Britton and Miss Nona McAdoo to San Remo, where they were going to serve as nurses in a hospital for wounded soldiers. Miss McAdoo's father, Secretary of the Treasury William G. McAdoo, and stepmother, Eleanor McAdoo (*née* Wilson)[20] came aboard to see her off. It took some doing to get the visitors ashore, but once this task had been carried out, the ship cast off. It was noted that she was "freighted deep into the water."[21] The "exchange of greetings between ship and shore continued until the liner was beyond [the] hearing of the crowd on the pier end."[22] What was not reported on in the press was that House was actually on a secret mission for President Wilson. The American President felt that with the war having reached a stalemate, the time had come for the United States to help mediate for peace. House was to investigate the possibilities for such a peaceful settlement.

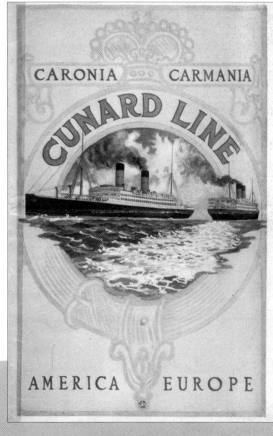

A very rare photograph of Captain Daniel Dow, taken in New York around 1914 or early 1915. This photograph may have been taken aboard the Lusitania, *as it looks very much like the port side of her forward Boat Deck, just where the Bridge wing stretched outboard to the ship's side. Captain Dow was an immensely popular skipper with passengers, but the strain of conducting the* Lusitania *through the new War Zone and being responsible for her safety in light of the threat from German U-boats was enormous and ultimately untenable.*

The press reported on Wednesday, February 3, 1915, that there was debate in shipping circles over whether the *Lusitania* was "in danger from a German submarine lurking in the Irish Sea." Those in authority who were interviewed for the report, however, seemed to show no real concern over submarine activity. Liverpool mercantile authorities showed no alarm. Cunard said it could not see any reason to make any alteration in its sailing schedule. Henry Concannon of the White Star Line said: "We have no reason to be seriously afraid, and propose to continue trade as usual." He said that the White Star Line had "every confidence the Admiralty [would] disperse hostile craft in Liverpool

bay as they [had] done elsewhere." They intended to maintain their sailing schedule. The manager of the Liverpool and London War Risk Association, which insured British vessels against war dangers, had the right to prohibit any sailings that it considered to involve excessive risk. The firm's manager, Sir Norman Hill, said: "We don't consider that the presence of one or two German submarines in Liverpool Bay involves any unreasonable risk to the safety of our ships."[23]

The next day after this information was circulated came the German announcement of the War Zone. Although it would not take effect until February 18, Captain Dow, still steaming east toward British waters, was deeply concerned by the new development when news came to him via the wireless. The crossing was rough; House recalled that the *Lusitania*, "big as she is [was] tossed about like a cork in the rapids." The closer the ship steamed to the British Isles, the more nervous Dow became. He ordered that the full size regulation American flag be raised at the stern, and also had the small American flag and mail pennant flown from the Forepeak. The lifeboats were prepared for immediate use if the situation became necessary. Colonel House recorded a second-hand account from another passenger, one who was related to Lord Charles Beresford and who had a naval background. Apparently on Thursday evening, as the ship was approaching the Irish coast, Captain Dow had asked this passenger to stay on the Bridge through the night with him, because he "expected to be torpedoed."[24] He reportedly felt that if the ship was torpedoed, and if the boilers didn't explode, that she could stay afloat for an hour or thereabouts, giving opportunity to get the passengers into the lifeboats. When dawn came on Friday morning, the ship "started at full speed up the Irish Channel and did not even stop to pick up a pilot." Captain Dow later said that he was not attempting to deceive the Germans into thinking that his ship was a vessel other than the *Lusitania*; everyone agreed that would have been impossible. However, he did say that he had been trying to inform any German submarines that spotted the ship that he was carrying United States citizens and mails.

There was a lot of talk on board about the situation, but the passengers were very pleased with the Captain's decision to fly the American ensign, and unanimously applauded Dow's every attempt to protect them. The British Government defended his choices. Germany protested the incident; the American Government sent a weak protest to Britain over the matter, and was given a rather bland response.

Passengers flocked to return to America by way of the *Lusitania* before the War Zone became active, and petitioned the Cunard Line to allow Captain Dow to fly the American flag again.

When the ship actually left Liverpool on February 13, she was flying the Cunard flag, the pilot flag, the Blue Peter and the British Ensign. The passengers and the large crowds that gathered to see her off were noted to be curious, but not apprehensive, about the German menace. She did not pause outside the Mersey Bar to drop off her pilot; he took the full crossing out to New York and returned to Liverpool aboard her again on the next. When the *Lusitania* arrived in New York safely at the conclusion of that voyage, it was noted that it was the first time she had arrived there flying the red British merchant marine flag rather than the blue British Royal Naval Reserve flag. Additionally, the U.S. flag had not been flown at any point during the voyage. The crossing had taken 6 days, 10 hours and 6 minutes, an eternity for the *Lusitania*; her paltry progress was blamed on poor weather, but had much more to do with the fact that Boiler Room No. 4 was still closed down.

Captain Dow was not particularly inclined to discuss the false-flag incident on his arrival in New York; he did allow for the possibility that he might again fly flags other than the Union Jack before the submarine menace was over. In point of fact, there was a more tangible sort of excitement as the *Lusitania* came into the pier; one of the hawsers snapped, and the severed end recoiled right into a seaman. It knocked him across the deck and broke his collarbone. In peace, the incident would have been widely reported in the press, but it was instead quickly forgotten, replaced in the papers by fresh war news. When the liner returned to Liverpool, she did not fly the American flag; indeed, she had flown no flag at all for two days of the voyage. The lights were extinguished during the trip up the Irish Channel, and the ship arrived in Liverpool safely on March 7, 1915.

The Cunard Line still seemed to be quite confident that the *Lusitania* was safe on the Liverpool-New York run. Even after the U-boat threat had begun to materialize, and even after the false-flag incident in February, they still felt confident enough to lower their Second Class fares to $50 (£10) in order to attract passengers. On the surface, this confidence may still have been justified. The submarines were only catching up with and sinking a relatively small portion of the overall traffic in English waters. From February of 1915, when the War Zone was declared, the U-boats' successes against merchant shipping were not catastrophic:

Month	Ships Sunk	Gross Tonnage	Lives Lost
February, 1915	14	36,372	30
March, 1915	23	71,479	161
April, 1915	11	22,453	38 [25]

There was another reason why Cunard might have felt confident about the *Lusitania*'s safety. From the start of the conflict up through April of 1915, no ship traveling at over fourteen knots had come under successful attack by a U-boat. Speed was certainly the best ally for a merchant vessel, and the *Lusitania* was the fastest on the Atlantic at the time, capable of eleven knots more than the fastest that any ship had been traveling when sunk – when under full steam. Numerous older, slower ships were plying the waters of the War Zone at speeds of 12-14 knots, and they were suffering little. Indeed, this margin was so large that Cunard still felt justified in maintaining the economizing measures they had instituted the previous November.

In addition to all of this, Cunard officials and the Admiralty may have felt the Germans simply wouldn't dare to sink the legendary *Lusitania*, speed-queen of the seas. Not when she was filled with civilian passengers; not when she was unarmed and had not been called up for military service; and certainly not when the Germans had already managed to acquire such a poor reputation on the international scene for invading neutral Belgium to attack France. Strictly speaking, Kaiser Wilhelm and some members of the German Government certainly felt that way. Even some of the U-boat commanders would most likely not have dared to sink the *Lusitania*; some were noted for their "gentlemanly" conduct in carrying out their warfare and would probably have felt that the ocean liner was not a proper target because of the high number of civilians that were sure to be aboard. Other U-boat skippers, however, did not seem to mind shooting unarmed targets with or without warning.

This was amply demonstrated on March 28, 1915, when the 4,806-ton British vessel *Falaba* ran afoul of the German *U-28* in the Irish Channel. Baron von Forstner, commanding the submarine, warned the ship to stop, but she ignored his warnings and attempted to escape. He gave chase, and closed in on the slow vessel, at which point she finally relented. Von Forstner gave the ship ten minutes to be abandoned, but fired a torpedo into her before the evacuation was complete; eight people died, including one

American. This case demonstrated a ghastly truth that was shown with remarkable regularity during the Great War, and in subsequent conflicts: humanity tends to go out the window when it gets in the way. This conflict taught the world that in modern war, the only crime was war itself.

In retrospect, from a twenty-first-century perspective, the decision by the Admiralty and the Cunard Line to keep the *Lusitania* sailing on the Atlantic at reduced speed seems quite poor. Some have pointed to the foolhardiness of this decision as evidence that the British Government or other entities were attempting to expose the *Lusitania* to greater danger in the hopes that she would be attacked and sunk by a U-boat. However, as we have already seen, such a decision would have had terrible repercussions for the British war effort, and it is far more logical to conclude that it was simply a bad choice. Hindsight is always twenty-twenty, and this is particularly true from our perspective, after two world wars as well as decades of submarine warfare and the evolution of anti-submarine defense tactics.

The danger posed to the *Lusitania* was quite real, however. Although not specifically a cargo-carrying freighter, the *Lusitania* did carry some amounts of cargo on each crossing. Once the war began and American munitions began to flow eastward toward England, the *Lusitania* is known to have carried this absolute contraband in her holds. In compliance with United States shipping regulations, this cargo would have been non-explosive in bulk, and clearly marked as such. She also carried items like foodstuffs, etc., that the British had categorized as absolute contraband after the outbreak of war. Once the German War Zone, in essence a blockade of England, began, this meant that the *Lusitania* was demonstrably, under International Law, a blockade runner. The Germans were keeping a close eye on the loading of cargo on many ships, including the *Lusitania*, in New York; they were aware of her cargo's nature. The *Lusitania* could not rely on a neutral flag for protection, either, for she was owned by a British steamship line, co-paid for by the British Government under the terms of the 1902 loan to Cunard. Even if she did fly a neutral flag, any German U-boat commander with a shred of sense would immediately be able to identify her correctly. Although she often carried neutral citizens, International Law still categorized her decks as an extension of British – and hence belligerent – soil. International Law simply did not allow neutral citizens to protect a British ship by their very presence.

Although not in active Government service at any time after the war began, the *Lusitania* and *Maure-*

Above: *Alfred A. Booth, Chairman of the Cunard Line beginning in 1909.*

Opposite: *Captain Turner returned to the* Lusitania *to replace Captain Dow in March of 1915.*

tania had been categorized in Brassey's 1914 edition of *The Naval Annual* as "Royal Naval Reserved Merchant Cruisers," which meant that they were subject to requisition at any time. Even if the British did not employ the *Lusitania* for use as an armed merchantman, there was always the possibility that they could use her as a troop transport or in some other militarily supportive role. Just days after the *Lusitania* arrived in New York after taking back the Blue Riband in 1907, *The New York Times* reported an interesting piece from Berlin:

> Naval officers here say they look upon the Cunard Line steamer *Lusitania* as being capable of transporting 10,000 troops from England to the Continent, so that the *Lusitania* and her sister ship, the *Mauretania*, could carry an expedition of 20,000 men. They said that, as all the officers of the two vessels and half the crews are members of the British Naval Reserve, the vessels could be taken over by the Government and placed in the service of the Admiralty in very short time.[26]

the *Aquitania* for the brief period of her career up to the outbreak of the war.

On March 10, only three days after the *Lusitania* had arrived in port, Turner boarded the ship for his full inspection. Turner had proven himself a meticulous commander during his tenures on the *Lusitania*, *Mauretania* and *Aquitania*. He drove both his crew and his vessel to attain their highest standards of efficiency and performance. Now he seemed quite disturbed by the conditions that had developed aboard the liner during his five-year absence. In short order, Turner had completed a report to Cunard, and to ensure that the matter was taken care of promptly, he also complained directly to the British Board of Trade's Liverpool Surveyor. Four new lifeboats were ordered to replace ones that Turner found unusable and irreparable, and other lifesaving equipment was carefully inspected; any defective items were to be replaced in short order.[29]

Turner was also quite alarmed by the poor level of the crew's morale and competence. Since the outbreak of war, many good men had left jobs like the *Lusitania* to enlist in the military and were now serving either on the fronts or in the Royal Navy in some capacity. Those that were left behind were not astoundingly experienced at their jobs; as it was, Cunard had difficulty in maintaining enough crew to man the ship and "had to take on the best men they could get and train them as well as might be in the time at their disposal."[30] The morale level was even worse, especially among the stokers and boiler room staff; they knew that their ship could be torpedoed, and that if it was, they would be the first to suffer the horrible consequences of such an attack.

While Cunard and the Board of Trade worked to replace the faulty equipment on the *Lusitania*, Turner took the ship out on her 199th crossing, beginning on March 20, with 536 passengers and 2,500 sacks of mail. That crossing of the Atlantic showed Captain Turner to be "cautious." The ship was studiously blacked out at night, and she encountered nothing more exciting than a westerly gale and a few icebergs. She arrived safely in New York on the evening of Friday, March 26.

Lusitania's departure from that port was scheduled for Saturday, April 3. That day brought a startling disruption to New York life and shipping in the form of a late-winter blizzard. The snow began to fall at 8:30 a.m., and it continued all through the day and into the early part of the night. Ten inches of the white substance had accumulated by 11:00 p.m. that night, and sixty-mile-per-hour winds, with gusts of up to seventy-five miles per hour, howled down the

The simple fact was that after February of 1915, there was a very real chance that if a German U-boat came across the *Lusitania*, he would fire on her without warning. No one felt this threat more acutely than her skipper, Daniel Dow. When Dow returned to Liverpool on March 7, 1915 – only one full round-trip voyage after the false-flag incident – it seems that he had had enough. On the day after the *Lusitania* tied up, he apparently informed Cunard Chairman Alfred Booth that although commanding a liner through the War Zone did not in particular bother him, he did not like the fact that the ship was carrying munitions and civilians.[27] Cunard immediately gave him leave, later explaining that he was "tired and really ill."[28] In his place, command of the *Lusitania* was returned to Captain William Thomas Turner, who had captained

A menu from Tuesday, April 6, 1915, during Crossing No. 200 East, the return leg of Turner's first round-trip since taking command from Captain Dow.

city's streets. It was reported that "in the North River it was impossible to see from one shore to the other." The city was virtually paralyzed by the weather. As bad as the situation was in New York, it was worse in the Boston area; in Virginia, there were reports of severe coastal flooding. The Washington, D.C. weather bureau reported that the storm had developed on Friday over Florida and then swept northeastward across the coast until it became a powerful snowstorm over the northeastern states.

In the middle of this mess, the *Lusitania* was due to sail at 10:00 a.m. The first delay of the day came because customs officials were enforcing new regulations regarding the examination of baggage prior to boarding; all small packages had to be examined on the pier to make sure that no saboteurs were attempting to smuggle an "infernal machine" aboard the liner. This was a very real concern; the Germans had taken to operating a clandestine team in the United States to divert British war materials away from the fronts. Sometimes they did this by placing large "dummy"

orders to clog up the manufacturing companies, and at times they did this by active sabotage. Passengers boarding the ship passed in a cue to the gangplank, and each had to show his or her ticket before boarding; pier detectives and Police Inspectors studied each one for any signs of trouble. All of this understandable caution led up to a delay, and it was 10:30 before all of the baggage and 830 passengers (including 405 in Second Class) were aboard. On the passenger list was Richard Croker and his bride, off to Ireland and saying he might never return. This was the same Richard Croker who had taken the *Lusitania*'s maiden voyage from Liverpool to New York in 1907. There was also Robert Bacon, a former U.S. Ambassador to Paris, and Madame Louise Vandervelde, the wife of the Belgian Minister of State, with over $300,000 in relief monies to aid those suffering in the conflict. George Sterling Ryerson was also traveling in First Class; he had been commissioned to make a survey of the work that the Canadian Red Cross Society in England was performing in the war effort.[31]

It was at 10:30, with all of the passengers and cargo aboard, that Captain Turner would normally have given the order to cast off. However, staring intently into the driving snow, it was clear to Turner that it would not be a terrific idea to try blindly maneuvering a thirty thousand ton ocean liner in the North River. The pilot and Captain D. J. Roberts, Cunard's New York Marine Superintendent, agreed with him. Roberts said that "it was one of the worst snowstorms he had seen in many years." At Sandy Hook, visibility was reported at twenty feet; at Quarantine, only twenty-five yards.

At 3:00 p.m., the wind shifted slightly and the snowfall tapered off for a bit, allowing a couple of ships to break from their piers and attempt to move out of harbor. None managed to make it past Sandy Hook, and they all had to remain in Gravesend Bay overnight. Captain Turner did not believe it safe to take his ship out even during that brief abatement, and remained at the pier throughout the afternoon, even though this put the liner quite behind schedule.[32] The next morning, Easter Sunday, 1915, she was finally able to depart, and made for England under Turner's watchful eye. Ryerson later recalled:

> During the voyage I had many conversations with the Commander, Captain Turner, a quiet, determined, and, as it proved, courageous man. He told me that the Admiralty absolutely declined to arm the ship, that in their opinion there was no necessity for it and the speed of the ship, twenty-five knots, was such that she could run away from any

undersea boat. He said very bitterly that he had not even a rifle on board, for if he had he could disable a submarine, submarines … being so lightly constructed that a rifle bullet would pierce their hulls.

From this account, we can see that Turner was certainly aware of the dangers of sailing his ship through the War Zone. We can also see that Turner apparently did not reveal to Ryerson the ship's reduced top speed. Despite the Captain's worry, Ryerson said of himself and his fellow passengers:

We were quite merry about [the dangers], for no one believed that any power would sink without warning a huge passenger vessel carrying a large number of women and children and many neutrals.[33]

Others felt the same way. Joseph Gallagher, a former resident of Lima, Ohio, had moved to Preston, England and was returning home on the same crossing. He later recalled that although a couple of Americans had canceled their bookings at the last minute, those who actually chose to take passage on the ship were "light-hearted," and that "there was as much joking and laughter on the subject of submarines as though they were nothing more than phantom 'Flying Dutchmen.' " Indeed, he commented:

… Nobody supposed for a moment that even a German submarine would attack without warning or that ample time would not be given all on board to escape … [The] worst we all anticipated was a few hours in an open boat and plenty to talk about for the rest of our lives.

On no day of the trip did the ship's run break the 500-mile mark, he later recalled. As she neared the War Zone, however, it was obvious that Captain Turner was serious about taking precautions to protect his ship. The liner was blacked out that night as they neared the Irish coast; every boat had been swung out, "ready to be launched at a moment's notice"; the lights in the First Class public rooms were extinguished early; passengers were requested to remain "indoors." Then it became obvious that the ship had sped up considerably; her vibration troubles were once again in evidence.

That night, a Third Class passenger foolishly attempted to light a pipe on deck; he apparently had trouble lighting the pipe, and determinedly struck several matches. He was immediately apprehended by Detective Inspector William Pierpoint, who believed

that he might have been trying to give the ship's position away. He was "kept under close supervision" until the ship reached Liverpool, and Gallagher knew of at least three other people who were detained as suspicious and later landed under custody at Liverpool. Over the night, some of the women in First Class were nervous enough to refuse to sleep in their cabins; they instead chose to spend "an uncomfortable night on sofas and cushions in the saloon."

At noon the next day, the ship's run was posted; it was only 460 miles, a decrease in mileage from her previous runs despite her obviously increased speed. The passengers were perplexed until the "mystery was explained (unofficially) later on." They were told that the actual mileage was 580, but that they "had been 'zig-zagging' out of [their] course for the express purpose of baffling any submarine that might be lying in wait for us." Although Gallagher could not vouch for the truth of that statement personally, he acknowledged that it was "the only explanation that [seemed] to fit the facts."[34]

Lusitania finished the voyage in safety despite the dangers, and without any serious incident, concluding her 100th round-trip voyage on the Atlantic. For a week, the *Lusitania* remained in Liverpool. Captain Turner was still reportedly not happy with his crew's overall morale, but it was something that he could work on during the upcoming crossing. Other than that, the turnaround period in Liverpool seemed relatively normal.

The *Lusitania*'s 101st departure from Liverpool was scheduled for Saturday, April 17, 1915. The ship departed the Landing Stage all right, but anchored in the Mersey until nightfall. In doing this, Captain Turner was applying an Admiralty directive, one of many that he was supposed to implement in the War Zone; later, he rather caustically remarked that he could have "papered the walls" with them, there were so many.[35] Among these were eight specific advices that would later prove important:

1. To avoid headlands, where U-boats typically hunted
2. To steer a mid-channel course
3. To operate at full speed off harbors
4. To preserve wireless silence within 100 miles of land, save for an emergency
5. To post extra lookouts
6. To maintain lifeboats ready for lowering and provisioned
7. To keep on the move outside ports and harbors
8. To steer a zigzag course

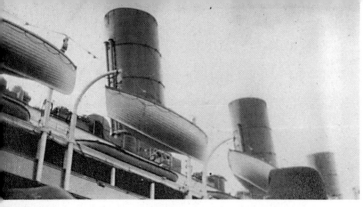

This page and the ones that follow show a selection of photographs from Crossing No. 201 West, the Lusitania's final westbound crossing.

The Lusitania *prepares for her 101st departure from Liverpool, England on Saturday, April 17, 1915. This photograph was taken from the Stage, looking up at her towering sides and mighty funnels. Her lifeboats are all swung out.*

The Lusitania *pulls away from the Prince's Landing Stage, leaving her home port of seven and a half years, bound for a tragic future. A large crowd stands on the quay bidding a fond, and permanent, farewell.*

The bow of the Lusitania *as it pulls away, seen from the Landing Stage.*

The stern half of the liner as she departed for the last time. Notice the alterations to her lifeboat configuration during the final stretch of her career. The stacks of three collapsibles, visible on page 240 (bottom) have been replaced with full lifeboats with collapsibles underneath. The pictures taken from shore were most likely taken by a relative or friend of those who were taking passage, and later found their way into the same album as the pictures taken aboard during the trip.

Top left: *The photographer who took these pictures was travel-ing in Second Class, and busily took snaps all over the Second Class decks during the crossing. Here a woman stands on the Sun Deck level astern, on the roof of the Lounge. The lady is dressed quite warmly for protection against the chill.*

Top right: *The woman is apparently in the midst of a game of shuffleboard. A Bull Board leans against the railing.*

Middle left: *The same lady, now standing against the forward rail of the Lounge Roof, overlooking the smokestacks and First Class spaces forward.*

Middle right: *The woman, having shed her overcoat, poses beside a container which holds life jackets; the ship's cat sleeps idly next to her arm. Was this the same cat that deserted the ship in New York at the end of this crossing?*

Bottom right: *Reading on the open decks of Second Class in the spring required warm clothing and a steamer rug in order to keep warm.*

Top left: A second view of the older lady reading on deck. She seems to be located on the port side of the Second Class Promenade, right aft, behind the stairs which led down from the Boat Deck. The windows behind her look out from the Second Class Smoking Room.

Top right: Standing on the starboard side of the Second Class Boat Deck, with Boat No. 21 plainly visible, and the walls of the Second Class Lounge visible on the left.

Middle left: A pair of Second Class passengers standing on the roof of the Lounge, port side, with the ratlines leading up the aft mast clearly visible behind them.

Middle right: Another container, apparently for life jackets, is visible behind the lady in this photograph on the Lounge roof.

Bottom left: A hardy pair of Second Class passengers in deck chairs on the Boat Deck. Not only are they dressed quite warmly, but they are also just aft of another locker for life jackets, which would most likely be helping to shelter them from the wind. The mainmast is visible behind them. Notice that all of the lockers on the deck are plainly marked to aid in their use during an emergency.

FATHER and MR TAINSH of Glasgow

Top left: *Relaxing on the starboard Boat Deck, just aft of the stairs leading to the Second Class Lounge roof, and next to the skylight for the Second Class Smoking Room.*

Top right: *This photograph was captioned "Father and Mr. Tainsh of Glasgow." According to the ship's manifest, this was 37-year-old Henry Tainsh, an Engineer of 98 Duke Street, Glasgow, Scotland.*

Above: *This may be what Mr. Tainsh was so eagerly viewing through his binoculars in the preceding photograph: another vessel on the horizon. Although the photograph is not exceedingly crisp, it appears to be a single-funnel vessel of small size.*

Bottom right: *This photograph shows several individuals standing on the roof of the Lounge; the man on the right may be the same Mr. Tainsh as in the previous photograph.*

Top left: *A slightly different group pose.*

Top right: *In this photograph, the group can be seen standing on the port side of the Lounge roof, just where the rail around the cowl ventilator jogs inboard.*

Middle left: *Several fresh faces can be seen in this group photograph.*

Below left: *In this photo, the photographer has moved from the Lounge roof, descended the stairs, climbed up to the Stern Docking Bridge, and has turned to look forward and photograph his group of traveling companions. Interestingly, we can see that the port staircase leading down from the Lounge roof remains missing. Its absence was first notable very early on in the ship's career.*

Opposite top: *A wonderfully unique photograph taken from the fantail of the ship, looking up at the Second Class decks above. On the Promenade Deck, the double doors leading to the vestibule, with the Smoke Room beyond, are open and resting against the bulkhead.*

Opposite bottom: *This view looks out over the fantail and shows the ship's wake stretching back toward war-torn Europe. No flag flies at the stern, but that is not unusual for when the ship was at sea, even in peacetime.*

Above: *An actual photograph of the Lusitania's final arrival in New York, on Saturday, April 24, 1915 – a week after her departure from Liverpool. Although Cunard was very quiet about the economization of the ship's powerplant during the war months, it was clear to everyone who took even a passing interest in the subject that the ship was not making pre-war speeds. Tugs are straining to get the ship in position to enter Pier 54. This photograph is also very important in that it proves without doubt or question that the ship's name was not painted black in an attempt to disguise her identity from German submarines; although just barely visible in the Liverpool departure photo from April 17, this view shows the name in all its stunning brilliance. One more long-held Lusitania myth laid to rest with finality. Like the pictures taken from shore back at Liverpool, this photo was most likely taken by friends or family of the passengers who took the shipboard photos, as it made its way into the same album as the other views.*

Right: Another passenger on that same crossing was Guglielmo Marconi, wireless inventor. He is pictured here on the First Class Boat Deck shortly after the ship had tied up at Pier 54.

The final one of these advices was given to Captain Turner on the day before the *Lusitania* departed Liverpool on this particular crossing.[36] Nevertheless, he did not use the zigzag technique as he steamed out of the War Zone, even though there was a submarine scare while she was clearing Irish waters.[37] Instead, Turner seemed to exude a "jovial," "typical" attitude for Captains of his stature, albeit mixed with an "air of authority."[38] On the other hand, the ship was blacked out while steaming at night, in accord with Admiralty directives. Once she had cleared the War Zone, the passengers could relax and settled in for a comfortable, almost typical crossing of the Atlantic. The liner arrived in New York safely on Saturday, April 24, 1915. She was tied up at Pier 54 with her starboard side resting against the north side of the dock, and her passengers were disembarked in the customary scene which had played out a hundred times before since September of 1907.

Once the passengers had disembarked, the turnaround process could begin in earnest; she was to spend a full week in New York, with her next departure scheduled for Saturday, May 1. The stay in the American port was eventful. The crew was clearly demoralized; even the German spies on the New York waterfront were aware of the fact, reporting that the liner's crew was not only in a "depressed mood," but that its members hoped that the upcoming crossing would be "the last Atlantic crossing during the war."[39] One must wonder where this little nugget of information was obtained, for the historical record clearly shows that Cunard had no plans to lay up the *Lusitania* upon her return to Europe. In fact, quite the opposite was true. On May 1, 1915, newspapers advertised her next sailing from New York as Saturday, May 29 at 10:00 a.m. On May 7, the sailing schedule went even further, showing that the *Lusitania* was also to begin east-bound crossings from New York on Saturday, June 26 and Saturday, July 24, also at 10:00 a.m. What is more, on May 5, Cunard announced that they would be returning the *Mauretania* – laid up in Liverpool since the previous autumn—to commercial service. She was scheduled to sail from Liverpool on May 29, and Cunard also announced that they were considering the option of placing the *Aquitania* back into commercial service, as well, 'if business demanded' her use.[40]

Certainly then, any hopes held by members of the Lusitania's crew that she would soon be laid up were certain to be dashed. Yet the Germans were correct in surmising that their morale was low. Indeed during the stay, some of the crew decided that they had had enough; a number of them walked down the gangplank into New York City once they had been given leave, never to return. The *Lusitania's* Staff Captain, James Clarke "Jock" Anderson, was forced to try to recruit replacements as the deadline for departure neared. Even the ship's mascot cat seemed to have decided that it was not a great idea to stay aboard for the upcoming crossing, deciding to set its paws on *Terra Firma* instead of the relative uncertainty of the *Lusitania's* decks.

The coal lighters tied up along the ship's port side, and the coal ports along the side were opened up. Now began the noisy, dirty, and eminently routine task of filling the ship's coal bunkers. When she arrived in port, the *Lusitania* had 900 tons of coal remaining, and she burned some 580 tons while tied up. The liner took on some 5,690 tons of coal from the lighters, for a total of 6,010 tons upon departure. This sum total was only 500 tons less than the fuel

that she had carried on her maiden voyage in 1907, and was more than enough to take her across the Atlantic with only three Boiler Rooms operating. The stewards and stewardesses busied themselves at freshening up the passenger cabins, changing the linens, making the beds, dusting and straightening, and taking particular care to return First Class cabins to absolutely pristine condition. The pace was quick, but having a full seven days to turn the ship around was certainly far less hectic when compared to a more typical stay in New York before the war had started.

Cargo began to come aboard the ship, and the liner's forward booms attached to the mast carefully lifted each batch and lowered it into the holds underneath the Forecastle, well forward of the Boiler Rooms. Staff Captain Anderson oversaw the loading, which continued up until the proverbial last minute before sailing. These shipments included much material that the British had designated as absolute contraband in the months since the outbreak of war. Among the list of items was a shipment of war materials: there were 4,200 cases of Remington rifle cartridges (.303 caliber), packed 1,000 to a box, for a total of 4.2 million. There was also a consignment of 1,248 empty shrapnel shells and 18 cases of non-explosive fuses. The shrapnel shells went into the after of the two cargo holds, just forward of the reserve coal bunker. The cartridges were stored just above, on the Lower Orlop Deck. By any reasonable measure, this was a good-sized shipment of munitions; however, in comparison with the amounts being carried on true cargo ships, it was diminutive. Its importance, in retrospect, had less to do with the size of the shipment than it did with the fact that it was being shipped on a British merchant liner carrying British and neutral civilians through a War Zone. Mixed in with the munitions was a good deal of less murderous items – furs stored on the Lower Deck, butter, cheese and lard on the Tank Top between the coal bunker and the shrapnel shells, with more stored in the forward cargo hold. In all, these items comprised a very average mixture of cargo for an Atlantic liner.

Despite the dangers of the War Zone, bookings for the Lusitania's 202nd crossing were strong; this was aided, no doubt, by the reduced rates which Cunard had offered to prospective passengers. Spring was also in the air, encouraging travel; fears of wartime dangers from Zeppelin attacks in English cities like London also seem to have been on the wane. Thus, the Lusitania's upcoming passenger list would be the longest since the onset of hostilities. Second Class was overbooked, and in the event, some Second Class passengers were given empty First Class cabins; First

Masquerade of an Icon

This photograph of the Lusitania's *final departure, on May 1, 1915, shows that her upper works were painted white, clearly shows the "gold" band around her superstructure, and also shows a stark contrast between the funnel bands and the main funnel segments. So the question is: were the funnels painted black? Were they in their traditional Cunard livery? Or were they painted something else?*

The *Lusitania* was arguably the most recognizable of the Atlantic liners when war erupted in August of 1914. Her size alone stood out among her peers. Her quartet of largely evenly spaced funnels was another quick identifying feature; only the Cunard trio and the *Olympic* could fit the bill up through May of 1915.[1] The smokestacks' orange-red and black paint scheme further narrowed the field to only the Cunard sisters. Because of the fame of these three liners, most mariners – indeed, even people with only a passing interest in steamships – could also easily distinguish which of the three was which.

To aid in concealing the *Lusitania's* iconic features, Cunard resorted to a masquerade of sorts. As the *Lusitania* returned to England immediately following the War's outbreak, her funnels and upper works were painted in a drab gray to make her less visible to any enemy commander searching for her; the paint had been acquired in New York prior to departure, and workmen had carried the task out at sea.[2]

Within a month or two, the drab gray on the funnels had been replaced with "black" paint. By November of that year, however, Cunard apparently felt that this disguise was no longer necessary. When the liner arrived in New York on the

evening of Friday, November 27, 1914, having completed Crossing No. 191 West, her black funnels had been returned to traditional Cunard livery. A headline in *The New York Times* proclaimed that the *Lusitania* had dropped her "disguise," and that smokestacks were again painted "red with black tops, the Cunard colors, after being painted black for the last two months as a disguise on account of the war."

The work had apparently been carried out prior to her November 21 departure from Liverpool; this is surmised from the fact that although she carried 825 passengers from Europe – including James G. Bennett, proprietor of the *New York Herald* – none of them reported seeing the ship repainted at sea.

The Cunard livery continued to adorn the funnels through mid-January of 1915. One passenger on Crossing No. 195 West recalled that before she boarded the ship, she could see the *Lusitania* "gleaming white in the distance, her yellow smokestacks proudly towering over those of all the other ships around her."[3] Although one could hardly call the *Lusitania's* ordinary funnel color "yellow," "yellow" is a far cry from gray or black. The ship's Cunard-red funnels were retained during the next eastbound crossing, No. 196.

On February 4, 1915, however, the Germans declared the War Zone around the British Isles. Although it would not take effect until February 20, Cunard apparently felt that it was necessary to resume their masquerade of the *Lusitania*. One of the passengers booked on Westbound Crossing No. 197, 26-year-old Nils Krook, later recalled that when the ship left Liverpool, concern was high among those aboard. As soon as the ship cast off, "painters made the vessel black, even to the funnels."[4] The ship ran at high speed out of Liverpool and into the North Atlantic, completely blacked out as she went. It was obvious that Captain Dow was seriously concerned about the submarine threat. In fact, it was on the return voyage that Dow flew the American flag, with all of the resulting controversy; once that crossing had been completed, Dow resigned his post as captain of the great ship. Her next trip was under the command of Captain Turner.

Krook wasn't the only one who remembered that the *Lusitania*'s funnels were painted black as her career wound down, particularly on her last trip. John Idwal Lewis later recalled that her main hull and funnels were black, while her superstructure remained white. Thomas Slidell described the funnels as "giant gray tubes."[5] Andrew Chalmers, the Assistant Marine Superintendent for Cunard, remembered that the ship was repainted before the final voyage.

Film footage taken as the *Lusitania* left New York on her last crossing, however, shows a noticeable contrast between the segments of the funnels and the black bands that separated them. There has been some doubt, in years past, as to whether the footage was taken on May 1, 1915, or on the date of her previous departure from New York. Since that departure took place just after a blizzard, however, and there is no evidence of snow in the film, it is quite clear that the footage was taken on May 1.

So what does the contrast shown in the film footage mean? Some have pointed out that due to the limitations of black and white photography at the time, the contrast may be misleading. Yet, if nothing else, the footage does show a contrast, that there is a difference between the bands and the primary segments. Indeed, the contrast is quite similar to that shown in pre-war photographs of the *Lusitania*'s funnels, when they were covered in traditional Cunard livery.

Could the dark lines visible in the film footage have been caused by shadows underneath the bands of the funnels? A close inspection of the images seems to show that the contrast shows along the top of the bands as well. This would tend to indicate a difference in the paint rather than a line caused by a shadow.

The presence of the dark bands in the May 1 departure footage thus means one of two things: the first option is that the funnels had been repainted in their famous "orange-red" color with black bands between early February and the end of April, 1915. This is quite possible, particularly since Cunard was attempting to revitalize bookings on the ship and a "business-as-usual" appearance would lend itself to that feeling. It also seems likely that at that point both the Admiralty and Cunard felt that the Germans simply would not have the chutzpah to torpedo the passenger liner; since her profile was so unique, it also seems likely that they had determined that any amount of disguise attempted to conceal her identity was a moot point. April 17 and 24, 1915 photographs (reproduced elsewhere in this chapter) of the ship show that her name was not obliterated, but remained gold-colored right up to the last voyage.

The second option, however, seems more likely. Because quite a few of the officers and crew on the last trip described the funnels as "black" or "gray," it is possible that the paint applied to the main funnel segments on the last voyage might not have been true black, but rather a dark shade of gray that appeared nearly black in some lighting conditions, but showed a contrast in other lighting conditions. This is the explanation that seems to best fit the evidence in hand at this time.

---

[1] *Lusitania* was the oldest of these ships. *Mauretania* was laid up in late October. *Aquitania* was at first requisitioned, but then laid up. *Olympic* was in service until early November, but was thereafter laid up. *Titanic* was at the bottom of the ocean, while the *Britannic* was as yet incomplete. The earlier German ships bearing four funnels were much smaller and presented a very different profile from that of the *Lusitania*.
[2] Reported in *The Illustrated London News*, 8/22/1914, and discussed elsewhere in this chapter. Photographs of the ship being repainted were published in *The Illustrated War News*.
[3] *Mission for Serbia; letters from America and Canada, 1915-1920*, by Helen Frothingham (*née* Losanitch). Edited by Matilda Spence Rowland. Walker (1970), pg. 3.
[4] Account provided by Jean Richards Timmermeister.
[5] Slidell's account was contained in *The New York Times*, May 10, 1915.

Class was slightly more than half full, while Third Class was – predictably for an eastbound crossing regardless of hostilities – only about one-quarter full. Some of these passengers had been rather apprehensive about taking passage on the liner through the War Zone, but invariably Cunard employees had allayed their fears by telling them that there was no risk involved. A good example of this was the experience of Rev. Charles C. Clarke, a First Class passenger. Before boarding, he stopped by the New York offices of the Cunard Line at 24 State Street.[41] He was later asked:

> - Did you make any enquiry about a threat to sink the *"Lusitania"* by submarines?
> - No, I only asked the man who gave me my ticket whether there was any extraordinary danger in travelling by the *"Lusitania"* he told me, no, there was none as far as he knew, and that the Cunard Company were not likely to risk a ship of such enormous value if there was any extra danger.[42]

His experience was by no means unique. Charles E. Lauriat, Jr., a Boston bookseller, bought his ticket at Cunard's offices in that city. When he asked if the *Lusitania* would be "convoyed through the war zone," he was told: "Oh yes! every precaution will be taken."[43] Lauriat and Clarke were not the only ones given this reassurance. Unfortunately, these promises were completely baseless; on one previous occasion, an escort had been arranged for the *Lusitania*, and the entire affair had fallen apart at the last minute, causing those in charge of the operation to send wireless transmissions to the liner in order to re-organize the rendezvous. These communications could easily have given her position away to any nearby U-boat.[44] Since that incident, the ship had never come under escort – under International Law, this would actually have made her subject to attack without warning. Additionally, because of a shortage of escort vessels, anything sent out to meet the *Lusitania* was bound to be slow and poorly armed. Such an escort would only have slowed down the speed queen, making her more vulnerable to a successful torpedo attack, and could have done very little to defend her against a submarine.

While the *Lusitania* was berthed in New York, Staff Captain Anderson had to see to a boat drill in accordance with regulations.[45] He was also successful in finding replacements for those who had "jumped ship" upon arrival; they weren't what could be called skilled seamen, but times were tough. Captain Turner lamented their lack of experience, but admitted that it didn't take a good seaman to push a wheelbarrow of coal.[46] In total, the crew would only amount to around seven hundred, far less than her standard complement.

While the *Lusitania*'s crew worked at preparing the liner for her next crossing, her next group of passengers was beginning to converge on New York, making their final arrangements to board the ship on the morning of Saturday, May 1. A few decided to cancel their passage at the last minute, still worried about the dangers of taking passage on the liner. Most, however, decided to forge forth. Some were traveling abroad for business or other necessary concerns; most, though, were booking passage for purely frivolous reasons. As usual, there would be a number of famous or familiar faces in First Class – millionaire Alfred Gwynne Vanderbilt was a prime example. Vanderbilt was a prominent member of *the* Vanderbilt family, and was well known for his love of fast automobiles and horses. Vanderbilt, who was traveling with his manservant, was still trying to put a scandal behind him; he had married Ellen French in 1901, but she had filed for divorce in 1908 alleging that he had committed adultery with the wife of the Cuban attaché in Washington, Mrs. Agnes Ruiz. Mrs. Ruiz took her own life in 1909 following the negative publicity, while Vanderbilt had remarried in 1911, to Margaret Emerson, a wealthy American woman who was also divorced. On the night before the sailing, Vanderbilt and his wife had seen a play entitled *"A Celebrated Case."*

That particular play was co-produced by one of Vanderbilt's fellow passengers on the upcoming crossing, Charles Frohman, impresario and personal friend to Sir James M. Barrie. He was making a trip to Europe to see the London and Paris "playmarkets." Some of his friends had advised him not to sail because of the dangers, but he ignored their pleas. "When you consider all the stars I've managed," he was reported to have said, "mere submarines make me smile." He was traveling with his valet, William Stainton. Additionally, as was the norm for a crossing on the *Lusitania*, there would be many others from theater circles traveling in First Class. Among these were actress Rita Jolivet and her brother-in-law George Vernon, actress Josephine Brandell, and playwrights Charles Klein and Justus Miles Forman.

Rita Jolivet had not originally booked passage on the *Lusitania*. Instead, she had booked passage on the *New York*, a neutral American liner. However the beautiful 25-year-old had at the last minute decided to switch her plans, and to take the *Lusitania* instead. The decision was motivated by the fact that her brother Alfred was preparing to ship out with his regiment; the actress knew that the *Lusitania* was a much faster ship than the *New York*, and thus offered a better chance of getting her to England in time to see her brother before he departed for the front. Once she had seen her brother off, she was planning to travel on to Italy to film a moving picture. Jolivet had already starred in several silent films, including *Fata Morgana* and *The Unafraid*, the latter film having been only just released in the United States. No doubt another factor in her decision to switch from the *New York* to the *Lusitania* was the fact that a number of other individuals involved in the stage and screen business would be aboard, as well.

That last Friday in New York was a busy one. Captain Turner took in a show and dined at his favorite restaurant, also paying a visit to his niece, Mercedes. Earlier in the day he had given testimony as an expert witness in the *Titanic* Limitation of Liability Hearings. He had come off rather gruffly, as a typically self-assured skipper. When he had been asked about the construction features of the *Titanic*, he had responded that he didn't "bother" with the details of ships' construction "as long as they float. If they sink I get out." When asked if he had learned anything from the *Titanic* disaster, he had replied: "Not the slightest. It will happen again."[47]

That night, the *Lusitania* sat quietly at Pier 54, her bright lights illuminating the dark New York waterfront, and giving only the faintest idea of her truly enormous size. Over the preceding years, she had become a regular fixture of the Fourteenth Street waterfront in Manhattan. Although work continued overnight to finish preparations for departure, the scene was overall quiet and peaceful – the antithesis of the pandemonium that would ensue the following morning, and wholly removed from the war-torn Europe that she would set her bow toward the following day.

Dawn on Saturday, May 1, 1915 arrived and the scene at Pier 54 began to liven with a building momentum. A drizzly mist hung over Manhattan, casting a gloomy, damp shadow over the normal activities of sailing. As the morning papers found distribution, a rumor began to spread that there was something unusual contained within their pages. Anyone curious enough to look for the source of the rumor would have found the item easily enough. Surrounded by a black border, and in most papers residing on the very page advertising the *Lusitania*'s sailing that morning, sat an eye-catching advertisement. It was a notice addressed to those contemplating an Atlantic voyage, reminding them of the War Zone, and that within that area of operations, "vessels flying the flag of Great Britain, or of any of her allies, [were] liable to destruction in those waters," and that anyone taking passage on those ships did so "at their own risk." It was signed: "IMPERIAL GERMAN EMBASSY, Washington, D.C., April 22, 1915."

Any sailing of the *Lusitania* had, during the preceding seven years, sparked great interest in New York papers and had invariably been cause for reporters' presence. However, this notice sparked a bona fide press frenzy. Although nowhere in the notice was the *Lusitania* specifically mentioned, by definition, it described the *Lusitania*. What could it all mean? German Ambassador Bernstorff was asked, and replied that it was merely a friendly warning. Some passengers congregating down at Pier 54 were caught off guard by the notice, suddenly nervous. Cunard's New York Agent, Charles Sumner, heard about the warning and hurried down to West Fourteenth Street to reassure passengers: "The truth is that the *Lusitania* is the safest boat on the sea. She is too fast for any submarine. No German war vessel can get her or near her. She will reach Liverpool on schedule time and come back on schedule time just as long as we are able to run her in the transatlantic trade."[48] In fact, he pointed out that sailing on her would not involve any "risk whatever."[49] Some of those present began calling this particular sailing the "Last Voyage of the *Lusitania*." A newsreel crew showed up and took footage of passengers arriving at Pier 54 and stayed around through the morning to film the ship's departure, as well.[50]

Similarly, Captain Turner was asked about the warning, and he retorted with a laugh: "I wonder what the Germans will do next. Well, it doesn't seem as if they had scared many people from going on the ship by the look of the pier and the passenger list."[51] Indeed, Cunard reported that there were no cancellations because of the warning, although this was not entirely true. As passengers began filing aboard through the stringent security that had been in place for some time, rumors began to spread that at least forty telegrams had reached them warning them not to sail; Cunard investigated the matter and categorically denied the telegrams.

Rita Jolivet found Pier 54 to be a hive of excitement that morning. She was cutting her timing a bit fine, and climbed aboard only just before 10:00 a.m. Because of the last-minute change in her plans, her cabin selection had been quite limited. When she finally reached the stateroom she had booked, D15, she judged it to be "a very bad room." It was located on the inside of the ship, and had no sea view.

Another First Class passenger who boarded the ship that morning was Michael Byrne. His wife and

two friends came aboard to see him off. Once the group had climbed aboard, they proceeded to his cabin, B64, which was an inside cabin just aft of the No. 2 Funnel casing. He found his baggage had arrived safely, and he next went to the Purser's Office, to inquire about purchasing baggage insurance. The staff responded by telling him that they did not insure baggage. Byrne and his party then began to tour the ship, viewing the Lounge, the Smoking Room, and then taking a walk on the Promenade Deck. A few minutes later, there came the cry of, "All ashore," the longstanding notification that it was time for anyone not booked for passage to return to shore. Byrne kissed his wife good-bye, he bade his friends farewell, and then he watched as they disembarked and stood down on the dock. Only after they had left did word come that the ship was going to be delayed.[52]

This delay was certainly quite unexpected. It took place because the Anchor liner *Cameronia* had been requisitioned by the British Admiralty, and a large number of her passengers were transferred to the *Lusitania*, along with their baggage. The transfer process took time, some two and a half hours in all; those passengers already aboard the *Lusitania* whiled away their time by getting settled in their accommodations, speaking with reporters, posing for photographs on deck, or just exploring the ship. There was plenty for passengers to do: seats in the Dining Sa-

loon had to be assigned by the Chief Steward; steamer chairs had to be acquired, for a fee of $1.00 each, before the most desirable locations were taken; and for many, arrangements with their Room Steward had to be made to reserve the use of the bathroom facilities for certain hours. Others took the opportunity to write letters to family and friends on the free stationary provided in the Writing Room, or on postcards which they purchased aboard, which would be sent off with the departure of the pilot at Ambrose light.

One First Class passenger, Dorothy Conner, took exactly this opportunity. She wrote a note to her mother which read in part: "The *Lusitania* is now being held up and there is a report that the Captain has lost his nerve, but I think we will get off alright."[53] Meanwhile Captain Turner found just enough time to dash off a note to Mrs. Seccombe, the widow of one of his fellow skippers, Captain W. S. Seccombe. Mrs. Seccombe's two children, Percy (aged 20) and Miss Elizabeth Ann (aged 38), were booked in First Class. Turner wrote in haste that he "would surely look after" her son and daughter. Sadly, in the ensuing disaster, both of her children were lost.

Rita Jolivet milled about the ship, and was surprised to find that her brother-in-law, 45-year-old George Vernon, was also aboard for the trip. Vernon was married to Rita's sister, Inez, a noted violinist who was a pupil of the Conservatoire of Paris and who had made

Top left: *Commander Joseph F. Stackhouse, United States Navy. He was traveling for the Belgian Relief effort, and had been involved in attempting to raise funds for a polar expedition.*

Top right: *Justus M. Forman, a friend of Charles Frohman and part of the "theater group" traveling in First Class.*

Lower left: *Elbert Hubbard, seen here on the Lusitania on May 1. He was traveling with his wife. All three of these men, as well as Mrs. Hubbard, perished in the ensuing disaster.*

Lower right: *A typical period photograph of a well-dressed First Class passenger settling in to a stateroom; she is being assisted by an ever-helpful Stewardess.*

her American debut in late 1905.[55] Her performances in Europe had garnered her enough attention that she had even been decorated by the Tsar of Russia and King Edward. Vernon himself had started life as a banker, but had eventually become a concert singer. He and Inez met and were married around 1906, even though she was seventeen years his junior. Unlike his notably talented wife, Vernon was apparently not a particularly gifted singer. After his first recital in 1901, one review wrote of him being "essentially a drawing-room singer."[56] Within a few short years, he had changed professions again, becoming an importer's agent and promoter. Some time before embarking on this voyage, he had become involved with the Russian Government, arranging munitions contracts for the war. He, like Rita Jolivet, had booked passage at the last minute, so much so that even some of his close family was not aware that he was aboard. His cabin selection had also been limited, and he found himself ensconced in E62, a cabin even smaller than Rita Jolivet's. His reasons for taking the crossing had to do with securing an arms contract for the Russians. At the same time, his wife was ill and staying with her family in Kew. Once he had conducted his business, he was planning to escort her back to the United States.

Meanwhile, First Class passenger Michael Byrne stood at the rail, looking down on his wife and friends. Finally at 11:30, he told them to leave so that they would not get chilled in the cool and damp air. Then he went below to unpack a few items from his luggage that he knew he would have use for in short order.

Outside, the early-morning drizzle had begun to fade away, and although it was still a bit damp and chilly on deck, the weather showed a definite improvement. By 12:00, when Byrne emerged back on deck, there were even a few rays of sun poking

Top left: *As the ship backed out of Pier 54, the Bridge wing, with Captain Turner standing on the end, passed the camera. Captain Turner turned to look at the film crew.*

Top right: *In this photo, Turner had turned away from the camera crew and can be seen looking down the length of the ship, ensuring the departure was going smoothly. The position of the telegraph handles is quite clear, and an officer with at least one stripe on his sleeves stands with his hands clutched in front of him in the doorway of the Bridge.*

Left: *The* Lusitania *glides away from the pier. Passengers can be seen on her Boat and Promenade Decks, and a careful examination of the film footage shows them lining the full length of the Shelter Deck, as well, waving handkerchiefs occasionally.*

Below left: *A good number of passengers are standing on the forward Boat Deck, underneath the Bridge, watching the departure.*

through the foreboding cloud cover overhead. It was just then that the liner was ready to depart. The last gangway was lowered, but Captain Turner appeared moments later, with his niece Mercedes at his side;

she had come aboard to visit her uncle once again, and now Turner gruffly ordered his men to bring the gangway back so that she could disembark. It was something of a scene, but the officers snapped to – no doubt with red faces – in order to meet Turner's demands. Then the Captain headed topside to watch over the departure from the Bridge.

The seven other ship's officers took up their positions in preparation for departure; there was Staff Captain James Clarke Anderson; (Senior) Chief Officer John F. Piper; "ex-Chief" Officer John Stevens;[57] First Officer Arthur Rowland Jones; Second Officer Percy Hefford; Senior Third Officer John Idwal Lewis; and Junior Third Officer Albert Arthur Bestic.[58] Bestic had become besotted with the *Lusitania* years earlier, and this was his first round-trip voyage on her – indeed, his first voyage on a large liner period.[59]

It was 12:15 p.m. As the liner cast off from Pier 54 and began to back slowly into the North River, Captain Turner walked onto the starboard Bridge wing

Top: *A pair of tugs presses into the port bow of the* Lusitania, *swinging her prow to the south, toward open water.*

Middle: *Before the war, friends and well-wishers were allowed onto the pier's end to bid farewell, as seen here at one of White Star's piers. With security concerns, however, admission - either to the ship or to the piers - was much more strictly regulated on May 1, 1915.*

Bottom: *Picking up speed in the North River, the* Lusitania *passes the German liner* Vaterland, *sitting immobile at her Hoboken, New Jersey pier.*

and eased himself into the inner curve of the bulwark. From this vantage point, he could clearly see down the entire fore and aft length of the ship as it slid past the dock. By this time the newsreel crew had taken up a position on the roof of the pier building, which was just higher than the ship's wing. Captain Turner glided by them quite closely, and he gave them a second glance as he passed; perhaps he was surprised to see that he was being scrutinized from this unusual vantage point.

The ship's five-man orchestra played "Tipperary" from the Boat Deck;[60] meanwhile, the Royal Gwent Male Voice Singers, a Welsh group which was wrapping up a tour throughout North America, sang "The Star-Spangled Banner." The tension of Europe seemed a long way off; the spirit seemed very nearly festive, almost as if nothing was out of the ordinary. However, mixed with this generally pleasant feeling, there was an undercurrent of concern about what lay ahead.

Once the ship was in the North River, the tugs eased her bow to starboard until she was pointed downstream. Then the telegraph bells jangled, and her ahead turbines were engaged. They started up faithfully, as they had so many times before, and as the thrust from her four props bit into the muddy water, she began to gain momentum. She soon passed the *Vaterland*, still interred in Hoboken, never to fly under the German flag again. Out through the Upper Bay, the Narrows, and to the Ambrose Lightship the *Lusitania* steamed. She paused to allow the pilot to clamber overboard, and then the ship started her engines once more. After about a half hour, she came up on the *Caronia*,[61] recruited for service by the Admiralty and now part of the British fleet "blockading" German ships in neutral American ports. The *Lusitania* slowed to a stop once again, and a cutter was sent out from the *Caronia* filled with a dozen of her crew. They were bringing out some mail to go back to England on the swift Cunarder.

James Bissett, later Sir James, was on the *Caronia* that afternoon. He would have a distinguished career with Cunard in the coming years, captaining both *Queens*. From his vantage point, he could see Captain Turner and Staff Captain Anderson on the port bridge wing of the *Lusitania*. He had served with both men previously and

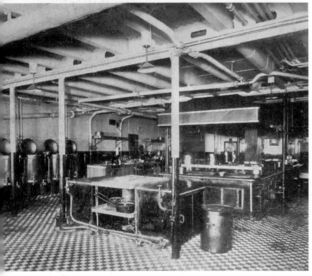

Top: *The last known photograph of the* Lusitania, *taken from the* Caronia, *as she steamed east toward Europe.*

Above: *The* Lusitania's *First Class Galley, where lunch was prepared even as the liner was departing New York. Passengers dined shortly after she had made open water.*

bines began their familiar whine for the last time; the next time they stopped, it would be permanently.

As the ship steamed away into the familiar North Atlantic, another photographer on the *Caronia* took a snapshot of her receding into the distance, with smoke ascending from her forward three funnels. More than seven years from the time she had entered service, she still looked clean and beautiful, every bit a greyhound of the Atlantic. While the *Lusitania* steamed east toward Europe, neutral New York receded into the distance, and finally disappeared together. In the *Lusitania*'s wake was a seven-and-a-half-year history comprised of well over half a million steaming miles on the Atlantic without any serious accidents or life-threatening incidents. Ahead of her lay an uncertain and, as events turned out, tragically brief future ...

Once the excitement of departing New York began to fade away, the passengers began to depart the decks and attend lunch, which was just then being served in the Dining Saloons of each class. From that point forward, for the most part, the crossing proved to be a typical one. Almost, but not quite. Just after clearing the Upper Bay, three stowaways had been found belowdecks. The Captain was duly informed; attempts at communication with the interlopers proved fruitless. It was believed that they were German spies or saboteurs who had managed to get aboard despite the stringent security precautions. They were locked up for the duration of the voyage; the Liverpool authorities could get to the bottom of the matter.

Passengers who were expecting the ship to ramp up to her full speed of 25 knots were disappointed. Charles Lauriat estimated that she was moving at only about twenty to twenty-one knots, and he was correct. Even so, he and another First Class passenger, fellow Bostonian Lothrop Withington, still felt comfortable that the ship was traveling fast enough to outrun any submarine in the German navy.

It was just as well that the ship wasn't flying at her maximum speed during this portion of the crossing; Second Class accommodations had always borne the brunt of her vibration troubles when she was flying, even though she had undergone significant improvements over the years to combat this problem. Second Class was overbooked and quite cramped on this particular crossing ... to add vibration into the mix could have proved the straw which broke the camel's back. The Saloon Stewards there had utilized not only the overflow area of the Saloon on the Shelter Deck, but also had set a few tables in the corridor just outside the Saloon; with arrangements thus in place, it was found that two sittings for each meal were enough

knew them quite well. He also spotted Second Officer Hefford, a good personal friend; Bissett recalled that it had always been Hefford's dream to serve on the *Lusitania*, and there he was. Hefford spotted Bissett, as well, and the two men took the opportunity to bid a cheerful farewell via semaphore: "Cheerio! Good Bye! Good Voyage! Good Luck!"[62] Meanwhile, a photographer on the *Caronia*'s deck snapped a shot of the *Lusitania* with the cutter between them. Once the small boat had left the speed queen's side, the *Lusitania*'s Engine Room telegraphs jangled to life. Chief Engineer Bryce and his team down below responded and the quartet of tur-

Top: *The First Class Entrance on the Boat Deck, looking from port to starboard. For those who had taken passage on the* Lusitania *before, finding their way around the ship was a simple matter; for newcomers, however, this prime people-mover in First Class was the easiest way to get around.*

Above: *The Entrance on the Promenade Deck, showing the Purser's Bureau. This is where passengers exchanged money, conducted shipboard business, turned valuables into the Purser's safe, and – in peacetime – sent telegrams to other ships or people ashore.*

to take care of all 601 passengers. Fortunately Staff Captain Anderson found, while making his rounds, that this particular batch of Second Class passengers seemed good-natured about their rather cramped conditions.

The afternoon passed quietly, and the sun began to set astern of the great Cunarder; there was tea in the Lounge & Music Room, where the ship's band played popular tunes of the day, like Carrie Jacobs Bond's "Just a-Wearyin' for You." Other popular tunes in the Cunard selection book of the period included: "The Merry Widow," "Song d'Automne," "Valse Septembre," "Alexander's Ragtime Band," "Oh, You Beautiful Doll," and "Moonlight Bay." Patriotic songs like "La Marseillaise," "God Save The King," "Rule Britannia," or "The Star-Spangled Banner" would have been heard frequently aboard, although considering the times "The Watch on the Rhine" would not have made an appearance. Interestingly, the Strauss waltz "The Blue Danube" was played during the crossing, despite its blatant Austrian origins.[63] Even once the clatter of fine china had ceased, the music continued, until finally the passengers began to drift off to their cabins to prepare for dinner. The band, meanwhile, took up their positions in the Dining Saloon, and began to prepare for the evening's repertoire of entertainment.

The customary rigors of dressing for dinner – a tradition at sea that had epitomized the dying Edwardian era – were typically eschewed for the first dinner aboard, so as not to overly exhaust passengers worn out from the rigors of boarding the ship earlier that day. As First Class passengers began to show up for dinner, most of them were still dressed in their day suits and dresses, but a few had apparently gone to the trouble of excavating their formal evening wear from their luggage. The sights and sounds of a dinner in First Class on the *Lusitania* were still unforgettable, even though she had been in service for years now. It was almost like a beautifully planned-out scene set on a lavish stage that was like none other. Other larger ships like the *Olympic* sported only a single-deck Saloon, but the *Lusitania*'s still felt superior in some respects, being two full decks in height and crowned off by the elegant dome on the third deck. The soothing strains of the band's music accompanied the soft murmur of voices in conversation, punctuated by occasional laughter and the clatter of silver against china. The smells of dinner wafted out from the Galley, heightening anticipation until the meal was actually served. Captain Turner even presided at his table, having decided to put his appearance in early and get it out of the way.

After dinner, passengers drifted off to the Lounge or to the Smoking Room, where there was talk of politics and the war over a cigar for the gentlemen, as well as the inevitable card-playing. Eventually everyone had retired for the night, and the ship sailed on quietly.

On Sunday morning, the liner encountered fog that forced her to reduce speed, as the Forecastle was not even visible from the Bridge windows. Ever since the first time she had traveled the Atlantic, fog had crossed the *Lusitania*'s path at frequent intervals, especially off the Grand Banks, which was notorious for its mists. Captain Turner remained vigilant on the Bridge throughout the morning, ever watchful for any other vessel which might blunder across his prow. The mists left everything feeling cold and damp; dew accumulated on the varnished teak rails on the Bridge wings, condensed to drops on the bulwarks, and tended to fog up the glass on the Bridge instruments. The foghorn sounded its continuous, precisely timed signal until, finally, the ship burst into the clear. Turner ordered the speed increased to full, then handed the watch back over to the watch officer and returned to his cabin.

At seven o'clock that morning, Michael Byrne was up and walking around the ship. This was his thirteenth crossing of the Atlantic, having taken passage on many of the great liners of the day; on previous trips, he had developed the habit of "inspecting" every liner early on in the voyage. He first "walked up to the bow and looked over it to see her cut through the water." Next, he turned to walk aft, taking "particular notice to see if they had any guns mounted or unmounted." Finding none there, he made his way all the way aft to the stern, scrutinizing everything in between. Having surveyed the ship from stem to stern, he was able to dismiss out of hand the very notion that the ship was carrying guns of any sort on board.

Later that morning, the Captain conducted the Sunday services in the First Class Lounge & Music Room; Turner was not noted to be a particularly gifted speaker, apparently reading the manuscript directly in a rather clipped fashion. The sermon was the standard mix of religion and politics – a prayer for those on the sea, coupled with a plea for God to bless the Royal family, all of which was followed by a hymn. That noon, the ship's run was calculated at 501 miles; on subsequent days, that figure dropped well below 500, disappointing passengers who were accustomed to hearing of the great liner's speed. Some passengers even approached the Captain and some of the officers, asking if everything was all right. To

Three photographs showing the crew of the Holland-America liner Rotterdam *while that liner was tied up in New York during a standard turnaround. This gives some idea of what it looked like to passengers on the* Lusitania *on the morning of May 6, 1915, as the crew turned the lifeboats out so that they were suspended over the water.*

these queries, the response invariably came that everything was fine.

The routine of shipboard life began to cement; mealtimes were the focal point of each day. Passengers could sit back and relax for a few days, trying to forget the stresses of everyday life and the war, and enjoying their passage at a time when "getting there" was "half the fun." For many, despite early reservations, it had turned into a rather ordinary crossing. Some others were still anxious over the dangers of a submarine attack. The first at-sea lifeboat drill was held on Sunday afternoon, and the passengers who witnessed this event – and the drills on each subsequent day – were not particularly impressed.

This drill consisted of a dozen or so seamen being assembled on the Boat Deck beside either Boat No. 13 on the starboard side, or Boat No. 14 on the port side, depending on what direction the wind was blowing from. After a quick inspection of this group, the officer in charge, Senior Third Officer John Lewis, would order: "Man the boats." At this point a curious thing would happen: instead of lowering the lifeboat down to the deck as they would normally do in an emergency, the crew members scrambled up the davits and into the boat, coolly tied on their life jackets, and sat down. Lewis, apparently satisfied, had the crew remove their life jackets, get back out of the boat, and return to their duties. The "so-called drill," as one passenger later referred to it, took less than five minutes, and none of the lifeboat handling gear was used. This was a pathetic and appalling display, "a pitiable exhibition to look at," as Michael Byrne recalled. A number of crewmen told him that this was their first crossing on the liner. Serious doubts about the crew's ability to lower and load the lifeboats in an emergency began to spring up among the passengers. Additionally, none of the passengers had received specific instructions about how to don their life jackets in an emergency, and Byrne recalled that many did not "even know where to find them," since "no one ever [showed] them where to look for them."

Passengers approached the officers, and even Captain Turner, with their concerns, only to be dismissed casually. Despite their protests, the efficiency of these 'drills' did not improve on succeeding days, nor was there any specific instruction to passengers about what to do in the event of an emergency – a possibility still fresh in the minds of all because of the German newspaper warning from sailing day. Turner's attitude was the complete antithesis of Captain Dow's remarkable caution on previous voyages, and is something that he no doubt regretted later.

Above left: *Actress Rita Jolivet.*

Above right: *Beatrice "Trixie" Witherbee and her son, Alfred S. Witherbee, Jr. The Witherbees spent some time with Rita Jolivet during the voyage eastbound, and Rita absolutely adored young Alfred and the other children aboard. Beatrice had taken the previous westbound crossing on the* Lusitania, *and was now escorting her mother – Mary Cummings Brown – and son back to England.*

Rita Jolivet was thoroughly enjoying her voyage. She had brought along her camera, and busied herself taking photographs of the "very beautiful" children aboard. During the crossing, perhaps through a mutual friend, Rita had met 24-year-old Beatrice Witherbee and her 3-year-old son Alfred, Jr. Beatrice Witherbee was the wife of Alfred Witherbee, the head of the Mexican Petroleum Solid Fuel Company. In addition to her son, she was traveling with her 55-year-old mother Mary "May" Cummings Brown. Her husband was moving the family to London on a permanent basis; she had taken the *Lusitania* on her last westbound crossing in order to make the final preparations for the move. Now they were taking the ship back to England, and were booked in cabin D52, on the same deck as Rita Jolivet. Beatrice had managed, although quite how is still an open question, to arrange with the Saloon Steward to have her young son to sit with her in the Dining Saloon at mealtimes. This arrangement was almost never allowed, as children had their own special Dining Saloon on C Deck. However, some fellow passengers remarked on what a fantastic little boy young Alfred was, and how his mother doted on him during the trip.

Second Class passengers, though more or less stuffed into public spaces designed to accommodate far fewer people, continued to prove an amiable lot as the voyage progressed. One Second Class passenger, Francis John Lucas, later recalled:

> It was beautiful weather and the early hours were spent in sighting warships outside New York, while later, several liners were passed. As usual there was plenty to interest the passengers after the first few days when *mal-de-mer* was the first concern. On Wednesday night, the members of the Welsh Choir who were returning after a long tour, gave a concert and a famous comedian provided a turn. Some idea of the success of this concert may be gleaned from the fact that in the second cabin there was a record collection on behalf of the Sailors' Orphanage at Liverpool, the amount realised being £36-16s-11d. No one knew how soon the work of the Orphanage was to be supplemented. On Thursday there were sports and in the evening there was a whist drive.[64]

Lucas took second prize at this latter activity, and was given a pearl-handled pocketknife with a very fine etching of the liner on the handle.

At 5:30 on the morning of that Thursday, May 6, Turner began to ready his ship preparatory to entering the War Zone. The passengers awoke to the none-too-reassuring sounds of the crew working on the lifeboats. They were in the midst of removing the canvas covers and uncoupling the chains holding the 22 davited boats to their decked positions atop the collapsibles. One after another, they were swung out over the water and snubbing chains were put into position to prevent them from swinging too far away from the ship as she moved through the water. Turner did not have the boats lowered until they were flush with the deck, and nothing was done to prepare the collapsible boats for launch, should the need arise. Yet Turner apparently felt that he had adequately complied with the Admiralty's instructions in this regard, and that he was thoroughly prepared for whatever lay ahead. The din roused all but the soundest of sleepers; there was much talk about submarines among the passengers that day, but there was reportedly no feeling of alarm or panic among them.

Meanwhile, in England, there was a growing level of concern within some quarters about the safety of the inbound *Lusitania*. In Room 40 of the Admiralty's Old Building in London, there was a Top Secret intelligence group reading German wireless traffic. The British were notorious in World War II for their code-breaking and intelligence work at Bletchley Park, but this particular team was less than a year old and far less efficient than their descendants would be. All the same, Room 40 had found good success since its inception the previous fall by Admiral Henry Oliver (Chief of Naval War Staff), albeit mostly through blind good fortune. The British had severed Germany's five cable lines running to other nations in the early months of the war, which forced the Germans to send almost all of their traffic via wireless on open frequencies. To prevent the Allies from reading these messages, they sent them in code; however, during the early months of the war, the British had acquired through "miraculous" coincidences three very important codes: the HVB, or Merchant Shipping Codebook; the SKM, the Signal Book of the Imperial Navy; and the VB, the "traffic book," by which the Germans communicated with their overseas naval attachés and also with their warships, including submarines. The German U-boat commanders, not realizing that their messages were being intercepted, frequently made contact with their superior officers in Germany to give them updates, apprise them of their positions, and also to receive fresh orders.

Unfortunately for the British, Room 40 was receiving far more than it could actually process in a timely manner; its hierarchy was hampered by inefficiencies. This meant that by the time information was processed, it might be out of date; additionally, just

because a certain U-boat's position was fixed at a given time did not mean that the entire Admiralty knew exactly where that U-boat was headed following its message – this often depended on the decisions that the submarine commanders made themselves. The new Director of Naval Intelligence, William Reginald Hall, was a smart man, though, and was slowly beginning to use Room 40 in effective ways.

Hall had recently begun a disinformation campaign to make the Germans believe that the movement of troops and supplies to the Dardanelles for the upcoming Gallipoli landings would not be weakening the strength of the BEF on the western fronts. To this end, he even created false reports of heavy sailings of troop transports out of southern and western British ports. When the Germans received this material on April 24, their reaction was immediate: they sent out U-boats to intercept these nonexistent transports. Three of the subs, the *U-20*, the *U-27*, and the *U-30*, were ordered out of Wilhelmshaven by Fregattenkapitän Hermann Bauer. The *U-20*, under the command of Kapitänleutnant Walther Schwieger, was to operate in the Irish Sea off Liverpool, the *U-27* in the Bristol Channel of the Irish Sea, and the *U-30* off of Dartmouth in the English Channel south of England. Bauer's instructions from the Admiralty in Berlin were quite clear: "Large English troop transports are to be expected starting from Liverpool, Bristol Channel, Dartmouth. In order to do considerable damage to the transports *U-20* and *U-27* are to be dispatched as soon as possible. Stations [to be] assigned there. Get to stations on the fastest possible route around Scotland; hold them as long as supplies permit … U-boats are to attack transport ships, merchant ships, warships." The *U-30*, already out of base, received her orders by wireless; the *U-27* was to depart on May 2; the *U-20* departed on April 30.[65]

The *U-20* was commissioned on August 5, 1913, one of four U-boats (*U-19* to *U-22*) in a class. She was 210 feet long, and had a submerged displacement of only 650 tons; her armament consisted of six torpedoes laid out in two bow and two stern tubes, as well as one 105mm deck gun with 300 rounds carried. She could operate at a maximum depth of 164 feet, and had a maximum surfaced speed of 15.4 knots, and of only 9.5 knots submerged. Her complement was thirty-five men, and she made her maiden patrol on August 1, 1914, under the command of Kapitänleutnant Otto Dröscher. Walther Schwieger had replaced Dröscher as commander of the *U-20* on December 16, 1914. Schwieger had just turned thirty in April of 1915, and had previously commanded the *U-14*. He was reportedly both well liked by his men

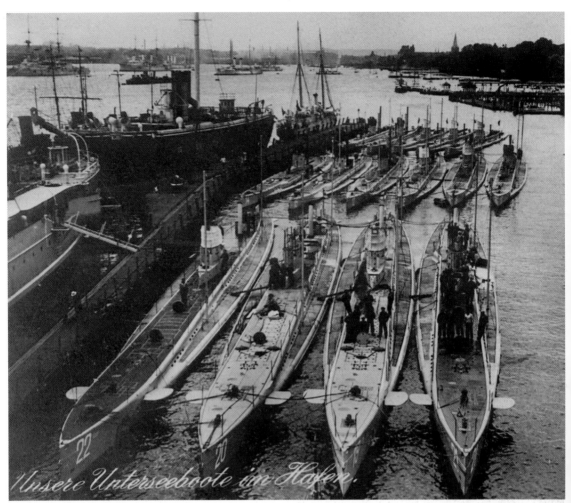

Opposite top: *A photograph of fourteen U-boats at rest. The four closest to the camera are, from left to right: U-22, U-20, U-19, and U-21. As the* Lusitania *steamed eastward, the U-20 was busy prowling the waters around Ireland.*

Above: *Kapitänleutnant Walther Schwieger, commander of the U-20.*

Opposite bottom: *The* Gulflight, *an American-owned tanker attacked by the U-30 on May 1, 1915 off the Scilly Isles. Although the ship survived, she took heavy damage, and three lives were lost. All of this transpired as the* Lusitania *was preparing to leave New York on her last crossing.*

should not risk letting a target get away even if there was question about her identity.

This particular cruise of the *U-20* proved rather frustrating. Upon departing Emden in the early morning of April 30, Schwieger took his vessel northwest between the Shetland and Orkney Islands, then turned and moved south along the west coast of Ireland. By May 5, he had rounded the southwest tip of Ireland and turned east into the Irish Channel, moving toward the Irish Sea and Liverpool, his pre-planned station. On May 3, he spotted a large neutral steamer which he concluded was Danish; he determined that "an attack on this ship [was] impossible," because she was running too fast and because of the two vessels' relative positions. Later that day, he attempted to torpedo a small steamer of about 2,000 tons without warning, but the torpedo jammed in its tube. This attack was made despite the presence of a Danish flag – Schwieger knew all too well the British misuse of neutral flags, but did not bother to legitimately identify the steamer's nationality before trying to carry out the attack. The next day, he tried to attack another ship without warning, but the steamer turned away quickly, apparently having spotted the submarine. Afterward Schwieger noted that she was a neutral Swedish vessel named *Hibernia*, but that she was not flying a flag. Again he had attempted to attack what could have been a legitimately neutral ship without first identifying her beyond doubt.

The next day, May 5, found the *U-20* in fog; even so, she managed to find and attack a small 132-ton schooner called the *Earl of Lathom* off the Old Head of Kinsale. This time, Schwieger followed cruiser rules, gave the crew time to abandon ship, and only then sent her to the bottom with a dozen rounds from the deck gun. She was not much of a prize, but neither was this patrol proving very fruitful. Schwieger attacked another vessel that night; she was about 3,000 tons in size, and bore neutral markings, but he apparently believed them to be fraudulent. The vessel got away and Schwieger dove to twenty-two meters so that he would not be rammed by any merchant vessels blinded in the fog.

On the morning of May 6, Schwieger managed to sink one vessel. The first ship that he attacked was the 5,858-ton *Candidate*, of the Harrison Line, out of Liverpool. Schwieger made a surface attack without warning. The crew took to the lifeboats in the middle of the assault, and Schwieger finished the steamer off with a torpedo to her Engine Room and more close-range gunfire. The attack was carried out some thirteen miles southeast of the Coningbeg Lightship,

and a capable submarine commander. Although he did not seem to have the barbaric streak of some U-boat skippers, he was not renowned for following the rules of cruiser warfare. His thinking seemed to be that his own crew's safety came first, and that he

Fastnet Light.

and directly in the *Lusitania's* typical steaming route for approaching Liverpool. After trying to attack the 15,801-ton White Star liner *Arabic* unsuccessfully (she would be sunk by the *U-24* off the Old Head of Kinsale on August 19, 1915, with the loss of 44 lives), the *U-20* next came across the 5,945-ton Harrison Line steamer *Centurion*, the *Candidate's* sister. Although he did not have any positive identification of this vessel, Schwieger fired a torpedo without warning, and the missile struck forward, causing the vessel to begin sinking by the bow. Her crew abandoned ship, but Schwieger still found that he had to finish her off with a second torpedo.

At this time, Schwieger decided to turn back to the east and return to Germany by the same route he had followed outbound, instead of proceeding up the Irish Sea toward Liverpool. He decided on this in part because he had only three torpedoes left; however, he compromised by deciding to linger in the Irish Channel until two-fifths of his fuel was consumed. He believed that the chances for "favorable attacks are better here and enemy defensive measures lesser than in the Irish Sea near Liverpool."[66] He was right ...

Meanwhile the fact that Schwieger had sunk three ships in two days was quite concerning to the British. Vice Admiral Sir Charles Coke, the Queenstown naval commander, sent communications to the Admiralty in London regarding the situation in the waters near his port. At 7:52 p.m. on the evening of May 6, the Naval Centre at Queenstown sent out a plain-language message which was received and acknowledged by the *Lusitania's* on-duty wireless operator. It read: "Submarines active off south coast of Ireland."[67] Clearly, the message had been inspired by the *U-20's*

attacks. The warning was serious and clear: there was trouble ahead.

At 8:05 p.m. that Thursday, an encoded message arrived in the Marconi Shack on the Sun Deck. It was addressed to all inbound British merchant vessels, and had originally been transmitted at 12:05 p.m. that day. The warning read: "Between South Foreland and Folkestone keep within two miles of shore and pass between the two light vessels. Take Liverpool pilot at bar. Avoid headlands; pass harbours at full speed; steer mid-channel course. Submarines off Fastnet." The first sentence of the message applied only to steamers in the English Channel near the Straits of Dover, but the rest of it applied directly to ships like the *Lusitania*. This message repeated six times during the night and the following morning. The content of the message, along with the fact that the Admiralty considered it important enough to send numerous times, should have left an alarming and lasting impression with Captain Turner and his officers – especially since the *Lusitania* was a mere eighteen hours from Fastnet.

Chairman Alfred Booth, of the Cunard Line, was aware of the U-boat activity and successes. He also knew that the *Lusitania* was closing on the danger area, and he was unwilling to leave her safety to chance. On the morning of Friday, May 7, he "went to the Admiral or the Senior Naval Officer in Liverpool and asked him to send a message. We, of course, did not venture to send any message to the captain as to how he should proceed, because the Admiralty might be doing that, or the captain might know a great deal more about it than we did. We merely asked the Admiralty to convey the fact that these ships [the *Earl of Lathom*, the *Candidate*, and the *Centurion*] had been sunk."[68]

Whether in response to Booth's request or just because concern about the *Lusitania* in particular was running high, the Admiralty in London opened another line of communication with the *Lusitania* via the Naval Centre at Queenstown. At 11:02 a.m., a message was sent consisting of a single word: "Questor." The *Lusitania's* wireless operator replied with another single word: "Westrona." The first word was a coded request of the *Lusitania* as to what edition of the Merchant Vessel Code she was holding. The response, also in code, meant that she held the "First Edition of the M.V. Code."[69] The Admiralty in London obviously had something very important to tell the *Lusitania*, and every attempt was being made to make sure that she would both receive and understand it. At 11:52 a.m., precisely fifty minutes after the first query, the important coded message came

The First Class Lounge & Music Room. It was here that many nervous First Class passengers slept during the night of May 6-7, 1915.

in: "Submarines active in southern part Irish Channel. Last heard of twenty miles south of Coningbeg Lightship." This particular message had originated with the Admiralty in London, not with Coke in Queenstown; it thus could have been sent in response to Booth's trip to the Admiralty that very morning. It also stood out from the other messages the *Lusitania* had received that morning and the previous night in that it was addressed specifically to her, not just to all inbound British merchant vessels. Indeed, the line "Make certain the *Lusitania* gets this" had gone with the message right from the Admiralty, although this addendum was, for obvious reasons, dropped in retransmission to the liner. More than any other previous communication, this warning should have alerted Captain Turner to the dangers waiting for him ahead.

Clearly, every reasonable effort was being made by the Admiralty to warn the inbound liner. Although they could, perhaps, have scrambled an escort to meet the liner – despite the obvious shortages of vessels to carry out such assignments – this would not have been a favorable idea to the Admiralty. Not only would it have made the *Lusitania* more vulnerable to an attack without warning under International Law, but it would also have been extraordinarily complicated to execute, as previous experience had shown.

At 1:00 p.m., Friday, May 7, yet another coded message came in from the Admiralty. It read: "Submarine five miles South of Cape Clear proceeding west when sighted at ten a.m."[70] There was only one submarine operating off the Irish coast that morning, the *U-20*, and she had not been anywhere near Cape Clear, which was at that time some 65 miles astern of the *Lusitania*. How did this erroneous report get filtered through and make its way to the *Lusitania*? Even with all of Room 40's advanced detection methods, the Admiralty was still relying on land-based spotters, as well. Apparently, someone at Cape Clear had made an all-too-common mistake, taking something that was not a submarine for a U-boat. However, the information should not have made Captain Turner feel confident: between 10:00 and 1:00, the "submarine" referred to could have turned back to the east and could have been in close proximity to his ship at that time. Additionally, the previous warnings mentioned "submarines," plural – this communiqué referred only to a single submarine. Although there was only one U-boat in those waters, Captain Turner had no way

of knowing that, and all of the other messages made direct reference to "submarines" being active in the waters ahead, not those behind. His vigilance should not have slacked.

The previous evening and night had been difficult for everyone aboard. On Thursday evening, the customary concert was held aboard the *Lusitania*. Normally, it would have been held on the last night of the crossing, but on this particular trip the decision had been made to move it to Thursday, due to the early arrival scheduled in Liverpool on Saturday morning. During the intermission, Captain Turner addressed the passengers, telling them that although there had been a submarine warning, there was "of course … no need for alarm." The next morning he would steam at full speed so as to arrive in Liverpool in good time – he did not tell them that "full speed" meant only twenty-one knots as opposed to twenty-five, but that didn't really matter because, in the end, he did not keep this promise. From the time that he finished and the concert began afresh, the atmosphere in the Lounge & Music Room was described as charged. As soon as the performances finished, anxious conversation about the dangers ahead began. From then on,

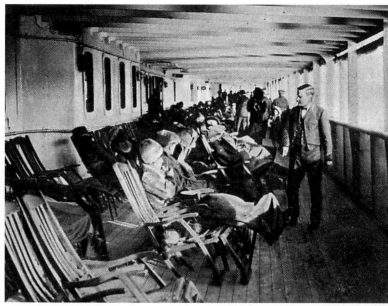

Left: *Josephine Brandell was one of many aboard who had trouble sleeping the night before the sinking.*

Above: *A typical scene along the Promenade Deck gives some idea of what it might have been like aboard on that Friday.*

the mood amongst many of the First Class passengers seemed to be one of great concern.

Even in Second Class, anxiety was evident. Arthur Jackson Mitchell, an American merchant with the Raleigh Cycle Company, later recalled that on that very evening a small committee was formed with the object of instructing everyone on how to put on and adjust the new style of life jacket that was provided aboard; it was not the first such committee to be formed during the crossing, but all of them met with limited success. He remembered that Turner had expressed his approval of the idea, on the stipulation that "no suggestion would be made to the passengers that the use of the preservers would be in any way imminent."[71]

That night, as passengers began to realize that it was time to turn in, these fears persisted. Some remained dressed when they went to bed; others refused to sleep in their cabins, but rather camped out in the public rooms on the upper decks. Josephine Brandell at first tried to sleep in her cabin, D30. She had been concerned with the submarine threat all through the crossing, but now she was so disturbed that she could only toss and turn. She had been aboard the *Lusitania* for a similar trip in February of that year, and although the passengers had been apprehensive about submarine dangers on that trip, they had come through all right ... but now? What would happen this time? Doubts and concerns surrounded her. Giv-

ing up on sleeping, she threw back the covers and decided to go up to see her friend, Mabel Crichton, who was in cabin A19. She asked if she could stay with her, and later recalled: "Poor soul, she was only too happy to be of any assistance to me and did all she could during the whole night to quiet my nerves."[72] Rita Jolivet also found herself sleeping only fitfully.

It wasn't just passengers who were having trouble with nerves about what the trip through the War Zone would bring. Captain Turner, who held the sole responsibility for the safety of everyone on board the ship, did not sleep well either.

Beginning at about 8:00 a.m. on May 7, the *Lusitania* encountered fog. For the next three hours, Captain Turner reduced his speed from twenty-one knots to eighteen, and at times to only fifteen; the fog horn was set to blow automatically once every minute. Captain Turner was being extremely cautious to avoid colliding with another steamship in these busy waters. Fog, however, was no guarantee that the liner would be concealed from any U-boat lurking in the area. Passengers at breakfast that morning, already nervous about the submarine situation, began to feel great annoyance for the ship's sluggish speed and the continual sounding of the foghorn. Oddly even after the fog let up, Captain Turner did not raise his speed from fifteen knots. Only near noon did he bring the speed up to eighteen knots,[73] but he never returned her to twenty-one knots throughout that early afternoon,

Inset: *This is a fascinating photograph in that it was purportedly taken on the Promenade Deck of the* Lusitania *on May 7, 1915. Although it certainly was taken aboard the* Lusitania, *one must wonder whether the dating was accurate, or whether it was merely captioned as a May 7 photograph, as many photographs were, even if they had been taken years before the sinking.*

Main: *This scene showing the Boat Deck of the* Lusitania, *from the port Bridge wing, dates to late in her career. Staff Captain James Clarke Anderson can be seen approaching the Bridge. The deck was certainly much more crowded than it had been in pre-Titanic years.*

even though the weather had become brilliantly clear. This was despite the fact that he had been receiving significant warnings of submarine dangers, and notwithstanding his orders to proceed at maximum available speed through the War Zone. He had also failed to implement all of the Admiralty orders, like zigzagging.

Turner did take some precautions. He had swung out his lifeboats the previous morning, and he was preserving almost absolute wireless silence. He had also posted a high number of lookouts in various positions. There were two on the Forecastle, two Quartermasters placed on each side of the Bridge, as well as the two standard Officers of the Watch and the two lookouts in the Crow's Nest. These eight official watch-keepers were ordered to "report anything" they saw, even "a broom handle."[74]

Rita Jolivet had slept so badly the night before that she was unable to get up the next morning for breakfast. She instead rested in her cabin, and was only able to pull herself together in time for lunch.

At noon, the ship's run was calculated and then posted for the passengers to see. They had been disappointed with her progress that morning, and sure enough, the run was an astoundingly low 462 miles. Charles Lauriat had bought the high field of 499 miles in the ship's pool the night before, expecting a dash of high speed through the War Zone into Liverpool; his £3 wager had proved fruitless. Captain Turner just wasn't driving his ship, in spite of his promises the night before, and in spite of the dangers that everyone knew were there. Michael Byrne noticed that a lot of passengers were distressed by the ship's slow speed. He recalled: "You could hear when ever you passed a group of passengers: 'Well, why are we not making full speed or twenty-five knots as Captain Turner told us[?]" At 1:00 p.m., the standard pre-meal bugle call was sounded, signaling that it was time for everyone to proceed to the Dining Saloon for lunch. This was at last a distraction from the dangers of submarines, and passengers soon found their way there to eat.

There was a reason why Captain Turner was moving at such a lazy pace that morning and afternoon, even after the fog had burned away. He had decided, in accord with Admiralty directions, to arrive at the Liverpool Bar at high tide the next morning, which was 6:53 a.m., and to proceed into the protected waters of Liverpool without stopping to take on the pilot. In order to accomplish this, Turner believed that he needed to shed some speed now; he could have accomplished the same thing, however, by steaming at twenty-one knots while engaged in zigzagging.

On the Bridge, there was a great amount of tension; Quartermaster Hugh Johnston, who took the wheel at noon, remembered that he could overhear officers speaking in hushed tones about the danger. "Oh we knew there were submarines around," he said.[75] Even some off-duty crew and passengers joined in the vigil looking for anything suspicious in the water. Just before noon, the Irish coast appeared, giving passengers a sense of relief. Mrs. Alice Loynd, a Second Class

passenger, wrote: "We can see Ireland quite well now. Thank God for a safe journey."[76]

Despite the fact that the *Lusitania* was traveling through familiar waters on a route that she had taken one hundred times before, Captain Turner was clearly confused as to his exact location. At first he seems to have thought that the point of land he was looking at was Brow Head, but he wasn't sure. He decided to close the shoreline, ordering the helmsman to turn hard to port, until he had settled on a course of 67° east. Just after 1:00, he thought he saw Galley Head – but this posed a problem. Galley was quite some distance from Brow, too far a gap for him to have covered ... so which one was which? At 1:40 p.m., Turner finally spotted the Old Head of Kinsale, an old and familiar friend. Now more confident of his position, he turned back to starboard, returning to course 87° east and running parallel to the shore. Next, apparently still unconvinced of his exact position, Turner decided to make a four-point bearing on the Old Head.

Top: *A view most likely taken c. 1910-1911 of the* Lusitania *steaming off the Old Head of Kinsale at high speed. Although she is westbound in this photograph, it gives at least some idea of what she would have looked like on that fateful afternoon.*

Above left: *The final edition of the* Cunard Daily Bulletin, *dated Friday, May 7, 1915.*

Right: *A c. 1910 photograph of the Old Head of Kinsale.*

Passengers on the Second Class deck playing quoits.

This required that the ship steam in a straight line for up to forty minutes at one speed while the officers took bearings on the landmark. A two-point bearing would have been nearly as accurate, and would have taken far less time, but Turner ordered the four-point bearing even though it was unnecessary. At 1:50 p.m., Junior Third Officer Bestic and Second Officer Hefford began this plot.

At about this same time, there came some fuss when the lookouts reported an object two points off the starboard bow, which caused "a little commotion on the bridge."[77] As the ship neared it, however, it was seen to be only a buoy. Just then, many of the passengers in First Class were just finishing their lunch in the Dining Saloon, lingering over a last cup of coffee or socializing; the band had finished playing the famous Strauss waltz "The Blue Danube." They next played "Tipperary." Some of the passengers had already gone back up on deck to enjoy the beautiful afternoon. Among these was Mrs. Mary Lobb, a 31-year-old British citizen traveling without her husband; she was sitting reading on the Boat Deck.[78] Rita Jolivet had left the Dining Saloon and headed back to her cabin. Beatrice Witherbee, her mother, and young Alfred had also left to go back to their cabin.

In Second Class, the second seating was well under way, and the Saloon there was heavily populated. Among those present was Miss Agnes Wild, travel-ing with her sister Evelyn; throughout the voyage, she had noted that the German submarine threat had been a common topic of conversation, 'but no one seemed to take the matter seriously.' Before lunch, she had chatted with one of the officers and three engineers who laughed at the idea of the ship coming to any harm ... the sea was beautiful, the day bright and clear, and she felt that no one could conceive of anything untoward happening to the mighty *Lusitania*.[79]

Mrs. Ellen Burdon, a 24-year-old resident of Winnipeg, Manitoba, Canada, was also at the second seating for lunch in Second Class. She had taken her 14-month-old son Robert with her into the Saloon, and was sitting at a table with a serviette in one hand, working her way through lunch.[80]

Michael Byrne had come up from the Dining Saloon at 1:30 p.m., and walked around the deck for some time smoking a cigar. He finally stopped on the starboard side, underneath the Bridge, looking out over the liner's bow. It was 2:09 p.m.

Just above Byrne, Captain Turner was on the port Bridge wing, according to his own testimony at the Mersey Inquiry; he had just returned from a trip to his cabin below on the Promenade Deck.[81] During the first few seconds of that minute, some of the passengers and crew noticed something quite odd. Michael Byrne noticed what he first thought was a porpoise, but then realized was a submarine, and soon enough he saw a white streak of foam speeding towards the

Top left: *A scene depicting the First Class Verandah Café in use. By the time of the sinking, some alterations had been made to alter it from the appearance shown here. Nevertheless the café was well used on that Friday afternoon.*

Above left: *A scene on the Boat Deck of the liner showing a typical afternoon during the ship's career.*

Above right: *A view taken from the conning tower of a period submarine, overlooking the vessel's bow as it cut through the surface of the sea.*

liner. Below and forward of Byrne, standing on the Forecastle, was Able-Bodied Seaman Leslie Morton. Morton had just come on duty a few minutes before as one of the extra lookouts. He had just glanced at his pocketwatch, which was apparently running just slightly fast and read 2:10 p.m. Satisfied, he replaced the watch in his pocket, "glanced round the starboard side and as roughly as I could judge, I saw a big burst of foam about 500 yards away four points[82] on the starboard bow. Immediately after I saw a thin streak of foam making for the ship at a rapid speed, and then I saw another streak of foam going parallel with the first one and a little behind it."[83] He picked up his megaphone and shouted to the bridge: "Torpedoes coming on the starboard side!"

The attack came from the *U-20*. Indeed, Schwieger had been watching the *Lusitania* for some time, unbeknownst to everyone on the liner. He had first spotted her at 1:00 p.m. at a range of about thirteen miles. "Four funnels and two masts of a steamer with course at right angles to us ... The ship is made out to be large passenger steamer." His heart must have throbbed in his chest as he sounded the alarm and took his submarine under the surface. Watching her for nearly twenty minutes through the periscope, he

was dismayed to see that she was steaming away at too great an angle for him to execute an attack. Then Captain Turner had made his thirty-degree turn to starboard, having closed land enough to begin his four-point bearing. This unwittingly brought the *Lusitania* right into Schwieger's range. As he studied her through his periscope, he must have known that she could be one of only two ships – the *Lusitania* or the *Mauretania*. Her profile was so well known to mariners and landsmen alike that there is no way he could have taken her for anything else. Both sisters were British vessels, both were liable to attack according to the orders he had in hand, and his custom during this voyage was to attack without warning. This was exactly what he did.

He ordered a G-type torpedo to be set to run at ten feet below the surface and launched it from a distance of about 700 meters or 2,300 feet. The missile ejected from the tube with a burst of foam at the surface, which is what caught Morton's eye at first, and then it sped toward an empty spot of the ocean about 500 yards in front of the liner at roughly forty knots. Over the next thirty-five seconds, the two objects inexorably converged. If the ship had been turned at that precise moment, there is every reason to believe that

Opposite top: *A period photograph of a submarine periscope cutting across the sea.*

Opposite middle: *Most likely from c. 1910-1911, and taken at the same time as the main photograph on pages 298-299, this view gives a good idea of what the* Lusitania *would have looked like to Schwieger as he studied her through his periscope.*

Opposite bottom: *This view of the Mauretania's Forecastle, taken in the early 1930s, shows a similar arrangement to that found on the Lusitania. The gun rings are visible at the end of the hose near the railing, and were installed in similar locations aboard the Lusitania. It was here, along the starboard rail, that Lookout Morton first spotted something odd in the water off the starboard bow.*

Right: *A period view showing a torpedo streaking toward its target.*

Next page: *An illustration of the scene on the starboard Boat Deck as passengers began to realize that they had been attacked without warning.*

she could have turned within the torpedo's track, but that is not what happened.[84]

Morton did not wait for the Bridge to acknowledge his single warning before he dropped his megaphone and ran below to warn his brother, John, who was off-duty at the time. Although a host of other passengers on the starboard side of the ship saw the torpedo inbound, none of the other lookouts or the men on the Bridge spotted it as early as Morton, Byrne, and some others. First class passenger Joseph Myers remarked to Frank Kellett on the matter when he first spotted the periscope, and then saw the torpedo launched. First Class Passenger Phillipe Yung looked up, noticing "a kind of white track in the water." He said to a couple of gentlemen standing nearby: "That seems to be a torpedo." One of these fellow passengers confirmed his supposition: "It is a torpedo."[85]

In the First Class Dining Saloon, William Pierpoint recalled that the band had finished "Tipperary"; his fellow passengers called for an encore, and the band responded. Suddenly, George Slingsby, a valet to Frederick Orr Lewis, shouted: "Look!" Pierpoint looked through the porthole, and "saw the torpedo coming straight at the ship." He immediately realized that there was no escape for the *Lusitania*, and stood there "spellbound and hopeless," watching the scene play out.[86]

Seconds ticked by ... ten, fifteen, twenty ... Then lookout Thomas Quinn on the starboard watch of the crow's nest spotted the torpedo, now about 200 yards away from the ship.[87] He shouted, "Here's a torpedo coming, Frank!" to his friend, Frank Hennessey, on the port side of the nest. Then he started to warn the Bridge by "word of mouth," probably via the telephone which communicated directly with the Bridge.[88] On the Bridge, Second Officer Hefford relayed the lookout's warning, shouting to Captain Turner: "There is a torpedo coming, sir!"[89] Turner spun on one foot and caught a glimpse of the torpedo wake out of the starboard windows. He took one step toward the Wheelhouse, where Quartermaster Johnston stood at the helm, now waiting for an order. Turner planned to order a crash turn to avoid the torpedo, but time had run out ...

The *U-20*'s torpedo struck home at roughly forty-five miles an hour, in the vicinity of the Bridge and forward funnel. Its 300-pound warhead exploded with a deafening, piercing bang that was over almost before it began – Captain Turner was reminded of the banging of a door on a windy day. In that instant, approximately 200 square feet of the *Lusitania*'s outer hull plating – which were a full inch thick – vanished in the blast. The hole has been estimated to be roughly twenty feet long and ten feet high. Based on damage done to other ships by similar torpedoes, a total of

Top left: *This photograph, taken on the Bridge of the* Mauretania, *gives some idea of how it would have looked as the ship's crew kept a watchful eye over the waters ahead and around their ship on that Friday afternoon. Unfortunately, word did not reach the Bridge in time to take evasive action.*

Top right: *Captain Turner standing on the Upper Bridge of one of his vessels, most likely the* Aquitania *in 1914. Turner was on the* Lusitania's *main Bridge when the word came in that a torpedo was streaking toward his ship.*

Bottom: *Impact. Although intended to show a second torpedo striking the* Lusitania, *it gives a good impression of the scene.*

5,000 to 10,000 square feet of the hull in the immediate area around the blast would have been exposed to severe damage as rivets failed and seams burst from the concussion of this explosion. A plume of water and debris shot up at least sixty feet into the air, and hung there suspended while the *Lusitania* passed by, before collapsing back onto the ship and into the sea along her side. It completely wrecked Boat No. 5.[90]

The starboard coal bunker of Boiler Room No. 1 was almost immediately inundated in the first few seconds after the blast, and water also began to flood the starboard coal bunker of Boiler Room No. 2.

According to Captain Turner's watch, it was exactly 2:10 p.m.

Michael Byrne likened the torpedo blast to "a million ton hammer hitting a steel boiler, a hundred feet

Above: *First Class passenger Oliver Bernard's sketch of his perspective at the time of the torpedo strike.*

Right: *A photograph of a period torpedo striking its target.*

high and a hundred yards in length." On the Boat Deck, Mrs. Lobb heard a "terrific booming explosion, followed by a torrent of water and coal dust" which rained down on her head. In the First and Second Class Dining Saloons, the explosion caused china and cutlery to leap off the tables. Mrs. Burdon recalled it as "a terrific crash." Everyone looked at each other in astonishment, as if asking one another just how on earth they could actually have been *torpedoed* … in that instant, the war went from a conflict hundreds of miles away to something very, *very* real. Miss Wild noted that a cry went 'round the Second Class Saloon that the ship had been torpedoed … Everyone came to their feet as if in one motion.

Rita Jolivet had only just reached her cabin when "the shock" came. She "was thrown about a great deal," and "all of the glasses and everything of a fragile nature" seemed to smash to pieces. "Well, the Germans have got us this time!" she exclaimed to the shambles of her stateroom.

Down in Boiler Rooms Nos. 1 and 2, the everyday activities of feeding the furnaces were stopped short with absolutely no warning. Although most of the explosion's force seems to have been contained within the two starboard bunkers flanking these compartments, the watertight doors leading into the bunkers were open. Some of the high-pressure shock wave from the blast would have traveled through

Top: *A view from that period showing the damage a single torpedo inflicted on a vessel. The damage shown here would have been very similar to that inflicted on the* Lusitania.

Bottom: *A view in one of the* Lusitania's *stokeholds. If the torpedo's impact and resulting second explosion seemed tremendous to those elsewhere on the ship, to anyone standing in Boiler Room No. 1, it would have seemed like the whole world had been turned on its ear.*

these apertures into the main stokehold. The sound must have been indescribable – what few men survived from Boiler Room No. 1 reported having difficulty hearing right after the explosion; those not thrown to the floor by the blast would instinctively have dropped what they were doing and clutched their ears in agony. It would have been a similar situation to that of a soldier on the battlefields of France having an explosive artillery shell land nearby. Disorientation, shock, and the temporary loss of hearing would have been overwhelming. The difference between that scenario and the scene playing out in the *Lusitania*'s stokehold was that, on the battlefield, such an incident might be expected, whereas these stokers were caught completely unawares. This lack of warning would only have compounded the shock they felt. Leading Fireman Albert Martin was so dazed and confused that he could have sworn that he saw the torpedo enter the Boiler Room and explode between a group of boilers, which was a physical impossibility.

Base human reactions to the blast would have been compounded by what followed next: the stifling 120° (F) heat of the stokehold was suddenly shattered as 50° seawater began to enter the Boiler Room through the damaged starboard coal bunker and its open watertight doors. With cold water pouring in and hot boilers nearby, Martin knew a steam explosion would probably follow in short order, and began to order his men out. Fireman Tom Lawson was in the starboard side of the Boiler Room when the blast came, and felt the frigidly cold water surge around him as he tried to escape. In Boiler Room No. 2, water also started to flood into the starboard bunker, and thence into the stokehold itself. This flooding indicates a tremendous amount of damage to the hull plating outboard of the bunker as well as to the transverse bulkhead between the two Boiler Rooms. Fireman Eugene Mc-Dermott[91], who was then on duty in that compartment, heard the torpedo explode, and "ran to about three parts of the way between the boilers, when a rush of water" knocked him right off his feet and had him struggling in the water for "two or three minutes;"[92] he would be the only survivor from that compartment.

Some distance away, Kapitänleutnant Schwieger could hardly believe that his torpedo had managed to find its target and detonate properly. He watched as the torpedo plume crashed back down on the decks of the liner, hearing the reverberation of the detonation as it came to his submarine through the water. If Schwieger was impressed in that moment, far more was to come in short order.

On the Bridge of the *Lusitania*, Captain Turner immediately ordered "Hard-a-starboard!" He clearly hoped, in those first few moments after the torpedo impact, that he could close the shore and beach his ship in shallower water. Then he ran to the starboard wing while Quartermaster Johnston put the helm hard over, and the ship began to turn to port, toward land. In Turner's mind, the damage was most likely serious, but not fatal. Running onto the wing, he began to order a damage report, but just then the ship reacted to the laws of physics. With seawater tearing into her starboard compartments at a phenomenal rate, the crippled liner began to roll onto her wounded side, groaning and protesting the indignity as she went. To those on her decks, it seemed as if she was never going to stop; Michael Byrne recalled that the ship started to roll over "almost immediately after … being hit." She swung through a list of five degrees,

then ten, and she just kept going … everyone clung to the nearest stationary object, leaning away from the roll in an effort to maintain their footing. About ten seconds after the explosion, the roll finally stopped and the ship stayed at a steep, disorienting angle.

Turner turned to Second Officer Hefford: "Have a look what list the ship has got." Hefford checked the indicator and reported back: "15° to starboard."[93] Turner replied: "Keep your eye on her to see if she goes any further."[94] Turner next gave orders to close any watertight doors that were still open. As he did so, the ship began to take a pronounced plunge toward the bow in addition to her starboard list. The damage was well forward of the ship's center, and the rush of incoming water was apparently moving forward into undamaged compartments, forcing the bow to dive deeper into the swells of the Irish Channel.

As if things were not already bad enough, there next came a new and terrifying sound: a strange, rumbling roar that built with frightening speed, emanating from deep within the ship's innards. It was a much more powerful sound than that of the first explosion, and it was far more prolonged than the initial stinging blow. The whole ship shuddered anew, as if trembling from fear of what was going on inside her tormented hull. The screech of tortured metal and shattering glass accompanied this new blast, which was so markedly different from the first. Michael Byrne remembered: "Then came that awful explosion, the expansion of which lifted the bows of the ship out of the water." To him it seemed nearly to rend the ship in half, as "everything amidship seemed to part and give way up to the superstructure."

Above Byrne, the telltale board on the Bridge that told which watertight doors were open and which were closed went berserk in tandem with this new explosion, then went dark altogether. Because a lit indicator light meant an open door and an unlit one meant a closed door, there was now no way of telling for sure whether the board was all dark because all the doors were closed or because the board had failed due to the turmoil below. Those on the Bridge must have known with a sinking feeling that there were a number still open.

Outside, on the starboard companionway between the Bridge and the Boat Deck, Junior Third Officer Albert Bestic had heard the warning cries, had watched the torpedo track in, and had braced himself against the two blasts which had come in short succession. He stood there, trying to reassure himself that this beautiful ship he was so fond of simply could not sink … even as the rumble of the second explosion faded into the distance, the entire ship fell into a

Above left: *Mrs. Ellen Burdon.*

Above right: *Young Robert Burdon, who was only fourteen months old at the time of the sinking.*

Right: *The menu from Wednesday, May 5, 1915, that Mrs. Burdon carried off of the ship in her pocket.*

R.M.S "Lusitania."   Wednesday, May 5. 1915

LUNCHEON

Hors d'Œuvres

Potage Fermiere

Fillets of Flounder—Portugaise

Macaroni—Napolitain   Navarin of Lamb

Corned Brisket of Beef & Vegetables
Yellow Squash   Baked Potatoes

TO ORDER FROM GRILL (15 minutes)
Veal Cutlet—Tomato Sauce

.   .   COLD   .   .
York Ham   Galantine of Veal   Oxford Brawn

Lettuce   Sliced Tomatoes

Zwieback Pudding   Blueberry & Apple Tart

Cheese & Crackers

Tea   Coffee

SECOND CABIN

strange, stunned, eerie silence. For a few seconds, no one spoke; they were all too shocked to. Then came the gruff voice of Captain Turner, the first sound that broke the momentary stillness: "Boat stations!"

Overhead, just after the order came, Bestic noticed rather abstractly the cry of a seagull; then, in the next second, everything melted away into chaos. On the *Titanic*, just three years before, the disaster had started slowly, quietly. Passengers had to be convinced of the danger, and the ship seemed stable and secure for a long time after she had struck the iceberg. Everything was so different on this bright sunny afternoon. In those first few moments, everyone realized that the ship was in serious trouble, and all began taking measures to ensure their survival and the survival of their loved ones.

Thirty-two-year-old Miss Violet Isabel James was in her Third Class cabin when the torpedo had struck; she "could scarcely believe" what her ears were telling her. "However, the fact had to be faced," she later recalled, "so I climbed up on the bunk and got my belt and put it on and then went along the alleyway, when the second explosion came." Some glass hit her, but she "kept quite calm and walked along the starboard side," climbing up to the Boat Deck. In the crowd, she somehow "grazed" her legs.[95]

In the Second Class Dining Saloon, Mrs. Burdon recalled that almost "at once" after the explosion, the ship listed, rolling to starboard and dipping forward toward the bow. She had a very clear memory of silver and plates sliding off the tables and onto the floor.

Next, there was a rush to get out and up on deck, which she described as "plenty of excitement." Without a second thought, she "seized" her baby and made for the exit. In her haste, she completely forgot that she was still holding the serviette she held in her hand just before the torpedo struck.

Miss Wild was seated quite close to the exit of the same Dining Saloon, and yet the "stampede" to get to the main stairway was so intense that she was blocked from making an easy escape. As the "commotion became something awful," the throng – which Miss Wild estimated to be some two hundred in number – managed to become wedged in the rush on the staircase and could hardly move. Mrs. Burdon was part of this terrified group; not only was she having trouble with the crowd, but because of the ship's list, she found that she had to climb the steps "hand over hand."

Behind Mrs. Burdon, Miss Wild sized up the situation for about three minutes, and then turned to her sister: "Evelyn, keep quiet; we will go the back way." She dragged Evelyn down a different route, running through a deserted passageway. The two women beat the crowd of passengers up the stairs and emerged onto the starboard side of the sun-drenched C Deck. The evacuation in the First Class

Above: *As Second Class passengers climbed the stairs from the Dining Saloon on D Deck, they would have been presented with this sight of the well over the Second Class Saloon on the Shelter Deck. During the last voyage, Second Class was booked so heavily that this area was in use for overflow Dining Saloon seating. Doubtless, due to the list, any furniture not secured to the deck would have slid down to the starboard side, on the right of the photograph. Also notice the upright piano in front of the well.*

Saloon was a bit more controlled, but only a few in either saloon seemed to notice that many of the 16-inch diameter portholes were open, and even fewer – a number of Saloon Stewards and several male passengers – stayed behind to begin the mammoth task of closing them all. Each porthole first had to be closed, and then dogged down securely by tightening its heavy brass bolt. There were a lot of them to look after.

Chief Marconi Operator Robert Leith was in the Second Class Dining Saloon, and had to run up to the Sun Deck before he could begin sending a distress call. Meanwhile, the ship's Carpenter, Robertson, knew that the collapsibles would need to be used shortly, and that they had not yet been loosed from their mounts. He now ran down the port side of the Boat Deck, stopping at each successive craft and unlashing each one … as he worked at the tedious, slow-going task, it quickly became apparent that time was not on his side.

Meanwhile, some were actually trying to get *below*, to their staterooms, to fetch their life jackets. Mrs. Lobb, who had been reading on the Boat Deck, was

one of these. As her cabin, B39, was just below, she thought that she could reach it quickly, and hurried toward the Grand Entrance. Before she reached her cabin, however, she was met by a steward who sternly charged her: "Take this belt and go up again." He paused to unapologetically strip off her fur coat, tie the life jacket onto her, and then send her back up to the Boat Deck.

Rita Jolivet had only stolen a quick glance outside her cabin door after the explosions. She had seen another female passenger in a nearby cabin coming out with her life jacket. Without any further ado, she climbed up on her bunk, grabbed her own life jacket, and quickly headed aft to the Entrance, then up the stairs bound for the Boat Deck. The ship was listing so badly that she had trouble making her way up.

Senior Second Engineer Andrew Cockburn was off-duty on the Engineer's Promenade of the Shelter Deck, outside his cabin. After the explosions, he went below to the "fan flat" on F Deck "to see if the bulkhead doors were closed," and the one that he could see from his vantage point was shut. He next made his way back topside to don a life jacket.

Above: *In the Engine Room of the* Lusitania, *seen here in 1907, it quickly became obvious that the ship's head of steam would not last long; any attempt to beach her was doomed to failure.*

Right: *A period photograph of a wireless operator using his set gives some impression of what it would have looked like as frantic distress calls were sent from the dying liner.*

After the second explosion, steam pressure began to drop steadily and noticeably in the Engine Room. This began to pose a problem ... if Captain Turner wanted to make an attempt at beaching the ship – which he did, and was in the process of attempting – it meant he only had a limited amount of time to do so. Additionally, the steam-generating plant was what kept the electrical power running on the ship. Chief Bryce, then in the Engine Room with the Second Engineer, must have known that time was running out for the *Lusitania* and everyone on board. With the steam pressure flagging, her speed slowly wilted away. Then she ceased to answer her helm ...

It took Leith about a minute and a half, in his estimation, to reach the Marconi shack. Upon entering, he found the Junior Operator, David McCormick, at the key. Immediately taking over, he knew that he didn't have to wait for official word from Captain Turner to request assistance. He began tapping quickly but methodically: "S.O.S. Come at once. Big list. Off South Head, Old Kinsale. MFA." An officer came by and told him the ship's rough position, which he quickly incorporated as he repeated the message. "S.O.S. Come at once. Big List. 10 miles south Old Head Kinsale. MFA." As he continued to tap, he watched the power gauge sink inexorably toward the zero mark.

Outside the Marconi shack, passengers were desperately trying to find loved ones in what had quickly become pandemonium. Life jacket lockers on the upper decks were raided first, and were fast depleted; the bravest of individuals dashed inside and fought their way below to their cabins to get the life jackets in their staterooms. Some male members of the crew and passengers were later remembered because they gave their jackets away to women and children. Even if one was fortunate enough to find a life jacket, however, it was not particularly easy to figure out just how to put it on – it would have been simple for the officers to instruct the passengers on this point during the crossing, knowing the dangers ahead, but now the passengers were forced to figure it out on their own in just a few minutes and under extreme psychological duress.

On the Bridge, at 2:13 p.m., Captain Turner ordered Second Officer Hefford to find the Carpenter to have him check the forward compartments for damage ... his ship's fate was still uncertain in his mind, and he needed to ascertain the damage quickly. Next, he tried to reverse the engines and slow the ship so the lifeboats could be lowered, but the ship did not respond to this command, either, and the liner continued to drift forward out of control.

The scene on the Boat Deck was a mess, with much "confusion" and "struggling," as Mrs. Lobb put it. Michael Byrne had moved aft to the Verandah Café, and was watching everything that transpired. The first order he had heard was, "Keep the boat deck clear," but that was impossible considering how many people were there and the general state of disorder. Next came word from the Third Officer: "It's all right now," and he kept repeating the statement in an attempt to reassure passengers. Next, however, came the attempt to launch the lifeboats.

The ship's list wreaked havoc with the lifeboats, complicating the evacuation process enormously. On the port, or high, side, the regular lifeboats now hung over the deck, not over the water. As Junior Third Officer Bestic and Staff Captain Anderson worked together on lowering Boat No. 10 down to the edge, they found it landed on the deck instead of hanging in the space alongside. This wouldn't do at all. Anderson promptly ordered Bestic to go to the Bridge and trim the ship's list with the port tanks. Bestic accordingly

Above: *A boat drill on the* Kaiser Wilhelm II, *just after the Ti-*tanic *disaster, gives some idea of how difficult it was for ladies to board the craft; add to this the terrible list and confusion, and it is easy to see why the scene at the lifeboats that Friday afternoon was so ghastly.*

Opposite: *An illustration showing the lifeboats being loaded on the* Lusitania *comes close to depicting the awful reality, but it was really far worse than even this.*

hurried to the Bridge and relayed the request, but he could not have known that it would be impossible to actually carry the procedure out.[96] Back on deck, passengers were climbing into the boats, unaware that they could not be lowered because of their inboard drift. The officers and crew tried desperately to convince them to get back out of the boats so that they could physically push the craft up to the edge of the deck, but the passengers were not particularly happy about leaving their imagined refuge and returning to the uncertainty of the listing Boat Deck. Some of the boats actually fell inboard against the deckhouse, injuring passengers and crew that happened to be standing nearby. Bestic's hopes were bolstered a little bit when the ship seemed to right herself slightly, but it wasn't a big enough difference to make the lifeboat loading significantly easier, and within a short time, the ship had begun to sag back onto her starboard side.[97]

On the starboard side, the story was just the opposite, with the lifeboats drifting away from the edge of the deck. They were restrained from going all the way out because of the snubbing chains which held them to the decks. Even so, there was a considerable gap of six feet between deck and gunwale, and passengers found it difficult to get into them; when the chains were released, this gap increased to ten feet. Once the crew tried to lower the boats on this side, they found another problem: the men assigned to lower the boats had no good footing to use their strength as leverage

Four minutes after the torpedo hit, at 2:14 p.m., the steam pressure had reached the point of no return, and the electricity failed all over the ship; the interior spaces had been hazardous before, even though brightly lit. Now the spaces belowdecks were plunged into smothering darkness. Any remaining communication between vital portions of the ship was lost. The loss of electrical power meant the loss of hydraulic power, as well, and with that went the ability to open watertight doors to allow crewmembers to escape into less critically damaged compartments; many of these men opted for the emergency ladders that led up to the Sun Deck, instead. Bob Leith's Marconi set failed, forcing him to switch to the emergency backup system to continue transmitting his electrifying message of distress. Anderson's idea of having the ship's port trim tanks filled to correct her list also went out the window with the loss of power.

Down below, the First Class lifts had been in operation immediately following the torpedo's impact. The two Lift Attendants, Alex Cowan and Stanley Rourke, should have been instructed not to operate the electric cars in an emergency; better judgment seems to have won out within the next couple of minutes, however, for both young men left their posts and were later rescued. Even so, there is some evidence that at least one of the cars was still in use up to the moment of power failure.[98] When the power failed, the car apparently came to a screeching halt on its tracks, with the mahogany lift becoming a cage for its now-helpless occupants. The foyer gates could not be opened unless the elevator car was directly opposite them, and the lift doors themselves had automated locks and electrical contacts to prevent accidental opening during use. Now these safety features signed the death warrants for anyone within the car at the time of the power loss ... if there had been time, the officers and crew would have tried to help, but things were happening so quickly that no one on the Bridge was even informed about the situation.

in operating the falls, and the deck ended in a precipice. One wrong move could send the seamen off the edge and into the sea, or make them lose control of the boat and let it slide away into the water – which is exactly what began to happen to one boat after another. Without warning the boats would fall out of control, with one end poised in mid-air and the other falling away into nothingness, spilling their freshly settled occupants into the sea. As a final insult, the other fall would invariably go, as well, dropping the craft into the water. The heavy craft then landed squarely on top of those that had just been tossed into the sea.

Despite all of these obstacles, and despite the crew's lack of experience in operating the lifeboats, the officers and men still worked feverishly at it – they knew lives were in their hands, and that time was slipping away. Meanwhile, crewmen and officers alike attempted to calm the passengers by telling them that the ship was completely safe, and that she was not going to sink. Most passengers remained unconvinced of these astoundingly optimistic statements.

Meanwhile, back on the Bridge, Turner ordered Second Officer Hefford to go down to the Forecastle head to try and close the watertight doors and portholes there. Before departing, Hefford popped into the Wheelhouse and said to Quartermaster Johnston: "Keep your eye on the indicator on the compass and the spirit level, and sing out if she goes any further." After Johnston began watching the list, the ship held at 15 °.[99] In short order, the Chief Officer left to help Hefford. Neither man was seen again. With their departure, a strange sort of quiet fell over the Bridge, oddly separate from the chaos on the decks aft. Johnston divided his attention between Captain Turner and the spirit indicator, determined not to leave his post without orders.

Senior Second Engineer Cockburn managed to get his life jacket from his C Deck cabin, and then he went to the Engine Room to see what was going on. It was dark when he re-entered the ship; he found Chief Engineer Bryce and the Second Engineer still at their posts, even though "nothing was working whatever." He stood on the first grating in the Engine Room, on the first ladder, and Bryce asked him what they could possibly do now. "Absolutely nothing," Cockburn replied. With nothing to do, the Senior Second Engineer went back topside ...[100]

Michael Byrne, still standing on the Boat Deck, noticed that, by this point, "people were nearly stark mad and screaming at the top of their voices, and the ship was listing very much." He watched as first one lifeboat and then still others were launched improperly, "ran afoul of the davits and tackle," and ended up in disaster. He busied himself, adjusting "several life jackets on people who did not know how to put them on." He noticed in dismay that "only a small percentage" of those on deck around him had found and donned their life jackets. He buttoned his own coat and put his own life jacket on, carefully making sure that all the straps were fastened correctly so that it would work properly if he had to go in the water. Just then, First Officer Jones came by, and Byrne asked him, "Are we badly damaged?"

Jones replied simply that they were planning to beach the ship.

This response didn't make any sense to Byrne. "How can you when your engines are gone dead?" he asked.

Rita Jolivet eventually managed to reach the Boat Deck Entrance. When she arrived, she spotted her friends on the port side, including Charles Frohman and George Vernon, and she noticed that Alfred Vanderbilt was standing with them.[101] Vernon saw her holding the single life jacket that she had brought

The First Class Entrance on the Boat Deck, where Rita Jolivet met up with her friends; the photo was taken from very near where they stood that afternoon.

with her from her cabin, and asked: "Did you bring any others?" She responded that she hadn't; when she had left her room, she was unable to reach the other jackets on top of the wardrobe.

In response, one of the other friends in her group, Alick Scott, "went downstairs to deck B," and returned with four additional life jackets. He kept one for himself, and gave one to Frohman. The theaterman was like the eye of the storm, quietly puffing on a cigar while his friend tied the jacket on him. While Scott was helping Rita get into her own life jacket, someone stole his own, and he was forced to make another trip below to get more. When he returned, he gave all of them away, including one which he gave to an elderly woman. "We all offered him ours," Rita recalled of Scott, "and he said no, he could swim better than any of us, and if we had to die we had to die; why worry?"

The group agreed to stick together. Frohman himself advised Rita to hold onto the rail and save her strength. Then he looked out at the azure waters of the Irish Channel, the same waters that harbored the submarine which had attacked them, and muttered: "I didn't think they would do it."

A gentleman who was a First Class passenger approached Mrs. Lobb on the Boat Deck. She did not know him by name, but he now told her: "I mean to get you out of this." Then he began moving her toward the next closest lifeboat, even though it already looked to be overcrowded.

Charles Lauriat had acquired life jackets for two other passengers, Mr. and Mrs. Hubbard, only to find that they had disappeared by the time he returned to their original location. He was unconvinced as he heard the officers' reassurances of the liner's safety, and soon found himself enveloped by a large family of Italian-speaking people who were desperately seeking assistance.

Miss Violet James had heard an order for the women to keep below and stay calm; she felt that those giving the orders feared a "terrible panic." Standing on the Boat Deck, she could see from the evidence at hand that the ship was lost, and tried to help push a lifeboat off the davits, but alas, found the craft chained. When she tried to get into another lifeboat that was already "too full," a sailor told her: "No more lady."

Below, two First Class passengers – William McMillan Adams and his father Arthur – had decided to go down to their D Deck cabins via the Grand Staircase. When they began descending the final flight of stairs, however, they found the starboard side of the Entrance to the Dining Saloon awash. The open portholes along the starboard side of the Saloon were now beginning to submerge, and each was admitting a deadly flow of seawater into the interior of the ship. This was a particularly strange scene … For over seven years, the Dining Saloon had catered to the cream of the world's society set. Now it was deserted, empty, alone, and it was being inundated by the sea … never again would the orchestra play from the balcony. It was the end of an era. Adams and his father turned from the bizarre scene, unwilling to continue to their cabin through the cold water and risk being trapped; William survived the sinking, but his father did not.

On the Boat Deck, one of the ship's bellboys, William Holton, was searching for a life jacket when he heard a Scotsman from the engineering department exclaim: "Och, but they can't sink a *Clyde*-built ship!" Holton, absorbing the scene around him, dismissed the engineer's comment as ridiculous … it was quite clear to him that the Germans just had.

Forward, the bow of the ship had plunged deeply into the sea, and now water began washing over the starboard rails, spilling onto the teak planking, washing around the bollards and capstans, and consuming the Forecastle. For the "couple of minutes" that Johnston had watched the indicator, the *Lusitania* had held steady at a list of 15°. Now, about ten minutes after the torpedo impact, and without any warning, the ship gave a long, protesting groan from every plate in her hull. Something seemed to give way within her, and the ship fell onto her starboard beam even further. The list indicator swung wildly past 15°, moving farther and farther away from the vertical until it finally stopped at 20°. Johnston quickly reported this new angle to Turner as he grasped a handrail for support. Although Turner had at first felt that his ship was savable, he must now have known that she was lost, and also that she was going to sink very soon. From that point forward, her angle steadily began to increase.

Miss Wild felt as "the vessel gave a still greater list," which almost pitched her into the sea. The past few minutes had been busy for her and Evelyn. It had taken them several minutes to gain the Second Class Boat Deck, and they had at first joined the crowds on the port side. However, she noticed the difficulties that the crew was having with launching the lifeboats there, so the pair had gone down to the starboard side, where they had run across an acquaintance, Toronto journalist Ernest Cowper. The 32-year-old journalist would become a hero that day, rescuing a young girl named Helen Smith, who had become separated from her parents in the confusion. Miss Wild, with her sister still in tow, now moved forward onto the

Above left: *This view of lifeboats in the water was purportedly taken during the* Lusitania's *final stay in New York, during a boat drill. Whether it was or not, it gives a good idea of how the lifeboats would have looked to those standing on the Boat Deck of the dying liner.*

Above right: *A scene of a lifeboat being lowered away from a period naval vessel, from round-bar radial davits similar to those fitted aboard the* Lusitania. *Add to the already complex scenario seen here the ship's strong list and the confusion, and it is easy to see why so many boats were upset, damaged, or swamped.*

Opposite: *This well-known illustration conveys some sense of what it was like to be in the water along the liner's starboard side as the ship was sinking.*

First Class Boat Deck, where they had just arrived when the ship's list increased. Now she was just about to give herself up as lost when a stoker put her and Evelyn into a nearby lifeboat, No. 13; her sister, she noticed, was now wearing a life jacket, even though she still did not have one. In the chaos, this newfound haven began to look less and less safe; the ship was continuing to sink and the lifeboat was coming inexorably closer to the sea, still attached to the ship by her falls ...

Ellen Burdon had managed to get to the Boat Deck, as well. Like Evelyn Wild, she had seen the chaos on the port side, and she had also decided to cross over to the starboard side. As she approached one lifeboat, she saw that it was filling. A man in the lifeboat called out to her to give him her baby, Robert. She did so, but could not climb into the same lifeboat, and moved toward another lifeboat nearby instead. Before she could board it, "someone cut the ropes that

were holding it up and [it] fell to the waves below. It upset. I think most of the people in it were drowned." She realized then that it "was no use trying for the lifeboats."

Frohman's small group must have known that the time had arrived to leave the First Class Entrance, so as not to be trapped inside the ship as she sank. They went through the port-side doors and emerged on the Boat Deck. The friends did not know exactly what the next few moments would bring as they watched the sea devour the liner, and eventually the Boat Deck forward of them, but they joined hands to face it together. Frohman's lips began to move as a famous line came to mind; it was from *Peter Pan*, the play that he had produced and which his good friend J. M. Barrie had written. The play was well-known to be his favorite. "To die would be an awfully big adventure."

Several hundred yards away from the crippled *Lusitania*, Kapitänleutnant Walther Schwieger watched

as the results of his torpedo attack played out. He was flabbergasted. Considering his experience on this patrol to date, he could hardly have hoped for the torpedo to actually hit the ship and explode ... even if it had, he had no reason to believe that it would pose any immediate threat to the ship's safety. After all, the small cargo ships which he had sunk on Thursday had each taken quite a bit of work to put on the bottom. He had watched and heard the "unusually heavy" second explosion; he believed that this could have been caused by any one of three things: a "boiler or coal or powder." He watched as, in no time at all, the bow of the liner began to settle, almost to the Forecastle, and as smoke enveloped the Bridge, he could have sworn that a fire had broken out on board. To his eye, it appeared "as if the ship were going to capsize very shortly."

The lens of his periscope also revealed the devastating confusion that immediately swept the liner. He watched as people crowded the Boat Deck, and saw as some boats were lowered full of passengers and went out of control, tossing their occupants into the sea before landing on top of them. The list might also have allowed him to see some of what was going on over on the port side of the ship, for his log reported that "fewer boats" were "made clear" there than on the starboard side "on account of the ship's list." If there was any question in Schwieger's mind as to what liner he had attacked, it was erased by now ... this was the ship that had taken the Blue Riband back from the German merchant marine in 1907. As he continued to watch the unfolding scene, he may have felt a strange sense of satisfaction in knowing that, at last, a German vessel had bested this proud British liner ... he must also have felt a deep sense of loss, knowing that he had sent a great ship and many people to the bottom.

Back on the *Lusitania*, water rushed over the starboard rail onto the Shelter Deck. It surged about the yellow pine decking in a green and white tide, smashing into the bulkhead which bordered the Chief Steward's cabin, the telephone exchange, the Doctor's Office, and the First Class Entrance, smashing out windows and tearing down the deck – everything not bolted down was picked up in the maelstrom and washed violently through the whirlpool.

To many, the ship did not feel as solid as she had even moments ago, just before her list had increased to 20 °; her decks were shaking wildly, and ominous bangs and thuds reverberated through her structure ... the poor old crippled speed queen was going down fast. Despite this, one officer was heard shouting: "The Captain asks everyone to keep calm. Don't worry. Everything will be all right." Those nearby

dismissed this fresh reassurance as preposterous. Many, sickened at the sight of lifeboats overturning, upending and spilling people into the sea, decided at this time to head for the stern and take their survival into their own hands. The ship's untrained, untested crew members continued working feverishly despite the deteriorating situation. They fought to get the heavy, unwieldy lifeboats away and save as many as they could in the limited time remaining. Passengers, too, were working heroically. Alfred Vanderbilt was seen in the last few minutes looking after others, and even giving his life jacket away to a woman.

In the Marconi Shack, Robert Leith was still tapping out his distress calls. Now he had switched to: "Send help quickly. Am listing badly." The Chief Electrician, George Hutchinson, poked his head into the shack, and looked at Leith and McCormick: "What about it, Bob?" he asked. Before Leith could reply, another crewman came running by, breathlessly reporting to Hutchinson: "The watertight doors are all right, quite all right, don't worry." The two telegraphists and Hutchinson merely grinned at each other over this curiosity.

On the starboard side of B Deck, 39-year-old First Class passenger Charles Jeffery – an automobile manufacturer from Wisconsin – spotted something unusual. Quite unbelievably, he saw a nearby gentleman balancing himself against the angle of the ship, busily snapping photographs of the unfolding disaster with his camera. "You better get off this boat!" Jeffery advised him. "These'll be the greatest pictures ever!" the man replied, and kept snapping away. Jeffery thought it was "the coolest thing" he had ever seen. He left the photographer behind, still taking photographs; Jeffrey survived the sinking, but the enthusiastic photographer and his treasure trove of historic pictures did not.[102]

On the port side of the Boat Deck, Staff Captain Anderson was still struggling to get the lifeboats loaded and away. However, at Boat No. 14, First Class passenger Robert W. Cairns noticed that there were "very few of the crew about ... and they could not get the boat off," which was at that time "swung right onto the deck." Cairns, sensing a vacuum of authority, called out: "The moment I rush the boat to the centre, push like wild." His fellow passengers in the vicinity followed his lead, and the group eventually succeeded in getting the boat over the edge. Women and children were placed aboard, and several gentlemen also climbed in, including Cairns, for a total of just over forty.

Meanwhile, Ship's Barber Lott Gadd was just emerging from the Smoking Room Entrance, which was just

Right: *Although this photograph was supposedly taken on the Lusitania's last voyage, the operators pictured are definitely not the operators who were on this journey. However, the photo does give some idea of how it would have looked to any pass-ersby as they peered in through the open door of the Marconi Shack as the liner was sinking.*

Below right: *Ship's Barber Lott Gadd. The photo dates to no later than February 14, 1914.*

astern of Boat No. 14. He was on his way to his as-signed lifeboat station, Boat No. 6, but he quickly found the scene of chaos surrounding Boat No. 14, and saw the difficulties that were being encoun-tered. Although the boat was now hanging free, no one seemed to know how to get her down to the water safely. Gadd apparently tried to explain, but no one could understand him, and they instead called him over for assistance, making a path for him to get to the boat and help. He jumped into the boat, put the block to right, and let go the ropes. He recalled a Quartermaster manning the forward fall with him, while someone else took care of the after fall.

Cairns remembered that the boat "went down very smoothly indeed," without any undue bump-ing or scraping along the steel plates and rivets of the liner. Once it reached the water, it became necessary to release the ship from the clutches of the dying liner quickly. Although Gadd managed to release the forward fall quite rapidly, the man at the after fall could not make heads or tails out of what to do with the equipment. Quick action needed to be taken; as the liner still had a slight headway on, and the forward fall was detached, the boat "slid around," until it was being dragged forward by its stern fall. Gadd kicked off his shoes

The Stokes Family

George Edward "Ted" Stokes, his wife Mabel Stokes (*née* Elliott) and two-year-old son Master William "Billy" Stokes were passengers on the *Lusitania*. They lived in Victoria, British Columbia, Canada, at 2846 Grahame Street. Mr. Stokes was a builder, and the family had decided to travel to England to visit his family, even though their relatives in Victoria had cautioned them against such a trip. Mrs. Stokes was expecting.

On the train trip down to New York, before boarding the *Lusitania*, Mrs. Stokes wrote a series of letters to her family in Victoria. The letters arrived at their destinations after the sinking of the *Lusitania*.

The last words of Mrs. Stokes' last letter were: "Now I must say goodbye for a little while. With lots of love from us all. xxxx – From Billie: Take care of yourselves and don't worry about us. Goodbye again and God bless you all. From Mabel, Ted & Billie."

The entire family was lost.

The Stokes family, in a photograph taken not long before they took passage on the Lusitania.

and climbed up onto the gunwale in an attempt to reach the after fall. Meanwhile, the boat's occupants began to feel cold water splashing into the boat's interior. Gadd suspected that no one had remembered to put the plug into the boat. The barber tried to direct them to bail the water with anything they had handy – even hats. Gadd had only traversed half the length of the boat when something happened, and he found himself tumbling into the sea.[103]

Cairns did recall the boat tilting and two of its occupants falling out, but whether he saw Gadd go over the side is unclear. Meanwhile, the boat continued to flounder. Soon Cairns realized that the craft was going to sink; he decided to abandon it while he could

An illustration of the scene as the great liner was settling head-first into the sea.

and struck out in the open water, as he was an excellent swimmer. Behind him, he watched Boat No. 14 succumb and capsize. "All had gone down with it with the exception of two or three who were hanging on to the keel."[104]

Most of the ship's complement of twenty-two standard lifeboats had by this time been launched, and their davits were empty with the falls trailing in the water as the ship eased forward at about five knots. Most of those boats had suffered calamity. The twenty-six collapsible lifeboats had proved almost totally useless; none of the eighteen that were stored under the regular lifeboats were launched, even though they were closest to the davits. The other eight, stored in relatively inaccessible locations, had virtually no chance of getting away under the circumstances. The way that the disaster was playing out, as well as the speed with which it was progressing, effectively cut the lifesaving capacity of the lifeboats and collapsibles from 2,605 persons – more than enough to accommodate all aboard – to less than 700. This reduced capacity was exacerbated as each lifeboat that had suffered disaster upon launch became useless.

Many passengers and crew still did not have life jackets ... the upper deck lockers and cabins had all been raided by those unwilling or unable to go below to get their own. Now the ship was really sinking fast ... the starboard B and C Deck Promenades were going under, and passengers and crew were being washed right off the decks. It was as if the sea had gotten hold of the ship and was pulling it down in its clutches ... the beautiful speed queen of the Atlantic tried valiantly to stay afloat, but everything – including the shortfalls of her own system of watertight subdivision – was fighting against her. It was becoming clear that she was dying, and that a lot of people were about to die with her.

In desperation, many of those left aboard were scrambling away from the onrushing sea, climbing up to the Sun Deck or running aft toward the imagined safety of the stern, which was the highest point above water. Then came the moment of truth in any sea disaster: the Boat Deck, the focus of all activity and usually at a great elevation above the sea, began to disappear under the surface. A wave like that on the seashore began to wash along the starboard side,

Water begins to wash over the Boat Deck, swamping the vessel and washing people into the sea.

eating the deck up hungrily as it continued moving aft.

With only a few seconds remaining, the crew attempted to release Boat No. 3, still hanging from its davits at the forward end of the Boat Deck, so that it could float away with the onrushing sea. By that point the craft was filled with women and children, but it was still connected to the ship by its falls and by its snubbing chain. Before anyone could free it, the sea arrived, and the boat was dragged under.

Mrs. Ellen Burdon had given her son Robert to a man in a lifeboat, but she was still on the sloping decks of the fast-dying liner. As the ship continued to sink, she slid to the edge of the deck, and then jumped over into the sea.

Nearby, Second Class passenger Miss Wild and her sister were still waiting in half-full lifeboat No. 13, hoping that someone would be able to free the craft from the sinking ship. "It was only at the last moment," she recalled, "that someone in the boat seemed to have the presence of mind to cut away the rope" holding the lifeboat fast to the ship, and they "just managed" to get clear of her.

For Ellen Burdon, the number "13" seemed to be uncharacteristically lucky, for Boat No. 13 came past her in the water, and she was pulled in. She thought that there could have been up to eighty people in the boat, including five who were dead or wounded. They were so close to the side of the *Lusitania* that Mrs. Burdon could clearly hear a man standing on the sloping deck calling to his wife, who was in one of the lifeboats. He was telling her: "Go to Birmingham. Go to my people there." The man's wife, as Ellen Burdon recalled, was "a young American girl who had no money and knew nobody at all in England."

On the Sun Deck, Bob Leith gave up on sending the distress calls ... a few more seconds would see the ship sink, and he knew he had done his duty. McCormick left as well, and paused to take a few snaps of the scene with his camera – which also seems to have been lost, even though he and Leith survived. The two men joined some others in descending to the Boat Deck to meet the sea.[105]

At about this same time, on the port side of the Boat Deck, the Irish Channel surged over the pine planks and swamped the area where Charles Frohman and his friends were standing, separating them from each other. Rita Jolivet remembered that her high-button boots were ripped off by the force of the water. Although she miraculously escaped drowning, she never saw Frohman, Scott or Vernon alive again.[106]

Mrs. Lobb, having failed to get into one lifeboat, found herself "pushed towards the last boat" to be launched on the port side. As it was being lowered, she noted that the "*Lusitania* heeled over and a great rush of black water came up towards us from the bows." She jumped, and "in falling, caught miraculously at" the lifeboat, which made it all the way to the sea without capsizing or upending. Mrs. Lobb clung doggedly to the craft, but was eventually parted from it. However, she did manage to get far enough away from the ship to avoid the worst of the suction.

Aft, on the starboard side of the same deck, First Officer Jones had filled Boat No. 15 with about eighty men, women and children. With no more time left, he jumped in and ordered the boat lowered away. Under Jones' careful command, it began pulling away from the quickly dying liner's side. When he spotted Boat No. 1 lying empty and upright not far away, he rowed over to the craft and divided his human cargo between the two boats.

When the water was washing over Michael Byrne's shoes, he dove from the ship and began swimming swiftly away from her. He was worried about getting caught in the suction when she went under, and he estimated that he had made about seventy-five yards before he turned over onto his back "and looked back at the fast disappearing ship." The liner's bow was by this time submerged. He saw Captain Turner "and an officer," perhaps Quartermaster Johnston, on the Bridge, and he also thought he saw the Assistant Surgeon climbing the gangway to the Bridge.

Back on the Bridge, Quartermaster Johnston was still watching the spirit indicator ... it now reported an angle of 25°, a development that Johnston quickly relayed to Captain Turner. At this point, Turner told the dutiful Quartermaster to save himself. Not wishing to argue this sensible command, Johnston grabbed a lifebuoy from the starboard wing and walked down to meet the sea as it poured over the bulwark rail.

This new angle was the farthest that the ship rolled onto her starboard side. With the bow well under water and the Bridge about to slip under, the buoyant stern was bobbing high enough to expose all four of her bronze quadruple-bladed props – the secret of her record-breaking speeds. Below, water was entering Boiler Room No. 3, reaching the hot boilers there and causing some of the last-minute explosions that passengers and

---

Opposite top: A dramatic illustration of the liner plunging into the sea.

Opposite bottom: As the ship sank lower and lower, passengers and crew remaining on board headed instinctively for the stern. This view of the Mauretania's *stern Boat Deck, by the Aft Docking Bridge, gives a good idea of what it would have looked like as people fled the water inundating the bow.*

Top: *Oliver Bernard's illustration showing the Boat Deck completely submerged and the funnels slipping into the sea.*

Middle: *The final plunge, in a sketch by Oliver Bernard.*

crew later reported. Now that water was flooding No. 3, the ship actually began to right herself slightly; at the same time, with water rushing aft, the last gasp of the vessel's buoyancy began to escape, and the stern started to settle slowly into the sea.

On the Boat Deck, Third Class passenger Violet James was watching the "captain and second in command," and suddenly found herself in the "nice warm water." Thanking God that she could swim, she struck out and managed to get clear of the ship, clutching at a spar to support herself in the water.

Back on the Bridge, Captain Turner shoved his cap tightly onto his brow and began climbing the line leading up to the signal halyards … he fully expected to be lost, but was not just going to give up. The water quickly began to catch up to him, swamping the Bridge completely; when he spotted an oar floating nearby, he let go the line and struck out for it, manag-

ing to get hold of it. Then he turned back and watched his ship's final moments. The forward funnel was sliding under the surface … the public rooms on the Boat Deck were swamped in quick succession – the Writing Room & Library, the Grand Entrance, the Lounge & Music Room … all of these rooms had been the focus of passenger activity for years, and all were destroyed in a matter of a few seconds. Next the wave rolled through the Smoking Room and thundered back out the Verandah Café.

The ship now began to roll to starboard again, and the funnels – still steadfastly attached to the ship by their guy wires and stays – began to settle their starboard sides into the sea. Captain Turner watched as, one after another, four people struggling in the water were all sucked down inside one of the gaping apertures: First Class passenger Detective Inspector William Pierpoint, Second Class passenger Margaret

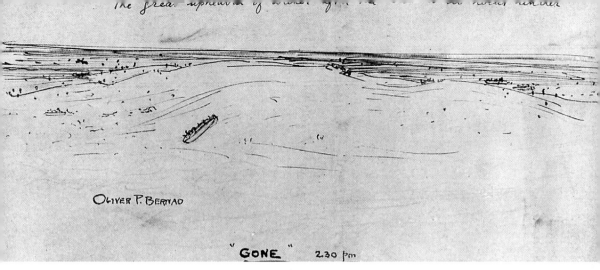

The final Oliver Bernard sketch. Entitled, "Gone", it shows the upheaval of water after the Lusitania went under.

Gwyer, First Class Bedroom Steward Edward Bond, and Third Class passenger Harold Taylor. This might have been the end of all four, but suddenly there came a rush of air belching up from the dark innards of the ship, and they were shot back out into the sea, covered in soot ... Turner noticed that Pierpoint was "swimming like ten men, he was so scared."

The ship now took her final plunge, emitting a "terrible moan" as she succumbed to the sea. Junior Third Officer Bestic was still working on the aft port lifeboats when he heard a noise like that of thunder and saw the sea rushing toward him, carrying all sorts of wreckage and human debris in it. Without a second thought, Bestic leapt over the edge of the deck, landing in the sea which was only a couple of feet below him at that time, and swam as hard as he could away from the ship. Just when he began to think he had escaped, he was caught in a vortex and dragged under; there, he was spun in every imaginable direction, almost completely disorienting him. He struggled to regain the surface, but the color of the water went darker, suggesting that he was going in the wrong direction. Finally, there came a sudden roar and he burst back into the fresh air, gasping for breath, but underneath a capsized lifeboat. He heard a terrible sound "like the despair, anguish and terror of hundreds of souls passing into eternity." Working quickly to get out from under the boat, he popped back up on the correct side and clutched the gunwale while watching the Lusitania sag into the sea.

There was still a good sliver of the ship's stern and port Second Class decks above the water ... people were hanging on through the wild ride of the vessel's last few, highly temperamental moments. Then, accompanied by the roar of all sorts of objects in the ship sliding toward the bow and the starboard sides, the last remnant of the Lusitania's buoyancy evaporat-

ed. She simply dropped from sight, washing everyone still on her decks into the water. The proud golden letters on her stern proclaiming her to be the mighty Lusitania – a name which had struck fear into the corporate officials of every competing transatlantic shipping line from 1906 onward – vanished under the foaming, raging sea. Then, with startling swiftness, the Cunarder was gone ...

... It was 2:28 p.m., Friday, May 7, 1915, a mere 18 minutes after the torpedo had struck the ship's starboard plates.

Michael Byrne watched as the "sea closed over where the Lusitania was fifteen minutes before." In her place was a large semi-circle of debris and human bodies, those of both the living and dead. Hundreds of voices pleading for help rose into the air off the Irish coast; the sounds of the drowning mingled with the diminishing roar of the ship as she settled onto the seabed roughly 300 feet below. A huge round mountain burst from the surface over the spot where the ship had sunk, churning white water containing the last collective bubble of air to escape the ship. Within this bubble was "all the wreckage such as spars, deckchairs, galvanized iron ventilators and every thing that was floatable," as Michael Byrne recalled.

Schwieger's official log, which was released after the war, reported that before the Lusitania had sunk, he had seen enough, and that he lowered the periscope, dove to 24 meters and ran out to sea. However, a number of survivors who were fighting for their lives told a different story. In their earliest accounts, many of them seemed to recall something very different. Michael Byrne was among these. He wrote:

After the waters closed over the ship I saw the submarine periscope then the manhole or entrance, at which a man's head appeared. He seemed to survey the ocean and the boats of people for about two minutes. Then the cover was closed and the submarine disappeared …

Some other accounts were far more dramatic, and far less believable; among these were tales of submariners machine-gunning survivors in the water. However, it seems that there is enough evidence to support at least the possibility that, contrary to later reports, Schwieger surfaced his submarine – perhaps only partially – to survey the results of his attack. It seems quite clear, however, that if Schwieger did surface, he did not stay there for long, and soon made his way away from the scene of the sinking. He would have known that rescue was not going to be long in coming for those struggling in the sea, and he would also have known that it would have been suicidal for him to remain there for any length of time.

Meanwhile, those who had only a little while before been enjoying life aboard the spacious grandness of the great *Lusitania* were struggling for their very lives. Although the weather was pleasant that day, the water was about fifty degrees (F), and it took time for the flotilla of small rescue vessels to arrive on the scene and begin to fish survivors out of the sea. Some who survived the actual sinking were in the water for three hours or more, and many of these individuals succumbed to hypothermia. Many of those who had donned life jackets had put them on incorrectly, and once they entered the water were drowned. Michael Byrne remembered swimming through numbers of dead bodies, including "the bodies of infants laid in life jackets, and floating around with their dead innocent faces looking towards the sky." Eventually, he made it to a lifeboat, and after a time he was pulled in.

Ship's barber Lott Gadd, who had been so mercilessly cast from Boat No. 14 before it sank, had man-

Above: *Beatrice Witherbee lost her mother and son in the sinking. Although she survived, she would never speak of her experiences that afternoon. She divorced her husband and eventually became Rita Jolivet's sister-in-law.*

Right: *Eventually rescue did come, but for some it was already too late. The living and the dead were placed aboard a veritable flotilla of small craft and most were brought to Queenstown, Ireland.*

aged to come across a life buoy, which he shared with four others. Finally, they happened across a floating, albeit damaged, collapsible boat, which they boarded. Gadd was selected to take charge of the craft, and those aboard it quickly got to work picking people out of the water.

What happened to Beatrice Witherbee, her son, and her mother during the sinking largely remains a mystery. Although Beatrice survived the sinking, her son and mother both perished. She never spoke of what had happened to them during those eighteen minutes.[107]

That evening, the rescue vessels began to bring both survivors and the bodies of the dead into Queenstown. Miss Violet James, Mrs. Lobb, as well as Agnes and Evelyn Wild all survived the sinking and were picked up by this flotilla of rescue craft. Ellen Burdon was reunited with her baby, Robert, and would always remember with fondness the kindness of the fishermen aboard the trawler that rescued them, as well as the hospitality of the Irish people in Queenstown. Captain Turner, recovered late in the afternoon, was seen walking the streets of the Irish coastal town that his ships had visited so often. His uniform was shrunken and looked awful, but it was obvious that he didn't really catch on to that fact. Turner was dazed, in a state of utter shock and not thinking clearly. Survivors who were missing friends and loved ones began the grim task of searching through the makeshift morgues over the coming days. All too frequently their search ended in a heartbreaking discovery. The sinking of the *Lusitania* and its aftermath was a tragic scene of civilian carnage in a war that removed with finality the distinct line between combatants and non-combatants. Never again would the world's residents be able to think that just because they were civilians or neutral citizens they could not be affected by the brutality of war ...

Albert J. Byington

Albert Jackson Byington was a 40-year-old American citizen traveling to London for business purposes. He was a native of Elmira, New York. Several years before, Byington, who was an electrical engineer, had moved his family to Brazil, where he worked with the Southern Brazil Electric Company of Sao Paulo.

From the outset of her husband's plans for this trip, Mrs. Byington expressed misgivings, but he had "not the least uneasiness" on his safety during the voyage. Although she did not accompany him on the actual trip to England, she did travel with him to New York. When the pre-sailing warnings were sent out, they did little to allay Mrs. Byington's fears. Her husband, however, "laughed at them," declaring that "the ship was unsinkable because of the watertight compartments." He was close friends with fellow passenger Frederick Edward Owen Tootal.

Albert Byington's passport photo.

Just before the torpedo impact, Byington and Tootal were waiting for the elevator outside the First Class Dining Saloon, having just come out from lunch. Tootal was talking with Margaret Mackworth and her father, D. A. Thomas. Byington survived the disaster. Upon arriving in Queenstown, he sent a quick cablegram back to his wife to let her know that he had survived. when he reached London two days after the disaster, he took the time to write her a letter, telling her about his experiences on the afternoon of May 7:

> We were steaming lazily into the Irish channel, with Ireland in sight, and had just finished lunch, standing talking outside of the dining saloon, when the first torpedo struck the ship with an unmistakable explosion and noise. We (referring to his friend Fred E. Tootal, who had been a visitor at his home here) ran to the promenade deck, and then to the boat deck. After the first few moments of natural hurrying to get the women and children up, Fred and I decided that the ship was not going to sink, and so went to work loading the people into the lifeboats that they might be lowered if necessary.
>
> The starboard boats owing to the list of the ship were hanging so far out that the women would not make the jump, so we two got into a

boat to take them as the other men held them out to us. There was such a rush of stokers, cooks, etc., for the boat that we couldn't get out, and the men on the boat started to lower it to avoid it being upset by the rush.

When we were about 25 feet from the water one rope broke or slipped and the whole boat-load was dumped into the water. I had kicked my shoes off so I found no difficulty in swimming and luckily about 30 yards away saw a boat that had been properly launched full of people. They were trying to get away, but not one knew which way to pull and they were going around in circles. After the ship sank they hauled me in and we started for shore – 63 souls and no room for more.

After rowing two and a half hours we were picked up by a fisherman trawler and again were transferred to a Government patrol boat and landed at Queenstown about 8 P. M. The only inconvenience I had was from wet clothes and the lack of shoes, which was speedily taken care of by the good people of Queenstown, where we were made comfortable.

I was worrying about Fred after I was hauled into the last boat, when all of a sudden, as I was being relieved at our oar and stood up to let the other men take my place, I saw him pulling away at his oar in the stern, and the

sight was good to the eyes. He behaved like a true sport through it all.

Due, I think, to the fact that nobody believed the boat would sink there was no panic and when the boats could not be pulled close enough to get into the women just sat down on deck and waited for orders.

The submarine could have given the ship two hours without any danger to themselves had they wanted to let the passengers save themselves. It was more than two hours and a half before the first fisher boat got to the place. Instead the submarine did not even come up out of the water or give any sign of its presence, but sent another torpedo into the wreck when women and children were jumping overboard.

When he left the *Lusitania*, Byington carried away a copy of his wine bill, which appears in the color section of this book.

Byington sailed back to Brazil after a stay of less than three weeks. Unfortunately, he was severely affected by his experiences. His skills as a manager deteriorated, and he exhibited symptoms of what we would now term post-traumatic stress disorder. He was awarded $10,000 by the Mixed Claims Commission in 1924.—*Contributed by Jon Kiger and Mike Poirier.*

A sketch which Byington drew depicting the Lusitania's *sinking.*

Above: *Crowds stand in the street, waiting for further details on the sinking, and eagerly scanning posted lists of survivors.*

Left: *Here a large sign, bearing a partial list of survivors, is held up in an open window for those outside to read.*

Opposite: *Other crowds also began to form across England immediately following the disaster, and with much more sinister intent. Looking to vent their wrath for the murder of so many innocent men, women and children, they attacked the shops of any naturalized Germans that they could find; even non-Germans with Teutonic-sounding names were not exempt from this frenzy of mob retaliation. This was in spite of the fact that the victims had nothing to do with the disaster and were, instead, law-abiding and innocent citizens. Yet the reputation of the Germans as "Huns", which had already been forming after the Belgian atrocities of 1914, was now indelibly cast.*

6
The End of the Road

News of the *Lusitania*'s sinking spread across the world in the hours following her loss. People were outraged, shocked, and incensed by this attack on an unarmed ship carrying civilians. There had been 1,959 passengers and crew aboard the ship when she left Pier 54 in New York on May 1. Of these, some 1,198 had perished.[1] There were only 761 survivors. Ironically, if the ship had been farther out in the Irish Channel when she was sunk – as she should have been according to the Admiralty's directives – there might not have been as many survivors. Then again, the ship would most likely have avoided her fateful encounter with the *U-20* in the first place.

In the days, weeks and months after the sinking, the survivors attempted to put their lives back together with varying degrees of success. Ellen Burdon was reunited with her young son, Robert, and later remembered with fondness the hospitality of the Irish in Queenstown. Some people were completely shattered by the experience, while others seemed relatively unfazed by their ordeal. Many had to deal with the loss of husbands, wives, children or parents under the most appalling of circumstances.

Meanwhile the political ramifications of the sinking were enormous.

There were three Inquiries into the loss of the *Lusitania*. The first was held almost immediately in Kinsale by a local group headed by the town coroner. Under local law, he had the authority to set up an inquest of this nature as several of the dead had been

The Voyage That Never Happened

The *Lusitania* was no stranger to the most prominent people of her day, including actresses, actors, inventors, playwrights, composers and extremely wealthy or otherwise socially prominent individuals. Some of the most famed sports players of the era also sailed on the great Atlantic liners, including the *Lusitania*. One of the most popular sports in England at the time was golf, and it was just catching on in the United States. English golfing legend Harry Vardon had taken the American liner *St. Paul* to America in 1900 for an extended tour of that country, trying to promote the sport and making headlines in the process. In 1913, he and his friend and fellow golfing legend Edward Ray had traveled to the United States to participate in the U.S. Open. It was there that Vardon was bested by 20-year-old amateur Francis Ouimet in one of the greatest games ever played. They made their round-trip voyage on the White Star liner *Celtic*.

In just two years since that match, the world had changed significantly. So it was a welcome break from war news when in the spring of 1915, *The New York Times* announced that Vardon and Ray would be returning to the States for another golfing tour. They would be coming with two other English golfers, George Duncan and C. H. Mayo. The group had booked passage on the *Lusitania*'s May 15 departure from Liverpool.

On May 8, the day after the *Lusitania* was sunk, it was announced that Vardon and Ray had canceled their plans to travel to America altogether. In the end, they did not return to America for another round of golf tournaments until after the war's end. When, in 1920, they actually did make the passage, they booked passage on White Star's *Celtic*.

Harry Vardon (the golfer on the right) and Ted Ray (making his putt) during their 1913 tour of the United States.

Famed golfer Harry Vardon; because of the Lusitania *disaster, Vardon and Ray canceled their plans to make a 1915 tour of the United States.*

landed there. Captain Turner was called to testify, and broke down on the stand. As the inquest ended, a representative from the British Government arrived, belatedly asking to stop the proceedings for fear that some sensitive or secret information might come to the attention of German sympathizers. In the end, there was no reason to worry; nothing secret was revealed. Quite surprisingly, considering the Irish hatred of just about everything British, the Kinsale Inquest placed the sole blame for the disaster on Germany's doorstep.

During June, there came the official British Inquiry, which was presided over by Lord Mersey, who had overseen the official investigation into the loss of the *Titanic* in 1912. This particular hearing was held partly on the open record and partly *in camera*, with the testimony being sealed to prevent sensitive information from falling into German hands. This particular investigation has been called a "sham" or "whitewash," terms that are not entirely without foundation, although in the end it was far

Top: *Five lifeboats made their way into Queenstown Harbour shortly after the sinking. Children can be seen playing in the craft in this photograph.*

Above: *Another view of the lifeboats sitting empty in Queenstown Harbour. Oars and life jackets can be seen abandoned inside the craft.*

Above: *Many of the Lusitania's victims ended up in mass graves just outside of Queenstown.*

Below: *A crowd pays their respects as one of the mass graves is filled in.*

Above: *A small sign is all that marks the mass graves' location.*

Above: *A photograph taken during the Mersey Inquiry, with Captain Turner on the witness stand.*

less sinister than is popularly believed today. It is quite clear that some within the British Government, including Winston Churchill, were justifiably outraged that Captain Turner had failed to adequately comply with all of the warnings and orders he had been sent both prior to and during that disastrous 202nd crossing. Despite this, Lord Mersey saw to it that all blame for the disaster was dumped on Germany's doorstep, and that Captain Turner was not censured or punished in any way for the way he had commanded the *Lusitania* as she entered the War Zone.

Turner retained his Masters' Licenses, and was subsequently given command of two other ships as a "relief" captain. He was not released from Cunard's employment, although Cunard and the Admiralty seemed understandably hesitant about giving him another crack ship during the war; he reached the age of retirement before the great liners returned to civilian service, and never regained his former status as one of the top Cunard skippers. Many have sought to defend his actions on that last crossing; to this day his defenders try to argue that he was scapegoated, caught up in some awful Government blame-game, and that in some way he received unfair blame for what happened on May 7. While it certainly was not Captain Turner watching the *Lusitania* through a submarine's periscope and deciding whether or not to fire on her, he was the Captain of the legendary liner. In the end, a Captain is entirely and solely responsible for the way he oversees his ship and for delivering her, the crew and his passengers to safety at the end of each crossing. Even without the benefit of hindsight, there were a good many preventive measures that Turner could have taken to minimize the potential for loss of life if the liner had been attacked, or to try to prevent a successful attack at all. Although he, his ship, and those aboard her were victims of an attack, in not maintaining maximum vigilance Captain Turner must inherently bear some burden of responsibility for the way events played out. Considering the notoriety of the disaster, it is actually rather surprising that he was simply allowed to retain his Masters' Licenses, was given command of two other ships during the war, and was thereafter allowed to retire and simply slide into obscurity.

In time, there came a third hearing into the sinking, this one held in the United States courts. Many

THE "LUSITANIA."

British Liner, torpedoed off Irish Coast by Sea Pirates, on May 7th, 1915, with a loss of over 1,100 lives.

The LUSITANIA is no more,
　　She plunged into the mighty deep,
Not far from dear old Ireland's shore,
　　And leaves a mourning crowd to weep.

The gallant liner steamed along,
　　With peaceful passengers aboard ;
The band played " Tipperary " song :
　　The spray danced and the seagulls soared.

Hark ! suddenly a mighty crash,
　　A huge explosion and a thud ;
The Sea Huns made a daring dash,
　　Thirsting to taste innocent blood.

Ah ! fiendish Hun, corrupt and vile,
　　Barbaric, cruel, on evil's spell,
Creator of a murderer's smile—
　　The warm confederate of Hell.

The crowd aboard the gallant ship
　　Met death in bitter agony :
Clenched tight within the pirates' grip,
　　'Midst fiendish grins of hideous glee.

Ah ! men and women met their doom,
　　And sank beneath the restless wave ;
The children found a chilly tomb :
　　Their spirits went to God, Who gave.

Sweet innocents have perished, yes !
　　And kindly women shared their lot ;
The family ties of tenderness
　　Are severed from affection's knot.

Toll for the brave, in death's long sleep,
　　And raise a prayer for mourners' needs ;
The Sea Huns, on the ocean deep,
　　Will reap remorse for foulest deeds.

Lyne Road, Kidlington, Oxon.　　　　Pte. W. WEST.

A commemorative poem about the loss of the Lusitania *printed for distribution. When Schwieger sent his single torpedo into the side of the* Lusitania, *it is very likely that he did not expect she would go to the bottom. Instead, he was most likely hoping to cripple the pride of the British merchant marine, the very vessel that had taken the Blue Riband back from Germany after it had been their special prize for an entire decade. When the ship sank, he might have had only the vaguest inkling that he had given the Allies the greatest propaganda victory of the war.*

had filed suit against the Cunard Company for loss of loved ones' lives or loss of property, or the like, and Cunard – like the White Star Line after the *Titanic* disaster – sought to limit its liability against such claims. The American court system, like both its predecessors, placed the blame squarely on German shoulders. However, by that point, the United States had entered World War One, and such a verdict was not, therefore, entirely unpredictable.

In school classrooms all throughout the United States, many are still taught that it was because of the sinking of the *Lusitania* that the U.S. entered the

MAY SEVENTH, 1918

This is the Anniversary of a Thousand Murders.

The lips of fathers, mothers, children, murdered in the Lusitania sinking, are stilled in death;
And yet, they call, call on us of the living,
That to-day we renew the high resolve to which we dedicated ourselves,
That they may not have died in vain.

We of the living should speak for them;
Must speak for them;
Only through the Mouths of Cannon—
Not in revenge, in no more than Righteous Anger, pray God—
In the divine knowledge that it is entrusted to us to teach the Hun of to-day and the possible Hun of to-morrow,
That, born of the Ages, there is, and ever shall be on earth the Kingdom of Humanity—
The Spirit of Right its Ruler—
Against which the forces of Barbaric Brutality shall not prevail.

Right is ever on the Scaffold; Wrong is ever on the Throne.
Whosoever will not fight for Right helps to enthrone Wrong.

THIS IS WHY WE FIGHT.

President Butterick Publishing Company.

"May Seventh, 1918: This is the Anniversary of a Thousand Murders." This third anniversary was taken out as an advertisement by the President Butterick Publishing Company, and ran in American magazines. Three years on, the Lusitania *was still a powerful tool to keep the Allies united in their "fight against evil" despite calamitous numbers of casualties. "Whosoever will not fight for Right helps to enthrone Wrong," the message stated. "This is why we fight."*

briefly if only to, once again, attempt to set the record of history straight.

President Wilson had sternly lectured the Germans about a "strict accountability" if American lives were lost as a result of submarine activity. However, his lecture had left out some important specifics on how such an event would have to take place in order to rouse American ire, and just what "strict accountability" actually meant. When 128 Americans were found to have perished in the sinking, Wilson and the American population were outraged. Strictly speaking, however, the Americans who boarded the belligerent *Lusitania* had taken their lives in their hands by choosing to take passage on a British ship carrying munitions to the Allies. In the heat of the moment, though, this fact was lost on the majority. Wilson could not back down from his heavy-handed policy because 1916 was an election year ... the American populace wanted to exact a diplomatic toll on the Germans, without actually breaking off diplomatic relations or declaring war. For Wilson to buck this tide would have meant almost certain defeat on the campaign trail, and so he 'stuck to his guns,' even though he was on uncertain footing in the eyes of International Law.

The diplomatic fracas was quite long-lived and hostile. Meanwhile, the British propaganda machine went into high-gear, making the Germans out to be barbarians for committing such an atrocity. Many Americans agreed with this sentiment. Losing face in the eyes of the world, Kaiser Wilhelm probably felt the need to give something back in the hopes of preserving at least a measure of pro-German sentiment. The upshot was, remarkably enough, that Kaiser Wilhelm's Government agreed to cease submarine activity in the War Zone. Much later, when his advisors convinced him that an unrestricted U-boat campaign could knock the British out of the war before the Americans could respond, a new campaign was launched. This campaign differed from the first in that it was entirely unrestricted ... any ship of any nationality found in the waters around Great Britain was subject to attack without warning. The muzzle had been removed from the submarine, and it wasted no time in baring its teeth. When Americans again began to perish in a German submarine blockade, and when shortly thereafter the British let the re-elected Wilson in

Great War. Simple chronology shows otherwise: it was about two years between the sinking and the American declaration of war. What happened in that two-year period was complicated and has been repeated often, but the general details are worth noting

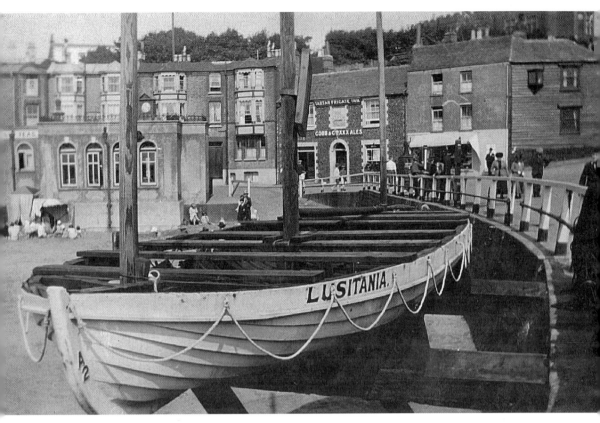

In remembrance of the May 7, 1915 disaster, one of the Lusitania's *collapsibles – which had washed ashore upside-down with several bodies underneath it – was placed on the jetty at Broadstairs in England. This photograph was taken in 1925. A sign mounted to the craft for some time gave a short version of the boat's story and concluded with the powerful words "Lest We Forget," which phrase was also the name of a 1918 film about the sinking starring* Lusitania *survivor Rita Jolivet.*

on the notorious Zimmerman telegram, the results were not hard to predict. On April 6, 1917, the United States Congress formally declared war on the government of Germany. The American expeditionary forces were sent to Europe to relieve Allied soldiers exhausted by two and a half years of stalemate and bloodshed. It took another year and a half, but eventually the tide was turned against the Germans. On the eleventh hour of the eleventh day of the eleventh month, 1918, a ceasefire came into effect ... the Germans surrendered, ending the war four and a quarter years after it had begun.

The resulting peace terms, settled upon in the Treaty of Versailles, were unjustifiably harsh on the Germans, however ... the ensuing poverty and unrest within the nation of Germany throughout the 1920s and early 1930s paved the way for the rise of a new leader for that nation: Fascist Adolf Hitler. The "War to End All Wars" was thus not the end of war at all, but rather the prelude – a dress rehearsal of sorts – to the worst conflict that the world has ever known, the 1939-1945 clash that became known as World War

Two. The world of today is still unsettled from the way those two conflicts shaped national, political and ethnic boundaries. Through all of this, it must be remembered that the *Lusitania* tragedy was merely one step on the path to American involvement in the First World War.

Whereas there was some hope of humanism during the Great War, there was no such nobility to the second, greater conflict. The illusion that an Atlantic liner was immune to the threat of submarines just because it was not actively engaged in fighting had been shattered by the loss of the *Lusitania* and, subsequently, other ships. Indeed, before the first crossing of the *Aquitania* out of Southampton after the British had declared war on Germany, a Cunard official was brought in to address neutral American passengers and to tell them that they sailed on the liner at their own risk.

As time drew on following the conclusion of The Great War, there was still a good deal of interest in the *Lusitania*. In May of 1932, the *Lusitania*'s former Junior Third Officer, Albert A. Bestic, now Lieutenant Bestic,

Above: *On November 4, 1916, during her seventh active-duty patrol, the U-20 grounded on the Danish coast. The following day, her crew attempted to blow her up using her own torpedoes. The attempt was only partially successful, and the submarine that had sent the* Lusitania *to the bottom of the Irish Channel was abandoned. She immediately became an attraction to the local populace.*

Right: *In April of 1917, Kapitänleutnant Walther Schwieger was given a newer boat, the U-88, as a replacement for the lost submarine. That September, on the newer sub's fourth patrol, she disappeared with all hands. It was presumed that she struck a mine and was totally destroyed.*

visited his former Master at his home in Liverpool. It had been seventeen years since the disaster, but Bestic found "the same alertness of manner and the same quick, penetrating look in his sharp blue eyes." However, Bestic noted that Turner's "abrupt quarterdeck manner [had] softened considerably."

"Did you expect we would be torpedoed?" he asked Turner.

"Yes," Turner replied. "I was distinctly worried. I was advised by the Admiralty that I was to keep a mid-channel course." At this point, Turner's memory seemed to fade a bit, as he said: "As you remember, we learned by wireless that there were six submarines waiting for us in mid-channel. That was the chief reason I closed in on the coast. I thought that if the ship were sunk nearer shore, the top deck might be above water after she had settled, allowing the passengers to escape. But apparently that was not to be." None of this corresponded with his actions on that fateful day, but in the intervening years, there was plenty of time for memories to become clouded.

When Bestic asked why the *Lusitania* had sunk so quickly, Turner replied that he was sure she was struck by two torpedoes. "What ship, however big, could withstand such wounds?" He recalled seeing a ship beached after being torpedoed. "There was a hole in her side 32 by 18 feet, although she had been hit only once." Turner was correct in surmising that the damage to the *Lusitania* had been profound, explaining her rapid demise, although he was mistaken in thinking she was sunk by two torpedoes.[2]

Just less than three years later, on the twentieth anniversary of the disaster, a small group of the *Lusitania*'s former officers gathered to mark the event. There was Captain John Lewis, former Senior Third Officer of the *Lusitania*, now the Assistant Marine Superintendent of Cunard-White Star; there was also Richard G. Wylie, the former Junior Third Engineer of the lost ship, who was now the Assistant Marine Engineer of the line; there was also William E. G. Jones, who had served as the Third Electrical Engineer on the *Lusitania* and who was at the time the Chief Electrical Engineer of the Cunarder *Scythia*. The three men met aboard Jones' ship in New York. "There was a moment of silent tribute and they touched glasses to the memory of their fellow-officers" who had perished with the ship. Alexander Duncan, the former Chief Engineer of the *Lusitania*, who was now serving as Chief Engineer of the *Berengaria*, had hoped to join them for the event, but his ship had not arrived in time for him to be present. The meeting was completely informal, but even twenty years after the loss of the great ship, the press had gotten wind of the small reunion and gathered to report the event in the next day's newspapers. Also on May 7, 1935, Karl Scherb, the man who purportedly first spotted the *Lusitania* from the *U-20* two decades before, lent weight to a "vigorous defense of the sinking of the *Lusitania*" in the Nazi press.[3]

There were rumors of some $4,000,000 in gold and silver bullion, as well as jewelry and specie, being locked within the tangled wreck of the liner; these rumors spurred interest in salvage operations. In late 1933 and early 1934, there were attempts to put together expeditions to find the wreck. It was not until 1935, however, that a team backed by the Tritonia Corporation actually got out to the area. A reconverted lighthouse vessel, the *Orphir*, set its nose into the waters of the Irish Channel, commanded by Captain Russell. It is easy to see why expectations were high that the expedition would find the ship in short order. An expert diver named Jim Jarrett was aboard, lending his assistance.[4] Additionally, three *Lusitania* survivors were involved, including Lieutenant Albert Bestic, who was serving as the Chief Officer of the *Orphir*. However, before the expedition got under way, Bestic alluded to the fact that since the ship's position had not been fully fixed when she was torpedoed, not to mention the fact that she had drifted for some minutes afterward, it might be a difficult task to find the site of the disaster. Even so, confidence was at a high level as the *Orphir* set out. Using sounding machines, they searched the seabed.

The first major return on the team's instruments raised high hopes, but turned out to be a sailing vessel. After a good deal of searching, the expedition had turned up nothing, and they began to confer with local fishermen in order to get a better idea of where the wreck might lie. Eventually, on October 6, toward the end of the season, they located a very large wreck, of the general dimensions of the *Lusitania*, approximately ten miles off the Old Head. Jarrett was sent to identify the wreck, and managed to get down to her. He reported the hull to be in good condition underneath a coating of slime. Due to the almost primeval state of the diving technology and underwater lighting he was using, Jarrett mistakenly reported that she was lying on her port side, not her starboard side. The press reported that there was still some question as to the wreck's identity. The expedition members felt confident that they had found the liner, however; on November 6, they held a memorial service over the site to commemorate the ship and those who had died when she sank. The team expected to return the next year, but did not. The ship that they had found was, indeed, the legendary liner; Jarrett had become the first person to stand on the *Lusitania* since she had sunk over twenty years before.

In point of fact no one visited the wreck again for a quarter-century. Then an American diver named John Light began a series of visits to the wreck, taking photographs and film footage of the lost liner as she appeared at the time. He became convinced that the ship's internal cargo had caused the second explosion, sending her to the bottom. It was this series of dives that really sparked another round of controversy over her loss, which will be discussed shortly. In 1982, yet another company did an expedition to the ship, recovering numerous items which were subsequently ill-cared for and poorly catalogued. Finally they were auctioned off to private collectors or disposed of entirely, rather than being placed in a museum exhibit available for the education and viewing pleasure of all.

In 1993, following his successes on the *Titanic* and the German World War Two battleship *Bismarck*, underwater explorer Dr. Robert Ballard set out to tackle the mysteries of the *Lusitania*. He was backed by the most powerful research equipment available, including R.O.V.s, divers, and a submersible; he also had at his disposal the knowledge base of widely respected maritime researchers and *Lusitania* specialists. Ballard and his team expected to find the liner in relatively good condition; they were horrified to discover her real state. Whereas the *Titanic* still retained a measure of her original beauty and the *Bismarck* still had the dignity of a warship, the wreck of the *Lusitania* had neither beauty nor dignity. Lying on her starboard side – not her port, as Jim Jarrett had reported – the ship retained only about half of her original breadth.[5] Her superstructure was mostly gone, slid away onto the seabed below; she was now a tangled mess only recognizable to those most familiar with her features. Her four proud smokestacks were gone, but the pipes which had been mounted on their fore and aft ends were still lined up neatly on the seabed just below their original locations – proof positive that the funnels did not fall off the ship on the surface as she sank. In addition to natural decay, the wreck was shrouded in fishing nets and littered with unexploded munitions, as her hull had been used in naval training exercises in the years since her sinking.

Ballard was able to accomplish much … reports of a gaping hole in the liner's side – which many suspected was caused by exploding cargo – were found to be wholly inaccurate. Ballard was even able to investigate the areas that would most likely have been damaged by exploding cargo, and found no evidence of such a blast. Although the theory that Ballard did propose as the cause of the second explosion, namely coal dust, has been demonstrated a near-impossibility, much was accomplished by this particular expedition.

In the years since the Ballard expedition, there have been many who have gone down to visit the *Lusitania*. Typically these have been free-divers, but they have returned with excellent photographs and footage of the wreck. A new docu-drama on the sinking of the *Lusitania* was released in the spring of 2007. While the show had some very nice high points and had a rather large budget, the portrayal fell into a number of well-known historical errors, including some long-debunked myths.

The following July, the wreck's owner, F. Gregg Bemis, led a well-equipped expedition to pay the liner a visit. Using sophisticated underwater exploration technology, including an R.O.V., the team documented the wreck and studied the rate of its deterioration. Bemis made it clear that one of the expedition's goals was to find evidence that secret high-explosives had caused the second explosion. No such evidence was found, but a number of the .303-caliber ammunition rounds the ship was carrying were found and retrieved. Naturally, it had been known for decades that the *Lusitania* had been carrying that ammunition, and portions of that cargo had been retrieved on previous expeditions. The press, however, reported the retrieval of these items as if it was some sort of revelation of new information. Although those familiar with the facts knew better, the unsuspecting could easily have been misinformed about the nature of how the salvaged ammunition fitted into the overall story of the lost liner. An hour-long documentary on the expedition was released in conjunction with The Discovery Channel.

While the ship's state is deteriorating quickly, there is yet hope that another expedition to the wreck can be undertaken in time to further document her remains, and make her current condition and her factual history more available to the public.

In April of 2008, Barbara Anderson McDermott – the next-to-last living survivor of the disaster, and the woman who so kindly penned the "Survivor's Note" for this book – passed away at the age of 95. The last-known survivor, Audrey Lawson-Johnston (*née* Pearl), was born on February 4, 1915, and was only three months old when the *Lusitania* went down. Sadly, she passed away on January 11, 2011, and with her loss the last voyage of that great ship has passed from living memory.

Even though a hundred years will have passed since the sinking when this volume reaches readers, the story of the *Lusitania* continues. Most likely inspired by the successes of the Light dives during the 1960s, from the 1970s onward there has come a new round of *Lusitania* conspiracy theories, which have renewed debate about the sinking to this day.

All of this controversy, political and otherwise, has tended, to a large extent, to crowd out the importance of the ship as the technological wonder that she was. For the most part the wonders of her career before the war, and the wonderful happy times that people enjoyed on her decks, were forgotten.

In those years between September 1907 and May 1915, the *Lusitania*'s breathtaking career had made her a household name, a ship of legendary splendor and speed, an old and reliable friend that was almost never missing from her scheduled stops at Pier 54 in New York and at the Landing Stage in Liverpool. When she sank, the victim of a war that ended the times into which she had been born, she left an irreplaceable gap in the minds and hearts of many. Eventually, after the war, Cunard purchased the German liner *Imperator* to replace the lost *Lusitania*. She was renamed the *Berengaria* and enjoyed a happy career through the "roaring twenties." One is forced to wonder, however, what the *Lusitania* could have done had she survived the war, converted to oil and matched back up with the *Mauretania* and *Aquitania* …

She was a stage upon which the end of the Gilded Age played out … passengers traveling upon her danced to the music of her band, gossiped about the latest social events, fell in love, honeymooned, made friends, and always kept a close eye on the latest ship's run posted in the main companionways; they willed her to go faster, hoping that she would beat out the

Mauretania and take the Blue Riband back as her own personal trophy. They braced themselves as the ship rolled and pitched in the frequently violent Atlantic weather; they watched in awe as the sea crashed over her Forecastle and Bridge, turning order into chaos; all the while, they fervently hoped that she really had been built to "Scotch-quality."

There were moments in that career that people would never forget. There was the beautiful scene in September of 1909, when the liner steamed into New York Harbor in the fading light of a late summer evening; her eight hundred Cabin passengers were celebrating the ship's record westbound passage and the fact that she had taken back the Blue Riband from the *Mauretania* for what would turn out to be the last time. Also not to be forgotten was the Christmas

Dinner in 1913 where Captain Dow sat down with his officers and engineers in the First Class Dining Saloon. They ate their turkey and plum pudding with a bottle of beer, ginger ale, or tot of grog, which had been magnanimously provided by Chief Steward Alison. No doubt, as they enjoyed each other's company in a rare "off-duty" moment, old "Fairweather" Dow took the opportunity to take out his pipe and begin telling one of his famous stories again. He no doubt used the pipe as a prop, thoroughly entertaining the officers that were under his command in his "racy Hibernian" style. Around the table sat a proud group of men; they took rightful satisfaction in the fact that they were privileged to serve on and operate one of the finest and most reliable ocean liners in the world: the mighty, vibrant and swift *Lusitania* ...

Both of the Lusitania's port-side propellers, and one of her starboard propellers, were recovered by salvage teams in 1982. Their method of detaching them from the wreck was simple: explosives. One of the propellers was melted down and turned into "commemorative" golf clubs. Another of them, however, is on display at the Merseyside Maritime Museum, not far from where the Lusitania tied up between each of her round-trip voyages. Each year a ceremony is held, commemorating her loss. A special exhibit and ceremonies were scheduled for the centennial anniversary of the disaster.

Appendix 1

Voyages & Crossings of the *Lusitania*

Voyage No.	Crossing No.	Date of Departure	Date of Arrival
1	1 West Liverpool–NY	Liverpool: Saturday, Sept. 7, 1907	**New York:** Friday, Sept. 13, 1907
	2 East NY–Liverpool	New York: Saturday, Sept. 21, 1907	**Queenstown:** Friday, Sept. 27, 1907 **Liverpool** Saturday, Sept. 28, 1907
2	3 West Liverpool–NY	Liverpool: Saturday, Oct. 5, 1907 **Queenstown:** Sunday, Oct. 6, 1907	**New York:** Friday, Oct. 11, 1907
	4 East NY–Liverpool	New York: Saturday, Oct. 19, 1907	**Queenstown:** Thursday, Oct. 24, 1907 **Liverpool:** Friday, Oct. 25, 1907
3	5 West Liverpool–NY	**Liverpool:** Saturday, Nov. 2, 1907 **Queenstown:** 11:30 a.m. Nov. 3	New York: Friday, Nov. 8, 1907
	6 East NY–Liverpool	New York: Saturday, Nov. 16, 1907	**Queenstown:** Friday, Nov. 21, 1907 **Liverpool:** Thursday, Nov. 22, 1907
4	7 West Liverpool–NY	**Liverpool:** Saturday, Nov. 30, 1907 / Sunday, Dec. 1, 1907 **Queenstown:** Monday, Dec. 2, 1907	**New York:** Sunday, Dec. 8, 1907
	8 East NY–Liverpool	New York: Saturday, Dec. 14, 1907	**Queenstown:** Friday, Dec. 20, 1907 **Liverpool:** Friday, Dec. 20, 1907
5	9 West Liverpool–NY	**Liverpool:** Saturday, Dec. 28, 1907 **Queenstown:** Sunday, Dec. 29, 1907	**New York:** Friday, Jan. 3, 1908
	10 East NY–Liverpool	New York: Saturday, Jan. 11, 1908	**Queenstown:** Thursday, Jan. 16, 1908 **Liverpool:** Friday, Jan. 17, 1908
6	11 West Liverpool–NY	**Liverpool:** Saturday, Jan. 25, 1908 **Queenstown:** Sunday, Jan. 26, 1908	**New York:** Saturday, Feb. 1, 1908

Voyage No.	Crossing No.	Date of Departure	Date of Arrival
	12 East NY–Liverpool	**New York:** Saturday, Feb. 8, 1908	**Queenstown:** Friday, Feb. 14, 1908 **Liverpool:** Friday, Feb. 14, 1908
7	13 West Liverpool–NY	**Liverpool:** Saturday, March 7, 1908 **Queenstown:** Sunday, March 8, 1908	**New York:** Friday, March 13, 1908
	14 East NY–Liverpool	**New York:** Saturday, March 21, 1908	**Queenstown:** Thursday, March 26, 1908 **Liverpool:** Friday, March 27, 1908
8	15 West Liverpool–NY	**Liverpool:** Saturday, April 4, 1908 **Queenstown:** Sunday, April 5, 1908	**New York:** Friday, April 10, 1908
	16 East NY–Liverpool	**New York:** Wednesday, April 15, 1908	**Queenstown:** Tuesday, April 21, 1908 **Liverpool:** Tuesday, April 21, 1908
9	17 West Liverpool–NY	**Liverpool:** Saturday, April 25, 1908 **Queenstown:** Sunday, April 26, 1908	**New York:** Friday, May 1, 1908
	18 East NY–Liverpool	**New York:** Wednesday, May 6, 1908	**Queenstown:** Tuesday, May 12, 1908 **Liverpool:** Tues, May 12, 1908
10	19 West Liverpool–NY	**Liverpool:** Sunday, May 16, 1908 **Queenstown:** Monday, May 17, 1908	**New York:** Friday, May 22, 1908
	20 East NY–Liverpool	**New York:** Wednesday, May 27, 1908	**Queenstown:** Tuesday, June 2, 1908 **Liverpool:** Late Tuesday, June 3, 1908
11	21 West Liverpool–NY	**Liverpool:** Saturday, June 6, 1908 **Queenstown:** Sunday, June 7, 1908	**New York:** Friday, June 12, 1908
	22 East NY–Liverpool	**New York:** Wednesday, June 17, 1908	**Queenstown:** Tuesday, June 23, 1908 **Liverpool:** Tuesday, June 23, 1908
12	23 West Liverpool–NY	**Liverpool:** Saturday, July 4, 1908 **Queenstown:** Sunday, July 5, 1908	**New York:** Friday, July 10, 1908
	24 East NY–Liverpool	**New York:** Wednesday, July 15, 1908	**Queenstown:** Monday, July 20, 1908 **Liverpool:** Tuesday, July 21, 1908

Voyage No.	Crossing No.	Date of Departure	Date of Arrival
13	25 West Liverpool–NY	**Liverpool:** Saturday, July 25, 1908 **Queenstown:** Sunday, July 26, 1908	**New York:** Friday, July 31, 1908
	26 East NY–Liverpool	**New York:** Wednesday, Aug. 5, 1908	**Queenstown:** Monday, Aug. 10, 1908 **Liverpool:** Tuesday, Aug. 11, 1908
14	27 West Liverpool–NY	**Liverpool:** Saturday, Aug. 15, 1908 **Queenstown:** Sunday, Aug. 16, 1908	**New York:** Thursday, Aug. 20, 1908
	28 East NY–Liverpool	**New York:** Wednesday, Aug. 26, 1908	**Queenstown:** Monday, Aug. 31, 1908 **Liverpool:** Tuesday, Sept. 1, 1908
15	29 West Liverpool–NY	**Liverpool:** Saturday, Sept. 5, 1908 **Queenstown:** Sunday, Sept. 6, 1908	**New York:** Friday, Sept. 11, 1908
	30 East NY–Liverpool	**New York:** Wednesday, Sept. 16, 1908	**Queenstown:** Tuesday, Sept. 22, 1908 **Liverpool:** Tuesday, Sept. 22, 1908
16	31 West Liverpool–NY	**Liverpool:** Saturday, Oct. 3, 1908 **Queenstown:** Sunday, Oct. 4, 1908	**New York:** Friday, Oct. 9, 1908
	32 East NY–Liverpool	**New York:** Wednesday, Oct. 14, 1908	**Queenstown:** Monday, Oct. 19, 1908 **Liverpool:** Tuesday, Oct. 20, 1908
17	33 West Liverpool–NY	**Liverpool:** Saturday, Oct. 24, 1908 **Queenstown:** Sun, Oct. 25, 1908	**New York:** Friday, Oct. 30, 1908
	34 East NY–Liverpool	**New York:** Wednesday, Nov. 4, 1908	**Queenstown:** Monday, Nov. 9, 1908 **Liverpool:** Wednesday, Nov. 10, 1908
18	35 West Liverpool–NY	**Liverpool:** Saturday, Nov. 14, 1908 **Queenstown:** Sunday, Nov. 15, 1908	**New York:** Friday, Nov. 20, 1908
	36 East NY–Liverpool	**New York:** Wednesday, Nov. 25, 1908	**Queenstown:** Tuesday, Dec. 1, 1908 **Liverpool:** Thursday, Dec. 3, 1908
19	37 West Liverpool–NY	**Liverpool:** Saturday, Dec. 5, 1908 **Queenstown:** Sunday, Dec. 6, 1908	**New York:** Friday, Dec. 11, 1908

Voyage No.	Crossing No.	Date of Departure	Date of Arrival
	38 East NY–Liverpool	**New York:** Wednesday, Dec. 16, 1908	**Queenstown:** Monday, Dec. 21, 1908 **Liverpool:** Tuesday, Dec. 22, 1908
20	39 West Liverpool–NY	**Liverpool:** Saturday, Dec. 26, 1908 **Queenstown:** Sunday, Dec. 27, 1908	**New York:** Saturday, Jan. 2, 1909
	40 East NY–Liverpool	**New York:** Wednesday, Jan. 6, 1909	**Queenstown:** Monday, Jan. 11, 1909 **Liverpool:** Tuesday, Jan. 12, 1909
21	41 West Liverpool–NY	**Liverpool:** Sunday, Feb. 7, 1909 **Queenstown:** Monday, Feb. 8, 1909	**New York:** Sunday, Feb. 14, 1909
	42 East NY–Liverpool	**New York:** Wednesday, Feb. 17, 1909	**Queenstown:** Monday, Feb. 22, 1909 **Liverpool:** Tuesday, Feb. 23, 1909
22	43 West Liverpool–NY	**Liverpool:** Saturday, Feb. 27, 1909 **Queenstown:** Sunday, Feb. 28, 1909	**New York:** Friday, March 6, 1909
	44 East NY–Liverpool	**New York:** Wednesday, March 10, 1909	**Queenstown:** Monday, March 15, 1909 **Liverpool:** Tuesday, March 16, 1909
23	45 West Liverpool–NY	**Liverpool:** Saturday, March 20, 1909 **Queenstown:** Sunday, March 21, 1909	**New York:** Friday, March 26, 1909
	46 East NY–Liverpool	**New York:** Wednesday, March 31, 1909	Queenstown: Tuesday, April 6, 1909 **Liverpool:** Wednesday, April 7, 1909
24	47 West Liverpool–NY	**Liverpool:** Saturday, April 17, 1909 **Queenstown:** Sunday, April 18, 1909	**New York:** Friday, April 23, 1909
	48 East NY–Liverpool	**New York:** Wednesday, April 28, 1909	**Queenstown:** Monday, May 3, 1909 **Liverpool:** Tuesday, May 4, 1909
25	49 West Liverpool–NY	**Liverpool:** Saturday, May 8, 1909 **Queenstown:** Sunday, May 9, 1909	**New York:** Friday, May 14, 1909
	50 East NY–Liverpool	**New York:** Wednesday, May 19, 1909	**Queenstown:** Monday, May 24, 1909 **Liverpool:** Tuesday, May 25, 1909

Voyage No.	Crossing No.	Date of Departure	Date of Arrival
26	51 West Liverpool–NY	**Liverpool:** Sunday, May 30, 1909 **Queenstown:** Monday, May 31, 1909	**New York:** Friday, June 4, 1909
	52 East NY–Liverpool	**New York:** Wednesday, June 9, 1909	**Queenstown:** Monday, June 14, 1909 **Liverpool:** Tuesday, June 15, 1909
27	53 West Liverpool–NY	**Liverpool:** Saturday, June 19, 1909 **Queenstown:** Sunday, June 20, 1909	**New York:** Friday, June 25, 1909
	54 East NY–Liverpool	**New York:** Wednesday, June 30, 1909	**Queenstown:** Monday, July 5, 1909 **Liverpool:** Tuesday, July 6, 1909
28	55 West Liverpool–NY	**Liverpool:** Saturday, July 17, 1909 **Queenstown:** Sunday, July 18, 1909	**New York:** Friday, July 23, 1909
	56 East NY–Liverpool	**New York:** Wednesday, July 28, 1909	**Queenstown:** Monday, Aug. 2, 1909 **Liverpool:** Monday, Aug. 2, 1909
29	57 West Liverpool–NY	**Liverpool:** Saturday, Aug. 7, 1909 **Queenstown:** Sunday, Aug. 8, 1909	**New York:** Friday, Aug. 13, 1909
	58 East NY–Liverpool	**New York:** Wednesday, Aug. 18, 1909	**Queenstown:** Monday, Aug. 23, 1909 **Liverpool:** Tuesday, Aug. 24, 1909
30	59 West Liverpool–NY	**Liverpool:** Saturday, Aug. 28, 1909 **Queenstown:** Sunday, Aug. 29, 1909	**New York:** Thursday, Sept. 2, 1909
	60 East NY–Liverpool	**New York:** Wednesday, Sept. 8, 1909	**Queenstown:** Monday, Sept. 13, 1909 **Liverpool:** Monday, Sept. 13, 1909
31	61 West Liverpool–NY	**Liverpool:** Saturday, Sept. 18, 1909 **Queenstown:** Sunday, Sept. 19, 1909	**New York:** Friday, Sept. 24, 1909
	62 East NY–Liverpool	**New York:** Wednesday, Sept. 29, 1909	**Fishguard, Wales:** Monday, Oct. 4, 1909 **Liverpool:** Tuesday, Oct. 5, 1909
32	63 West Liverpool–NY	**Liverpool:** Saturday, Oct. 16, 1909 **Queenstown:** Sunday, Oct. 17, 1909	**New York:** Thursday, Oct. 21, 1909

Voyage No.	Crossing No.	Date of Departure	Date of Arrival
	64 East NY–Liverpool	**New York:** Wednesday, Oct. 27, 1909	**Queenstown:** Monday, Nov. 1, 1909 **Liverpool:** Tuesday, Nov. 2, 1909
33	65 West Liverpool–NY	**Liverpool:** Saturday, Nov. 6, 1909 Queenstown: Sunday, Nov. 7, 1909	**New York:** Thursday, Nov. 11, 1909
	66 East NY–Liverpool	**New York:** Wednesday, Nov. 17, 1909	**Queenstown:** Monday, Nov. 22, 1909 **Liverpool:** Tuesday, Nov. 23, 1909
34	67 West Liverpool–NY	**Liverpool:** Saturday, Nov. 27, 1909 **Queenstown:** Sunday, Nov. 28, 1909	**New York:** Friday, Dec. 3, 1909
	68 East NY–Liverpool	**New York:** Wednesday, Dec. 8, 1909	Fishguard: Monday, Dec. 13, 1909 **Liverpool:** Tuesday, Dec. 14, 1909
35	69 West Liverpool–NY	**Liverpool:** Saturday, Dec. 18, 1909 **Queenstown:** Sunday, Dec. 19, 1909	**New York:** Friday, Dec. 24, 1909
	70 East NY–Liverpool	**New York:** Wednesday, Dec. 29, 1909	**Fishguard:** Tuesday, Jan. 4, 1910 **Liverpool:** Wednesday, Jan. 5, 1910
36	71 West Liverpool–NY	**Liverpool:** Saturday, Jan. 8, 1910 **Queenstown:** Sunday, Jan. 9, 1910	**New York:** Saturday, Jan. 14, 1910
	72 East NY–Liverpool	**New York:** Wednesday, Jan. 20, 1910	**Queenstown:** Monday, Jan. 25, 1910 **Liverpool:** Tuesday, Jan. 26, 1910
37	73 West Liverpool–NY	**Liverpool:** Saturday, Feb. 26, 1910 **Queenstown:** Sunday, Feb. 27, 1910	**New York:** Friday, March 4, 1910
	74 East NY–Liverpool	**New York:** Wednesday, March 9, 1910	**Fishguard:** Monday, March 14, 1910 **Liverpool:** Tuesday, March 15, 1910
38	75 West Liverpool–NY	Liverpool Saturday, March 19, 1910 Queenstown Sunday, March 20, 1910	**New York:** Friday, March 25, 1910
	76 East NY–Liverpool	**New York:** Wednesday, March 30, 1910	Fishguard: Monday, April 5, 1910 **Liverpool:** Tuesday, April 5, 1910

Voyage No.	Crossing No.	Date of Departure	Date of Arrival
39	77 West Liverpool–NY	Liverpool: Saturday, April 9, 1910 Queenstown: Sunday, April 10, 1910	New York: Friday, April 15, 1910
	78 East NY–Liverpool	New York: Wednesday, April 10, 1910	Fishguard: Monday, April 25, 1910 Liverpool: Tuesday April 26, 1910
40	79 West Liverpool–NY	Liverpool: Saturday, May 7, 1910 Queenstown: Sunday, May 8, 1910	New York: Thursday, May 12, 1910
	80 East NY–Liverpool	New York: Wednesday, May 18, 1910	Fishguard: Monday, May 23, 1910 Liverpool: Tuesday, May 24, 1910
41	81 West Liverpool–NY	Liverpool: Saturday, May 28, 1910 Queenstown: Sunday, May 29, 1910	New York: Thursday, June 2, 1910
	82 East NY–Liverpool	New York: Wednesday, June 8, 1910	Fishguard: Monday, June 13, 1910 Liverpool: Tuesday, June 14, 1910
42	83 West Liverpool–NY	Liverpool: Saturday, June 18, 1910 Queenstown: Sunday, June 19, 1910	New York: Thursday, June 23, 1910
	84 East NY–Liverpool	New York: Wednesday, June 29, 1910	Fishguard: Monday, July 4, 1910 Liverpool: Tuesday, July 5, 1910
43	85 West Liverpool–NY	Liverpool: Saturday, July 9, 1910 Queenstown: Sunday, July 10, 1910	New York: Thursday, July 14, 1910
	86 East NY–Liverpool	New York: Wednesday, July 20, 1910	Fishguard: Monday, July 25, 1910 Liverpool: Tuesday, July 26, 1910
44	87 West Liverpool–NY	Liverpool: Saturday, Aug. 6, 1910 Queenstown: Sunday, Aug. 7, 1910	New York: Thursday, Aug. 11, 1910
	88 East NY–Liverpool	New York: Wednesday, Aug. 17, 1910	Fishguard: Monday, August 22, 1910 Liverpool: Tuesday, August 23, 1910
45	89 West Liverpool–NY	Liverpool: Saturday, Aug. 27, 1910 Queenstown: Sunday, Aug. 28, 1910	New York: Thursday, Sept. 1, 1910

Voyage No.	Crossing No.	Date of Departure	Date of Arrival
	90 East NY–Liverpool	**New York:** Wednesday, Sept. 7, 1910	**Fishguard:** Monday, Sept. 12, 1910 **Liverpool:** Tuesday, Sept. 13, 1910
46	91 West Liverpool–NY	**Liverpool:** Saturday, Sept. 17, 1910 **Queenstown:** Sunday, Sept. 18, 1910	**New York:** Thursday, Sept. 22, 1910
	92 East NY–Liverpool	**New York:** Wednesday, Sept. 28, 1910	**Fishguard:** Monday, Oct. 3, 1910 **Liverpool:** Tuesday, Oct. 4, 1910
47	93 West Liverpool–NY	**Liverpool:** Saturday, Oct. 8, 1910 **Queenstown:** Sunday, Oct. 9, 1910	**New York:** Thursday, Oct. 13, 1910
	94 East NY–Liverpool	**New York:** Wednesday, Oct. 19, 1910	**Fishguard:** Monday, Oct. 24, 1910 **Liverpool:** Tuesday, Oct. 25, 1910
48	95 West Liverpool–NY	**Liverpool:** Saturday, Nov. 5, 1910 **Queenstown:** Sunday, Nov. 6, 1910	**New York:** Thursday, Nov. 10, 1910
	96 East NY–Liverpool	**New York:** Wednesday, Nov. 16, 1910	**Fishguard:** Monday, Nov. 21, 1910 **Liverpool:** Tuesday, Nov. 22, 1910
49	97 West Liverpool–NY	**Liverpool:** Saturday, Dec. 17, 1910 **Queenstown:** Sunday, Dec. 18, 1910	**New York:** Friday, Dec. 23, 1910
	98 East NY–Liverpool	**New York:** Wednesday, Dec. 28, 1910	**Fishguard:** Monday, Jan. 2, 1911 **Liverpool:** Tuesday, Jan. 3, 1911
50	99 West Liverpool–NY	**Liverpool:** Saturday, Jan. 7, 1911 **Queenstown:** Sunday, Jan. 8, 1911	**New York:** Thursday, Jan. 12, 1911
	100 East NY–Liverpool	**New York:** Wednesday, Jan. 18, 1911	**Fishguard:** Monday, Jan. 23, 1911 **Liverpool:** Monday, Jan. 23, 1911
51	101 West Liverpool–NY	**Liverpool:** Saturday, Jan. 28, 1911 **Queenstown:** Sunday Jan. 29, 1911	**New York:** Friday, Feb. 3, 1911
	102 East NY–Liverpool	**New York:** Wednesday, Feb. 8, 1911	**Fishguard:** Monday, Feb. 13, 1911 **Liverpool:** Tuesday, Feb. 14, 1911

Voyage No.	Crossing No.	Date of Departure	Date of Arrival
52	103 West Liverpool–NY	Liverpool: Saturday, Feb. 18, 1911 Queenstown: Sunday, Feb. 19, 1911	New York: Friday, Feb. 24, 1911
	104 East NY–Liverpool	New York: Wednesday, March 1, 1911	Fishguard: Monday, March 6, 1911 Liverpool: Thursday, March 7, 1911
53	105 West Liverpool–NY	Liverpool: Saturday, March 11, 1911 Queenstown: Sunday March 12, 1911	New York: Thursday, March 16, 1911
	106 East NY–Liverpool	New York: Wednesday, March 22, 1911	Fishguard: Monday, March 27, 1911 Liverpool: Tuesday, March 28, 1911
54	107 West Liverpool–NY	Liverpool: Saturday, April 8, 1911 Queenstown: Sunday, April 9, 1911	New York: Thursday, April 15, 1911
	108 East NY–Liverpool	New York: Wednesday, April 19, 1911	Fishguard: Monday, April 24, 1911 Liverpool: Tuesday, April 25, 1911
55	109 West Liverpool–NY	Liverpool: Saturday, April 29, 1911 Queenstown: Sunday, April 30, 1911	New York: Thursday, May 4, 1911
	110 East NY–Liverpool	New York: Wednesday, May 10, 1911	Fishguard: Monday, May 15, 1911 Liverpool: Tuesday, May 16, 1911
56	111 West Liverpool–NY	Liverpool: Saturday, May 20, 1911 Queenstown: Sunday, May 21, 1911	New York: Thursday, May 25, 1911
	112 East NY–Liverpool	New York: Wednesday, May 31, 1911	Fishguard: Monday, June 5, 1911 Liverpool: Tuesday, June 6, 1911
57	113 West Liverpool–NY	Liverpool: Saturday, June 10, 1911 Queenstown: Sunday, June 11, 1911	New York: Thursday, June 15, 1911
	114 East NY–Liverpool	New York: Wednesday, June 21, 1911	Fishguard: Monday, June 26, 1911 Liverpool: Tuesday, June 27, 1911
58	115 West Liverpool–NY	Liverpool: Saturday, July 8, 1911 Queenstown: Sunday, July 9, 1911	New York: Thursday, July 13, 1911

Voyage No.	Crossing No.	Date of Departure	Date of Arrival
	116 East NY–Liverpool	**New York:** Wednesday, July 19, 1911	**Fishguard:** Monday, July 24, 1911 **Liverpool:** Tuesday, July 25, 1911
59	117 West Liverpool–NY	**Liverpool:** Saturday, July 29, 1911 **Queenstown:** Sunday, July 30, 1911	**New York:** Thursday, Aug. 3, 1911
	118 East NY–Liverpool	**New York:** Wednesday, Aug. 9, 1911	**Fishguard:** Monday, Aug. 14, 1911 **Liverpool:** Tuesday, Aug. 15, 1911
60	119 West Liverpool–NY	**Liverpool:** Monday, August 28, 1911 **Queenstown:** Monday, August 28, 1911	**New York:** Saturday, Sept. 2, 1911
	120 East NY–Liverpool	**New York:** Sunday, Sept. 3, 1911	**Fishguard:** CANCELLED **Liverpool:** Saturday, Sept. 9, 1911
61	121 West Liverpool–NY	**Liverpool:** Monday, Sept. 11, 1911 **Queenstown:** Tuesday, Sept. 12, 1911	**New York:** Saturday, Sept. 17, 1911
	122 East NY–Liverpool	**New York:** Wednesday, Sept. 20, 1911	**Fishguard:** Monday, Sept. 25, 1911 **Liverpool:** Tuesday, Sept. 26, 1911
62	123 West Liverpool–NY	**Liverpool:** Saturday, Oct. 7, 1911 **Queenstown:** Sunday, Oct. 8, 1911	**New York:** Thursday, Oct. 12, 1911
	124 East NY–Liverpool	**New York:** Wednesday, Oct. 18, 1911	**Fishguard:** Monday, Oct. 23, 1911 **Liverpool:** Tuesday, Oct. 24, 1911
63	125 West Liverpool–NY	**Liverpool:** Saturday, Oct. 28, 1911 **Queenstown:** Sunday, Oct. 29, 1911	**New York:** Friday, Nov. 2, 1911
	126 East NY–Liverpool	**New York:** Wednesday, Nov. 8, 1911	**Fishguard:** Monday, Nov. 13, 1911 **Liverpool:** Tuesday, Nov 14, 1911
64	127 West Liverpool–NY	**Liverpool:** Saturday, Nov. 18, 1911 **Queenstown:** Sunday, Nov. 19, 1911	**New York:** Friday, Nov. 24, 1911
	128 East NY–Liverpool	**New York:** Wednesday, Nov. 29, 1911	**Fishguard:** Monday, Dec. 4, 1911 **Liverpool:** Tuesday, Dec. 5, 1911

Voyage No.	Crossing No.	Date of Departure	Date of Arrival
65	129 West Liverpool–NY	**Liverpool:** Saturday, Dec. 8, 1911 **Queenstown:** Sunday, Dec. 9, 1911	**New York:** Friday, Dec. 15, 1911
	130 East NY–Liverpool	**New York:** Saturday, Dec. 16, 1911	**Fishguard:** Friday, Dec. 22, 1911 **Liverpool:** Saturday, Dec. 23, 1911
66	131 West Liverpool–NY	**Liverpool:** Saturday, Dec. 30, 1911 **Queenstown:** Sunday, Dec. 31, 1911	**New York:** Friday, Dec. 5, 1911
	132 East NY–Liverpool	**New York:** Wednesday, Jan. 10, 1912	**Fishguard:** Monday, Jan. 15, 1912 **Liverpool:** Tuesday, Jan. 16, 1912
67	133 West Liverpool–NY	**Liverpool:** Saturday, Feb. 17, 1912 **Queenstown:** Sunday, Feb. 18, 1912	**New York:** Saturday, Feb. 24, 1912
	134 East NY–Liverpool	**New York:** Wednesday, Feb. 28, 1912	**Fishguard:** Monday, March 4, 1912 **Liverpool:** Tuesday, March 5, 1912
68	135 West Liverpool–NY	**Liverpool:** Saturday, March 9, 1912 **Queenstown:** Sunday, March 10, 1912	**New York:** Friday, March 15, 1912
	136 East NY–Liverpool	**New York:** Wednesday, March 20, 1912	**Fishguard:** Tuesday, March 26, 1912 **Liverpool:** Tuesday, March 26, 1912
69	137 West Liverpool–NY	**Liverpool:** Saturday, April 27, 1912 **Queenstown:** Sunday, April 28, 1912	**New York:** Friday, May 3, 1912
	138 East NY–Liverpool	**New York:** Wednesday, May 8, 1912	**Fishguard:** Monday, May 13, 1912 **Liverpool:** Tuesday, May 14, 1912
70	139 West Liverpool–NY	**Liverpool:** Saturday, May 18, 1912 **Queenstown:** Sunday, May 19, 1912	**New York:** Friday, May 24, 1912
	140 East NY–Liverpool	**New York:** Wednesday, May 29, 1912	**Fishguard:** Monday, June 3, 1912 **Liverpool:** Tuesday, June 4, 1912
71	141 West Liverpool–NY	**Liverpool:** Saturday, June 8, 1912 **Queenstown:** Sunday, June 9, 1912	**New York:** Saturday, June 15, 1912

Voyage No.	Crossing No.	Date of Departure	Date of Arrival
	142 East NY–Liverpool	**New York:** Wednesday, June 19, 1912	**Fishguard:** Monday, June 24, 1912 **Liverpool:** Tuesday, June 25, 1912
72	143 West Liverpool–NY	**Liverpool:** Saturday, July 6, 1912 **Queenstown:** Sunday, July 7, 1912	**New York:** Friday, July 12, 1912
	144 East NY–Liverpool	**New York:** Tuesday, July 16, 1912	**Fishguard:** Monday, July 22, 1912 **Liverpool:** Tuesday, July 23, 1912
73	145 West Liverpool–NY	**Liverpool:** Saturday, July 27, 1912 **Queenstown:** Sunday, July 28, 1912	**New York:** Saturday, Aug. 3, 1912
	146 East NY–Liverpool	**New York:** Wednesday, Aug. 7, 1912	**Fishguard:** Tuesday, Aug. 13, 1912 **Liverpool:** Tuesday, Aug. 13, 1912
74	147 West Liverpool–NY	**Liverpool:** Saturday, Aug. 17, 1912 **Queenstown:** Sunday, Aug. 18, 1912	**New York:** Friday, Aug. 23, 1912
	148 East NY–Liverpool	**New York:** Wednesday, Aug. 28, 1912	**Fishguard:** Monday, Sept. 2, 1912 **Liverpool:** Tuesday, Sept. 3, 1912
75	149 West Liverpool–NY	**Liverpool:** Saturday, Sept. 7, 1912 **Queenstown:** Sunday, Sept. 8, 1912	**New York:** Friday, Sept. 13, 1912
	150 East NY–Liverpool	**New York:** Wednesday, Sept. 18, 1912	**Fishguard:** Monday, Sept. 23, 1912 **Liverpool:** Tuesday, Sept. 24, 1912
76	151 West Liverpool–NY	**Liverpool:** Friday, Sept. 27, 1912 **Queenstown:** Saturday, Sept. 28, 1912	**New York:** Friday, Oct. 4, 1912
	152 East NY–Liverpool	**New York:** Wednesday, Oct. 9, 1912	**Fishguard:** Monday, Oct. 14, 1912 **Liverpool:** Tuesday, Oct. 15, 1912
77	153 West Liverpool–NY	**Liverpool:** Friday, Dec. 13, 1912 **Queenstown:** Sunday, Dec. 15, 1912	**New York:** Saturday, Dec. 21, 1912
	154 East NY–Liverpool	**New York:** Tuesday, Dec. 24, 1912	**Fishguard:** Monday, Dec. 30, 1912 **Liverpool:** Tuesday, Dec. 31, 1912

Voyage No.	Crossing No.	Date of Departure	Date of Arrival
78	155 West Liverpool–NY	**Liverpool:** Saturday, Aug. 23, 1913 **Queenstown:** Sunday, Aug. 24, 1913	**New York:** Saturday, Aug. 30, 1913
	156 East NY–Liverpool	**New York:** Wednesday, Sept. 3, 1913	**Fishguard:** Monday, Sept. 8, 1913 **Liverpool:** Tuesday, Sept. 9, 1913
79	157 West Liverpool–NY	**Liverpool:** Saturday, Sept. 13, 1913 **Queenstown:** Sunday, Sept. 14, 1913	**New York:** Thursday, Sept. 18, 1913
	158 East NY–Liverpool	**New York:** Wednesday, Sept. 24, 1913	**Fishguard:** Monday, Sept. 29, 1913 **Liverpool:** Monday, Sept. 29, 1913
80	159 West Liverpool–NY	**Liverpool:** Saturday, Oct. 4, 1913 **Queenstown:** Sunday, Oct. 5, 1913	**New York:** Friday, Oct. 10, 1913
	160 East NY–Liverpool	**New York:** Wednesday, Oct. 15, 1913	**Fishguard:** Tuesday, Oct. 21, 1913 **Liverpool:** Wednesday, Oct. 22, 1913
81	161 West Liverpool–NY	**Liverpool:** Saturday, Oct. 25, 1913 **Queenstown:** Sunday, Oct. 26, 1913	**New York:** Friday, Oct. 31, 1913
	162 East NY–Liverpool	**New York:** Wednesday, Nov. 5, 1913	**Fishguard:** Monday, Nov. 10, 1913 **Liverpool:** Tuesday, Nov. 11, 1913
82	163 West Liverpool–NY	**Liverpool:** Saturday, Nov. 22, 1913 **Queenstown:** Passed (Did Not Call) Monday, Nov. 24, 1913	**New York:** Friday, Nov. 28, 1913
	164 East NY–Liverpool	**New York:** Wednesday, Dec. 3, 1913	**Fishguard:** Monday, Dec. 8, 1913 **Liverpool:** Tuesday, Dec. 9, 1913
83	165 West Liverpool–NY	**Liverpool:** Saturday, Dec. 13, 1913 **Queenstown:** Sunday, Dec. 14, 1913	**New York:** Friday, Dec. 19, 1913
	166 East NY–Liverpool	**New York:** Wednesday, Dec. 24, 1913	**Fishguard:** Monday, Dec. 29, 1913 **Liverpool:** Tuesday, Dec. 30, 1913
84	167 West Liverpool–NY	**Liverpool:** Saturday, Jan. 3, 1914 **Queenstown:** Sunday, Jan. 4, 1914	**New York:** Friday, Jan. 9, 1914

Voyage No.	Crossing No.	Date of Departure	Date of Arrival
	168 East NY–Liverpool	**New York:** Wednesday, Jan. 15, 1914	**Fishguard:** Monday, Jan. 19, 1914 **Liverpool:** Tuesday, Jan. 20, 1914
85	169 West Liverpool–NY	**Liverpool:** Saturday, Jan. 31, 1914 **Queenstown:** Sunday, Feb. 1, 1914 CANCELLED	**New York:** Friday, Feb. 6, 1914
	170 East NY–Liverpool	**New York:** Wednesday, Feb. 11, 1914	**Fishguard:** Monday, Feb. 16, 1914 **Liverpool:** Tuesday, Feb. 17, 1914
86	171 West Liverpool–NY	**Liverpool:** Saturday, Feb. 28, 1914	**New York:** Friday, March 6, 1914
	172 East NY–Liverpool	**New York:** Tuesday, March 10, 1914	**Fishguard:** Monday, Mar. 16, 1914 **Liverpool:** Monday, Mar. 16, 1914
87	173 West Liverpool–NY	**Liverpool:** Saturday, March 21, 1914	**New York:** Friday, March 27, 1914
	174 East NY–Liverpool	**New York:** Tuesday, March 31, 1914	**Fishguard:** Monday, April 6, 1914 **Liverpool:** Monday, April 6, 1914
88	175 West Liverpool–NY	**Liverpool:** Saturday, April 11, 1914	**New York:** Friday, April 17, 1914
	176 East NY–Liverpool	**New York:** Tuesday, April 21, 1914	**Fishguard:** Monday, April 27, 1914 **Liverpool:** Monday, April 27, 1914
89	177 West Liverpool–NY	**Liverpool:** Saturday, May 9, 1914	**New York:** Friday, May 15, 1914
	178 East NY–Liverpool	**New York:** Tuesday, May 19, 1914	**Fishguard:** Monday, May 25, 1914 **Liverpool:** Monday, May 25, 1914
90	179 West Liverpool–NY	**Liverpool:** Saturday, June 13, 1914	**New York:** Friday, June 19, 1914
	180 East NY–Liverpool	**New York:** Tuesday, June 23, 1914	**Fishguard:** Tuesday, June 30, 1914 **Liverpool:** Tuesday, June 30, 1914
91	181 West Liverpool–NY	**Liverpool:** Saturday, July 4, 1914	**New York:** Friday, July 10, 1914

Voyage No.	Crossing No.	Date of Departure	Date of Arrival
	182 East NY–Liverpool	New York: Tuesday, July 14, 1914	Fishguard: Monday, July 20, 1914 Liverpool: Monday, July 20, 1914
92	183 West Liverpool–NY	**Liverpool:** Saturday, July 25, 1914	**New York:** Friday, July 31, 1914
	184 East NY–Liverpool	**New York:** Tuesday, Aug. 4, 1914	**Liverpool:** Tuesday, Aug. 11, 1914
93	185 West Liverpool–NY	**Liverpool:** Saturday, Sept. 12, 1914	**New York:** Thursday, Sept. 17, 1914
	186 East NY–Liverpool	**New York:** Wednesday, Sept. 23, 1914	**Liverpool:** Tuesday, Sept. 29, 1914
94	187 West Liverpool–NY	**Liverpool:** Saturday, Oct. 3, 1914	**New York:** Friday, Oct. 9, 1914
	188 East NY–Liverpool	**New York:** Wednesday, Oct. 14, 1914	**Liverpool:** Monday, Oct. 19, 1914
95	189 West Liverpool–NY	**Liverpool:** Saturday, Oct. 24, 1914	**New York:** Saturday, Oct. 31, 1914
	190 East NY–Liverpool	**New York:** Wednesday, Nov. 4, 1914	**Liverpool:** Tuesday, Nov. 10, 1914
96	191 West Liverpool–NY	**Liverpool:** Saturday, Nov. 21, 1914	**New York:** Friday, Nov. 27, 1914
	192 East NY–Liverpool	**New York:** Saturday, Dec. 5, 1914	**Liverpool:** Friday, Dec. 11, 1914
97	193 West Liverpool–NY	**Liverpool:** Wednesday, Dec. 16, 1914	**New York:** Wednesday, Dec. 23, 1914
	194 East NY–Liverpool	**New York:** Wednesday, Dec. 30, 1914	**Liverpool:** Tuesday, Jan. 5, 1915
98	195 West Liverpool–NY	**Liverpool:** Saturday, Jan. 16, 1915	**New York:** Saturday, Jan. 23, 1915
	196 East NY–Liverpool	**New York:** Saturday, Jan. 30, 1915	**Liverpool:** Saturday, Feb. 6, 1915
99	197 West Liverpool–NY	**Liverpool:** Saturday, Feb. 13, 1915	**New York:** Saturday, Feb. 20, 1915
	198 East NY–Liverpool	**New York:** Saturday, Feb. 27, 1915	**Liverpool:** Saturday, March 6, 1915
100	199 West Liverpool–NY	**Liverpool:** Saturday, March 20, 1915	**New York:** Saturday, March 27, 1915
	200 East NY–Liverpool	**New York:** Saturday, April 3, 1915	**Liverpool:** Saturday, April 10, 1915
101	201 West Liverpool–NY	**Liverpool:** Saturday, April 17, 1915	**New York:** Saturday, April 24, 1915
	202 East NY–Liverpool	**New York:** Saturday, May 1, 1915	Sunk, Friday, May 7, 1915

Note: No list of this nature has ever before been compiled and published. Because of its groundbreaking nature, there may be some incidental errors or omissions. For corrections, please contact the author via his website: http://www.atlanticliners.com.

Appendix 2
Masters of the *Lusitania*

Master	Date took Command	Date left Command	Voyages	Crossings	Length of Tenure
James B. Watt	September 7, 1907	November 10, 1908	1-17	1-34	1 year 2 months 3 days 17 voyages 34 crossings
William T. Turner	November 14, 1908	January 26, 1910	18-36	35-72	1 year 2 months 12 days 19 voyages 38 crossings
James Charles	February 26, 1910	October 15, 1912	37-76	73-152	2 years 7 months 19 days 40 voyages 80 crossings
Daniel Dow	December 13, 1912	December 31, 1912	77	153, 154	19 days 1 voyage 2 crossings
James Charles	August 23, 1913	October 22, 1913	78-80	155-160	1 month 29 days (2 mos less 1 day) 3 voyages 6 crossings
Arthur H. Rostron	October 25, 1913	November 11, 1913	81	161, 162	18 days 1 voyages 2 crossings
Daniel Dow	November 22, 1913	March 31, 1914	82-87	163-174	3 months 9 days 6 voyages 12 crossings
William T. Turner	April 11, 1914	April 27, 1914	88	175, 176	13 days 1 voyage 2 crossings
Daniel Dow	May 9, 1914	March 6, 1915	89-99	177-198	9 months 25 days 11 voyages 22 crossings
William T. Turner	March 20, 1915	May 7, 1915	100, 101	199-202	1 month 17 days 2 voyages 4 crossings
5 masters, 10 tenures					

Masters' Facts & Figures

- James Charles was in command of the *Lusitania* for the longest aggregate period of her career. His first tenure was 2 years, 7 months, 17 days; his second tenure was 1 day short of 2 months, for a total of 2 years, 9 months, and 16 days (40 voyages/80 crossings, 3 voyages/6 crossings = 43 voyages/86 crossings).
- James Charles' first tenure was also the longest single tenure that any master held aboard the *Lusitania*.
- Captain Daniel Dow's first tenure was 19 days (1 voyage/2 crossings); his second tenure was 1 year, 3 months, 12 days (18 voyages/36 crossings), for a total of 1 year, 4 months (19 voyages/37 crossings).
- Captain William Thomas Turner's first tenure was 1 year, 2 months, 12 days (19 voyages/38 crossings); his second tenure was 1 month, 17 days (2 voyages/4 crossings), for a total of 1 year, 3 months, 29 days (21 voyages/41 crossings).
- The shortest command of the *Lusitania* was by Arthur H. Rostron: 18 days, 1 voyage, 2 crossings. Captain Dow's first tenure was one day longer – 19 days, 1 voyage, 2 crossings.

Appendix 3
First Class Passenger List
Crossing No. 1

Name	Age	Gender	Married	Ethnicity/Residence
A				
Abbott, Frank	48	M	M	English/Kilmarnock, Scotland
Abelson, Abe	39	M	M	USA
Ackerman, Ernest R.	44	M	M	USA
Ackerman, Nora L.	40	F	M	USA
Adams, Winifred, *Maid*	22	F	S	English/London, England
Akahoshi, Fetsuma	20	M	S	Japanese/London, England
Alexander, Kenneth D.	19	M	S	USA
Alexander, Ralph	34	M	S	USA
Anderson, Mary	60	F		USA
Antoine, Gustave	41	M	M	English/London, England
Arnott, Hermione Louise	35	F	M	English/Bexhill, England
Arnott, Neil	37	M	M	English/Bexhill, England
Atkins, William Hugh	29	M	M	English/England
Atkinson, Francis Herbert	27	M	S	English/Liverpool, England
Attay, James Buesford	46	M	M	English/London, England
Ausoategui, Sabas	54	M	M	Cuban, Spanish/San Iguano, Havana
Austin, Frank Edward, *Valet*	33	M	S	English/London, England
B				
Badell, C., *Maid*	29	F	S	France/London, England
Bailey, Anna M.	14	F	S	USA
Bailey, Charles	77	M	M	USA
Bailey, Geo H.	66	M	M	USA
Bailey, Grace L.	15	F	S	USA
Bailey, Mrs. Geo H.	44	F	M	USA
Baird, E.	74	F	S	USA
Balfour, Josephine Marie	54	F	M	English/London, England
Balfour, Robert	63	M	M	English/London, England
Bansman, Thomas F.	25	M	S	USA
Barber, Ohio C.	66	M	M	USA
Barnett, William J.	28	M	S	English/London, England
Bateman, James	37	M	M	English/Dartford, England
Baxter, Blanche	28	F	S	USA

Name	Age	Gender	Married	Ethnicity/Residence
Beeton, Mayson M.	42	M	M	English/Woodbridge, England
Bell, James Wood	53	M	M	English/London, England
Bell, Thomas J.	53	M	M	USA
Benn, Harrisire	54	M	M	English/Bradford, England
Bentley, Wm John	39	M	S	English/Waterloo, Liverpool, England
Bevan, Anna	45	F		USA
Bevan, Arthur	46	M		USA
Bierce, Ellen D.	48	F	M	USA
Bierce, Wm. W.	52	M	M	USA
Black, Frances	23	F	S	USA
Blood, Aelish A.	18	M	S	USA
Blood, Edward	52	M	M	USA
Blood, Florie E.	22	F	S	USA
Blood, Mary H.	52	F	M	USA
Blood, Nancy	19	F	S	USA
Blount, Hilda M.	23	F	S	USA
Boron, Adelaide	50	F	M	USA
Boron, Constance E.	13	F	S	USA
Boron, Marjorie	20	F	S	USA
Boston, Charles Fred	41	M	M	English/Huyton, England
Bovee, Arthur Gibbon	25	M	S	USA
Boyce, Cramer R.	28	M	M	USA
Boyce, Hollie W.	28	F	M	USA
Boyd, Hugh	59	M	M	USA
Boyle, Frank Whelace	40	M	M	English/London, England
Branson, William George, *Valet*	24	M		English
Bromwick, Francis Henry	38	M	M	English/London, England
Brown, Kirk				USA
Brown, Peter Stuart	65	M	M	British-Scotch/Bothwell, Scotland
Browne, Lowell Huntington	22	M	S	USA
Browne, Muriel Gore	38	F	M	Scotch/London, England
Bulland, George Edwin	68	M	M	USA
Butler, Fannie Marie	50	F	M	USA
Butler, John William	65	M	M	USA
Butsen, Henry H. Van	21	M	S	English/London, England
Butsen, Richard E. G. Van	31	M	S	English/London, England
C				
Campbell, Hon. Cecil Arthur	38	M	M	English/London, England
Capewell, George Joseph	64	M	M	USA
Carson, Charles George	22	M	S	English/London, England

Name	Age	Gender	Married	Ethnicity/Residence
Carteu de Marchieium, Mr. G., *Secretary*	35	M		Belgium/London, England
Cary, F. Stanley	30	M	S	English/London, England
Chafman, Clarence C.	34	M	M	USA
Chafman, Evelyn S.	30	F	M	USA
Charlesworth, A. H.	55	M	M	English/London, England
Charlesworth, Miss Eleanor	16	F	S	English/London, England
Charlesworth, Miss Mary	3	F	S	English/London, England
Charlesworth, Mrs A. H.	40	F	M	English/London, England
Chase, Frances Gertrude	35	F	S	USA
Chetwynd, Amelie Mary	15	F	S	English/Beal, England
Child, Calvins	45	M	M	USA
Chivers, Cedric	54	M	M	English/Bath, England
Christian, Rose	38			USA
Christmas, Rose, *Nurse*	37	F	S	English/London, England
Clark, Charles W.	41	M	M	USA
Clark, Ernest L.	39	M	M	USA
Clark, George	38	M	M	Scotch/Kilmarnock, Scotland
Clark, Jacobin Smith	35	F	M	Scotch/Kilmarnock, Scotland
Clark, Melville	31	M	M	USA
Clark, Mrs. Ernest L.	38	F	M	USA
Clark, Ronald B.	14	M	S	USA
Clarkson, Samuel	26	M	S	English/London, England
Clendenning, John	52	M		USA
Clendenning, John J.	18	M		USA
Cockshutt, Euiento Lisien	44	M	S	English/London, England
Colley, William H.	55	M	M	USA
Collie, Alexander	29	M	M	US Citizen/Liverpool, England
Cooper, Huntting	40	M	M	USA
Costijan, Lillian	23	F	S	USA
Costijan, Miss Margaret	25	F	S	USA
Costijan, Mrs. Margaret	55	F	M	USA
Crane, Elizabeth T.	23	F	S	USA
Crane, Jas. A.	59	M	M	USA
Crane, John B.	20	M	S	USA
Crane, Mrs.	57	F	M	USA
Crater, George E.	37	M	M	USA
Croker, Elizabeth	42	F	M	USA
Croker, Miss Ethel	12	F	S	USA
Croker, Richard	32	M	M	USA
Cunard, Ernest Haleburton	44	M	M	English/London, England

Name	Age	Gender	Married	Ethnicity/Residence
Cunningham, William C.	45	M	M	USA
Cushner, Mrs. Samuel	50	F	M	USA
Cushner, Samuel	60	M	M	USA
D				
Dahl, Rudolph	50	M	M	German/Bremen, Germany
Davidson, Margaret B.	37	F		USA
Davies, Arthur Henry	31	M	S	English/London, England
Davies, Earl B.	26	M	S	English/Birmingham, England
De Haven, Alexander Henry	70	M	M	USA
De Haven, Mrs. Alexander Henry	58	F	M	USA
de Normandie, James	70	M	M	USA
Dean, Henry Samuel	45	M	M	English/London, England
Denehy, Miss M.	34	F	S	USA
Dilnot, Frank	32	M	M	English/London, England
Dixon, William	65	M	M	USA
Dodge, Ethel	25	F	M	USA
Dodge, Matthew H.	26	M	M	USA
Doherty, Henry L.	37	M	S	USA
Doherty, John P.	65	M	M	USA
Dolan, Henry Gale	38	M	M	USA
Donovan, John F.	45	M	M	USA
Donovan, Robert F.	35	M	M	USA
Doyle, Edward H.	58	M	M	USA
Doyle, Mary E.	25	F	S	USA
Doyle, Sarah J.	55	F	M	USA
Drake, William	42	M	M	USA
Dresser, Grace Forbush	34	F	M	USA
Dresser, Miss De la Roy	13	F	S	USA
Dresser, Miss Sue F.	16	F	S	USA
Dresser, Mrs. De la Roy	38	F	M	USA
Dribbon, Henry J.	28	M	S	USA
Dunbar, James R.	59	M	M	USA
Dunbar, Lucilla Harris	38	F	M	USA
Dunlap, Mrs.	35	F	M	USA
Dunlap, Robert	45	M	M	USA
Dunmore, Gertrude	68	F	W	English/London, England
E				
Edgar, Catherine Beatrice	2	F	S	Canadian/London, England
Edgar, Charlotte	30	F	S	English/Montreal, Canada
Edgar, Edward Mackay	31	M	M	Canadian/London, England
Edgar, Ethel Brocadale	25	F	S	Canada, English/Montreal, Canada

Name	Age	Gender	Married	Ethnicity/Residence
Edgar, John Fraser Mackay	4	M	S	Canadian/London, England
Edgar, Mrs. Edward Mackay	31	F	M	Canadian/London, England
Edwards, Alury H. B.	40	M	M	USA
Ettlen, Marie, *Maid*	40	F	S	Swiss, Scandinavian/Leamington, England
F				
Fesler, James K.	42	M	M	USA
Fibush, Aron	52	M	M	USA
Flaitz, Albert	32	M	M	German/Liverpool, England
Forbes, George D.	46	M	M	English/London, England
Fow., Jenine R.	54	F	M	USA
Fowlie, Miss Coutts	44	F	S	English/London, England
Fraser, Charles Lacklan	47	M	M	British-Scotch/Berwick, England
Freeman, Albert	38	M	M	USA
Freeman, Fannie	34	F	M	USA
Frick, Lena Jeffres	21	F	M	USA
Frick, Master Hunter Jeffres	11	M	S	USA
Frick, Mrs. Hunter W.				USA
Frost, Edwin P.	55	M	M	USA
Frost, Mary C.	50	F	M	USA
Frost, Ramelle M. K.	22	M	S	USA
Furman, Mrs. P. F.	36	F	M	USA
G				
Gadsdue, Arthur	34	M	M	English/Framlington, England
Gallard, Joseph Adams	29	M	S	English/Harrow, England
Gibb, David Eric	25	M	M	English/London, England
Giles, Anne, *Maid*	66	F	S	English/London, England
Gill, Archie	30	M	M	USA
Gillingham, Edward	37	M	M	USA
Gillingham, Elsie	32	F	M	USA
Glove, Chas F.	18	M	S	USA
Goelet, Mrs. Robert	27	F	M	USA
Goelet, Robert	27	M	M	USA
Goldmann, Robert	28	M	S	Austrian, Hebrew/London, England
Graham, Mildred P.	29	F	M	USA
Gray, Edith	22	F	S	USA
Gray, James C.	47	M	M	USA
Gray, Jessie C.	25	F	M	USA
Green, George Harry	33	M	S	English/London, England
Grieve, Richard A.	21	M	S	English/London, England
Grimley, H. G.	42	M	M	English/Liverpool, England

Name	Age	Gender	Married	Ethnicity/Residence
Grogan, Bridget	47	F	M	USA
H				
Hands, Aaron A.	43	M	M	USA
Hands, Anna S.	40	F	M	USA
Hansen, Jos O.	20	M	S	USA
Harde, Herbert Spencer	37	M	M	USA
Harde, Mrs. Herbert Spencer	25	F	M	USA
Harriman, Herbert M.	36	M	M	USA
Hay, Jennie B.	42	F		USA
Hay, Louis C.	47	M		USA
Hay, Wellington B.	19	M	S	USA
Heath, Edward	42	M	M	USA
Heber, Juliet E.	39	F	M	USA
Hersey, Mrs. Dudley H.	53	F	M	USA
Higgenson, Frances Lee J.	30	M	M	USA
Higgenson, Francis L.	14	M	S	USA
Higgenson, Mrs. Hetty	30	F	M	USA
Hill, Edith		F		USA
Hitchcock, Alfred Edwin	41	M	M	English/London, England
Hobbs, Walter Edward	38	M	S	English/Norbury, England
Hodgeman, Lucy H.	4	F	S	USA
Hodges, John S. Bach	77y 6m	M	M	English/London, England
Holt, Philip D.	30	M	S	English/Liverpool, England
Holt, William R.	37	M	M	English/London, England
Homewood, Ernest		M		
Homewood, William Thos.	23	M	M	English/London, England
Hood, Joseph	44	M	M	English/Bromfield, England
Hook, Thos G.	38	M	M	USA
Hope, Robert, *Valet*	25	M		English/London, England
Hormis, Geo	34	M	M	USA
Hubbard, Hermon Milton	23	M	S	USA
Hubble, Maria	29	F	M	USA
Hunt, William Floyd	35	M	M	USA
J				
James, Frederick, *Valet*	30	M	S	English/Fromington, England
Jean, Isaac	45	M	M	English/Streakham, England
Jefferies, Jenny	38	F	M	USA
Jefferies, Robert	37	M	M	USA
Jeffries, Thomas	39	M	M	USA
Jenny, William George	27	M	S	Swiss/Basle, Switzerland
Jockura, William, *Valet*	45	M	S	English/London, England

Name	Age	Gender	Married	Ethnicity/Residence
Joerinsen, Gertrude L.	30	F	M	USA
Jones, Ernest Rae	29	M	S	English/Charles, England
Jones, George Albert	40	M	M	English/London, England
Jones, Lewis J.	41	M	M	USA
Jones, Simeon	79	M	S	English/London, England
Jones, Wellington D.	21	M	S	USA
Jonssen, Carl	36	M	M	USA
K				
Kellen, William Vail	55	M	M	USA
Kelley, E. B.	40	M	M	USA
Kelly, Mrs. Elza	30	F	M	USA
Kiernan, Stephen M.	59	M	M	USA
Knight, Charles Y.	40	M	M	USA
Knowles, John Thomas	51	M	M	English/London, England
Knowles, Mrs J. T.	49	F	M	English/Chigwell, Essex, England
Kowaki, Geryiro y	40	M	M	Japan/London, England
L				
Lacompte, Francis D.	70	M	M	USA
Lajan, Hugh	37	M	M	USA
Latham, Eleanor	27	F	S	English/Caernarfon, Wales
Lever, Marty Edythe	30	F	M	English/London, England
Lever, Samuel H.	37	M	M	English/London, England
Leyand, Helen Dora		F		USA
Leyland, Christopher Digby	14	M	S	English/Beal, England
Leyland, Christopher John	57	M	M	English/Beal, England
Leyland, Dorothy	13	F	S	English/Beal, England
Leyland, Helen Dora	47	F	M	English/London, England
Liberfierie, Marie, *Maid*	35	F		French/Lives in England
Lindsay, William J.	43	M	M	English/Toronto, Canada
Litchfield, Edward H.	61	M	M	USA
Little, Jan Piteairie	23	M	S	Scotch/Ecclefechan, Scotland
Loel, Herman	44	M	M	USA
Lomas, Frank E.	43	M	M	USA
Lovegrove, Mrs. Thomas G.	49	F	M	USA
Lovegrove, Thomas G.	54	M	M	USA
Low, Eliza	54	F	M	Scotch/Dundee, Scotland
Low, John C.	55	M	M	Scotch/Dundee, Scotland
Lowry, John A.	38	M	M	Irish/Belfast, Ireland
Ludlow, Thomas, *Valet*	32	M	S	English/London, England
Luke, Ellen	44	F	M	English/Glasgow, Scotland
Luke, Elsie Ellen	20	F	S	English/Glasgow, Scotland

Name	Age	Gender	Married	Ethnicity/Residence
Luke, William Joseph	45	M	M	English/Glasgow, Scotland
M				
Mabson, Richard R.	60	M	M	English/Britain
MacBozis, Mrs.	21	F	M	USA
MacBozis, S. P. Rand	11m	M	S	USA
Macfee, Anne, *Nurse*	46	F	S	English/London, England
MacHugh, Robert Joseph	42	M	S	English/London, England
Mackay, Alexander	51	M	M	Scotch/Broughty Ferry, Scotland
MacKenzie, George Richard	60	M	M	Celtic/Glasgow, Scotland
Mackey, Frank J.	55	M	M	English USA
Mackey, Mrs. Frank J.	46	F	M	USA
Magnus, Anna	26	F	S	USA
Mahan, Charlotte	36	F	M	USA
Majima, Tomoyoshi	48	M	M	Japanese/London, England
Mallach, John	42	M	M	Scotch/Scotland
Mallory, Albert	29	M	S	USA
Markanian, Bedros H.	35	M	M	USA
Marsh, Wilber W.	44	M	M	USA
Mason, Alfred Darius	38	M		English/London, England
Masuda, Nobuyo	20	M	S	Japanese/London, England
Masuda, Takashi	59	M	M	Japanese/London, England
Mayhew, Cornelia	35	M	M	USA
Maynard, Frank H.	67	M	M	USA
Maynard, Mrs. F.	54	F	M	USA
McCabe, Joseph L.	41	M	M	USA
McCargo, Grant	38	M	S	USA
McCargo, Mary	32	F	M	USA
McCormick, Cyrus H.	40	M	M	USA
McCormick, Gordon	13	M	S	USA
McFadden, Geo H.	62	M	M	USA
McFadden, Mrs. Geo H.	56	F	M	USA
McMormick, Cyrus H.	17	M	S	USA
McNiell, Daniel	29	M	M	USA
Mendes, Edyard Pereica	26	M	S	Brazil, Portuguese/London, England
Mendes, Octaviano	50	M	M	Brazil, Portuguese/London, England
Millar, Charles	18	M	S	USA
Millar, Eleanor	22	F	S	USA
Millar, Florence	27	F	S	USA
Millar, Gertrude	20	F	S	USA
Moore, George F.	58	M	M	USA
Moore, Samuel Wallace	45	M	M	USA

Name	Age	Gender	Married	Ethnicity/Residence
Morrill, John F.	29	M	M	USA
Morrison, D. L.	32	M	M	USA
Morrissey, Daniel A.	43	M	M	USA
Murphy, Dorothy	25	F	S	English/Buxton, England
Murphy, Eugene	45	M	M	USA
Murray, Lady Victoria		F	S	English/London, England
Myers, George	43	M	M	English/Bradford, England
Myers, Mrs. George	41	F	M	English/Bradford, England
N				
Nicholls, Joseph	42	M	M	USA
Nielson, John Frederick	32	M	M	English/Bothwell, Scotland
North, Hugh M. James	34	M	M	USA
Norton, E. Hope	34	M	M	USA
Norton, Lily M.	28	F	M	USA
O				
Ogilvie, Thomas	62	M	M	Scotland/Aberdeen, Scotland
Onterbudge, Cyril N.	17	M	S	USA
Owen, Alice	45	F	M	USA
Owen, Samuel	56	M	M	USA
P				
Page, Howard	45	M	M	USA
Paine, George F. D.	70	M	M	USA
Paine, Margaret Elizabeth	50	F	M	USA
Palmer, Mrs. Potter	31	F	M	USA
Palmer, Potter	58	M	M	USA
Patten, Alexander	15	M	S	USA
Patten, Edith B.	17	F	S	USA
Patton, Mrs. Alexander E.	38	F	M	USA
Payne, George	9	M	S	English/Southall, England
Payne, Harriet	28	F	M	English/Southall, England
Payne, John	10m	M	S	English/Southall, England
Payne, Rosa	3	F	S	English/Southall, England
Payne, Thomas	6	M	M	English/Southall, England
Peabody, George	18	M	S	USA
Peter, John	39	M	S	English/Liverpool, England
Phillips, James Alexander	41	M	S	English/London, England
Pinder, Muriel	25	F	S	Canadian/London, England
Plank, Milton H.	41	M	M	USA
Plank, Mrs. Mary	35	F	M	USA
R				
Ralston, Kate J.	38	F	M	USA

Name	Age	Gender	Married	Ethnicity/Residence
Ralston, William Johns	47	M	M	USA
Ralston, Wm. J.	19	M	S	USA
Rankin, Alexander	25	M	M	USA
Rankin, Mrs. Alexander	25	F	M	USA
Reeves, Mary T.		F		USA
Reeves, Mary T.	31	F	M	USA
Reeves, Samuel J.	27	M	S	USA
Reidel, Anna	29	F	S	USA
Reitleuger, Alexander	58	M	M	USA
Reynolds, Mrs. Charles G.	39	F	M	USA
Rice, Isaac L.	11	M	S	USA
Rich, Clayton E.	16	M	S	USA
Rich, Mrs. J.	48	F	M	USA
Roberts, Eileen	30	F	M	USA
Ross, James	31	M		English/Cheshire, England
Rudd, Anthony George	57	M		English/Stockton on Tees, England
Rudd, Anthory G.				USA
S				
Sandermann, David Thomas	69	M		Scotch/Glasgow, Scotland
Saunders, Elva	34	F	M	USA
Saunders, Minerva	10	F	S	USA
Sawyer, Samuel Woodson	28	M	S	USA
Seccombe, Elizabeth	29	F	M	USA
Sewell, Maria	36	F	M	USA
Sewell, Marion, *Maid*	36	F	S	English/London, England
Shavin, John H.	82	M		USA
Shaw, Charles G.	56	M	M	USA
Shaw, Charles G. Jessie	15	M	S	USA
Shaw, Frank D. 2nd	15	M	S	USA
Shaw, Frank D. Esq.	59	M	M	USA
Sheedy, Mary	29	F	S	USA
Shirra, Charles	38	M	M	Scotch/Glasgow, Scotland
Shirra, Edith Mercedes	11m	F	S	Scotch/Glasgow, Scotland
Shirra, Mrs. Charles	33	F	M	Scotch/Glasgow, Scotland
Shraker, Margurite	28	F		USA
Sidebottom, Mrs. William	56	F	M	USA
Sidebottom, William	58	M	M	USA
Simpson, Gertrude	36	F	S	English/Birkenhead, England
Simpson, William	54	M	M	English/Birkenhead, England
Sims, Harold Haig	26	M	S	Canadian/London, England
Smith, Grace M.	39	F	M	USA

Name	Age	Gender	Married	Ethnicity/Residence
Smith, Harold H.	22	M	S	USA
Smith, James Nicoll	56	M		Scotch/Dundee, Scotland
Somerset, Mrs. Thomas	29	F	M	Irish/Belfast, Ireland
Somerset, Thomas	30	M	M	Irish/Belfast, Ireland
Soule, Beach C.	6			USA
Soule, Carry J.	50	F		USA
Soule, Ernest B.	4	M		USA
Soule, Henry B.	18	M		USA
Soule, Mrs. E. Bacon	52	F	M	USA
Stewart, Louis	17	M		USA
Still, Andrew	40	M		English/London, England
Stimson, Miss Cordelia	46	F	S	USA
Stimson, Mrs. George W.	48	F	M	USA
Stone, Henry A.	46	M		English/Liverpool, England
Stuart, Horatio	39	M	M	Scotch/Edinburgh, Scotland
Sullivan, James	40	M	M	USA
Suter, Hermann	28	M		German/London, England
Sutherland, George	45	M	M	USA
T				
Tabbersfield, Gerald	8	M		USA
Tabbersfield, Kube Jos.	40	M		USA
Tabbersfield, Olga	11	F		USA
Tabbersfield, Percival	47	M		USA
Tanakaa, Keishui	39	M	M	Japanese/London, England
Tayler, Edith	31	F	S	English/Buxton, England
Taylor, Arthur James	45	M		English/London, England
Taylor, Geo S.	21	M		USA
Taylor, Janet, *Maid*	35	F	S	Scotch/London, England
Thompson, Ralph C.	30	M	M	USA
Thompson, William Payne	34	M	M	USA
Thomson, Benjamin Thomas	57	M	M	English/Wimbledon, England
Thomson, Robert Bruce	49	M		English/Liverpool, England
Thorn, Charles E.	35	M	M	USA
Thorn, Mrs. Charles E.	30	F	M	USA
Tiedmann, Tuder J. A.	43	M		English/San Francisco, USA
Travers, Wm Richard	53	M	M	Irish/London, England
Triscott, Emily	26	F	S	English/London, England
Trumbull, Gertrude	40	F	M	USA
Trumbull, Walter H.	48	M	M	USA
Turner, Harold Rupert	23	M		English/Rochdale, England
Tweedle, Robert	39	M	M	USA

Name	Age	Gender	Married	Ethnicity/Residence
V				
Vallee, Sarah, *House Keeper*	40	F	M	Irish/New York, USA
Van Liew, Harry	45	M	M	USA
Verdon, Frederick A.	52	M	M	USA
Verdon, Mr. F. A.	52	M	M	USA
Vogel, Martin	30	M		USA
W				
Wallbrook, Henry Mackinius	42	M		English/London, England
Walls, Annie	25	F	S	USA
Walls, John	40	M	M	USA
Walls, Reina		F		USA
Ward, John	32	M	M	USA
Ward, Mrs.	31	F	M	USA
Ward, Mrs. Cordelia E.	48	F		USA
Ward, Reginald H.	45	M	M	USA
Warren, Julia P.	66	F		USA
Warren, Louise	37	F		USA
Warren, Moses A.	30	M		USA
Watts, Ruth Budd	36	M	M	USA
Webster, William	51	M		Scotch
Weir, William	30	M	M	Scotch/Glasgow, Scotland
Welch, George, *Valet*	30	M		English/London, England
Wellman, Frederick S.	19	M	S	USA
Wellman, Julien A.	60	F	M	USA
Wellman, Samuel T.	60	M	M	USA
Wells, Harry W.	37	M	S	English/Kent, Beckenham
Wells, Sydney Clarke	32	M	S	English/Kent, Beckenham
Wenbury, Frank, *Valet*	26	M		English/Lives in London
Werthinia, Jules	25	M	S	USA
Wheeler, Arthur	58	M	M	USA
Whippell, Sherman L.	45	M	M	USA
Whitaker Gribben, Robert	43	M	M	English/England
White, Archibald S.	40	M	M	USA
White, Mrs. Archibald S.	27	F	M	USA
Whittaker, Christopher Joseph	42	M		English/Lytham, England
Whyham, Walter	29	M	S	Scotch/London, England
Wigram, W. G.	30	M		English/Leeds, England
William, Frank B.	54	M	M	USA
Williams, Mrs. F. B.	48	F	M	USA
Williams, Richard	48	M	M	English/London, England
Wilson, Luke J.	35	M	M	USA

Name	Age	Gender	Married	Ethnicity/Residence
Winterbotham, Lindsey Dillon	46	M	M	English/London, England
Wiseman, Sir George Eden	23	M		English
Wishart, George	44	M	M	USA
Witherspoon, Preston	30	M		USA
Wolfenden, Chas F.	42	M		English/Liverpool, England
Wood, Emersen	49	M		English/Rose Hill, England
Worthington, H. Edward		M		USA
Worthington, Henry E.	46	M		English/Liverpool, England
Wotton, Henry	50	M	M	English/London, England
Wulff, Deller Friedrich	62	M	M	German/Brevini, Germany
Wylie, Herbert	39	M		USA
Wylie, Mrs. Herbert	36	F		USA
Y				
Young, Wm H.	24	M	S	USA

Appendix 4

Crew List, *Lusitania*
Crossing 202

Last Name	Title	First Name	Age	Fate	Nationality	Function	
A							
Adamson	Mr.	Thomas	32	Saved	British	First Waiter	S
Aindow	Mr.	Charles		Died		Night Watchman	S
Allan	Mr.	Ashley		Died		Third Waiter	S
Allen	Mr.	Norman Frederick		Died		Second Waiter	S
Allport	Mr.	Harry		Saved		Saloon Steward	S
Almond	Mr.	John		Died		First Waiter	S
Anderson	Mr.	James Clarke	49	Died		Staff Captain	D
Anderson	Mr.	John		Died	Norwegian	AB Seaman	D
Anderson	Mr.	James		Saved		Second Class Cabin Bed Steward	S
Anderson	Mr.	William		Saved		Boots	S
Anderson	Mr.	William Affleck		Died		Senior Fifth Engineer	E
Archer	Mr.	Joseph		Saved		First Waiter	S
Ashcroft	Mr.	Gordon Ernest		Died		First Waiter	S
Ashe	Mr.	John		Died		Trimmer	E
B							
Bain	Mr.	Duncan Campbell		Died		Waiter	S
Baldwin	Mr.	Edgar		Saved		First Waiter	S
Baldwin	Mr.	Thomas	28	Saved	British	First Waiter	S
Banner	Mr.	A.		Died		Waiter	S
Barnes	Mr.	William	44	Saved	British	First Class Cabin Bed Steward	S
Barrnet	Mr.	Daniel		Died		Fireman	E
Barry	Mr.	W.		Died		Fireman	E
Bates	Mr.	George	17	Died		Steward's Boy	S
Batt	Mr.	George		Saved		Trimmer	E
Battle	Mr.	James		Saved		AB Seaman	D
Beattie	Mr.	James		Died		Fireman	E
Beckett	Mr.	Henry	38	Saved	British	Passenger Cook	S

Last Name	Title	First Name	Age	Fate	Nationality	Function	
Beesley	Mr.	George William Alfred		Died		Junior Assistant Purser	D
Beggs	Mr.	John		Died		Senior Sixth Engineer	E
Bestic	Mr.	Albert Arthur	23?	Saved	British	Junior Third Officer	D
Betrand	Mr.	Maurice (Laparge)		Died		Extra Second Cook	S
Bird	Miss	Marian May		Saved		Stewardess	S
Bird	Mr.	Walter		Died		Chief Butcher	S
Blend	Mr.	John Henry		Died		Waiter	S
Blythyn	Mr.	Robert William		Died		Smokeroom Steward	S
Bond	Mr.	Edward		Saved		First Class Cabin Bed Steward	S
Bostock	Mr.	Joseph James		Died		Assistant Engineers' Mess Steward	S
Bowden	Mr.	Joseph	19?	Saved	British	AB Seaman	D
Bowen	Mr.	Henry		Died		Fireman	E
Boyd	Mr.	Fullerton R.	37	Saved	British	Barkeeper	S
Bradley	Mr.	Thomas		Died		Trimmer	E
Breen	Mr.	James		Died		Leading Fireman	E
Brennan	Mr.	Patrick		Died		Greaser	E
Brennan	Mr.	John		Saved		Trimmer	E
Brennan	Mr.	Thomas		Saved		Trimmer	E
Bridge	Mr.	William		Saved		Fireman	E
Brooke	Mr.	George		Died		Third Waiter	S
Brown	Mr.	John		Died		Joiner	D
Brown	Mr.	James H.	29	Saved	British	First Waiter	S
Brown	Mr.	Patrick		Died		Trimmer	E
Brown	Mr.	John		Saved		Fireman	E
Brown	Mr.	James		Died		Fireman	E
Browne	Mr.	E. Bennett		Died		First Waiter	S
Bryce	Mr.	Archibald	54	Died		Chief Engineer	E
Burden	Mr.	Arthur Howell		Died		Assistant Purser	D
Burke	Mr.	James		Died		Trimmer	E
Burns	Mr.	John James		Died		Leading Fireman	E
Burns	Mr.	Peter		Died		Trimmer	E
Burns	Mr.	Joseph		Saved		Fireman	E
Burrows	Mr.	Francis		Died		Waiter	S
Burrows	Mr.	William	15	Saved		Steward's Boy	S
Butler	Mr.	Joseph		Died		Fireman	E

Last Name	Title	First Name	Age	Fate	Nationality	Function	
C							
Cain	Mr.	Thomas	54	Died		Fireman	E
Caldecutt	Mr.	Samuel	32	Saved	British	Assistant Smokeroom Steward	S
Cameron	Mr.	Charles W.	38	Died	British	Bandmaster	B
Campbell	Mr.	Charles		Died		Trimmer	E
Campbell	Mr.	Patrick		Died		Fireman	E
Cannon	Mr.	Robert Henry		Died		Inspector	D
Carribine	Mr.	Bernard	43	Saved	British	Fireman	E
Carr-Jones	Mr.	E.	37	Died	British	Bandmember	B
Carroll	Mr.	Thomas		Saved		Leading Fireman	E
Cartwright	Mr.	Harry		Died		Second Class Cabin Bed Steward	S
Casey	Mr.	Martin		Died		Second Class Cabin Bed Steward	S
Casey	Mr.	Joseph		Saved		Fireman	E
Casey	Mr.	James		Died		Fireman	E
Casey	Mr.	Patrick	48	Died		Fireman	E
Cassels	Miss	Nora Isabel	44	Died		Stewardess	S
Cassidy	Mr.	Bernard		Died		Fireman	E
Chadwick	Mr.	Jacob		Saved		Fireman	E
Chamberlain	Mr.	Richard		Died		Night Watchman	S
Charlton	Mr.	George J.	53	Saved	British	First Class Cabin Bed Steward	S
Chester	Mr.	Michael		Died		Fireman	E
Chisholm	Mr.	Robert Daniel Fletcher	33	Saved	British	Second Steward	S
Christian	Mr.	K.		Died		Second Class Cabin Bed Steward	S
Christian	Mr.	William Edward		Died		Third Baker	S
Clark	Mr.	Robert James	15	Saved		Steward's Boy	S
Clarke	Mr.	James		Saved		Second Waiter	S
Clegg	Mr.	Arthur		Died		First Class Cabin Bed Steward	S
Clinton	Mr.	George		Saved		AB Seaman	D
Clyde	Mr.	Neil		Saved		AB Seaman	D
Coady	Mr.	James	53	Died		Fireman	E
Cockburn	Mr.	Andrew	44	Saved	British	Senior Second Engineer	E
Cole	Mr.	William Henry		Died		Second Intermediate Third Engineer	E
Collins	Mr.	James		Saved		First Class Cabin Bed Steward	S

Last Name	Title	First Name	Age	Fate	Nationality	Function	
Collins	Mr.	James Lord		Died		Trimmer	E
Collins	Mr.	Patrick		Died		Fireman	E
Colwell	Mr.	William J.		Saved		Trimmer	E
Comerford	Mr.	Thomas	31	Saved	Irish	First Waiter	S
Conlon	Mr.	Bernard		Saved		Trimmer	E
Connelly	Mr.	Owen		Died		Trimmer	E
Connertin	Mr.	Thomas		Died		Extra Third Cook	S
Conway	Mr.	Richard		Died		First Waiter	S
Cooney	Mr.	Michael Sr.	40	Died		Fireman	E
Cooney	Mr.	Michael Jr.	20	Died		Fireman	E
Cooper	Mr.	Frederick		Saved		Fourth Baker	S
Corby	Mr.	Michael		Died		Fireman	E
Costello	Mr.	Thomas		Died		Fireman	E
Cowan	Mr.	Alex		Saved		Lift Attendant	S
Coyle	Mr.	Patrick		Died		Trimmer	E
Craigie	Mrs.	Margaret	40	Saved	British	Stewardess	S
Crank	Mr.	John		Died		Baggage Master	D
Cranston	Mr.	George		Died		Night Watchman	S
Crawford	Mr.	Thomas		Saved		Third Butcher	S
Critchley	Mr.	David		Died		First Class Cabin Bed Steward	S
Cross	Mr.	Andrew		Saved		Fireman	E
Crumby	Mr.	Stephen		Saved		Fireman	E
Culshaw	Mr.	William		Saved		Fireman	E
Cummings	Mr.	John		Died		Scullion	S
Cunningham	Mr.	Edward		Saved		AB Seaman	D
Curran	Mr.	Patrick		Died		Fireman	E
Currie	Mr.	George		Saved		First Waiter	S
Cushion	Mr.	Michael		Saved		Trimmer	E
D							
Daley	Mr.	Daniel		Died		Fireman	E
Dalrymple	Mr.	James		Saved		Refrigeration Greaser	E
Danson	Mr.	Richard	45	Saved	British	Assistant Pantry Steward	S
Darcy	Mr.	John		Saved		First Waiter	S
Davies	Mr.	John		Saved		Bosun	D
Davies	Mr.	Fred		Died		Ship's Printer	S
Davies	Mr.	Charles		Saved		Assistant Panrty Steward	S

Last Name	Title	First Name	Age	Fate	Nationality	Function	
Davies	Mr.	Kenneth		Died		Assistant Engineers' Mess Steward	S
Davies	Mr.	John		Died		Trimmer	E
Davies	Mr.	J.		Saved		Trimmer	E
Davis	Mr.	Frederick		Saved		Trimmer	E
Dawes	Mr.	Thomas George		Died		First Class Cabin Bed Steward	S
Deiner	Mr.	John Frederick	32	Saved	British	First Waiter	S
Delvin	Mr.	Henry		Died		Fireman	E
Denton	Mr.	Jonathan S.	47	Saved	British	Barber	S
Dewhurst	Mrs.	Elizabeth Ross Morris	32	Saved	British	Stewardess	S
Dewrance	Mr.	Sydney		Died		Sculleryman	S
Dickinson	Mr.	John Faulkner		Died		Third Waiter	S
Dimmond	Mr.	John		Died		Scullion	S
Dingley	Mr.	H. J.		Died		Waiter	S
Dodwell	Miss	Eleanor	26	Died		Stewardess	S
Donnelly	Mr.	John		Died		Fireman	E
Donnelly	Mr.	Peter		Saved		Fireman	E
Donoghue	Mr.	Peter		Died		Greaser	E
Donovan	Mr.	William		Saved		Fireman	E
Dougherty	Mr.	William (Pitchford)		Died		Fireman	E
Downey	Mr.	Edward		Saved		Trimmer	E
Doyle	Mr.	Peter		Died		Leading Fireman	E
Doyle	Mr.	Joseph		Saved		Trimmer	E
Doyle	Mr.	John		Died		Fireman	E
Drakeford	Mr.	Ernest Dixon	30	Saved	British	Bandmember	B
Draper	Mr.	Percy	30	Saved	British	Second Purser	D
Driscoll	Mr.	Cornelius	20	Died		Third Waiter	S
Duckworth	Mr.	Thomas		Died		Fireman	E
Duggan	Mr.	John		Died		Trimmer	E
Duncan	Miss	Christina Campbell	36	Died		Stewardess	S
Duncan	Mr.	Joseph		Saved		Assistant Cook	S
Duncan	Mr.	Alex		Saved		Junior Second Engineer	E
Duncan	Mr.	Robert Henry	34	Saved	British	First Senior Third Engineer	E
Duncan	Mr.	Peter Robinson		Died		Senior Fourth Engineer	E
Dunn	Mr.	Albert Charles	30	Saved	British	Intermediate Sixth Engineer	E
Dunn	Mr.	Thomas		Died		Fireman	E

Last Name	Title	First Name	Age	Fate	Nationality	Function	
Dwyer	Mr.	James		Saved		Trimmer	E
Dwyer	Mr.	John		Saved		Fireman	E
Dyer	Mr.	John		Died		Trimmer	E
E							
Eastwood	Mr.	William Henry		Died		Second Class Cabin Bed Steward	S
Edgar	Mr.	William Henry		Died		Second Waiter	S
Edwards	Mr.	Joseph		Died		Third Waiter	S
Edwards	Mr.	Henry		Died		Sculleryman	S
Edwards	Mr.	Thomas		Saved		Fireman	E
Egan	Mr.	William		Saved		Bosun's Mate	D
Elliott	Mr.	Fred		Saved		AB Seaman	D
Elliott	Mr.	Arthur Graham		Died		AB Seaman	D
Elliott	Mr.	James		Died		Fireman	E
Enderson	Mrs.	Anna	45	Died	Norwegian	Matron	S
English	Mr.	Michael		Saved		Fireman	E
Ennis	Mr.	John		Died		Greaser	E
Evans	Mr.	Thomas		Died		AB Seaman	D
Evans	Mr.	David		Saved		Leading Fireman	E
Evans	Mr.	Robert		Saved		Trimmer	E
F							
Fairclough	Mr.	Robert		Saved		Donkeyman	E
Fairhurst	Mr.	Wilfred George		Died		First Intermediate Third Engineer	E
Farrell	Mr.	John		Saved		Fireman	E
Farrell	Mr.	John		Saved		Fireman	E
Fayle	Mr.	Edward		Saved		AB Seaman	D
Fearon	Mr.	Peter		Died		Greaser	E
Fenton	Mr.	Colin Stanley Morehouse		Died		Deck Engineer	E
Fernandez	Mr.	Eduardo		Saved		Fireman	E
Ferris	Mr.	John		Saved		Assistant Steward	S
Fields	Mr.	William		Died		Trimmer	E
Finnegan	Mr.	Edward		Died		Trimmer	E
Finucane	Mr.	Noel	24	Saved		First Waiter	S
Fitzgerald	Mr.	John		Saved		Electric Attendant	E
Flemming	Mr.	Herbert		Died		AB Seaman	D

Last Name	Title	First Name	Age	Fate	Nationality	Function	
Fletcher	Mr.	George		Saved		First Waiter	S
Fletcher	Mr.	William S.		Saved		First Class Cabin Bed Steward	S
Foden	Mr.	Robert E.		Saved		Waiter	S
Ford	Mr.	Arthur Hugh		Died		Extra Chief Steward	S
Ford	Mr.	John	45	Died		Fireman	E
Forrest	Mr.	John		Saved		Fireman	E
Foster	Mr.	John		Died		First Waiter	S
Foulkes	Mrs.	Margaret Elizabeth Hughes	42	Died		Stewardess	S
Francom	Mr.	James		Saved		Extra Second Baker	S
Freeman	Mr.	Matthew		Saved		Waiter	S
French	Mr.	Edward Stanley		Died		Fireman	E
G							
Gadd	Mr.	Lott	45	Saved	British	Barber	S
Gallagher	Mr.	George		Died		Fireman	E
Gardner	Mr.	William George	45	Died		Second Waiter	S
Gardner	Mr.	Alfred		Died		Trimmer	E
Garry	Dr.	Joseph		Died		Assistant Surgeon	D
Gaul	Mr.	Bart		Saved		Second Waiter	S
Gaul	Mr.	Richard		Died		Greaser	E
Gavan	Mr.	Peter		Died		Trimmer	E
Geraghty	Mr.	Martin		Died		Assistant Butcher	S
German	Mr.	Samuel K.		Died		Assistant Pantry Steward	S
Giftenburg	Mr.	Anton		Died	Dutch	Extra Third Baker	S
Gilroy	Mr.	Charles Stuart	22	Died		Second Waiter	S
Glancy	Mr.	James Wilson		Died		Assistant Steward	S
Glover	Mr.	George Alfred		Died		First Waiter	S
Glover	Mr.	Edwin		Saved		Officers' Mess Steward	S
Godley	Mr.	Thomas G.		Saved		First Waiter	S
Goodman	Mr.	B.		Saved		Trimmer	E
Gorst	Mr.	Frederick William		Died		First Waiter	S
Gouder	Mr.	Charles (Gontes Cloules)	24	Saved	Maltese	Waiter	S
Gould	Mr.	Richard	34	Died		Senior Boilermaker	E
Gowan	Mr.	G.		Died		Waiter	S
Grainger	Mr.	Robert		Saved		Waiter	S
Grant	Mr.	James	26?	Saved	British	First Class Cabin Bed Steward	S

Last Name	Title	First Name	Age	Fate	Nationality	Function	
Grant	Mr.	Michael		Died		Fireman	E
Gregory	Mr.	John Henry		Died		Trimmer	E
Griener	Mr.	Oscar		Saved		Roast Cook	S
Griffith	Mr.	George		Saved		Second Waiter	S
Griffiths	Mr.	John Humphrey	38	Saved	British	Chief Steward Third Class	S
Griffiths	Mr.	William Henry		Died		Refrigaration Greaser	E
Griffiths	Mr.	Samuel Herman		Died		Trimmer	E
Grisdale	Mr.	Harry	26	Saved	British	Library Steward	S
Grundy	Mr.	George		Saved		Leading Fireman	E
Gunn	Mr.	C.		Saved		AB Seaman	D
Gunther	Mr.	Charles		Saved		Fireman	E
H							
Hagen	Mr.	Francis J.	30	Saved	British	First Waiter	S
Hale	Miss	Sadie		Died		Typist	D
Hall	Mr.	Edwin		Saved		Assistant Engineers' Mess Steward	S
Hallam	Mr.	Ernest	38	Saved	British	Second Class Cabin Bed Steward	S
Hamel	Mr.	George James		Died		Trimmer	E
Handlin	Mr.	David Cowell		Died		Second Class Steward	S
Hanlon	Mr.	Patrick		Died		Trimmer	E
Hannah	Mr.	Thomas		Died		Waiter	S
Hannan	Mr.	John	56	Saved	British	AB Seaman	D
Harkness	Mr.	William H.	25	Saved	British	Assistant Purser	D
Harries	Mr.	George Edward		Died		Assistant Baker	S
Harris	Mr.	John Lewis		Died		Assistant Butcher	S
Harris	Mr.	Edward James		Died		Trimmer	E
Harrod	Mr.	Alfred		Died		Junior Assistant Purser	D
Hawkins	Mr.	Handel	25	Saved	British	Bandmember	B
Haybyrne	Mr.	James Benedict		Died		First Waiter	S
Hayes	Mr.	John Henry L.		Died		Junior Fith Engineer	E
Heap	Mr.	Harry		Died		Boots	S
Hefford	Mr.	Percy		Died		Second Officer	D
Heighway	Mr.	Edwin John	41	Saved	British	AB Seaman	D
Hemingway	Mr.	John William	27	Saved	British	Bandmember	B
Henderson	Mr.	John	31	Saved	British	First Waiter	S
Hendry	Mr.	William		Saved		First Waiter	S

Last Name	Title	First Name	Age	Fate	Nationality	Function	
Hennessey	Mr.	Frank		Saved		AB Seaman	D
Herman	Mr.	Albert		Died		AB Seaman	D
Heston	Mr.	Patrick		Died		Fireman	E
Hetherington	Mr.	Walter Lewis		Died		Third Senior Third Engineer	E
Heyes	Mr.	J.		Saved		AB Seaman	D
Higgins	Mr.	John		Died		Sculleryman	S
Hillhouse	Mr.	Hugh		Died		Trimmer	E
Hilton	Mr.	George Percival		Died		First Waiter	S
Hine	Mr.	John Benjamin	24	Died		Extra Vegetable Cook	S
Hodder	Mr.	James		Died		Fireman	E
Hoey	Mr.	James		Died		Trimmer	E
Holden	Mr.	James William		Died		First Waiter	S
Holman	Mr.	Frank		Saved		Third Waiter	S
Holton	Mr.	Benjamin R.H.	16	Saved		Steward's Boy	S
Hopkins	Mr.	Patrick		Died		Fireman	E
Horden	Mr.	Joseph Thomas		Died		Greaser	E
Horncastle	Mr.	William Alfred		Died		Trimmer	E
Horrigan	Mr.	Cornelius	16	Saved		Steward's Boy	S
Horrigan	Mr.	Michael		Died		Greaser	E
Hotchkiss	Mr.	Charles		Saved		First Waiter	S
Houghton	Mr.	Thomas Johnson		Died		Barkeeper Smokeroom	S
Howdle	Mrs.	Jane Ellen (Jane Ellen Hughes)	33	Died		Stewardess	S
Hughes	Mr.	John Edward		Died		Hospital Attendant	D
Hughes	Miss	Ellen		Saved		Stewardess	S
Hughes	Mr.	Edward		Saved		Assistant Pantry Steward	S
Hughes	Mr.	William Wilson		Died		Steward's Boy	S
Hughes	Mr.	William		Died		Assistant Cook	S
Hughes	Mr.	Thomas Owen		Died		Assistant Storekeeper	S
Hughes	Mr.	Owen		Died		Greaser	E
Hughes	Mr.	W.		Saved		Fireman	E
Hull	Mrs.	Margaret		Saved		Stewardess	S
Hume	Mr.	James		Saved		AB Seaman	D
Hume	Mr.	Archie		Died		Trimmer	E
Hussey	Mr.	John		Saved		Fireman	E
Hutchinson	Mr.	George		Saved		Chief Electrician	E
Hutchinson	Mr.	George		Saved		Fireman	E

Last Name	Title	First Name	Age	Fate	Nationality	Function	
Huther	Mr.	Edwin Arthur		Died		First Class Cabin Bed Steward	S
I							
Ipsen	Mr.	Owen Alfred		Saved		Third Waiter	S
Irving	Miss	Catherine	30	Died		Stewardess	S
Iverson	Mr.	Ambrose		Died		Sculleryman	S
J							
James	Mr.	Oswald		Died		First Class Steward	S
Jenkins	Mr.	James		Died		Fireman	E
Jessop	Mr.	Robert Nelson		Died		Second Class Cabin Bed Steward	S
Johnson	Mr.	James Andrew S.		Died		Assistant Engineers' Mess Steward	S
Johnston	Mr.	Hugh Robert		Saved		AB Seaman	D
Jones	Mr.	Arthur Rowland	33	Saved	British	First Officer	D
Jones	Mr.	William		Died		AB Seaman	D
Jones	Mr.	John Frederick Valentine		Saved		Chief Steward	S
Jones	Miss	Mary Elizabeth	43	Died		Stewardess	S
Jones	Mr.	William		Died		Second Waiter	S
Jones	Mr.	Charles (Cann Cooper Lann)		Died		Second Butcher	S
Jones	Mr.	Alfred		Died		Night Watchman	S
Jones	Mr.	Richard Ellis	31	Died		Junior Fourth Engineer	E
Jones	Mr.	William Ewart Gladstone	29?	Saved	British	Third Electrician	E
Jones	Mr.	Hugh		Died		Greaser	E
Jones	Mr.	Michael		Saved		Trimmer	E
Jones	Mr.	John		Died		Fireman	E
Jorgenson	Mrs.	Karen	35	Died	Danish	Assistant Matron	S
Joynson	Mr.	Edgar H.	19	Saved		Steward's Boy	S
K							
Kearney	Mr.	Patrick		Died		Trimmer	E
Kearney	Mr.	Thomas		Died		Fireman	E
Keating	Mr.	Philip		Died		Fireman	E
Keegan	Mr.	John Ernest		Died		Trimmer	E
Kehoe	Mr.	Denis		Died		Trimmer	E
Kelly	Mr.	Alfred Aloysius		Died		Scullian	S
Kelly	Mr.	Sidney Crawford		Died		Intermediate Fifth Engineer	E

Last Name	Title	First Name	Age	Fate	Nationality	Function	
Kelly	Mr.	John		Died		Fireman	E
Kelly	Mr.	Thomas		Died		Fireman	E
Kennedy	Mr.	John		Saved		Extra Fourth Baker	S
Kennedy	Mr.	John		Saved		Trimmer	E
Kennedy	Mr.	John James		Died		Trimmer	E
Kenny	Mr.	Joseph		Died		Fireman	E
Kenrick	Mr.	Henry		Died		Sculleryman	S
Kent	Mr.	John George		Died		Lounge Steward	S
Keogh	Mr.	P.		Saved		Fireman	E
Kewley	Mr.	Ernest Alexander	38	Died		First Waiter	S
Kidd	Mr.	Frank	40	Saved	British	Second Class Cabin Bed Steward	S
King	Mr.	Michael		Died		Trimmer	E
Kinshott	Mr.	William Henry		Died		Waiter	S
Knight	Mr.	C.T.		Saved		AB Seaman	D
Knight	Mr.	Charles	65	Saved		Night Watchman	S
Knill	Mr.	George		Saved		Sculleryman	S
Kupfenagel	Mr.	Alfred		Saved		First Waiter	S
L							
Laffey	Mr.	Thomas		Died		Fireman	E
Lake	Mr.	William		Died		Second Class Cabin Bed Steward	S
Lamont	Mr.	Charles	28	Saved	British	Third Waiter	S
Lapphane	Mr.	Charles	19	Died		Third Waiter	S
Larkin	Mr.	James J.		Died		Greaser	E
Latham	Mr.	George		Died		Second Electrician	E
Lawrence	Mr.	William		Saved		Fireman	E
Lawson	Mr.	Percy		Saved		First Waiter	S
Lawson	Mr.	Thomas		Saved		Trimmer	E
Lawton	Mr.	John		Died		Trimmer	E
Le Touzel	Mr.	Sydney Gibbon	32	Saved	British	First Waiter	S
Lea	Mr.	James		Died		Senior Seventh Engineer	E
Leach	Mr.	John F.	35	Saved	British	Waiter	S
Leach	Mr.	John Neil	25	Died		Waiter	S
Leathers	Mr.	Samuel		Died		Leading Fireman	E
Ledene	Mr.	Thomas		Died		AB Seaman	D
Ledger	Mr.	James		Died		Third Waiter	S

Last Name	Title	First Name	Age	Fate	Nationality	Function	
Ledson	Mr.	John		Died		Extra Extra Second Baker	S
Lee	Mr.	Richard	21	Saved	British	First Waiter	S
Lee	Mr.	William		Died		Trimmer	E
Lee	Mr.	Daniel	50	Died		Fireman	E
Leech	Mr.	T.		Saved		First Junior Third Engineer	E
Leitch	Mrs.	M.		Saved		Matron	S
Leith	Mr.	Robert		Saved		Telegraphist	D
Lemburg	Mr.	Ferdinand		Died		Confectioner	S
Lemon	Mr.	John		Saved		Trimmer	E
Lewis	Mr.	John Idwal	29	Saved	British	Senior Third Officer	D
Lewis	Mr.	Fred		Died		Second Waiter	S
Lewis	Mr.	Joseph		Saved		Trimmer	E
Lewis	Mr.	F.		Died		Fireman	E
Linton	Mr.	Isaac	48	Died		Fireman	E
Little	Mr.	George		Saved		Second Senior Third Engineer	E
Livermore	Mr.	Vernon		Saved		First Waiter	S
Lockett	Mr.	H.		Saved		AB Seaman	D
Lockhart	Mr.	Peter		Died		Fireman	E
Loughran	Mr	Peter		Died		Trimmer	E
Lyons	Mr.	Archibald		Died		Trimmer	E
M							
Machell	Miss	Elizabeth		Saved		Stewardess	S
MacKenzie	Mr.	Henry		Died		Waiter	S
MacKenzie	Mr.	Kenneth		Died		Waiter	S
MacPherson	Mr.	John		Died		Waiter	S
Madden	Mr.	John	43	Died		Fireman	E
Madden	Mr.	Thomas		Saved		Fireman	E
Malfiat	Mr.	Shef (may have been lost)		Saved	Belgian	Trimmer	E
Mallin	Mr.	William		Died		Fireman	E
Malone	Mr.	F.		Died		AB Seaman	D
Manan	Mr.	Andrew		Died		Trimmer	E
Manning	Mr.	John		Died		Trimmer	E
Manning	Mr.	Peter		Saved		Fireman	E
Markey	Mr.	Patrick		Died		Trimmer	E
Marrion	Mr.	John		Died		Trimmer	E
Marshall	Mr.	James		Died		First Waiter	S

Last Name	Title	First Name	Age	Fate	Nationality	Function	
Martin	Mr.	Albert		Saved		Leading Fireman	E
Matthews	Mr.	Henry		Saved		Second Waiter	S
Maylor	Mr.	George		Saved		Boots	S
McAdam	Mr.	Michael		Died		Fireman	E
McAleavey	Mr.	Thomas		Saved		Fireman	E
McAleer	Mr.	James		Died		Trimmer	E
McAlteer	Mr.	Matthew		Died		Vegetable Cook	S
McArthur	Mr.	William George		Died		Assistant Cook	S
McAteer	Mr.	Francis		Died		Fireman	E
McBride	Mr.	Peter		Died		Trimmer	E
McCabe	Mr.	John Alexander		Died		Trimmer	E
McCabe	Mr.	Andrew		Died		Fireman	E
McCabe	Mr.	Richard		Died		Fireman	E
McCann	Mr.	Owen		Died		Trimmer	E
McCann	Mr.	Thomas Michael		Died		Fireman	E
McCarthy	Mr.	Patrick		Saved		Greaser	E
McCarthy	Mr.	Bartholemew		Died		Fireman	E
McClean	Mr.	Robert		Died		Plumber	E
McClelland	Mr.	David		Saved		Extra Extra Second Cook	S
McCleod	Mr.	William		Died		First Class Cabin Bed Steward	S
McConkey	Mr.	Christopher Evans		Died		Second Waiter	S
McCormick	Mr.	David		Saved		Assistant Telegraphist	D
McCormack	Miss	Margarita Christina	34	Died	Indian	Stewardess	S
McCormick	Mr.	James		Died		Fireman	E
McCubbin	Mr.	James A.	50	Died		Purser	D
McCutcheon	Mr.	Thomas		Died		Fireman	E
McDermott	Dr.	James Farrell	38	Died		Surgeon	D
McDermott	Mr.	Eugene		Saved		Trimmer	E
McDermott	Mr.	Thomas		Died		Fireman	E
McDonald	Mr.	Charles		Saved		First Waiter	S
McDonald	Mr.	James		Died		Trimmer	E
McDonald	Mr.	John		Died		Fireman	E
McEvoy	Mr.	John		Saved		Refrigeration Greaser	E
McFarlane	Mr.	Malcolm John		Died		First Waiter	S
McGinty	Mr.	Thomas		Saved		Trimmer	E
McGlade	Mr.	George		Died		Seaman	D

Last Name	Title	First Name	Age	Fate	Nationality	Function	
McGough	Mr.	Michael		Died		Fireman	E
McGowan	Mr.	Joseph		Saved		Fireman	E
McGregor	Miss	Agnes	43	Died		Stewardess	S
McGugan	Mr.	Donald		Saved		Trimmer	E
McGugan	Mr.	Walter		Died		Trimmer	E
McGuiness	Mr.	Bernard		Saved		Trimmer	E
McIver	Mr.	John		Saved		Assistant Steward (Waiter)	S
McKenna	Mr.	Frank		Saved		Trimmer	E
McKenna	Mr.	John		Died		Trimmer	E
McKenna	Mr.	Bernard		Died		Trimmer	E
McKenna	Mr.	Patrick		Saved		Fireman	E
McKenzie	Mr.	Henry		Saved		Night Watchman	S
McKinley	Mr.	Andrew		Saved		Trimmer	E
McLauhglin	Mr.	Joseph		Died		Sculleryman	S
McLeod	Mr.	Victor		Died		O Seaman	D
McLoughlin	Mr.	John		Died		Greaser	E
McMahon	Mr.	P.		Saved		Fireman	E
McMahon	Mr.	Patrick		Died		Fireman	E
McNally	Mr.	Peter		Died		Seaman	D
McNulty	Mr.	Peter		Died		Trimmer	E
McParland	Mr.	Terence		Died		Fireman	E
McSane	Mr.	Patrick		Saved		First Waiter	S
McStay	Mr.	John		Saved		Fireman	E
Melia	Mr.	Patrick		Died		Greaser	E
Mills	Mr.	John		Died		First Waiter	S
Mitchell	Mr.	William		Saved		Linenkeeper	S
Mitchell	Mr.	George		Saved		Ship's Printer	S
Mitchell	Mr.	John		Died		Fireman	E
Moffatt	Mr.	John H. B. H.		Died		First Waiter	S
Molden	Mr.	James		Died		Fireman	E
Moore	Mr.	Daniel		Saved		Seaman	D
Moran	Mr.	James		Saved		Greaser	E
Moran	Mr.	Patrick		Saved		Fireman	E
Morecroft	Mrs.	Fannie	36	Saved	British	Stewardess	S
Morrice	Mr.	David		Died		Junior Sixth Engineer	E
Morris	Mr.	John		Died		Trimmer	E

Last Name	Title	First Name	Age	Fate	Nationality	Function	
Morrow	Miss	Isabel Harding	42	Died		Stewardess	S
Morse	Mr.	Robert	40	Saved	British	First Class Cabin Bed Steward	S
Morton	Mr.	John Clifford		Saved		AB Seaman	D
Morton	Mr.	Leslie Noel	18	Saved		AB Seaman	D
Moss	Mr.	John Barrow		Died		Second Waiter	S
Mudge	Mr.	John		Saved		Night Watchman	S
Murphy	Mr.	John Henry	32	Died		First Waiter	S
Murphy	Mr.	James		Saved		Fireman	E
Murphy	Mr.	Matthew		Died		Fireman	E
Murphy	Mr.	Dennis	23	Saved	British	Fireman	E
Mylaska	Mr.	C.		Died		Fireman	E
Myles	Mr.	Peter	17	Died		Trimmer	E
N							
Needham	Mr.	Patrick	47	Saved	British	Leading Fireman	E
Needham	Mr.	John		Died		Trimmer	E
Neems	Mr.	William F.		Died		First Waiter	S
Newbold	Mr.	Hubert H.		Saved		Cellarman	S
Newby	Mr.	John		Saved		Fireman	E
Newport	Mr.	William		Saved		Smokeroom Steward	S
Nice	Mr.	Reginald Bertie S.		Died		Barber	S
Niemann	Mr.	Robert		Saved		Waiter	S
Nixon	Mr.	Harold		Saved		Storekeeper	S
Norman	Mr.	Arthur William		Saved		Fireman	E
Norton	Mr.	Bernard		Died		Fireman	E
Nussbaum	Mr.	Samuel		Died	Swiss	Soup Cook	S
O							
O'Brien	Mr.	Patrick		Died		Fireman	E
O'Connell	Mr.	John	19	Saved		Fireman	E
O'Hare	Mr.	Owen	42	Died		Engineers' Store	E
O'Mahoney	Mr.	Thomas	21	Saved	British	Seaman	D
O'Neill	Mr.	F. H.		Saved		AB Seaman	D
O'Neill	Mr.	Bernard		Died		Trimmer	E
O'Neill	Mr.	James		Saved		Fireman	E
O'Neill	Mr.	Michael		Died		Fireman	E
O'Neill	Mr.	Paul		Saved		Fireman	E
Orange	Mr.	John		Died		Fireman	E

Last Name	Title	First Name	Age	Fate	Nationality	Function	
Ormrod	Mr.	James	41	Died		Greaser	E
Ormrod	Mr.	Thomas	40	Died		Greaser	E
Orwins	Mr.	Nicholas		Died		Deck Steward Second Class	S
Osborne	Mr.	J.		Died		Fireman	E
Osterburg	Mr.	August		Saved		Fireman	E
Osterman	Mr.	Jacob		Saved		Waiter	S
Ottino	Mr.	John		Saved		Larder Cook	S
Owen	Mr.	Thomas		Saved		Linenkeeper	S
Owens	Mr.	Owen		Died		AB Seaman	D
Owens	Mr.	Richard		Died		Engineering Storekeeper	E
P							
Palmer	Mr.	Thomas		Died		Trimmer	E
Parry	Mr.	Joseph	26	Saved	British	AB Seaman	D
Parry	Mr.	Frank	45	Saved	British	Assistant Deck Steward	S
Paton	Mr.	J. F.		Died	Brazilian	Steering Engineer	E
Payne	Mr.	Michael		Died		Fireman	E
Pederson	Mr.	Johan Adolph		Saved		Interpreter	S
Penkeyman	Mr.	Samuel J.		Died		Pantry Steward	S
Penny	Mr.	Algernon Percy	33	Saved	British	First Class Cabin Bed Steward	S
Perry	Mr.	John		Died		First Class Cabin Bed Steward	S
Phillips	Miss	Mary	33	Saved	British	Stewardess	S
Pimblett	Mr.	James		Died		Refrigaration Greaser	E
Pinkerton	Mr.	Robert		Died		Chief Baker	S
Piper	Mr.	John P.		Died		Chief Officer	D
Plummer	Mr.	Leslie		Saved		Fireman	E
Potter	Mr.	Benjamin		Died		Waiter	S
Powell	Mr.	Edward		Saved		Trimmer	E
Power	Mr.	Daniel		Saved		Fireman	E
Pratt	Mr.	Richard		Saved		Grill Cook	S
Price	Mr.	C.		Died		Waiter	S
Pringle	Mr.	Thomas		Saved		First Waiter	S
Prowse	Mr.	Thomas		Died		Assistant Pantry Steward	S
Q							
Quarrie	Mr.	Walter Scott		Died		Ventilation Engineer	E
Quinn	Mr.	Thomas John (father of Thomas)		Saved		AB Seaman	D

Last Name	Title	First Name	Age	Fate	Nationality	Function	
Quinn	Mr.	Thomas	17	Died		Bosun's Boy	D
Quin	Mr.	Alfred J.		Saved		Second Waiter	S
Quinn	Mr.	George		Died		Greaser	E
Quirk	Mr.	William Eduard	33	Died		AB Seaman	D
R							
Rafferty	Mr.	P.		Saved		Trimmer	E
Rafferty	Mr.	Joseph		Died		Fireman	E
Ralph	Mr.	M.		Saved		Fireman	E
Randall	Mr.	Charles	53	Saved	British	First Class Cabin Bed Steward	S
Ratcliff	Mr.	Peter		Died		Fireman	E
Redmond	Mr.	James		Saved		Vegetable Cook	S
Reid	Mr.	James		Died		Seaman	D
Reid	Mr.	Alfred		Died		Third Waiter	S
Reynolds	Mr.	Patrick		Saved		Fireman	E
Rice	Mr.	Edward		Died		Fireman	E
Rice	Mr.	Michael		Died		Fireman	E
Rice	Mr.	Stephen		Saved		Fireman	E
Richardson	Miss	Annie	37	Died		Stewardess	S
Rigby	Mr.	G.		Died		Fireman	E
Riston	Mr.	Issac		Died		First Waiter	S
Roach	Mr.	John		Saved		First Waiter	S
Roache	Mr.	James	24	Died		Fireman	E
Robb	Mr.	Joseph	27	Died		AB Seaman	D
Roberts	Mr.	Charles A.	25	Saved	British	AB Seaman	D
Roberts	Miss	Annie Jane	35	Died		Stewardess	S
Roberts	Mr.	John		Died		Assistant Engineers' Mess Steward	S
Robertson	Mr.	Neil		Saved		Carpenter	D
Robins	Mr.	T. (Edward Kyle)		Died		AB Seaman	D
Robinson	Mr.	William		Saved		Fireman	E
Rogan	Mr.	John		Died		Trimmer	E
Ronnan	Mr.	George	16	Died		Assistant Butcher	S
Roper	Mr.	John		Saved		AB Seaman	D
Rose	Mr.	William		Saved		Second Waiter	S
Ross	Mr.	Henry		Died		Barkeeper	S
Ross	Mr.	E.W.		Saved		Fireman	E
Rossiter	Mr.	Laurence		Saved		Fireman	E

Last Name	Title	First Name	Age	Fate	Nationality	Function	
Rourke	Mr.	Stanley	21?	Saved	British	Lift Attendant	S
Rowan	Mr.	Fred		Saved		Fireman	E
Rowbottom	Mr.	Harold E.		Saved		Second Waiter	S
Rowe	Mr.	John		Died		Trimmer	E
Ruddan	Mr.	Thomas		Saved		Trimmer	E
Ruffels	Mr.	William Samuel		Died		First Class Cabin Bed Steward	S
Rushton	Mr.	George		Saved		First Waiter	S
Russell	Mr.	Frederick		Saved		First Waiter	S
Rylands	Mr.	William Deakin		Died		First Waiter	S
S							
Saultry	Mr.	William		Died		Ship's Cook	S
Savage	Mr.	Frank		Died		Fireman	E
Scanell	Mr.	Charles		Saved		Fireman	E
Scantlebury	Mr.	Samuel		Saved		Sculleryman	S
Scott	Mr.	C.		Died		Fireman	E
Seagraves	Mr.	Patrick		Died		AB Seaman	D
Septon	Mr.	William		Saved		Night fireman's Cook	S
Settle	Mr.	Vincent	55	Saved	British	First Class Cabin Bed Steward	S
Seurre	Mr.	Etienne Pierre		Died	French	Chef	S
Shalvey	Mr.	Gerald		Saved		Waiter	S
Shanley	Mr.	J.		Saved		Fireman	E
Shann	Mr.	Sydney James		Died		Third Waiter	S
Sharkey	Mr.	John		Saved		Electric Attendant	E
Sharp	Mr.	Philip Archibald		Died		Steward's Boy	S
Sheil	Mr.	Michael S.	32	Saved	British	Saloon Steward	S
Shepherd	Mr.	Ralph Alfred		Died		Fireman	E
Sherridan	Mr.	Jeffrey		Died		Fireman	E
Sherridan	Mr.	Patrick		Died		Fireman	E
Shevland	Mr.	John		Died		Second Waiter	S
Sikking	Mr.	James	24	Saved	British	AB Seaman	D
Sikking	Mr.	Florence		Saved		Bosun's Mate	D
Simpson	Mr.	Malcolm	34	Saved	British	First Waiter	S
Sinnot	Mr.	William		Saved		Fireman	E
Skay	Mr.	Edward	16?	Saved	British	Kitchenporter	S
Slavin	Mr.	Owen		Saved		Trimmer	E
Sloane	Mr.	Leonard Hanson		Died		Junior Assistant Purser	D

Last Name	Title	First Name	Age	Fate	Nationality	Function	
Smith	Mr.	Peter		Died		Master-At-Arms	D
Smith	Mr.	William		Saved		First Waiter	S
Smith	Mr.	Oliver Barrow		Died		Ship's Cook	S
Smith	Mr.	William Thomas		Died		Intermediate Second Engineer	E
Southwold	Mr.	Henry		Died		Greaser	E
Spendley	Mr.	David March		Died		Waiter	S
Stafford	Mr.	Thomas		Saved		Trimmer	E
Stanley	Mr.	David H.		Saved		First Waiter	S
Stanley	Mr.	H.		Saved		Fireman	E
Stansfield	Mr.	Leslie		Died		Second Waiter	S
Stark	Mr.	Robert Lucas		Died		Second Class Cabin Bed Steward	S
Steinberg	Mr.	Arthur Valentine		Died		Steward's Boy	S
Sterberg	Mr.	R. A.		Died	Finnish	Fireman	E
Stevens	Mr.	John		Died		Chief Officer	D
Stewart	Mr.	Thomas Edgar	23	Died		Assistant Steward	S
Stringer	Mr.	Harry	26	Died		First Waiter	S
Suttan	Mr.	Nugent Moore		Died		Pantry Steward	S
Sutton	Mr.	Frank		Saved		Second Waiter	S
Sweeney	Mr.	Jeremiah		Died		Fireman	E
Swift	Mr.	Edward		Died		Third Cook	S
T							
Taylor	Mr	Chris		Saved		Trimmer	E
Taylor	Mr.	Thomas		Died		Trimmer	E
Tear	Mr.	Joseph Edward		Died		Trimmer	E
Thomas	Mr.	John		Saved		Second Waiter	S
Thomas	Mr.	William Stanford		Died		Second Class Cabin Bed Steward	S
Thomas	Mr.	George Henry		Died		Assistant Officers' Mess Steward	S
Thompson	Mr.	Leo Henry		Saved		AB Seaman	D
Thompson	Mr.	John		Died		O Seaman	D
Thompson	Mr.	John		Died		Trimmer	E
Thompson	Mr.	John E.		Saved		Trimmer	E
Thompson	Mr.	Michael		Died		Trimmer	E
Thorn	Mr.	Alfred Richard		Died		First Waiter	S
Thornley	Mr.	George		Saved		Assistant Pantry Steward	S

Last Name	Title	First Name	Age	Fate	Nationality	Function	
Tierney	Mr.	Michael		Saved		Fireman	E
Todd	Mr.	James		Saved		AB Seaman	D
Toder	Mr.	Ernest		Died		Waiter	S
Toner	Mr.	Frank		Saved		Fireman	E
Toole	Mr.	James		Died		Fireman	E
Trainor	Mr.	A.		Died		Trimmer	E
Traynor	Mr.	Philip Henry		Died		Trimmer	E
Turner	Mr.	William Thomas	58	Saved		Commander	D
Turner	Mr.	Joseph		Died		Trimmer	E
U							
Ulgar	Mr.	Jean		Died	Spanish	Sauce Cook	S
V							
Van Hocke	Mr.	Julius E.	27	Saved	Dutch	First Waiter	S
Varney	Mr.	John		Died		Waiter	S
Verdin	Mr.	Francis		Died		Sculleryman	S
Vose	Mr.	George		Died		Trimmer	E
W							
Wallace	Mr.	James		Saved		Second Waiter	S
Walsh	Mr.	R.		Saved		Greaser	E
Ward	Mr.	John		Saved		Fireman	E
Ward	Mr.	Michael		Died		Fireman	E
Weaving	Mr.	Richard		Died		Fireman	E
Webb	Mr.	James		Died		Trimmer	E
Weigh	Mr.	Edward		Saved		Waiter	S
Weir	Mrs.	Margaret	51	Died		Stewardess	S
Welsh	Mr.	Martin		Died		Trimmer	E
Welsh	Mr.	Christopher	36	Died		Trimmer	E
Whalley	Mr.	Leslie		Saved		Third Waiter	S
Wheelhouse	Mr.	Alfred Faulkner		Died		Junior Seventh Engineer	E
Whelan	Mr.	John James		Died		Fireman	E
Whitmore	Mr.	George		Saved		Fireman	E
Wiencke	Mr.	Paul		Died		Greaser	E
Wiencke	Mr.	Paul Frederick		Died		Trimmer	E
Wiggins	Mr.	William	23	Saved	British	Deck Steward	S
Wilkinson	Mr.	James		Died		Engineers' Mess Steward	S
Williams	Mr.	William		Saved		Master-At-Arms	D

Last Name	Title	First Name	Age	Fate	Nationality	Function	
Williams	Mr.	Robert Neptune		Died		First Waiter	S
Williams	Mr.	Harold		Died		Second Waiter	S
Williams	Mr.	John		Died		Third Waiter	S
Williams	Mr.	William H.		Saved		First Class Cabin Bed Steward	S
Williams	Mr.	Robert		Died		Night Watchman	S
Williams	Mr.	Sydney		Died		Trimmer	E
Wilmin	Mr.	William		Saved		Pantry Steward	S
Wilson	Mr.	James Robert		Died		First Waiter	S
Wiseman	Mr.	James		Died		Second Baker	S
Wood	Mr.	Henry Edward	35	Died		Assistant Pantry Steward	S
Wood	Mr.	Walter	31	Saved	British	First Class Cabin Bed Steward	S
Wood	Mr.	Alfred		Saved		First Class Cabin Bed Steward	S
Wood	Mr.	Wallace Edkin		Died		Barkeeper Smokeroom Second Class	S
Wood	Mr.	John H.		Died		Greaser	E
Woods	Mr.	Joseph		Saved		Fireman	E
Wright	Mr.	Harold Joseph		Died		Steward's Boy	S
Wylie	Mr.	Richard G.	31	Saved	British	Third Junior Third Engineer	E
Wynn	Mr.	Peter		Died		Trimmer	E
Wynne	Mr.	George	16	Saved	British	Assistant Cook	S
Wynne	Mr.	Joseph D.	37	Died	British	Sculleryman	S
Y							
Yetts	Mr.	William R.		Died		AB Seaman	D

Note: The list contains the names of four people who died soon after the disaster; one came on the official list of dead, but died later than the other three, but since they lived long enough to be rescued, all four appear on this list as saved. They are:

Clarke, Mr. Alfred Russell (died on June 20, 1915)
McKetchan, Master Campbell (died on September 15, 1915, and appeared on the official list among the victims)
Plank, Mrs. Harriet (died on August 3, 1915)
Knigh, Mr. Charles (died one day after the disaster)

Right column symbol key:
B= Member of the Ship's Band
D= Deck Department
E= Engineering Department
S= Stewards Department

Crew list for Crossing No. 202 East kindly provided by Mike Poirier. Compiled by Mike Poirier, Jim Kalafus, Hildo Theil, Paul Latimer, Geoff Whitfield, and Craig Stringer.

Appendix 5

Passenger List, *Lusitania*

Crossing 202

Last Name	Title	First Name	Age	Fate	Nationality	City	Country
					FIRST CLASS		
A							
Adams	Mr.	Arthur Henry	46	Died	U.S.C.		England
Adams	Mr.	William McMillan	19	Saved	U.S.C.		England
Adams	Mr.	Henry		Died	British	London	England
Adams	Mrs.	Henry (Annie Elizabeth)	46	Saved	British	London	England
Allan	Lady	Montague (Marguerite Ethel)	42	Saved	British	Montreal	Canada
Allan	Miss	Gwendolyn Evelyn	16	Died	British	Montreal	Canada
Allan	Miss	Anna Marjory	15	Died	British	Montreal	Canada
Davis	Miss	Emily, *Maid*		Saved	British	Montreal	Canada
Walker	Miss	Annie, *Maid*	30	Saved	British	Montreal	Canada
Alles	Mr.	Nicholas Naftel	50	Saved	U.S.C.	New York	USA
Ayala	Mr.	Julian de	45	Saved	Cuban	Liverpool	England
B							
Baker	Mr.	James	50	Saved	British		England
Baker	Miss	Margaret Anne 'Millie'	27	Died	U.S.C.	New York	USA
Baldwin	Mr.	Harry Bradley	48	Died	U.S.C.	New York	USA
Baldwin	Mrs.	Harry Bradley (Mary Margaret)	38	Died	U.S.C.	New York	USA
Barnes	Mr.	Allan Byron	43	Saved	British	Toronto	Canada
Bartlett	Mr.	George Walter Bowers	42	Saved	British	London	England
Bartlett	Mrs.	George Walter Bowers (Irma Florine)	31	Saved	British	London	England
Bates	Mr.	Lindon Wallace Jr.	32	Died	U.S.C.	New York	USA
Battersby	Mr.	James Johnson	40	Saved	British	Stockport	England
Bernard	Mr.	Clinton Percival	27	Saved	U.S.C.	New York	USA
Bernard	Mr.	Oliver Percy	34	Saved	British	Boston	USA
Bilicke	Mr.	Albert Clay	54	Died	U.S.C.	Los Angeles	USA
Bilicke	Mrs.	Albert Clay (Gladys)	50	Saved	U.S.C.	Los Angeles	USA
Bistis	Mr.	Leonidas M.	33	Died	Greek		Greece
Black	Mr.	James Joseph	39	Died	British	Liverpool	England
Bloomfield	Mr.	Thomas	48	Died	U.S.C.	New York	USA
Bohan	Mr.	James	38	Saved	British	Toronto	Canada

Last Name	Title	First Name	Age	Fate	Nationality	City	Country
Boulton	Mr.	Dennis Duncan Harold Owen Jr.	23	Saved	British	Chicago	USA
Bowring	Mr.	Charles Warren	44	Saved	British	New York	USA
Braithwaite	Miss	Dorothy Douglas	24	Died	British	Montreal	Canada
Brandell	Miss	Josephine Mary	23	Saved	U.S.C.	New York	USA
Brodrick	Mr.	Carlton Thayer	28	Died	U.S.C.	Boston	USA
Brooks	Mr.	James Ham (Jay)	41	Saved	U.S.C.	Bridgeport	USA
Brown	Mrs.	F. C. (Mary "May")	51	Died	U.S.C.	New York	USA
Brown	Mr.	William Henry Helm	34	Died	U.S.C.	Buffalo	USA
Bruno	Mr.	Henry Augustine	45	Died	British	Montclair	USA
Bruno	Mrs.	Henry Augustine (Annie)	45	Died	British	Montclair	USA
Burgess	Mr.	Henry George	37	Saved	British		England
Burnside	Mrs.	Thomas David Meldrum (Josephine Smith)	49	Saved	British	Toronto	Canada
Burnside	Miss	Iris Margaret	20	Died	British	Toronto	Canada
Waites	Miss	Martha Pinda, *Maid*	36	Died	British	Toronto	Canada
Buswell	Mr.	Peter	26	Saved	British		England
Byington	Mr.	Albert Jackson	40	Saved	U.S.C.	London	England
Byrne	Mr.	Michael G.	47	Saved	U.S.C.	New York	USA
C							
Cairns	Mr.	Robert Wishart	49	Saved	British		
Campbell	Mr.	Alexander	43	Died	British		England
Campbell-Johnston	Mr.	Conway Seymour Godfrey	56	Died	British	Los Angeles	USA
Campbell-Johnston	Mrs.	Conway Seymour Godfrey (Ida Amelia)	57	Died	British	Los Angeles	USA
Chabot	Mr.	David Louis	49	Died	British	Montreal	Canada
Chapman	Mrs.	William Henry (Ellen Elizabeth)	59	Saved	British	Toronto	Canada
Charles	Mr.	Joseph Henry	48	Saved	British	Toronto	Canada
Charles	Miss	Doris Maud	21	Saved	British	Toronto	Canada
Clarke	Mr.	Alfred Russell	55	Saved	British	Toronto	Canada
Clarke	Reverend	Charles Cowley	64	Saved	British	London	England
Cloete	Mr.	William Brodrick	60	Died	British	San Antonio	USA
Colebrook	Mr.	Herbert Gladstone	35	Saved	British	Toronto	Canada
Conner	Miss	Dorothy	25	Saved	U.S.C.	New York	USA
Copping	Mr.	George Robert	52	Died	British	Toronto	Canada
Copping	Mrs.	George Robert (Emma Louisa)		Died	British	Toronto	Canada
Crichton	Mrs.	William C. (Mabel)	42	Died	U.S.C.	New York	USA
Crompton	Mr.	Paul	44	Died	British	Philadelphia	USA
Crompton	Mrs.	Paul (Gladys Mary)	40	Died	British	Philadelphia	USA
Crompton	Mr.	Stephen Hugh	14	Died	British	Philadelphia	USA
Crompton	Miss	Alberta	13	Died	British	Philadelphia	USA
Crompton	Master	Paul Romelly	9	Died	British	Philadelphia	USA

Last Name	Title	First Name	Age	Fate	Nationality	City	Country
Crompton	Master	John David	6	Died	British	Philadelphia	USA
Crompton	Master	Peter Romelly	9m	Died	British	Philadelphia	USA
Allen	Miss	Dorothy Ditman, *Nurse*	26	Died	U.S.C.	Philadelphia	USA
Crooks	Mr.	Robert Williams	39	Died	British	Toronto	Canada
Cross	Mr.	Ambrose Betham	38	Saved	British		F. Malay States
D							
Daly	Mr.	Harold Mayne	35	Saved	British	Ottawa	Canada
Dearbergh	Mr.	Robert Edward	48	Died	British	New York	USA
DePage	Mrs.	Antoine (Marie)	43	Died	Belgian	Brussels	Belgium
Dingwall	Mr.	Charles Arthur	62	Died	British	London	England
Dougall	Miss	Catherine	24	Died	British	Guelph	Canada
Drake	Mr.	Bernard Audley Mervyn	21	Died	British	Detroit	USA
Dredge	Mr.	Joseph Allan	43	Died	British		British Honduras
Dredge	Mrs.	Joseph Allan (Evelyn)	39	Died	British		British Honduras
Dunsmuir	Mr.	James A.	21	Died	British	Toronto	Canada
E							
Emond	Mr.	Wilfrid Alfred	46	Died	British	Quebec	Canada
F							
Fenwick	Mr.	John	44	Died	British		Switzerland
Fisher	Dr.	Howard Lowrie	49	Saved	U.S.C.	New York	USA
Forman	Mr.	Justus Miles	39	Died	U.S.C.	New York	USA
Fowles	Mr.	Charles Frederick	49	Died	British	New York	USA
Fowles	Mrs.	Charles Frederick (Frances May)	38	Died	British	New York	USA
Freeman	Mr.	Richard Rich Jr.		Died	U.S.C.	Boston	USA
Friedenstein	Mr.	Joseph	48	Died	British	London	England
Friend	Professor	Edwin William	28	Died	U.S.C.	Farmington	USA
Frohman	Mr.	Charles	54	Died	U.S.C.	New York	USA
Stainton	Mr.	William, *Valet*	36	Died	U.S.C.	New York	USA
G							
Gauntlett	Mr.	Frederic John	45	Saved	U.S.C.	New York	USA
Gibson	Mr.	Matthew Orr	48	Died	British	Glasgow	Scotland
Gilpin	Mr.	George Arthur	47	Died	British	London	England
Gorer	Mr.	Edgar Ezekiel	43	Died	British	London	England
Grab	Mr.	Oscar Frederick	30	Saved	U.S.C.	New York	USA
Grant	Mr.	Montagu Tassell	47	Died	British	Chicago	USA
Grant	Mrs.	Montagu Tassell (Chastina Jane)	43	Died	British	Chicago	USA
H							
Hammond	Mr.	Frederick Sydney	29	Died	British	Toronto	Canada
Hammond	Mrs.	Frederick Sydney (Kathleen Saunders)	29	Saved	British	Toronto	Canada
Hammond	Mr.	Ogden Haggerty	46	Saved	U.S.C.	New York	USA

Last Name	Title	First Name	Age	Fate	Nationality	City	Country
Hammond	Mrs.	Ogden Haggerty (Mary Picton)	29	Died	U.S.C.	New York	USA
Hardwick	Mr.	Charles Cheever	50	Saved	U.S.C.	New York	USA
Harper	Mr.	John Henry	55	Died	British	New York	USA
Harris	Mr.	Dwight Carlton	31	Saved	U.S.C	New York	USA
Hawkins	Mr.	Frederick William		Died	British	Winnipeg	Canada
Hickson	Miss	Catherine	57	Died	U.S.C.	New York	USA
Hill	Mr.	Charles Tilden	38	Saved	U.S.C.	London	England
Hodges	Mr.	William Sterling	33	Died	U.S.C.	Philadelphia	USA
Hodges	Mrs.	William Sterling (Sarah)	35	Died	U.S.C.	Philadelphia	USA
Hodges	Master	William Sterling Jr.	8	Died	U.S.C.	Philadelphia	USA
Hodges	Master	Dean Winston	6	Died	U.S.C.	Philadelphia	USA
Holt	Mr.	William Robert Grattan	15	Saved	British	Montreal	Canada
Home	Mr.	Thomas	50	Saved	British	Toronto	Canada
Hopkins	Mr.	Albert Lloyd	43	Died	U.S.C.	New York	USA
Houghton	Dr.	James Tilley	29	Saved	U.S.C.	Saratoga Springs	USA
Hubbard	Mr.	Elbert Green	55	Died	U.S.C.	East Aurora	USA
Hubbard	Mrs.	Elbert Green (Alice)	53	Died	U.S.C.	East Aurora	USA
Hutchinson	Miss	Phyllis	24	Died	British		England
J							
Jacobaeus	Mr.	Sigurd Anton	55	Died	Swedish		Sweden
Jeffery	Mr.	Charles Thomas	39	Saved	U.S.C.	Chicago	USA
Jenkins	Mr.	Francis Bertram	29	Saved	British	New York	USA
Jolivet	Miss	Marguerite Lucile	25	Saved	French	Paris	France
Jones	Miss	Margaret Drutler	41	Died	British	Honolulu	USA
K							
Keeble	Mr.	Wilfrid R.	31	Saved	British	Toronto	Canada
Keeble	Mrs.	Wilfrid R. (Fannie Maud)	32	Saved	British	Toronto	Canada
Kellett	Mr.	Francis Cranston	47	Died	U.S.C.	Tuckahoe	USA
Kempson	Mr.	Maitland	55	Saved	British	Toronto	Canada
Kenan	Dr.	Owen Hill	42	Saved	U.S.C.	New York	USA
Kennedy	Mrs.	(Caroline)	53	Died	U.S.C.	New York	USA
Keser	Mr.	Harry J.	41	Died	U.S.C.	Philadelphia	USA
Keser	Mrs.	Harry J. (Mary Bringhurst)	40	Died	U.S.C.	Philadelphia	USA
Kessler	Mr.	George A.	52	Saved	U.S.C.	New York	USA
King	Mr.	Thomas Boyce	49	Died	U.S.C.	New York	USA
Klein	Mr.	Charles	48	Died	British	London	England
Knight	Mr.	Charles Harwood	39	Died	U.S.C.	Baltimore	USA
Knight	Miss	Elaine Harwood	42	Died	U.S.C.	Baltimore	USA
Knox	Mr.	Samuel Mclhenny Knox	57	Saved	U.S.C.	Philadelphia	USA
L							
Lane	Sir	Hugh Percy	39	Died	British		England

Last Name	Title	First Name	Age	Fate	Nationality	City	Country
Lassetter	Mrs.	Harry Beauchamp (Elisabeth Anne)	43	Saved	British	London	England
Lassetter	Lieutenant	Frederick Macquarie	22	Saved	British	London	England
Lauriat	Mr.	Charles Emelius Jr.	40	Saved	U.S.C.	Boston	USA
Learoyd	Mr.	Charles Alfred	46	Died	British	Sydney	Australia
Learoyd	Mrs.	Charles Alfred (Mabel Kate)	41	Saved	British	Sydney	Australia
Hurley	Miss	Margaret, *Maid*	25	Saved	British	Sydney	Australia
Leary	Mr.	James Joseph	36	Saved	U.S.C.	New York	USA
Lehmann	Mr.	Isaac	36	Saved	U.S.C.	New York	USA
Leigh	Mr.	Evan Arthur	64	Died	British	Liverpool	England
Letts	Mr.	Gerald Arthur	45	Died	British	New York	USA
Levinson	Mr.	Joseph	36	Saved	British		Canada
Lewin	Mr.	Frederick Guy	45	Died	British		England
Lobb	Mrs.	Reginald Popham (Mary Beatrice)	31	Saved	British	New York	USA
Lockhart	Mr.	Reginald Raphael	49	Saved	British	Toronto	Canada
Loney	Mr.	Allen Donnellan	43	Died	U.S.C.	New York	USA
Loney	Mrs.	Allen Donnellan (Catherine Wolfe)	36	Died	U.S.C.	New York	USA
Loney	Miss	Virginia Bruce	14	Saved	U.S.C.	New York	USA
Boutellier	Mrs.	Paul, *Maid* (Elise)	47	Died	French	New York	USA
Luck	Mrs.	Arthur Courtland (Charlotte)	34	Died	U.S.C.	Worcester	USA
Luck	Master	Eldridge Courtland	9	Died	U.S.C.	Worcester	USA
Luck	Master	Kenneth Field	7	Died	U.S.C.	Worcester	USA
M							
Macdona	Mrs.	Henry D. (Amelia)	59	Died	U.S.C.	New York	USA
Mackworth	Lady	Humphrey (Margaret Haig)	32	Saved	British	Cardiff	Wales
MacLennan	Mr.	Frederick Ebenezer	44	Died	British	Glasgow	Scotland
Mason	Mr.	Stewart Southam	30	Died	British	Boston	USA
Mason	Mrs.	Stewart Southam (Leslie Hawthorne)	28	Died	British	Boston	United States
Mathews	Mr.	Arthur Thomas	38	Saved	British	Montreal	Canada
Maturin	Reverend	Basil William	66	Died	British	Holywell, Oxford	England
McConnell	Mr.	John Wanklyn	60	Saved	British	Manchester	England
McLean	Mr.	Walter	38	Died	British		France
McMurray	Mr.	Leonard Lethes	48	Saved	British	Toronto	Canada
McMurtry	Mr.	Frederick	45	Died	British	Toronto	Canada
Medbury	Mr.	Maurice Benjamin	50	Died	U.S.C.	New York	USA
Miller	Captain	James Blaine	32	Died	U.S.C.	Washington DC	USA
Mills	Mr.	Charles Veitch	33	Died	U.S.C.	New York	USA
Mitchell	Mr.	James Duncan		Died	British		England
Moody	Mr.	Ralph Troupe		Died	British	Gainesville	USA

Last Name	Title	First Name	Age	Fate	Nationality	City	Country
Morell	Mrs.	Moses Samuel (Goldiana "Georgina")	76	Saved	British	Toronto	Canada
Morrison	Mr.	Kenneth John	48	Died	British		Canada
Mosley	Mr.	George Gordon	30	Saved	British		England
Munro	Mrs.	Charles (not aboard) (Alexandria)			British	Liverpool	England
Myers	Mr.	Herman Abraham	44	Died	U.S.C.	New York	USA
Myers	Mr.	Joseph Lewis	48	Saved	U.S.C.	New York	USA
N							
Naumann	Mr.	Frank Gustavus	61	Died	British		England
Nyblom	Mr.	Gustaf Adolf	29	Died	Swedish		Canada
O							
Orr-Lewis	Sir	Frederick	49	Saved	British	Montreal	Canada
Slingsby	Mr.	George, *Valet*	26	Saved	British	Montreal	Canada
Osborne	Mrs.	Alexander B. (Alexandra Mary)	49	Saved	British	Hamilton	Canada
Osbourne	Mrs.	T.O. (Ella)	31	Died	British	Glasgow	Scotland
P							
Padilla	Mr.	Frederico G.	34	Died	Mexican	Liverpool	England
Padley	Mrs.	Charles (Florence May)	23	Saved	British	Liverpool	England
Page	Mr.	John Harvey	40	Died	U.S.C.	New York	USA
Pappadopoulo	Mr.	Michael N.	43	Died	Greek	Athens	Greece
Pappadopoulo	Mrs.	Michael N. (Angela)	32	Saved	Greek	Athens	Greece
Partridge	Mr.	Frank E.	42	Saved	British	New York	USA
Paynter	Mr.	Charles Edwin	63	Died	British	Liverpool	England
Paynter	Miss	Irene Emily	30	Saved	British	Liverpool	England
Peardon	Mr.	Frank Arthur	35	Died	British	Toronto	Canada
Pearl	Mr.	Frederic Warren	46	Saved	U.S.C.	New York	USA
Pearl	Mrs.	Frederic Warren (Amy Lea)	34	Saved	U.S.C.	New York	USA
Pearl	Master	Stuart Duncan Day	5	Saved	U.S.C.	New York	USA
Pearl	Miss	Amy Whitewright	2	Died	U.S.C.	New York	USA
Pearl	Miss	Susan Warren	1	Died	U.S.C.	New York	USA
Pearl	Miss	Audrey	3m	Saved	U.S.C.	New York	USA
Lines	Miss	Alice Maud, *Nurse*	18	Saved	British	New York	USA
Lorenson	Miss	Greta, *Maid*	23	Died	Danish	New York	USA
Pearson	Dr.	Frederick Stark	54	Died	U.S.C.	New York	USA
Pearson	Mrs.	Frederick Stark (Mabel)	52	Died	U.S.C.	New York	USA
Walker	Mr.	David, *Secretary*	32	Died	British	New York	USA
Perkins	Mr.	Edwin	41	Died	British		England
Perry	Mr.	Frederick John	25	Saved	British	Buffalo	USA
Perry	Mr.	Albert Norris	28	Died	British	Buffalo	USA
Phillips	Mr.	Wallace Banta	29	Saved	U.S.C.	New York	USA
Pierpoint	Mr.	William John	51	Saved	British	Liverpool	England
Pirie	Mr.	Robinson	59	Saved	British	Hamilton	Canada

Last Name	Title	First Name	Age	Fate	Nationality	City	Country
Plamondon	Mr.	Charles Ambrose	57	Died	U.S.C.	Chicago	USA
Plamondon	Mrs.	Charles Ambrose (Mary Letitia)	57	Died	U.S.C.	Chicago	USA
Pollard	Mr.	Henry	30	Died	British	Washington DC	USA
Pope	Miss	Theodate (Effie) Brooks	48	Saved	U.S.C.	Farmington	USA
Robinson	Miss	Emily, *Maid*		Died	British	Farmington	USA
Posen	Mr.	Eugene Henry	41	Saved	British	New York	USA
Powell	Mr.	George A.	55	Died	British	Toronto	Canada
R							
Rankin	Mr.	Robert	33	Saved	U.S.C.	New York	USA
Ratcliff	Mr.	Norman Albert	36	Saved	British		England
Robinson	Mr.	Charles E.	54	Died	U.S.C.	Philadelphia	USA
Robinson	Mrs.	Charles E. (Prudence Mary)	59	Died	U.S.C.	Philadelphia	USA
Rogers	Mr.	Frank Albert	34	Died	British	Toronto	Canada
Rogers	Mrs.	Frank Albert (Agnes Bloor)		Died	British	Toronto	Canada
Rogers	Mr.	Percy William	46	Saved	British	Toronto	Canada
Rumble	Mr.	Thomas Walter	27	Died	British	Toronto	Canada
Ryerson	Mrs.	George Sterling (Mary Amelia)	56	Died	British	Toronto	Canada
Ryerson	Miss	Laura Mary	23	Saved	British	Toronto	Canada
S							
Schwabacher	Mr.	Leo M.	41	Died	U.S.C.	Baltimore	USA
Schwarcz	Mr.	Max M.	52	Died	U.S.C.	New York	USA
Schwarte	Mr.	Friedrich Wilhelm August	44	Saved	British	New York	USA
Scott	Captain	Alick John		Died	British	Manila	Philippines
Seccombe	Mr.	Percy W.	20	Died	U.S.C.	Petersboro	USA
Seccombe	Miss	Elizabeth Ann	38	Died	British	Petersboro	USA
Shields	Mr.	Victor E.	45	Died	U.S.C.	Cincinnati	USA
Shields	Mrs.	Victor E. (Retta)	44	Died	U.S.C.	Cincinnati	USA
Shymer	Mrs.	Robert D. (Anne C. Patterson)	36	Died	U.S.C.	New York	USA
Silva	Mr.	Thomas James	27	Died	U.S.C.	Temple	USA
Slidell	Mr.	M. Thomas	40	Saved	U.S.C.	New York	USA
Smith	Mrs.	John W. (Jessie)	39	Saved	U.S.C.	Braceville	USA
Soloman	Mr.	George	43	Died	British	London	England
Sonneborn	Mr.	Henry Becker	41	Died	U.S.C.	Baltimore	USA
Stackhouse	Commander	Joseph Foster	41	Died	British	London	England
Stephens	Mrs.	George Washington (Frances Ramsey)	65	Died	British	Montreal	Canada
Stephens	Master	John Harrison Chattan	18m	Died	British	Montreal	Canada
Millen	Miss	Caroline, *Nurse*		Died	British	Montreal	Canada
Oberlin	Miss	Elise, *Maid*		Died	Swiss	Montreal	Canada
Stewart	Mr.	Duncan	52	Died	British	Montreal	Canada

Last Name	Title	First Name	Age	Fate	Nationality	City	Country
Stone	Mr.	Herbert Stuart	43	Died	U.S.C.	New York	USA
Strauss	Mr.	Julius	39	Died	British	Hamilton	Canada
Stuart	Mr.	Alexander		Died	British	Glasgow	Scotland
Sturdy	Mr.	Charles Frederick	38	Saved	British	Montreal	Canada
T							
Taylor	Mr.	Richard Lionel	31	Saved	British	Montreal	Canada
Tesson	Mr.	Frank B.	60	Died	U.S.C.	Philadelphia	USA
Tesson	Mrs.	Frank B. (Alice Lowe)	49	Died	U.S.C.	Philadelphia	USA
Thomas	Mr.	David Alfred	59	Saved	British	Cardiff	Wales
Rhys-Evans	Mr.	Arnold Leslie, *Secretary*	23	Saved	British	Cardiff	Wales
Thompson	Mr.	Elbridge Blish	32	Died	U.S.C.	Seymour	USA
Thompson	Mrs.	Elbridge Blish (Maude)	32	Saved	U.S.C.	Seymour	USA
Tiberghien	Mr.	Georges	32	Died	French		France
Timmis	Mr.	Robert James	51	Saved	British	Gainesville	USA
Tootal	Mr.	Frederick Edward Owen	39	Saved	British	London	England
Townley	Mr.	Ernest Ethelbert	56	Saved	British	Toronto	Canada
Trumbull	Mr.	Isaac B.	38	Died	U.S.C.	Bridgeport	USA
Turner	Mr.	Scott	34	Saved	U.S.C.	Lansing	USA
Turton	Mr.	George Henderson	45	Saved	British	Melbourne	Australia
V							
Van Straaten	Mr.	Martin	49	Died	British/ Dutch	London	England
Vanderbilt	Mr.	Alfred Gwynne	38	Died	U.S.C.	New York	USA
Denyer	Mr.	Ronald, *Valet*	30	Died	U.S.C.	New York	USA
Vassar	Mr.	William Arthur Fisher	44	Saved	British	London	England
Vernon	Mr.	George Ley Pearce	45	Died	British	London	England
W							
Wakefield	Mrs.	Alfred Thomas (Mary Gertrude)	38	Saved	British	Honolulu	USA
Wallace-Watson	Mrs.	William (Florence)	49	Died	British	Montreal	Canada
Watson	Mrs.	Anthony (Katherine)	52	Died	British		England
Willey	Mrs.	Cameron (Catherine E.)	57	Died	U.S.C.	Lake Forest	USA
Williams	Mr.	Thomas Henry	32	Died	British	Liverpool	England
Williamson	Mr.	Charles Francis	44	Died	U.S.C.	New York	USA
Winter	Mr.	William Henry	28	Died	British	Liverpool	England
Witherbee	Mrs.	Alfred Scott (Beatrice Wilhemena Theodora "Trixie")	24	Saved	U.S.C.	New York	USA
Witherbee	Master	Alfred Scott Jr.	3	Died	U.S.C.	New York	USA
Withington	Mr.	Lothrop	58	Died	U.S.C.	Boston	USA
Wood	Mr.	Arthur John	37	Died	British		England
Wright	Mr.	Robert Currie	54	Saved	U.S.C.	Cleveland	USA
Wright	Mr.	Walter		Died	British		Scotland

Last Name	Title	First Name	Age	Fate	Nationality	City	Country
Y							
Young	Mr.	James M.	60	Died	British	Hamilton	Canada
Young	Mrs.	James M. (Georgina Ann)	56	Died	British	Hamilton	Canada
Yung	Mr.	Philippe Joseph	33	Saved	Belgian	Antwerp	Belgium
SECOND CLASS							
A							
Abas	Mrs.	Philip Robert (Beatrice)	26	Died	Dutch	New York	USA
Abas	Miss	Isabel	6	Died	Dutch	New York	USA
Abas	Miss	Beatrice	2	Died	Dutch	New York	USA
Abercromby	Mr.	Ralph Frank	21	Died	British	Cincinnati	USA
Abramowitz	Mr.	Samuel	36	Saved	Russian	Paris	France
Ackroyd	Mrs.	(Hannah)		Died	British	Brooklyn	USA
Ackroyd	Master	Frederick	3	Died	British	Brooklyn	USA
Adams	Mr.	Allan H.	42	Saved	British	Winnipeg	Canada
Adams	Mrs.	Albert E. (Gertrude)	25 ?	Saved	British	Edmonton	Canada
Adams	Miss	Joan M.	2	Died	British	Edmonton	Canada
Aiston	Mr.	Joseph	20?	Saved	British	Brooklyn	USA
Aitken	Mr.	James		Died	British	Merritt	Canada
Aitken	Mr.	Jarvie Sr.		Died	British	Merritt	Canada
Aitken	Master	Jarvie Jr.	3	Died	British	Merritt	Canada
Aitken	Miss	Christina 'Chrissie'	16	Saved	British	Merritt	Canada
Allen	Mr.	John		Saved	British	Philadelphia	USA
Amory	Mrs.	Alfred Howard (Phoebe)	60	Saved	British	Toronto	Canada
Anderson	Mrs.	Rowland (Emily Mary)	26	Saved	British	Bridgeport	USA
Anderson	Miss	Barbara Winifred	2	Saved	British	Bridgeport	USA
Anderson	Mrs.	George R. (Margaret Armstrong)	30	Died	British	Pittsburg	USA
Armitage	Mrs.	Martin ? (Florence Gertrude)	27	Died	British	New York	USA
Arnott	Mr.	Robert		Died	British	Kerney	USA
Arter	Mr.	James Sydney	33	Saved	British	Seattle	USA
Arthur	Mr.	George Henry		Died	British	Minneapolis	USA
B							
Bailey	Mr.	Walter George	53	Died	British	Nelson	Canada
Bailey	Mrs.	Walter George (Jessie Annie)	45	Died	British	Nelson	Canada
Bailey	Miss	Ivy	15	Died	British	Nelson	Canada
Baker	Miss	Eva		Died	British	New York	USA
Bancroft	Mr.	William Blanchard Jr.	27	Died	U.S.C.	New York	USA
Barber	Miss	Constance		Died	British	Winnipeg	Canada
Barbour	Miss	Elizabeth 'Bessie'		Saved	British	Victoria	Canada
Barchard	Mr.	Edmund E.	39	Died	British	Columbus	USA
Barker	Mrs.	Thomas (Martha Ann)	39	Saved	U.S.C.	Trenton	USA

Last Name	Title	First Name	Age	Fate	Nationality	City	Country
Barker	Miss	Winifred	9	Died	U.S.C.	Trenton	USA
Barr	Mr.	James (John)		Died	British	Toronto	Canada
Barr	Mrs.	James (John) (Catherine Symington)	40	Died	British	Toronto	Canada
Barrett	Miss	Mae	25	Saved	British	New York	USA
Barry	Mr.	Edward	38	Saved	British	New York	USA
Bartlett	Mr.	Edmund Thomas	56	Saved	British	New York	USA
Baxter	Mr.	William		Died	British	Welland	Canada
Baxter	Mrs.	William (Annie Elizabeth)	39	Saved	British	Welland	Canada
Baxter	Master	William Jr.	6	Died	British	Welland	Canada
Beattie	Reverend	James Anderson	55	Died	British	New York	USA
Beattie	Mrs.	James Anderson (Margaret White)	58	Saved	British	New York	USA
Beattie	Mrs.	John A. (Grace S.)	58	Died	British	Winnipeg	Canada
Beattie	Mr.	Allan Martin	18	Saved	British	Winnipeg	Canada
Beaumont	Mr.	James		Died	British		England
Bingham	Miss	Alice Winifred	35	Died	British	Toronto	Canada
Bilbrough	Mr.	George W.	36	Saved	British	Smith Fall	Canada
Birchall	Mr.	Henry		Saved	British	Roslyn	USA
Bird	Mrs.	Lyndon (Rose)		Died	British		England
Booth	Mr.	John	35	Died	British	Alexandria	USA
Booth	Mrs.	Charles Henry (Emily Eliza)	30	Died	British	Ottawa	Canada
Booth	Master	Nigel Frederick	8m	Saved	British	Ottawa	Canada
Booth-Jones	Mr.	Edward	38	Died	British	New York	USA
Booth-Jones	Mrs.	Edward (Millichamp Letton)	25	Died	British	New York	USA
Booth-Jones	Miss	Ailsa Georgina	8	Died	British	New York	USA
Booth-Jones	Master	Percival	4	Died	British	New York	USA
Bourke	Mrs.	(Mabel Juliet)		Died	British	Winnipeg	Canada
Boyd	Miss	Margaret L.		Died	British	Hamilton	Canada
Braddick	Mr.	Sidral William	32	Died	British	Minneapolis	USA
Brammer	Mrs.	Richard H. (Elizabeth Jane)	32	Saved	British	Trenton	USA
Brammer	Miss	Edith	8	Saved	British	Trenton	USA
Bretherton	Mrs.	Cyril Herbert Emanuel (Norah Annie)	32	Saved	U.S.C.	Santa Monica	USA
Bretherton	Master	Paul	3	Saved	U.S.C.	Santa Monica	USA
Bretherton	Miss	Elizabeth	15m	Died	U.S.C.	Santa Monica	USA
Brilly	Mr.	Louis	43	Died	Italian	New York	USA
Brown	Mr.	Daniel Taylor	43	Saved	British	Los Angeles	USA
Brownlie	Mr.	Thomas		Died	British	Freeport	USA
Brownlie	Mrs.	Thomas (Margaret)	41	Saved	British	Freeport	USA
Bryce	Mr.	Hugh B.	33	Saved	British	Syracuse	USA
Bryce	Mrs.	Hugh B. (Annabelle)	33	Saved	British	Syracuse	USA

Last Name	Title	First Name	Age	Fate	Nationality	City	Country
Buchanan	Miss	Mary	30	Died	British	Pottstown	USA
Bull	Mrs.	John Henry (Elizabeth)	62	Died	British	Hamilton	Canada
Bullen	Mr.	Henry Garnet		Died	British	Winnipeg	Canada
Burdon	Mrs.	Andrew Thompson (Ellen Mary)	24	Saved	British	Winnipeg	Canada
Burdon	Master	Robert P.	14m	Saved	British	Winnipeg	Canada
Burley	Mr.	Reuben	39	Died	British	Hamilton	Canada
Burley	Mrs.	Reuben (Florence)	38	Died	British	Hamilton	Canada
Burley	Miss	Doris Florence	9	Died	British	Hamilton	Canada
Burley	Master	Reginald	Infant	Died	British	Hamilton	Canada
Busvine	Mr.	William Robert	34	Died	British	New York	USA
Butler	Mr.	Thomas O'Brien	43	Died	British		Ireland
Butler	Mrs.	W. (Margaret)	40	Died	British	Whitfish Manchester	USA/ England
Butters	Miss	Margaret	39	Died	British	Toronto	Canada
C							
Callan	Mr.	Patrick		Died	U.S.C.	Chicago	USA
Campbell	Mr.	Kennedy		Died	British	Boston	USA
Campbell	Mr.	William	31	Died	British	Chicago	USA
Campbell	Mrs.	William (Amy E.)	33	Saved	British	Chicago	USA
Campbell	Miss	Ada Mena	31	Saved	British	New York	USA
Campbell	Miss	Christina Fraser		Died	British	Calgary	Canada
Candlish	Mr.	Arthur	33	Died	U.S.C.	Pawtucket	USA
Candlish	Mrs.	Arthur (Ellen)	30	Saved	U.S.C.	Pawtucket	USA
Carson	Miss	Henrietta	19	Died	British	Sherbrooke	Canada
Catherwood	Mr.	John	41	Died	U.S.C.	Philadelphia	USA
Catherwood	Mrs.	John (Maria)	40	Died	U.S.C.	Philadelphia	USA
Cattley	Mr.	Colin		Died	British	Edmonton	Canada
Chalmers	Mrs.	Adam (Blanche)		Died	British	Winnipeg	Canada
Chambers	Mr.	Guy Winstaney P.	36	Saved	British	Boston	USA
Chambers	Mrs.	Guy Winstaney P. (Ethel)	30	Died	British	Boston	USA
Chantry	Mr.	Harold	22	Died	British	Nelson	Canada
Chantry	Mrs.	Harold (Mina)	21	Died	British	Nelson	Canada
Chantry	Miss	Elizabeth Ellen	3/4m	Died	British	Nelson	Canada
Charles	Miss	Eleanor		Died	British	New York	USA
Chatt	Miss	Anna		Died	British	New York	USA
Chirgwin	Mrs.	Frederick (Maud Gertrude)	31	Died	British	Havana	Cuba
Chirgwin	Master	Richard	Infant	Died	British	Havana	Cuba
Clarke	Mrs.	Francis William (Nore)		Died	British	Toronto	Canada
Clay	Miss	Elizabeth Alice	44	Died	British	San Francisco	USA
Clayton	Mr.	William		Died	British	Vancouver	Canada
Clayton	Mrs.	William		Died	British	Vancouver	Canada
Cockburn	Mr.	Guy Rosebery	31	Saved	British	Pasadena	USA

Last Name	Title	First Name	Age	Fate	Nationality	City	Country
Colbert	Mr.	William	51	Died	U.S.C.	New York	USA
Colbert	Mrs.	William (Helena)	45	Died	U.S.C.	New York	USA
Coleman	Miss	Susan	22	Saved	British	Brooklyn	USA
Collis	Mr.	Edwin Martin	38	Saved	U.S.C.	Riverside	USA
Condon	Mrs.	Terence (Della Josephine)	28	Died	U.S.C.	New York	USA
Costello	Miss	Mary		Died	British	New York	USA
Cowper	Mr.	Ernest Sedgwick	32	Saved	British	Toronto	Canada
Cox	Mrs.	Samuel J. (Margaret Elizabeth)	27	Saved	British	Winnipeg	Canada
Cox	Master	Desmond Francis	17m	Saved	British	Winnipeg	Canada
Critchison	Mr.	Stanley Lascelles	31	Saved	British	Hamilton	Canada
Critchison	Mrs.	Stanley Lascelles (Lillian)		Died	British	Hamilton	Canada
Critchison	Master	Bernard	13m	Died	British	Hamilton	Canada
Crosby	Miss	Ellen 'Nell'	36	Died	British	Vancouver	Canada
Crosby	Miss	Annie		Died	British	Vancouver	Canada
Crossley	Mr.	Cyrus	37	Saved	British	Toronto	Canada
Crossley	Mrs.	Cyrus (Sylvia Ellen)	34	Saved	British	Toronto	Canada
D							
Dale	Mr.	William		Died	British	Toronto	Canada
Dalrymple	Mr.	David	32	Saved	British	Hoboken	USA
Davies	Mr.	George F.	43	Died	British		Wales
Davis	Mrs.	(Anna)	52	Died	U.S.C.	Welland	Canada
De Broissierre	Mr.	Etienne T.		Died	Belgian	San Francisco	USA
Dewhurst	Mr.	William		Died	British	Fall River	USA
Dingley	Mrs.	Edward (Katherine S.)	38	Died	British	New York	USA
Dixon	Mr.	Arthur		Died	British		England
Dixon	Mrs.	Arthur (Bertha)		Saved	British		England
Dixon	Master	Stanley	6	Died	British		England
Docherty	Mrs.	William (Mabel)	29	Saved	U.S.C.	New York	USA
Docherty	Master	William Thomas	2m	Saved	U.S.C.	New York	USA
Dodd	Miss	Dorothy		Saved	British	Edmonton	Canada
Dolphin	Miss	Avis Gertrude	12	Saved	British	St. Thomas	Canada
Donahue	Miss	Sarah	35	Died	British	Boston	USA
Donald	Mr.	Archibald Douglas	26	Saved	British	Cambridge	USA
Duguid	Mr.	George Davie		Saved	British	Toronto	Canada
Duncan	Mrs.	Robert		Saved	British	Montreal	Canada
Dyer	Mr.	Robert	47	Saved	U.S.C.	Pittsburg	USA
E							
Egana	Mr.	Vicente	19	Saved	Spanish	New York	USA
Ehrhardt	Mr.	Herbert Wilfrid	21	Saved	British	Toronto	Canada
Elliott	Mr.	Arthur W.	30	Died	British	Calgary	Canada
Elliott	Mrs.	Arthur W. (Annie Louise)	25	Saved	British	Calgary	Canada
Ellis	Mr.	Herbert	45	Died	British		England
Ellis	Miss	Hilda		Died	British	St. Thomas	Canada

Last Name	Title	First Name	Age	Fate	Nationality	City	Country
Ellis	Mr.	John		Saved	British	Edmonton	Canada
Ewart	Mr.	Robert James	37	Saved	U.S.C.	Brooklyn	USA
Exley	Miss	Ida	19	Died	British	N. Braintree	USA
F							
Fentiman	Miss	Nellie	33	Died	British	Manchester	USA
Ferguson	Mr.	John	49 ?	Died	U.S.C.	New York	USA
Ferrier	Mr.	Alexander Hubert Buxton		Died	British	Penticton	Canada
Ferrier	Mrs.	Alexander Hubert Buxton (Beata Elizabeth Margaret)		Saved	British	Penticton	Canada
Ferrier	Miss	Sheila	1	Died	British	Penticton	Canada
Finch	Mrs.	William (Eva Eliza)	29	Died	British	Lynn	USA
Fish	Mrs.	Joseph (John E.) (Sarah Mary)		Saved	British	Toronto	Canada
Fish	Miss	Sadie Eileen	10	Saved	British	Toronto	Canada
Fish	Miss	Marion Enid	8	Saved	British	Toronto	Canada
Fish	Miss	Joan	05-m	Died	British	Toronto	Canada
Foley	Mr.	Arthur Richard	50	Died	U.S.C.	Trenton	USA
Foss	Dr.	Carl Elmer	27	Saved	U.S.C.	New York	USA
Fox	Mr.	Francis Edwin	30	Died	British	Trenton	USA
Fox	Mrs.	Francis Edwin (Emily)	28	Died	British	Trenton	USA
Freeman	Mr.	John	37	Saved	British	Falklain	Canada
Freeman	Mrs.	John (Rachel)	30	Saved	British	Falklain	Canada
French	Miss	Grace Hope	24	Saved	British	Passaic	USA
Friedman	Mr.	Samuel	28	Died	U.S.C.	Brooklyn	USA
Frost	Mr.	Harry Robinson	42	Saved	British	Regina	Canada
Fulton	Mr.	John Napier	59	Died	British	Montreal	Canada
Fyfe	Mrs.	James (Jennie)	65	Saved	British	Holyoke	USA
G							
Gadsden	Mr.	Arthur	39	Saved	British	Chicago	USA
Galligan	Miss	Margaret	22	Saved	British	New York	USA
Gardner	Mr.	James Andrew		Died	British		New Zealand
Gardner	Mrs.	James Andrew (Annie)		Died	British		New Zealand
Gardner	Mr.	Eric Clarence	16	Saved	British		New Zealand
Gardner	Master	William Gerard 'Willie'	11	Saved	British		New Zealand
Garry	Mr.	Christopher	51	Died	U.S.C.	Cleveland	USA
Gauthier	Mr.	Carlos		Died	Argentinian	Montreal	Canada
Gilhooly	Mrs.	(Catherine)		Saved	British	New York	USA
Gill	Mrs.	James (Catherine)	40	Died	British	Gillespie	USA
Gilsenan	Mr.	Hugh	60	Died	U.S.C.	Long Island City	USA
Glancy	Mr.	Joseph	43	Saved	British	Toronto	Canada

Last Name	Title	First Name	Age	Fate	Nationality	City	Country
Goodman	Mr.	Arthur		Died	British	Rochester	USA
Grandidge	Mrs.	Arthur (Nancie B.)	26	Died	British	Yonkers	USA
Grandidge	Miss	Eva Mary	3	Died	British	Yonkers	USA
Gray	Mr.	James Paul	64	Saved	British	San Francisco	USA
Gray	Mr.	Robert Duncan	35	Saved	British	Brooklyn	USA
Gray	Mrs.	William Hiram (Terence Florence)	24	Died	U.S.C.	Los Angeles	USA
Gray	Master	Stuart James	3	Died	U.S.C.	Los Angeles	USA
Greenwood	Master	Ronald Sutcliff	11	Died	U.S.C.	Lawrence	USA
Griffiths	Mr.	Christopher William	32	Saved	British	Winnipeg	Canada
Grimshaw	Mr.	Arthur	18	Died	British	Brooklyn	USA
Groves	Mr.	Sidney Frederick	28	Died	British	Toronto	Canada
Groves	Mrs.	Sidney Frederick (Clara)	27	Died	British	Toronto	Canada
Groves	Master	Frederick	1.5	Died	British	Toronto	Canada
Gwyer	Reverend	Herbert Linford	32	Saved	British	Saskatoon	Canada
Gwyer	Mrs.	Herbert Linford (Margaret Inglis Adams)	26	Saved	British	Saskatoon	Canada
H							
Haigh	Mr.	James Harold	38	Died	British	Winnipeg	Canada
Haldane	Mr.	James Cargill	36	Saved	British	Boston	USA
Hamilton	Mrs.	John (Isabella)		Died	British	New Haven	USA
Hampshire	Miss	Elizabeth Eleanor	36	Saved	British	Boston	USA
Hanes	Mr.	Duncan Arthur Walpole	32	Saved	British	Saskatoon	Canada
Hanson	Mr.	Samuel	51	Died	British	Central Falls	USA
Hanson	Mrs.	Samuel (Mary)	59	Died	British	Central Falls	USA
Hardy	Miss	Elsie	25	Saved	British	Montclair	USA
Hare	Miss	Bessie	27	Died	British	New York	USA
Harris	Mr.	Reuben	51	Died	British	Toronto	Canada
Harris	Mrs.	Reuben (Emma)	61	Died	British	Toronto	Canada
Harrison	Mr.	Herbert Kesteven	37	Died	British	Chicago	USA
Harrison	Mr.	James	48	Died	British	New York	USA
Hastings	Mrs.	(Margaret)	40	Died	British	New Rochelle	USA
Henderson	Mrs.	Harris Reginald (Violet Alice)	32	Saved	British	Montreal	Canada
Henderson	Master	Harris 'Huntley' Reginald	10	Saved	British	Montreal	Canada
Hendrickson	Mr.	Knud I.		Died	British	Edmonton	Canada
Henn	Mr.	Ernest George	35	Died	British	Saskatoon	Canada
Henn	Mrs.	Ernest George (Edith Mabel)	27	Died	British	Saskatoon	Canada
Henshaw	Mrs.	George (Mabel Iris)	27	Saved	British	Saskatoon	Canada
Henshaw	Miss	Constance	05-m	Died	British	Saskatoon	Canada
Herbert	Mrs.	E.V. (Florence)	26	Died	British	London	England
Hertz	Mr.	Douglas Grant	32	Saved	British	St. Louis	USA
Higginbotham	Miss	Mary "Polly"		Died	British	Fall River	USA

Last Name	Title	First Name	Age	Fate	Nationality	City	Country
Hill	Mr.	William Spencer	29	Saved	British		Wales
Hill	Mrs.	Richard (Emmie Jane)	31/32	Saved	British	Schenectady	USA
Hogg	Mrs.	(Ellen)	28	Saved	British	New York	USA
Holbourn	Professor	Ian Bernard Stoughton	43	Saved	British	Yonkers	USA
Holland	Mrs.	H. Hedley L. (Nina)	34	Saved	U.S.C.	New York	USA
Homewood	Mr.	William Thomas	30	Died	British	Toledo	USA
Hopkins	Miss	Alice	33	Died	British	Boston	USA
Hopkins	Miss	Kate	35	Died	British	Boston	USA
Hopkins	Mr.	David Thomas	25 ?	Died	British		Wales
Horsburgh	Miss	Martha	21	Died	British	Bernardsville	USA
Horton	Mrs.	Edwin (Elizabeth)	51	Died	British	Cleveland	USA
Hoskins	Mr.	Arthur		Saved	British	Montreal	Canada
Hounsell	Mr.	Edgar Cyril	28	Saved	British		England
Hubbard	Mr.	Frederick Cole Amos	23	Died	British	New York	USA
Hull	Mrs.	George (Winifred)	33	Saved	British	Winnipeg	Canada
Hume	Mrs.	Samuel E. (Mary Agnes)		Died	U.S.C.	Harrison	USA
Humphreys	Mr.	Henry St. Giles	29	Died	British	Los Angeles	USA
Hunt	Miss	Isabella Gertrude	37	Died	British	Haverford	USA
Hunter	Mr.	George H.		Died	British	Atlanta	USA
Hunter	Mrs.	George H. (Maggie)		Died	British	Atlanta	USA
Huston	Miss	Nellie	31	Died	British	Chicago	USA
I							
Inch	Mr.	William Ernest	27	Saved	British	New York	USA
J							
Jackson	Mr.	Isaac		Saved	British	Patterson	USA
Jackson	Mr.	Percy Thornton		Died	British	Buffalo	USA
Jones	Mrs.	Alfred (Ellen)		Died	British	Toronto	Canada
Jones	Master	William Edward	15m	Died	British	Toronto	Canada
Jones	Miss	Gwendolyn	29	Died	British	San Francisco	USA
Jones	Mr.	Fred		Died	British	Winnipeg	Canada
Jones	Mr.	Isaac Talbot		Died	British		Wales
Jones	Mr.	Patrick Llewellynn	28	Died	British		England
Jones	Mr.	William Gwynne	24	Saved	British		Wales
Judson	Mr.	Frederick Sheldon	25	Saved	U.S.C.	New York	USA
K							
Kaltenbach	Miss	Alice Margaret (Calterback)		Died	British	Toronto	Canada
Kay	Mrs.	James (Marguerita)	31	Died	British	New York	USA
Kay	Master	Robert Belsher	7	Saved	British	New York	USA
Kaye	Miss	Kathleen	14	Saved	British	Toronto	Canada
Keely	Miss	Annie		Died	British	Toronto	Canada
Kelly	Mr.	James Robert	42 ?	Died	British	New York	USA
Kelly	Miss	Margaret S.	34	Died	U.S.C.	Pittsburg	USA
Kenney	Mrs.	Peter (Margaret)		Died	British	Charlestown	USA

Last Name	Title	First Name	Age	Fate	Nationality	City	Country
Kenney	Miss	Mary Bridget	2	Died	British	Charlestown	USA
Kinch	Mrs.	William (Eunice)	45	Died	British	Cleveland	USA
Kinch	Mr.	William Mustoe	19	Died	British	Cleveland	USA
King	Mrs.	Sidney (Martha Frances)	59	Died	British	Lockport	USA
Kuebellick	Mr.	Max Samuel	31	Died	British	Montreal	Canada
L							
Ladd	Mr.	Owen	33	Died	British	Winnipeg	Canada
Lakin	Miss	Martha Maria	40	Died	British	Saskatoon	Canada
Lambie	Mrs.	Daniel (Mary)	27	Died	British	Roslyn	USA
Lambie	Miss	Elizabeth	8	Died	British	Roslyn	USA
Lambie	Miss	Mary	2	Died	British	Roslyn	USA
Lancaster	Mr.	Frank William	50	Died	British	Toronto	Canada
Lancaster	Miss	Annie		Died	British	Montreal	Canada
Lancaster	Miss	Dorothy		Died	British	Montreal	Canada
Lander	Mr.	Edward Harris	32	Saved	British	New York	USA
Lane	Mr.	George Benjamin	26	Saved	British		England
Lawranson	Mr.	Edward		Died	British	Michel	Canada
Lawranson	Mrs.	Edward (Elizabeth)		Died	British	Michel	Canada
Lawrence	Miss	Ella Woods	50	Died	British	Winnipeg	Canada
Lee	Miss	Bridget	51	Saved	British	New York	USA
Leipold	Miss	Catherine Estella M.	27	Saved	British	Chicago	USA
Leverich	Mrs.	William Edward (Rosina)	60	Died	U.S.C.	New York	USA
Leverich	Miss	Rosina Philip	28	Died	U.S.C.	New York	USA
Lewis	Mr.	Isaac 'John'	31	Saved	British	New York	USA
Lewis	Mrs.	Isaac 'John' (Jane)	31	Saved	British	New York	USA
Lewis	Miss	Edith	5	Saved	British	New York	USA
Lines	Mr.	Stanley Llandolf Burnett	30	Saved	British	Toronto	Canada
Lines	Mrs.	Stanley Llandolf Burnett (Ethel Moore)	34	Saved	British	Toronto	Canada
Lintott	Mr.	Roy Iver	21	Died	British	Calgary	Canada
Little	Mrs.	J.	24	Died	British	Brooklyn	USA
Little	Miss	Alice Laura (Margaret)	14m	Died	British	Brooklyn	USA
Lohden	Mrs.	H. (Sarah Rose Mary)	38	Saved	British	Toronto	Canada
Lohden	Miss	Rose Elsie	11	Saved	British	Toronto	Canada
Longdin	Mr.	Arthur	39	Died	British	Toronto	Canada
Longdin	Mrs.	Arthur (Matilda)	30	Died	British	Toronto	Canada
Lovett	Miss	Mary		Died	British	Fall River	USA
Loynd	Mr.	David	51	Died	British	Ottawa	Canada
Loynd	Mrs.	David (Alice)	49	Died	British	Ottawa	Canada
Lucas	Mr.	Francis John	22	Saved	British	Pittsburg	USA
Lund	Mr.	Charles Henry	29	Died	U.S.C.	New York	USA
Lund	Mrs.	Charles Henry (Sarah Jane)	28	Saved	U.S.C.	New York	USA
M							
MacFarquhar	Mrs.	John (Jane Ann)	52	Saved	U.S.C.	Stratford	USA

Last Name	Title	First Name	Age	Fate	Nationality	City	Country
MacFarquhar	Miss	Grace Marie	16	Saved	U.S.C.	Stratford	USA
MacGregor	Mrs.	(Betsy)	63	Died	British	New York	USA
MacGregor	Mr.	Arthur L.	31	Died	British	New York	USA
Mackay	Mr.	Hamish	33	Died	British	New York	USA
Macky	Mr.	Joseph		Died	British		New Zealand
Macky	Mrs.	Joseph (Mary)	56	Died	British		New Zealand
Maclay	Miss	Bessie		Died	British	Ridgefield Park	USA
Mainman	Mr.	Alfred Reid	56	Died	British	Edmonton	Canada
Mainman	Mrs.	Alfred Reid (Elizabeth)		Died	British	Edmonton	Canada
Mainman	Mr.	John V.	21	Died	British	Edmonton	Canada
Mainman	Mr.	Alfred S.	19	Died	British	Edmonton	Canada
Mainman	Miss	Mary Frances 'Molly'	16	Saved	British	Edmonton	Canada
Mainman	Miss	Elizabeth Sarah	7	Saved	British	Edmonton	Canada
Mainman	Master	Edwin Richard	7	Saved	British	Edmonton	Canada
Manby	Miss	Ada	36	Saved	British	Montreal	Canada
Mannion	Mr.	Martin		Saved	British	Albany	USA
Marichal	Mr.	Joseph Phillibert Rene	38	Saved	French	Kingston	Canada
Marichal	Mrs.	Joseph Phillibert Rene (Jessie)	39	Saved	French	Kingston	Canada
Marichal	Miss	Yvonne Jessie	5	Saved	French	Kingston	Canada
Marichal	Miss	Phyllis Renee	4	Saved	French	Kingston	Canada
Marichal	Master	Maurice	2	Saved	French	Kingston	Canada
Martin	Mr.	Charles D.	21 ?	Died	British	Pittsburg	USA
Martin	Miss	Ruby	26	Saved	British	New York	USA
Martin-Davey	Mr.	William		Died	British	Vancouver	Canada
Martin-Davey	Mrs.	William (Elizabeth Cumbe)	53	Died	British	Vancouver	Canada
Martin-Davey	Mr.	Arthur	18	Died	British	Vancouver	Canada
Matthewson	Mrs.	Joseph (Maud E. S.)		Died	British	Springfield	USA
Matthewson	Master	Joseph Jr.	8m	Died	British	Springfield	USA
Matthews	Mr.	Robert	34	Died	British	Winnipeg	Canada
Matthews	Mrs.	Robert (Annie) *This was his mistress; the real Mrs. Matthews didn't travel with him.*		Died	British	Winnipeg	Canada
Maycock	Miss	Mary	23	Saved	British	Harrison	USA
McClintock	Miss	Margaret	31	Saved	British	New York	USA
McClure	Miss	Margaret		Died	British	New York	USA
McColm	Mrs.	James A. (Christina Harrow S.)	38	Saved	British	Ottawa	Canada
McCorkindale	Mrs.	Daniel (Elizabeth)	33	Died	British	Chromo	USA
McCorkindale	Master	Duncan	7	Died	British	Chromo	USA
McCorkindale	Miss	Mary	Infant	Died	British	Chromo	USA
Mecredy	Dr.	Ralph R. J. R.	26	Saved	British	Battle Creek	USA

Last Name	Title	First Name	Age	Fate	Nationality	City	Country
McDonnell	Miss	Kate 'Kitty'	25	Saved	British	New York	USA
McEvoy	Mr.	Henry		Died	British	New York	United States
McFayden	Mr.	Hugh	24	Saved	British	Galt	Canada
McGinley	Mr.	Patrick Vincent	32	Saved	British	New York	USA
McGovern	Miss	Mazie		Died	U.S.C.	Bloomfield	USA
MacHardy	Mrs.	Peter Kenneth (Annie)		Died	U.S.C.	New York	USA
McIlroy	Mr.	Archibald		Died	British	Edmonton	Canada
MacKenzie	Mrs.	Robert (Mary A.)		Died	U.S.C.	New Bedford	USA
McKechan	Mrs.	Robert (Elizabeth)	32	Saved	British	Gillespie	USA
McKechan	Master	James	5	Died	British	Gillespie	USA
McKechan	Master	Campbell	10-m	Saved	British	Gillespie	USA
McKinnon	Mrs.	Robert		Died	British	Toronto	Canada
McLellan	Miss	Sarah	36	Saved	British	Lake Forrest	USA
McPartlin	Mr.	Myles		Died	U.S.C.	New York	USA
Menzies	Miss	Isabella	57	Died	British	Yakima	USA
Meriheina	Mr.	William Uno	26	Saved	Russian	New York	USA
Michael	Mr.	Dewi	38	Saved	British		England
Middlemast	Mrs.	Edward (Isabella L.)	32	Saved	British	Regina	Canada
Middleton	Miss	Alice	25	Saved	British	New York	USA
Milford	Mr.	Frederick John	36	Saved	U.S.C.	Hancock	USA
Millar	Mrs.	Aubrey M. (Margaret)		Died	British	New York	USA
Mitchelhill	Mr.	William		Died	British	St. Joseph	USA
Mitchell	Mr.	Arthur Jackson	45	Saved	U.S.C.	Toronto	Canada
Mitchell	Mr.	Walter Dawson	27	Died	British	Newark	USA
Mitchell	Mrs.	Walter Dawson (Jeanette Elizabeth)	27	Saved	British	Newark	USA
Mitchell	Master	Walter Dawson Jr.	10-m	Died	British	Newark	USA
Moffatt	Mr.	William		Died	British	Winchester	Canada
Molloy	Miss	Margaret		Died	British	New York	USA
Moody	Mrs.	(Martha)	70	Died	British	San Francisco	USA
Moody	Miss	Martha	32	Saved	British	San Francisco	USA
Moore	Dr.	Daniel Virgil	36	Saved	U.S.C.	New York	USA
Moore	Mr.	Ernest		Died	British	Moose Jaw	Canada
Moore	Mr.	Edwin		Died	British	Central Falls	USA
Moore	Mr.	John	24	Saved	British	Manchester Green	USA
Morris	Reverend	Hugh Carlton Syddall	32	Saved	British	Toronto	Canada
Mounsey	Mr.	William Edgar	58	Died	U.S.C.	New York	USA
Muir	Mr.	Matthew	63	Saved	British	Philadelphia	USA
Murdoch	Miss	Jessie	34	Saved	British	Westbury	USA
Murray	Mrs.	Christopher (Rose Ellen)	30	Saved	U.S.C.	New York	USA

Last Name	Title	First Name	Age	Fate	Nationality	City	Country
Myers	Mr.	William Ellason G.	16	Saved	British	Hamilton	Canada
N							
Naish	Mr.	Theodore	59	Died	U.S.C.	Kansas City	USA
Naish	Mrs.	Theodore (Belle)	49	Saved	U.S.C.	Kansas City	USA
Neatby	Miss	Winifred	29	Saved	British	Saskatoon	Canada
Needham	Mr.	Henry E.		Saved	British	New York	USA
Negus	Mr.	Edward	27	Saved	British	New York	USA
Neilson	Mr.	Henry	41	Died	British	Brooklyn	USA
Neilson	Mrs.	Henry (Frances)	40	Died	British	Brooklyn	USA
Neilson	Mr.	Charles H.	18	Died	British	Brooklyn	USA
Neimark	Mr.	Abraham		Died	Russian	New York	USA
Neville	Mr.	Albert Charles	40	Died	British	Toronto	Canada
Neville	Mrs.	Albert Charles (Mabel Frances)	35	Saved	British	Toronto	Canada
Neville	Miss	Evelyn	14	Died	British	Toronto	Canada
Neville	Master	Charles	11	Died	British	Toronto	Canada
Neville	Miss	Muriel	4	Died	British	Toronto	Canada
Nicholson	Mr.	Charles Duncan	27	Died	British	Edmonton	Canada
Nichol	Miss	Mary F.	22	Died	British	Chicago	USA
Nicholl	Mr.	George		Died	British	Philadelphia	USA
Norman	Mr.	Robert	39	Died	British	New York	USA
North	Miss	Olive	25	Saved	British	Saskatoon	Canada
O							
O'Donnell	Mr.	Patrick		Saved	U.S.C.	Hoboken	USA
Owens	Mrs.	Hubert Isaacs (Cecilia Mildred)	33	Saved	British	Elwood City	USA
Owens	Master	Ronald Hubert	10	Died	British	Elwood City	USA
Owens	Master	Reginald	8	Died	British	Elwood City	USA
P							
Page	Mr.	Andrew	30	Saved	British	Medicine Hat	Canada
Palmer	Mr.	Albert		Died	British	Toronto	Canada
Palmer	Mrs.	Albert (Annie)	33	Died	British	Toronto	Canada
Palmer	Master	Edgar	6	Died	British	Toronto	Canada
Palmer	Miss	Olive	4	Died	British	Toronto	Canada
Palmer	Master	Albert	06-m	Died	British	Toronto	Canada
Palmer	Miss	Kathleen	41	Died	British	N. Augusta	USA
Palmer	Mr.	Frank Arthur		Died	British	N. Augusta	USA
Partlett	Mrs.	Frank (Amy)	35	Died	British	New York	USA
Partlett	Miss	Enid	13	Died	British	New York	USA
Parsons	Mr.	Archibald Ernest	30	Died	British	New York	USA
Pavey	Miss	Lorna Mary	28	Saved	British	Fort Qui Appelle	Canada
Payne	Mr.	Martin Sylvester	19	Saved	British	Springfield	USA
Peacock	Mrs.	Thomas Edward (Elizabeth L.)	48	Saved	British	Jerome	USA

Last Name	Title	First Name	Age	Fate	Nationality	City	Country
Peacock	Mr.	Thomas Edward Jr.	17	Saved	British	Jerome	USA
Pells	Mr.	Cyril Elmore	24	Saved	British	Vancouver	Canada
Pells	Mrs.	Cyril Elmore (Mary Anita)	32	Saved	British	Vancouver	Canada
Pells	Master	John	Infant	Died	British	Vancouver	Canada
Phair	Reverend	Ernest Edward Maxwell	44	Died	British	Winnipeg	Canada
Pirie	Mrs.	Arthur (Annie)	35	Died	British	Lynn	USA
Pirie	Miss	Margaret	10	Died	British	Lynn	USA
Pirie	Master	Arthur	4	Died	British	Lynn	USA
Pirrie	Miss	Henrietta		Died	British	Ottawa	Canada
Plank	Mrs.	David (Harriet)	61	Saved	British	Toronto	Canada
Poole	Mrs.	Thomas William (Gertrude Kate Elizabeth)	45	Died	British	New York	USA
Potter	Mr.	Walter		Died	British	Calgary	Canada
Prescott	Mrs.	George (Bertha)	30	Died	British	Toronto	Canada
Press	Miss	Mary Jane		Died	British	New York	USA
Prichard	Mr.	Richard Preston	29	Died	British	Montreal	Canada
Proudfoot	Mr.	Samuel Lamond		Died	British	Belle Vernon	USA
Purse	Mr.	Reginald		Died	British	Chattanooga	USA
Purse	Mrs.	Reginald (Gertrude Alice)		Died	British	Chattanooga	USA
Pye	Mrs.	William Samuel (Charlotte Lillian)	28	Saved	British	Edmonton	Canada
Pye	Miss	Marjorie	18-m	Died	British	Edmonton	Canada
R							
Readdie	Mr.	James Robert	29	Saved	British	Brooklyn	USA
Reid	Mr.	Peter (Ellen)		Died	British	Little Rock	USA
Richards	Mr.	Thomas Henry	40	Saved	British	Butte	USA
Richards	Mrs.	Thomas Henry (Phillipa "Phyllis")	38	Saved	British	Butte	USA
Richards	Master	Thomas Percy	7	Saved	British	Butte	USA
Richards	Master	Cecil Henry	4	Saved	British	Butte	USA
Richards	Miss	Dora Millicent	18-m	Died	British	Butte	USA
Richardson	Mrs.	James (Annie)	39	Saved	British	Philadelphia	USA
Ritchie	Mr.	William Joass		Died	British	Winnipeg	Canada
Robertson	Mr.	Andrew		Died	British	New Orleans	USA
Robinson	Mr.	Thomas H.		Died	British	Vancouver	Canada
Robinson	Mrs.	Thomas H. (Edith)		Saved	British	Vancouver	Canada
Robson	Miss	Annie	30	Died	British	Mount Vernon	USA
Robson	Mr.	Kenneth Hamilton Stewart	29	Died	British	Mount Vernon	USA
Rogers	Miss	Elizabeth		Saved	British	Toronto	Canada
Rogers	Mr.	Richard James	41	Died	British	Toronto	Canada
Rolfe	Mr.	George Sommerville	31	Died	British	Hamilton	Canada
Rooney	Miss	Mary		Died	British	Brooklyn	USA

Last Name	Title	First Name	Age	Fate	Nationality	City	Country
Rose	Mr.	Fred J.		Saved	British	Baltimore	USA
Rowell	Mr.	Thomas Reuben		Died	British	New York	USA
Ryan	Miss	Mary		Died	British	New York	USA
S							
Salt	Mr.	Henry Jordan		Died	U.S.C.	Boston	USA
Samoilescu	Mr.	David (Dave Samuels)	32	Died	U.S.C.	New York	USA
Sandells	Mr.	Thomas	50	Saved	British	Winnipeg	Canada
Scott	Mr.	George	27	Saved	British	Toronto	Canada
Scrimgeour	Mr.	William		Saved	British	New York	USA
Secchi	Mrs.	Herbert (Edith Helen)	35	Saved	British	New York	USA
Semours	Mr.	Charles T.		Died	British	Buffalo	USA
Semple	Mrs.	Andrew (Agnes)	29	Died	British	Toronto	Canada
Semple	Master	John	Infant	Died	British	Toronto	Canada
Shaw	Miss	Emily	32	Died	British	Winnipeg	Canada
Shineman	Mr.	James	29	Died	U.S.C.	New York	USA
Shineman	Mrs.	James (Margaret)		Died	U.S.C.	New York	USA
Simpson	Reverend	Henry Wood	37	Saved	British	Roseland	Canada
Slater	Mr.	Frank William		Died	British	New York	USA
Slattery	Mr.	Patrick John	27	Saved	U.S.C.	New York	USA
Smart	Mr.	George Mercer		Died	British	Vancouver	Canada
Smith	Mr.	Albert R.	35	Died	British	New York	USA
Smith	Mrs.	Albert R. (Gladys E.)	31	Died	British	New York	USA
Smith	Miss	Dorothy	Infant	Died	British	New York	USA
Smith	Mr.	Alfred F.		Died	British	Elwood City	USA
Smith	Mrs.	Alfred F. (Elizabeth A.)		Died	British	Elwood City	USA
Smith	Miss	Helen	6	Saved	British	Elwood City	USA
Smith	Miss	Bessie	06-m	Died	British	Elwood City	USA
Smith	Mr.	David J.		Died	British		England
Smith	Mr.	George Arthur	32	Died	British	Rochester	USA
Smith	Mr.	Harry		Died	British	Toronto	Canada
Smith	Mr.	John Preston	28	Saved	British		England
Smith	Miss	Sarah		Died	British	St. Thomas	Canada
Sorenson	Mr.	Soren	33	Saved	British	Edmonton	Canada
Spillman	Mr.	John Bowen	33	Died	British	Wyandotte	USA
Spillman	Mrs.	John Bowen (Eliza)		Died	British	Wyandotte	USA
Stanley	Mr.	Henry William		Died	British	Trenton	USA
Stevens	Mr.	Charles Henry	57	Died	U.S.C.	Atlantic City	USA
Stevenson	Mrs.	William (Janet M.)		Died	British	Cleveland	USA
Stevenson	Miss	Elizabeth	Infant	Died	British	Cleveland	USA
Stewart	Mrs.	James (Christina)	30	Saved	British	Toronto	Canada
Stewart	Master	John Knox	05-m	Saved	British	Toronto	Canada
Stokes	Mr.	George Edward "Ted"		Died	British	Victoria	Canada
Stokes	Mrs.	George Edward (Mabel)		Died	British	Victoria	Canada
Stokes	Master	William "Billie"	2.5	Died	British	Victoria	Canada

Last Name	Title	First Name	Age	Fate	Nationality	City	Country
Stones	Mr.	Norman	28	Saved	British	Vancouver	Canada
Stones	Mrs.	Norman (Mary Hilda)	29	Died	British	Vancouver	Canada
Storch	Mr.	Walter Reinhold	29	Saved	British	San Francisco	USA
Stroud	Mr.	Edward Percy Wallace	38	Saved	British		Mexico
Stroud	Mrs.	Edward Percy Wallace (Constance Eda)	31	Saved	British		Mexico
Stroud	Miss	Helen	3	Died	British		Mexico
O'Sullivan	Mr.	Florence	26	Saved	British	Boston	USA
O'Sullivan	Mrs.	Florence (Julia)	25	Saved	British	Boston	USA
Sullivan	Mr.	George		Died	British	Groton	USA
Sullivan	Mrs.	George (Emily)		Died	British	Groton	USA
Sumner	Mr.	Thomas		Saved	British	Quincy	USA
Surman	Mrs.	Henry George (Mabel Annie)		Died	British		England
Sutherst	Mr.	Thomas		Died	British		England
Sweeney	Mr.	John Martin		Saved	U.S.C.	Watertown	USA
Sweet	Mr.	Frank H.	22	Saved	British	Toronto	Canada
T							
Taft	Mr.	Sidney	31	Saved	British	Needham	USA
Tarry	Mr.	Edward	27	Saved	British	Toronto	Canada
Taylor	Mrs.	Stanley Robert (Annie Sarah)	41	Died	U.S.C.	Boston	USA
Taylor	Mr.	Stanley Robert Jr.	14	Saved	U.S.C.	Boston	USA
Thomas	Mr.	Ernest	33	Died	British	Winnipeg	Canada
Thomas	Mrs.	Ernest (Mary Ann)		Died	British	Winnipeg	Canada
Thompson	Mr.	Albert	37	Died	British	Toronto	Canada
Thompson	Miss	Muriel		Died	British	Miami	USA
Thompson	Mr.	Robert Joseph	37	Died	British	Holdridge	USA
Thurston	Mr.	John		Died	British	Bridgeport	USA
Tierney	Mrs.	James (Mary)	26	Died	British	Vandegrift	USA
Tierney	Miss	Nina	5	Died	British	Vandegrift	USA
Tijou	Mr.	Walter Edgar	44	Saved	British	Toronto	Canada
Tijou	Master	Howard Walter	10	Died	British	Toronto	Canada
Todd	Mr.	David	28	Died	British	Philadelphia	USA
Treverrow	Mrs.	(Caroline)	62	Died	British	Butte	USA
Tulloch	Mr.	James		Died	British	Kendall	USA
Tulloch	Mrs.	James (Agnes)	21	Died	British	Kendall	USA
Tulloch	Miss	Hannah	11m	Died	British	Kendall	USA
Turpin	Mr.	Thomas Keith	30	Saved	British	Victoria	Canada
Turpin	Mrs.	Thomas Keith (Maud)		Saved	British	Victoria	Canada
Twigg	Mr.	Frederick Alexander		Died	British	Winnipeg	Canada
Tyers	Mr.	Frederick Charles		Died	British	Nottingham	England
V							
Vance	Mr.	John		Died	U.S.C.	New York	USA

Last Name	Title	First Name	Age	Fate	Nationality	City	Country
Varcoe	Mrs.	John Francis (Lavinia)	70	Died	British	Kansas City	USA
Varley	Miss	Alice Mercy	50	Died	British	East Northfield	USA
Venn	Mr.	Harold Stanley		Died	British	San Francisco	USA
de Vescovi	Dr.	Silvio Bruno	28	Saved	Italian	New York	USA
W							
Walker	Mr.	John	28	Died	British	Toronto	Canada
Walker	Mrs.	John (Gertrude)	26	Died	British	Toronto	Canada
Walker	Miss	Mary Jane		Died	British	San Francisco	USA
Wallace	Mr.	Cyril John George	20	Saved	British	Holyoke	USA
Wallace	Miss	Delia		Died	British	New York	USA
Wallace	Miss	Margaret		Died	British	New York	USA
Walsh	Miss	Ellen		Died	British	New York	USA
Ward	Mr.	James Langmuir		Died	British	Wilkie	Canada
Ward	Mr.	Michael		Died	U.S.C.	Pittsburg	USA
Waring	Mr.	Charles		Died	British	Winnipeg	Canada
Warner	Mr.	Tertius Selwyn	21	Died	British	London	Canada
Waters	Miss	Katherine W.	25	Died	British	Elcentra	USA
Waters	Miss	Margaret	29	Died	British	Elcentra	USA
Webb	Miss	Minnie	34 ?	Saved	British	New York	USA
Webster	Mr.	Frederick G.	28	Saved	British	Toronto	Canada
Webster	Mrs.	Frederick G. (Margaret)	24	Died	British	Toronto	Canada
Webster	Master	William	3	Saved	British	Toronto	Canada
Webster	Master	Frederick	11m	Died	British	Toronto	Canada
Webster	Master	Henry	11m	Died	British	Toronto	Canada
Weir	Mr.	Cecil Hamilton	31	Died	British	Victoria	Canada
Whaley	Mr.	Robert William	33	Saved	British	Victoria	Canada
Whitcombe	Mr.	Hugh Martin Donald Gore	25	Saved	British	Havana	Cuba
Whitehead	Miss	Florence	41	Saved	British	Boston	USA
Whyatt	Mrs.	Aaron Taylor (Martha Ann)	60	Saved	British	New Bedford	USA
Wickham	Mrs.	(Nina)	50	Died	British		New Zealand
Wickings-Smith	Mr.	Cyril	27	Saved	British	Victoria	Canada
Wickings-Smith	Mrs.	Cyril (Phyllis)	24	Saved	British	Victoria	Canada
Wickings-Smith	Miss	Nancy Eileen Fenn	8m	Saved	British	Victoria	Canada
Wickings-Smith	Mr.	Basil Guilford	29	Died	British	Victoria	Canada
Wiggins	Mrs.	Arthur Vaughan (Sarah Helena)	49	Saved	British	Toronto	Canada
Wild	Miss	Evelyn Norbury	25	Saved	British	Paterson	USA

Last Name	Title	First Name	Age	Fate	Nationality	City	Country
Wild	Miss	Agnes	21	Saved	British	Paterson	USA
Williams	Miss	Beatrice	24	Saved	British	Rock Island	USA
Williams	Mrs.	(Jane)	55	Died	British	Toronto	Canada
Williams	Mr.	Robert		Saved	British	Calgary	Canada
Williams	Mr.	Thomas J.	32	Saved	British		Wales
Wilson	Mr.	John		Saved	British	Cambridge	USA
Wilson	Mrs.	Patrick (Inez Minnie)	46	Saved	British	Moosejaw	USA
Wilson	Miss	Sarah		Died	British	Brooklyn	USA
Winter	Miss	Thirza	31	Saved	British	New York	USA
Wise	Sister	Isabelle Eloise	59	Died	British		Jamaica
Wolfenden	Mr.	John Charles	51	Died	British	Pawtucket	USA
Wolfenden	Mrs.	John Charles (Dora)	49	Saved	British	Pawtucket	USA
Woodcock	Miss	Sarah Emma		Died	British	Fall River	USA
Woolven	Mrs.	Emond Victor (Helen)		Died	British	Edmonton	Canada
Worden	Mrs.	Charles E. (Jane)		Died	U.S.C.	Lowell	USA
Wordsworth	Mr.	Osmund Bartle	27	Saved	British	Toronto	Canada
Wordsworth	Miss	Ruth Mary	37	Saved	British	Toronto	Canada
Wright	Miss	Mary		Died	British	New York	USA
Wylie	Mrs.	(Emma)		Died	British	Jersey City	USA
Y							
Yardley	Mr.	Lewis Frank		Died	British	Toronto	Canada
Yeatman	Mr.	Charles Aylmer Luttrell	36	Died	British	New York	USA
Yeatman	Mrs.	Charles Aylmet Luttrell (Cora Rose)	33	Died	British	New York	USA
THIRD CLASS							
A							
Agnew	Mr.	Thomas W.	27	Died	British	Monessen	USA
Agnew	Mrs.	Thomas W.	27	Died	British	Monessen	USA
Alexan	Mr.	Babajan	30	Saved	Russian	New York	USA
Ameraiof	Mr.	Benjamin	37	Died	Persian	Chicago	USA
Andersdotter	Mrs.	(Carolina B.)	54	Died	Swedish	Walden	USA
Andreatos	Mr.	Marinos	39	Died	Greek	New York	USA
Andrijine	Mr.	Anisyon	22	Died	Russian	New York	USA
Antila	Mrs.	(Aino)	25	Saved	Finnish	Deported	USA
Antila	Master	Carl	4	Saved	U.S.C.	Deported	USA
Antila	Master	Jan	3	Saved	U.S.C.	Deported	USA
Aprin	Mr.	Joseph	45	Died	Russian	Gary	USA
Ashman	Mr.	Henry Clifford	27	Saved	British	Butte	USA
B							
Baba	Mr.	Abraham	45	Died	Persian	Chicago	USA
Baba	Mr.	Frank	30	Saved	Persian	Chicago	USA
Baba	Mr.	George	39	Died	Persian	Chicago	USA
Babeicz	Mr.	Jakim	33	Died	Russian	New York	USA

Last Name	Title	First Name	Age	Fate	Nationality	City	Country
Babiczuk	Mr.	Siemion	39	Died	Russian	Windsor	Canada
Babka	Mr.	Matthew	28	Saved	Russian		Canada
Bailey	Mr.	Frederick R.	40	Saved	British	Orange	USA
Ballantyne	Miss	Margaret	29	Saved	British	New York	USA
Bannerji	Mr.	Induprakas	30	Died	Indian	Princeton	USA
Barclay	Mr.	George	30	Saved	British		Canada
Barrow	Mr.	Donald George M.	25	Saved	British	Maple Creek	Canada
Barrow	Mrs.	Donald George M.	20	Died	British	Maple Creek	Canada
Bartley	Mr.	George Noble	38	Died	British	Welland	Canada
Bartley	Mrs.	George Noble	28	Died	British	Welland	Canada
Bartley	Master	Arthur	4	Died	British	Welland	Canada
Bartley	Master	Gordon	3m	Died	British	Welland	Canada
Beauchamp	Mr.	William	36	Saved	British	Otsego	USA
Benjamin	Miss	Queenie	30	Saved	British	Roland Park	USA
Bennett	Mr.	William	39	Died	British		Canada
Bevan	Mr.	Jack	26	Died	British	Bellaire	USA
Bialans	Mr.	Stefan	30	Saved	Russian	Waterbury	USA
Bishop	Mr.	Joseph	50	Died	British	Hamilton	Canada
Bishop	Mrs.	(Alice)	49	Died	British	Hamilton	Canada
Bishop	Mr.	William	44	Died	British	Hamilton	Canada
Blackburn	Mr.	George	42	Died	British		Canada
Blackshaw	Mrs.	Fred (Alice)	29	Died	British	St. Thomas	Canada
Blackshaw	Master	John J.	1	Died	British	St. Thomas	Canada
Blankman	Mr.	Judka	37	Saved	Russian	New York	USA
Bodell	Mr.	Thomas	32	Died	British	Toronto	Canada
Bodell	Mrs.	Thomas (Florence)	36	Died	British	Toronto	Canada
Bodell	Master	Thomas Jr.	3	Died	British	Toronto	Canada
Boreskevecs	Mr.	Folop	28	Died	Russian	Palmerton	USA
Bottomley	Mr.	Fred	26	Saved	British	New York	USA
Boyle	Mr.	James	28	Saved	British		Canada
Boyle	Miss	Nicholas	24	Died	British	Chicago	USA
Bozenof	Mr.	Dennis	34	Saved	Russian	Chicago	USA
Bozenof	Mr.	Philate	35	Saved	Russian	Chicago	USA
Brown	Miss	Constance	38	Died	British	Philadelphia	USA
Brown	Miss	Evelyn	28	Died	British	Philadelphia	USA
Brown	Mr.	William	31	Saved	British	Toronto	Canada
Budrin	Mr.	Antoni	50	Saved	Russian	Greaville	USA
Burke	Mr.	Ernest James	48	Died	British	Central Falls	USA
Butler	Mr.	William M.	38	Died	British	New York	USA
Byrne	Miss	Nellie M.	45	Died	British	Boston	USA
C							
Caracitsos	Mr.	George	38	Died	Greek	New York	USA
Carlson	Mr.	C. J.	57	Died	Swedish	Chicago	USA

Last Name	Title	First Name	Age	Fate	Nationality	City	Country
Carrigan	Miss	Margaret	28	Died	British	Boston	USA
Cattew	Miss	Emily	37	Died	British	New York	USA
Charkowski	Mr.	Porflri	41	Died	Russian	E. St. Louis	USA
Chwysink	Mr.	Pawel	21	Died	Russian	Chicago	USA
Clift	Mr.	Horace	23	Died	British	Chicago	USA
Connolly	Mr.	Michael	39	Died	British	New York	USA
Cook	Mr.	William George	38	Saved	British	Toronto	Canada
Cooper	Mrs.	(Nellie Elizabeth)	33	Died	British	New Bedford	USA
Cooper	Master	Joseph E.	3m	Died	U.S.C.	New Bedford	USA
Coughlan	Mr.	John	40	Died	British	Butte	USA
Coughlan	Mrs.	John (Katherine)	40	Saved	British	Butte	USA
Coughlan	Master	John Jr.	3	Saved	U.S.C.	Butte	USA
Coughlan	Miss	Margaret	2	Died	U.S.C.	Butte	USA
Coughlan	Master	Jeremiah Bernard	11m	Saved	U.S.C.	Butte	USA
Coxon	Mr.	Geoffrey Thornley	18	Died	British	New York	USA
Crosbie	Miss	Agnes	24	Saved	British	Wilmette	USA
Cross	Mr.	Charles Ivor	21	Died	British	Camden	USA
Crurchley	Mr.	William Henry	47	Died	British	E. Liverpool	USA
Cunniffe	Miss	Hannah	30	Died	British	Brooklyn	USA
Curley	Miss	Alice	22	Died	British	New York	USA
Czertowiczx	Mr.	Marcin	48	Saved	Russian	Philadelphia	USA
D							
Dowsley	Dr.	David H.	54	Died	British	New York	USA
Dawson	Mr.	Walter	23	Saved	British	Lowell	USA
Deickey	Mr.	Ewstafey	24	Died	Russian	New York	USA
Delaney	Miss	Mary	34	Saved	British	New York	USA
Dhenin	Mr.	Thomas	31	Saved	British	New York	USA
Dhenin	Mrs.	Thomas (Evelyne)	33	Died	British	New York	USA
Dhenin	Master	Thomas Jr.	10	Died	British	New York	USA
Dhenin	Miss	Isabella	2	Died	British	New York	USA
Diamandis	Mr.	Theodore	41	Saved	Greek	New York	USA
Dick	Miss	Annie	24	Died	British	New York	USA
Dixon	Mr.	Alfred	29	Died	British	El Paso	USA
Doyle	Miss	Anna	24	Died	British	New York	USA
Doyle	Mr.	Michael	31	Saved	British	Gt. Barrington	USA
Driscoll	Mr.	Timothy	45	Died	U.S.C.	Boston	USA
Duckworth	Mrs.	Mrs. Alfred (Elizabeth Ann)	49	Saved	British	Norwich	USA
Duncan	Mrs.	(Kate Cassie)	43	Saved	British	New York	USA
Dunn	Mr.	Thomas W.	34	Died	British		Canada
Duplex	Miss	Kate M.	34	Died	British	New York	USA

Last Name	Title	First Name	Age	Fate	Nationality	City	Country
E							
Edwards	Mr.	Isaac	28	Died	British	Greenburg	USA
Eshoo	Mr.	Benjamin	35	Died	British	Yonkers	USA
F							
Farrow	Mr.	Robert	32	Saved	British		Canada
Faulds	Mr.	Andrew	28	Saved	British	Yonkers	USA
Faulds	Mrs.	Andrew (Margaret)	27	Saved	British	Yonkers	USA
Feeley	Mrs.	(Teresa)	34	Died	British	New York	USA
Feely	Mr.	Joseph	29	Died	British	New York	USA
Ferguson	Mrs.	Samuel James (Mary Agnes)	23	Died	U.S.C.	Newark	USA
Ferguson	Master	Edward	14-m	Died	U.S.C.	Newark	USA
Ferrick	Mr.	John	26	Died	British	New York	USA
Ferrick	Mrs.	John (Margaret)	22	Died	British	New York	USA
Flaherty	Mr.	Thomas	29	Died	British	Brooklyn	USA
Flynn	Mr.	John	37	Died	British	New York	USA
Frankum	Mr.	Joseph William	36	Saved	British	Detroit	USA
Frankum	Mrs.	Joseph (Annie Mariah B)	36	Died	British	Detroit	USA
Frankum	Master	Francis	6	Saved	British	Detroit	USA
Frankum	Master	Frederick George	4	Died	U.S.C.	Detroit	USA
Frankum	Miss	Winifred Annie	10-m	Died	U.S.C.	Detroit	USA
G							
Galvin	Mr.	Michael	30	Died	British	New York	USA
Gately	Mr.	John	27	Saved	British	New York	USA
Gibbons	Mr.	Michael	36	Died	U.S.C.	Chicago	USA
Gililen	Mr.	Ellie	36	Saved	Persian	Yonkers	USA
Gleason	Miss	Catherine	23	Died	British	Chicago	USA
Goodall	Mr.	William	30	Died	British	Kearny	USA
Goodall	Mrs.	William (Beatrice)	33	Died	British	Kearny	USA
Goodall	Master	Leonard	7	Died	British	Kearny	USA
Goodall	Master	Jack	10m	Died	U.S.C.	Kearny	USA
Goode	Mr.	George	23	Died	British		Canada
Goodwin	Miss	Rose	30	Saved	British	Baltimore	USA
Gordon	Mr.	George		Saved	British	Calgary	Canada
Graham	Mr.	Gordon	26	Died	British	San Francisco	USA
Granahan	Mr.	Michael	52	Saved	British	Chicago	USA
Greenshields	Mr.	A. J.		Died	British		
Grigorian	Mr.	Majlim	37	Saved	Russian	New York	USA
Grinsted	Mr.	Cyril	27	Saved	British	New York	USA
Griwaczewski	Mr.	Michael	28	Died	Russian	New York	USA
Groves	Mr.	George	70	Died	U.S.C.	New York	USA
Gryszkiewicz	Mr.	Antoni	26	Saved	Russian	Three Rivers	USA

Last Name	Title	First Name	Age	Fate	Nationality	City	Country
H							
Hancock	Mr.	Thomas	36	Died	British	Bisbee	USA
Hanly	Mr.	Patrick		Saved	British	Brooklyn	USA
Hanus	Mr.	Charles	37	Died	British	Chicago	USA
Hanus	Mrs.	Charles (Mary)	37	Died	British	Chicago	USA
Harkens	Mr.	Alexander	41	Died	British	Philadelphia	USA
Harrison	Mr.	George Wraith	24	Saved	British	Fernie	Canada
Harvey	Mr.	William	53	Died	U.S.C.	New York	USA
Hebden	Mr.	Robert	35	Saved	British	New Bedford	USA
Hebden	Mrs.	Robert (Clara)	27	Died	British	New Bedford	USA
Henry	Mrs.	John (Catherine)	24	Saved	British	New York	USA
Hesketh	Mr.	Alfred W.	31	Saved	British	Welland	Canada
Hogan	Miss	Jane	39	Saved	British	New York	USA
Hook	Mr.	George	47	Saved	British		Canada
Hook	Miss	Elsie	12	Saved	British		Canada
Hook	Master	Frank	11	Saved	British		Canada
Houston	Mr.	Frank	27	Died	British	Auburn	USA
Howard	Mr.	William	36	Died	British	St. Louis	USA
Howley	Mrs.	Edward (Rose)	42	Saved	British	New Rochelle	USA
Hurley	Mr.	Charles Edwin	33	Died	U.S.C.	Boston	USA
I							
Inman	Mr.	John Edward	26	Died	British	Park City	USA
Ireton	Mr.	Edward	36	Died	British	New York	USA
Isherwood	Mr.	Fred	29	Died	British	New York	USA
Ivannik	Mr.	Peter	34	Died	Russian	Jamaica	USA
Iwanuk	Mr.	Emilian	27	Saved	Russian	New York	USA
J							
Jacobs	Mrs.	Abraham (Liba Bella)	67	Died	British	Chicago	USA
Jackson	Mr.	William	40	Died	British	Medforth	USA
Jackson	Mrs.	William (Sarah)	32	Died	British	Medforth	USA
James	Miss	Violet Isabel	32	Saved	British	Edmonton	Canada
Jenkins	Mr.	Alfred	73	Died	British		Canada
Johannsen	Mr.	Sven	36	Died	Swedish	Chicago	USA
Johnson	Mr.	Albert E.	72	Died	British		Canada
Johnson	Mr.	Herbert K.	24	Saved	British	New York	USA
Johnson	Mr.	John	27	Died	British	New York	USA
Jones	Mr.	Evan	59	Died	U.S.C.	Chicago	USA
Junczyk	Mr.	Egor	24	Saved	Russian	Hoosick Falls	USA
K							
Kaperalia	Mr.	Nikola	33	Died	Persian	Chicago	USA
Kasiaran	Mr.	Mirja	50	Died	Russian	New York	USA

Last Name	Title	First Name	Age	Fate	Nationality	City	Country
Kelly	Miss	Annie	19	Died	British	Deported	Passenger
Kelly	Miss	Marie	30	Died	British	Boston	USA
Kenny	Miss	Agnes	26	Saved	British	New York	USA
Kevorke	Mr.	Ahajan	28	Died	Russian	New York	USA
Kilkenney	Miss	Annie	22	Died	British	New York	USA
Kilkenney	Miss	Delia	33	Saved	British	Cambridge	USA
Killawe	Miss	Winifred	30	Saved	British	Pittsburg	USA
King	Mr.	George	32	Died	British	W. Frankfort	USA
King	Mr.	Harry	24	Died	British	Chicago	USA
King	Miss	Sarah	24	Died	British	Deported	Passenger
Koczurko	Mr.	Wilkenti	59	Died	Russian	Chicago	USA
Komaryshyn	Mr.	Hryhory	43	Saved	Russian	S. Ste. Marie	USA
Kornejczyk	Mr.	Andrej	25	Died	Russian	Clarksburg	USA
Koweretz	Mr.	Naum D.	29	Died	Russian	Chicago	USA
Kozlowski	Mr.	Kost	26	Died	Russian	Clarksburg	USA
Kulicz	Mr.	Stegan	32	Died	Russian	Chicago	USA
L							
Lambert	Mrs.	John (Delia)	25	Died	British	New York	USA
Lambert	Master	William Patrick	5	Died	U.S.C.	New York	USA
Leyland	Mr.	William	44	Died	British	San Francisco	USA
Lichaczow	Mr.	Ignatii	23	Died	Russian	Windsor	USA
Barks	Mr.	Herbert Light	32	Saved	British	Camden	USA
Lindley	Mr.	Harry	24	Died	British	Toledo	USA
Lizawczuk	Mr.	Alexaj	26	Died	Russian	Philadelphia	USA
Lockhart	Mr.	James	30	Died	British	New York	USA
Lockwood	Mrs.	Dick (Florence)	35	Died	British	Harrison	USA
Lockwood	Master	Clifford	11	Died	British	Harrison	USA
Lockwood	Miss	Lily (Lillian)	7	Died	U.S.C.	Harrison	USA
Logan	Mrs.	James (Ruth)	27	Saved	British	New York	USA
Logan	Master	Robert	11m	Died	U.S.C.	New York	USA
Lognunietz	Mr.	Wasili	23	Died	Russian	Chicago	USA
Long	Mr.	Harry	21	Died	British	Detroit	USA
Losevicz	Mr.	Fadej	32	Died	Russian	Woodhaven	USA
Lucko	Mr.	Timofej	32	Died	Russian	Hastings	USA
Luker	Mr.	Francis John	32	Saved	British		Canada
Lukianowicz	Mr.	Wawren	39	Died	Russian	Chicago	USA
Lyons	Miss	Annie	26	Died	British	Newark	USA
M							
Mackenzie	Mr.	Robert Anderson	40	Saved	British	New York	USA
Malicz	Mr.	Pawel L.	34	Saved	Russian	Chicago	USA
Marchewka	Mr.	Josef	50	Died	Russian	Three Rivers	USA

Last Name	Title	First Name	Age	Fate	Nationality	City	Country
Marks	Mrs.	G. (Elizabeth)	50	Died	British	Chicago	USA
Marks	Miss	Georgina	24	Died	British	Chicago	USA
Marsh	Mr.	Thomas	29	Died	British		Canada
Marsh	Mrs.	Thomas (Annie)	26	Saved	British		Canada
Marsh	Master	Thomas Jr.	11m	Died	British		Canada
Marshall	Mrs.	(Fannie E.)	35	Saved	British		Canada
Martin	Mrs.	Albert (Laura)	54	Saved	British	New Philadelphia	USA
Mason	Mr.	Joseph Howard	31	Died	British	Detroit	USA
Matthews	Mr.	Thomas	27	Saved	British	Calumet	USA
Mazurak	Mr.	Iwan "John"	22	Saved	Russian	Waterbury	USA
McAfee	Mr.	Thomas	28	Died	British		Canada
McAnemy	Mr.	John	23	Died	British	New York	USA
McCallum	Mr.	Albert Alexander	27	Died	British	New York	USA
McClammond	Mr.	Samuel	32	Saved	British	New York	USA
McCormick	Mr.	Thomas	30	Saved	British	Nashua	USA
McCready	Mr.	Robert G.	28	Died	British		Canada
McDermott	Mr.	Andrew	22	Saved	British	Boston	USA
McKeon	Miss	Jane	24	Died	British	New York	USA
McLoughlin	Mr.	Patrick J.	35	Saved	British	Hartford	USA
McNulty	Mr.	Steve	30	Died	British	New York	USA
Meaney	Mr.	George Peter	30	Died	British	Thomas	USA
Michalkowicz	Mr.	Iwan	26	Died	Russian	Chicago	USA
Molloy	Mr.	Robert J.		Died	British	Deported	Passenger
Moses	Mrs.	George (Janet)	42	Saved	British	Wilkinsburg	USA
Muirhead	Mr.	William	31	Saved	British	New York	USA
Muraszko	Mr.	Boris	24	Died	Russian	Oxford Furnace	USA
Murray	Mrs.	James (Margaret)	26	Died	British	Chicago	USA
Murray	Master	Walter	4.5	Died	British	Chicago	USA
Murray	Mrs.	(Mary)		Died	British		Cuba
N							
Neiborski	Mr.	Gregory	22	Died	Russian	Oxford Furnace	USA
Neilson	Miss	Gerda Theoline	29	Saved	British	Brooklyn	USA
Nielson	Miss	Violet		Saved	Norwegian	Deported	Passenger
Nikander	Mr.	Gunnar		Died	Finnish	Deported	Passenger
Norman	Mr.	Jasper	27	Died	British	Rochester	USA
O							
O'Connor	Mr.	John	23	Died	British	New York	USA
Oginski	Mr.	Danil	27	Died	Russian	Hartford	USA
Ohannia	Mr.	Aziz	35	Died	Persian	Chicago	USA
O'Kelly	Mr.	John J.	28	Died	British	New York	USA
Oleszko	Mr.	John	22	Died	Russian	Chicago	USA
Olivar	Mr.	Diego	46	Died	Mexican	New York	USA

Last Name	Title	First Name	Age	Fate	Nationality	City	Country
Ordyniez	Mr.	Andrej	48	Died	Russian	Syracuse	USA
Owens	Mr.	Patrick	29	Died	British	St. Louis	USA
P							
Palmer	Mr.	Charles	21	Died	British	Camden, NJ	USA
Parkes	Mr.	William Henry	23	Saved	British		Canada
Perka	Mr.	Maxim Antanow	27	Saved	Russian		Canada
Petrenok	Mr.	Andrej	34	Died	Russian	Mechanicville, NY	USA
Petronsian	Mr.	Kahraman	16	Saved	Russian	New York, NY	USA
Phillips	Mr.	William	40	Died	British	Hillcrest	Canada
Pickard	Mr.	Fred	30	Saved	British	New York, NY	USA
Podrubleny	Mr.	Aleksij	38	Died	Russian	Niagara Falls, NY	USA
Polubinski	Mr.	Mikentii	44	Saved	Russian	North Easton	USA
Pryor	Mr.	John	25	Died	British	New York, NY	USA
Pulik	Mr.	Mychail	34	Saved	Russian	S. Ste. Marie, MI	USA
R							
Ruane	Miss	Annie	29	Saved	British	Chicago	USA
Reid	Mrs.	(Ellen)	26	Died	British	New York	USA
Reid	Mr.	John	50	Died	British	Trenton	USA
Riley	Mr.	Eddie	30	Saved	British	Boston	USA
Riley	Mrs.	Eddie (Annie)	29	Saved	British	Boston	USA
Riley	Miss	Ethel	4	Saved	British	Boston	USA
Riley	Mr.	Sutcliffe	4	Saved	British	Boston	USA
Robinson	Mr.	Allan William	26	Died	British	Clay Centre	USA
Robshaw	Miss	Edith	26	Died	British	Kearney	USA
S							
Sargis	Mr.	Pera	28	Died	Persian	Gary	USA
Scott	Mrs.	Arthur (Alice Ann)	29	Died	British	No. Adams	USA
Scott	Master	Arthur Jr.	8	Saved	British	No. Adams	USA
Seferien	Mr.	Levon	29	Saved	Persian	Troy	USA
Seisian	Mr.	Karatioum	35	Died	Persian	Troy	USA
Self	Mr.	James	33	Died	British		Canada
Self	Mrs.	James (Florence)	30	Died	British		Canada
Sergis	Mr.	George	37	Saved	Persian	Yonkers	USA
Shackell	Mr.	George William	50	Saved	British	New York	USA
Sharp	Miss	Annie	32	Saved	British	Boston	USA
Sharp	Mr.	Samuel S.	53	Saved	British	Crooksville	USA
Sharp	Mrs.	Samuel S. (Mary Jane)	53	Saved	British	Crooksville	USA
Sharp	Mr.	George	15	Saved	British	Crooksville	USA
Sheedy	Mr.	Patrick	30	Died	British	Deported	Passenger

Last Name	Title	First Name	Age	Fate	Nationality	City	Country
Shepperson	Mr.	Arthur George	26	Saved	British	New York	USA
Shirras	Mr.	Robert Brown	26	Died	British		Canada
Shkredoff	Mr.	Archie	21	Died	Russian	Pittsburg	USA
Shkredoff	Mr.	Jacob	19	Saved	Russian	Pittsburg	USA
Sidwell	Mr.	George	48	Died	British	Hamilton	Canada
Sikiwicki	Mr.	Andro	25	Died	Russian	Franklin Furnace	USA
Sikora	Mr.	Joseph	32	Died	Russian	Buffalo	USA
Simpson	Mr.	Edward	50	Saved	British	Lawrence	USA
Skelton	Mr.	Frederick	30	Died	British	Hamilton	Canada
Smethurst	Mr.	Harold	27	Saved	British	New Philadelphia	USA
Smethurst	Mrs.	Harold (Alice)	24	Saved	British	New Philadelphia	USA
Smith	Miss	Agnes	24	Died	British	Chicago	USA
Smith	Mr.	George	33	Saved	British		Canada
Smith	Mrs.	William (Minnie)	28	Died	British	Hamilton	Canada
Snowden	Mr.	Fred A.	30	Died	British	Toronto	Canada
Snowden	Mr.	Thomas	30	Saved	British	Lynn	USA
Sobolowski	Mr.	Mitrofan	29	Saved	Russian	Lyndora	USA
Solonina	Mr.	Stefan	37	Died	Russian	E. St. Louis	USA
Spendley	Mrs.	David March (Kate)	28	Saved	British	New York	USA
Stacey	Mr.	Joseph Nelson	22	Died	British		Canada
Stachula	Mr.	Michael	30	Died	Russian	Buffalo	USA
Standfast	Mr.	Noel	40	Died	British	Nanaimo	Canada
Stankicwicz	Mr.	Anthony	46	Died	Russian	Trenton	USA
Steele	Mr.	George	29	Saved	British	New York	USA
Stenson	Miss	Delia	40	Died	British	Boston	USA
Stephen	Mr.	Thomas Ohan	23	Saved	U.S.C.	Chicago	USA
Stevens	Mr.	George	28	Saved	British	Olean	USA
Stevenson	Mr.	Hugh	31	Died	British	Yonkers	USA
Stockton	Mr.	Alfred	23	Saved	British	Marion	USA
Stolarenic	Mr.	Vasili	26	Died	Russian	Chicago	USA
Strulz	Mr.	Theodor	27	Died	Russian		Canada
Strynechuk	Mr.	Save	26	Saved	Russian	Palmerton	USA
Swallow	Mr.	Allan	17	Died	British	Hamilton	USA
T							
Tadus	Mr.	Asset	38	Died	Persian	Yonkers	USA
Taracsewics	Mr.	Iwan	42	Saved	Russian	Palmerton	USA
Taylor	Mr.	Arthur		Died	British		Canada
Taylor	Mr.	Harold William	24	Saved	British	Niagara Falls	USA
Taylor	Mrs.	Harold William (Lucy)	19	Saved	British	Niagara Falls	USA
Thompson	Mr.	Joseph	40	Saved	British	Canton	USA
Thompson	Mrs.	Joseph (Sarah Ann)	40	Died	British	Canton	USA

Last Name	Title	First Name	Age	Fate	Nationality	City	Country
Thompson	Mr.	Norman	18	Died	British	Canton	USA
Tobin	Mrs.	(Nora)	25	Saved	British	Boston	USA
Tomaszewicz	Mr.	Iwan	28	Saved	Russian	Bayonne	USA
Tomms	Miss	Elizabeth		Died	British	Toronto	Canada
Topping	Mrs.	Albert (Margaret)	40	Died	British	Brooklyn	USA
Topping	Miss	Hilda	10	Died	British	Brooklyn	USA
Travers	Mrs.	(Jane)	30	Died	British	Newark	USA
Tucker	Mr.	Albert	25	Died	British	Hamilton	Canada
Tuohey	Miss	Margaret	25	Saved	British	New York	USA
Twinning	Mr.	Edwin	21	Died	British	New York	USA
Tyler	Mr.	Samuel	28	Died	British	Whitehall	USA
V							
Veals	Mr.	Albert Edward	31	Saved	British	Orange	USA
Veals	Mrs.	Albert Edward (Agnes Maud)	27	Saved	British	Orange	USA
W							
Waaranen	Miss	Elli M.	22	Died	Finnish	Worcester	USA
Ward	Mr.	George	48	Saved	British	Newark	USA
Ward	Mrs.	George (Ellen)	43	Saved	British	Newark	USA
Ward	Mr.	Joseph	41	Died	British	Blakely	USA
Wardle	Mrs.	Frank (Cissie)	22	Died	British	Adamsdale	USA
Watson	Mrs.	(Kate)		Died	British	Seaforth	Canada
Webb	Mrs.	(Elizabeth)	69	Died	British	Medforth	USA
Welsh	Mr.	John	34	Saved	British	New York	USA
Wilks	Miss	Alice Kaye	30	Saved	British	Chicago	USA
Williams	Mrs.	Harry (John) (Elizabeth "Annie")	37	Died	British	Newark	USA
Williams	Master	John	10	Saved	British	Newark	USA
Williams	Miss	Edith	9	Saved	British	Newark	USA
Williams	Master	George	6	Died	British	Newark	USA
Williams	Miss	Ethel	5	Died	British	Newark	USA
Williams	Miss	Florence	4	Died	British	Newark	USA
Williams	Master	David	3m	Died	U.S.C.	Newark	USA
Williams	Mr.	David	27	Died	British	Edmonton	Canada
Williams	Mr.	James	38	Died	British	New York	USA
Williams	Mr.	Thomas	45	Died	British	Johnstown	USA
Wilson	Mrs.	William (Emily)		Died	British	Toronto	Canada
Wilson	Master	Frank	4	Died	British	Toronto	Canada
Wilson	Miss	Dorothy	2	Died	British	Toronto	Canada
Woodward	Mr.	Robert	22	Saved	British	Niagara Falls	USA
Worrell	Mr.	Fred A.	45	Died	British	New York	USA
Y							
Yocab	Mr.	Baba Jan	33	Saved	Persian	Chicago	USA
Yohama	Mr.	Envia	40	Died	Persian	Chicago	USA

Last Name	Title	First Name	Age	Fate	Nationality	City	Country
Yohanan	Mr.	Alvaretz	32	Saved	Persian	Chicago	USA
York	Mr.	William		Died	British	Brantford	Canada
Young	Mrs.	Charles (Elizabeth)	27	Died	British	Chicago	USA
Z							
Zaliachanoff	Mr.	Khaeho	37	Died	Russian	New York	USA
Also							
Domingues	Mr.	Manuel		Died			D.B.S.
Genanselm	Mr.	A.		Died			D.B.S.
Slight	Mr.	H.		Died			D.B.S.

Passenger list for Crossing No. 202 East kindly provided by Mike Poirier. Compiled by Mike Poirier, Jim Kalafus, Hildo Theil, Paul Latimer, Geoff Whitfield, and Craig Stringer.

Note: Maids, valets, manservants, etc. are listed with the individuals/families that they traveled with. Known spelling errors have been corrected.

Appendix 6
Annual Service Log, *Lusitania*

1907	9 Crossings (4½ voyages)
1908	30 Crossings
1909	31 Crossings
1910	28 Crossings
1911	33 Crossings
1912	23 Crossings
1913	12 Crossings
1914	28 Crossings
1915	8 Crossings

TOTAL   202 Crossings

(Sunk at end #202)

Conclusions:

- 1911 was the *Lusitania*'s busiest year, with 33 crossings; this was two full crossings more than her second-best year, namely 1909, with 31 crossings.
- Her third-busiest year was 1908, with 30 crossings.
- In two separate years, 1910 and 1914, she made the same number of crossings – 28. These two years thus tied for her fourth-busiest years.
- Her fifth-busiest year was 1912, with 23 crossings.
- During the first nine months of 1907 and the last seven months of 1915, the ship was not in service. Her numbers of crossings for these years are thus unusually low.
- During the first eight months of 1913, the *Lusitania* was out of commission due to turbine difficulties. This is thus her slowest full year in service.

Note: At times, a crossing would start one year and end during the following calendar year. In such cases, the year that starts the crossing is given credit for the full crossing.

Acknowledgements

It never ceases to amaze me just how much work is involved in putting together a project such as this. Material for this book was found on both sides of the Atlantic Ocean, and much of it would never have found the light of day without the assistance that others have given me.

Mike Poirier and Jim Kalafus – the authors of the *"Lest We Forget"* articles on the *Lusitania* – deserve special recognition. Not only did they open their personal collections of *Lusitania* material to my use and reproduction, but they were also ever-willing to help me through some of the more muddled areas of the ship's last voyage and fate. Mike in particular managed to save me from a few pitfalls which other researchers of the subject have fallen into. Their proofreading on the manuscript as well as their comments, criticisms and suggestions were infinitely helpful. I am also eternally indebted to both of them for penning an introduction on extremely short notice. This book truly would not have been what it is now without their help.

Mrs. John E. Roosevelt, for taking an interest in my work over the years.

Mark Chirnside was ever-willing to dig through archives in England to aid my research into the ship's least-told stories. Bruce Beveridge, Scott Andrews, Art Braunschweiger, and Jerry Davidson of the *Titanic* Research & Modeling Association were also extremely helpful to me, particularly in technical issues of ship construction. Also helpful were Shelley Dziedzic and Barb Shuttle of the *Titanic International Society*. Not to be forgotten is Mark Warren, for his proofreading and for permission to use material from *The Shipbuilder*. Digital artist Tom Lear, who toiled laboriously to create the remarkable three-dimensional graphic model of the *Lusitania* which graces the pages and cover of this book, deserves special mention. Roger Hull of the Liverpool Record Office was extremely helpful to me, as was M. Scott Visnjic. Enda Ryan and Martin O'Neill of the Mitchell Library, Glasgow City Council, who jumped at my request for assistance with obtaining the photograph of Architect James Miller. Everyone who opened their personal photographic and illustrative collections to me for use in this project are also due the heartiest of thanks – for a complete list of these individuals, make sure to check the photographic credits. Mel Watkins for suggesting some corrections for the passenger and crew list; my editor Campbell McCutcheon for jumping at the chance to publish this volume, for contributing generously from his maritime collection to help illustrate its pages in all its finished glory, and for his patience as we approached the final deadline.

Then there are the people who have helped me personally, my friends and family. This list is longer than space will allow for, but briefly: Dave, Cherie and Elyse; Beatrice & Gertrude; the extended Layton family, including all of my aunts, uncles, & cousins – a wonderful family to be part of; Bob & Carolyn Henry; my old Auburn posse, especially including Eric & Laura and the new little one (adopted niece), Elizabeth Ann Marie. Also Rich & Leanna; Ed, Ellie, Crystal, & Sarah; Steve & Jamie Wheatley & clan; Jesse & Andrew; Bob, Mary & Jaimy; Ron & Sharon; the Browns and the entire King Ferry clan – good friends, all of them; Don & Ann; Aaron & Michelle; Craig & Amy; Harry & Arthur C.; Jerry & Linda; Michelle; Bill, Colleen & Rachel. Oscar & Fran; Clay & Barb; Dennis & Mary; Butch, Chris & Hannah; Ken & Deb; Greg, Donnetta & Evan; Lona & my adopted grandmother Rita; the rest of my Wolcott clan; Mark & Deb; the Ron & Kayln; Dani, Annie, Jade, Anita (and Lindsay, too), Lonnie, Nate, Martin, Jim, & the rest of my 2009 class – good friends, all (including my new Binghamton friends). Everyone else that won't fit on this list or that I am forgetting …

Also: Although I have been meticulous in my research, if errors have crept into the text, please let me know so that I can make the alterations in future editions of this volume. Any mistakes in the research are also mine alone, and should be attributed to no one else.

PHOTOGRAPHIC CREDITS

Author's Collection: 2, 4, 8, 13 (top, btm left), 16, 20, 21, 22 (top, mid), 23, 24, 25, 26 (top), 27, 28 (btm), 29 (top, mid), 31 (btm), 33 (btm), 34, 36, 37, 38, 39 (top, btm), 40, 41, 43, 44 (plans © 2010 by J. Kent Layton), 45 (plans © 2010 by J. Kent Layton), 47, 48, 49 (top), 52, 56 (mid right, btm left), 57 (btm right), 58 (top right), 59 (top), 61 (all but top), 63 (top), 64, 65, 67, 68 (plans © 2010 by J. Kent Layton), 70-75 (plans © 2010 by J. Kent Layton), 78, 79 (btm right), 84, 85 (top), 87 (right), 88, 89 (plans © 2010 by J. Kent Layton), 92, 93, 99, 101, 102, 107 (right), 108 (left), 109 (right), 110 (top), 112 (top), 115, 116, 117 (top), 118 (btm), 119, 120, 121, 122, 123, 124, 125, 127 (top left, top right), 129 (btm right), 130, 131, 133 (top left & right), 134 (btm), 136 (top), 137 (top), 138 (top left), 139 (top), 145, 147 (lower right), 155 (btm), 156 (top), 158 (btm), 162, 163 (btm), 164, 167 (btm), 172, 174-175, 183, 186, 187, 192 (top left), 193 (top), 201, 202 (btm, mid left), 209, 212 (btm), 223, 224 (top), 225 (top), 229, 230 (top), 243, 246, 250, 251, 252, 253, 259, 265, 276, 282 (btm right), 283, 284, 285, 286, 27 (btm), 292 (btm), 294, 297, 298-299, 299, 301 (top left, lower left), 302, 303, 306 (lower), 307 (lower), 311, 316 (right), 319 (top), 320 (btm), 335 (btm), 338, 340 (btm)

Library of Congress, Prints & Photographs Division: 6, 12 (top), 14, 15, 18, 83 (all except 2nd from btm), 91, 109 (left), 132, 133 (btm), 134 (top), 135, 136 (btm), 137 (btm), 138 (top right), 139 (btm), 140-141, 150-151, 152-153, 155 (top), 156 (btm), 178-179, 180-181, 184 (left), 197, 207 (btm), 208, 210-211, 212 (top), 214 (btm), 224 (btm), 228, 236 (top), 239 (top and btm), 240, 241, 242, 245, 247, 254, 255, 256, 258, 260, 260-261, 262, 274 (btm), 280, 282 (all except btm right), 289, 292 (top), 305 (btm), 332, 333, 340 (top), 361 (all except top left)

J&C McCutcheon Collection: 12 (btm), 50, 51, 54 (top), 55 (all except top), 56 (top, mid left, btm right), 57 (top, btm left), 58 (top left), 60 (top), 61 (top), 62 (top and btm left), 63 (btm), 96, 110 (btm), 113 (top), 117 (btm), 147 (top), 154 (top), 158 (top), 165 (top), 167 (top), 171, 188-189, 192-193, 194 (top left, btm left), 199, 202 (top), 203, 204, 205, 206 (top), 214 (top), 220, 226 (btm), 244, 305 (top right), 335 (top), 336 (top), 337, 343, 344

Ioannis Georgiou Collection: 10, 13 (btm right), 59 (btm left and right), 62 (right), 142, 191, 287 (top), 293, 295, 296 (right), 304, 306 (top), 310, 313, 314, 316 (left) 317, 321, 323, 324, 325, 326, 327, 330, 331, 334, 336 (btm)

Mike Poirier Collection: 103, 107 (left), 127 (btm right), 152 (btm), 182, 184 (right), 192 (top right), 194 (btm), 195, 196 (except btm right), 198 (top right, btm right), 206 (btm), 215, 222, 226-227, 236 (btm), 237, 238, 239 (mid right), 261, 264, 266, 268-273, 274 (top), 290, 296 (left), 300

Lawrence Jolivet Collection, Courtesy Mike Poirier: 326

Jim Kalafus Collection: 83 (2nd from btm), 95, 221, 225 (btm), 226 (top left), 230 (btm), 232-235, 297 (inset), 339

Jonathan Smith Collection: 28 (top), 30, 53, 54 (btm, left and right), 85 (btm left), 86 (btm), 112 (middle), 138 (btm), 149, 165 (btm), 170, 185, 200, 207 (top), 301 (right), 305 (top left)

Richard Smye Collection: 22 (btm), 31 (top), 55 (top) 58 (btm), 159, 161, 231

Georgiou/Chirnside/Klistorner/Layton Collection: 312

Liverpool Record Office: 57 (middle), 60 (btm), 112-113, 118 (top), 154 (btm), 163 (top), 190

Russ Willoughby Collection: 26 (btm), 29 (btm), 33 (top), 35, 39 (middle), 46

Bruce Beveridge Collection: 79 (top right), 87 (left), 108 (right), 307 (top)

Michael & Elizabeth Gibson Collection: 49 (btm), 361 (top left)

Courtesy Peter Davies-Garner: 216

Richard Burdon Collection: 309

Courtesy Shelley Dziedzic: 9 (middle, right)

Courtesy Cliff Barry: 9 (left)

By Courtesy of the Mitchell Library, Glasgow City Council: 32

U.S. Naval Historical Center: 81

Courtesy Jerry Davidson: 86 (top)

Courtesy Art Braunschweiger: 129 (top)

Bill Young Collection: 176-177

Caroline Windsor Collection: 319 (btm)

Troy & Jeanette White Collection: 320 (top)

Steven B. Anderson Collection: 196 (btm right)

Courtesy of LostLiners.com: 281

Courtesy Jon Kiger: 328, 329

Color Section: Artwork by Tom Lear: 1, 16, 17, 24, 26, 27; **Artwork by Stuart Williamson:** 11, 21, 25, 28; **Author's Collection:** 2, 3, 5, 6, 10; **Courtesy Rob Johnston:** 32; **Courtesy Jon Kiger:** 33; **Jim Kalafus Collection:** 4, 15; **Ioannis Georgiou Collection:** 18, 19, 20, 23; **Liverpool Record Office:** 7; **Mike Poirier Collection:** 13, 14; **Peter Davies-Garner Collection:** 31; **Photos by Dave Evans:** 29, 30; **Photos by Omar Khokkar:** 8, 9; **Stuart Williamson Collection:** 12; **Trevor Powell Collection:** 22

RECOMMENDED READING

Bailey, Thomas A. & Ryan, Paul B. *The Lusitania Disaster* (The Free Press, 1975)

Ballard, Robert D. *Exploring the Lusitania* (Warner/Madison Press, 1995)

Bestic, Captain A. A. *Kicking Canvas* (Evans Brothers, Ltd., 1957)

Fitch, Tad & Poirier, Mike. *Into the Danger Zone: Sea Crossings of the First World War.* (The History Press, 2014)

Garzke, William H., Dulin, Robert O., Jr., Hsu, Peter K.; Powell, Blake; Bemis, F. Gregg (Members of Panel SD-7, Marine Forensics Panel). *The Saga of the RMS Lusitania: A Marine Forensic Analysis.* January 8, 1998.

Gould, John H. *Outward Bound* (Outward Bound Company, 1905/1913)

Glyn, Elinor. *Elizabeth Visits America* (Duffield & Co., 1909)

Hoehling, A. A. & Mary. *The Last Voyage of the Lusitania*, Bonanza Books, 1956/1991

Hopkins, Albert A. *The Scientific American Handbook of Travel* (Munn & Co., 1910)

Kalafus, Jim & Poirier, Mike. *Lest We Forget*, Parts 1-3. (Online articles hosted by Encyclopedia Titanica.)

Keegan, John. *An Illustrated History of the First World War* (Alfred A. Knopf, 2001)

Layton, J. Kent. *The Edwardian Superliners* (Amberley, 2013)

Layton, J. Kent. *The Unseen Mauretania (1907): The Ship In Rare Illustrations.* (The History Press, 2015)

Molony, Senan. *Lusitania: An Irish Tragedy* (Mercier Press, 2004)

Ocean Liners of the Past, Volume 2. *The Cunard Express Liners Lusitania and Mauretania* (Reprinted from *The Shipbuilder & Marine Engine Builder.*) (Patrick Stephens, 1970)

Preston, Diana. *Lusitania: An Epic Tragedy.* (Walker & Co., 2002)

Sauder, Eric. *Lusitania: The Ship & Her Record.* (The History Press, 2009)

Sauder, Eric. *The Unseen Lusitania: The Ship in Rare Illustrations.* The History Press, 2015)

Warren, Mark D. *The Cunard Turbine-Driven Quadruple-Screw Atlantic Liner Lusitania* (Reprinted From *Engineering* Magazine). (Patrick Stephens Ltd., 1986)

Endnotes

CHAPTER 1: A Matter of Honor

1   *The New York Times*, June 8, 1906, page 8. The correct launch date of the *Lusitania* was June 7, 1906, not June 6, as is often quoted.
2   *Ocean Liners of the Past*, Vol. 2 (reprinted from *The Shipbuilder*), pgs. 15-16.
3   *Outward Bound*, by John Gould (1905/1913), pgs. 1-2.
4   *The Scientific American Handbook of Travel*, (Munn & Co., 1910), pgs. 2-3.

CHAPTER 2: The Birth of the *Lusitania*

1   A ship's length between perpendiculars (b.p.) is a measurement between the forward and aft perpendiculars. The forward perpendicular is a vertical line that intersects the forward side of the stem at the waterline; the after is a similar vertical line that intersects the after edge of the stern post at the waterline. The actual overall length of a ship would include additional portions of her structure that would extend beyond each of these points. This is thus very different from the measurement of a ship's overall length, her waterline length, her registered length, and her Length by Lloyd's rules.
2   *Glasgow Today*, 1909 pg. 23.
3   University of Glasgow Archives; Ian Johnston, *Ships For A Nation: John Brown & Company, Clydebank* (Argyll Publishing, 2008), pg. 337. For many years, the keel-laying date of the *Lusitania* has been recorded as June 16, 1904, and this was similarly recorded in the 2007 volume, *Lusitania: An Illustrated Biography of the Ship of Splendor*. More recently, however, more detailed information has come to my attention which points to August 17, 1904 as the correct date.
4   It is important to note the difference between an Imperial ton and a ton as it is commonly referred to today: a modern-day ton is equal to 2,000 lbs., whereas an Imperial ton is equal to 2,240 lbs. Sir William Arrol & Co. Ltd. is well known for building the "Great Gantry" over Slips Nos. 2 and 3 at the Harland & Wolff shipyards, where the *Olympic* and *Titanic* were later built.
5   *The New York Times*, July 9, 1908.
6   In *Engineering*, July 19, 1907, the architect who designed the *Lusitania*'s interior décor is referred to as "James Millar, R.S.A., F.R.I.B.A." Some modern books on the *Lusitania* also refer to him as Millar. At the same time, at least one volume spells his name as Millar and Miller in the same paragraph, and still other books on the subject spell his name Miller.

Meanwhile, a number of reference works on architecture, including numerous references to Scottish and Glasgow architecture, refer to him as Miller. Included among this list is a more modern reference work, *C.R. Mackintosh: The Poetics of Workmanship (Essay in Art and Culture)*, by David Brett (Harvard University Press, 1992). In an article on his work for the Glasgow Exhibition, *The New York Times* of May 12, 1901 reported: "The man building, Industrial Hall, and the adjacent Machinery Hall, testify to the skill and taste of James Miller, one of the foremost Scotch architects." The architectural firm that he later ran with his son, George, was also called Miller & Son, as opposed to Millar & Son.

It seems that all of the confusion over the spelling of his name, as regards the *Lusitania*, comes from an original spelling mistake within the *Engineering* special number on the liner, and that this spelling mistake has been repeated time after time over the decades.
7   *The New York Times*, Saturday, November 23, 1907.
8   *Engineering*, July 19, 1907.
9   Only the First Class Smoking Room fireplaces actually operated, burning coal and ventilating up through the No. 4 funnel. The other fireplaces in First Class were nonfunctioning *objets d'art*.

10 A full description of these public rooms was made in the July 19, 1907 issue of *Engineering* magazine.

11 These prices come from a Cunard Line brochure of the era. The seasons were described as follows. Eastbound: Out of Season: Mid-August to end-March; Intermediate Season: April and early August; Full Season: May, June and July. Westbound, they were: Out of Season: November through March; Intermediate Season: April through July; Full Season: August through October. $1,250 US dollars in 1912 would be the equivalent of just over $27,500 US dollars in 2008; $2,250 would amount to almost $50,000.

12 This information comes from the same Cunard Line brochure as the previous endnote. In 2008 U.S. dollars, that would range between $15,400 and $33,000. Each additional person would have cost $2,200 by the same inflationary standard.

13 The passage, as well as the quotation in the preceding paragraph, was taken from the *Journal of Commerce*, (apparently from Liverpool, England) of Saturday, August 31, 1907. A copy of this fascinating article was kindly given to me by Alec Watt, who is a member of the late Captain Watt's family. The photograph of Captain Watt is held in the collection of the Captain's great-grandchildren Michael & Elizabeth Gibson. Mr. Watt was kind enough to secure the copy of the picture for use in this volume, and he also kindly obtained their permission to use it in this book. My deepest thanks to Mr. Watt and Mr. and Ms. Gibson for their assistance and generosity.

14 *Star*, August 20, 1907, pg. 2.

15 *Ibid.*

16 *Engineering*, July 12, 1907. Papers that reported she had grounded included brief statements like that in the *Otago Witness*, July 3, 1907, pg. 69, among others.

17 *Engineering*, July 12, 1907.

18 *Engineering*, July 12 & 19, 1907.

19 Mrs. Tweedie's recollections were published in her 1916 volume, *My Table Cloths: A Few Reminiscences*, Chapter XXVI. My thanks go to Mike Poirier of the *Titanic* International Society (TIS) for bringing my attention to this terrific account.

20 *Nelson Evening Mail,* September 19, 1907, pg. 1.

21 For a complete breakdown on the issues surrounding the *Mauretania's* cost over-runs and the resulting tension, please see my book *The Unseen Mauretania [1907]: The Ship in Rare Illustrations.* (2015, The History Press).

CHAPTER 3: *Lusitania*: A Closer Look

1 This figure is not a determination of weight, per se, but rather a determination of enclosed space. 100 cubic feet = 1 ton. Gross tonnage is a measurement of the entire internal cubic capacity of a vessel.

2 Net tonnage is a measurement of the internal cubic capacity of a vessel remaining after the capacities of certain specified spaces (i.e., crew's quarters, machinery compartments and working spaces, etc.) have been deducted from the gross figure. As in the gross measurement, 100 cubic feet = 1 ton. At the Mersey Inquiry into the loss of the *Lusitania*, Cunard's Assistant Superintending Engineer, Alexander Galbraith, testified that the net tonnage of the liner was 12,611 tons, a figure somewhat higher than that which was originally registered for the ship, as cited in the statistics list.

3 This figure was measured at a total equal to ¼ the depth from the weather deck at the side (amidships) to the bottom of the keel. The displacement is the quantity of water displaced by a vessel when afloat. It exactly equals the weight of the vessel itself with whatever is on board at the time that the measurement is recorded. Displacement can be shown in cubic feet or tons. 1 cubic foot of seawater weighs 64 pounds, and 1 ton is equal to 35 cubic feet of sea water.

4 This measurement basically means that it would take 112.4 tons of additional weight to lower the *Lusitania* by one inch in draft. The approximate tons per inch of immersion (for salt water) is equal to the area of the waterplane in square feet divided by 420.

5 The Orlop and Lower Orlop Decks were only present at the extreme bow and stern sections of the ship; for the length of the Boiler, Engine and Auxiliary Machinery Rooms, the vertical space where they would have stood was left open to accommodate the ship's propulsive equipment.

6 No better demonstration of these very different reports can be found than by

comparing the two great British technical journals of the period, *Engineering* and *The Shipbuilder*. *Engineering* magazine, in its series of special articles on the *Lusitania* in 1907, referred to her as being 785 feet in length overall. *The Shipbuilder*, meanwhile, was also very specific in quoting her length overall at 790 feet. Both journals referred to the *Mauretania* as being 790 feet in length over all.

7   The draught measurement given in this instance is incorrect for both vessels, as they both were registered with a draught of 33 feet, 6 inches.

8   The *Mauretania*, by comparison, was 88 feet 0 inches in extreme breadth, and had a moulded depth of 60 feet 3 inches and a "depth to shelter deck" measurement of 60 feet 6 inches. According to the registry details of both ships, the *Lusitania*'s "depth from top of beam amidships to top of keel" was 61.72 feet, while the same measurement for the *Mauretania* was 62.23 feet. All of this is included to show that there was a variation in their depth measurements, as well as in their width measurements, which tends to help show that the above citation was taking the *Lusitania*'s dimensions and mistakenly applying them to both ships.

9   Citations include the *Poverty Bay Herald*, May 12, 1906, pg. 6, and November 7, 1907, pg. 5; the *Otago Witness*, November 20, 1907, pg. 64; *Star*, December 7, 1907, pg. 4; the *Wanganui Herald*, July 31, 1907, pg. 5; *The Daily Mirror*, November 18, 1907, pg. 3. As recently as August 16, 1993, the *Pittsburgh Post-Gazette*, on pg. 6, had an article about the Ballard expedition to explore the liner's wreck. Therein, the author referred to her as the "787-foot passenger liner." Although it is unclear where that reference was obtained, it seems that no previous book on the liner has ever clearly specified her length to this degree of accuracy.

10 The *Mauretania* had the same two expansion joints cut into her superstructure. Interestingly, she also bore a third expansion joint, which was placed just forward of her No. 3 funnel.

11 Many thanks to Bruce Beveridge and Scott Andrews for their assistance with sorting out the pine vs. teak deck planking issues on ships of the period. The specifics on plank layout

originally were found in the ship's Builder's Specification Book, while the ship's plans were quite clear on what kind of deck materials would be used in what areas.

12 According to the original Builder's Specification Book of the *Lusitania*, this deck was to be 10 feet in height; by the time the ship had been constructed, however, this had been increased by one foot.

13 All four funnels measured approximately the same height from the Sun Deck to their peaks, a distance just shy of 65 feet. Although the No. 1 funnel was mounted on a slightly lower portion of the Sun Deck, because of the ship's sheer line, it was no shorter than the other funnels at the ship's designed load draft. Naturally, as the ship's fuel and stores were consumed during a voyage, her draft would change. If her bow rode higher than her stern, this would have tended to make the forward funnel the highest by a small margin.

14 Indeed, the Cunard Line specified to John Brown that all rails within a 10-foot radius of any compass were to be of brass construction in order to prevent magnetic interference. All of the ship's rails along the Promenade, Shelter and Boat Decks were of four rails each, topped off with a teak rail. Each rod of these rails was ¾" in diameter. On the Forecastle, the rails were comprised of five rods each, with the top rod being 1½" diameter, with the lower four being 7/8" diameter. No teak top was fitted to the Forecastle rails. All of the rails were galvanized.

15 Rates varied considerably based on what shore stations had to relay the message. The services offered by the Marconi Company worked in conjunction with Inland Telegraphs and International Cables throughout the world. Telegrams sent from the *Lusitania* would go through Marconi stations, and "through rates," travelers were advised, "can be obtained from the Pursers ..." The exact rates thus depended on how many times the message would need to be re-transmitted. "A charge is made for the first ten words or less, and at a reduced rate for each word over ten." However, the "address and signature are not charged for," and passengers were thus encouraged to write out the address as fully and clearly as possible to avoid trouble in delivery. – *The Scientific American Handbook of Travel*, (Munn & Co., 1910), pgs. 84-86.

16 As originally reported, the rudder weighed 56 tons 8 centerweight. Imperial tons were some 2,240 lbs, while a centerweight was some 112 lbs. The total weight of the rudder was thus 125,440 lbs + 896 lbs, for a total of 126,336 pounds or 63.168 modern tons. The American measuring system, by comparison, defines a ton as 2,000 lbs, while an American centerweight is exactly 100 lbs. This description of weight in tons is not to be confused with the term "tons" as applied to a ship's gross or net tonnage, which was a measurement of enclosed space, rather than weight.

17 A closer breakdown of these passengers and crew shows: 186 First Class, 66 Second Class and 389 (or 395 according to some accounts) Third Class passengers. There were also 205 officers and crew aboard.

18 According to some accounts, she sank up to eight hours after the collision.

19 Excerpted from the transcripts of the Board of Trade Inquiry into the sinking of the *Titanic*.

20 *The Saga of the RMS Lusitania, A Marine Forensic Analysis* (William H. Garzke, Jr., Robert O. Dulin, Jr., Peter K. Hsu, Blake Powell, F. Gregg Bemis), January 8, 1998.

21 By way of comparison, the *Kaiser Wilhelm II* of 1903 sported only 40,000 horsepower; the *Olympic*-class ships – which were launched starting in late 1910 – had two four-cylinder triple-expansion reciprocating engines each, with each engine supplying a nominal yield of 15,000 horsepower.

22 The placement of the *Mauretania*'s propellers was somewhat different: the centers of her inner props sat 12 feet 10 inches forward of the after perpendicular, while the centers of the outer props sat 78 feet 11 inches forward of the inner props, or 91 feet 9 inches forward of the after perpendicular.

23 When the *Mauretania* was launched, she had similar propellers, except that the blades were slightly narrower and longer than those on the *Lusitania*. The propellers of the *Lusitania* and *Mauretania* were replaced several times during their careers to improve performance, as it was found that the original propellers were far from ideal.

24 In another source, a slightly different set of data is given, mainly a diameter of 16′ 6″ for both sets, and a mean pitch for the inner propellers of 14′ 6″, while for the outer props

the mean pitch was 15′ 9″. A root thickness of 9.75″ and a tip thickness of .75″ were also specified in this document.

25 A different approach was taken to the *Mauretania*'s turbines. Her discs, gudgeons, shafts and drums were constructed of Whitworth fluid-pressed steel. To achieve the maximum strength with as little weight as possible, it was decided to reduce the number of parts to the bare minimum. All stiffeners were solid and formed part of the drums. When all of the three large low-pressure drums were screwed together and the gudgeons and discs were bolted to the lathe, the combination was found to be perfect; there was not even any need for testing the balance by spinning the turbines in the shop after they were completed. The first turbine rotations were done aboard the *Mauretania* in their final position.

26 It is interesting to note the depth below the waterline at which these steam lines ran, for the torpedo that doomed the ship in 1915 was running ten feet below the surface; if the second explosion was indeed caused by a failure of the ship's high-pressure steam lines, it is possible that they suffered initial damage due to the torpedo's impact or the vibration of the ship in response to the torpedo's detonation.

27 Some other sources cite 23.993 knots as the average speed for this voyage, but I agree more readily with Cunard's official statement.

28 I must emphasize that this comparison refers to the period of time that the two ships served together between late 1907 and late 1914, since the average speed of the *Mauretania* increased significantly through the years as improvements were made to her powerplant and propellers; these were improvements that the *Lusitania* never saw because she was lost during the war. Pre-war, the *Mauretania* was still faster, but only by a small margin.

29 *Colonist*, June 18, 1910, pg. 2.

30 By way of comparison, the *Mauretania* had 53 thermo-tanks, 29 in First Class, 9 in Second Class, and 15 for the Third Class, officer and crew spaces.

31 These regulations were out-dated almost as soon as they went into effect. White Star's *Majestic* of 1890 was some 9,965 gross tons, but before the decade was out, the *Kaiser Wilhelm der Grosse* of 1897 had topped that

out at 14,349 gross tons, and the tonnage of the *Lusitania* had more than doubled that by 1907.

CHAPTER 4: A Distinguished Career

1   "A Trip Round Ireland," *Nelson Evening Mail*, Sept. 19, 1907, pg. 1.

2   From a published interview with Ernest Wighton. Newspaper account provided by Mike Porer.

3   *Poverty Bay Herald*, Sept. 5, 1907, pg. 6.

4   *The New York Times*, November 3, 1907.

5   Listing from the *Dawson Daily News*, Nov. 5, 1907.

6   *Poverty Bay Herald*, October 19, 1907, pg. 1.

7   *Engineering: An Illustrated Weekly Journal*, Edited by W. H. Maw and B. Alfred Raworth, Vol. LXXXIV (July–December, 1907), pg. 170 (originally Aug. 2, 1907 issue).

8   *The New York Times*, 11/1/1930

9   At times, these figures could vary. These figures represent the original designed complement when the ship first entered service.

10   *Poverty Bay Herald*, October 26, 1907, pg. 11.

11   *Poverty Bay Herald*, October 26, 1907, pg. 11.

12   *Poverty Bay Herald*, October 26, 1907, pg. 11.

13   *Poverty Bay Herald*, October 25, 1907, pg. 4.

14   *Outward Bound*, by John Gould, Outward Bound Co. (1905/1913), pgs. 13-14.

15   *Poverty Bay Herald*, October 26, 1907, pg. 11.

16   *Ibid.*

17   *Poverty Bay Herald*, October 26, 1907, pg. 11.

18   Although she had passed the *Lucania* on the trip to Queenstown, the *Lusitania* was deliberately slowed to give the older vessel the honor of pulling in first. Calculating the exact arrival time is complicated by vague and apparently contradictory reports. The Cunard Company reportedly stated that the *Lucania*'s arrival time was 10:20 a.m., while the *Lusitania*'s was 10:25 a.m. This time was supposedly given in Irish Time (*Poverty Bay Herald*, October 26, 1907, pg. 11). Up until 1916, Ireland had not standardized with Greenwich Mean Time (GMT), which was a full five hours ahead of New York. Instead, Ireland used Dublin Mean Time, or Irish Time, which placed them behind GMT by 25 minutes and put the nation 4 hours and 35 minutes ahead of New York Time (NYT) (*The Scientific American Handbook of Travel*, 1910, pg. 12). During the *Lusitania*'s career, her abstract of log cards recorded events in Ireland at both Irish Time (IT) and GMT. The 10:25 a.m. arrival time for the *Lusitania*, if given by Cunard in IT, would thus have equated to 10:50 a.m. GMT.

So far things seem clear enough, though complicated. However, another source put the *Lusitania*'s arrival 10 minutes after the *Lucania*'s, rather than five minutes, and gave the *Lusitania*'s arrival time at 9:25 a.m., without specifying what time zone was being referred to (*The Daily Mirror*, September 9, 1907, pg. 3). If reporting in Irish Time, this would give GMT arrival time of 9:50 a.m. Meanwhile, *The New York Times* correspondent aboard the *Lusitania* reported that she had arrived in Queenstown at "10 A.M.," in his September 8 report; the paper later cited the *Lusitania*'s arrival time at precisely 9:53 a.m., again, without specifying what time zone this was recorded in. If recorded in Irish Time, this would have translated to 10:18 a.m. GMT; if this report was given as GMT time, then that would have translated back to 9:28 a.m. – which is very close to *The Daily Mirror*'s 9:25 a.m., if that time was reported in Irish Time rather than GMT. It would also have been close enough on the clock that the initial report from *The New York Times*' correspondent could have been a "guesstimate" when read at the clock and roughed-in to GMT.

If the report given in the *Poverty Bay Herald* was mistaken in stating that the times were given in Irish Time, and the report was actually citing GMT, then this report would – instead of being wholly contradictory – again agree closely with the other estimates when studied carefully.

As *The New York Times* account is the most specific to the precise minute, I tend to believe its accuracy more than that of the other reports, and it appears to have been given in GMT. If true, then the ship's precise arrival time at Queenstown was 9:28 a.m. (Irish Time), 9:53 a.m. (GMT), 4:53 a.m. (NYT), Sept. 8, 1907.

19   *Outward Bound*, by John Gould, Outward Bound Co. (1905/1913), pgs. 15-16.

20   It was subsequently recommended that an extra steward be assigned to groups of certain numbers of tables in order to care specifically for the passengers' drink requests; this would leave the stewards already assigned available to

focus specifically on the passengers' food with an improvement in overall service.

21 *Bush Advocate*, November 23, 1907, pg. 3.

22 *The Scientific American Handbook of Travel* (Munn & Co., Inc., NY, 1911), pg. 6.

23 To further show that the *Lusitania* was not driven during the maiden voyage, a comparison with the *Aquitania's* maiden westbound crossing, May 31 – June 5, 1914, is enlightening. From Liverpool to the Ambrose Channel Lightship, the larger, slower liner took 5 days, 17 hours and 43 minutes over a course of 3,181 miles at an average speed of 23.17 knots. Her two best days' runs were of 602 miles each, and her best day's average was 24.3 knots.

24 *Outward Bound*, by John Gould (1905/1913), pg. 14.

25 Frederick A. Talbot, *Steamship Conquest of the World* (William Heinemann Company, London, 1912). Excerpt kindly provided by Art Braunschweiger.

26 This groundbreaking research was carried out by Mark Chirnside, who was given unprecedented access to some original source documents that revealed the figures. Mr. Chirnside subsequently published an article on the subject, entitled "*Lusitania* and *Mauretania* – Perceptions of Popularity." It was contained within the *Titanic Commutator* 2008, Volume 32, Number 184, pgs. 196-200. The article is also available on his website, http://www.markchirnside.co.uk. Full figures and statistics for each year of the ships' service are also available therein. My deepest thanks to Mr. Chirnside, not only for ascertaining the truth of the matter through some great detective work, but also for giving me permission to publish his findings in this volume.

27 *The Scientific American Handbook of Travel*, (Munn & Co., 1910), pg. 191.

28 *The New York Times*, January 16, 1910.

29 "Safer Navigation," *Poverty Bay Herald*, June 7, 1911, pg. 7.

30 Details of this series of problems will be covered later in this chapter.

31 "*Butter With My Bread: The Memoirs of Olga Petrova*," by Mme. Petrova (1942), pgs. 245-246.

32 According to numerous sources, including *Mauretania*, by Humfrey Jordan, and *Outward Bound*, by John Gould (1905/1913). One other reference, namely *The Scientific American Handbook of Travel* (Munn & Co., Inc., NY, 1911), pg. 102, notes that the first watch of each day began at noon. In either case, the watch breakdown was the same.

33 Testimony of Fifth Officer Harold G. Lowe to the U.S. Senate Inquiry into the loss of the *Titanic*, day five of proceedings.

34 *The New York Times*, June 8, 1912/The Cunard Archives, University of Liverpool Library/*The Daily Gleaner*, 6/18/1912.

35 *The Scientific American Handbook of Travel*, (Munn & Co., Inc., NY, 1911) pg. 100.

36 *The Scientific American Handbook of Travel*, (Munn & Co, 1910), pg. 270.

37 Reported in *The New York Times*, 12/28/1911.

38 *The New York Times*, 1/1/1913

39 *Ibid*, 8/23/1913 / Cunard Archives, University of Liverpool.

40 The information on this story was taken from a variety of sources, including *Trial of Oscar Slater* (1929) by W. Teignmouth. Within that volume are transcriptions of original sworn testimony from the witnesses called for the case, including that of Cunard Agent John Forsythe, Stewardess Beryl Bedford, Bedroom Steward Thomas Atherton, and of Slater's partner, Andrée (or Andrea, or Anna, depending on the account) Junio Antoine. Information on the arrest aboard the *Lusitania*, including Miss Antoine's statement to the press, was also gleaned from *The New York Times* of January 3, 1909.

Certain questions regarding Slater's history, and his relationship with Miss Antoine, remain unanswered in my mind. Although many sources cite the date of his first marriage in 1902, some place it in 1901; Miss Antoine said in her statement to the press that she married Slater on July 12, 1901. Since it is known that Miss Antoine did not meet Slater until much later, was this perhaps the actual date of his marriage to his first wife? There are other questions, as well, worthy of a full investigation by modern researchers. The basic facts of his case, however, seem quite clear, as is Slater's innocence insofar as the murder of Miss Gilchrist.

41 *The New York Times*, 11/21/1911; 11/25/1911.

42 *The Scientific American Handbook of Travel* (Munn & Co., Inc., NY, 1911), pg. 115.

43 Reported in *The New York Times*, 5/27/1911.

44 *The Scientific American Handbook of Travel* (Munn & Co., Inc., NY, 1911), pgs. 98-99.

45 *Outward Bound*, John H. Gould (Outward Bound Company, NY, 1905, 1913), pg. 22.

46   *Ibid.*

47   A wealth of information on the *Olympic* and her sisters is available. The best and most comprehensive books include: *Titanic: The Ship Magnificent*, Volumes 1 & 2, by Bruce Beveridge, with Steve Hall and Daniel Klistorner; and *The Olympic-Class Ships* by Mark Chirnside.

48   This account of Mr. Guggenheim's statement was later recalled by his Steward, Henry Samuel Etches, who survived the sinking of the *Titanic*. When he reached New York, Etches was able to personally give Guggenheim's family the account of his final hours. Their meeting, including the quotation in the text, was reported in *The New York Times* of 4/20/1912.

49   Wyn Craig Wade, *Titanic: Death of a Dream.*

CHAPTER 5: The Last Days

1   *The Illustrated London News*, 8/22/1914.

2   *RMS Olympic: Titanic's Sister*, Mark Chirnside, pg. 122.

3   This account was published in *The Illustrated London News*, 8/22/1914. All original spelling and punctuation has been preserved.

4   *The Manitoba Free Press*, Saturday, August 29, 1914.

5   *The Toronto World*, August 7, 1914.

6   *The Toronto World*, August 7, 1914.

7   *The Manitoba Free Press*, Saturday, August 29, 1914.

8   *The Manitoba Free Press*, Saturday, August 29, 1914.

9   *Naval Operations, I*, Julian S. Corbett, (London, 1920) page 51.

10   Voyages Nos. 94 (Liverpool–New York, August 29/New York–Liverpool, Sept. 9), 95 (Liverpool–New York, Sept. 19/New York–Liverpool, Sept. 30) and No. 96 (Liverpool–New York, Oct. 10/New York–Liverpool, Oct. 21).

11   *The New York Times*, February 7, 1915; also an article entitled "The Sensible Romance of Marshall Field III 'The Richest Boy in the World,' supplied by Jim Kalafus. Sadly, the union was not to last. Eventually, Mr. Field went to the fronts. Although he survived the conflict and came home safely, the couple was divorced in 1930 (*Time* magazine, July 8, 1935).

12   The westbound crossing to New York that Mr. Field and Miss Marshall were on carried a high number of passengers. According to *The New York Times* of September 18, there were 1,502 passengers aboard, divided between 605 First, 387 Second, and 510 Third Classes. According to Ellis Island records for the same trip, there were some 1,712 passengers aboard. But from there forward, the numbers began to fall quickly. Crossing 187 West carried 1,477 passengers (*The New York Times* figures) or 1,601 passengers (Ellis Island Records). Crossing 189 West carried 918 passengers (*The New York Times* figures) or 1,029 passengers (Ellis Island Records), and Crossing 191 West carried 825 passengers (*The New York Times* figures) or 913 passengers (Ellis Island Records). Whichever figures are more accurate, the drop was pronounced, and harmonized with the end of the summer traveling season. This standard drop-off in traffic was no doubt exacerbated by the war.

13   *The New York Times*, 9/18, 9/19/1914

14   *Ibid*, 10/31/1914; 11/1/1914.
      In his book, Colin Simpson tried to show that the *Lusitania* had, by October of 1914, been thoroughly gutted by the Admiralty and that, as a result, she was very top-heavy and unstable. He cited a conversation that was supposed to have taken place during this particular crossing between Captain Dow and George Booth, cousin of Cunard Chairman A. A. Booth, as to why the *Lusitania* was giving such a wild ride. (Simpson suggested that this was the *Lusitania*'s first voyage after the Admiralty released her from Government service; in point of fact it was her third round-trip voyage of the war.)
      According to Simpson, Captain Dow had told Booth that the reason for the ship's poor behavior was some new extra strengthening of the ship's structure to support 6-inch guns, as well as the gutting of F Deck forward, alterations done by the Admiralty. Additionally, Dow reported that all passenger accommodations on C Deck and below, forward, had been closed down, and that everything forward of the No. 2 funnel on C Deck was in the control of the Admiralty and no one was allowed there; this reportedly necessitated the closing of the Third Class Smoking Room and Dining Saloon, and meant that Third Class passengers had to dine in the Second Class Saloon because their own saloon had been closed down.

It is true that, for the sake of economy, some of the *Lusitania's* passenger accommodations had been closed down during the fall of 1914; however, these areas were later reopened and were in use at the time of the *Lusitania's* last voyage. The concept that Third Class passengers were allowed to eat in the Second Class Dining Saloon would have been completely against immigration laws of both the United States and Great Britain, and can therefore be dismissed as unreliable; at any rate, the Third Class Saloon was on D Deck, not C Deck – so someone, somewhere along the line, was grossly unfamiliar with the ship's layout in making such a report. The report that everything forward of the No. 2 funnel on C Deck was under the control of the Admiralty also seems dubious because of the fact that this would have required the closing of the Third Class and Crew's Galley, the Third Class Entrance (a primary people-mover within the ship), and a number of other key portions of the ship, including a number of lavatories and bathrooms for the crew and petty officers, which were not duplicated anywhere else on board.

Although Simpson cited George Booth's correspondence with Alfred Booth to back up this story, specific dates of these letters are not cited, and even if the letters exist and do contain such statements, it seems clear that Booth was very much mistaken. Attempts have been made over the years to take from this account the idea that the *Lusitania*, because of Admiralty alterations, was still dangerously light and top-heavy on her final voyage. However, tremendous evidence on the point comes from a photograph of the ship's final arrival in New York (pg. 265), when compared with a similar photo taken on November 20, 1908, of the ship in the same light (arrival) condition (pgs. 172-3). The comparison shows that the ship was no lighter in the water at the end of her final complete crossing than she had been before the war; if anything had been "gutted," for whatever reason, it was also not affecting the ship's weight in any apparent way; it is also the only evidence I can find of such alterations. Indeed, several score American travelers were returning from Europe in Third Class, and upon arrival there are no accounts of them being inconvenienced by alterations to the ship. Finally the *Lusitania* was built with

the required structural strength to hold 6-inch guns, so one is also forced to wonder why the Admiralty would have needed to make hasty modifications on the *Lusitania* to support such guns when the ship was not in Government service and was going to remain in commercial service for the foreseeable future.

So why was the *Lusitania* giving such a terrible, harsh ride to her passengers during that October crossing? Quite simply, the weather during the crossing was ghastly; the ship was delayed in leaving the Mersey by twenty-four hours, and waves were actually breaking over the Bridge during the worst of the gale according to Captain Dow. The weather remained foul throughout the whole crossing, right through to Nantucket, again according to Captain Dow. The *Lusitania* had always had a reputation for a spirited ride even during the best of weather, so it is not surprising that she was giving her passengers a wild ride yet again during weather that was on a par with some of the worst she had ever steamed through.

15 *The Lusitania: Unravelling the Mysteries*, Patrick O'Sullivan, pgs. 129-130.
16 *Lusitania: An Epic Tragedy*, Diana Preston, pgs. 78-81.
17 *Winston S. Churchill, Companion Vol. III*, Martin Gilbert, 1973, part 1, p. 501..
18 *Lusitania: An Epic Tragedy*, Diana Preston, pgs. 395-6.
19 Recollections of Miss Losanitch's experiences aboard the *Lusitania* on that trip were written by her in letters to her family back home in Serbia. She was married to one John W. Frothingham in January of 1921. She later collected her letters of that voyage on the *Lusitania*, among many others, and published them in book format under the title *Mission for Serbia*. It is from these letters that the stories and excerpts in this passage are drawn. My thanks to Mike Poirier for drawing my attention to this account for its inclusion in this volume. Her name, as given to authorities at Ellis Island at the conclusion of that voyage, was one "Miss Helene Lozanitch," and her occupation was listed as "Secretary."
20 Nona's mother had passed away in 1912, and her father had remarried President Wilson's daughter the previous year.
21 The fact that she was sitting so low in the water as she left New York on this late-January

1915 crossing also tends to dispel the Simpson argument that the liner was top-heavy, as mentioned in endnote 14 of this chapter.

22 *The New York Times*, 1/31/1915 .

23 *The Manchester Guardian / The New York Times*, 2/3/1915.

24 *The Intimate Papers of Colonel House*, Charles Seymour, (1926) I, pgs. 359-361.

25 *The Merchant Navy, III*, Archibald Hurd (1929), pgs. 378-9.

26 *New York Times*, 10/13/1907

27 *The Lusitania*, Colin Simpson (1972), pgs. 87-88. Many of Simpson's conclusions were very poor, but this particular tidbit of information has, to the best of my knowledge, never been refuted by other researchers.

28 Testimony of Alfred A. Booth, Cunard Chairman, at the Mersey Inquiry.

29 These complaints were referred to in Colin Simpson's book, as well. Curiously, Simpson also made reference to a defect in the changeover valves to the astern turbines. He states that Turner was warned that putting the turbines astern could lead to a steam feedback explosion; however, Simpson does not specify his source for this very clearly. One would think that if the ship's astern turbines were in serious disarray that Cunard might have canceled the upcoming voyage or that Lloyd's of London or the Board of Trade would have made a reference to such, but I have not been able to find any further evidence on this to date.

30 *Report on the Loss of the "Lusitania,"* Mersey, 1. The Ship.

31 All references to Mr. Ryerson's account on this passage come from his autobiography, *Looking Backward*, published in 1924. It was provided by Mike Poirier.

32 *The New York Times*, 4/4/1915.

33 From Ryerson's autobiography, provided by Mike Poirier. Spelling and punctuation have been corrected.

34 Account published in the *Lima Sunday News*, 5/30/1915, and provided by Mike Poirier.

35 *New York Liability Hearings*, pg. 95.

36 This has become a hotly debated issue in *Lusitania* lore. The simple truth of the matter is that Captain Turner personally admitted – at both the Mersey Inquiry and the New York Liability Hearings – to having received the zigzagging advice. In addition, although zigzagging was relatively new in the maritime community, other merchant skippers were known to have used the practice long before May 1915. For example, Captain Haddock of the *Olympic* implemented this tactic during four round-trip voyages between August and October of 1914. Thus, this method of evasion was certainly known to Captain Turner. Indeed, according to Gallagher's account of the 200th crossing, Turner had apparently implemented zigzagging even before the official advice from the Admiralty reached him.

37 *The New York Times*, May 10, 1915.

38 *The Lusitania Disaster*, Bailey & Ryan, excerpted from their correspondence with Albert Worley (3/11/1973), a passenger on that crossing, which is contained in the Bailey/Ryan Collection of the Hoover Institution.

39 From a report made by German Naval Attache Captain Boy-Ed to Berlin on April 27, 1915. Referred to in *Lusitania: An Epic Tragedy*, by Diana Preston, pg. 111.

40 The *New York Tribune*, *The Richmond Times-Dispatch*, 6/5/1915; sailing schedules published in *The New York Times* of 5/1/1915 and 5/7/1915, also *The Sun*, 5/6-10/1915.

41 From a report made by German Naval Attaché Captain Boy-Ed to Berlin on April 27, 1915. Referred to in *Lusitania: An Epic Tragedy*, by Diana Preston, pg. 111.

42 The sailing advertisements referred to were contained in *The New York Times* of 5/1/1915 and 5/7/1915. At times, these advertisements were subject to alteration at short notice, depending on the situation; I feel that it is possible that Boy-Ed's sources were correct, but at this time I find that the evidence does not support a firm conclusion.

43 *The Scientific American Handbook of Travel* (Munn & Co.), pg. 38. The telephone number given therein was 3300 Broad, while the dock telephone was 6780 Chelsea. The company leased piers 53, 54 and 56.

44 The Mersey Hearings, testimony of Reverend Clarke (cited incorrectly as Clark), examined by the Attorney General.

45 *The Lusitania's Last Voyage*, Charles E. Lauriat, Jr., (1915), Part 1.

46 This incident took place between Friday, March 5 and Saturday, March 6, 1915. The escorts *Laverock* and *Louis* were tasked for the assignment, but no one had bothered to inform Cunard of the escort, and no one in the Admiralty had managed to inform the escorts' commanders of when and where precisely to

rendezvous. The frustrated commanders tried everything in their power – from phoning Cunard's Liverpool offices on poor-quality lines to sending a wireless to Captain Dow personally asking him where they should meet. Dow on the *Lusitania* was concerned that it could be an enemy trap, and quite rightly so; he did not reveal his position, and sailed into Liverpool unescorted. As they approached England, Dow and the *Lusitania* had just missed the *U-27*, under the command of Kapitänleutnant Bernhard Wegener; Wegener had been lurking off Liverpool waiting for the *Lusitania*, but had decided to call it quits on March 5, having mistakenly expected the Cunarder the previous day.

47 Some authors have tartly pointed out that Anderson would not have been able to carry out a boat drill with coal lighters tied up alongside the liner, and that he thus must have falsely signed off on that point in the documents to clear the ship from port. However, this argument does not hold water. On June 7, 1912, when the *Mauretania* arrived in New York, Staff Captain McNeil had lowered all the lifeboats to the water, something reported on in the press the next day. Such lifeboat drills were a regular feature of the *Lusitania*'s stays in New York. Coaling was also a constant feature while tied up there, and yet lifeboat drills had been successfully executed in the past ... so why not during this stay? Additionally, the ship's turnaround in New York between Crossings Nos. 201 and 202 was rather longer than a normal pre-war stay in that port, giving more than usual opportunity to conduct a lifeboat drill.

48 *Seven Days to Disaster*, pg. 47.

49 *The New York Times*, May 14, 1915.

50 *The New York World*, May 2, 1915.

51 *The Washington Post*, May 8, 1915.

52 We can now be certain that this departure footage was obtained on May 1, 1915, due to the aforementioned blizzard which swept New York City at the time of the *Lusitania*'s previous departure from that port. All evidence of said storm is entirely lacking in the footage, and the film could not have been taken before the spring of 1915.

53 *The New York Times*, May 2, 1915

54 Michael Byrne's account is contained in a letter that he wrote to Secretary of State William Jennings Bryan on June 22, 1915, and which is contained in the National Archives and Records Administration's files. A copy of this letter was kindly loaned to me by researcher Mike Poirier. Unfortunately, the original letter is absolutely chock full of spelling and grammatical errors. These have been repaired where direct quotations have been made in the narrative.

55 Dorothy Conner letter excerpt provided by Mike Poirier.

56 Information on the *Cameronia* from Paul Latimer.

57 *The New Music Review*, Volume 4 (November, 1905-November, 1905), pg. 523. It was said of Inez that she was possessed of "excellent technical equipment, especially a strong and free bow arm. She also has much dash and spirit, and her attention is largely directed toward brilliancy, even to the neglect of intonation, which was frequently noticeable in her playing. She has the further strong point of a most possessing appearance."

58 This review is available in a link from *Lest We Forget*, Part 2. The exact link is: http://www.encyclopedia-Titanica.org/images/lusi_vernon_art.jpg.

59 Stevens had been serving on the *Cephalonia* when he was informed that his wife had passed away. His transfer to the *Lusitania* was thus rather hasty; he was basically working his passage back to England. The term "Ex-Chief' is an abbreviation of "Extra Chief." My thanks to Mike Poirier for some of the details on both Stevens' back-story and for information on the precise title of his post.

60 This arrangement differs from the ship's standard pre-war complement in both number and rank assignments. Obviously it was not only the lower ranks of the ship's crew that were suffering from the attrition of war.

61 Testimony of Albert Bestic (mistakenly referred to as Bestwick) at the Mersey Inquiry.

62 There were five members of the band: Bandmaster Charles W. Cameron (aged 38, died); Mr. E. Carr-Jones (aged 37, died); Mr. Edward Drakeford (aged 30, saved); Mr. Handel Hawkins (aged 25, saved); and Mr. John William Hemingway (aged 27, saved). Mr. Hemingway played the double bass. Based on other similar bands on liners of the period, I would be tempted to believe that Bandmaster Cameron played violin, but this is mere speculation. Mr. Hemingway's daughter, Josephine Lucie, was named after the lost liner. Hemingway had

previously survived the sinking of the *Republic*, and Hawkins was supposed to have been one of the musicians on the ill-fated *Titanic*, but changed out at the last minute.

63 Some books have mistakenly referred to this converted Cunarder as the *Carmania*, which was the *Caronia*'s sister; the two were siblings that had earned the nickname the "Pretty Sisters." These had been Cunard's test bed to compare reciprocating engines to turbine engines before the *Lusitania* and *Mauretania*. The *Caronia* had reciprocating engines, whereas the *Carmania* had been fit with turbines. The *Carmania* was the ship involved with the *Cap Trafalgar* early in the war, and was nowhere near New York on May 1; the *Caronia*, on the other hand, had been on patrol off New York for some six months, with her station being Halifax, Nova Scotia. She would be returning to Liverpool before the month was out for a complete overhaul, and survived the war.

64 *Commodore*, by Sir James Bissett, also quoted in *The Cunard Story*, by Howard Johnson, pgs. 86-87.

65 *Lusitania* researcher Mike Poirier has a copy of a Cunard music book from January of 1915, and most of these pieces are listed therein, along with some others. Special thanks to Mr. Poirier for access to his materials on this point.

66 Account provided by Peter Kelly.

67 *The Lusitania Disaster*, Bailey & Ryan, pgs. 117-118.

68 *The Lusitania Disaster*, Bailey & Ryan, pg. 127.

69 Punctuation has been supplied to these messages for ease of reference. The originals of all four are found in an official transcript in the Public Record Office, ADM 137/1058, Frs. 28-29, and match a reproduction in *The Lusitania*, by Colin Simpson, pgs. 152-3.

70 Testimony of A. A. Booth, Mersey Inquiry.

71 Some have tried to assert that this single word "Questor," was an Admiralty order for the *Lusitania* to put into Queenstown. This is incorrect, however. PRO, ADM 186/678 contains the First Edition Merchant Vessel Code. Right on the first page two special code words, "Questor," and "Westrona," appear, along with their meanings as given in the narrative.

72 Frequently, this is quoted as "submarines," plural, not singular. However, decoding the original copy of this message, Bailey & Ryan found that the singular form of the word was originally transmitted, but that the plural was used in later official documents.

73 Account provided by Mike Poirier.

74 *Lest We Forget*, Part 1, by Mike Poirier and Jim Kalafus.

75 Testimony of Senior Second Engineer Andrew Cockburn at the Mersey Inquiry; he was in charge of the Engine Room from 8-12 a.m.

76 Wynne Hearings, pg. 198.

77 *Lusitania: An Epic Tragedy*, Diana Preston, pg. 180, from an interview he gave to the BBC.

78 Note retrieved from Mrs. Loynd's body after the sinking.

79 Reported by Able Bodied Seaman Thomas O'Mahoney.

80 This and subsequent references to Mrs. Lobb's experiences are taken from her own account of the disaster, kindly provided to me by fellow *Lusitania* researcher Mike Poirier.

81 This and subsequent references to Miss Wild's experiences are taken from an account of her experiences during the disaster, kindly provided to me by Mike Poirier. Further details have been gleaned from her testimony at the Mersey Inquiry.

82 Copies of Mrs. Burdon's account, photographs, and ephemera were kindly provided to me by her grandson, Richard Burdon for inclusion in this book. My thanks to Mr. Burdon, and to Mike Poirier for putting us in touch.

83 Quartermaster Johnston reported in his Mersey Inquiry testimony that Turner was in his cabin at 1:30 p.m., because he had to take a message to him at that time. However, some have suggested that Captain Turner was still in his cabin when the torpedo was spotted, and that he made it up to the Bridge before the torpedo impact. This does not seem likely, however. On the first day of his testimony in the Mersey Inquiry, Turner was asked where he was when the ship was struck. He responded: "On the port side of the lower bridge," – apparently "lower" as opposed to the roof of the Bridge with the compass platform on it. When he heard the last-moment warning of the approaching torpedo, he "went across to the starboard side and saw the wake, and there was immediately an explosion ..." This last warning was only a few seconds before the impact ... if Turner was still in his cabin below the Bridge, how would he have had time to leave the cabin, and whatever he was in the middle of at the time, and climb the stairs to the Bridge

in time to see the wake of the torpedo before the impact? The confusion may come from the testimony he gave immediately afterward, that after he ordered the lifeboats lowered to the rails, he "went up to the navigation bridge," in the words of the examiner. However, this was clearly after the torpedo impact, when Turner had already ordered the lifeboats lowered.

84 A point is $1/32$ of a compass card, or 11.25°. Four points thus equaled a 45° angle, according to Morton's observation.

85 Testimony of AB Morton, Mersey Inquiry.

86 The *Mauretania*, for example, successfully performed this maneuver just a few months later, while serving as a troopship under the command of Captain Dow. It was estimated that the torpedo missed by no more than five feet.

87 Account provided by Mike Poirier.

88 *Lest We Forget*, Part 1, by Mike Poirier & Jim Kalafus.

89 Quinn's testimony on this point is difficult to understand; he at first said it was about 200 yards off the starboard side. Then he said that it was fully 100 yards off when he first spotted it. At a speed of forty knots, the torpedo was moving at about 46 m.p.h., covering roughly 4,048 feet every minute, or about 67.4 feet per second. At a range of 2,300 feet, this gives a travel time of just over 34 seconds. If Quinn's distance estimate of 100 yards is accurate, this means that he spotted the inbound torpedo about four and a half seconds before it struck, or just about thirty seconds after it was launched. By this point, roughly 85% of the time between the torpedo's launch and its impact would have elapsed. Warning the Bridge would have taken a few seconds however, and leads me to believe that the distance between the torpedo and the ship would be more like his original estimate of 200 yards when he first spotted it. Either way, the Lookouts' lapse in this critical moment seems shocking.

90 Testimony of Thomas Quinn at the Mersey Inquiry.

91 Testimony of Captain Turner at the Mersey Inquiry – the exclamation point has been added to supplement the inadequate punctuation supplied in the transcripts of the Captain's testimony; I can not imagine any more correct form of conveying the urgency of Hefford's remark. According to the Mersey Inquiry testimony of Quartermaster Johnston – who

was at the helm – Hefford's warning came in response to the lookout's.

92 Many of these details were calculated in a forensic analysis by the Society of Naval Architects and Marine Engineers; see Recommended Reading for full reference.

93 McDermott was signed on as a Trimmer, but according to his testimony at the Mersey Inquiry, had been "promoted" to Fireman.

94 Testimony of McDermott at Mersey Inquiry.

95 This is the exact angle of roll that Leonard Peskett had calculated the ship would go over to with two coal bunkers flooded on one side. Some, like Michael Byrne, thought that the list was even greater, but it is very easy to feel that a list is greater than it really is to one who is standing on the sloping deck hanging on for dear life. Far more trustworthy are the reports from the Bridge read directly from the list indicator.

96 This exchange was quoted in the testimony of Quartermaster Johnston, who was at the helm.

97 This and later references to Miss James' story are taken from her own account, kindly provided me by Peter Kelly.

98 Testimony of Bestic, Mersey Inquiry.

99 According to evidence, the ship's list rectified slightly – or "a small bit" – about ten minutes after the torpedo impact. However, Bestic quite clearly agreed that the ship never lost her big list to starboard. Quartermaster Johnston watched the list from 15°, increasing from there – the slight recovery must have taken place while Second Officer Hefford was watching the indicator, before he left to go below to the Forecastle.

100 This evidence comes from James Leary, Harold Boulton, and from a reference by twenty-three-year-old Florence Padley. Exactly who was operating this car in the absence of the Lift Attendants is still a mystery.

101 Testimony of Johnston, Mersey Inquiry.

102 Testimony of Andrew Cockburn, Mersey Inquiry.

103 According to some of the earliest recollections of Rita Jolivet. Vanderbilt was also seen in other locations by other passengers; it seems pretty apparent that he did not stay in one place for any great length of time during the sinking. The position of this group (namely, Boat Deck, port side) is at variance with most accounts (namely, starboard side, Promenade Deck) in other books. However, it is taken from Jolivet's very lucid 1917 Limitation of Liability Hearings

testimony, as reproduced in *Lest We Forget*, Part 2, by Mike Poirier and Jim Kalafus. She was very clear and specific in this position – both in regards to what deck and what side of the ship. She was also clear in stating that they were quite close to the Entrance.

104 Some books have identified the photographer in Jeffery's account as twenty-eight-year-old Patrick Jones, a Second Class passenger and London resident who was a photographer with the International News service. Jeffery's original account, however, does not identify Jones by name, so this assumption is rather dubious.

105 Mr. Gadd's written experiences were kindly forwarded to my attention by Mike Poirier. They are housed in the Mariners' Museum of Newport News, Virginia, United States. Although Mr. Gadd referred to the lifeboat he was lowered away in as "Boat No. 16," from the details of the account, it is clear that he was actually aboard Boat No. 14. Mr. Poirier also kindly obtained permission for the use of Mr. Gadd's photograph in this volume from Gadd's relatives.

106 Testimony of Robert W. Cairns at Mersey Inquiry. The fate of Boat No. 14 has become distorted in many other works on the disaster, but Cairns' highly specific testimony reveals the truth of the matter. Further details on this lifeboat's story can be found in Mike Poirier's excellent article on Boat No. 14.

107 There has often been confusion on McCormick's fate, but he gave an account to the newspapers after the sinking and two photographs attributed to him appeared in *The Daily Sketch*.

108 The loss of George Vernon severely affected his wife, the violinist Inez. She traveled to the United States and spent some time visiting friends in New Jersey, and she was according to many severely depressed. She next booked passage back to England on the *New York*, did some shopping for the trip, and had her trunks sent to her West Eleventh Street apartment. She was last seen on Monday, July 19, 1915. On Thursday, July 22, her landlord went into the apartment to show it to a prospective tenant, thinking that Mrs. Vernon was out of town. Instead, he found her crumpled form at the foot of the bed. She had dressed herself in black, knelt on the floor, and shot herself in the head. A coroner examined her body, and declared that she had been dead for at least

three days, meaning that she had most likely chosen to end her life on Monday, July 19. The loss of her husband had simply been too much for the beautiful twenty-eight-year-old musician to bear. Thus, without ever having stepped foot on the decks of the *Lusitania* during her last voyage, Mrs. Vernon had become a victim of the tragedy. She was buried with her husband in Queenstown.

109 Beatrice Witherbee traveled to Dublin following the sinking, to recuperate. She was joined by her husband, and they set off traveling. Very quickly, however, they broke up. Beatrice stayed with the family of her shipboard friend, Rita Jolivet. In time, she met Rita's brother, Alfred, who Rita had been traveling to see before he had shipped out for the fronts. She quickly fell in love with Alfred, divorced her husband, and in 1919 she became Rita's sister-in-law.

CHAPTER 6: The End of the Road

1   Neither of these figures take into account the three stowaways who were found aboard the ship after leaving her pier and all of whom were apparently lost in the subsequent disaster.

2   This account was referenced in an article Bestic wrote for *The New York Times*, published in *The Daily Gleaner* on Thursday, May 19, 1932. It was also referred to extensively in *Seven Days to Disaster*, by Des Hickey and Gus Smith, although some details of the conversation were apparently reconstructed for dramatic effect in that book.

3   Both news stories were run on the same page in *The New York Times* of May 8, 1935.

4   I have seen Jarrett's name spelled every conceivable way – from Jarrat to Garret and everything in between. This was the spelling originally given in numerous period press reports. At least in part due to his breakthrough dives to the wreck of the *Lusitania*, the deep-water JIM suit was named in his honor.

5   Interestingly, at the time of the Tritonia expedition, Lieutenant Bestic had expressed the feeling that the ship would be lying on her side, and that she would most likely have been "considerably flattened"; this is the exact state of the wreck as she was found in 1993.

SEVEN DAY LOAN

This book is to be returned on
or before the date stamped below

2 6 APR 1999	2 3 MAR 2001
CANCELLED	2 1 OCT 2003
1 5 NOV 1999	2 9 OCT 2003
2 8 JAN 2000	1 0 NOV 2003
2 3 MAR 2000	2 0 NOV 2003
1 3 FEB 2001	11 NOV 2004 .
22·2·01	

UNIVERSITY OF PLYMOUTH

PLYMOUTH LIBRARY

Tel: (01752) 232323
This book is subject to recall if required by another reader
Books may be renewed by phone
CHARGES WILL BE MADE FOR OVERDUE BOOKS